Practical Pursuits

Practical Pursuits

Religion, Politics, and Personal Cultivation in Nineteenth-Century Japan

Janine Tasca Sawada

University of Hawai'i Press HAWAI Honolulu

09 08 07 06 05 04   6 5 4 3 2 1

Library of Congress Cataloging-in-Publication Data

Sawada, Janine Anderson.
    Practical pursuits : religion, politics, and personal cultivation in
nineteenth-century Japan / Janine Tasca Sawada.
        p.   cm.
    Includes bibliographical references and index.
    ISBN 0-8248-2752-X (alk. paper)
    1. Religion and politics—Japan—History—19th century.   I. Title.
BL2211.S73S29   2004
200′.952′09034—dc22   2003023963

Publication of this book has been assisted by a grant from the
Japan Foundation.

Designed by University of Hawai'i Press production staff in Sabon, with
        display type in Hiroshige
Printed by The Maple-Vail Book Manufacturing Group

For Ryoichiro

CONTENTS

ACKNOWLEDGMENTS

THE GOODWILL and expertise of many scholars, friends, and mentors made this book possible. Stephen Vlastos read through a version of the entire manuscript at a critical juncture, before I submitted it for publication; I thank him for his excellent advice and his warm friendship. Michel Mohr has served over the years both as my keenest critic and as a fellow traveler in the labyrinth of Japanese Zen history; several chapters of this book as well as the bibliography and glossary benefited immeasurably from his erudition. Helen Hardacre has given me generous support throughout my studies and intelligent suggestions for improving the book. Richard Jaffe assisted me from the earliest stages of my research on Meiji Buddhism and gave the manuscript an incisive reading. I am especially grateful to Ogihara Minori, who unstintingly shared his unique knowledge of nineteenth-century religious movements with me and procured research materials for me on countless occasions; without his assistance during the past several years, this book would never have come to be.

Inoue Zenjō was a special source of inspiration for me during the early stages of my research. He met with me several times in Kamakura and generously supplied me, not only with copies of rare Engakuji documents, but with invaluable help in reading them. The late Morinaga Sōkō inspired me to take the Confucian side of Imakita Kōsen seriously. Wendi Leigh Adamek helped me enhance both the content and the style of my chapters on Meiji Buddhism; Sarah E. Thal's perceptive reading improved my discussion of Shinto-related phenomena of the Meiji period. John Allen Tucker offered me indispensable advice on Tokugawa Confucian matters, and Hayashi Makoto's gentle criticism improved the accuracy of my treatment of Edo-period divination. Richard Rubinger gave me encouraging feedback on my review of Meiji educational policy. Paul B. Watt, James H. Foard, and Mary Evelyn Tucker have sustained me over the years with their friendship and intellectual openness. My thinking and writing in various sections of the book have also benefited from conversations with Timothy H. Barrett, Martin Collcutt, W. Theodore de Bary, T. Griffith Foulk, Victor S. Hori, Christopher Ives, James E. Ketelaar, John Lobreglio, Peter Nosco, Herman Ooms, Scott Schnell, Robert Sharf, Frederick Smith, Tu Wei-ming, Duncan R. Williams, Samuel Hideo Yamashita, and Michiko Yusa. I am greatly indebted to Koyama Shikei for supplying me with numerous Shingaku and Zen Buddhist materials; and I am continually obliged to Yokoyama Toshio for helping me obtain research materials and facilitating my visits to Kyoto. Pat Crosby of the University of Hawai'i Press has supported me throughout the writing this book; I also wish to thank Barbara Folsom for her careful editing of the manuscript. Needless to say, any errors that remain in the book are entirely my responsibility.

Portions of the research for this volume were presented at the Center for East Asian Studies of Stanford University in 1997 and at the Conference on Confucian Spirituality, held at the Harvard-Yenching Institute for East Asian Studies of Harvard University in the same year; at the American Academy of Religion meetings of 1995 and 2002; at the International Association for Buddhist Studies of 1999; and at the Symposium on New Perspectives in the Study of Shinto, held at Columbia University in 2002. The comments I received from participants in each of these meetings helped me rethink and improve the pertinent sections of the book. Portions of my essay, "The Confucian Linguistic Community in Late Tokugawa Japan," to be published by Crossroad Press in a volume called *Confucian Spirituality,* appear in revised form in chapters 1 and 3. Abridged sections of my "Political Waves in the Zen Sea: The Engakuji Circle in Early Meiji Japan," published in the *Japanese Journal of Religious Studies* 21.1–2 (Spring 1998), are contained in chapter 9. I wish to express my appreciation to both of these publishers for allowing me to use this material here.

Part of the research that contributed to this book was carried out under the auspices of a Japan Foundation fellowship in 1993–1994; I am indebted to the foundation and to the Kyoto University Research Institute for the Humanities for facilitating my studies in Kyoto during that period. A grant from the Japan Society for the Promotion of Science and the Social Sciences Research Council made it possible for me to complete another phase of the research in 1998–1999; I am grateful to James Heisig and the Nanzan University Institute for Religion and Culture for helping me to work productively in Nagoya during that time. An award from the University of Iowa Arts and Humanities Initiative in the summer of 2001 permitted me to carry out research for chapter 10. Ellen Hammond, the former Japanese studies librarian of the University of Iowa, Maeda Naomi of Hanazono University Library, and the librarians of the Kanagawa Prefectural Library and the Kamakura city Library gave me crucial assistance in obtaining needed documents. I also wish to thank the Department of Religious Studies at the University of Iowa for supporting the preparation of the illustrations in this book.

My children, Emilia Roma Sawada and Xavier Gian Sawada, my sisters, Loredana Anderson-Tirro and Michela Anderson, and my parents-in-law, Ryoya and Teruko Sawada, supported and loved me throughout the long years of researching and writing this book. Ryoi-chiro Sawada offered valuable suggestions for difficult readings of Japanese names, conversed with me frequently about my work as it progressed, accompanied me on research jaunts in Japan, and helped me correspond with Japanese scholars when time was at a premium. All the while he remained a lovable father and husband, regularly chauffeuring young musicians and soccer players, taking out the dog, and best of all, bringing me coffee early in the morning.

CONVENTIONS

JAPANESE AND CHINESE names are given in the customary order with surname first. In general, I use the name by which the individual is best known; in some cases I give alternative names in parentheses when the person is first mentioned. After the first use, I refer to those who died before the Meiji Restoration of 1868 by their literary or personal names but to later figures by their surnames, following modern convention. Age is based on traditional Japanese reckoning, which is usually one year more than the Western count. Lunar months are cited for dates prior to January 1, 1873, when the solar calendar came into use in Japan. Romanized terms are Japanese, unless the term applies primarily to a Chinese text or context, in which case the Chinese romanization is given. Common place-names, such as Tokyo, Kyoto, and Kyushu, and well-known proper nouns and terms such as Shinto, Mahayana, and sangha are written without macrons or diacritical marks. All translations are mine, except where noted.

Introduction

THE NINETEENTH CENTURY was an era of extraordinary religious ferment in Japan. Popular thought and culture underwent a surge of creativity, especially during the last several decades of the Tokugawa shogunal order. New religious groups, revivals of older ones, mass pilgrimages, devotional gatherings, and moralist associations of various types proliferated. The religious restlessness, which the governing authorities periodically suppressed with indifferent success, is often interpreted as part of the larger social turmoil that led to the Meiji Restoration or (in the case of movements that first appeared after 1868) as a manifestation of popular dissatisfaction with the dramatic changes that accompanied that transition. In this book, while recognizing the importance of the Restoration as a turning point in the history of nineteenth-century Japan, I concentrate on apparent continuities across the period —specifically, on the ways in which a family of Tokugawa interpretive groups reproduced itself in the Meiji in the form of a political network led by Buddhist and Shinto activists.

Chartier has remarked that intellectual history is the tension between the belief that one can conceptualize the past and the reality that "to conceptualize an object cut out of the past implies that one cannot simultaneously conceptualize all objects."[1] I have certainly cut an object out of the past and thereby sacrificed the rest of the historical brocade to which it "belonged." The object of my conceptualization, however, is not necessarily a single idea or practice, or how this presumably developed over time, but a conversation that actor-thinkers of different affiliations carried on with each other about a common area of concern during the period in question. The participants in this discussion did not necessarily query and respond to each other directly, whether orally or in writing; in some cases they were only dimly aware of each other's existence, if at all. The debate I sketch here is therefore rather disjointed, reduplicative, and sometimes dissonant—more like a prolonged town-hall meeting than an ordered academic panel.

In focusing on this intercourse, my aim is not to present an over-arching history of Japanese religion from the late Tokugawa through the early Meiji, but to explore the religion and thought of this time on the scale of individuals and small groups. My immersion in the particular complements recent European and American studies of the religious phenomena of this pivotal epoch, which until very recently have painted pictures of "Buddhism" and "Shinto" on broad canvases.[2] Instead of assaying a general history of these presumed entities, here I offer detailed analyses of the ideas and actions of single agents and the modest communities they represented. These individuals and their associates maintained some level of contact with each other throughout the nineteenth century. They took up new partners in dialogue, found different opponents to debate, were represented by spokespersons of more than one generation, and ultimately used channels of communication that did not exist at the beginning of the parley. Yet the basic set of players remained connected enough to warrant a construction of their relationship as on-going quite apart from any resonances among the ideas and practices they promoted.

Scholars have long underscored the overlapping or syncretic nature of Japan's religious culture, but in practice historical connections between different systems are often left unexplored in favor of intensive study of a single group or discourse. The neglect of the interstices between past religious formations has led to a disjunction between the common perception of contemporary Japanese religious life as one of variegation and multiple affiliation, on the one hand, and the representation of past phenomena as a set of discrete, insular "traditions," on the other.[3] This book moves in the direction of a multiplex history of Japanese religion by stressing interactions and commonalities between distinct systems and communities in their historical contexts. A metaphor used by Norbert Elias captures the thrust of this model of ongoing interrelatedness. He explains how a set of individuals playing a game together are fully interdependent during that particular game, whether they are positioned as allies or adversaries. By virtue of their interdependence, the players form what Elias calls a "figuration"—that is, a changing pattern of interaction that the players constitute as a whole. Elias uses the specific example of a soccer game to illustrate his meaning:

> We can only understand the constant flux in the grouping of players on one side if we see that the grouping of players on the other side is also in constant flux. If the spectators are to understand and enjoy the game, they must be able to understand how the changing dispositions of each side are interrelated—to follow the fluid figuration of each team....

The process of interaction, in this view, is a fluctuation of power that reaches equilibrium first in one figuration and then in another.[4] The power of the "fluid figurations" treated in this book became palpable in the early Meiji era, when several members of the network in question, though diverse in the details of their religious practices and ideas, formed coalitions based on political and economic interests. Winston Davis has spoken of the centripetal force of multiple religious affiliation in modern Japan;[5] under some conditions, religious difference may serve, paradoxically, as an integrating force in society. The "game" or figuration process described in the following chapters suggests ways in which multireligious connections have contributed to the strengthening of social and political ties in Japan's past. My aim is therefore not only to elucidate intellectual and ritual idiosyncrasies, but also to characterize the broader dispositions of the participants in this evolving network with an eye to how they may or may not have changed over time.[6] The distinctive ideas and practices that the players in this socio-intellectual soccer game produced and reproduced during the nineteenth century differed from and sometimes conflicted with each other, but their creators shared key premises, and in their writings and speeches drew on a common (yet evolving) stock of textual allusions, lexicons, phraseology, and rhetorical patterns. In short, the multiple partners in this conversation relied on a common mental grammar in any particular historical moment—a logic that is marked in their discourse by similar linguistic elements.

This shared logic provides the heuristic framework for my treatment of several interpretive groups. The ideas and practices that were elaborated by the spokespersons of these associations converged on the definition of "personal cultivation" *(mi o osameru; shūshin),* or as some advocates called it, "learning" *(gakumon)*—that is, the moral, ritual, physiological, and/or educational processes by which individuals were believed to attain well-being. The delineation of the enterprise of cultivation is pervasive to the point of banality in nineteenth-century Japanese religious and intellectual discourse, and as such provides a convenient template for gauging differences and affinities between the various interpretive positions of the time. The terminology of personal cultivation is also broad enough to comprehend phenomena that are implicitly channeled into distinct fields of study by the English-language rubrics "religion," "morality," "divination," "health," and "education," but that in Japanese texts of the time are often presented as a unified human endeavor.

The present work encompasses to a modest degree consideration of phenomena pertinent to more than one social stratum. My aim is to infringe as much as possible on the old boundary between "popular" and "learned" culture, a distinction that still endures in the study of Japanese

religion despite the application of more fluid interpretive models in religious histories of other parts of the world. The ideas and actions of
highly educated thinkers, on the one hand, and of semiliterate religious
adepts, on the other, are placed on the same playing field and viewed as
interdependent. I originally aspired to give equal attention to the details
of thought and practice generated or interpreted by persons of a wide
range of social origins within a particular geohistorical context, and to
highlight the movement and interaction among them. While rummaging
through the documents associated with the lesser-known units that I selected for this analysis, however, I realized that the core members of the
understudied groups were not as socially subordinate as I had surmised
from these movements' "popular" image in the few pertinent secondary
accounts available. When examined closely in terms of their relations
with other individuals and communities from the late Tokugawa into the
1880s, the leading practitioners of these systems (those for whom records are available) turn out to be rather well-connected. Village headmen, craftworkers, tradesmen, unemployed samurai, and other middle-
level Tokugawa estates developed into educational elites, some of whom
wielded significant influence in Meiji society.

Since the scope of this study is defined by relevance to a single network of persons and groups, in the course of my research I have ultimately maintained the bias of the traditional intellectual historian for
documents that can be identified with individuals. Nevertheless, with the
exception of the few chapters in which I deliberately discuss the ideas
of well-known scholars and thinkers in order to create an intellectual
backdrop for the analyses of diffusers and dissenters that ensue in each
case, the book draws mostly on interpretations that are valuable for their
representativeness of the general mentality or "world vision" of the particular community in question, rather than for their originality.[7] The best
of such discourses, like that of Carlo Ginzburg's sixteenth-century miller,
directly illuminate how persons of rudimentary education appropriate
and transform the stock of religious knowledge available to them in
their own era.[8] Most of the sources I use in this book, however, are less
vivid in this regard, and indeed somewhat conventional in form: essays,
biographies, records of sermons and speeches, eulogies, personal letters,
the occasional poem or playscript, government documents, political pro-
nouncements, denominational registers, and newspaper articles. The
ideas and practices elaborated and recorded in these texts do not directly
reveal the appropriations of the "masses." The voices in the texts interpreted here are for the most part one step or more away from the interests of the less articulate people who made up the larger chorus of the
time. Nevertheless, precisely because of their authors' intermediary position in the socio-educational process, some of the records left behind by

the spokespersons treated here (especially those of the Tokugawa era) shed light on forms of practice and thought that never came to be associated with the mainstream religious and educational institutions of modern Japan, and that are accordingly under studied today. Although the available information about these little-known interpretive systems in their formative stages is fragmentary, it provides a modicum of insight into a side of Japanese religious history that tends to be left out or sublimated in modern textbook accounts. I should add that the absence in my later chapters of extended analysis of these groups' practices and theories marks my own perception of the displacement of the religious creativity of the earlier practitioners by the ideological frenzy of the systemizers and proselytizers who succeeded them in the Meiji era.

The debate over personal improvement that transpired in nineteenth-century Japan is illustrated with specific reference to a social circuit that operated mostly (though not exclusively) in the Edo/Tokyo and eastern Kanagawa areas. In order to display the duration and range of this network, the book adopts a "skip-stop" approach, dwelling in turn on religious and ideological discourses produced in three distinct subcontexts (roughly, 1830s–1860s; 1870s–early 1880s; and late 1880s –early 1890s). The first part of the book describes systems of moral and religious development that were elaborated by precursors of this circuit from about the Tenpō era (1830–1843) to the Bakumatsu (1853–1867). By way of introducing the intellectual climate in which these proposals emerged, in chapter 1 I sketch the textualist trends that marked the Confucian scholarly world during the late Tokugawa and the related ambivalence of diverse educators about the ultimate meaningfulness of the classical Chinese texts. In chapters 2 and 3 I consider three cultivation programs, two of which originated in divination systems (Tōkyūjutsu and Nanboku physiognomy), while the third became a "new religion" (Misogikyō). I present a considerable amount of historical information in narrative form about each of these little-known communities and their teachings, but return in each case to the ways in which their spokespersons redefined the Confucian-associated enterprise of "learning" to accord with their own notions of practicable self-improvement. The available historical sources for these groups (especially the first two) are limited to a few unannotated, uncritical editions of primary texts, but taken together their content suggests characteristic patterns in the thought and practices of nonmainstream interpretive communities during a critical phase in the history of early modern Japan.

The survey of Tokugawa groups is followed by a transitional discussion in chapter 4 of the institutional and ideological processes of the first Meiji years that shifted the parameters of the continuing debate over personal development and social well-being. Notions of practicality or "practical learning" *(jitsugaku)* took on a pressing interest for so-called enlightenment thinkers, government officials, educators, and newspaper writers. I describe in this chapter how "learning" in the sense of adult moral cultivation was displaced in the 1870s—both institutionally, in the Meiji higher education system, and discursively, by modern constructs of meaning such as "education" *(kyōiku)* and "religion" *(shūkyō)*. In a related process, both critics and supporters of "Confucianism" *(Jukyō)* argued that it was completely distinct from the phenomenon that was now designated "religion." In the last part of the chapter I cite the fate during these years of Shingaku, a syncretic religious movement that had flourished in the late Tokugawa period, in order to illustrate the implications of this renegotiation of terms for unofficial concepts of learning that did not fit the categories of the new age.

Chapters 5 and 6 pursue the quest for practical forms of cultivation into the world of established Buddhism. My concern here is not to characterize the state of Meiji Buddhism in general, nor to explicate the ideas and practices of the particular Buddhist system that I discuss, Rinzai Zen; excellent Japanese and Western scholarship on these topics is already available. I aim rather to illuminate the way in which representatives of a single, well-established Buddhist community assimilated elements from contemporary discourse about practicality into their own debates over monastic education, on the one hand, and the role of the lay practitioner, on the other.[9] Chapter 5 examines the "practical" Zen education that Imakita Kōsen, the abbot of the Kamakura temple, Engakuji, proposed in the early Meiji period in response to the current vogue for "doctrinal" or Western-influenced utilitarian studies. Chapters 6 and 7 transport the discussion from the educational to the social dimensions of the Engakuji program as it developed during the 1870s and 1880s. I suggest that two East Asian models of human fulfillment, the Confucian gentleman-official and the Buddhist lay bodhisattva, coalesced in a new idealization of the lay practitioner during the mid-Meiji. It is well-known that laypeople played a prominent role in the reinvigoration of Japanese Buddhism in the decades following the anti-Buddhist drive of the first Meiji years. My emphasis here is that the rise of lay activism was not simply the result of a reconstruction strategy devised by clerical leaders in the aftermath of the anti-Buddhist campaign; it was also driven by an elite form of voluntarism that had precedents in Tokugawa systems of social and religious practice.

The growing prominence of lay forms of religious life in eighteenth- and nineteenth-century Japan was part of a general trend toward greater public access to religious knowledge. In the late Edo period, people played an increasingly active role in creating and controlling their own religious lives, both inside and outside the clerical and scholarly establishment. This trend was marked, for example, by the multiplication of religious associations or *kō*—groups of laypeople who met together to study, pray, or practice rituals. The development of these lay groups facilitated voluntary participation in religion by individuals of various social origins, though usually still within the larger administrative hierarchy of the established institutions. The gradual spread of ways of thinking that emphasized the moral autonomy of the individual and the value of communalism, whether mediated by Confucian-inspired educators, rural nativists, or divinely inspired leaders of new religions, also marked a rising discomfort with clerical and scholastic restrictions on religious knowledge.[10] The lay appropriation of ritual and educational functions that had traditionally been reserved to priests and scholars in fact characterizes several new movements of the time. Many early-nineteenth-century groups presented themselves as nearly autonomous subworlds that downplayed reliance on the expertise of Buddhist, school-Shinto, and Confucian professionals—figures who for the most part were formally associated with the Tokugawa order.[11] The new forms of practice did not require the direct intervention in religious life of ritual experts, much less entrance into a monastery or other formal training; ordinary family life and work were often depicted in popular discourse of the time as the ideal context for personal and social improvement.

The development of a new level of lay religious participation made itself felt in the monastically oriented Buddhist sects especially after the institutional changes of the first Meiji years. The process was complex. One cannot speak of an anticlerical spirit in the Tokugawa and early Meiji periods along the lines of the early modern European phenomenon; what emerges in nineteenth-century Japan is not massive lay opposition to priestly control of socioreligious practices, but rather an overall reinterpretation by both the clerical and lay sectors of their mutual relations —a process that was greatly accelerated by direct government intervention.[12] Each phase of this reinterpretation involved economic, territorial, gender, and other issues specific to the sectarian context. Chapters 6 and 7 show how some of these issues came into play in the development of the lay program at the Rinzai temple, Engakuji.

The successors of the nonmainstream religious and divinatory groups that are treated in the early chapters of this book rearranged themselves in the Meiji under the auspices of "sect Shinto" *(shūha Shintō)*. The conventional view of the so-called Shinto sects is that they were artificial groupings, marshaled together in response to the centralizing pressures of the Meiji state. In chapter 8 I stress, rather, the voluntaristic dimension of the sect-Shinto phenomenon, as illustrated by the formation and early history of a sect called Shintō Taiseikyō. My larger purpose in chapters 8, 9, and 10 is in fact to delineate the spontaneous participation across religious boundaries of diverse proponents of personal cultivation (whether associated with a long-established Buddhist monastery or with a newly constructed Shinto sect) in the ideological coalition building that swept over Japan in the years just prior to the establishment of the Meiji constitution and the national diet. Ideals of personal development that prevailed among the educated classes in Japan invariably included the notion that, for men, moral cultivation should culminate in public service, especially government service. In the Meiji context, political activity, whether in or out of the government, was part of everyday life for many educated males who lived in the vicinity of the capital.

The discussion in the last part of this book accordingly shifts gears, moving away from the earlier description of religious and educational programs to the identification of their spokespersons' political dispositions and ideologizing activities. While the early-nineteenth-century participants in this evolving figuration debated the relative efficacy of concrete practices of cultivation, their Meiji successors concentrated on how to spread ideologies of personal and social improvement. In chapter 9 I take up this aspect of the Engakuji community, characterizing diverse currents in its fluid political culture by sampling the organizational and ideological initiatives of its leading members and associates during the early Meiji decades. I highlight especially the crescendo of conservative voices in this circle in the 1880s, which arose in response to the liberalizing and Westernizing arguments that had dominated public discourse in the preceding years. The chapter concludes with a discussion of the informal political cooperation of key members of both the Buddhist and Shinto-associated groups treated earlier. The collaboration of the leading members of this circuit (another round in a figurational spiral that originated in the late Tokugawa period) suggests that multireligious groupings, ostensibly outside the public domain, functioned as effective political forces in late-nineteenth-century Japanese society.

Chapter 10 pushes the story line a few years further, describing how the members of this socioreligious network, along with other moralists of the day, defined their views on the correct path to human fulfillment by demonizing the teachings of less conventional religious interpreters. The least orthodox member of the Taisei organization, Renmonkyō, became a prime target in this polemical process. A popular healing movement brought to the Tokyo area by a little-educated woman from Kyushu, Renmonkyō was systematically discredited in the 1890s by a brash new Meiji press in collaboration with religious professionals across the sectarian spectrum. The campaign against this movement (which later ceased to exist) and other new religions of the time helped form modern journalistic conventions for writing about religious phenomena that are still employed in Japan today (most notably in the copious coverage of the new religion AUM Shinrikyō, whose members carried out the notorious sarin gas attack in the Tokyo subway system in 1995). The drive to disband Renmonkyō more than a century ago marks the foundational role of the Japanese press in constructing modern notions of religion and morality. It also invites consideration of the peculiar and often insidious relationship between the construction of religious orthodoxy and the rise of nationalism that is so familiar to us today across cultural contexts. In the early nineteenth century, the Tokugawa shogunate had swiftly suppressed movements characterized by devotional excitement, charismatic leadership, healing practices, female authority, and, above all, the potential to control large numbers of people. In 1894, as Japan was poised to enter its first modern war, ordinary citizens inspired by the vision of a powerful nation followed the lead of journalists and established religious leaders in voluntarily excluding these elements from their definition of an acceptable path of personal cultivation.

CHAPTER 1

The Fertility of Dead Words

THE ASSUMPTION THAT the psychological, physiological, social, and cosmic conditions of an individual's existence were closely related to each other, with changes in the more personal or particular spheres reverberating progressively in the larger, more universal ones, was rarely disputed in late Tokugawa religious discourse. For many, the key to an auspicious existence at all levels was the reality closest at hand—their own inner state or moral condition. Others felt that although one's state of mind was indeed paramount, it was in turn affected by other, more external aspects of existence. Even these components of reality, however, were still "personal" enough to be susceptible to individual control— here I mean especially bodily processes, such as eating, breathing, and sexual intercourse. To be sure, many ordinary citizens believed that the larger levels of their universe, particularly the configuration of cosmic forces or deities under which they purportedly lived, powerfully affected their personal situations; but at the same time they often conceived of these forces as somehow amenable to their own actions and attitudes. Personal development invariably occupied a prominent place in the theories and praxes advocated by religious spokespersons of the time.

The quest for well-being played itself out in a spectrum of diverse discourses, each of which represented a slightly different combination of emphases on state of mind, health, social relations, and material welfare. In this and the following chapters I shall introduce several theories of practice, all of which purported to offer Tokugawa subjects the possibility of better controlling their lives (and, ultimately, of benefiting others). These proposals do not represent a broad sampling of all the systems that arose during this time, but they do illustrate specific fields of concern that were shared by members of the middle strata of late Tokugawa society (shopkeepers, traders, landed peasants, village headmen, and samurai in reduced circumstances). Common among these groups, whether samurai or commoner, were a number of identifiable preoccupations. It is often pointed out, for example, that a sanctification of economy and work, or of "common values" such as loyalty and filial piety, was a characteristic feature of the texts produced and consumed by members of these sectors.[1]

In the following pages I highlight a related but slightly different motif in the religious discourses of the time—a strong interest in the practical, accompanied by an ambivalence toward textual learning and language. Exaltation of practicality was nearly universal in the lower and middle estates of later Tokugawa Japan. Systems of knowledge advocated by professional scholars (whether Confucian, Buddhist, nativist, or other) were often characterized in popular literature as dull and irrelevant. A teaching of personal cultivation that did not offer a workable schedule of disciplines for attaining well-being did not easily gain affirmation in these sectors. Particularly in view of the economic instability and social unease that characterized the late Tokugawa world, seemingly concrete, reliable methods to preserve personal tranquility, health, and, if possible, wealth, exerted more appeal than ever.

Distrust of language was the corollary of this concern with practice. For some, all linguistic expression was at issue, but most focused their discontent on the language that dominated the education and intellectual discourse of male elites of the time—the Chinese of the Confucian classics. The tendency to deprecate Confucian textual language had well-established precedents in the interpretations of Motoori Norinaga (1730–1801), Hirata Atsutane (1776–1843), and several other nativist (Kokugaku) thinkers. In the eighteenth and early nineteenth centuries, nativist scholars argued that language usage was the key to bringing about transformation in other spheres of reality. Harootunian has spoken in this regard of the nativists' "linguistic alienation"; it seemed to them that language had become a "commodity" that was used without an awareness of the conditions under which it originated.[2] Their polemics were of course directed entirely at the Chinese linguistic system and Sino-Japanese locutions. Motoori Norinaga was persuaded that Chinese textual learning obstructed understanding of the way of the gods. He characterized the foundation of Japanese language as "living words" *(ikita kotoba),* whereas foreign languages such as Chinese, he averred, were composed of "dead words" *(shinda kotoba).*[3] Atsutane for his part believed that linguistic usages were intimately related to daily practices and customs, and thus significantly influenced people's thinking and behavior. Chinese, in his view, was a set of static and opaque ideographs that had had a detrimental impact on the Japanese people, preventing them from grasping the sacred truths with which the gods had endowed ordinary life and work.[4] The nativists' linguistic alienation was therefore closely connected to their view of learning *(gakumon).* Some of Norinaga's followers maintained that Japan appeared to possess no ancient learning of its own only because of the conventional definition of learning as Confucian or Buddhist.[5] In their view, true learning was a natural understanding endowed in human beings by the gods; the abstract knowledge of the Chinese texts was irrelevant to the concerns of common people.

Harootunian suggests in this regard that "the content of life [the nativists] were defining related to the life of the ordinary person, who had remained outside the Neo-Confucian field of knowledge."[6] The implication is that the latter field was inhabited only by those who did *not* live the "life of an ordinary person"—members of the upper or samurai classes, who constituted a minority of the Tokugawa population. In contrast to the nativists and their constituents (in the nineteenth century, mostly peasant leaders), in this view people who created and utilized Neo-Confucian forms of knowledge (and thus presumably cultivated its "field") were somehow oblivious to the "texture of daily life." Harootunian clarifies his perspective further in the following passage:

> In the late-Edo period, activity everywhere attested to and signified how theory was contradicted at every turn by experience, so that it could no longer be discounted as mere anomaly.... Neo-Confucianism, in whatever form, sought to resolve the contradiction between representation and experience by heaping theory upon theory to bridge the widening separation between principle or reason *(ri)* and social life.[7]

The difficulty here is the parameters of "Neo-Confucianism, in whatever form." In the remainder of this chapter I will seek to clarify these parameters by sampling the discourses of selected representatives of the late-Edo Confucian world.

Textualists and Eclectics

The Japanese Confucian schools as a whole, not only Neo-Confucianism in the sense of the Zhu Xi and Wang Yangming schools, produced "theory upon theory" informed by one or another textual hermeneutic.[8] Textual studies or textualism˙ (in this context, the close, even critical analysis of the language of the Chinese classics) was by now firmly entrenched in many Confucian academies. A wave of textualist scholars of various stripes had appeared beginning in the mid-eighteenth century in the aftermath of the so-called ancient learning (Kogaku) movement associated with Itō Jinsai (1627–1705) and Ogyū Sorai (1666–1728).[9] These later scholars were generally critical of Sorai's ideas, although their own emphases on philologically correct readings of ancient Chinese texts were invariably indebted to his approach. They associated themselves with such movements as Kochūgaku (ancient commentary studies) or, especially in the Bunka and Bunsei periods (1804–1829), Kōshōgaku (evidential studies).[10]

The sheer number and accessibility of the Chinese texts in Japan had burgeoned by this time. Numerous editions of primary works had been imported earlier in the period, and later Tokugawa students could also consult multiple Japanese commentaries on these earlier imports. After the emergence of the ancient learning movement, many Japanese Confucian scholars became less focused on the Four Books and other standard Neo-Confucian compilations, and more interested in producing their own commentaries on the Five Classics and other ancient Chinese texts. Several, notably Minagawa Kien (1734–1807) and Ōta Kinjō (1765–1825), put out their own annotated editions of the Chinese classics.[11] The shogunal college in Edo, for its part, sponsored publication of about two hundred classical texts between the beginning of the nineteenth century and the Meiji Restoration; in 1842 it also ordered the domains to publish official versions of the Chinese classics.[12]

This material and intellectual drive for textual accuracy, regularized in academies that promoted exegetical analysis, engendered a proportional reaction. Some of the early proponents of evidential studies grew disenchanted with the emphasis on textual analysis that they had inherited from scholars of the Qing period (1644–1912). In his late years Ōta Kinjō took to calling the evidentialist approach to learning "bookstore studies" *(shoshi no gaku)*. It seemed to him that his evidentialist colleagues were more interested in issues of scholarly method than in what he considered the ultimate aim of learning: moral practice.[13] Kinjō had criticized Zhu Xi–style Neo-Confucian learning in his youth, but he now reversed himself and promoted "real" or "practical learning" *(jitsugaku)* in opposition to the textually based activities that he associated with Sorai's followers.[14]

> The [teaching of] rites and music that Sorai advocated cannot be put into practice today; thus, although it appears to be practical learning, its substance *(jitsu)* is in fact empty theory *(kūron)*. Lecturing on moral principles [on the other hand] appears to be empty and abstract, but [the principles] can be put into practice today; hence they constitute the *true* practical learning.[15]

Kinjō was not alone among late Tokugawa textualists in pointing out the impracticability of the learning in which they had been trained. The Kyoto scholar Igai Keisho (1761–1845) was also schooled in the critical textual methods of the time and expressed dissatisfaction with contemporary articulations of Zhu Xi Neo-Confucianism.[16] Yet he ultimately returned to the paradigm of the *Great Learning (Daxue)*—an emblem of the Song redaction of the classics that Jinsai and Sorai had discredited: "In my view, the path of the ancient [sage-]kings and Confucius is simply to place priority on moral relations and to practice correcting one's mind, cultivating one's person, bringing order to one's family, governing the nation, and bringing peace to the empire."[17]

This reversion by post-Sorai scholars to a morally oriented interpretation of the Confucian classics did not necessarily translate into support for practical programs of personal development for the common people. Kinjō reportedly opposed the spread in Izu of the Confucian-inspired religious movement Shingaku on the grounds that there was no need for a separate school that proclaimed itself the "learning of the mind (or heart)" *(shingaku),* since Confucian study itself was the "learning of the mind."[18] A more practicable system of personal cultivation that could be carried out by people unversed in the Chinese classics was apparently not within the scope of his *"true* practical learning." "Practicality" in this sense remained primarily a theoretical concern for Kinjō and numerous other Confucian scholars of the time.

Igai Keisho, on the other hand, perceived a connection between popular forms of moral improvement and his own emphasis on the experiential dimension of learning. Although he cited such texts as the *Great Learning,* he suspected that only a few people were capable of implementing its vision at the highest levels. In the end Keisho concluded that "real learning" consisted in working hard at one's occupation.[19] He believed that the Shingaku teachings of Teshima Toan (1718–1786), which he had studied in his youth, encouraged this more realistic approach to self-discipline.[20] Yet by 1833 Keisho had decided that even the Shingaku teachers were failing in their practice of the "art of the mind" *(shinjutsu)* and had lapsed into a superficial, secondhand type of learning *(kōji no gaku).*[21] He agreed with Kinjō, in any case, that a separation had taken place between book learning and practice in their time that was not true to the Confucian spirit. Both scholars attributed the origins of this separation to the vogue for text-critical methods to which they themselves had once contributed.

I cite these views simply to highlight a general disposition among Confucian scholars of the time to characterize the perceived decline in moral practice as a legacy of the Sorai school. It was thus not only "Neo-Confucianism" that sought to resolve the perceived separation between theory and experience in the late Edo period, but the erstwhile followers of Sorai. In fact, the spokespersons of several interpretive and religious communities premised their programs on the notion of a disjunction between social reality and theoretical activity (or between "practical" and "empty" learning).

Contemporary Confucian scholarship was criticized in several quarters of society, not only for its overpreoccupation with texts, but also for its fragmentation into numerous schools based on trivial theoretical differences. The rise of so-called eclectic studies or Setchūgaku in the late Tokugawa probably contributed to this perception of divisiveness. Ironically, the eclectic movement first arose among Confucian scholars as a strategy for dealing with their own intellectual multiplicity. The literal meaning of *setchū* is to decide the mean or middle between things that are perceived as either excessive or deficient, particularly between different theoretical points of view. In practice the *setchūgaku* approach was not a random grouping of unrelated ideas, but rather a process of choice based on the individual scholar's particular criteria. The eclectics advocated selecting the most appropriate interpretation of the ancient texts through judicious consideration of all the pertinent commentarial traditions, regardless of school. In his *Keigi setchū* (A Reconciliation of Interpretations of the Classics, 1764), usually cited as the inaugural work in this movement, Inoue Kinga (1739–1784) thus proposes his own views after comparing and selecting ideas from the works of Zhu Xi, Wang Yangming, Itō Jinsai, and Ogyū Sorai.[22] His contemporary Katayama Kenzan (1730–1782), another former member of the Sorai school, adopted a similar procedure.[23]

The idea of evaluating the contrasting textual commentaries of the time offered late Tokugawa students a method for coping with the proliferating Confucian discourses. In the final analysis, the criteria for selecting and synthesizing existing interpretations were necessarily subjective. However, by undergoing the process of surveying the field and developing a critical perspective on a range of scholarly proposals, the eclectics were forced to come to terms with opposing positions and to articulate their own thinking on the matter. Moreover, these scholars were under less pressure to exhibit loyalty to school lineages; their constant comparing, selecting, and borrowing paradoxically led them to establish relatively independent positions.[24] Many set up their own academies and trained their students to use similar methods of textual interpretation: whether strictly evidentialist or simply eclectic, the use of comparative, multitextual approaches to Confucian learning remained popular throughout the rest of the Tokugawa period. The number of eclectic schools steadily increased in the last decades of the shogunate — a well-known example is the Kangien academy, established by Hirose Tansō (1782–1856), which attracted over four thousand students between 1801 and 1871.[25] According to Tansō's own account, during his time "among well-known Confucian scholars, seven or eight out of ten were [proponents of] Setchūgaku."[26]

Reading Wordless Books

The tendency to select from among a variety of interpretations of an accepted canon was not peculiar to the eclectics and/or textualists; a great deal of interchange took place across school lines among the older Japanese Confucian lineages as well. In the aftermath of ancient learning, advocates of both Yōmeigaku (Wang Yangming learning) and Shushigaku (Zhu Xi learning) explicitly acknowledged their common concern with personal cultivation, even though they disagreed sharply on several specific issues.[27] Many Neo-Confucian scholars of both schools studied under the shogunal school director in Edo, Satō Issai (1772–1859), who "never accepted the notion of a single lineage or school," and who purportedly held to the ideas of Wang Yangming privately, even though he officially professed the learning of the Cheng brothers and Zhu Xi, which the late Tokugawa regime sanctioned.[28] Like Ōta Kinjō and other disenchanted evidentialists, but with greater intensity, Wang and Zhu followers of this period continually voiced the refrain that too much concern with textual niceties had led to moral turpitude among their professional colleagues. A number of these reformists proposed rehashed versions of the "learning of the mind" (Ch. *xinxue*, J. *shingaku*), a system of inner discipline that had occupied Neo-Confucian scholars in the Song, Ming, Yi Korea, and earlier Tokugawa Japan.[29] Unlike earlier versions of mind learning, however, the late Tokugawa interest in the spiritual authority of the subject defined itself in relation to the recent wave of encyclopedic, objectivist analyses of ancient classical texts.[30]

Satō Issai typifies this response to the trends of the time.[31] "People today read books containing words with their eyes," he reflected, "as a result they are held back by the words and are incapable of proceeding beyond them. What they should do is read wordless books with their hearts. Then their self-understanding will be [as deep as] as a cave."[32] Issai disapproved of contemporary scholars' intellectualism and their penchant for fixating on and defending one particular school. He reiterated the familiar Neo-Confucian cautions against overemphasis on book learning (and its associated evil, academic disputation), depicting these habits as veritable threats to the individual's personal integrity. Issai's disciple, Yoshimura Shūyō (1797–1866), formulated guidelines for reading books that faithfully pinpoint his teacher's concerns:

(1) Do not fall into the pettiness of textual exegesis.
(2) Do not establish school views.
(3) Do not rely on the minute details of intellectual understanding.[33]

In his youth, Issai had studied under the creative textualist scholar

Minagawa Kien, among others; he was not oblivious to the philological interests of his times. His statement about "wordless books" is not a denial of the value of book learning, but simply a reaffirmation of the priority of the personal dimension of learning. Unlike his textualist peers, Issai felt that reading the classics was primarily a means of dispelling erroneous thoughts (he also promoted writing as a method of self-reflection).[34] The ultimate aim of learning, as he implies above, was the acquisition of a knowledge that was beyond words and texts. He asserted that the Confucian tradition included both a "transmitted" (articulated) dimension and an "untransmitted" (unarticulated) dimension, and that the latter was more fundamental. "The untransmitted tradition," he noted, "is the mind, not words."[35]

In his lifework, *Genshi shiroku* (A Statement of My Aspirations: Four Records), Issai repeatedly takes up the subjective dimension of personal cultivation and the value of individual experience, implying almost a "self-esteem" mentality: one must respect oneself in order to become an authentic human being. The shogunal college professor clearly echoes earlier Neo-Confucians when he speaks of "studying for the sake of oneself" rather than for the sake of impressing others, but as Sagara Tōru notes, Issai pushes the argument for individuality further, insisting that a man who is committed to learning should rely entirely on himself, not on others—an approach that Issai contrasts with the "learning of recent times."[36]

The insistence on self-reliance was not simply a regurgitation of past Confucian discourses on this theme (which, to be sure, were multiple), but a conscious response to what Issai considered to be the superficiality of current scholarship.[37] Mere textual erudition, regardless of its purported accuracy, could not guarantee the maintenance of physical health, economic prosperity, and political order—ideals that were increasingly elusive during the late Tokugawa. Issai argued that the progress of affairs in society and/or the phenomenal world depended on one's internal state. "If you lose your self," Issai warned, "then you lose people. If you lose people, then you lose things."[38] This kind of progressive linkage of the inner and outer, the personal and the social, is, needless to say, a hallmark of the mode of thinking outlined in such Neo-Confucian classics as the *Great Learning*. Amid the diverse Confucian perspectives that circulated in the late Edo, not to mention the proliferation of nativist, Western-learning, and other intellectual and religious proposals that accompanied the gradual dissolution of the shogunal order, the deliberate return by some scholars to this well-worn language of personal cultivation was an attempt to maintain a plausible world of meaning within the growing plurality of interpretations.

Disenchantment with the philological orientation and divisiveness of the Confucian schools was expressed, then, not only by late nativists, but also by intellectuals who were central figures in the Tokugawa establishment, whether they were employed (like Issai) by the shogunate itself or (like Kinjō and many other Confucian scholars) by the domains. Moreover, the leaders of mainstream educational and religious institutions that were *not* formally identified with Confucian studies expressed similar disaffection with contemporary intellectual trends. Imakita Kōsen (Sōon, 1816–1892) is a case in point. Trained in Chinese studies under a Sorai disciple (Fujizawa Tōgai, 1794–1864), Imakita later rejected the textualist approach and began to explore the theories of Zhu Xi and other Neo-Confucian thinkers. In 1834 Imakita opened a Confucian studies school in Osaka, where he propagated his own "eclectic learning" *(setchūgaku)*. During these years of study and teaching, Imakita was exposed to a wide range of approaches to the Chinese classics, and ultimately developed a dim view of the contemporary Confucian world.[39] After five years of teaching, he reportedly encountered the well-known Zen Buddhist saying, "specially transmitted outside the teachings, without setting up written words" *(kyōge betsuden furyū monji)*, which seems to imply that the truth cannot be fully communicated in words (or, more broadly, intellectual discourse), and that in order to grasp it, one must forgo reliance on the authority of any text. According to his own account, Imakita felt that this passage represented exactly the perspective he had been seeking; soon afterward he became a Zen monk (1840).[40]

After about eighteen years of training, Imakita was appointed abbot of Yōkōji, a temple in Iwakuni (in today's Yamaguchi prefecture).[41] During this period the Zen master recorded his view of the contemporary state of Confucian scholarship in his well-known work, *Zenkai ichiran* (One Wave in the Zen Sea), a Buddhist apologetical treatise addressed to the Confucian-schooled daimyo and samurai-officials of Iwakuni domain.[42] The text confirms that Imakita's negative view of the intellectual climate of the time, like that of his fellow eclectics, was fueled by his reaction to Sorai-style textualism and the divisions to which it seemed to have given rise in the Confucian scholarly community. The abbot complained that scholars of the day were excessively absorbed in literary activities and as a result failed to cultivate "the reality" *(jitsu)* of moral values. These scholars were incapable of moving beyond their trivializing, abstruse exegetical methods, and as a result, he concluded, their teachings would never satisfy people.[43] Imakita also perceived the Confucian world as hopelessly divided; scholars merely elaborated their peculiar theories and were intolerant of those with whom they disagreed.[44] Not unlike Satō Issai, the Zen master felt that Confucian learning had declined in Japan since the time of Nakae Tōju (1608–1648) and Fujiwara Seika (1561–1619); especially with the emergence of ancient learning scholars Itō Jinsai, Itō Tōgai (1670–1738), and Ogyū Sorai, he asserted, "the learning of the art of the mind *(shinjutsu no gaku)* became obsolete and rote learning developed." Lost in superficial and frivolous matters (textual exegesis and literary composition), scholars had grown proud and self-indulgent, and no longer bothered to cultivate their own moral integrity, much less edify others. From Imakita's perspective, contemporary Confucian scholars' priority was simply to attain philological and literary skills; they pursued no program of personal discipline to back up these external types of study.[45]

The abbot further lamented that scholars and exegetes influenced by Sorai had lost appreciation, both aesthetic and spiritual, of the transverbal truth that he believed was at the heart of Confucius' message. In *Zenkai ichiran* Imakita cites the passage of the *Analects* (11:26) in which one of the sage's disciples pinpoints an aspect of the Confucian path that is often overlooked:

> [Tian said:] "In late spring, after the spring clothes have been newly made, I should like, together with five or six adults and six or seven boys, to go bathing in the River Yi and enjoy the breeze on the Rain Altar, and then to go home chanting poetry."
> The Master sighed and said, "I am all in favour of Tian."[46]

The Zen teacher interprets this anecdote as evidence that the ineffable, delightful realm of truth is accessible in the Confucian mode of being as well the Buddhist.[47] It was especially important to the erstwhile Confucian scholar to persuade his readers that the Zen transmission "beyond words" was identical to *authentic* Confucianism. In response to a rhetorical questioner in *Zenkai ichiran* who asks why Imakita downplays the Confucian emphasis on "relying on [book] learning and enjoying the arts," the Zen master retorts that these activities are merely part of the "elementary stage" of the path (to Buddhahood). He directs the questioner's attention instead to what he sees as the nondiscursive dimension of Confucian learning: "The most profound teaching of the Confucian school consists in clarifying the virtuous nature. Therefore, its true meaning does not lie in books."[48]

This interpretation of Confucius' message is confirmed, paradoxically, by the texts. Confucius' admission that he was not "the kind of man who learns widely and retains what he has learned in his mind," but simply possessed "a single thread binding it all together" is proof, according to the abbot, that the followers of Confucius, like those of the Buddha, have a "special transmission outside the teachings."[49] This creative reading of Confucius culminates in the Zen master's gloss on *Analects* 17:19:[50]

The Master said, "I am thinking of giving up speech." Zigong said, "If you did not speak, what would there be for us, your disciples, to transmit?" The Master said, "What does Heaven ever say? Yet there are four seasons going round and there are the hundred things coming into being. What does Heaven ever say?"[51]

Imakita concludes that this passage conveys the gist of Confucius' teaching: the truth, in the end, is beyond verbal discourse.[52] Just as the sage's "single thread" was not merely an oblique reference to the fundamental virtues of the way, so Confucius' impulse to "give up speech" was not simply a reverent acknowledgment of the marvelous efficacy of the natural order. The Zen master depicts these and other famous passages in the *Analects* as signposts to a religious truth that is free of all linguistic restrictions.

Pursuing the same line of reasoning, Imakita further implies in *Zenkai ichiran* that the Zen message could be a critical lifesaver for the community of scholars who, in the aftermath of the Sorai school's textual-ritual extravagances, had lost sight of the true Confucius.[53] In his critique of late Tokugawa Confucian trends, Imakita indeed presents himself as an authentic Confucian who is seeking to revive a nearly moribund system of spirituality. He takes it upon himself to shore up the deteriorating Confucian world with Zen Buddhism and documents his qualification for this salvific role by means of his own biography. Having found his own first inspiration in the Confucian way, he avows, he could not bear to sit back and watch its "system of the mind" fall out of use in the world.[54] In a gloss on a passage from the *Doctrine of the Mean* *(Zhongyong)*, Imakita uses an anecdote about his early Zen training to illustrate the vital role that Confucian texts can play in the Buddhist life of faith:

The Master [Confucius] said, "Men all say, 'We are wise'; but being driven forward and taken in a net, a trap, or a pitfall, they know not how to escape. Men all say, 'We are wise'; but happening to choose the course of the Mean, they are not able to keep it for a round month."[55]

Master [Daisetsu Jōen, 1797–1855] asked me, "If suddenly an enormously powerful demon-king caught you from behind and threw you into a fire-hole that was erupting in flames, how would you get yourself out?" I could not answer, and the sweat caused by my shame ran down my back. I agonized over this for many days. One day, all of a sudden, I recalled the [above] words, "net, trap, or pitfall," and had a tremendous insight. It was like drinking sweet nectar. Then I entered Master's room and presented my understanding. The Master laughed quietly and rested. At that point, I understood privately that the Sage had helped me along my path of learning.[56]

Imakita adds that he did not understand the last part of the above passage from the *Mean* until after he completed several *more* years of Zen practice. At that point he fully realized that Confucius' words were "not easy" to grasp.[57] In other words, according to this testimony, Zen practice is a clearinghouse for genuine engagement with the words of Confucius. In order to understand the full meaning of the Confucian teaching, one needs to undergo a regimen of meditation and consultation with a Zen master.

In response to the philological currents that coursed through academies in the late Tokugawa, intellectuals across religious and scholastic affiliations argued for a source of interpretive authority that transcended the limitations of the Chinese exegetical enterprise. Disenchanted Confucian textualists and eclectics like Ōta Kinjō, Igai Keisho, and Katayama Kenzan called for a return to personal moral cultivation. Satō Issai, a leading figure in the Tokugawa educational establishment, publicly promoted an orthodox course of Neo-Confucian book learning but wrote profusely about the ultimate value of inner personal experience. Zen master Imakita Kōsen, abbot of a temple patronized by domain officials, wisely affirmed the universality of the teachings of the sage but at the same time proclaimed that a Zen-type "special transmission" was the only hope for the survival of authentic Confucian learning. All of these figures were "organic intellectuals" in Gramsci's sense; they drew on their textual expertise to elaborate values deemed integral to the dominant social order, and in their role as professional educators they helped develop and administer its institutions.[58] Yet the perception among these and other thinker-administrators that contemporary scholars "let their minds become drunk with ornate words and make their living from perusing literature" (as Imakita put it) ironically fueled an intense spate of arguments that the truth of the classic texts was not really susceptible to linguistic analysis.[59]

It was thus not "Neo-Confucianism" in some abstract, generalized sense, but specific individuals, often associated with official or semi-official institutions, who "sought to resolve the contradiction between representation and experience by heaping theory upon theory."[60] The identity of the presumed entity "Neo-Confucianism" must be extended still further, however. For during the second half of the Tokugawa period, spokespersons of a wide range of intellectual and religious views that circulated outside formal institutions were actively involved in the same discursive quest. "Neo-Confucianism," in this sense, must be stretched to include interpretive systems that were propagated, not only by intellectuals educated in self-identified Confucian schools, but by humbler thinkers as well. The latter also associated their teachings with the program of personal cultivation set out in Zhu Xi's editions of the classics, though far more loosely.

Dead Words and Living Words

As rural nativists, Shingaku teachers, and street preachers of sundry affiliations often reminded their audiences during the late Edo period, for most people the Chinese texts were indeed abstract to the point of insignificance. Harootunian aptly says that "[r]eading the Great Learning provided only the rules with which to govern and tranquilize all under heaven."[61] Precisely because of this schematic, abstract quality, however, the oft-recited passages of the *Great Learning* and other Neo-Confucian canons maintained a powerful presence in popular discourse in the late Tokugawa. Many of the "small" thinkers of this time shared the nativists' concern with the inadequacy of Confucian linguistic usage. They concurred that Neo-Confucian *gakumon* (learning) was unworkable, and similarly envisioned systems of knowledge that cohered with natural processes and ordinary work rhythms. In the process of formulating their own proposals, these popularizers also "reworked" earlier cultural traditions that were on the margins of the official Tokugawa ideology.[62] Yet it was because Neo-Confucian learning involved, in Harootunian's parlance, "concentrating on the totality" and the "privileging of the paradigmatic," that these independent thinkers were able to identify with as well as exploit that learning.[63] Several religious and prognosticatory thinkers valued the *Great Learning* as a kind of blueprint for their own non-Confucian programs—a phenomenon that will occupy us in the subsequent chapters.

People in any differentiated society bring diverse cultural, economic, and political interests to their engagement with the common linguistic system, and in the process they place various, sometimes contrasting, claims on the same words. "The paradox of communication," Bourdieu notes, "is that it presupposes a common medium, but one which works ... only by eliciting and reviving singular, and therefore socially marked, experiences."[64] A shared terminology accordingly may take on quite different, even opposite meanings within the same "linguistic community"—that is, within a set of individuals who use the same vocabulary, phraseology, and other linguistic elements to enunciate their ideas.[65] The "paradox of communication" is especially evident in the case of philosophical or religious discourse, which often exploits the several possible meanings that inhere in the conventional language used by a particular society.[66]

The ambiguity of the Confucian lexicon in the context of late To-kugawa Japan allowed it to be diversely appropriated in this sense by spokespersons of the various social and interpretive groups that participated in the Confucian linguistic community of the time. Gumperz notes that "classical administrative and liturgical languages" (especially classical Chinese, in the Tokugawa context) "are quite distinct from and often unrelated to popular speech, and the elaborate ritual and etiquette that surround their use can be learned only through many years of special training. Instruction is ... limited to a privileged few who command the necessary social status or financial resources."[67] Nevertheless, in the Tokugawa case, people of different social origins were able to exploit the polysemy of the classical administrative language, not infrequently in the interests of critiquing professional Confucian preoccupations with that very same language (particularly in its written form). For it was not only academy teachers and learned Buddhist priests who displayed an ennui with Confucian textual scholarship during this period. Many low-ranked samurai, rural notables, successful merchants and artisans, and members of other middle-level social groups learned to "read off" Zhu Xi's edition of the Four Books in domain, local, or private schools, and were apprised, even if cursorily, of ancient-learning, textualist, and eclectic approaches to the classics. Like the late nativists, the representatives of several religious movements that originated in these social strata in the eighteenth and early nineteenth centuries asserted the priority of practical and work needs over theoretical forms of learning. At the same time, however, they referred explicitly to Neo-Confucian notions of personal development in their discourses.

A vivid example of this phenomenon is the Shingaku movement, founded by the dry-goods clerk Ishida Baigan in the early eighteenth century. In the early nineteenth century the movement spread widely in both urban and rural areas; its teachers not infrequently were commissioned by the shogunate and various daimyo to hold sermon tours in local areas in order to shore up what the authorities perceived as a decline in moral values among their subjects. Shingaku teachers had originally drawn much of their inspiration from the Neo-Confucian canon, but as the period wore on, several began to produce more idiosyncratic readings of these texts. During the nineteenth century, the earlier, more contemplative version of Shingaku, which had centered on the aim of "knowing one's original mind" *(honshin o shiru)*, lost ground in the face of its teachers' constant involvement in free-wheeling sermons and of the growing internal divisions in the movement. By the Bakumatsu period, Shingaku preachers had become best known for the lively, playful narratives they used to convey axioms of filial piety and frugality.

Ostensibly, the training of Shingaku teachers continued to be regulated by the movement's headquarters in Kyoto (Meirinsha), which adhered to the group's original Neo-Confucian curriculum.[68] There had always been tensions between the official Shingaku message propagated by Meirinsha and its regional elaborations, but by the 1850s these differences reached an irreversible disjunction in eastern Japan.[69] At about this time Sanzensha, the Kantō headquarters of Shingaku, located in Edo, began to identify its religious and educational concerns concertedly with those of Rinzai Zen Buddhism. This shift was not simply a revival of the Zen predilections of earlier Shingaku leaders (particularly the Sanzensha founder, Nakazawa Dōni, 1725–1803). The Edo school of Shingaku became, in effect, an unofficial lay Zen group, staffed by teachers who regularly practiced under nearby Rinzai masters. The transformation was spearheaded by a man named Takahashi Kōsetsu (Tokusaburō, 1819–1876).

Takahashi was the son of an Edo gold-lacquer craftsman, but he was adopted into a samurai family at the age of nine and was thus able to acquire an education in the literary and martial arts.[70] He is said to have become well versed in the Chinese classics and was appointed a Confucian scholar in the domain of his adopted family when only eighteen years old. After two years, however, he resigned this position (for unknown reasons) and returned to Edo to take up the occupation of his birth family.[71] Evidently Takahashi's business responsibilities were not overly demanding, for he continued to study Confucian texts and to investigate other intellectual systems and practices. In 1857 he heard about the Edo Shingaku school, Sanzensha, became a member, and before long was initiated into the "method of the mind of the Ishida school" *(Sekimon no shinpō)* by his teacher, Kumatani Tōshū (b. 1814).[72] After diligent practice of the group's disciplines (according to Takahashi's official biography), he at length attained the essence of "no self" *(muga)*. His teacher nevertheless urged Takahashi to advance beyond this "enlightenment" experience (called *hatsumei* or "discovery" in Shingaku). Reminding Takahashi of Confucius' counsel that "one should 'be widely versed and integrate [one's learning],'" Kumatani sent his disciple off to study the Way under a more "distinguished" teacher.[73]

Kumatani's advice was probably an imprimatur of Takahashi's own plans. The biography implies that Takahashi had become restless with the Shingaku system because of his abiding concern about the significance of written words *(moji)*. He reportedly felt that

> Shingaku transmits the living mind which is apart from written words, but what we call the "venerable replies" *(okotae)* of our former teacher [Ishida Baigan] are also written words.[74] The answers given by our former teacher were living words *(kakku)*, but once they were recorded in writing and

transmitted to later generations, they became traces of the mind, that is, written words.[75] In the Confucian texts as well, when Ziyou, Zixia, and others each ask about filial piety, their question remains the same, but Confucius answers each one differently....[76] Confucius' answers were living answers, and the fact that they were different, depending on the time and person, is truly [evidence of his] living mind. Nonetheless, once his [answers] were put in writing and handed down to today, they, too, became merely written words.[77]

With the idea of words as traces of a more "live" reality or of a "living mind apart from written words," we are evidently back to the Zen rhetoric of a "special transmission outside the teachings" that does not involve "setting up words." This parlance seems to mark the Zen Buddhist orientation of Takahashi (and/or his Meiji biographer).[78] At the same time, however, the Shingaku adept's ruminations on the significance of the written word resonate with the concern for meaning in language that had been articulated by Tokugawa thinkers across the board. The fact that Takahashi uses the same binomial nomenclature ("living words" versus "dead words") to contrast written and oral language that Motoori Norinaga had employed much earlier to distinguish between Chinese and Japanese is not purely coincidental. The two men operated in entirely distinct intellectual and historical frameworks, but they were both concerned with the problem of authenticity in linguistic communication. In *haikai* poetics (with which Motoori presumably was more familiar than he was with Zen), *kakku* or *ikita kotoba* denotes words that are suggestive: they point to a meaning beyond the immediate referent itself. For Takahashi, the value of "living words" in the Zen sense was, similarly, their power to point beyond themselves.

In Sorai's proposal and its derivatives, on the other hand, there was no assumption of a transcendent, ineffable truth or "way" that subsisted eternally in the mind or in an intangible realm beyond the written texts.[79] As we have seen, post-Sorai Confucian scholars (as well as Confucian-educated nativists, Buddhists, and Shingaku teachers) faulted ancient learning and evidential studies precisely for this failure to allow for a transtextual reality with which individuals could identify their moral and religious ideals. Takahashi's insight into the particularity of discursive expressions of truth (his realization that Confucius' remarks were meaningful, as he put it, "depending on the time and person") led him, like the more elite thinkers discussed above, to produce a discourse on personal cultivation that pointed, not toward the text, but away from it. Once Confucius' (or Baigan's) answers were written down, they were no longer authoritative sources of truth—they might even distract one from the pursuit of the way. One therefore had to look elsewhere for the "living mind."

Takahashi accordingly concluded, much like Igai Keisho, that Shingaku was declining in his time because its members "all vainly ponder the dregs of the ancients, mistakenly believing that they are being assiduous [in learning], and overlook the direct truth of knowing the nature."[80] Evidently the Neo-Confucian canon—the Four Books, the *Elementary Learning (Xiaoxue)*, and *Reflections on Things at Hand (Jinsilu)*—had become material for intellectual dissection rather than spiritual inspiration not only in the halls of contemporary Confucian academies but also in the neighborhood study groups run by Shingaku teachers.

After coming to this realization, Takahashi reportedly "resigned" from Sanzensha and proceeded to Kamakura to practice Zen, first under Tōkai Shōshun (1796–1865) of Engakuji, then for a protracted period under Gan'ō Genshi (1815–1875) of Kenchōji and Chōtokuji.[81] In early 1867, we are told, Takahashi attained enlightenment while "sitting motionless" *(gotsuza)* in Gan'ō's training center.[82] The adept continued to practice Zen avidly thereafter, commuting between his home in Edo, Kenchōji in Kamakura, and Chōtokuji (in today's Saitama prefecture). Following Gan'ō's wishes, however, Takahashi also began to frequent Sanzensha again. One day he happened to peruse some writings of Ishida Baigan that he had "overlooked" for some time. As he was reading, "every word seemed to release rays of wisdom and conveyed a very different meaning from what he had formerly perceived."[83] As if echoing Imakita Kōsen's rediscovery of Confucius, Takahashi suddenly realized that Shingaku was extraordinarily profound: "not something that one could easily grasp."[84] From then on, Takahashi devoted himself to propagating Shingaku with extraordinary zeal. His biographer reports in near-Pauline terms that "those who were sleeping woke up, and those who had died became alive."[85] The Shingaku community began to attract members once more, and in response to the new demand, in 1869 Takahashi set up a new meetinghouse (Kaiseisha) in the Fukagawa area of Tokyo.[86]

If we are to trust the official Shingaku rendition of Takahashi's life, the gold-lacquer dealer was a conscientious seeker who reached the culmination of his religious practice only after first denying the meaningfulness of Shingaku-Confucian language and subsequently "restoring" it from a Zen perspective. We are being told once more, in other words, that serious Zen practice is a prerequisite for understanding Confucian discourse—indeed, that the true Neo-Confucian "learning of the mind" is in reality Zen Buddhism. It was only after Takahashi adopted this perspective that he was able to redeem the Confucian linguistic codes in which he had been versed in his youth. His Zen practice qualified him to marshal this lexicon in the interests of reaffirming a transverbal source of religious authority that was putatively beyond the domain of Confucian learning.

Numerous educated persons in the late Tokugawa were eager to point through and beyond the Confucian texts to hermeneutical niches that they carved out and infused with their own meanings. The thinkers discussed in this chapter did not question the fundamental worth of textual learning itself; their writings lack the derogatory references to scholarship that punctuate the discourses of religious leaders who operated in more popular social contexts. Shingaku as a whole is a borderline case. Many of its preachers disparaged book learning in their public sermons even while drawing copiously on Confucian and Neo-Confucian texts in their writings. Takahashi Kōsetsu, in any case, like Imakita Kōsen, was a gifted student of the classical Chinese texts, a former Confucian scholar who ultimately recommitted himself to the enterprise of learning from a Zen Buddhist perspective. All the thinkers treated above were in fact educational and religious professionals, schooled in the Confucian texts and commentaries. All, moreover, were employed or at least implicitly sanctioned by the shogunal-domain establishment— whether as educators, abbots, or morality preachers. Yet by insisting that the meaning of Confucian passages depended on a personal understanding that was grounded in a particular form of cultivation, each of these interpreters helped render multivalent the cultural codes that had come to be associated with the Tokugawa order. These core members of the Confucian linguistic community thus created their own interpretive enclaves, negotiated between the textual systems of knowledge with which they had been imbued and the reality of their social and religious experience.

CHAPTER 2

Divination as Cultivation

THE POLEMIC AGAINST textualism was carried out at all levels of the Confucian linguistic community—by professional scholars and educated religious leaders, such as those already discussed, and by popular interpreters of personal cultivation. In this and the next chapter I take up theories and systems of practice that were generated by some of the lesser-known thinkers of the early nineteenth century: diviners and the founder of a new religion. All of these individuals shared energetically in the task of creating a hermeneutics that promised resolution of the perceived discontinuity between the dominant cultural discourse, much of which was articulated in Confucian lexicons, and the realities of people's lives. At the same time, all relied on Confucian allusions and rhetorical patterns to communicate their proposed paths to well-being. Their programs illustrate the continuing power as well as the frangibility of Confucian discourse in late Tokugawa society.

The resonance among the various contributors to this discussion was not a matter of lineal influence or deliberate reformulation. The people introduced here were not representatives of any formal nativist, Confucian, or Buddhist school—indeed, they took a dim view of scholars in general, whom they often called (in a rather deprecatory tone) "savants" *(monoshiri)*. The decision of these popular thinkers to bypass formal Confucian learning, in particular, is justified in their writings primarily by derogation of what they perceived as its overly intellectual, bookish nature, which they depicted as lying beyond the ken of their less-educated constituents. However, for the most part these figures' proposals were not heavily charged with anti-Confucian polemics; indeed, they used the Neo-Confucian paradigm of self-improvement as a mental grammar for their various elaborations. This almost systematic ambivalence toward the Confucian enterprise was a regular part of the rhetorical self-definition of these groups.

Upon first consideration, the logic of divination as practiced in Edo Japan appears straightforward. Everyone had a destiny; the function of the diviner was to inform people of the main features of that fate, so that they could prepare for it as best they could. The premise of the prognostication, whether based on interpretation of the hexagrams in the *Book of Changes (Yijing)*, or on physiognomy, astrology, or other methods of discernment, was that the individual had limited power to effect change in the "fortune" with which she or he had been born. The divining arts were no doubt often patronized by a clientele that had little notion of actively bringing about such changes. Nevertheless, during the late Tokugawa other trends were also at work. In some cases, long-established forms of prognostication were reformulated by their practitioners in the direction of full-fledged systems of personal improvement. Leaders arose within the world of fortune-telling who criticized the fatalistic perspective that had informed past divination practices. These reformists did not deny the validity of the traditional systems completely, but astutely transformed them by introducing a novel emphasis on the power of the client while at the same time retaining the older systems' lexicons. The customers of these new diviners were encouraged to be self-reliant: after the "fortune-teller" provided an initial analysis of a client's inherited destiny, it was the latter's responsibility to modulate his or her life toward the better (regardless of the prognosis).

The historical relationship between divination, religion, and moral practice in Japan is intricate (and little-studied). Divining services were (and are) made available for a fee at Buddhist temples and Shinto shrines, among other sites, and have been included in the repertoires of the founders of several new religions.[1] In the late Tokugawa context, purportedly ancient prognostication traditions lent the new groups a framework of respectable continuity with the past—and thus an argument for legitimacy that proved useful when their activities caught the attention of the shogunal or domain authorities.

The intersection between divination and religious cultivation was not always a matter of expedience or economics, however. The thinkers discussed in this chapter did not offer prognostication services as an addendum to their main ritual or doctrinal program; they created new systems of personal development by consciously reinterpreting past fortune-telling practices. In these cases the divination act functioned as a kind of hook to draw people into the project of cultivation, whether under the direct guidance of the diviner or the auspices of a separate religious community. Ian Reader and George Tanabe have called attention to the moral dimension of "luck" in contemporary Japanese society. "In the conceptual framework of practical benefits *[genze riyaku]* little is said about *kōun*, which is good luck understood as a lucky break that just happens without any cause or deliberate effort.... But *kaiun* is the opposite: luck affected and even created by morality and religious ritual."[2]

This way of thinking was already at work in the Tokugawa; people who called on the emerging breed of diviners were more interested in *kaiun* than *kōun*. They consulted prognosticators not simply to map out their future but to review the legacy of their past, and thereby identify areas of possible self-improvement that could lead to benefits at all levels of existence.

Tōkyūjutsu is a little-known example of the marshaling of divination traditions to promote personal cultivation. The movement was founded in 1834 by Yokoyama Marumitsu (Shunkisai, 1780–1854), ostensibly as a revised version of Tengenjutsu.[3] The latter was a long-established method of prognostication that synthesized various Chinese augury practices with yin-yang ideas and the theory of the five phases or agents *(wuxing;* J. *gogyō)*. The Tengen diviner reportedly predicted people's fortunes by identifying their personality characteristics based on an analysis of their dates of birth (calculated according to the Chinese system of "stems and branches") and their physical appearance. According to tradition, the Tengen system originated in ancient China during the period of the legendary cultural founders and later inspired Daoist and Confucian philosophers, as well as Śākyamuni Buddha. In Japan, Tengen practices are said to have been advocated by such great religious leaders as Hōnen (1133–1212) and Nichiren (1222–1282), though the Tendai priest and shogunal advisor Tenkai (1536–1643) is credited with their systemization. Legend has it that Tokugawa Ieyasu (1542–1616) held the Tengen method in such awe that, fearing its misapplication, he banned its use in the early seventeenth century. The art was nevertheless transmitted secretly, we are told; such Confucian worthies as Nakae Tōju (1608–1648) and Arai Hakuseki (1657–1725) allegedly drew on it to supplement their teachings.[4]

Tengenjutsu, in short, was popularly associated with a distinguished pedigree of patrons dating from antiquity to late Tokugawa times. Apparently following the account constructed by contemporaneous Tōkyū spokespersons, however, a Meiji newspaper writer summarized the later history of the Tengen teaching as follows:

> The teaching [of Tengenjutsu] was said to be mystical and people were not easily allowed access to it. It advocated a method by which one could cultivate oneself and one's family; applied more broadly, it was a tool for governing the country. However, with the change of the times, it developed into [a way of] telling fortunes based on the directions and people's countenances, and ended up not differing at all from divination based on the *Book of Changes*.[5]

According to this rendition, Yokoyama Marumitsu's reformulation saved the Tengen system from complete degeneration by reviving its original aim of moral cultivation.

The nineteenth-century history of the Tengen-Tōkyū movement is more factual in tone, though still shaped by the preferences of modern denominational writers. Original documentation of the early Tōkyū teaching itself is sparse, no doubt partly because of the group's stress on oral transmission.[6] The founder's family was of peasant origins, but his father acquired a low samurai rank when he was employed as a guard in the shogunal quarters in Edo. Marumitsu became visually impaired in his childhood; an eye disease reportedly prevented him from reading or writing much, and at his mother's urging he compensated for this cultural deficiency by learning the art of the *tsuzumi* drum. He nevertheless succeeded to his father's position and not long afterward (1821) met a fellow shogunal employee called Okuno Nanboku (Marumichi Genkisai; Seijirō), who doubled as a Tengenjutsu diviner. Nanboku's exact prediction of certain upcoming events in Marumitsu's life convinced the latter to study the art of prognostication himself. He became Okuno Nanboku's disciple and is said to have mastered his teacher's fortune-telling methods within two to three years.

In the meantime, however, Marumitsu (now married with three children) found that he was unable to make ends meet. He had risen to the rank of guard captain *(kumigashira)* by the early 1820s, but his stipend was so low that he had to supplement his income by playing the drum and the flute. Marumitsu had become highly proficient in these arts, but (as he later related) felt ashamed of having to make a living from his musical skills. Evidently he believed that the work of a diviner was more respectable for a man of his rank—as a fortune-teller Marumitsu could independently command a field of knowledge, while as a musician he was simply a hired performer. Like other semieducated thinkers of his time, Marumitsu was impelled to create a system of practice that held at least the promise of reconciling the tension between his economic reality and the prevailing status ideology.

After Okuno Nanboku died in 1823, Marumitsu succeeded to the Tengen master's position and inherited his clientele. From this point the diviner is said to have invested himself completely in creating a "discipline for changing one's inherited dispositions" *(kishitsu henka no shugyō)*. He apparently succeeded. Before long, people heard about his novel methods of self-improvement, and by the mid-1830s several had begun to seek his guidance. Marumitsu's living conditions improved vastly. He initially called the new interpretive system Tengen Tōkyūgaku —the "Learning of Tengen and Tōkyū," but after a few years he changed its name to Kaiun Tōkyūjutsu—the "Tōkyū Art of Improving One's Fortune" (the meaning of "Tōkyū" is discussed below).

The addition of the term "kaiun"—which denotes a process or event in which one's fortune "opens up" or improves—is significant. In contemporary Japan, as Reader and Tanabe emphasize, *kaiun* is often believed to occur in conjunction with a deliberate change in the subject's efforts or attitudes.[7] Assuming that a similar nuance characterized late Edo usage, it may well have inspired Marumitsu's new title for his divination system, which placed a novel priority on personal responsibility. The substitution of *"jutsu"* (art, skill) for *"gaku"* (learning, study) in the title of the group was even more explicitly motivated. Marumitsu reportedly felt that the character *gaku,* or learning, had theoretical, academic overtones that obscured his exclusive emphasis on *practical* application.[8] He insisted that his teaching was not a philosophy or doctrine of any sort, but simply a practicable method of self-improvement.

Marumitsu professed this modest view of his teaching and social role throughout his life. According to one anecdote, when a follower asked him to produce calligraphic specimens that she could bequeath as talismans to her descendants, he angrily refused, saying: "I am neither a Shinto nor a Buddhist priest, and I am not versed in even one section of the *Great Learning.* How would I know how to write the calligraphy for a talisman?"[9] Judging from such accounts, it was integral to Marumitsu's sociopsychological identity not to be viewed as a professional representative of any established body of textual or theoretical knowledge. The Tōkyū founder maintained that he had taken up divination simply to improve his own situation in life and that he therefore felt "ashamed" whenever people called him "teacher" *(sensei)* (figure 1).[10]

Disclaimers of professional status were not uncommon among low-ranked or non-samurai teachers during the Edo period. Such statements functioned both as an oblique way of proclaiming the superiority of the simple, nonintellectual Way over the learning that was mediated by recognized experts (scholars and educated clergy) and as a strategy by which teachers who disseminated knowledge outside mainstream institutions might defend their precarious social status.[11] In any event, the growing numbers of Marumitsu's followers nonetheless caught the attention of the Tokugawa authorities, who summoned him to a hearing in the ninth month of 1848.[12] During the 1830s and 1840s, when the shogunate was promoting the so-called Tenpō reforms, it instituted a number of social controls in Edo, including strictures against religious groups that were unaffiliated with mainstream Buddhist and Shinto institutions.[13] The leaders of several obscure groups were imprisoned, sent into exile, or banned from their home areas, during the 1840s in particular. Marumitsu's close disciples were necessarily anxious about the possible outcome of their teacher's interrogation. Records of the interview have evidently survived in Tōkyūjutsu archives; reports of their content afford

FIGURE 1. Yokoyama Marumitsu, the founder of Tōkyūjutsu. A painting by contemporary artist Iwase Shunga, based on a wood-block print. Courtesy of Nihon Tōdōkai.

a rare glimpse into the late Tokugawa regime's treatment of heterodox groups.[14] Marumitsu was interrogated with regard to six points. The authorities began by demanding that he explain the nature of the activities that he engaged in, and the circumstances under which he had come to advocate "Tengenjutsu." In response, the founder recounted his personal history:

> After I exerted myself and tried to change my destined nature *(unsei)*, it improved beyond my expectations. I was not able to recover from my eye disease, but otherwise, my headaches, depression, hemorrhoids, stomach spasms, and irritability were cured. Moreover, the members of my family, who were constantly quarreling, became peaceful. I therefore designed [a method] that even illiterate people can use to control their bodies and manage their families; I gave it the name "Kaiun Tōkyūjutsu" and have been teaching it to people who wish [to learn it]. This method is not one of the Three Teachings; no one [formally] transmitted it to me. I simply worked it out, taking the universe as my model and trying [the method] out on myself.[15]

Marumitsu identifies the principal virtue of his new teaching as its efficacy in curing minor illnesses and harmonizing family relations. This representation of his system may have been, in part, a rhetorical tactic to legitimize Tōkyūjutsu in the eyes of the investigating authorities, but it is also a fairly straightforward statement of the fundamental aims of his teaching, which were eminently compatible with prevailing notions of personal and family well-being.

The Tōkyū founder claimed in his deposition that he had two thousand and some hundred disciples, with about one hundred enrolling each month of the year. If we are to credit his account, by the late 1840s Marumitsu was the head of a significant organization in the local Edo area. No doubt because of the growing scale of the diviner's enterprise, his interrogators were exquisitely interested in its financial aspects; three of their six questions concern the amount of money he received from followers. He was asked how much disciples were required to pay when they were initiated into each level of the teaching (beginning, intermediate, and advanced), how much they were expected to give at the two seasonal payment times (Bon and New Year's), and even how much he had received from donors when his house recently burnt down.[16] The authorities were also interested in the group's initiation procedures. According to Marumitsu's description, new members were expected to submit a written affirmation of the truth of the "Twelve Personalities," to pay obeisance to the venerable deity Nikkō (the apotheosis of Tokugawa Ieyasu), and to recite the names of the "Twelve Branches" (the numerary system used in Tōkyū prognostication).[17] The deposition's modern editor and Tōkyū practitioner, Yokoyama Masamitsu, argues that Nikkō was not in fact worshiped in Tengen or Tōkyū during the Edo period, and that Marumitsu probably inserted this (as well as other laudatory references to Nikkō) in his account in order to appease the Tokugawa authorities.[18] The founder also informed his questioners that in accordance with ancient Tengen tradition, new members pledged their commitment to the Tōkyū teaching by offering up written pledges, sealed in blood, in a ritual fire to the gods, the Buddha, and Confucius.[19]

Marumitsu was also required to report the names of the shogunal officials and daimyo who were numbered among his followers, and of the townspeople who had been formally initiated into his teaching. The names of over forty persons reportedly appear in the founder's response to this question, ten of whom held the rank of daimyo.[20] Several of the latter had enrolled in the Tōkyū program along with their entire households (including wives and daughters, retainers and their spouses, maids-in-waiting, and so forth). The Tōkyū founder claimed numerous additional followers of samurai rank (especially *hatamoto* or bannermen), as well as government officials, artists, teachers, and laborers. We have no knowledge of the relative proportion of each of these social groups in the early Tōkyū organization, but it is safe to conclude that Marumitsu's teachings appealed to practitioners from the lower-middle through the upper ranks of Edo society.

In the month after the hearing, Marumitsu received notice that henceforth he was prohibited from accepting disciples and from holding meetings to propagate his teachings. He was also required to submit all Tengen and Tōkyū texts to the authorities.[21] The fact that the leader himself was not exiled or otherwise punished may indicate that the shogunate did not regard his activities as particularly pernicious. Tōkyū-jutsu's lack of social activism, its roots in traditional divination practices, and its dearth of discourse about all-powerful deities, salvation, and world transformation apparently persuaded shogunal officials that the organization did not pose a threat to the existing order—in contrast to contemporaneous heterodoxies such as Tohokami (discussed in chapter 3), which was treated more harshly during this period. Judging from the questions put to Marumitsu, the authorities were more interested in controlling Tōkyū revenue than in the details of its doctrine or praxis.

The verdict was nevertheless something of a setback for the divination group. Marumitsu duly enjoined his followers from accepting disciples or holding meetings in their houses, and from 1848 until the early Meiji the Tōkyū movement remained more or less underground. Most of the founder's less-committed followers abandoned the movement in the aftermath of the 1848 restrictions,[22] but a vital core of practitioners apparently remained loyal during the last Tokugawa years; the group underwent a veritable revival in the Meiji. Moreover, Marumitsu's claim in 1848 that his followers included many people of middle to high social standing was not proffered, like his allusion to Tokugawa Ieyasu, simply to allay the authorities' suspicions about the group; extant records confirm that Tōkyūjutsu indeed appealed to educated and/or privileged members of later Tokugawa society. Of the six direct disciples who were first initiated into Tōkyūjutsu at the advanced level, and who are therefore regarded as Marumitsu's legitimate successors (the so-called *roku kaiden*), four were shogunal retainers of high rank (mostly bannermen): Sano Kazumaru (1807–1888); the latter's younger brother, Aoki Sugan (1815–1888); Iida Katsumi (1817–1883); and Niinomi Harumitsu (1814–1890). The fifth successor, Kurushima Maruichi (d. 1850), was the lord of Mori domain (today's Ōita prefecture).[23]

Like a number of other systems of knowledge that circulated in the Tokugawa period, Tōkyūjutsu at the advanced level was communicated orally, in the form of a secret transmission. Marumitsu avowed in his 1848 statement that he did not teach Tōkyūjutsu indiscriminately, because it concerned "profoundly secret matters" *(shinpi no koto)*.[24] The practice of Tōkyū at the highest level may well have been dominated by

high-ranking shogunal officers and other Edo elites.[25] The program attracted members of this milieu during the late Tokugawa period partly
because they found themselves unexpectedly reduced in circumstances. In
the early nineteenth century the shogunate's financial basis deteriorated
significantly and its retainers experienced corollary difficulties in maintaining their households.[26] The Tōkyū founder, himself of low samurai
rank, had been unable to meet his living expenses without engaging in
work that was, in theory, the domain of the common classes. His highly
ranked disciples were in some cases worse off. Niinomi Harumitsu was
so poor (allegedly because of debts left by his deceased father) that he
performed manual labor to make ends meet. Indeed, Niinomi's penury is
explicitly identified in traditional accounts as the reason he first enrolled
in Tōkyūjutsu: he hoped that by adhering to Marumitsu's teachings he
would be able to improve his pecuniary fate (and at length, we are told,
he did).[27]

The involvement in the group of Marumitsu's sixth (and only female) successor, Aibara Teisan (1793–1865), represents a similar dynamic. After her husband, a *fudasashi,* took ill, she endeavored to make
a living by playing the shamisen publicly in Edo, but was stopped by the
local performers' guild because she could not afford to pay the requisite
membership fee.[28] When her husband subsequently died, Teisan tried to
resolve her personal and financial difficulties by taking the tonsure, but
to no avail: even as a Buddhist nun, in order to survive she was reduced
to begging in front of Sensōji, the popular Edo temple.[29] It was not until
Teisan began practicing under Marumitsu that her personal circumstances improved, according to Tōkyū accounts; she soon became active
in teaching Tōkyūjutsu to the wives of daimyo who resided in Edo.[30]

The Three Rings

The initial attraction of Tōkyūjutsu was evidently the hope it held out to
potential recruits of improving their lot in life in tangible ways—leading
to economic prosperity, social respectability, health, family happiness.
The fulfillment of this expectation, however, required Tōkyū clients to
reform themselves thoroughly. The level of commitment required of the
individual seems in fact to have been the main point of difference between Tōkyūjutsu and the Tengen teachings from which it derived. The
aim of the earlier method had been simply to determine clients' fates and
thereby help them prepare for what would inevitably take place, be it
good or bad. Modern Tōkyū historians, seeking to set off Marumitsu's
teachings from earlier formulations, have argued that the people who
patronized the older Tengen diviners lived in a paralysis of fear: customers believed that if they attempted to modify their predicted destinies,

ill effects would ensue and might even extend to their descendants. Marumitsu is credited with the liberating insight (for a diviner) that as long as people genuinely endeavor to improve themselves, they can change the cards they have been dealt, as it were.[31] We cannot assess the extent of determinism that characterized the older Tengenjutsu without a full-fledged study of this divination theory as it developed in the Edo period.[32] However, it is probably true that changing one's destiny by reforming one's personality was not the main thrust of the older Tengen system. Marumitsu, at least, was confident that his emphasis on personal transformation was eminently novel. He taught that the process of self-reform would disclose one's "true heart" or "original mind" *(honshin)* and restore the proper circulation of one's vital energies, thereby leading to spiritual and physical well-being.[33]

This approach to cultivation was original as an interpretation of the meaning of divination, but as a framework for self-development it was of course not new, and indeed pervaded much Tokugawa religious discourse.[34] Marumitsu's popular-style writings do not allude to specific sources, but his premises closely resemble long-established Neo-Confucian theories about the origins of moral differences among people. The Song thinkers had argued along Mencian lines that all people are born with moral goodness, which resides in their "original mind" *(ben-xin,* J. *honshin)* or "nature" *(xing,* J. *sei).* At birth each person is endowed with a unique configuration of vital energy or "material force" *(qi,* J. *ki),* which then determines her or his psychological and physiological dispositions. Zhu Xi had enunciated the gist of this idea as follows:

> The nature of all people is good, and yet there are those who are good from their birth and those who are evil from their birth. This is because of the difference in the material force with which they are endowed. The revolutions of the universe consist of countless variety and are endless. But these may be seen: If the sun and moon are clear and bright, and the climate temperate and reasonable, the person born at such a time and endowed with such material force, which is clear, bright, well-blended, and strong, should be a good person. But if the sun and moon are darkened and gloomy, and the temperature abnormal, all this is evidence of violent material force. There is no doubt that if a person is endowed with such material force, that person will be evil. The objective of learning is to transform this material endowment.[35]

The notion that one's "endowment" of vital energy or material force is influenced by the climatic conditions at the time of one's birth no doubt long predated the Song Neo-Confucian revival. The cited passage, however, represents the classical Neo-Confucian moralization of this notion, which was popularized in Edo Japan and evidently contributed to the stock of knowledge upon which Yokoyama Marumitsu drew when he formulated Tōkyūjutsu.

The name Marumitsu gave to his revised version of Tengenjutsu was a deliberate allusion to the methods he proposed for improving the aforementioned "material endowment"—that is, the inborn legacy of each individual, which includes psychological dispositions as well as physical energies and fluids. *Tō (yonageru)* originally connoted the separating out of impure bits in the process of washing rice. *Kyū (miya)* usually means the shrine or dwelling-place of a divine being, but in this context it refers to the twelve divisions of the zodiac, *jūnikyū* (twelve "realms"). The divisions correspond to constellations that are in ascendance at particular times of the calendar year and, by extension, to twelve distinctive configurations of vital energy that were (and are) believed to circulate at these times. In Tōkyūjutsu these configurations are further associated with twelve types of human nature or personality. The thrust of the compound "tōkyū," then, is to purify, refine, or cleanse one's character or personal dispositions.

As mentioned above, the founder's formal education was somewhat limited, and whether for this or other reasons, he did not leave a substantial written corpus to posterity. Aside from a selection of his verses, later compiled by his disciple Sano Kazumaru under the title *Tōeishū* (A Collection of Tōkyū Poems), the only extant work that Marumitsu is believed to have written is *Aki no arashi*, "Autumn Storm," a dialogue written in two parts (dated 1833 and 1836). This piece, which has the status of scripture in the modern Tōkyū organization, is short but nevertheless useful for understanding the founder's premises.[36]

Marumitsu identified the twelve zodiacal realms taught in Tengenjutsu with twelve cosmic energy configurations or personality characteristics. In "Autumn Storm" he says that when a child is created, the energies in force at that time meet and congeal to form its body and mind, thereby producing a set of physical and spiritual characteristics that reflects the cosmic configuration of the moment. He compares the constant revolution of the twelve energies in the universe to the different-sized wheels that gyrate inside a clock; the speed with which the wheels revolve accords with their size, just as the energies that happen to be circulating when a person comes into existence determine his or her bodily features, mental dispositions, and so forth. According to Marumitsu, each human being may be identified with "Three Rings" *(sanrin)*—that is, a set of three energy combinations that are associated with the individual's date of conception or birth (determined by means of a numerary calculation based on the Ten Stems and Twelve Branches).

The Tōkyū founder's characterization of the crucial moment in the reproductive process—which decides the individual's endowment—is ambiguous. He associates the stage at which the Three Rings are determined with the "one drop of water inside the mother's womb," and thus is probably referring to the moment in which the embryo is conceived rather than the time of its birth. (Today's Tōkyū practitioners in fact believe the essential date is that of conception, which they calculate by subtracting ten months from one's birthday.) In Marumitsu's view, the Three Rings (large, medium, and small) or configurations of vital energy that come together at conception provide a kind of blueprint for a person's eventual physical dimensions, complexion, temperament, health, and material fortune. The outcome does not depend on any one of the three configurations alone (though the "large ring," *dairin,* is weighted more heavily than the others), but on the ways in which they combine with each other.[37]

This convergence was not the only factor that affected a person's fate, however; otherwise, as Marumitsu points out in his dialogue, people born at the same time would have the same destiny, which is manifestly not true. In addition to one's own Three Rings, one's endowment is affected by one's father's and mother's rings; in other words, an individual's psychophysical constitution is influenced by six configurations of vital energy in addition to the three that are ascendant at the time of his or her own birth. The parental endowment is known as the "Field" *(hatake)* in Tōkyūjutsu. Since inherited factors affect a person's appearance and character quite palpably (children resemble their parents), according to Marumitsu it is important for a diviner to estimate a person's endowment based not only on the date of birth/conception, but also on her or his physical appearance. The latter task requires a physiognomic analysis *(kansō).*

The determination of the Three Rings and the Field was only the initial step in Marumitsu's program, however. The bulk of it lay with the practitioner. According to the Tōkyū founder, bad fortune—whether illness, poverty, or other troubles—is caused by the obfuscation of one's original, pure nature by inherited dispositions that ultimately derive from a poor endowment of vital energy. The solution is, first, to identify these characteristics and tendencies, based on an understanding of the Three Rings and the Field, and subsequently to engage in a disciplined effort *(kufū)* to change them.[38] One can improve the shape of a tree if one prunes it correctly, as Marumitsu puts it. In an allusion to the *Great Learning,* he avers that revealing the goodness inherent in the tree's trunk (one's original mind or spirit, *seishin*) by pruning the branches (one's inherited dispositions, *kishitsu*) is the meaning of the phrase "illuminating the bright virtue" *(meitoku o akiraka ni suru).* He also identifies this cultivation process with Buddhist and Shinto teachings. The founder assumed that these religious discourses were all concerned with the same issue: "This matter of 'branches' is called 'defilement and impurity' *(kegare fujō)* in the way of the gods, 'evil nature and selfish mind' *(akushō shishin)* in the Confucian way, and 'worldly passion and delusion' *(bonnō mayoi)* in the Buddhist way."[39]

Marumitsu thus unhesitatingly translated his ideas on personal cultivation into the established religious idioms of the day; but at the same time he engaged in a polemic against the systems of learning with which these locutions were associated. In "Autumn Storm" he criticizes "savants" who become caught up in their own theories and as a result neglect practical application of moral and religious teachings.

> For many years I, too, believed that these Twelve Branches were a code for the date and time. I did not know that the essence of the gods and the Buddhas, their punishments and their manifest blessings, and my own self *[waga mi]* arose from them. Regrettably, I passed [my time] looking for something else. The source of the various teachings is the principle of heaven-and-earth, and that principle lies in myself.
>
> However, if one observes people of the world,... [one sees that] when they hear about the [way of the] gods, they think it concerns things of the past; [when they hear about] the way of the Buddha, they think it has to do with the next life; and [when they hear about] heaven, [they think] it is far away and vast, and completely empty. They do not understand the difference between right and wrong. Absorbed by what they see and hear, they become distracted—the more they know, the more their minds run away. Even if they become savants, they are unable to keep their own bodies or their families in good order; and even if they plan to go to paradise, they are pursued by their inborn demons. In addition, they struggle to fulfill their morning and evening tasks and their family business.
>
> What, then, is the purpose of becoming versed [in these teachings]? It is for the sake of one's own self. You should study the various paths from this perspective. Without self, there are no gods or Buddhas, no masters or parents, nor anything at all.[40]

The Tōkyūjutsu founder viewed current religious systems as potential pitfalls for the unwary truthseeker. Involvement in the doctrines and rituals associated with these traditions, he felt, tended to distract weak people from authentic self-reform and thus to have a deleterious effect on their personal and family well-being. He lists the Confucian tradition along with others in this regard, without singling it out as more or less "intellectualistic" than native or Buddhist teachings. Yet Marumitsu's ideas on inherited dispositions resonate most strongly with Neo-Confucian theories about the origin of moral deviance. Furthermore, although his premise—that the central problem of human life is to disclose one's innate goodness and allow it to operate freely—was an assumption shared by many thinkers of his time, regardless of affiliation, Marumitsu chose to frame his own solution to this problem most often in Confucian language: "When one eliminates the things that conceal one's virtue, it should naturally become clear, without one having to seek for it."[41]

Like other members of the Confucian linguistic community, Marumitsu and his immediate disciples accepted the authority of the conventional framework of personal improvement, whereby rectification of the inner self is the basis of physical and social well-being. Indeed, in his insistence that the fundamental principle of religious teachings lies in one's self, and that one should study such traditions only "for the sake of one's own self," the Tōkyū leader echoes (or previews) Satō Issai and the host of other Confucianizing professionals of the time who placed priority on individual experience in the cultivation process. However, the Tōkyū founder's understanding of "self" was more explicitly shaped by a genuine preoccupation with the tangible and the practical than were the conceptions of these highly educated theorists. "Self" in the passage quoted above does not denote simply a sense of agency, or the mind, or even a configuration of inner states; it means the complete physical and psychological person, composed of specific material and spiritual energies. Although Confucian scholars of the time shared the premise that internal and external states are intimately related, most paid only lip service to the need for workable, individualized methods of modulating that relationship.

Yokoyama Marumitsu and his successors interpreted dates of conception (or birth) and the appearance of people's faces in concrete fashion. The Tōkyū teachers conveyed to their followers the specifics of each individual's moral endowment rather than abstractions drawn from Chinese texts. The latter applied to everyone in general but no one in particular. Instead of merely advising clients in a general way to practice sincerity, frugality, or filial piety, the Tōkyū diviner first informed them of the peculiar fate they had inherited. A person born on January 17, 1952, for example, would be identified with the Three Rings, *ho, fu,* and *re.* Based on Tōkyū lore, an individual born with this particular configuration may be generous and open-hearted to a fault, but inclined to eat too much. An analysis of the same individual's countenance based on the principles of physiognomy might further reveal that he or she had inherited a predisposition to be loyal but also to overindulge his or her sexual desires. Equipped with knowledge of such particulars about themselves, Tōkyū patrons could focus more realistically on cultivating their positive attributes and diminishing their deficiencies rather than risk losing themselves in the less determinate processes of "learning" intimated in the classical Chinese texts. The promise of Tōkyūjutsu, then, was the ability to understand and thus transform one's person by means of a "science of the particular": estimations of specific conditions based on predictable rules. The *Great Learning* and other Confucian texts provided a schematic framework for improving oneself, but Tōkyū supplied the personalized, practical details of how to do so.

Ironically, the specific methods of cultivation that Marumitsu advocated, if any, are unclear: as mentioned above, by tradition they are transmitted only orally. Even today, the surviving group, Tōdōkai, does not publicize or circulate written descriptions of approved practices. Modern members seem to choose from a variety of common Japanese cultivation systems, depending on their particular needs and inclinations, ranging from diet modulation (as inspired by the ideas of Mizuno Nanboku, discussed below) to Zen-type meditation. One notable feature of modern Tōkyū practice is the custom of having individuals give oral testimonies upon request in the presence of other members (or in written form, in the group's in-house publications). These testimonies are mildly confessional in character, focusing on problems that practitioners have encountered in their attempts to overcome their personality defects. Group discussion, self-reflection, and repentance *(zange)* are commonly practiced in Tōkyūjutsu today, much as they are in the new religions.

The Destiny in One's Body

Unlike Yokoyama Marumitsu, who did not require that his clients practice one particular method of self-improvement, other little-known teachers of the late Tokugawa stressed specific, concrete practices, and in so doing pushed cultivation theory further in the direction of the physiological. A case in point is Mizuno Nanboku (Kumata; 1760?–1834?), popularly considered the father of modern Japanese physiognomy *(sōhō* or *kansōhō)*—the art of predicting people's fortunes by analyzing their physical features.[42] One often sees practitioners of this traditional East Asian art offering their services for a fee in busy shopping centers and subway stations in urban Japan today; they usually sit in little stalls decorated with diagrams of the human face and charts for the other kinds of prognostication in which they specialize. Ironically, in his later years Nanboku radically revised the traditional physiognomic emphasis on inherited physical features. The diviner's early writings are still a resource for aficionados of Japanese physiognomy, but his final interpretations constitute a truly original contribution to Japanese thinking about dietary health and natural conservation.

Popular traditions about Mizuno Nanboku's life abound, but his own writings remain the only reliable source of information about him.

He is believed to have been the son of an Osaka playwright who wrote scripts for the Awaza puppet and Jōruri theaters, but he lost his parents at an early age and was raised by his uncle, a locksmith—hence his early sobriquet, Kagiya Kumata (Kumata the Locksmith). He reportedly was a rowdy youth, and at one point ended up in prison because of his involvement in a violent incident while on a drunken spree. The experience of confinement seems to have precipitated his efforts to reform himself.[43] According to one account, after his release from jail Nanboku met a physiognomist who told him that his face (which was genuinely ugly, judging both from an extant portrait and from Nanboku's own remarks) contained signs that he would die a violent death in the near future unless he changed his ways (figure 2). Impressed by this warning, Nanboku decided to take up Zen Buddhist practice, but the temple priest to whom he applied for instruction requested that the erstwhile miscreant abstain completely from rice products for a year as a prior condition for admittance to the training program. Nanboku duly restrained himself, consuming only soy products and grains for a year, though he continued to

FIGURE 2. Mizuno Nanboku, teacher of physiognomy and dietary cultivation, at the age of fifty. 1812 wood-block print by Nanboku's disciple Haruna Ippeki. From the frontispiece of *Naniwa no sō hijiri—Mizuno Nanboku to sono shisō*, by Makino Masayasu and Tanaka Ichiro. Courtesy of Ōsaka Shunjūsha.

drink sake and to gamble. Subsequently, we are told, he happened to meet the diviner who had made the dire prediction a year earlier: the latter marveled, for the fatal signs in Nanboku's face had now completely disappeared.

Whether this story is reliable or not, it successfully conveys that Nanboku's restriction of his eating habits, quite apart from any other behavioral changes, effectively improved his destiny—or his "record in heaven" *(tenroku)*, as he calls it. At this juncture Nanboku became personally interested in the practice of physiognomy and before long dedicated himself entirely to mastering the art. Tradition has it that he sought to perfect his divining skills by working for three years in a barbershop (in order to observe people's faces), three years in a public bath (in order to study the shape of people's bodies), and three years in a crematorium (in order to investigate the bone structure of corpses). We have no hard evidence that Nanboku actually pursued this fascinating nine-year regimen.[44] However, his own testimony indicates that when he was twenty-five, after much traveling and searching, he encountered a master of the Daoist art of longevity on Kinkazan (a mountain island in today's Miyashiro prefecture). Kinkazan was an important Shugendō site, and Nanboku's teacher may well have been a mountain ascetic of that genre. In any event, the physiognomist later claimed that he practiced under this master for one hundred days, learning how to cultivate long life—an art that he identifies in his writings as "the secret of physiognomy." Nanboku attributed the considerable length of his own life to his personal mastery of this practice.[45]

Nanboku recounts that he also studied under "Precept Master Kaijō," a Shingon or Shingon-Ritsu Buddhist priest who offered instruction in physiognomy along with a smattering of moral and religious education. Kaijō expounded to Nanboku (who was barely literate) the *Shenxiang quanpian* (Complete Manual of Spiritual Prognostication), a standard Ming work on physiognomy that circulated widely during the Tokugawa era in various annotated and translated editions.[46] Physiognomy was one of several systems of knowledge that Buddhist priests included in their repertoires of popular instruction during the Tokugawa period.[47] (Nanboku's students, after he established himself as a diviner in his own right, encompassed a number of Buddhist and Shinto priests, who probably sought his guidance in order to meet their parishioners' demand for fortune-telling services.)[48] The physiognomist himself became a dedicated Buddhist practitioner; he donated his divining services as well as copies of his written works to the sangha on various occasions. He also took to wearing Buddhist clothing, though he did not take the tonsure.[49] In 1803, after Nanboku had been a professional physiognomist for several years, the Shingon-Ritsu master, Jiun (Onkō, 1718–

1804), reportedly granted him the title of *"koji"* (lay Buddhist practitioner) in acknowledgment of the diviner's commitment to Buddhism.[50]

In his first years practicing divination, however, Nanboku lived from hand to mouth, traveling about and struggling to establish himself. He had difficulty in building a clientele, according to his own account, partly because his own face was so inauspicious-looking that it deterred prospective clients.[51] His 1788 work, *Nanboku sōhō zenpen* (Nanboku's Manual of Physiognomy, part 1), articulates his concern with mastering the fundamental skills of divination during this early period; in it he discusses the phases of the fortune-telling act and gives specific interpretations of facial and bodily features.[52] Eventually, Nanboku began to attract some customers, but he continued to make mistakes in his prognostications and nearly despaired of finding a reliable system for predicting people's destinies.[53] He became convinced that physiognomy must be founded on underlying, cosmic principles rather than simply on piecemeal analyses of clients' physical features. "Physiognomy," he reflected in a rather Neo-Confucian vein in 1802, "is called *kansō* [seeing forms] because one sees [people's forms] by abandoning oneself and becoming one body with heaven-and-earth."[54] However, this lofty insight did not solve the problem of divination errors and as a last resort Nanboku decided to visit the Ise shrines, where he carried out fasting and cold-water austerities at the Isuzu River for a period of fifty days. According to his later account, upon completing the stint he received a vital insight from the god Toyouke, the deity who is believed to dwell in the Outer Shrine of the Ise complex. The oracle (fittingly, as Toyouke is considered the god of food) declared that "people's destiny lies in their food."[55]

Nanboku concluded that he had erred in his predictions of people's destinies because he had not fully comprehended that people's fortunes can change if they exercise restraint in their eating and drinking. From then on, Nanboku enquired thoroughly into his clients' eating habits in addition to investigating their physical features. If their physiognomic prognoses were poor, he advised them to restrict their food—not only in quantity, but also in quality. Eating small amounts of plain, unrefined food would ensure a good fortune. Overeating or partaking of tasty, elaborately prepared foods would have a negative impact, as would irregular eating habits, such as switching back and forth from simple to rich foods. Nanboku avers in his writings that, to set an example for his followers, he made it a rule to eat only grains (up to about one cup a day) and vegetables; and to exclude rice and rice products completely from his diet. He also limited his intake of alcoholic drink to less than a cup each day, and diluted this daily ration by half with water in order to avoid becoming attached to its taste (he admitted a weakness for sake).[56]

Limited eating and drinking were directly related, in Nanboku's view, to the attainment of a serene state of mind. People who strictly regulated their food intake, he taught, had disciplined minds; because they controlled both their minds and their bodies, they were able to manage their daily affairs well.[57] The spirits *(seishin)* of people who ate indiscriminately, on the other hand, were not calm. Like others of his time, Nanboku understood the linkage between personal habits and overall well-being in terms of vital energies or *ki;* he would have agreed with the Tōkyū proposal, for example, that the condition of one's energies plays a central role in determining one's fate. However, the physiognomist's advice for attaining the correct balance of these psychophysical forces was more concrete and specific than that of Yokoyama Marumitsu:

> Diet *(shoku)* corresponds with vital energy. One's energies become disordered because one's diet is unsettled. If one's daily diet is uneven, one's affairs become uneven and fail to proceed smoothly, and as a result losses and disasters arise. If [one's affairs] are out of order, one is unable to prosper. Consequently, people should place priority on establishing their diet. When one's diet is settled, one's vital energies naturally become calm, and one's mind naturally attains order. Moreover, once one's mind is ordered and does not waver, disasters do not arise, and as a matter of course it becomes easy to manage one's family.[58]

The idea that the proper cultivation of *ki* is critical to one's well-being at broader physical and social levels was a long-established premise of East Asian health theory. In early Tokugawa Japan, Kaibara Ekiken (1630–1714) had advised his readers that "the fundamental vital energies are the basis of life; drink and food are the nourishment of life."[59] The Confucian scholar had also warned that eating or drinking too much could result in a blockage of one's vital energies, and thus, illness.[60] Nanboku draws on a popularized form of the same discourse in his insistence that "food is the basis for nourishing one's life."[61] The difference between these two articulations is the degree of implied emphasis on physical vis-à-vis more internal forms of cultivation. For Ekiken and other Neo-Confucian scholars of the Tokugawa period, ordering one's mind and heart, and thereby one's vital humors, was generally a precondition of successful physical discipline (such as dieting). In Nanboku's cited remarks on diet, however, the sequence is slightly altered. Eating habits determine the condition of one's vital forces, which then determine one's physical health and state of mind; these in turn affect one's family and social life.

The paradigmatic view that mind cultivation preceded and indeed directed one's progress in larger spheres of existence (health, family, society) was thus rearranged in the physigonomist's program. Regulation of the physiological processes of eating and drinking was now the absolute priority; mental/emotional states were influential in their own right, but in the final analysis they were determined by diet. Eating and drinking correctly were not simply temporary disciplinary exercises that could be bypassed once inner calm was attained; the quality and quantity of one's dietary intake, in Nanboku's view, directly affected the material energies and humors that constitute the human body and mind. It was because of this direct connection between food and one's person (or self), Nanboku believed, that one could actually transform the "destiny" that had already been inscribed on one's face and body.

Digestible Capital

Nanboku's insight into the value of diet as a means of self-betterment was closely related to his belief that the enactment of "hidden virtue" *(intoku)* is required to change one's life course.[62] The physiognomist understood "virtue" to be charity offered to others and believed that authentic virtue was necessarily "hidden"—an act of goodness performed without anyone's knowledge. This idea contrasts with Reader and Tanabe's emphasis on the public quality of contemporary rituals aimed at acquiring practical benefits.[63] For Nanboku, traditional Buddhist acts of merit, such as setting animals free in a formal liberation ceremony or sponsoring sutra readings, did not qualify as effective forms of virtue because they were publicly carried out and therefore inevitably tinged with self-interest. The genuine emancipation of animals, as far as Nanboku was concerned, was refraining from eating them all together.[64] (He cautioned in any case against eating meat for health reasons, as had Kaibara Ekiken.)[65]

The highest type of hidden virtue, for Nanboku, was giving up one's food. One could presumably do this without other people knowing about it. In his *Shūshinroku*, Nanboku recommends quietly offering one-third of each meal to the gods and Buddha: "When one offers [food to the gods], one is in fact offering up one's own life."[66] The idea was not simply to eat one's fill and offer up the leftovers, but to reduce deliberately the amount that one would normally wish to eat and give the remaining portion away. Nanboku does not specify the ultimate recipient of the offered food, but he calls this act of hidden virtue *hodokoshi*, a term that connotes the distribution of alms or charity. Possibly the diviner was advocating an informal type of social welfare as well as a cultivation-oriented interpretation of the act of making offerings to deities.

Ultimately, however, Nanboku's program of food restraint seems to have been less informed by a Buddhist sense of compassion or an impulse to gain merit in the eyes of the gods than by a profound sense of frugality and its presumed benefits. His concern with reducing human consumption—which may appear marvelously forward-looking from today's ecological perspective—extended beyond food and beverages to a variety of other natural resources and products, including water, fire, wood, oil, and paper. He recommended, for example, using discarded bits of wood for fuel, and repeatedly reusing paper (especially white paper, which he believed should never be discarded). People who carefully conserved the products of nature would be assured of good fortune and long life, even if their facial features boded poorly. "When one refrains from using up all the things of nature and maintains frugality, in every case one will be able to succeed in the world *(risshin shusse)....*"[67]

One might conclude from such statements that Nanboku was simply reiterating the argument, well known in Japanese merchant sectors more than a century earlier, that personal frugality is the basis of social and economic prosperity. Mizuno Nanboku sometimes seems to imply that restraint in consumption is merely one step in an overall program of personal cultivation that begins (as in Shingaku) with modulating one's state of mind and ends with the embodiment of common moral values. However, the physiognomist's stress on diet was more thoroughgoing and radical in its implications than earlier merchant discourses. Although he advised his followers to treat money with care, for example, he also allowed that as long as people conserved food, water, and other products of nature, they could spend their money freely without damaging their prospects for health and happiness. Indeed, for Nanboku, gambling and splurging in the pleasure quarters were in themselves irrelevant to the progress of one's cultivation.[68] This perspective of course conflicted with Confucian and other religious arguments that true personal and social success derives from moral circumspection, not from mere physical self-restraint.

For Nanboku, grain was more valuable than money. This judgment was on the one hand simply a hardheaded observation of the facts. As the diviner rightly observed, samurai counted their stipends in measures of rice, not gold and silver, and social disorder originated, not in the fluctuation of market prices, but in the changing outcomes of the yearly grain harvest.[69] At the same time, Nanboku's high valuation of grain (especially rice) expressed an agrarian idealism that pervaded a number of social movements in the late Tokugawa. In his writings Nanboku depicts food as a deity (Shoku Bosatsu, the Food Bodhisattva) who assists laborers, an idea that resonates, for example, with "grain-spirit" *(kokurei)* themes in Fuji devotionalism.[70] For the diviner, eating food was a cosmic transaction: with each meal, the consumer incurred a debt to nature, which would need to be repaid sooner or later. Farmers and working people, who necessarily ate a great deal, according to Nanboku, were more heavily indebted to the universe than others, and as a result they spent their entire lives working to pay back their debts. If they stopped working, they would run out of food (nature did not "loan" food to those who had no prospect of paying it back).[71] In fact, it was not they, but the Food Bodhisattva who did their work through them, and in order for the Bodhisattva to perform this service, the workers had to eat sufficiently (to feed the deity, as it were). Thus, in a rare exception to his strict eating regimen, Nanboku allowed that people who did heavy physical work could eat heartily.

The diviner's view of the intimate relations between eating, working, and repaying one's obligations to nature or nature gods recalls the interpretations of his contemporary, Hirata Atsutane, who similarly depicted food, clothing, and shelter as blessings from the gods, and their consumption as a type of religious devotion.[72] Both Nanboku and Atsutane saw eating and working as segments of a cosmic transaction among human beings, deities, and nature. Nanboku, however, was more concerned with devising a purposive program of personal betterment that could be tailored to the individual client rather than with diffusing a generalized discourse. The Osaka physiognomist understood self-improvement not only as a cosmic-religious endeavor, but also as a social and economic process governed by a daily regimen of concrete rules.

Nanboku's reversal of the mind–body hierarchy of conventional cultivation theory—in other words, his prioritizing of dietary restraint over, say, meditation or moral self-examination as the path to well-being —did not imply any questioning of the Tokugawa social order. Indeed, the physiognomist differentiated his program hierarchically according to the rank, occupation, and sex of the practitioner. Refined, tasty food was meant for highly ranked people, while plain food was for those of lower status.[73] Even while reiterating the social framework of the day, however, Nanboku suggested an intriguing mechanism for circumventing it: one's rank and stipend would rise or decline in inverse proportion to the amount of food that one consumed. He proposed the following theory of social mobility within the samurai estates:

> One's daily meals correspond to the limits of one's status and stipend *(roku)*. . . . When one is filled with food, one's stipend naturally diminishes. When a person who has no office at all consumes the food of a high-ranked officer, he fills that [high] office in terms of food, so in the end he cannot [actually] advance to that office and its stipend. . . . Moreover, one who consumes the food of a low-ranked officer while he is in a

middle-ranked position does not fill [his office] in terms of food; thus his stipend gradually fills up, and in the end he rises to a high office. In this way, one who controls his food intake and is not extravagant will be able to succeed in the world *(risshin shusse)*.[74]

Food was thus a material resource, convertible into various other kinds of capital; its conservation not only enhanced physical health and family relations but also enabled the elevation of social rank and the augmentation of income. Following the right diet, in this view, constituted a religious, social, and economic investment.[75]

The idea that one could attain "success in the world" by restricting one's diet applied not only to samurai but also to physical laborers and other social groups.[76] Even though working people needed to eat substantially, Nanboku advised, they should reduce their intake whenever they happened not to be working, and limit their consumption of rich foods. If workers controlled themselves in these ways, they, too, would set in motion the cosmic mechanism that led to a better endowment *(roku)* in life. People of all classes were thus engaged in a continuous process of exchange with the universe. When the physiognomist said "heaven and earth and human beings are all one body," he meant it in a far more literal sense than did Neo-Confucian anthropocosmic theorists.[77] Food, rather than a mystical sense of the unifying principles of the universe, was the immediate link between nature and humankind, and therefore the key to well-being at all levels.

Mizuno Nanboku's teachings on the exchangeability of food and socioeconomic status were addressed primarily to men. The diviner's writings are punctuated with misogynistic remarks; he depicts women in general as an uncontrollable, ever-present threat to male self-discipline and well-being. Yet Nanboku apparently believed that under the proper circumstances even women could improve their destinies incrementally through dietary restraint. They were held to a stricter standard than men, however: they were to eat less. The physiognomist warned his disciples that women who ate a great deal would overwhelm their husbands. If a woman consumed too much, Nanboku taught, she would be usurping the dietary allotment of a man; as a result, her vital spirit *(ki)* would grow violent and she would "conquer" her husband. On the other hand, unlike men aspiring to high office, women who ate little would not advance to a higher status vis-à-vis their men—they would simply become better at serving their husbands.[78] Nanboku's philosophy of restraint in eating was a male-oriented discourse: whereas frugal eating would enhance men's social and economic possibilities, it would ensure the restriction of women's.

Physiognomy and Learning

Mizuno Nanboku drew on a wide variety of interpretive traditions less from a premeditated plan than because he simply encountered these elements and found them stimulating and useful at that particular time in his life. His resultant theories might be taken to illustrate what Lévi-Strauss once called intellectual bricolage—a process in which the agent's "universe of instruments is closed and the rules of his game are always to make do with 'whatever is at hand.'..."[79] At hand, in this case, were Daoist-Shugendō longevity lore, breathing techniques, Kaibara Ekiken's dietary cautions, Chinese physiognomic traditions, Shingon-Ritsu Buddhist ideas, Ise oracles, Neo-Confucian cultivation paradigms, and agrarian grain-spirit beliefs, among other bits of knowledge. Moreover, the diviner professed to see little substantial difference between the three established religious teachings of the day (Buddhist, Confucian, Shinto); like the Shingaku teachers, the Tōkyū founder, and the leaders of the incipient new religions, Nanboku easily identified concepts from each of these systems with his own understanding of the truth: "In the way of the gods it is called the primeval chaos [*konton*], in the Confucian school it is called the bright virtue [*meitoku*], and in Buddhism it is called [A]mida.[80] Amida arises from the primeval chaos, chaos in its turn arises from the bright virtue, and the bright virtue arises from Amida. These are one, and there is no distinction between them."[81]

Nanboku's interpretation of the various ideas and practices from which he drew was limited by their "particular history"—that is, by their meanings in preexisting contexts of praxis and/or communication.[82] To be sure, he was considerably less aware of the details of this history than teachers who possessed a more formal education. Nevertheless, the physiognomist's employment of seemingly unrelated elements was by no means random or serendipitous in nature. He deliberately researched and eventually formulated a theory of personal cultivation from the knowledge that he encountered. Unlike a true bricolage, Nanboku's teaching was a "project" (in Lévi-Strauss' parlance) that mandated more emphasis on some elements than others.

The purposive character of this theoretical activity informed the diviner's encounter with Neo-Confucian cultivation discourse. Late in his career, Nanboku began to profess that his physiognomy program shared the same aim as the *Great Learning*. On one occasion, a listener complained that Nanboku talked only about self-restraint in eating and drinking, and that he did not actually divine people's fortunes. If this were the case, what was the point of his continuing in the profession of a diviner? The questioner challenged Nanboku to study ancient divination texts and to devote himself to actual prognostications. Nanboku's response reveals much about the conditions under which he came to identify his message with the dominant learning of his age.

> From when I was young, my father and mother were poor and I did not learn my letters; because of that, I cannot read books.... I dislike "licking the dregs of the ancients,"[83] but three years ago a scholar among my disciples read to me the Three Principles of the *Great Learning*.[84] I first heard this [passage] when I was forty-seven years old, and for the first time I understood the "bright virtue" of physiognomy. And I realized on my own that ... physiognomy is the great path for governing one's person and the empire. Consequently I practice divination in order to bring people together and explain that path to them. Because of this, in recent years I have only guided people [along this path] and have rarely spoken about their fortunes. I simply consider diet to be the foundation and the beginning of the Way, and therefore I speak a great deal about food and drink. In every case, I do this in order to [encourage people to] govern their minds and bodies.[85]

According to this account, Nanboku had been practicing divination for many years before he was exposed to the Neo-Confucian paradigm of personal cultivation. Perhaps he had unknowingly heard popular renditions of the concept earlier in his life. In any event, after the exposure in his late forties, he inserted the notion of "clarifying bright virtue" into his evolving theory of self-discipline, consciously translating the aims of his program into the prevailing cultural idiom of the time. Educated listeners could now identify in his teachings a logic of personal improvement with which they were already familiar.

Nanboku was nevertheless ambivalent about the value of classical Confucian learning. When asked how persons of little capacity or low rank *(shōjin)* could possibly understand how to discipline themselves and their families without studying the teachings of the sages, Nanboku responded (momentarily eliding his usual emphasis on diet) that self-discipline was based in the first place on correcting one's internal attitude *(kokoro)*, not simply on book learning. He pointed out that even people who were deeply learned did not necessarily know how to be frugal in conducting their businesses or running their households. Echoing a common refrain in *chōnin* (townspeople) discourse of the Edo era, Nanboku warned that too much attention to studies could result in financial and moral loss to one's household.[86] The physiognomist extended this ambivalence toward learning to professional Confucian scholars in general, as did so many other popular teachers of the time. When asked whether the great Confucian thinkers Ogyū Sorai and his disciple Dazai

Shundai (1680–1747) were indeed "men of great virtue," Nanboku demurred.

> Sorai and Dazai were not men of virtue. Since they studied the Way with a strong spirit and surpassed a myriad other people in committing it to memory, we call them "heroes" *[gōketsu]*. We do not call them "men of virtue" [just] because they were great Confucian scholars.... To be a genuine person of virtue means that you do not dispute over written words and that singlemindedly, in all your actions, you regard your self as the Way and all things as your texts—and that you concentrate only on mastering this principle in its entirety.[87]

The diviner here sounds the same theme that preoccupied Confucian educators of his time: one must look into oneself for the "Way" and avoid becoming caught up in textualist debates. Unlike professional scholars, however, Nanboku and other thinkers of his ilk refused to identify their ideas with "learning" *(gakumon)* per se, preferring simply to sprinkle their discourses with selected phrases from a few well-known classical texts. When one critic asked why Nanboku placed all his emphasis on eating and drinking and not on the five Confucian "constants" *(gojō)* or virtues, he averred that these moral standards were simply the branches (as opposed to the root). He preferred to speak of the "various principles" of the universe (by which he meant, in the first place, the conservation of natural resources).

> Life is the virtue of heaven; the things that nourish this [life] are the virtues of earth. Therefore, the virtues of heaven and earth are what give us life and nourish us. When one is apprised of these blessings of heaven and earth, one naturally realizes one's obligation to one's parents [because one has received life and nourishment from them]. A person who appreciates this [obligation] has respect for life, food, and drink—the Five Constants are included within this.[88]

This kind of individual, or "person of virtue," was evidently one whose understanding of the unity of life, nature, and morality transcended the conceptualizations of Confucian scholars like Ogyū Sorai and Dazai Shundai.

Nanboku's polemic against professional scholars, like that of Yokoyama Marumitsu, also functioned as an assertion of his own social identity. Fortune-tellers of various types proliferated in the late Tokugawa period; they included hexagram *(Book of Changes)* diviners, physiognomists, Onmyōdō (yin-yang) experts, and an assortment of other prognosticators who specialized in analyzing tombs, swords, dreams, and more. The boom in divination was stimulated by the importation and widespread dissemination of Chinese prognostication manuals in annotated Japanese editions. The city of Edo at one point is said to have boasted at least one diviner for every *chō* (city ward)—altogether about one thousand professional fortune-tellers; Kyoto and Osaka were no doubt similarly equipped.[89] Physiognomy in particular, which before Tokugawa times had been the prerogative of Buddhist priests and other ritual specialists, attracted a growing clientele after the Genroku era (1688–1703); by the close of the eighteenth century professional physiognomists were very much in demand.[90]

The multiplication of diviners in the late Tokugawa provoked a corresponding rise in criticism of their activities, which some viewed as money-making scams. We recall that the shogunate's primary concern about Tōkyūjutsu was its revenue. The Neo-Confucian scholar Arai Hakuga (1714–1792), who himself practiced hexagram divination, vituperated prognosticators whose methods were not also based on the *Book of Changes*. In 1789 Hakuga listed what he considered "devices that mislead the ignorant and the vulgar in the world": "Geomancy, physiognomy, ink-hue divination, character-stroke divination; [beliefs in] Konjin and Buddha, curses from the gods, sword divination, *nisshu seiten,* possession spirits *[tsukimono],* incantations, and inauspicious days; fortune-telling at intersections; and [beliefs in] spirits of the dead and of the living...."[91] Educated figures tended to view the divination arts with ambivalence at best; many associated prognostication with other popular customs of which they disapproved. Senior shogunal councilor Matsudaira Sadanobu (1758–1829), for example, repeatedly questioned the merit of physiognomy in his writings; the merchant-scholar Yamagata Bantō (1748–1821) reportedly pronounced it useless.[92]

In its mature form, as we have seen, Nanboku physiognomy moved quite beyond simple fortune-telling, but educational elites of the time seem to have lumped it together with other divination practices. Nanboku was keenly aware of such criticisms. In the preface to his *Shūshinroku,* he remarks that "vulgar Confucians" who chose to deride his book would make enemies among those who followed the "path of goodness," and indeed would "contradict the principles of heaven." Such critics, he predicts, would never succeed in the world, because they regarded themselves as lofty and brilliant, and thus were "useless to people."[93] In the body of his text as well, Nanboku harshly criticizes teachers who, in his view, failed to cultivate a genuine understanding of the "principles of the universe" *(tenchi no ri)* and to realize that all things ultimately derive from nature. Because of their lack of understanding, these people were wont to waste natural resources and dissipate themselves in drinking, meat eating, and sexual immorality. They also attacked the views of others and used their learning to impress ignorant people and inflate their own images.[94] Needless to say, the physiognomist considered his own approach to learning far superior to that offered by professional Confucian scholars. In his view, it was these men of "learning" who distracted people with their abstruse theories from the real task at hand: taking control of one's life through authentic self-discipline.

Like the Tōkyūjutsu founder, then, Nanboku adopted a view that was eminently *not* fatalistic; changing one's life course was very much within one's power. Neither of these teachers was unique among diviners in this regard; several other fortune-tellers of the late Edo period promoted individual responsibility and personal discipline. The writer Ban Kōkei made the following report, for example, about a physiognomist called Nakamura Ryōtai:

> When he divined the features of ordinary people, he consistently explained the art of [cultivating the] mind to them, saying: "Although your physiognomic appearance is auspicious, you will not profit because your resolve is not good;" [or,] "although your physiognomic appearance is inauspicious, by means of determination and effort you can overcome it...." In recent times, numerous people discourse on physiognomy, and many vulgar customers, for their part, delight in it. However, the outstanding characteristic of this person is that he teaches [his clients] the workings of the mind based on physiognomy.[95]

Despite some scholars' blanket accusation that divination was misleading and pernicious, a number of fortune-tellers apparently encouraged their clients to exercise self-discipline in order to overcome the material and spiritual handicaps that they had presumably inherited. Nanboku's program is our best-documented example of this divination-as-cultivation approach in the early modern period. He transformed the merchant ethic of frugality into a system of personal conservation that promised empowerment (especially to men) at all levels of society. Adherence to it would result most immediately in the improvement of one's health, understood as the unimpeded circulation of vital energies throughout one's mind and body, and ultimately in the amelioration of the moral, social, and economic aspects of one's life.

While intellectuals of the time classed physiognomy with other forms of knowledge that they considered superstitious nonsense—such as the belief that people can be possessed by evil spirits who take the form of foxes and badgers *(tsukimono)*—popular figures like Nanboku ironically saw their own teachings as countering, if not the superstitions themselves, the ill effects that the latter were believed to bring about in people's lives. The physiognomist promoted the ultimate power of personal discipline even while affirming the validity of popular beliefs.

> Even if people have physiognomic features that indicate they will go mad, if they always regulate their diet correctly, we cannot say they will become insane. But if people have features that indicate insanity and their food intake is limitless and indiscriminate, they will definitely go mad. Moreover, they will suffer harm from foxes and badgers....
>
> If people constantly run off at the mouth as if mad or possessed, do not make an issue of this; treat them as you normally would and do not offer them food or drink more than three times [a day]. If you do this for a hundred days, things like foxes and badgers will retreat of their own accord.
>
> In addition, when people have been afflicted for several years, if they carry this [regimen] out for three years, they will naturally be cured. This [cure] is definitely not caused by the withdrawal of the possessing spirits. When their diet is strictly regulated, people's natures and minds become sound of themselves and their gut energies *[kanki]* naturally settle down; the affliction is thereby cured. Even if things like foxes and badgers take hold of [a person], if [that person's] nature and mind are sound, the [possessing spirits] will not be able to inflict any harm and will depart of their own accord. You should realize that in every case this [insanity] arises from lack of discipline in eating and drinking.[96]

Nanboku thus accepted the existence of possessing spirits, but at the same time viewed them as susceptible to human administration. By advocating dietary restraint as a means of repelling evil influences, he placed control of personal well-being directly into the hands of the ordinary individual (as opposed to a professional exorcist or other ritual expert). In a similar vein he subsumed benevolent deities within the self-transforming subject. "The gods are gods everywhere. Therefore, they [also] dwell within the hearts of the people. As such, the gods do not possess exceptional virtue: the exceptional virtue is all in oneself."[97] While paying due respect to the spiritual "others" in which some of his clients placed their faith, Nanboku in fact dedicated the bulk of his discourse to exhorting people to determine their own lives.

The duty of the physiognomist, in this view, was to identify and "clarify the bright virtue" of his clients.[98] In other words, the diviner should aim first at discerning the inborn spiritual makeup of the individual—or, in popular Buddhist terms, the person's karmic inheritance.[99] Nanboku had concluded early on that "physiognomy must be based on observation not of external appearances but of the formless features *[musō]* that lie concealed in the depths [of a person]."[100] In order to "see" these invisible features clearly, he believed, diviners had to cultivate a state of selfless unity with the universe (become "one body with heaven-and-earth") or, as he expressed it in devotional terms, rely on the help of the gods. It was only after establishing this state of piety and inner clarity, which would permit accurate perception of people's characters, that physiognomists could successfully lead their clients to cultivate themselves. The Nanboku physiognomist, like the Tōkyūjutsu diviner, was thus not simply a fortune-teller, but a teacher who taught clients how to "cultivate one's person and bring order to one's family."[101] The act of divination, in short, provided the occasion for a didactic discourse on self-discipline that Nanboku associated with the Neo-Confucian paradigm.

Both Marumitsu and Nanboku exploited the popular appeal of divination, a service that traditionally placed the client in a passive position vis-à-vis the diviner, and at the same time drew on existing stocks of religious knowledge to formulate a method of active self-improvement that could be used by people from a range of social classes. The physiognomist's proposal outdid Tōkyūjutsu, however, in terms of tangibility and practicality. Few areas of self-discipline are closer at hand than eating. According to the most common interpretation of the *Great Learning* during this time, the internal steps of "making one's thoughts sincere" and "correcting one's mind" were preliminary (in causal if not temporal sequence) to "cultivating one's person" *(shūshin)*. The latter endeavor was generally understood to involve modification of one's inner states as well as of one's physical condition, demeanor, and conduct. The title of Nanboku's *Shūshinroku* (Records of Personal Cultivation) duly connotes this broader sense of personal cultivation, but the book concentrates on the physiological dimension of self-improvement.

Nanboku physiognomy may contain a hidden premise: one cannot really succeed in restricting one's diet until one first disciplines one's mind. However, this interpretive possibility becomes a logical nicety in the face of the diviner's constant exhortations to control one's consumption; the sheer repetition of this message in Nanboku's written discourse has the effect of rearranging the paradigm of cultivation for his readers in the direction of the physiological and the concrete. By identifying specific bodily disciplines more than the refinement of mental and emotional states as the foundation of overall well-being, Nanboku in effect upset the canonical sequence of learning that was inculcated in most male members of the privileged classes during his time, and that was widely diffused among members of lesser estates as well. Despite his rhetoric of identification with the Neo-Confucian framework of personal development, Nanboku clearly differentiated his program from the system of learning he associated with Confucian scholars.

CHAPTER 3

Breathing as Purification

THE THINKERS DISCUSSED in the preceding pages universally relied on the Neo-Confucian cultivation paradigm as a point of reference in their discourses on the pursuit of happiness and success in life. Core members of the Confucian linguistic community—who were well versed in the classical texts—such as Ōta Kinjō, Satō Issai, Imakita Kōsen, and Takahashi Kōsetsu, respected the power of those texts, and each in his own way interpreted them for a public audience. At the same time, these scholars created special interpretive enclaves in which they depicted the texts not as sources of absolute truth but as provisional articulations— stepping-stones to a higher realm of meaning. Yokoyama Marumitsu and Mizuno Nanboku, on the other hand, were less concerned with creatively rereading the classical texts than with constructing workable methods of self-improvement to compensate for what they perceived as the inherent abstractness of current modes of scholarship. These and other popular interpreters—who were literate or semiliterate but not professional scholars—assumed the value of Confucian-style moral cultivation, but qualified it and to varying degrees transformed it through their emphasis on the practical (and often physiological) dimensions of self-development.

The interpretation of personal cultivation in the direction of tangible, physically oriented practices is characteristic of the early "new religions" as well. One of these movements emerged in the Edo area during the same period in which Marumitsu's and Nanboku's teachings began to attract sizable followings. The founder, Inoue Masakane (1790–1849), spent several years traveling around Japan and studying under Buddhist and Shinto priests, Confucian teachers, Chinese-medicine practitioners, and diviners. The system of religious practices and ideas that he eventually produced, Tohokami, later became the "Shinto-type" new religion Misogikyō.[1] This chapter treats the early history and teachings of the Tohokami movement, ultimately with an eye to the issues raised in the preceding pages: the conception of authentic cultivation and its relationship to Confucian logic. The concluding portion of the chapter situates Tohokami within the larger interreligious network discussed in this book. As we shall see, the Bakumatsu movement was one part of a social and interpretive figuration that continued to function through a series of shifting and overlapping connections into the modern period.

Inoue Masakane began his search for religious and medical knowledge in his late teens.[2] He is said to have practiced Zen Buddhism for a time under an Ōbaku nun called Tetsuyo Zenni, and to have studied Chinese medicine under the physician Isono Kōdō (b. 1772).[3] Of Masakane's various teachers during this early period, however, the most important for the development of his religious practice was probably Mizuno Nanboku, whom he met during a trip to Ise in 1814. Under Nanboku's supervision, Masakane not only learned the art of physiognomy, but also a great deal about self-discipline.[4] While training in Nanboku's Kyoto residence, the future Tohokami leader carried out cold-water ablutions early in the morning, performed manual labor, ate only small amounts of plain food (mostly grains, supplemented by greens), wore simple clothing, slept on a thin futon, and stood under the waterfall at Kiyomizudera every day.[5] Like his teacher, Masakane would come to advocate giving up a portion of one's repasts, not only as an offering to the gods and a concrete form of charity to others, but also as a means of purifying oneself, both physically and spiritually. Nanboku may also have taught Masakane how to breathe while focusing his energies in the lower abdomen, a method of personal cultivation that would become central to the Tohokami program.

Masakane moved back to Edo in late 1815 and began practicing hexagram divination (under the name Shūeki),[6] although he continued to support himself by practicing Chinese medicine; during this period he married Itoko (1802–1878), the daughter of a samurai named Anzai Masahisa. Under the guidance of a physician called Asai Sen'an, Masakane also mastered finger-pressure therapy *(shiatsu ryōhō)* and a healing technique called *kantsū*. He gradually began to attract students, notably Honjō Munehide (Matsudaira Hidejirō, 1809–1873), the future domain lord of Miyazu, who would remain an important supporter of the Tohokami community through the Restoration period.

Inoue Masakane believed that his personal search for the truth was intimately connected to that of his father, Andō Magane (1753–1827), a samurai who served in the Edo residence of the lord of Tatebayashi. According to Masakane's account, his father was intensely concerned about the suffering and unhappiness he observed in the world around him; Edo in fact underwent significant famine and social unrest during Magane's lifetime. From about 1794 until his death, Magane is said to have shut himself up in a second-story room, pondering how best to succor the sick and the poor.[7] Shortly before he died, Masakane's father allegedly attained the realization he had been seeking and commissioned his son to teach it to others, at all costs.[8]

Andō Magane's ruminations may have been imbued with nativist strains of thought. His son later claimed that the first syllable of Magane's name was inspired by that of the great nativist scholar Kamo Mabuchi (1697–1769), of whom his father had considered himself a follower.[9] In fact, Magane was in his teens when Mabuchi died, and it is unlikely that the latter instructed him directly. Inoue Masakane himself was no doubt familiar with the works of Mabuchi, Motoori Norinaga, and possibly Hirata Atsutane or other nineteenth-century nativists, but his writings exhibit only a generalized Kokugaku perspective; the Tohokami founder did not present himself as a spokesperson of any particular nativist school.[10] Andō Magane's "transmission" to his son more likely centered on the meaning of certain Shinto ritual prayers *(norito)*, especially the well-known formula *To ho kami emi tame* (discussed below).[11]

Inoue Masakane later recounted that he did not immediately understand what his father had tried to teach him and continued to travel in search of further understanding. He realized before long that the teachers he encountered were "capable and possessed wide learning and many talents; [but] they simply spoke about their own individual teachings, and did not cultivate their persons, bring order to their families, or extend this [care] to their relatives."[12] Not finding a reliable exemplar of this ideal, framed in the familiar phraseology of the *Great Learning,* Masakane reportedly tried to attain a higher level of understanding on his own—by fasting, confining his diet to fruit and nuts, performing cold-water austerities, and meditating. None of these disciplines produced the desired result, however.[13] Later, Masakane commented about this phase of his life that

> for numerous years, I had been initiated into and studied several kinds of teachings. However, when I served my father and mother, I could not give them peace of mind; when I attempted to bring order to my family, I was unable to give my wife and children peace; when I tried to regulate my body, I could not succeed in doing so; when I tried to quiet my mind, it would not calm down; and when I tried to confirm my resolve, I was unable to achieve a serene mind.[14]

If we are to credit this account, Masakane's chief problem was the lack of a form of personal cultivation that would fulfill the aims of the Neo-Confucian paradigm. Just as he began to feel that he had exhausted, to no avail, virtually all possible methods for enacting this ideal, according to his account, two events changed his outlook. In 1833, Masakane had a revelatory dream in which a female "messenger of the gods" appeared to him and gave him the power to dispel his delusions and attain the insight he was seeking. He realized that his previous way of thinking had been completely mistaken, and determined to preserve the "sacred teachings of our imperial land."[15] The second pivotal episode of this period was Masakane's encounter with an obscure teacher who imparted to him the "mind of faith" *(shinjin);* he allegedly "attained the truth" *(tokudō)* at this point, along with one of his followers, Sugiyama Shūzan (d. 1878).[16] According to one account, this awakening took place after an elderly woman called Teishō initiated Masakane into a form of Shinto.[17]

Not much is known about Teishō, not even the extent to which her teaching should be characterized as Shinto rather than Buddhist. The identity of the transmission that the Misogi leader received at this point may well have been a version of Pure Land Buddhism. A travel diary that Masakane wrote in 1826 contains evidence of his early Pure Land sympathies.[18] Moreover, a mid-Meiji Misogikyō text states that Teishō was the member of the Okura or "hidden *nenbutsu*" community (an underground group of Pure Land Buddhist practitioners).[19] To further complicate the question of the relationship between Tohokami and Pure Land Buddhism, some of Masakane's later followers reportedly chanted the Pure Land formula *Namu Amida Butsu* in order to conceal the true identity of their religion after it was banned. Masakane's writings do not indicate that he understood his teaching to be a form of Pure Land Buddhism, but the resemblance between his notion of a transmission of faith or mind of faith *(shinjin)* and the True Pure Land idea of Amida's transfer of faith to human beings *(shinjin ekō)* is probably not coincidental.[20] Devotion to a compassionate, powerful deity who saves believers by granting them the capacity for faith would become a central emphasis in the Tohokami leader's writings.

In any event, soon after Masakane received this transmission, he reportedly began to notice an improvement in his mental and physical condition. He also began to see a connection between his new understanding and the Shinto-based teaching that his father had tried to convey to him.[21] He enrolled in the Shirakawa (Hakke) school of Shinto in Kyoto the next year, when he was forty-five.[22] There he learned the formal details of two key rituals, *misogi* (cleansing) and *harae* (expurgation), as well as other ceremonial forms that shrine priests of the time were expected to master.[23] In late 1836 the Shirakawa house conferred on Masakane a license to perform shrine rituals as well as permission to wear the black cap and white vestments of the shrine priest (figure 3).

FIGURE 3. Inoue Masakane, founder of Misogikyō. Woodblock print contained in *Inoue Masakane shindenki,* ed. Inoue Sukekane (1877).

The Quest for Legitimacy

The Tohokami founder's 1833 dream is consistently presented in his and his followers' retrospective narratives as the force that propelled him to enroll in the Shirakawa school. The decision to study school Shinto is thus "explained" and indeed sanctified in these histories by the mechanism of an oracular dream (a device not infrequently used in traditional Japanese literature to justify inexplicable leaps in the narrative). Nevertheless, other factors figured in the decision. The Yoshida and Shirakawa houses controlled Shinto shrines during the Edo period; some leaders of nonestablished religious groups gained legitimacy and thus permission to proselytize by formally associating with these schools. In the late period the Shirakawa school was especially liberal in granting such licenses. Masakane's affiliation with the latter may in fact have deflected unwelcome shogunal attention from his own activities, at least for a time. Some historians have accordingly argued that the affiliation was a preventive strategy on Masakane's part, even though his enrollment in the school predated his troubles with the shogunate by several years. By this

FIGURE 4. The Umeda Shinmei Shrine in Tokyo today. (Photo by the author).

account he would already have been worried about possible government hostility in the early 1830s.[24]

Ogihara Minori, the leading modern scholar of Tohokami/ Misogikyō history, believes that Masakane enrolled in the Shirakawa house because of a genuine interest in Shinto ritual—unlike the founding figures of Konkōkyō and Tenrikyō, whose affiliations with formal Shinto schools were clearly designed to legalize their religious activities.[25] Yet the Tohokami leader's decision to become a shrine priest was surely also related to his proselytizing ambitions: it was only after he became priest of the Umeda Shinmei Shrine in Musashi in 1840 (under the name Shikibu) that he began propagating his own teachings openly and regularly in the Edo area (figure 4).[26] Shinto shrine personnel, like Buddhist priests, were part of the shogunal-domain establishment, and their public status as religious professionals was thus relatively secure. The Kurozumikyō founder's case provides an instructive comparison in this regard. Kurozumi Munetada (1780–1850) was affiliated with a Yoshida shrine for some time before he began actively proselytizing, but after resigning his post as priest, he apparently lost his image of legitimacy, especially among his samurai followers.[27] It is unlikely that Inoue

Masakane, for his part, was unaware of the social and political value of being a licensed Shirakawa priest before he enrolled in the Kyoto school.

Indeed, after the founder received the Shirakawa license and bought the rights to the Shinmei Shrine, several wealthy farmers and headmen from the vicinity began supporting his activities by donating funds and other resources. Masakane opened the shrine to the ill, elderly, and indigent, transforming the precincts into a kind of sanctuary for the downtrodden, and began to give sermons on the "Way of the Gods" *(Shintō)*. A disciple later recounted that the people who congregated at the Shinmei Shrine during this period included "the sick, the poor, people who had lost themselves in sake and sexual desire and could not control their bodies, and people who were a source of distress to their relatives. [Inoue Masakane] had pity on every one of them and lodged them inside the shrine" (presumably while he guided them back to a state of well-being).[28] In addition to helping care for his clients' fundamental health needs, the Tohokami leader imparted practices of self-purification to individuals who were seriously interested in his teachings. These more committed followers regularly met to chant *To ho kami emi tame—* loudly and in time to a bell rung by the group leader *(osa)*.[29]

The status of shrine priest did not provide infallible protection from government suppression. Before long, Masakane's use of the shrine as a center for social relief and unconventional rituals attracted the attention of the shogunate's religious control bureau, the Office of Temples and Shrines *(jisha bugyō)*. Masakane was arrested in late 1841, along with his wife, Onari, and his two close followers Miura Hayato (1791–1841) and Uneme (Chizen, 1798–1856). At this juncture, the Shirakawa affiliation served Masakane well, if only as a stalling mechanism. The Kantō representative of the Shirakawa house, Minamiōji Sahyōe, submitted a letter to the government in Masakane's defense, arguing that the priest's teaching conformed with the Shirakawa tradition.[30] After this intervention, the authorities ordered Masakane to deliver a written summary of his teachings to them and in early 1842 released him to the custody of his village (Umeda). The disquisition that Masakane subsequently presented to the Office of Temples and Shrines, *Shintō yuiitsu mondō sho* (Questions and Answers on the One Shinto), duly enhances the connection between his ideas and the Shirakawa teachings. The emphasis on school-Shinto terms and rituals is notably absent from Masakane's later writings (mostly letters that he smuggled to his followers from exile), in which he no longer needed to downplay the novel aspects of his teachings.[31]

Shirakawa sources reveal that many of Masakane's followers affiliated with and provided financial support to the school, especially in the years just before and after the shogunate's actions against the Toho-

FIGURE 5. Inoue Masakane's followers bid him farewell as he departs for a life of exile in Miyakejima. Wood-block print. Contained in *Inoue Masakane shindenki,* ed. Inoue Sukekane (1877).

kami leader. When the founder was arrested a second time in late 1842, these members again appealed to the Shinto school for support.[32] Honjō Munehide and his associates requested that Masakane be transferred to the custody of the Office of Temples and Shrines in Edo, perhaps in the hope that they could wield more influence through their Shirakawa liaisons there.[33] In response, the school asked the authorities for leniency, citing Masakane's poor health and reiterating that his teachings cohered with Shirakawa traditions.[34] This second petition proved fruitless, however, and in the second month of 1843 a verdict of exile was handed down. Masakane was sent to the island of Miyakejima, where, despite his followers' subsequent petitions to the shogunate, he remained until his death in 1849 (figure 5).

Several aspects of Masakane's religious activities were unacceptable to the shogunate. The purported reasons for the government's suppression of the group are delineated in the verdict against him. The authors of the document describe the founder's activities as follows:

> [Inoue Masakane] became a Shinto priest of the Shirakawa school, was initiated into the Nakatomi Triple Purification *[Nakatomi sanshu no*

harai], and understood it to be the same in intent as his breathing system *(kokyū no hō)*. Moreover, he interpreted the Shinto, Confucian and Buddhist [teachings] that he had learned on his own in such a way as to tally with each other, point for point. He attracted numerous people by giving Shinto lectures and had them loudly chant the purification [formula] day and night until their breath gave out. He transmitted his breathing system to them and taught them that through disciplined practice of this one method of breathing, they would recover completely from their afflictions and fulfill in a natural manner their obligations to lord, father, and country. To those who became well versed [in this practice], he transmitted the significance of the purification rite and, based on his own insight, the innermost meaning of the Shirakawa house teaching, calling it the "Revered Law" *(Gohō)*. He did not distribute medicine to the homeless, the debauched, or the ill, but lodged them for lengthy periods and encouraged them, saying he would dispel their evil thoughts, sickly dispositions, and impurities. He received rice, money, and so forth from [his followers], in accordance with their position in society....

The statement goes on to describe how Masakane's followers visited neighboring villages in Shinto priestly garb and healed the ill, whereupon "overcome with joy, [people] chanted the purification [formula] and danced." The authors conclude that Masakane was "relying entirely on his own idiosyncratic ways *(kuse)*," which were *not* part of the Shirakawa teachings, and that he was "leading people astray by means of these novel interpretations and heterodox currents *(shingi iryū)*."[35]

Some have speculated that Inoue Masakane's exile was provoked by his alleged predictions of the shogunate's collapse, but as Sakata Yasuyoshi notes, there is no firm evidence of anti-Bakufu thought in his writings.[36] The Tohokami founder reportedly believed that the world had become disordered after the third generation of Tokugawa shoguns, but he did not pursue the implications of this premise in any explicit way. Masakane spoke often of the importance of Amaterasu and her "vow" to save ordinary people; he shared the prevailing view that she had designated the imperial family to rule Japan, a belief that was no doubt reinforced during his stint at the Shirakawa school. However, these tenets did not translate into an anti-shogunal ideology. The founder's pointed explanations of his breath-control and healing practices in the semi-apologetic *Shintō yuiitsu mondō sho* indicate at least his own belief that it was his departures from conventional shrine practice that had provoked the government's suspicions.

At the same time, despite the language of the verdict and the implications of Masakane's own discourse, the authorities' concern did not derive simply from their perception of his religious heteropraxy. The Shirakawa school had authorized Masakane's priestly status and affirmed that his seemingly unconventional practices—chanting ritual formulae, conducting breathing exercises, and healing—all conformed with Hakke Shinto teachings. Even if the shogunate did not accept the Shirakawa arguments at face value, other issues were clearly at stake in the its decision to take action against him. Masakane's ability to elicit the devotion of large numbers of people within the Edo area, especially the underprivileged, was probably a greater source of alarm to the government; as I noted earlier, the shogunate issued strictures against popular movements with increasing frequency during the 1840s. The chanting and healing practices were viewed as dangerous because they appeared to encourage an autonomous form of communal action outside the existing socioeconomic order rather than primarily because of their religious novelty.

The apparent sympathy of Shirakawa representatives for Masakane and his followers was, in turn, not based purely on doctrinal or ritual considerations. During the late Tokugawa, the Shirakawa house came into conflict with the Yoshida school of Shinto because of the latter's growing influence over shrine priests. In an effort to expand their control over shrine personnel, from the second half of the eighteenth century both schools pursued strategies of expansion; the Shirakawa in particular increasingly authorized the priestly qualifications of religious agents who were not traditionally part of the school-Shinto establishment, such as pilgrimage guides and shamans.[37] Granting the status of shrine priest to Masakane, encouraging the affiliation of his followers, and defending the Tohokami leader to the shogunate were part of the Shirakawa drive to assert itself as an alternative power within the Tokugawa socioreligious arrangement.[38]

The Purification Discipline

The distinguishing feature of Inoue Masakane's teaching is the value he imputed to breathing as a means of personal improvement. I noted earlier that the Tohokami founder may have learned how to control his breath while studying under Mizuno Nanboku.[39] The exercise of regulating one's breathing was common to numerous religious communities of this time, both Buddhist and other, but as we have seen, Nanboku's insights were probably inspired mostly by the Daoist-type longevity praxis with which he had experimented during his mountain travels. The physiognomist recommended that before carrying out a prognostication, diviners should stabilize themselves internally by sitting calmly in an upright posture and breathing seven times, while mentally focusing on the part of the body in which the vital energies are stored—namely, the abdominal area just below the navel (commonly called the "field of cinnabar," J. *tanden,* in East Asian health discourse).[40] The process of inhaling and exhaling, in this view, was integral to the discipline of preserving one's life force. "When people settle their spiritual energies *(shinki)* in their abdomens," Nanboku once remarked, "we call this the longevity of immortals. The preservation of fortune, wealth, and long life depends entirely on one's lower abdomen. The reason why it depends on one's lower abdomen is that in each case it depends on discipline in eating and drinking."[41]

Inoue Masakane shared this way of thinking, in which life, breath, food, vital energy, and success in life are all inextricably related to each other. However, instead of giving priority to diet, as did his teacher Nanboku, the Tohokami founder identified breathing as the critical focus of self-modulation (though he duly advocated restraint in eating and drinking). Masakane reportedly justified his emphasis on breathing by citing passages from the ancient Japanese chronicles and the Nakatomi priestly liturgies.[42] Borrowing Hakke Shinto nomenclature, he referred to the breathing exercise as *Nagayo no den* (the eternal tradition) and instructed his followers to carry it out daily in preparation for their main religious practice, the purification ritual. Nagayo breathing involved inhaling deeply through the nose while directing the breath to the abdominal area below the navel (using diaphragm rather than lung movement), and exhaling slowly through the mouth. The breathing was meant to be moderate and gentle, not strained or violent. Masakane advised his followers to practice Nagayo "in front of the gods" *(shinzen)* every day for the amount of time it took to burn one stick of incense.[43] Like certain preliminary Buddhist meditational exercises and Neo-Confucian quiet sitting *(seiza),* the practice was intended in the first instance to calm the mind and body.

The purification ritual itself, usually called the "discipline of purification" *(harae shugyō)* in Masakane's writings, centered on the chanting of a prayer formula that was declaimed in major seasonal ceremonies at Shinto shrines during the Edo period: *to ho kami emi tame.*[44] In the founder's view, this formula was closely related to the three divine regalia *(sanshu no kandakara)* that Amaterasu had bequeathed to her descendant Ninigi when she commissioned the latter to rule Japan.[45] Masakane believed that the string of sounds had a mysterious power to drive away personal impurities (caused by sins, offenses, or curses) and to imbue one with the virtuous qualities of Amaterasu.[46]

The Tohokami leader claimed that his teachings were different from those of ordinary Shinto priests. In his writings he carries on a veritable polemic against established ritual learning. He implies that many shrine priests of the time were trained merely in the niceties of ritual purification and were not cognizant of the practice's deeper religious significance—they lacked an internal grasp of the gods' teachings.[47] In contrast to the highly formalized recitation of *norito* ordinarily carried out at shrines, Masakane advised his followers simply to repeat the chant in its full version *(To ho kami emi tame, harae tamae kiyome tamau)* in conjunction with rhythmic breathing.[48] The practitioners' exhalations were to be understood as a "blowing away" of their accumulated defects, offenses, and impurities. After a prolonged period of intensive chanting/breathing of the sound syllables, when the followers were barely able to breathe and their voices were hoarse, they would reach a spiritual climax. At that juncture, Masakane promised, they would feel a great sense of well-being and profound gratitude toward their country, masters, teachers, and parents. They would no longer be troubled by the "mind of delusion"—self-centered dispositions and desires for material goods such as food, clothing, and shelter—but would be imbued with the mind of faith *(shinjin).*[49]

Inoue Masakane defined the attainment of *shinjin* as the third and highest stage of his religious regimen: a direct, personal experience of salvation, granted by Amaterasu to the individual.[50] The event is depicted in Tohokami and Misogikyō writings as a turning point in practitioners' religious lives, after which they begin to live (and proselytize) their faith in earnest. I indicated earlier that Masakane's understanding of *shinjin* may have been inspired by the True Pure Land notion of *shinjin ekō*, an event that is similarly believed to reorient one's religious life toward the expression of gratitude to one's deity (in the latter case, Amida Buddha). In practice as well, the enunciation of the Tohokami formula in tandem with abdominal breathing served as a devotionally oriented contemplative exercise not unlike the meditative use of the *nenbutsu* by some Pure Land Buddhists. However, in the Tohokami founder's written discourse, the idea of a divine transfer is usually identified with the Japanese belief that human beings are the children of the gods and as such inherit their divine inner qualities.

The repetition of the *norito* was understood in the Tohokami community as facilitating this transfer. Masakane implies in his writings that repeated enunciation of the sacred formula activates *kotodama,* the mysterious power traditionally believed to inhere in Japanese words. It was precisely because of their *kotodama* that the sounds "to ho kami emi tame" could purge adepts of spiritual defilements and allow the gods to revive in them the "true heart" *(magokoro)* of faith.[51] In other words, the utterance of the syllables of the *norito* mysteriously cleansed the practitioner of self-centered psychological residue and restored the mental and emotional pristineness requisite for authentic union with the gods. Subsequent enactments of the discipline served to maintain the individual in this state of purity and communion with the *kami*.

The mystical and magical nuances of this breathing/chanting practice characterized other Tohokami rituals as well.[52] A striking example of Masakane's own magical use of the purification formula is his rain-making in Miyakejima. After he arrived on the island in 1843, the Tohokami leader offered his ritual and medical services to the island people and his fellow exiles (who allegedly included arsonists, pickpockets, and other petty criminals). In one letter, he relates that during a severe drought local officials asked him to petition the gods for rain. According to one report, Masakane considered this sort of activity to lie beyond the purview of his teachings, but the founder himself testifies that he immediately consented and proceeded to carry out seven days of ritual abstinence *(monoimi)* dedicated to the tutelary deity of the area (Kisaki Daimyōjin).[53] He then went into confinement in the nearby mountains and began fasting, having vowed to starve himself to death if the gods failed to respond to his request for rain.[54] A few drops fell on the first night of his fast, but the following day was sunny, so Masakane persevered. He recounts that on the third day of his fast, as he was engaged in continuous repetition of the purification formula, dark clouds gathered, thunder rolled, and torrents of rain poured down. The village people were reportedly so delighted that they welcomed the Tohokami leader back from the mountains by dancing and chanting *To ho kami emi tame* (figure 6). Masakane relates that after this incident, many island dwellers came to listen to his teachings.

Not unlike the Pure Land Buddhist chant, *Namu Amida Butsu,* which possesses multiple possible functions and levels of significance depending on the context of its use, the enunciation of the Tohokami formula was evidently not only a device for mental concentration, a purposeful prayer to Amaterasu, and an evocation of *kotodama* that enabled mystical union with the goddess; it was also a dhāraṇī-like articulation of spiritual power that, when correctly enunciated, could effect changes in the physical world. The Tohokami purification discipline was used by its Tokugawa-era practitioners both as a means of achieving personal serenity and moral perfection in daily life, *and* (when the occasion demanded) in order to obtain (or confer) concrete "worldly benefits" *(genze riyaku).*[55]

The putative benefit of Tohokami practice that appealed most to its constituents, however, was probably its healing effects. Teachings about the body occupy a prominent place in the letters that Masakane wrote to his followers from exile. He shared with Confucian scholars, Buddhist priests, and physicians of his time the belief that the well-being of the body was intimately related to that of the mind and heart; but the To-

FIGURE 6. The people of Miyakejima rejoice as Inoue Masakane brings rain to the island. Wood-block print. Contained in *Inoue Masakane shindenki,* ed. Inoue Sukekane (1877).

hokami founder identified care of health *(yōjō)* with religious discipline in a far more detailed and practical way than many other professional scholars and doctors were disposed to do.[56] Taking inspiration from his teacher Mizuno Nanboku, Masakane recommended self-control with regard to food, drink, and general lifestyle, advising all of his followers to consume only small, plain meals and counseling some to abstain completely from drinking sake.[57] Nevertheless, in the final analysis the purification ritual was all that one needed to attain moral probity, physical health, and by implication, long life.[58] Masakane's promotion of breathing exercises and of the purification *norito* as the best treatment for any illness is well documented in his letters to followers who were suffering from a range of emotional and physical ailments. Whether they were affected by scabies, a short temper, or fear of thunder, the Tohokami founder unfailingly advised them to concentrate on breathing properly and chanting the formula.[59] By doing so they would learn to entrust themselves to the power of Amaterasu—an approach guaranteed to destroy the very root of illness.[60]

Masakane's therapeutics was rooted in long-established East Asian medical-cosmological theories, elements of which originated in ancient China. Like the diviners treated in chapter 2, the Tohokami leader believed that disease comes about when the vital energies of one's mind and heart are "inverted" or upset, or else when the vital fluids and humors *(kekki)* of one's body fail to circulate properly. "If the vital energies of one's mind are upset and unstable, one's eating and drinking will inevitably be disordered.... [O]ne's food will necessarily stagnate in one's spleen and stomach; the vital fluids of one's body will not circulate and will thus lead to illness."[61] This analysis of the interaction of psychological and physical energies was part of a larger discourse that, through a series of identifications, ultimately returned to Masakane's understanding of the gods. The basis of one's physical energies was blood; if it (and other bodily fluids) circulated well, one's body would function properly. The founder assumed that blood (and its "form," the body) derived from the food one ingested, and that food in turn was generated by the earth (or the products of the earth.) Breath, on the other hand, was the foundation of one's mental or spiritual energies, and derived from the vital forces of the universe—in other words, according to Masakane, from the gods. Discipline of the breathing process thus permitted the adept to make contact with the source of the universe—and to restore the primal unity of gods and human beings *(shinjin gōitsu)*. As long as one did not deviate from this "mind of the universe" (the will of the gods), one would remain healthy in both body and mind.[62]

Breathing was thus pivotal to the entire cultivation process; it was the link between the gods and the innermost part of the individual. Masakane declared in this vein that "if one's breathing is correct, one's mind will be correct and one's actions will be correct. If one's breathing is not correct and is defiled, one's mind will be evil and one's actions will be incorrect."[63] The restoration of a pure, moral condition that conformed with the intent of Amaterasu depended, in short, on the quality of the practitioner's breathing. It is true that Masakane sometimes seems to suggest in his writings that the mind and heart are themselves the primary field of cultivation. He states explicitly in the passage quoted in the preceding paragraph that the state of one's mind affects one's eating habits rather than the reverse, as Nanboku had often implied. Yet both the Tohokami leader and his teacher understood the beginning of personal development as a specific physiological process—in the one case, breathing, and in the other, eating. I should add that Masakane interpreted the exercise of breathing very much in "spiritual" terms: breathing was a way of uniting one's mind with the gods or heaven, as opposed to eating, which he correlated with the earth and its products. For the Tohokami leader, ritualized breathing was itself a form of mental and emotional cultivation.

Inoue Masakane's dual emphasis on devotion to Amaterasu and personal cultivation through breathing led to a fruitful ambiguity in his attitude toward healing. In his writings he does not encourage his followers to seek others' help in curing their ailments but emphasizes their own responsibility in the matter. He expected his disciples to grasp for themselves the "great foundation" of healing that had been bequeathed to humanity by the gods, and to learn to apply it.[64] The founder insisted that the best way for the individual to take care of inversions of vital energy was to practice Nagayo breathing. Nevertheless, the group's members also engaged in healing people, as noted in the shogunal verdict cited earlier. Masakane allowed that if an individual was unable to perform the breathing exercises for some reason, other methods were acceptable. Another person could assist in the healing process by applying the art of *kantsū* (literally, "seeing through") to the patient.[65] The method involved having advanced Tohokami practitioners place their hands on the patient's abdomen and synchronize their breathing with the sick person's in such a way as to transfuse their own life energies *(ki)* into his or her body.[66] Followers were encouraged to use other curative therapies as well. Masakane variously suggests in his letters that his correspondents pronounce incantations to stir up their vital energies when the latter become stagnant, that they try aromatic medicines to restore their internal physiological equilibrium, and that they use purgatives to eliminate large quantities of rich food that have accumulated in their digestive systems.[67]

These therapeutic techniques were not dissimilar to those used by members of other Japanese religious communities of the time, though Masakane's overall approach to recovery from illness may have placed somewhat more emphasis on the role of the patient as subject in the healing process.[68] Because breathing was the key to the health of the entire psychophysical complex of an individual (as well as the mystical link between humankind and the divine order), given the requisite faith and effort, in this view, any follower could control her or his personal well-being. As long as one was diligent in the breathing and chanting practices, one would have no need either to receive *kantsū* from senior Tohokami members, or indeed to undergo treatment at the hands of any other professional healer or physician.[69] Masakane states in his writings that healing ultimately depends on the favor of the gods, not on one's own power, but in the final analysis activation of divine power depended on the initiative of the individual practitioner. The Tohokami founder thus presented his teaching as a method that members could use to cure themselves, not as a form of faith healing in which they would passively submit to a "laying on of hands," even though the latter remained an option for the weak or uninitiated.[70] Tohokami differs in this regard from such later new religions as Mahikarikyō, which promotes healing as a "magical" process that can succeed even without the patient's conscious volition.[71]

The Grammar of Personal Cultivation

Taken together, the details of Inoue Masakane's program provide a bird's-eye view of the plethora of religious, intellectual, and medical lore that circulated during his time. The Tohokami leader had a penchant for organizing these bits of knowledge under the motto of Confucian moral cultivation. He carries out this process on more than one level in his written works. The explicit Confucian analogies and identifications in *Shintō yuiitsu mondō sho,* which Masakane wrote with the express aim of defusing the shogunate's charges of heteropraxy against him, could be read as apologetical attempts to show that Tohokami ideas and practices were within the bounds of accepted ethical and religious ideologies of the time. However, similar allusions are also scattered throughout the Tohokami founder's personal letters, which were secretly sent to his followers from Miyakejima and thus not written with an eye to the reaction of the authorities.[72] The frequent use of Confucian idioms in Masakane's writings was not a conscious tactic; passing reference to the classical texts and their commentaries was a routine feature of popular didactic writing during this period.

The Confucian language probably came more easily to the Tohokami leader than it did to the diviners discussed in Chapter 2, given his samurai education. He was relatively well schooled in the Neo-Confucian editions of the classics; he cites the Four Books and refers to the Cheng brothers and Zhu Xi, as well as to later Confucian thinkers.[73] Nevertheless, like Yokoyama Marumitsu and Mizuno Nanboku, Inoue Masakane usually refers not to detailed, text-based commentaries but to the overall Neo-Confucian logic of cultivation. I suggested earlier that it was precisely during the late Tokugawa, when various Confucian proposals, elaborated and reelaborated, seemed to many people to be losing their plausibility, that the fundamental premises of the Song Neo-Confucian synthesis imbued Japanese thought most profoundly. Well-endowed merchants, village headmen, and others who possessed a modicum of schooling in Chinese texts sometimes deplored the apparent trivialization of Confucian scholarship, but they rarely questioned the idea that learning in the sense of moral cultivation is the true basis of social well-being. Inoue Masakane typifies this mentality. Although not a scholar, he was distinctly conscious of the contemporary surplus of Japanese school interpretations (if not of their detailed content). It seemed to him, in fact, that "the learning of China" had degenerated from the time of Confucius into a fragmented spectrum of conflicting propositions—he complains in his writings that this learning had splintered into the teachings of the Chengs and Zhu Xi, the teachings of Wang Yangming, and so-called ancient learning (Kogaku), among others. Yet the Tohokami leader nonetheless maintained that all these interpretations were "the teachings of the Sage, the precious teachings of cultivating one's person and bringing order to one's family."[74]

It was this pithy rendition of the Confucian program that informed the Misogi teacher's program most conspicuously. His religious and therapeutic teachings are all subsumed in his discourse within the ordered steps of the *Great Learning:* internal rectification, personal cultivation, family harmony, and the security of Japan as a whole.[75] This grand project is presented as the overarching aim of all Tohokami rituals, prayers, breathing exercises, dietary disciplines, and healing practices. Indeed, Masakane describes the purpose of his "teaching of the gods" in terms of this paradigm so repeatedly throughout his writings that reference to it functions, not simply as a statement of belief, but as an integral component of his rhetorical style—a kind of rhythmic pattern of speech that gives added meaning to all the subsidiary details. The following example typifies the founder's organization of "Shinto" ideas according to the prevalent cultivation grammar of his time.

> As the great land of Japan is a country that originated in the gods, if one simply worships these gods, one's person will be cultivated, one's family will be in order, and the country will be governed.... Those who wish to cultivate their persons and bring order to their families should first respect the power of the great goddess Amaterasu and worship her every morning and evening.[76]

In a letter to a man who was thinking of becoming a Shinto priest, Masakane similarly iterates that the "teaching of the gods" is to attain peace in one's body, in one's mind, and in one's family.[77] By the same token, not being able to ensure the security and well-being of one's parents, wife, or family was due, in the final analysis, to insufficent practice of that teaching.[78]

Even while repeatedly advocating the conventional sequence of the cultivation paradigm, however, Masakane questions and very nearly subverts it. The success of the Tohokami purification ritual, as we have seen, depended on a transmission of faith from Amaterasu to the practitioner. Masakane allows that Amaterasu and the other gods are the same as what the Chinese (in the *Great Learning*) call "bright virtue," and that when this inner virtue is revealed, one realizes the true scope of one's personal defects and family problems. The drawback, in the founder's view, is that once people attain this insight into their moral potential, they tend to make strenuous efforts to improve themselves and their relations with others. They invariably assume that as long as they rely on their own intelligence, their lives can be put in order. But in the process of striving to reform themselves, Masakane warns, people often ignore and confound the power of the gods. He accordingly advises his correspondents to bypass the procedure envisioned in the Confucian texts (which assumes the initiative of the self as agent) in order not to lapse into this delusory, self-centered state, and to entrust the entire project to the gods through worship and ritual disciplines.[79]

The Tohokami leader reiterates this skepticism about the workability of the Neo-Confucian program in his various comments about famous Confucian passages. In a reference to the *Doctrine of the Mean,* he warns that "the Chinese say to take hold of the mean (J. *chū o toru*); [but] when one attempts to take hold of that mean, one becomes deluded in various ways, things multiply, and one isn't able to do so...."[80] Even in the apologetical *Mondō,* where he is presumably attempting to depict his teachings in the most uncontroversial light possible, Masakane points out the inapplicability of Neo-Confucian notions of self-improvement. He draws on the *Great Learning* to illuminate his ideas, but cannot help adding that while "the wise" know very well that one must "return to oneself" *(onore ni kaeru)* in order to solve problems in one's social relations, they do not enact this axiom in their own lives—they simply theorize about it.[81] The Tohokami discipline, on the other hand, can definitely be put into practice, even if a little at a time. Shinto, as Masakane conceived it, was eminently more doable than Neo-Confucian learning.[82]

Yokoyama Marumitsu and Mizuno Nanboku similarly elevated tangible methods of personal development above the abstract vision that all three teachers associated with the classical Chinese texts. However, Masakane's ambivalence toward Confucian learning was also colored by nativist sentiments. In one letter he remarks that in both China and Japan people had become involved in the "study of principles" (Zhu Xi–style Neo-Confucian studies), but that few had ever succeeded in embodying those principles. Those who possessed an intellectual grasp of the principles often labored under the illusion that they had mastered this type of learning, but as far as Masakane was concerned, their understanding remained superficial because they did not put these principles into practice.

The emphasis on moral enactment, not infrequently designated by the rubric "practical learning" *(jitsugaku),* was a familiar refrain in East Asian Neo-Confucian discourse; as we have seen, it fueled antitextualist arguments particularly in the late Tokugawa. Yet Masakane's solution to the problem of an overly theoretical approach to learning was radically different from that proposed by professional scholars such as Ōta Kinjō or Satō Issai. The Tohokami leader advises one correspondent simply to "abandon the study of principles, not rely on the wise or on the foolish, and learn the law of the gods"; he expressly advocates not knowing "the principles" until *after* one has become proficient in the purification discipline. Otherwise, Masakane implies, knowledge of these ideas will slow down or hinder one's religious quest. "If one knows the principles in advance, one obscures the power of the gods, and the power of one's own person becomes weak."[83] In short, if one became versed in various (in this context, Neo-Confucian) theories, one would become stuck in an abstract, intellectualized realm and would be unable to enact the sacred teaching in the natural, spontaneous way that the gods intended.

Tohokami practitioners were not generally encouraged to engage in book learning. Masakane's own writings are the only works that he seems to have recommended to his members with any frequency. He advised his followers to read passages, one at time, from his *Mondō*, in conjunction with performing prayers and the purification ritual every day in front of an altar to the gods, and to write to him whenever they had questions about the content of the tract. This limited reading was regarded not as doctrinal study but as part of a daily regimen of ritual exercise and contemplation.[84]

Judging from an exchange with one of his rhetorical questioners, Masakane anticipated Confucian-type objections to his approach to "learning":

> Q: You do not rely on written words, you do not have [others] read books, and you do not teach the way of the Five Constants of humaneness, rightnesss, decorum, wisdom, and trust. What do you rely on, in teaching people?
>
> A: Teaching the way of the Five Constants of humaneness, rightness, decorum, wisdom, and trust by means of words and books is the teaching of China, it is not the teaching of our Imperial Land.[85]

The Japanese teachings, as the founder goes on to explain, had been transmitted by the gods. Just as Mizuno Nanboku claimed that his rather diffuse "principles of nature" encompassed the Five Constants, so his student Masakane asserted that the sacred Shinto traditions, articulated through worship rituals and musical performances, already comprehended these Confucian virtues (as well as government laws and all other Chinese formulations). There was no need, therefore, to rely on the Confucian canon or, for that matter, on any other complicated, foreign system of knowledge.[86]

The Tohokami leader depicted the teachings of the gods, on the other hand, as eminently accessible; they did not require scholarly knowledge or even the ability to distinguish between good and evil.[87] Amaterasu would bestow whatever insight one might need for the fulfillment of moral obligations: one had only to follow the divinely endowed mind of faith.[88] Moreover, as long as one kept that faith, the power of the gods would ensure the success of one's affairs in the world, without any elaborate efforts on one's own part.[89] Masakane did not thereby advocate an absolute surrender of individual initiative, as we have noted. He warned his followers that if they failed to practice breath regulation and the purification ritual every morning and evening, they would never attain authentic inner peace—on the contrary, they would become vulnerable to a host of evils.[90]

Physical and spiritual equilibrium—achieved by breathing properly, exerting restraint in personal consumption, and above all by intoning the Tohokami *norito*—was indeed a precondition for activating the gods' blessing. Masakane explains in his *Mondō* that the "realization of faith" *(shinjin tokudō)* simply means receiving the gods' *promise* of salvation. The gods would never violate this pledge, but human beings might fail to fulfill their part of the contract. In other words, even after one had gained an attitude of faith, external distractions and one's own thought processes could lead to neglect of the essential regimen.[91] The divine endowment would remain dormant without continuing acts of faith by the recipient—hence the importance in the Tohokami system of ongoing purification rituals. Masakane's fervent emphasis on completely surrendering oneself to the gods' power was thus partly rhetorical; on closer scrutiny, it gives way to a contractual view of human–divine relations. The mind of faith could not become authentic unless one *cultivated* it by breathing/chanting the purification formula.[92] The ideal Tohokami practitioner maintained a delicate balance between self-reliance and dependence on the gods.

Kobayashi Junji differentiates two poles in Tokugawa discourse about the mind or heart *(kokoro no gensetsu): shinpō,* a method of actively cultivating one's inner states; and *shinjin,* placing one's faith entirely in the power of an Other (and becoming purified through identification with that Other). He groups Inoue Masakane together with Shingaku leader Teshima Toan and Zen master Bankei Yōtaku (1622–1693) as promoters of a faith-oriented or *shinjin* mode of discourse, which they constructed in response to their audiences' needs.[93] In their writings and sermons, as Kobayashi correctly points out, all three speakers negatively depict systems of cultivation that depend on individual judgment or power.[94] However (and paradoxically), Masakane and Toan also advocated specific techniques for allowing or encouraging one's mind to return to a pristine state of purity. Such religious programs are probably best characterized, not in terms of binary oppositions (such as the contrast between self-power and other-power, to borrow Pure Land terminology), but in terms of their ever-shifting syntheses of personal cultivation and devotional faith—emphases that their teachers variously promoted in accordance with the need of the moment. Inoue Masakane, perhaps even more than his predecessors, maintained wide-ranging contacts with diverse religious and medical practitioners, and his teachings were open-ended enough to allow for divergent understandings of the religious project that he advocated.

Masakane's disciples in the Kantō area maintained this interpretive flexibility during the Tokugawa period. The aforementioned Uneme—who took the name Chizen when she became a Buddhist nun in the mid-1840s—reinforced Masakane's stress on the role of the individual subject in the religious process.[95] She apparently disapproved of Tohokami followers' involvement in the exorcistic type of healing practices that contemporary Shugendō and/or Ontake mountain ritualists were allegedly carrying out in the Kōzuke area.[96] She also tended to rationalize phenomena that others viewed as miraculous or inexplicable. Her disciple Murakoshi Morikazu reports an incident in which one of Chizen's followers pitied a woman who was believed to be insane. One day the woman stood upright and began abusing the follower in a loud voice, proclaiming that she herself was the deity Shinmei (Amaterasu). The Tohokami member wondered whether the woman had in fact been possessed by the god or, on the other hand, by an evil spirit (commonly believed to take the form of a fox or a badger). Chizen calmly responded that the madwoman had been possessed by neither. "Human beings are the leaders of all things [in nature]. Therefore, they are not the sort of beings that can be possessed by foxes and badgers."[97] The nun explained that, because the woman was deranged, her mind did not contain any thoughts or desires of her own—it simply reflected other people's thoughts and feelings. It was critical, therefore, that the Tohokami member control her own feelings and thoughts whenever she was taking care of her patient; if the latter heard some one say that a god or a fox or badger had possessed her, she would become even more ill. The right approach to this sort of case, according to Chizen, depended entirely on the caregiver's attitude and thus, in the final analysis, on the latter's cultivation of the Tohokami discipline.[98]

This anecdote sets up a contrast between a magical mentality that presupposes the objective reality of inexplicable forces that are able to control human beings, on the one hand, and a humanistic perspective that views such phenomena as imaginary projections, on the other. Chizen is depicted as representing the latter point of view: she coolly shifts the burden of the problem back to the religious subject, arguing that the patient's condition somehow "reflects" the state of mind of the Tohokami practitioner.[99] Masakane's teaching of purification was to be understood as a system of personal development and theistic worship, not as an exorcistic method for dispelling evil spirits.

Helen Hardacre has tentatively linked the worldview of the new religions with Neo-Confucian modes of thought.[100] Yet the humanistic approach to possession and other spiritual phenomena adopted by Tohokami practitioners in the late Edo period was not accompanied by affirmation of Neo-Confucian cultivation theory. Indeed, in the 1850s and 1860s some members were even more skeptical about the workability of the classical paradigms than the founder had been. In his 1860 *Nakatomi no harai ryakuge* (An Abbreviated Expanation of the Nakatomi Purification), Masakane's disciple Nozawa Kanenori (1814–1875) baldly states that it is impossible to serve one's lord as well as one's parents, or to serve one's parents while taking good care of one's spouse and children. People can never fulfill these moral demands, he claims, because they are born into a world that is defiled, and thus have inherited a degenerate, self-centered mentality. Echoing the reformist diviners whom we discussed earlier, Nozawa notes that even religious experts and educators are unable to cultivate their persons, harmonize their families, and take loving care of their relatives, much less guide others in these endeavors. Professional teachers inevitably end up adopting an intellectualist approach to learning: they focus on the writings of the ancient sages, but because they interpret these works from their own individual, distorted point of view, they are never able truly to embody the moral ideals contained in these texts. In contrast to the (Confucian) "learning of the sages," avows Nozawa, the purification ritual bestowed by the gods involves the entire person: "If one firmly believes in this blessed purification, enunciates it with one's mouth, listens to it with one's ears, and enacts with one's body, then one will be comfortable in body and mind, one's person will be perfected, one's family will be cultivated, the country will be governed, the empire will be brought to peace...."[101] As had his teacher decades earlier, Nozawa appeals to the overarching aims of Neo-Confucian learning even while redefining it in terms of workable, concrete practices.

Inoue Masakane and his followers were able to exploit the classical language of personal improvement in this way, even while cautioning followers not to lapse into what they considered a Confucian-style mentality of self-reliance, because they used this language merely to indicate the grammatical outline of their message rather than any specific content. In their view, the outline badly needed filling up with concrete, practical details. It was the very generality of the well-known passages of the

Neo-Confucian canon that allowed both the Tohokami founder, who
was relatively educated in the Chinese texts, and his less-schooled contemporaries, Yokoyama Marumitsu and Mizuno Nanboku, to employ
these locutions as codes that both communicated and legitimated their
various ideas within the larger Confucian linguistic community. As
Gumperz notes, command of the stylistic conventions associated with
classical languages "may be more important in gaining social success
than substantive knowledge of the information dispensed through these
languages."[102]

A Web of Memberships

Our survey of late Tokugawa movements in this and the preceding
chapters brings two points into relief. First, spokespersons of diverse religious groups and intellectual communities utilized a common vocabulary and/or phraseology, composed of words taken from the Confucian
textual corpus, in order to enunciate their various programs. Satō Issai's
scholarly ruminations in *Genshi shiroku,* Imakita Kōsen's apologetical
legerdemains in *Zenkai ichiran,* Takahashi Kōsetsu's rereadings of Shingaku texts, and Yokoyama Marumitsu's, Mizuno Nanboku's, and Inoue
Masakane's broad interpretations of classical passages mark these individuals' continuing respect for the power of Confucian language in the
waning years of the Tokugawa regime. Second, these and other educators and religious leaders of the time articulated their views on the ultimate truth and the means to attain it partly in response to specific trends
in the scholarly world—particularly to what they perceived as an obses-
sion with philological and literary minutiae to the neglect of personal
experience. Although on one level their proposals merely carry forward
the conventional arguments of Neo-Confucian mind-learning, Zen Buddhism, and popularized nativism on the limitations of the written word,
on another their elaborations were part of a shared "discussion" that
was evolving in the Confucian linguistic community as a whole. The rejection of the utility of the Confucian language of "words and books"
(often, paradoxically, expressed in that very language), the concomitant
proclamation of the ultimate authority of the inner self (or, as the case
may be, of the gods who "endowed" the self), and the focus on practical
spheres of reality believed to be under the individual's immediate control,
all signaled a growing ambivalence within this community toward its
own raison d'être.

The convergence of concern over these issues across interpretive
groups illustrates what Harootunian calls the "cultural overdetermina-
tion" of the late Tokugawa—that is, the appearance during this period
of multiple discourses, "whereby the same elements appear time and

again in different form."[103] Natural disasters, economic stresses, peasant rebellions, and the threat of foreign incursions all contributed to the perception of dissonance and instability in the existing social order in the early nineteenth century. The cultivation arguments I have discussed may be seen as singular articulations of this perception—variations on a theme performed, albeit unwittingly, in a kind of counterpoint.

Although I have focused here on popular reinterpretations of Neo-Confucian ideals, it must be emphasized that not all religious discourses of the late Tokugawa arose in dialectic with these modes of thought; representatives of some interpretive communities did not share these ways of thinking or become even minimally competent in the associated linguistic system. Bourdieu has suggested that "[s]peakers lacking the legitimate competence are *de facto* excluded from the social domains in which this competence is required, or are condemned to silence."[104] Yet members of late Tokugawa society who were unversed in the Confucian lexicon were condemned to silence only within certain educated spheres. Those whose schooling was limited to a few years of copybook and abacus practice at the local *terakoya* (so-called temple school) may have possessed little facility in the classical administrative language of the era, but through informal educational channels they became versed in other cultural idioms, some of which were highly specialized. The latter codes, in contrast to the Confucian vocabulary and phraseology, were fully exploited only within the small, relatively bounded communities that generated them, but each nevertheless provided a medium for its members to debate issues that were universal to the time.

The members of the middle social estates probably had greater rhetorical versatility than individuals whose extremely high or low rank prevented them from acting and speaking in a wide range of social venues; modern sociolinguistic research indicates that people whose social sphere is rigidly confined generally have less ability to discourse in a wide variety of linguistic styles.[105] Masakane, Marumitsu, Nanboku, and other middle-level theorists commanded diverse lexicons, each of which signaled participation in a distinctive world of meaning; at the same time they were also able to demonstrate the compatibility of their aims with the prevailing ideology of the day by utilizing well-known classical phrases.

The core members of Tōkyūjutsu, Tohokami, and other movements, such as Shingaku, that grew popular in the Edo area during the early nineteenth century were often village headmen, established merchants and artisans, or low-ranked or impoverished samurai. Under the Tokugawa social system, members of these milieux enjoyed a certain status and respect within their communities; they had access to spheres of knowledge that were for the most part closed to the less-privileged, and thus played a critical role in the mediation of new forms of thought and practice. Village headmen, for example, were commoners who shared some of the interests of their constituents, but they were also beholden to the domain government, which authorized them to collect taxes and administer laws. These and members of other intermediary groups tended to interpret the available stock of knowledge in ways that not only promised to improve their own lives but also could be used to edify or modulate the attitudes of the workers and peasants under their jurisdiction.

I do not mean to imply that when the leaders of these groups professed concern for the physical and material welfare of their followers they were simply seeking to maintain their authority in the face of the restlessness of the lower classes. Members of the early Tohokami community actively assisted the poor and infirm (especially during Inoue Masakane's lifetime).[106] A number of these religious practitioners were themselves penurious, and keenly aware of other people's economic and health needs. The leading members of the Tōkyū and Nanboku divination communities struggled to attain financial and physical betterment long before they systematically facilitated others' pursuit of well-being. The emphasis on bodily health and success in life that characterizes the discourses of these and similar spokespersons was directly informed by their own experiences in seeking to reach these goals. The groups that originated under these circumstances thus possessed a dual character; their discourses and practices often originated in personal quests for self-fulfillment, but once systemized they could also be used to edify others. This pattern is perhaps best exemplified by the Shingaku movement, which over the course of the eighteenth century was transformed from Ishida Baigan's personal ideas about cultivation into a system of moral education that ultimately proved useful to shogunal and domain administrators.

The interpretive groups surveyed in this and the last chapter never acquired the semiofficial status enjoyed in some parts of Japan by Shingaku teachers, who advocated a syncretic but fundamentally orthodox version of Neo-Confucian moral improvement. Yet the newer groups catered to the same constituencies that the Shingaku movement served, and indeed the leaders of these groups display an expository style in their written discourses that is reminiscent of Ishida Baigan and his successors. Like Shingaku preachers, for example, Inoue Masakane drew not only on Confucian works but also on such sources of early modern Japanese inspiration as the *Warongo* (Japanese Analects), the homilies of famous Buddhist teachers (Hōnen, Shinran [1173–1262], Ippen [1239–1289], and Nichiren), the *Kokin waka shū* (Collected Japanese Verses of the Past and Present), and the poems of Bashō (1644–1694).[107] The Tōkyū founder was similarly eclectic in inspiration, judging from the sparse writings that he left behind.

Given their affinities of social context, style, and general moral purpose, it is not surprising to find that Tohokami, Tōkyūjutsu, and Shingaku shared personnel within certain geographical areas during the late Edo period. Some of this overlap dates back to the early 1840s, but it was probably during the Bakumatsu period that connections among the practitioners of the three groups became regularized. The Tohokami movement seems to have occupied a central position in this expanding network of affiliations.

Little is known about the activities of Inoue Masakane's followers after he died and his letters from Miyakejima ceased. The leading members were restricted in their movements; some followers apparently became fearful and passive in the face of continued government pressure, while others simply lost interest in the teachings. Efforts to gain a pardon for the founder met with no success. Kawajiri Hōkin's later dramatic rendition of the group's history documents its members' painful collective memory of this period of suppression and low morale. In one scene, the eight-year-old son of a follower is in tears because his companions have called him a "Tohokami hungry ghost" and pushed him into a ditch. Other characters in the play lament that they are despised by the people of the world.[108]

At first the community retained some cohesion through the exchange of letters among members,[109] but before long the scattered small cells that constituted the underground movement lost touch with each other. One of the most enduring factions proved to be the Murakoshi/ Sakata family and its associates. Murakoshi Masahisa, the headman of Shimo-kinegawa village (in Musashi), had met Masakane soon after the latter became priest of the Shinmei Shrine in Umeda—the shrine was about an hour's walk from the Murakoshi residence. Masahisa and several members of his family soon committed themselves to the teaching, including his brothers, Murakoshi Morikazu and Sakata Masayasu (1802–1873).[110] Masayasu's son, Sakata Kaneyasu (1820–1890), joined Masakane's group in the early 1840s and corresponded closely with the founder during the latter's exile.

Chizen, for her part, helped maintain connections among various groups of members, clandestinely visiting them in the Edo area (from which she had been banned in 1842) during the late 1840s and early 1850s. Her death in 1856 seems to have galvanized the remaining Tohokami followers. Masayasu, Masahisa, Morikazu, and several other immediate disciples of the founder became more active in their religious activities and enrolled in the Shirakawa Shinto school.[111] Itō Kaname (Sukekata, 1806–1877), who converted to Tohokami in 1840 while spying on the group for the shogunate, began to work for the Shirakawa house in the capacity of an itinerant official. Like the Honjō household members fifteen years earlier, these followers may have hoped that their Shirakawa affiliation would protect their religious activities from further shogunal action. In any event, they now began to proselytize in several parts of the country and to produce teaching materials.[112] However, their activities once again attracted the government's notice, and in early 1862 the Office of Temples and Shrines summoned twenty-six Tohokami followers to a hearing. Masahisa, Morikazu, Masayasu, the latter's son, Sakata Kaneyasu, and two other members were charged with propagating "novel and heterodox" teachings and were banned from their home communities in the larger Edo area.

Proselytizing efforts nevertheless continued, underground in Edo and more openly in areas such as Okayama, Kyoto, and Echigo.[113] Sakata Masayasu and his son Kaneyasu became Shirakawa priests shortly after they were banned from their village, Hokima.[114] They and other members managed to pursue their religious activities relatively freely under Shirakawa auspices, but the prohibition of the movement weighed more heavily on those who remained in Edo. Murakoshi Morikazu's disciple, Tōgū Chiwaki (1833–1897), enjoyed the status of a Yoshida head priest and perhaps for this reason was not directly affected by the 1862 suppression. But Tōgū remained cautious: in 1864 he built a large earthen mound in the guise of a storage cellar so that members could chant the purification formula without being heard by outsiders.[115]

The most prominent Tohokami practitioner of the Bakumatsu period was the aforementioned Honjō Munehide, a member of the Matsudaira (Tokugawa) family who reportedly became acquainted with Inoue Masakane when Honjō was still a young boy, in 1822.[116] Later accounts indicate that Honjō's religious preference initially provoked dissension in his household; two retainers were dismissed from service for the part they played in introducing the young lord to Masakane.[117] The young man nevertheless remained one of the founder's most committed followers, even after he took over as daimyo of Miyazu in 1840. During Masakane's exile Honjō is said to have sent money to his teacher regularly.[118]

Little else is known about Honjō's involvement in the Bakumatsu Tohokami community—perhaps not unexpectedly, given his high rank and the official ban on the movement. His importance to the group ultimately derived more from the influence he came to wield in ruling circles than from his personal involvement in religious proselytization. Honjō Munehide was appointed, in succession, Superintendent of Temples and Shrines (from 1858 until at least 1860), governor of Osaka (*Ōsaka jōdai,* 1860), acting governor of Kyoto (*Kyōto shoshidai,* 1862), and senior councilor to the shogun (*rōjū*, 1864). In the last years before the Restoration, the daimyo negotiated with foreign envoys on behalf of the shogunate and served in its punitive expeditions against Chōshū domain.[119]

The Honjō household was a key player in the interaction between the Tohokami and Shingaku movements throughout the nineteenth century. A biographical document associated with Kōshinsha, an Edo Shingaku meetinghouse, states that in 1841 Honjō (who by this time had been a Tohokami practitioner for almost twenty years), supported Shingaku activities in Edo and personally practiced under the Shingaku teacher, Kondō Heikaku (a disciple of Ōshima Urin, 1735–1836).[120] The document also reports that in the same year Matsudaira Muneaki (Honjō's adopted father and his predecessor as lord of Miyazu) hired Kondō Heikaku to teach "Shingaku practice" *(Shingaku shugyō)* to the women who resided in the domain's Edo residence.[121] Ishikawa's exhaustive research into domain employment of Shingaku preachers during the late Tokugawa further demonstrates that from 1849 until 1858, a period of nearly ten years, Honjō employed the skilled Shingaku preacher Shibata Yūō (1809–1874) to carry out lecture tours in Miyazu.[122] Another Shingaku source lists Honjō Munehide ("the lord of Hōki") as one of 211 samurai and daimyo who were initiated into Shingaku practice between 1848 and 1859 by Nakamura Tokusui (1800 –1856), a well-known Shingaku teacher associated with the Sanzensha meetinghouse in Edo.[123]

The Miyazu daimyo and other highly ranked samurai probably attended Shingaku sessions not simply for their own self-improvement but to learn how to become effective moral instructors; Ishikawa compares Sanzensha in this regard to a kind of teaching college.[124] My point here, however, is that Honjō was simultaneously a Tohokami stalwart and a regular supporter, if not practitioner, of Ishida Baigan's teachings. Moreover, he is only the most prominent exemplar of the overlap between these two movements during the nineteenth century. Shingaku records show that several samurai from Tatebayashi domain, where Inoue Masakane originated, enrolled in a Shingaku study course at Sanzensha in 1854. Numerous retainers of this domain attended Shingaku meetings in 1855 as well.[125] One of these men, Tarasawa Okaemon, attained the Shingaku "Three Seals" teaching certification and became an important instructor at Sanzensha.[126] Yet Okaemon was also a direct disciple of Masakane; Tohokami documents show that he had been actively propagating Tohokami teachings since 1842.[127]

The simultaneous affiliation of figures like Honjō Munehide and Tarasawa Okaemon with both religious movements is not anomalous. A close look at the leading Kantō members of Tohokami and Shingaku, as well as Tōkyūjutsu (which also operated in Edo at this time, despite the shogunate's restrictions), reveals an almost regular imbrication among members of these groups during the last decades of the Tokugawa period. Takahashi Kōsetsu, the Shingaku leader who questioned the value of Baigan's written discourse (discussed in chapter 1), reportedly was learned in "Tengengaku"—an alternate appellation for Tōkyūjutsu. Takahashi also "entered the Shinto school" during the Bakumatsu period.[128] The type of Shinto he practiced is not identified, but considering subsequent patterns among his immediate disciples (discussed below), it is likely that the group he joined was Tohokami (which at the time identified itself simply as "Shinto"). Takahashi's involvement with Tōkyūjutsu and "Shinto" preceded his encounter with Shingaku by some years; it was not until 1857 that the gold-lacquer craftsman was initiated into the Shingaku "method of the mind" *(shinpō)* by his teacher, Kumatani Tōshū.[129] However, even after joining Shingaku, Kōsetsu continued his involvement in at least one of the interpretive systems he had studied earlier; his biography reports that he included "Tengengaku" in his teachings and that his Shingaku disciples followed his example, using it to supplement their own practice of mind cultivation.[130]

Kawajiri Hōkin (Yoshisuke, 1842–1910), the son of a tortoiseshell artifacts dealer of Edo, joined Inoue Masakane's followers in the ninth month of 1861, just a few months before its leaders were banned from Hokima and other Edo vicinities. He is said to have practiced the founder's teachings diligently and to have mastered the "divine transmission" *(shinden)*—probably a reference to the Tohokami "transmission of faith" ritual. One year later, Kawajiri began to frequent Shingaku meetings in Edo and to study Ishida Baigan's teachings under Takahashi (who was now a fully certified Shingaku teacher), as well as under an instructor called Kikuchi Tōsai (1804–1873).[131]

The Edo merchant Mitani Ken'ō (Sōyaku, 1817–1886) followed a similar course. As a young man, he immersed himself in both Buddhist and Confucian forms of learning, but in his "middle years" (presumably corresponding to the late 1850s and 1860s), became well-versed in "Tengen Tōkyūjutsu." Like Takahashi, he allegedly continued to rely on the latter for assistance in his daily life even after he became involved in other religious groups.[132] Mitani also joined a "Shinto" school in 1865, where he practiced under a teacher named Fukuda Kanetomo (1836–1893). Fukuda, for his part, was the ninth son of Murakoshi Masahisa and Fukuda Saku—in other words, Mitani's "Shinto" teacher was the cousin of the emerging Misogikyō leader, Sakata Kaneyasu.[133] Like Kawajiri in 1861—and probably Takahashi in the 1840s or 1850s—Mitani was drawn into the Murakoshi/Sakata branch of the Tohokami movement that subsisted in the Edo area during the last years of the shogunate. The merchant's rapid progress in the Tohokami disciplines soon qualified him to become a teacher, and he is said to have attracted many followers, especially in Ōshū, Aizu, and Yonezawa.[134] A few years after the Restoration, however, Mitani decided to enroll in the Shingaku school in Tokyo; before long he reportedly became a skilled teacher in that tradition as well.[135]

Personal acquaintances among Tōkyū practitioners, Tohokami followers, and Shingaku members in the Edo area no doubt encouraged some of these multiple affiliations, though, judging from the above chronologies, a number of individuals made their way to these groups quite independently of each other. In any event, from approximately the 1840s to the 1860s, these practitioners (and probably others who left no records) created a social network bound together by similar ideals and interests. It is true that, in contrast to Tōkyū and Tohokami, the Shingaku movement advocated contemplative practices rather than divination, therapeutic arts, ritual chanting, or physiological disciplines. Nevertheless, Shingaku practitioners agreed with members of the newer groups that, in the final analysis, physical and social well-being depended on the fulfillment of practicable regimens of personal development—and that the study of Confucian texts was of limited value in accomplishing that aim.

The network of religious practitioners, fortune-tellers, and moral preachers outlined here operated not only during the last decades of the Tokugawa period but also in the Meiji period. Before the Restoration, the spokespersons of these various groups used Confucian language to organize, translate, and legitimate the diverse ideas and practices they advocated for self-development and for the edification of dependents and employees. Even as that language lost currency and the worldview associated with it was explicitly challenged in the Meiji, however, the remnants of these groups continued to participate in ongoing socioreligious figurations. It would be inaccurate to say that the Tokugawa teachers' critiques of the seemingly abstract learning of the Confucian texts and their affirmation of more practicable programs prefigured the early Meiji debate over practicality and learning—at least not in any simple, direct way. That debate was dominated, as we shall see in the following pages, by public intellectuals who operated in a highly politicized context. Yet the popular interpretive fermentation that we have sampled thus far was not unrelated to the intellectual fragmentation and cultural openness that characterized the first Meiji years. When Confucian textual learning was finally turned under, it left a rich compost for the elaboration of new models of personal cultivation.

CHAPTER 4
The Parameters of Learning

THE FESTERING PREOCCUPATION with linguistic renewal and everyday practicability that marked late Tokugawa religious discourse broke into an efflorescence of new proposals after the collapse of the shogunal order. Language was now actively and openly created. It was through language that people first took possession of the growing influx of ideas and objects from abroad; they interpreted the new phenomena and created new lexical codes to express those interpretations.[1] Neologisms, formulated in rapid succession, expressed novel insights but at the same time revised old ones, for with the circulation of the new rubrics, the meanings of related older terms changed irrevocably. The characters *kyō* (teaching, doctrine, religion) and *gaku* (learning, study) exemplify this process of lexical rearrangement. They became pivotal elements in a reformulation that not only produced fundamentally new Japanese compounds, such as *kyōiku* (education) and *shūkyō* (religion), but also led to reinterpretations of older compounds, such as *gakumon* (learning) and *jitsugaku* (practical or real learning). The construction and revision of terms was in fact a redrawing of the boundaries between different spheres of knowledge and power in the new society, for the application of terms to particular phenomena was inevitably ideologically interested.[2] In this chapter I discuss the shifts that took place during the first two Meiji decades in the usage of several of these terms, with particular reference to the circumscription of the system of knowledge that has come to be designated Confucianism *(Jukyō, Judō)*. The parameters of Confucianism, like Buddhism, Shinto, and numerous other "traditions," were reset during the Meiji era.[3]

The debates over educational and religious policy that took place in the early Meiji are well known to students of this period. I review them here selectively, insofar as they bear on the changing identity of Confucian learning during this period; in doing so I am much indebted to the research of the Japanese and Western scholars whose works are cited in my notes. I highlight three interrelated moments in the early Meiji process of sociocultural rearrangement: (1) the displacement of Confucian studies in the emerging public university curriculum; (2) the initial derogation of Confucian-style learning vis-à-vis "practical" or "specialized" education in public discourse; and (3) the drive to dissociate Confucian-inspired programs from "religion" and to promote them under other names in the public domain. During this process the familiar idea of "learning" *(gaku* or *gakumon)* was revived by parties of diverse interests and defined as a mature form of personal improvement, in contrast to the inculcation of knowledge in others, which was associated with "doctrine," "teaching," or "religion" *(kyō)*. In conclusion I use the case of Shingaku to illustrate the impact of the differentiation of "learning" and "religion" on one Tokugawa-era system of personal cultivation. In later chapters we shall see how the larger socioreligious network to which Shingaku belonged contributed in turn to this post-Restoration debate over learning.

The convoluted story of how Confucian learning was removed from public higher education marks the first phase in the emergence of new ideologies of personal development during this period. Immediately after the Restoration, officials began taking steps to establish new schools, beginning with institutions intended to educate the nobility. The courtier Iwakura Tomomi (1825–1883) appointed nativist advocates to oversee this early educational drive, allegedly because he felt their emphasis on "the unity of rites and government" *(saisei itchi)* would counter the residual influence of the Confucian modes of thought that he associated with the discredited shogunal polity. Samurai leaders in the new government agreed that the nobles, given their historical association with the court, would be the most appropriate representatives of the new imperial power vis-à-vis the still restless domains; moreover, an educated nobility could help fend off what officials perceived as the impending influence of Christian ideas in Japan.[4]

The main impetus behind the nativist superintendents' educational (and ritual) policy—delineated in their 1868 "College Statutes" *(Gakushasei)*—was indeed the desire to counter the threat of Christianity, but they also aimed to eliminate Confucian and Buddhist influences from the educational sphere.[5] They accordingly called for the establishment of a school of advanced learning modeled after the ancient Daigakuryō, complete with a built-in shrine dedicated to the Japanese ancestral gods.[6] The college head would double as its chief priest, and all faculty and students would be required to participate in seasonal Shinto-type rituals, which would replace the original Daigakuryō's seasonal rites in honor of Confucius and his disciples *(sekiten)*. The curriculum, too, was to be dominated by the study of Japan's "original teachings" *(honkyōgaku)* rather than the Confucian classical course.[7] Chinese textual studies would be relegated to one segment of the foreign studies program.

The plan was not well received. Pragmatically inclined officials criticized the omission of Confucian and Western statecraft from the curriculum as well as the particularistic emphasis on Shinto-type subjects.[8] Before long, Iwakura reversed himself and threw his weight behind the Gakushūin, a Confucian-oriented school for nobility that had originated in Kyoto in 1847.[9] Against the objections of the nativist administrators, Gakushūin was now renamed the Daigakuryō-dai, a rubric that again signaled the school's special status.[10] The struggle for control of the nation's educational policy continued after the capital was moved to Tokyo in 1869. The former Edo shogunal college (Shōheikō) had been revived in 1868 under the name Shōhei Gakkō and was staffed mostly with teachers from the pre-Meiji facility. Unlike the Gakushūin in Kyoto, however, it aimed to educate former shogunal retainers rather than members of the nobility. In the summer of 1869 this school was renamed the Main College (Daigaku Honkō) and, along with the revived shogunal medical and Western-studies schools, became the Meiji state's most advanced institution of learning (the Daigakkō or "University").[11] Its proposed curriculum nonetheless provoked further discord among the various interested parties, since the Study of the Imperial Way (Kōdōgaku)—a Shinto-type ideology that purported to be more universalistic than current nativist conceptions—still took precedence over Confucian and Western forms of knowledge.[12] As in the earlier proposal, the envisioned shift was ritual as well as academic in nature. In the new arrangement both Confucian and Buddhist ceremonies would be eliminated, and newly designated Japanese "gods of learning" would be installed as the objects of worship.[13]

The conflict between the Shinto/nativist and Confucian studies factions grew bitter, with both faculty and students taking sides in the struggle for control of the school's curriculum and ritual practices.[14] Nativist-inspired revisions, such as the elimination of instruction in "reading off" Chinese texts, were stoutly resisted by Sinologically oriented students who identified with the established practices of the earlier Shōheikō. Tensions came to a head in late 1869 and effectively prevented the university from functioning. Early the next year, by order of the Council of State (Dajōkan), both nativist and Chinese studies teachers at the Main College were reduced in number, while the other two former shogunal schools were made integral parts of the university and thus elevated in importance.[15] A set of rules issued the following month

betrayed significant European influence in the overall curricular organization of the university—most notably, the courses of study were no
longer formally divided among Sinological, Western, and Japanese systems of knowledge.[16]

The battle over the curriculum of the nation's top educational facility now spiraled into a new figuration: nativists and Confucians joined
forces and presented administrators with a jointly signed critique of the
new rules in which they strongly objected to the dominant role played by
Westernizers in devising the university curriculum. Attempts to reach a
compromise among the different groups were of no avail, and in the
eighth month of 1870 the institution was forced to close.[17] This event
marked the end of any public basis for Tokugawa-style classical learning
(whether Confucian or nativist) at the postsecondary level. Whatever else
gakumon would come to mean in modern Japan, at the state's flagship
university it clearly would not denote the study of Chinese texts as a
means of moral improvement.

Motoyama Yukihiko and other Japanese scholars have shown that
educational policy during the first Meiji years was driven by political
considerations, especially by preoccupation over the possibility of conflict between the residual shogunate-domain power structure and the
centralizing forces of the new Meiji state.[18] The displacement of Confucian studies at the state's highest educational institution was the result,
not so much of a devaluation of the particular ideas that were associated
with the Sinological curriculum, but of the perception that these ideas
lacked "universality"[19]—and thus, I would add, practicality. The administrators of the short-lived Main College had attempted to implement
a moral education that would train the nation's elite to become "paragons of talent and virtue" by inculcating them with familiar Confucian
values while at the same time exposing them to new, putatively more
universalistic modes of thought. But in the face of political pressures the
compromise failed to create a unified, industrialized Japan. Rather than
an exalted vision of philosopher-leaders who would personally embody
the Way, the early Meiji government opted for a utilitarian model of
technician-administrators who would be sufficiently trained in Western
disciplines to create an efficient, "modern" nation.

Higher educational policy at government institutions continued to
be guided by political and pragmatic sensibilities in the ensuing years.
After the final abolition of the domains and the institution of the prefectural system in 1871, the new Ministry of Education (Monbushō)[20] announced that it expected the university to promote "the cultivation of
talent useful for building an industrial nation and a state governed by
laws."[21] Admission to the university no longer required any preparation
in classical textual studies; the ability to read ordinary documents was

deemed sufficient. The replacement of Confucian-style learning by law, science, and technology in the public university system now seemed complete.[22]

Private Chinese studies academies, which had spawned the most creative Confucian schools of the Tokugawa period, were unable to compensate for this displacement, especially after the Ministry of Education issued the first national "Code of Education" *(Gakusei)* in the spring of 1872. The code was a direct blow to Confucian-oriented schools of all levels; they were now required to meet the curricular standards and educational goals set by the government, which were "quite different from the stress on Confucian morality found in the official schools of the Tokugawa period."[23] In 1876, one Confucian scholar turned middle-school teacher lamented in this vein that "there are many students who enroll in my family academy, but for the most part they aspire to enter the [public] teachers' college *(shihan gakkō),* and since they study with the aim of preparing for that, none of them succeed in cultivating themselves in the Confucian classics."[24] A wide variety of private schools thrived in the first Meiji decade (before public middle schools were systemized by the state), but training in old-style *gakumon* at these schools declined dramatically.

The Debate over Learning

The *Book of Changes (Yijing)* defines *gakumon (xuewen)* in terms of its two components as follows: "The gentleman learns [J. *gaku*] in order to gather material; he questions [J. *mon*] in order to sift it."[25] The *Doctrine of the Mean* defines these components of learning as the first two steps in its program of intellectual and moral discipline: "study [J. *gaku*] extensively, enquire [J. *mon*] accurately, think carefully, sift clearly, and practice earnestly."[26] Questioning what one studies is thus depicted as an integral part of the process of learning in classical texts that were familiar to educational elites in Tokugawa Japan. In other well-known Chinese works, however, the compound *"gakumon"* has wider connotations of a process of personal cultivation. *Mencius* 6A:11 argues that the entire purpose of learning is to find one's true heart or mind, understood as the source of moral perfection. In a similar vein, Chinese Neo-Confucian commentators highlighted the individual dimension of learning by citing such sayings as "getting it for oneself" *(zide)* or "learning for the sake of oneself" *(wei ji zhi xue).*[27] Tokugawa scholars of various schools were also keen on reviving the personal, self-reflective meaning of learning as opposed to mere textual analysis, as we saw in Chapter 1.

Kyō or *oshie* (Ch. *jiao*), which in accordance with the context may be translated as teaching, doctrine, education, or religion, is not

unexpectedly represented in early Confucian texts as closely related to
the learning process. The *Doctrine of the Mean* opens with the statement: "What heaven endows is called the nature. Following one's nature
is called the Way. Cultivating the Way is called education (J. *kyō*)."[28] In
contrast to *gaku* or *gakumon,* however, the term *kyō* implies a social
transaction—a transmission of knowledge from one party to another.
The compound *kyōiku,* which came into wide use as a translation of
"education" in the early Meiji, strengthened the hierarchical connotations of *kyō* by adding a character *(iku)* that indicates the raising or
nourishing of a younger party by a senior or more knowledgeable person.[29] The thrust of *kyō* in comparison with *gaku* as these word elements came to be used in Japan informed the distinction between *kyōiku*
and *gakumon* made by education minister Mori Arinori (1847–1889) in
the mid-1880s. He suggested that *kyōiku* was "that intellectual, moral
and physical education which is imparted entirely by older persons to
younger persons who have not yet achieved maturity and are still in a
dependent status." *Gakumon,* on the other hand, was "for men of maturity, a matter in which one follows one's own inclinations, freely
choosing a subject and performing research on it."[30] Mori's idea of *gakumon* was not conceived in association with the Neo-Confucian project
of moral cultivation (against which he argued in policy debates on education). Nevertheless, in his view *gakumon* was the preserve of "men of
maturity" precisely because it allowed scope for pursuing "one's own
inclinations." Ironically, his "modern" definition of learning is reminiscent both of the term's classical Chinese sources, which explicitly emphasize the element of doubt or questioning, and of the later Neo-
Confucian insistence that genuine learning must involve "getting it for
oneself."[31]

     In fact, although Confucian studies as an identifiable discipline fell
by the wayside in the first Meiji years, a more generic-sounding *gakumon*
appealed strongly to the new generation of elites. Soon after the Restoration, a chorus of educated persons—both government officials and
forward-looking members of the private sector—began to polemicize
publicly against (in Harootunian's parlance) "the Confucian conceit that
had identified learning with Confucianism."[32] The model of the Confucian scholar who pursued classical learning as a form of moral cultivation was stereotyped in these circles as impractical and unsuited to
the new age.[33] In fact, not only Confucian studies, but most other pre-
Meiji intellectual and religious systems were now categorized as abstruse forms of learning, divorced from utilitarian concerns. Fukuzawa
Yukichi was outspoken in his early derogation of Tokugawa-era ideas
and institutions—whether Confucian, Buddhist, or Shinto. Yet he and
other advocates of "civilization and enlightenment" *(bunmei kaika)* were

especially critical of the system of knowledge that had dominated Japanese schools during their youth.

The word *"gakumon"* underwent a precipitous shift in connotation in public discourse during the early Meiji years; as one modern historian comments, "just as learning *[gakumon]* meant Confucian studies in the Tokugawa era, from about the first through the second Meiji decade, it simply meant Western academic skills."[34] Fukuzawa explicitly redefines the term in his writings, most notably in his early best-seller, *Gakumon no susume* (An Encouragement of Learning): "Learning does not essentially consist in such impractical pursuits as study of obscure Chinese characters, reading ancient texts which are difficult to make out, or enjoying and writing poetry.... The object of one's primary efforts should be practical learning that is closer to ordinary human needs."[35]

Needless to say, by "practical learning" *(jitsugaku)* Fukuzawa did not mean the contemplation and enactment of classical Confucian ideals, as many Tokugawa scholars had understood it, but academic study of a "useful" sort, such as arithmetic, geography, physics, or economics. This understanding of *jitsugaku* was not new; many earlier Confucian scholars had occupied themselves with "practical" matters ranging from botany to economic reform.[36] In the late Edo period in particular, several had acknowledged the value of a "real learning" that was informed by Western scientific knowledge.[37] It was not until the post-Restoration period, however, that the technological interpretation of *jitsugaku* overtook other meanings of the term in public discourse. In the following much cited passage from an early issue of the *Meiroku zasshi* (Meiji Six Magazine), Tsuda Mamichi (1829–1903) expresses a perspective similar to that of Fukuzawa. Tsuda employs the time-honored convention of denouncing undesirable forms of knowledge by designating them "empty" learning *(kyogaku),* as opposed to "real" or "practical" learning *(jitsugaku):*[38]

> There is empty learning *(kyogaku)* that is devoted to such lofty doctrines as nonexistence and Nirvana, the five elements and the principles of human nature, or intuitive knowledge and intuitive ability. And there is practical learning that solely explains factual principles through actual observation and verification, such as astronomy, physics, chemistry, medicine, political economy, and philosophy of the modern West. We may call a society truly civilized when the reason of each individual has been illumined by the general circulation of practical learning throughout the land.[39]

Members of the central government were at the forefront of the disavowal of the impractical. A proposal submitted to the Council of State in late 1871 by a senior education official singled out traditional

Chinese learning as a major obstacle to Japan's progress in the modern age:

> What clarifies the law and details regulations? That is the canonical duty of the state. Who prospers the industrial arts and masters rational knowledge? That is the all-important obligation of mankind. In our Imperial Land, however, studies remain afflicted by the lingering bad habits of sinology *[kangaku]*, whose essence is rhetorical flourish on the outside and sophistry inside. Time that should be utilized profitably is squandered frivolously, and the self-indulgent, far from wasting only their own lives, even seduce others into imitating them.... The harmful influence released thereby upon the public is by no means small. Unless this very day they are rescued from their evil ways, these good-for-nothings are sure to disgrace the nation. And there is no means to effect this rescue other than hiring many teachers of specialized subjects and vigorously supporting specialist schools *[senmon no gakkō]*.[40]

The last sentence is telling. The redemption of these Sinological good-for-nothings would be effected by having them undergo "specialized" schooling. "Specialized" *(senmon)* was a key word in early Meiji debates over the relative value of higher educational systems. Arguments frequently revolved around the utility of vocational or specialized training as opposed to humanistic or general education.[41] The phrases "specialized studies" *(senmongaku)* and "ordinary studies" *(futsūgaku)* were commonly understood in the Meiji era to indicate the advanced and elementary levels of schooling, respectively.[42] The 1872 Code of Education accordingly characterized universities as "schools with a specialized curriculum that offer instruction in the various forms of higher learning."[43] A set of 1873 guidelines further specified that the state university's special schools or colleges *(senmongakkō)* should aim to educate students *only* in scientific and technological disciplines, not in religion and ethics. Shinto teachings and moral cultivation *(shinkyō shūshin)* were explicitly excluded.[44] Specialized, higher, and utilitarian types of education were thus placed in opposition to general, ordinary, and impractical forms of learning.[45]

While the state system was taking shape, private schools of various stripes—middle schools, language schools, and vocational colleges—also proliferated under the rubric of *senmongakkō*. These schools did not universally offer the technologically oriented advanced education that government officials promoted; they included academies along the lines of Fukuzawa's Keiōgijuku, as well as Buddhist seminaries, Christian institutions, and Chinese studies schools.[46] Regardless of the type of school, however, "specialized" was understood to mean a level of education more advanced than the "general" or "ordinary." The educated man came to be seen as one who had received some sort of special training—in the 1870s at one of the higher-level private schools that abounded in Tokyo and, after the public system took over, at the new state university.

Learning for the Public Good

The government annointed the model of a skilled, economically productive citizen in the preamble to the 1872 Code of Education. It announced that pre-Restoration learning had been mistaken in its aims: whereas the samurai educated under the old system had simply "indulged in poetry, empty reasoning, and idle discussions," men should now pursue forms of knowledge such as "language, writing, and arithmetic" that were essential to "military affairs, government, agriculture, trade, arts, law, politics, astronomy, and medicine." This kind of *gakumon* was indeed "the key to success in life"—the "capital" *(zaihon)* that one needed in order to establish oneself in the world.[47]

The idea that learning is the key to prosperity was not discontinuous with notions of education that had prevailed among the privileged classes during the late Tokugawa.[48] However, the learning that was understood to be the domain of these elites had often been defined *in contrast to* labor skills and commercial activities, and thus, at least ostensibly, was far from the "study of the industrial arts" envisioned by the Meiji oligarchs. "Learning" in the new age accordingly required redefinition. Motoyama suggests that the promulgation of the preamble to the Code of Education and other "civilizing" policies in language that played on people's self-interest was a deliberate tactic that government bureaucrats used in their campaign to implement social and economic change.[49] But many outside the government also participated in the creation of this new discourse on learning. It was during these years, for example, that educated young men were avidly reading the Japanese rendition of Samuel Smiles' *Self-Help (Saigoku risshi hen)* by Confucian scholar Nakamura Masanao (Keiu; 1832–1891). Members of the Meiji Six Society (Meirokusha) were much taken with the work. Nishimura Shigeki (1828–1902) admired it greatly; Katō Hiroyuki (1836–1916) lectured on it; and the progressive political association Risshisha took both its name and some of its founding ideals from the book. Masses of lesser-known readers shared the same approbation. Kinmonth concludes that Nakamura's version of *Self-Help* and Fukuzawa's *Encouragement of Learning* attained a wide circulation in the early Meiji because these works catered to the desire of the offspring of samurai and wealthy peasants to rise in the world through new forms of learning.[50]

As the years passed, government leaders continued to promote the idea that old-style *gakumon* had little practical value. Some intensified the attack on Confucian studies, charging that it led not only to useless intellectualizing but also to undesirable political debate among the young people of the time. In 1879 Itō Hirobumi declared that

> our students usually come from the Confucian schools, and whenever they open their mouths it is to babble political theory and argue about the world situation. Thus, when they read Western books, they are unable to set about their tasks with calm and cultivated minds. Rather, they plunge themselves into the radical schools of European thought, delighting themselves with empty theory and chattering themselves up a wind, so that city and countryside are clamorous with politics. In order to remedy this situation, we should spread the study of industrial arts....[51]

These remarks were part of Itō's argument against Confucian moral instruction in schools in general; he was responding to Motoda Eifu's 1879 manifesto in support of such instruction.[52] However, the above comments also betray Itō's apprehensions about the role of private schools in the popular rights movement of the 1870s.[53] He implies that training in the Confucian texts perpetuated an unproductive intelligentsia that fed on politically questionable strains of Western thought and threatened to defy the authority of the central government. His rationale for diminishing Confucian studies was thus political as well as pragmatic.

The Confucian enterprise was repeatedly depicted in public discourse during the first Meiji years as outdated and "conservative," but some members of the ruling elite nevertheless perceived it as a potential challenge to the new social order, a form of intellectual activity that allowed the individual more scope than was desirable for the purpose of creating a "rich country and strong army" *(fukoku kyōhei)*. That goal required technicians, not lifelong students who might take the "questioning" aspect of *gakumon* too seriously. Learning in the Confucian sense was therefore characterized in some contexts as almost ominous in its impracticality. The nation would be better off, if we are to judge by Itō's rhetoric, if young people of educated parentage simply relinquished the moral idealism grounded in classical studies with which their parents had been imbued.

Some forms of Confucian study prevalent in the Bakumatsu period had encouraged a sense of independence, not necessarily of a political nature, but a kind of intellectual inquisitiveness that roamed beyond institutionalized lineages and authoritative texts. Satō Issai's marked emphasis on the value of self-reliance and his insistence that "learning is to be carried out for the sake of oneself" without regard for others' approbation is a typical expression of this outlook.[54] The eclectics and evidentialists, for their part, had invested themselves energetically in developing independent hermeneutical perspectives from among the plurality of possible readings of the classics. These late-Edo approaches to learning, though necessarily tied to the Confucian textual enterprise, had allowed for a degree of individuality and critical judgment that contrasts sharply with the type of schooling envisioned by the Meiji oligarchs.

Outside official circles, the new generation marshaled their Confucian heritage in a variety of ways, transforming it in the process. Kishida Toshiko (1863–1901), a forerunner of the Japanese feminist movement, identified *gakumon* as the prerogative of young women.[55] While still in her teens Kishida was appointed to the educational staff of the imperial court, where her responsibilities included lecturing on Chinese texts to the empress. The latter is said to have been particularly impressed by Kishida's lectures on the *Mencius*.[56] Perhaps the young tutor had a talent for making the ideals recorded in this text seem relevant to the contemporary social context. While employed at court Kishida reportedly felt, in fact, that she was inhabiting "an enchanted land, far from the real world, filled with a sense of *ennui* and beautiful women."[57] She may well have interpreted the *Mencius* in such a way as to alert her listeners to the disorder and difficulty of ordinary people's lives in society at the time.

In any event, Kishida soon resigned her post and began to speak out on women's rights under the auspices of the popular rights movement. Her preoccupation with the correct definition of learning is notable in a speech she gave at Ōtsu in late 1883, entitled "Daughters Confined in Boxes" *(Hakoiri musume)*. She warned that contemporary mothers were gravely misled in their belief that learning would have a harmful effect on their daughters' marriages.

> If you hold learning to be reciting *waka*, alluding to *hokku* and *haikai* [forms of Japanese poetry], and enjoying elegant pleasures, not to mention reading the Four Books, the Five Classics, the Eight Great Poets or the writings of Han Tuizhi, and intoning the poems of the various great writers—that is a great misconception.[58] ... What I mean by learning is that while living in this promising nation you should not pass your time idly, but should at least learn the responsibility of a woman. In short, I hope that you will cultivate learning—the most important part of a woman's marriage trousseau....
>
> And in what does that learning consist? I suggest [that it is] the study of economy and the study of personal cultivation *(keizaigaku to shūshingaku)*. Even if you expect to receive the protection of your husband for your entire life, should your husband depart from this world, at that time

you will need to take care of yourself by using your learning of personal
cultivation and to manage your livelihood by using your learning of
economy. That is why I say learning is the most important part of your
trousseau.[59]

Kishida went on to censure parents of the Osaka-Kyoto region who
in her view had no understanding of the importance of true learning and
as a result prepared their daughters for marriage simply by training them
to clean the house well. Another, relatively exalted type of "box" to
which these women were confined when they were still young and unmarried, declared Kishida, was "a box in which their parents make
them study the writings of long ago—books like the *Elementary Learning for Women [Onna shōgaku]* and the *Greater Learning for Women
[Onna daigaku]*—a box in which they study [the teachings] handed
down by sages and gentlemen."[60] Even well-meaning parents who ar-
ranged for their daughters to learn tea ceremony, flower arranging, poetry, shamisen, or dancing were oblivious to the fact that this sort of education would never allow the girls to develop themselves in any serious
way. Kishida argued that authentic parents should instead teach their
daughters "morality" *(dōtoku)*.[61] Instead of restricting their development by having them focus only on how to please men with various superficial skills, parents who genuinely cared for their daughters should
foster their intellectual and ethical growth. Parents should strive to overcome the weight of tradition in this regard, Kishida cautioned, for "today is a time in which all daughters know very well that the heavenly
ruler *[tentei]* has granted them freedom."[62] Bringing up girls in the
1880s, when new forms of knowledge were more accessible than ever
before, required creating a "box," if any, that was as "vast and free as
the world."[63]

Gakumon, in Kishida's view, was a broad educational process
through which young women could enrich their individual potential and
develop their sense of autonomy. Many voices are at work in her discourse, representing not only Western notions of equal rights and freedom but also a native feminist perspective, a familiar polemic against the
impracticality of literary and aesthetic pursuits in favor of "real learning" *(jitsugaku),* and not least, a Confucian-style respect for individual
moral cultivation. Like other thinkers we have discussed, Kishida was
interested in Confucian cultivation more as a general framework for
personal betterment than in terms of its detailed ethical content; for
many women in the Tokugawa period, Confucian moral instruction had
been closely associated with the very manuals of female education that
Kishida rejected in her Ōtsu speech. She was drawn rather to the language of the early classical texts, which more easily allowed for creative

readings in the direction of human rights. The *Mencius,* famed for its implication that people have a natural right to overthrow unjust rulers, is particularly amenable to such interpretations.[64] Kishida's affinity for Mencius, whose doctrine of innate moral goodness had been a major source of Neo-Confucian inspiration, also tallied with her concern for personal autonomy and ethical integrity. In this case at least, Itō Hirobumi was not far wrong in linking Confucian textual studies, moral idealism, and political dissent. After the Ōtsu speech, police charged Kishida with giving a political speech instead of the announced educational lecture: she was arrested and imprisoned for eight days.[65]

The notion of a practical kind of learning thus encompassed highly diverse agenda. Private educators as well as makers of public policy seemed to agree that a new, pragmatic type of education was essential to prosperity in the modern age, but they disagreed on the meaning of the implied "practicality." The Confucian program seems to have functioned as a lightning rod in this debate. Some defined practical studies in opposition to what was depicted as overly abstract Confucian ideas; others acknowledged the need for technological training in particular fields but insisted that it remain subsidiary to the *truly* practical learning— Confucian moral cultivation.[66] In the end, however, the rejection of Confucian learning proved to be, as Martin Collcutt puts it, "a temporary and rather superficial phenomenon."[67] After the first Meiji decade, public opinion shifted; well-known figures such as Nishimura Shigeki and Motoda Eifu lobbied energetically for the reintegration of a Confucian-based ethical component in school curricula.[68] Itō Hirobumi and the other pragmatists who continued to lament the inadequacies of Confucian studies during this period were reacting precisely to these latter-day attempts to reintroduce Confucian moral content into primary-school curricula.[69]

Ultimately, the 1890 Imperial Rescript on Education *(Kyōiku chokugo)* vindicated the advocates of traditional moral education; it sanctified not only the nativist premise of divine imperial succession but also the Confucian virtues of the five moral relations. The rescript specifically urges Japanese citizens to "pursue learning," yet in the next line advises them to "advance the public good."[70] "Learning" now encompassed both a morally oriented quest and a utilitarian form of study, each to be pursued for the benefit of the nation.[71] The thrust of the rescript and in deed of mid-Meiji educational policy in general was thus the exhortation, on the one hand, to be loyal to the empire, filial to one's parents, affectionate to one's brothers and sisters, harmonious in one's marital relations, and true to one's friends; and, on the other, to educate oneself in order to further the national good.

Despite echoes of classical texts such as the *Great Learning,* this synthesis of moral and civic axioms contrasts with the *gakumon* that had occupied scholars in the Tokugawa period. The Learning in the Neo-Confucian sense had always been depicted in terms of its benefit to larger social levels of existence, but at the same time it purported to be a holistic program of personal cultivation that required reading classical texts, scrutinizing one's daily behavior in light of the virtues enunciated in those texts, and, as often as not, engaging in contemplative practices. The difference between the learning of the rescript and the old-style Confucian variety lay in the degree of emphasis placed on individual experience, or on following one's own "inclinations," as Mori had phrased it. In the official 1890 version, learning was identified almost entirely with its social and political benefits—the harmony of the family and the success of the nation. This new civic interpretation of learning would have lasting effects; it became a dominant theme in the state-sponsored ethics textbooks that were used in primary schools throughout Japan in the first half of the twentieth century.[72]

The Separation of Religion and Learning

The mid-Meiji reinstatement of Confucian ethics was part and parcel of the ongoing definition of "religion" *(shūkyō)*. The term had been used in pre-Restoration texts primarily to denote the Buddhist teaching, or more precisely, the doctrine of a particular Buddhist sect.[73] However, the translators of Western texts who faced the task of rendering the term "religion" into Japanese in the late 1860s and 1870s were not necessarily Buddhist in orientation, and at first they simply generated a variety of terms to render what they took to be the meaning of "religion" in Western-language works—a broad phenomenon that included Buddhism, Christianity, Shinto, Islam, and so forth. *Shūshi, shinkyō, shūmon, kyōmon, kyōhō,* and *hōkyō* all appeared along with *shūkyō* as renditions of "religion" in the translations and writings of Japanese intellectuals of the time who concerned themselves with Western culture.[74] Most of these early variations included the character *kyō* (teaching, doctrine) and as such connoted a social transfer of knowledge. The multiple usages eventually coalesced in the term *"shūkyō,"* which gained wide currency in the mid-1870s after it appeared in the writings of Mori Arinori and Fukuzawa Yukichi (though the other terms remained in use throughout the early Meiji).[75]

Whether translated as *shūkyō* or otherwise, diverse conceptions of religion were now formulated by representatives of several interested groups—not only the so-called enlightenment thinkers, but also sectarian leaders and, of course, government officials. The various definitions of religion were then used in public discourse to designate systems of thought and practice as religious or not religious and, on that basis, to characterize their relationship to the state.[76] Ketelaar astutely remarks in this regard that in the early Meiji the construction of the meaning of the term

> was carried out by means of a series of negative definitions of religion in order to "separate" religion from all other major conceptual fields. In the quest for definition, "religion" was placed in opposition to politics ..., in opposition to education ..., in opposition to the discipline of science ..., in opposition to cultural enlightenment ..., in opposition to the prevailing articulation of Imperial authority, and in opposition to contrasting definitions of "religion" itself.[77]

"Religion" was also placed in opposition to "Confucianism" *(Jukyō)* and its common self-presentation, "learning" *(gakumon)*. Tokugawa Confucian scholars had set their theories and ritual activities off from popular belief systems; Meiji educational elites followed suit by creating boundaries between "Confucian learning" and the newly generic "religion"—although they now had the added incentive of countering the Christian component of the latter. Several enlightenment writers viewed Confucian learning more positively than other Tokugawa interpretive systems; they believed that it had helped to liberate the Japanese people from irrational beliefs and practices. The journalist Fukuchi Gen'ichirō (1841–1906), for example, argued that Buddhism in medieval times and Confucianism during the Tokugawa period had each in turn contributed to the development of Japanese civilization. He claimed that members of the upper levels of pre-Meiji society, who were educated in Confucian thought, had not even needed religion, and that Japan was now able to become an enlightened "society without religion" precisely because of its Confucian heritage.[78]

It is worth noting at this juncture that some of the writers in this circle placed Zen Buddhism on a par with Confucian learning in the higher tiers of their religious-evolutionary scales. Tsuda Mamichi averred that Confucius and the putative Zen founder Bodhidharma were a cut above other ancient figures who had generated religious legends, because "their imagination was somewhat different and more elevated."[79] The creative powers of Confucius and Bodhidharma were evidently less encumbered by irrational (and impractical) beliefs.

Fukuzawa Yukichi's early writings on religion were especially influential. He described himself as an inveterate skeptic who regarded religion as a form of superstition that was suited only to the needs of the uneducated. He argued in the early 1870s that reliance on religious systems was antithetical to the spirit of "independence and self-respect" that he advocated.[80] Fukuzawa's view of religion was closely related to his idealization of the "gentleman" *(shijin)*—that is, the man of status and education. Such a man, Fukuzawa said, is "indifferent to religion." He described the gentleman as one who "regards the creed of loyalty and morality as the foundation for 'finding peace of mind and fulfilling heaven's will' *[anjin ryūmei]*. He diffuses this creed and uses it to conduct his personal life, to abide with his family, to associate with his friends, and to organize society. Moreover, he preserves these virtues [of loyalty and morality] without relying on religion."[81] Fukuzawa's derogation of religion was part of his larger polemic against the view held by some at this time that Japan's assimilation of Western civilization would necessarily involve the acceptance of Christianity.[82] The model that Fukuzawa counterproposed, however, was an adapted version of the *Great Learning* paradigm: the gentleman is a person who disciplines himself, enhances his family life, and thereby brings order to the larger levels of society.

Fukuzawa coined the phrase "follower of loyalty and sincerity" *(chūsei no shinto)* to describe his notion of the modern Japanese gentleman. He claimed that his model was significantly different from the undercivilized "feudal religion of lords and retainers" of the Tokugawa period, which in his view had fostered a rigid moralism that led to excesses of inhumanity. Yet, as is often noted, Fukuzawa's vision of a moral paragon untainted by religious belief closely resembles the perspective of pre-Meiji Confucian scholars.[83] In late Tokugawa times, even though popular preachers faulted the Confucian enterprise of learning for its impracticality and irrelevance to people's lives, few questioned the ideal of personal cultivation. In the early Meiji as well, educated persons dismissed Confucian studies in favor of "practical learning" but at the same time assumed the need for a model of personal and social improvement. Despite his dissatisfaction with classical Confucian studies, Fukuzawa viewed the sequence of the *Great Learning* as a viable standard, given some critical revisions to suit the new age.

> If it were possible to revive these ancient sages [the Duke of Zhou, Confucius, and Mencius], and let them observe the circumstances of international intercourse today, they would certainly perceive that the security of a nation is not affected so much by its internal conditions as by its international relations. Then they would certainly add another article on foreign intercourse to the four stages of personal discipline, family management, national government, and world pacification. Rather, the sages would find it difficult to apply their doctrine to society without a fifth article [on foreign relations].[84]

The Confucian blueprint, in other words, was still workable, but needed to be expanded to encompass the new geopolitical reality.

Nishimura Shigeki also joined in the debate on religion. He shared with Fukuzawa, Nishi Amane (1829–1897), and other public intellectuals of the time an evolutionary perspective on religious history that was inspired by the works of Auguste Comte (1798–1857) and other European theorists.[85] Nishimura assumed from the outset that the key to modern Japanese progress was moral education, but unlike other enlightenment writers he insisted that this educational function should ultimately be assumed by a nonreligious system. He argued that as the Japanese "enlightenment" progressed, religion would be purified of supernatural beliefs and, in effect, turn into philosophy. Genuine morality was to be found, not in "otherworldly teachings" *(segaikyō)*, but in "the teachings of this world" *(seikyō)* that placed priority on ethics. By "teachings of this world" Nishimura meant a combination of the best elements of Confucian thought and Western philosophy, which he dubbed the "true principles of the universe" *(tenchi no shinri)* or simply "sincerity" *(makoto, sei)*. As people became more educated, this reason-based moral teaching would naturally come to replace the established religions.[86] Sakatani Shiroshi (1822–1881), another contributor to the *Meiroku zasshi,* similarly suggested that an official moral doctrine (which he called *seikyō,* "government teachings") should be used to spread values among the people; he argued that the propagation of ethical ideas was a legitimate government domain as long as the ideas were not specifically identified with any religion.[87]

We catch a glimpse here of the ideological dimension of the differentiation between "Confucianism" and "religion." The process paralleled the ongoing debate over the meaning of "Shinto," in which nativists argued that Shinto-type beliefs and rituals belonged to the civic domain and thus were not religion. The Tosa scholar Okunomiya Zōsai (Masayoshi, 1811–1877), to cite one example, asserted that Shinto was simply the "royal way of the ancient past," which was recorded in the *Kojiki* and the *Nihongi.* These works were ancient histories, not the canonical texts of a religious creed *(shūshi).*[88] Japan had no such scriptures, said Okunomiya, because the ancient imperial government used only rituals to rule the people. To call this practice "religion" *(shūkyō)* was a misnomer, he argued in a rather Protestant-sounding mode, for it did not encompass any doctrinal formulation *(kyō).*[89] Based on this definition of religion, Okunomiya thus managed to advocate freedom of religion and Shinto indoctrination at the same time. His reasoning typifies that disingenuous yet ingenious mode of thought, characteristic of the early Meiji ideological process, whereby selected ideas and rituals were defined as nonreligious and therefore legitimate material for government propagation.[90] Renaming the Confucian enterprise "the creed of loyalty and morality," "the teachings of this world," or "official moral doctrine" and setting it off from "religion" was a similar ideological move, though far less visible and awkward than the creation of "state Shinto" *(kokka Shintō)*. The enlightenment interpreters of Confucianism in effect laid the groundwork for the state's later establishment of Confucian-type values in primary education.

Dim views of religion were of course not the prerogative of the well-known writers associated with *Meiroku zasshi*. The Meiji press played an important role in the public division of religion and Confucian learning. An 1876 essay in *Chōya shinbun* adopts a rationalist tone similar to that of the Meiji Six writers. According to the author, gods do not serve any purpose and worship of them had best be eliminated: their status is entirely dependent on the whims of human beings, who created them in the first place.[91] Asano Ken, who later became an active debater in Kaishintō circles, contributed a series of pieces on religion to the same paper during the mid-seventies.[92] He argued that although religion was fundamentally irrational superstition, people of the lower estates were heavily influenced by it, and it therefore constituted an obstacle to "civilization and enlightenment."[93] The fulfillment of Confucian morality, in Asano's view, would suffice to establish the equivalent of heaven on earth, obviating the need to seek for an ephemeral paradise after death.[94] The same perspective apparently inspired the Kyoto municipal government's 1872 public denunciation of the new Ministry of Doctrine (Kyō-bushō) that Ketelaar highlights in his study of this debate. Sounding the early Meiji refrain on utility and practicality, the author of this statement (which was addressed to the administration and later released to the press) relegated both Buddhism and Christianity to the sphere of the irrational: "In this age of the flowering of international civilization, deceptive and grotesque religions must be discarded and the people must be trained in reasoning and the importance of fulfilling their occupations...."[95]

These and other educated members of early Meiji society, most of whom had been schooled in the classical Chinese texts, made a remarkable effort to reinforce the boundary between Confucian learning and the disparate phenomena that only now were grouped under the rubric *shū-kyō*. Drawing ammunition from Western philosophical theories as well as from Tokugawa models, they succeeded in establishing a binary opposition between "Confucianism" and "religion" in Meiji public discourse. The immediate impetus for this drive was a defensive move against Christianity, the seemingly paradigmatic Western religion that threatened to encroach on Japan's cultural territory. However, the division was also part of a "wide-ranging exercise in signification," as Ketelaar puts it.[96] The marking off and classifying of spheres of knowledge seems to have been a regular disposition of the educated sectors of the time. The constant discussing and defining of key terms was not necessarily an organized campaign, but it was not simply a random process, either—Bourdieu's directorless orchestra is an apt metaphor.[97]

The contrast between popular devotional practices and individual cultivation of the moral values recorded in the Chinese classics had been a characteristic feature of Tokugawa scholarly discourse. Although a sizable percentage of Confucian-educated persons undoubtedly pursued both tracks without any sense of contradiction, fervent worship of gods and Buddhas was at least ostensibly excluded from the repertoire of many professional Confucian scholars.[98] Early Meiji intellectuals replicated this pattern. They initially denounced Confucian learning as impractical and outdated, but in the context of the debate over religion they frequently depicted Confucian cultivation theory as relatively enlightened—indeed, as a veritable evolutionary foundation for the civilized, religionless era they now envisioned. In comparison with the newly imported scientific forms of knowledge, Confucian studies per se no longer seemed "real" or "practical" enough to take Japan into the new age; but if presented in the right guise, in combination with selected "modern" elements, some Confucian themes would do nicely.

The adaptation of these themes required frequent iteration of the suitability to modern Japanese needs of the Confucian mode of thought vis-à-vis Christian, Buddhist, and other interpretive systems—a suitability that was ascribed to the nonreligious quality of this mode. Gluck points out that from the mid-1870s the Meiji official Inoue Kowashi "supported Confucian ethics precisely because he wished to avoid all semblance of a 'national doctrine' and the kind of religious strife that the link between Christianity and the state had engendered in the West."[99] Motoda Eifu, in contrast, agitated exactly for such a Confucian national teaching. Both men, however, justified their positions on the same grounds—namely, that Confucianism was by its very nature different from religion. Inoue spoke approvingly of Confucianism "both as a 'teaching that does not rely on the deity' and as the closest counterpart in Japan to 'the science that in the West is called "philosophy."'"[100] The imperial advisor, Motoda, not only sharply distinguished Confucianism from religion, but promoted it as a remedy for the latter's dangerous influence on the populace: "While the errors of Buddhism and Christianity render them unworthy of belief, their concern with life and death, misery and happiness, and gain and loss strikes a kindred note in the human mind, people become superstitious, and the disease becomes rooted and immovable."[101] In a memorandum directed in 1887 to Mori Arinori (who rejected the use of Confucian-based ethical texts in primary schools), Motoda reiterated that the type of Confucian program he envisioned was not a religion like Buddhism or Christianity, but a moral system that would foster family values and allegiance to the nation of Japan.[102] It is worth noting that Motoda also distinguished his vision of a modern Confucian system from the textualist activities that had alienated late-Tokugawa educators: the *gakumon* he advocated was not that of "the China-loving literary stylists and the slaves of evidential studies."[103]

Sectarian leaders, needless to say, did not easily accept the relegation of *shūkyō* to a lower order of reality or its concomitant exclusion from public education. They came to the defense of religion—understood, of course, as a phenomenon that in its most authentic and intelligent form was identical only with their own faith. Zen master Imakita Kōsen took issue with the view, popularized by Fukuzawa, Fukuchi, and other public intellectuals of the time, that religion had become superfluous in Japan's newly civilized society.[104] Along with numberless other Buddhist spokespersons, Imakita argued instead for renewed government sponsorship of the Dharma.

The Zen priest agreed with his contemporaries that learning and religion were distinct spheres of activity. He even conceded that religion was "no match for Confucian learning" in terms of intellectual and spiritual depth. Nevertheless, in the 1880s he claimed (in contrast to Motoda) that religion surpassed other forms of knowledge because it not only provided clear guidelines for behavior—"enabling even ignorant husbands and wives to grasp its teachings"—but also engendered faith.[105] Confucian teachings were an appropriate form of learning for people who already possessed considerable education, said Imakita, but not for the majority, who had barely mastered an ordinary school curriculum. Like other educated persons of his generation, the abbot did not understand *Jukyō* to be simply a set of moral (or civic) values, like those that came to be associated with the 1890 Rescript on Education or that were emphasized in the late-Meiji *shūshin* primers. He correlated the Confucian field of knowledge, rather, with an advanced phase in the educational sequence. Unlike Mori Arinori, he never doubted that *gakumon* should be centered on the classical Chinese texts; but at the same time he agreed with Mori that it should be reserved for the advanced, mature student.[106] As the abbot put it, "the world is large and the unlearned are numerous"—and civilizing the "unlearned" through Confucian studies simply would not work. The only effective means for developing people's moral lives, he insisted, was religion (by which he undoubtedly meant Buddhism). *Gaku* (learning) could not be facilitated on a large scale—in order to edify large numbers of people, one needed *kyō* (religion). Despite his own extensive Confucian training, Imakita rejected the proposal put forth by Nishimura, Motoda, and others that Confucian ideas be made the centerpiece of moral education in Japan.

Sectarian leaders like Imakita thus differed with enlightenment advocates and government pragmatists about the educational value of religion, but at the same time they agreed that religion was quite distinct from Confucianism; as in Elias' soccer game, the players in this debate all abided by the same rules. Most also concurred that the Confucian program, or some part of it, should play a role in modern Japanese education precisely because of its nonreligious quality. A consensus further emerged that the guise of the new Confucian learning was critical. Nishimura, perhaps the most persistent proponent of Confucian moral education of his time, was keenly aware of the need to reidentify this heritage for the new age. He recommended in 1889 that "when the Confucian Way is used, its spirit alone should be taken, and I hope that the name Confucianism will not be used. The name Confucianism has for some time been disliked by the people, so that there are many who would not believe in the substance because of the name."[107] As Gluck has shown, when the Rescript on Education was finally issued in 1890, a spectrum of interpreters, each representing his or her own interests, rushed to disassociate its ethical content from the Confucian stigma.

> Although the name ["Confucianism"] did not indeed appear in the Rescript, Tokutomi [Sohō (1863–1957)], who had earlier opposed Confucianism as fusty and antiquated, was quick to assert that the "Way" mentioned in the Rescript did not refer to Confucianism alone, but to "the ordinary morality of the Japanese that has been transmitted from earliest times, even before there was Confucianism or Buddhism." And another journalist explained that "although the five virtues are also taught in Confucianism, since the Rescript describes the subjects' loyalty and filialty as the principle of our *kokutai* [national polity], here they are not Confucianism but *kokutai*-ism." Moreover, he argued that where Confucians valued morality at the expense of knowledge, the Rescript expressly urged the development of knowledge and skills. Even Inoue Kowashi minimized the Confucian connection. . . .

Gluck concludes that during the 1890s many "self-consciously forward-looking intellectuals" shared this tendency to disclaim the Confucian sources of the Rescript.[108] Given the various proposals for an official ethical doctrine under such rubrics as "teachings of this world" that appeared in the pages of the *Meiroku zasshi* and other forums of public opinion, the drive to rename Confucian teachings was common among intellectuals back in the 1870s and early 1880s as well, though it was expressed in more muted tones. These earlier advocates had also presented Confucian morality as a rational form of knowledge that was peculiarly adaptable to the needs of the newly modern Japan, paralleling contemporary Buddhist leaders' efforts to reinterpret their own systems in this way.

A Case in Point: *Religion or Learning?*

Thinkers who had been educated in their youth in the Confucian texts thus defined religion in diverse ways, depending on their interests, but all seemed to agree that it excluded Confucian learning. Intellectuals who had once identified the latter as their domain in contraposition to the sectarian teachings and folk practices that appealed to the masses of Tokugawa society now drew on Western rationalisms to reproduce and enhance the opposition, and indeed to establish its social reality through government policies and public education. With the popularization of a general term for religion in the early Meiji, the division between the two modes of thought and practice was marked by a convenient nomenclature. For enlightenment advocates, who envisioned a new, practical type of learning, *shūkyō* included all those phenomena which, in their view, lacked universal relevance and reasonability—Buddhism, Shinto, folk traditions, and for many, Christianity. Nativist/Shinto activists argued that their program was not religion but, in effect, a set of civic rituals. Buddhist leaders, for their part, strove mightily to except Buddhism from the view of religion as a lower order of human endeavor by depicting it as rational, enlightened, and modern in comparison with foreign traditions.[109]

When the new Ministry of Doctrine (Kyōbushō) inaugurated its Great Teaching Campaign *(Taikyō senpu undō)* in 1872, Shinto and Buddhist priests, and eventually teachers, storytellers, performing artists, and other professional communicators were drafted into the campaign as "doctrinal instructors" *(kyōdōshoku)*. Centered on an institution in Tokyo called the Great Teaching Academy (Daikyōin), the preachers were organized into an elaborate system of fourteen ranks. The promulgation of the ministry's generalized Shinto ideology in the form of the so-called Three Standards of Instruction *(Sanjō no kyōsoku)* was carried out through a nationwide network of supporting institutions, modeled after the Great Teaching Academy: regional head temples and shrines were designated "middle teaching academies" *(chūkyōin)*, while smaller institutions became "elementary teaching academies" *(shōkyōin)*.[110]

A critical feature of this system was its defining function: groups that participated in the Great Teaching Campaign were ipso facto "religions." For groups like Shingaku that had functioned under the Tokugawa neither as mainstream sectarian bodies nor as educational institutions, however, reality was less clearly segmented. Shingaku was a grass-roots movement that purported to foster personal cultivation in the Zhu Xi mode; its members had long depicted their program as a highly accessible form of "learning." The Shingaku pursuit of the "true heart" or "original mind" (J. *honshin*), as they were fond of pointing out, had been defined by Mencius as the "sole concern of learning."[111] Nevertheless, during the decades prior to the Restoration, Shingaku was best known for its preaching events and proselytizing tours; many of its teachers were employed in these capacities by shogunal and domain authorities. Under the circumstances, Shingaku members were obvious candidates for enlistment in the Great Teaching Campaign, along with sundry other preachers, storytellers, and performers of the time. It was partly because of its reputation as a cadre of public speakers, rather than as an individually oriented system of "learning" centered on Confucian texts, that in 1873 the group was involuntarily designated a religious teaching.

Given their historical self-image as a conveyors of Confucian learning, the Meiji followers of Ishida Baigan found themselves in an awkward position. The dilemma derived from Shingaku's double identity as both *gaku* and *kyō*. *Gakumon* in the Mencian sense of a quest for one's innate goodness could perhaps be preached as an ideal in public sermons, and no doubt made to cohere with the ideology of the Three Standards, but in the final analysis it was inevitably a personal affair. The Shingaku teachers' Neo-Confucian mentors had insisted, after all, that learning was to be carried out "for the sake of oneself" rather than with the thought of gaining acclaim from others. At the same time, judging from the frequency with which the group's leaders reminded their preachers of the dangers of aiming for popular success in their teaching, the pursuit of learning as a personal quest devoid of such ulterior motives was probably more an ideal than a reality in the movement during the years leading up to the Restoration.[112]

In any case, Ministry of Doctrine officials had a rather different perspective on Shingaku preaching skills. As practiced public speakers and, in some cases, official moral instructors during the Tokugawa, Baigan's followers were among the most qualified candidates of the available pool to carry out the new government's ideological campaign. Before the Restoration, the famous Shingaku preacher Nakazawa Dōni and his disciples in the Kantō area had regularly introduced or concluded their sermons with readings from the *kōsatsu*, or notice boards that the Tokugawa shogunate erected in public places in order to edify the populace. The official postings were largely ethical in content, exhorting people to fulfill the Confucian virtues associated with the five moral relations, or at times prohibiting contact with Christian or other heterodox forms of knowledge.[113] During the first half of the nineteenth century, Shingaku teachers had preached regularly at the Edo *ninsoku yoseba* (a labor camp for released convicts and homeless people established by the shogunate); their *kōsatsu* readings were an established part of the program, encouraged by the camp authorities. When the preachers read off the maxims displayed on the plaques, "all the members of the audience would lower their heads and listen respectfully." This practice allegedly continued right up to 1872, when the Ministry of Doctrine was established. Shingaku sources state that it was only after the preachers began working as doctrinal instructors in the following year that they "no longer read off the official notice boards. In place of these, they read off the Three Standards of Instruction."[114]

The Shingaku chroniclers' almost casual homologization of the shogunate's Confucian-flavored postings with the Meiji government's nativist-Confucian injunctions accords with the testimony of other sources that, for ordinary Japanese citizens, the role of the government in religious-ethical affairs in the early 1870s initially seemed to have changed little. However, the modifications in the government's moral-religious vocabulary were far from unimportant to the spokespersons of the religious groups involved. Meiji records indicate considerable anxiety among the Shingaku leadership over the new nomenclature that the Ministry of Doctrine imposed on the group. For example, the use of the trademark Shingaku term *"dōwa"* (talk on the Way) was discontinued in 1872 and replaced by the ministry's preferred *"sekkyō."* The latter term (which like *"shūkyō"* first came into wide use in the early Meiji) is usually rendered as "sermon" in English, but in the 1870s it referred in the first place to the "explication of the doctrine" of the Three Standards.[115] Yet the content of the *dōwa* rather than its name was the most pressing issue for Shingaku leaders in the early 1870s. The movement had long prided itself on being open to all the "Three Teachings" (Shinto, Confucian, Buddhist). Statements of the fundamental compatibility of these (as well as Daoist) ideas and of the error of intersectarian conflict appear frequently in late Tokugawa Shingaku writings.[116] From the perspective of Meiji Shingaku narrators, the establishment of the Ministry of Doctrine marked the loss of official approval of the group's interreligious nature.

The problem for Shingaku was not the forcible separation of Buddhist and Shinto elements, as it was for most other syncretic systems of the time.[117] The sea change for Shingaku in the Restoration was rather that "the Confucian Way was separately allocated to the education section *(kyōiku no bubun)* [of the Meiji government]," while Shinto and Buddhist teachings were assigned to the "religion section *(kyōhō no bubun)."*[118] This division had originated earlier, when the new public university or Daigakkō (prefiguring the Ministry of Education) was charged with the administration of education that took place inside formal schools throughout the country, while the Department of Shinto or Jingikan (prefiguring the Ministry of Doctrine) was assigned the supervision of education that took place outside these institutions. In other words, the Ministry of Doctrine inherited control of the informal, oral channels of education understood in the broadest sense—which in the Tokugawa had included not only Buddhist and Shinto sermons, but also the activities of raconteurs, performing artists, village readers, fortune-tellers, and Shingaku preachers, among others. The division of the two spheres of activity was reinforced by a series of edicts that led to the exclusion of sectarian instruction from general education. Despite various policy reversals and reiterations, by late 1873 religious professionals were not permitted to establish or teach in nonsectarian primary schools.[119]

The latter-day followers of Ishida Baigan were thus confronted head-on with the question of their modern identity. Were they training people how to engage in *gakumon* (as Baigan had invariably referred to his teachings), or were they leading a movement of religious believers? And if the latter, was the movement Shinto or Buddhist? Needless to say, these questions were meaningless to members of an interpretive community that had thrived for more than a century in a world where such distinctions held no sway. The answers, in any case, were supplied willy-nilly by the government, as they were for other religious groups of ambiguous identity during this time—although, given Shingaku's muted Confucian-type presentation, without the iconoclastic furor that accompanied the "cleansing" of Buddhist-Shinto ritual complexes.

Contemporary advocates of "civilization and enlightenment" exulted over the centralization and redefinition of non-mainstream groups like Shingaku. One commentator wrote:

> In our Imperial Land, several kinds of religious creeds circulate. Shinto, Confucianism, and Buddhism, and popularly, Munetada Shintō [Kurozumikyō], Tohokami-kō, Oharai-kō, Fuji-kō, Kaseki-kō, Ontake-kō, Yudonosan-kō, Tōkyūjutsu, Shingaku, and Seigaku....[120] Right now, through the moral transformation of the Restoration, one hundred rivers are merging with the great ocean—what a delight [to see] the power of all of them about to arrive, like waters and currents mixing together![121]

Regardless of its claim to be a form of Confucian learning, Shingaku was thus swept along with other "popular" groups—including the aforementioned Tohokami and Tōkyūjutsu—into the tidal wave of the Great Teaching Campaign.

The Tokyo Shingaku leadership did not welcome the group's new identity as a religion, if we are to credit its in-house records. Soon after the Ministry of Doctrine was founded, we are told, a senior government official invited the Shingaku leader Takahashi to his private residence. The official proceeded to discuss what he perceived as the decline of Shingaku since the Restoration and rather disingenuously recommended as a solution that henceforth its leaders advocate "the Way of the Gods" *(Shintō)*. They should start, he suggested, by replacing the character *shin* (mind; heart) in the name Shingaku with the character *shin* (god); in other words, the group should rename itself the "Learning of the Gods" *(shingaku)*. In addition, the official allegedly advised, Takahashi and his colleagues should stop quoting from Confucius and Mencius in their talks; they should also remove the calligraphy scrolls hanging in Shingaku meetinghouses that displayed the words "humaneness, rightness, propriety, wisdom, and trust" (the five Confucian virtues) and replace them with altars to the Japanese gods. In sum, the ministry official concluded, as long as Shingaku teachers invested themselves in spreading "Shinto teachings," they most assuredly would be able to reverse their group's fortunes.[122]

Takahashi is said to have politely replied that Shingaku teachers had no understanding of the "Japanese classics" *(kokuten)*.[123] They were not learned people, he averred. They merely endeavored to lead ordinary men and women to "the path of loyalty and filiality," and could not possibly consider themselves on a par with "stately Shinto priests." Takahashi further emphasized that none of the group's lecturers made their living by teaching; they all supported themselves through their regular occupations and pursued Shingaku studies only in their spare time.[124] In making this distinction, Takahashi was echoing Teshima Toan, Nakazawa Dōni, and other past Shingaku leaders who had insisted on identifying themselves as amateurs rather than as paid professionals. The disclaimer had sometimes served in the past as an oblique way of criticizing the shallow, self-interested approach of professional teachers and scholars of all affiliations.[125] In the early Meiji, however, the insistence that Shingaku teaching was not a profession also served as a strategy to establish the movement's identity as a voluntarist form of personal cultivation rather than as a religion that would be proselytized en masse. The learning of the mind, in short, was a learning *(gaku)*, not a teaching *(kyō)*.

Takahashi's interlocutor did not take kindly to the Shingaku leader's resistance to the nativist/Shinto makeover.[126] We are told that the official's face "hardened" and that Takahashi was reduced to silence. Ultimately the Shingaku teacher persisted, however, declaring that he "could not by any means comply" with the official's request to change the character "mind" to "god" in the group's name, or to replace the Confucian calligraphy scrolls with altars to the gods. Taking the official's line of reasoning at face value, he reportedly argued that changing Shingaku's name and associating it with Shinto "for the sake of success" would be dishonest. Should the group accede to the ministry's demand, the public would conclude that Shingaku was untrustworthy. If the government forced the group to adopt the proposed measures, Takahashi intrepidly concluded, its preachers would resign their appointments as doctrinal instructors and the group would dissolve.[127]

The threat was effective, according to this account: the official's demeanor "softened" and he changed the subject. Soon after this interview, Takahashi followed up by submitting a memorial to the Ministry of Doctrine in which he reiterated his position. Before long he was summoned for another interview.[128] On this occasion, however, Takahashi was interviewed by Honjō Munehide, the Tohokami stalwart, Shingaku supporter, and Shirakawa priest discussed earlier.[129] By late 1872, Honjō was a prominent figure in the Shinto world. The commentator cited earlier lists him as one of the itinerant instructors who had been specially selected to serve in the ministry's proselytizing campaign during the early 1870s.[130] Honjō had also been appointed head priest of the Ise shrines and in that capacity conducted preaching tours around the country on behalf of Jingū Kyōkai (later called Jingūkyō), a new Shinto organization composed of pilgrimage groups that were associated with the Ise shrines. The scale of Honjō's preaching activities was significant: over nine thousand listeners attended a six-day series of his talks held in July 1873 at Chion'in in Kyoto; a four-day sequence held at Myōkenji in Kyoto the following month attracted over five thousand.[131]

The former daimyo was able to wield enough influence not only to legitimize the Tohokami movement (an event discussed in chapter 8), but also to have Shingaku assigned to his division of the ministry. I noted earlier that the Tohokami elder and members of his household had practiced and sponsored Shingaku as early as the 1840s, and that the overlapping of Tohokami and Shingaku in the Edo area had continued throughout the Bakumatsu period; Takahashi and his Sanzensha comrades were personally involved in Tohokami during the 1860s. In other words, the established connections between the two groups and Honjō's prominence in the ministry gave Ishida Baigan's followers an edge in the complex process of negotiating the preservation of their group's identity.

Shingaku chronologers depict Takahashi's and Honjō's consultation at the Ministry of Doctrine as exquisitely cordial. The former daimyo acknowledged that Shingaku had always been a "learning of the heart" *(kokoro no manabi)* that was inspired by all "three teachings." However, he carefully explained, the recent government prohibition of "the mixing of Shinto and Buddhism" made it necessary that Shingaku associate itself with a single, distinctive tradition. Honjō reasoned as follows:

> Shingaku [members'] social position is said to be that of Confucian scholars; but insofar as they take responsibility for religious doctrine, they are not under the jurisdiction of the Confucian school. They lecture on Buddhist theories, but insofar as they are laypeople who eat meat and marry, they do not personally belong to the Buddhist monastic order, either. Consequently, Shingaku will be assigned to the Shinto division [of the Ministry of Doctrine].[132]

Here, too, Confucian-type learning is assumed to exclude religion. Whether the premise that Shingaku members "took responsibility for religious doctrine" originated with other ministry officials or with Honjō himself, it was probably based on Shingaku's public image as an organized company of proselytizers rather than on any particular aspect of its teachings. Moreover, although according to this account Shingaku was designated "Shinto" almost by default, the group's connection with Honjō was clearly the key factor in the decision. The record depicts him in a mediating role: in the end, he told Takahashi, Shingaku teachers could propagate their teachings just as they had always done, as long as they "upheld the Way of the Gods" in their talks.[133] Evidently the ritual of reading off the Three Standards, perhaps acompanied by a few brief explanatory comments, would suffice. As far as the Meiji Shingaku chroniclers were concerned, in the end "our former teacher [Ishida Baigan]'s style of learning was entirely preserved."[134]

The claim that Shingaku's doctrinal integrity was maintained is not implausible, but it is more a retrospective affirmation of the Meiji movement's authenticity than an exact statement of fact. Similar claims are contained in the modern accounts of other non-mainstream groups that were involuntarily designated "Shinto" during this time, as we shall see. In any event, the identity of Shingaku as religion rather than learning remained an issue for the group throughout the Meiji era. In 1895, Shingaku leaders were still seeking to persuade the authorities that the group possessed no "religious followers and believers" *(kyōto shinto)*. The Sanzensha spokesperson of the time (probably Kawajiri Hōkin) insisted that Shingaku members were simply "scholars" or "students" *(gakusha)*, and that the group was not a religious institution but a school of learning.[135] Sanzensha members were taught to "practice quiet sitting, to exert themselves in self-discipline and training, and to come to know their innate natures—that is, their original minds.... Therefore, we call our students 'school members' *[monjin]*. This is different from so-called 'religious followers' or 'religious believers'; calling [our members] 'pupils' *[seito]* is more appropriate."[136]

This interpretation of the Shingaku enterprise was eventually accepted. The movement took its place alongside other modern Japanese groups that advocated "religionless" forms of personal cultivation. As such, it may have preserved more autonomy vis-à-vis the government in the ensuing decades than overtly devotional groups. Today, Shingaku still carefully maintains its image as an organization dedicated to learning rather than matters of faith. We shall see in a later chapter, however, that the identity of the Shingaku program in Tokyo in fact extended beyond both its "nonreligious" Confucian presentation and its nominal sect-Shinto affiliation.

After the Restoration, Confucian scholars for the most part ceased to exist as an identifiable social group, and the learning with which they had been associated was reduced at the university level to the academic study of Chinese texts. Both government officials and forward-looking thinkers agreed that modern education could no longer be delimited by the "box" of ancient Confucian texts, as Kishida Toshiko had put it. Nevertheless, the idea that the cultivation of the person is the foundation of a prosperous society did not lose ground. As we shall see in the subsequent chapters, a synthesis of established disciplines of inner cultivation with the new practical learning became a persuasive model of personal development among educated members of early Meiji society. With the disappearance of the institutions that promoted traditional Confucian learning, however, the new versions of *gakumon* had to be not only renamed but also grounded in different social venues. Just as Meiji advocates of primary moral education were reluctant to identify Confucian moral codes as their principal source of inspiration, so proponents of learning in the sense of adult cultivation also endeavored to "forget" the Confucian sources of their theories—whether they had promoted nonreligious enlightenment philosophies, like Fukuzawa and the other intellectuals already discussed, or explicitly religious models for personal improvement, which we shall now proceed to examine.

CHAPTER 5

Practical Learning in the
Meditation Hall

THE PREOCCUPATION among educated people in the early Meiji to create and institutionalize forms of learning that were "practical" and "real" in contradistinction to traditional Chinese textual studies might be interpreted as the final tidal wave of dissatisfaction with the Confucian scholarly project that washed over the mid- to upper levels of Japanese society during the first half of the nineteenth century. Yet it was driven in a more immediate sense, as we have seen, by the pressing demand for a unified, industrialized Japan. The identification of practical forms of knowledge now became a matter of political debate, in which the definition of utility differed according to the interpreter. Women's rights activist Kishida Toshiko argued that a productive education for young women should include personal economy and applied Mencian idealism, rather than housekeeping and tea ceremony. Government officials and public intellectuals asserted that technical and scientific instruction, devoid of ethical or religious content, was the only sure route to personal and national prosperity. Court educator Motoda Eifu, for his part, insisted that education was "real" only insofar as it *was* morally directed.

Representatives of sectarian religious interests also laid claims to practical learning. This chapter describes one such claim, put forward by Rinzai master Imakita Kōsen while he was abbot of the Kamakura temple, Engakuji. By way of introducing the context in which Imakita made his argument, I begin the chapter with a summary of the effects of the new Meiji state's policies on the Rinzai Zen community, with special attention to the revival in Rinzai discourse during this time of the image of the meditation hall as a symbol of the ideal Buddhist lifestyle. The second half of the chapter details the abbot's proposals for higher Zen education. Imakita, ever the Confucian scholar, resurrected the pre-Meiji meaning of *jitsugaku* as personal cultivation, but interpreted it from a Buddhist perspective. The chapter concludes with an account of how the younger generation of Zen practitioners reacted to the abbot's program of practical learning.

FIGURE 7. Engakuji. A photograph of the approach to the main gate, taken during the Meiji period. Reproduced from *Engakujishi,* by Tamamura Takeji and Inoue Zenjō. Courtesy of Engakuji.

Even after the Meiji government began to operate and the capital was transferred to Tokyo, for a time life continued as usual at Engakuji, without any disruption (figure 7). Soon after the Restoration, under the nativist rubric of "unifying rites and governance" *(saisei itchi),* the central state promulgated the "Edict on Clarifying the Distinction between Gods and Buddhas" *(Shinbutsu hanzen rei),* which inspired a popular movement to "separate gods and Buddhas" *(shinbutsu bunri).* The newly established Department of Shinto (Jingikan) fermented with the anti-Buddhist sentiments of its nativist staffers, while localized drives to eliminate Buddhist influence and infrastructure erupted, sometimes violently, in various parts of Japan.[1] However, Engakuji belonged to a class of large, well-established Rinzai temples that survived the separation of gods and Buddhas without incident. The ritual assimilation of *kami* worship into Rinzai monastery life in general had been relatively modest, or at least not visible enough to provide a convenient target for the religious cleansing inspired by nativist zealots.

Rather than anti-Buddhist iconoclasts, it was the bureaucrats of the first Meiji years who took effective aim at long-standing monastic institutions like Engakuji. In the early 1870s Buddhist temple personnel throughout Japan underwent a dramatic transformation in their social status, educational function, and economic resources. The prerogatives they had enjoyed under the shogunate were withdrawn. They were required to register as ordinary citizens and therefore lost their tax and conscription exemptions. Their guaranteed constituencies were severely weakened by the elimination of the *terauke* (temple registration) system, which had required all villagers to belong to and support the local Buddhist parish. The personal identity of monastics was most profoundly affected in the long term by the Council of State's announcement in early 1872 that Buddhist priests were legally free to eat meat and marry, if they so desired.[2] A similar ordinance for nuns followed in 1873. These measures initially provoked strong resistance from most Buddhist leaders; a flurry of intrasectarian activity ensued, aimed at exhorting the priestly rank-and-file not to break the precept of celibacy. Clerical marriage remained a controversial issue for priests for the next several decades, as Jaffe has demonstrated; it was a lightning rod for debate that brought into relief a wide diversity of perspectives within the Meiji Buddhist community.[3]

Rinzai Zen is representative of the monastic sangha's response to the new policies. In the immediate aftermath of the decriminalization of clerical marriage, the Gozan leadership in Kyoto issued a stern statement to all branch temples to the effect that, henceforward, Rinzai head temples would "cooperate" in enforcing the precept of celibacy among the priesthood: violators would be relieved of their clerical status.[4] Rinzai reaction in the east was similar. Two months after the marriage decree was issued, the Engakuji abbot of the time, Yūhō Zetan (1806–1882), warned Engakuji-line priests not to misunderstand the "broad-minded" *(kandai na)* government measure and to exercise self-discipline. Temple personnel evidently failed to discipline themselves sufficiently, for several weeks later Yūhō sent out a similar memorandum to the branch temples in which he again enjoined strict obedience to the precepts.[5]

Engakuji chronicles do not record specific instances of clerical marriage within the head temple community during the nineteenth century.[6] But the problem was real enough, especially in smaller, regional temples. More than a decade after the clerical marriage decree was issued, Imakita Kōsen professed intense concern about the massive return to lay life of monks who had wavered in their religious commitment. By his own account, he willingly stretched monastery protocol when he believed it would help stem the outflow of priests from the sangha. On one occasion, a young monk from Yamaguchi appeared at Engakuji, hoping to participate in the summer retreat. The session had already begun, however, and when questioned, the monk admitted that he did not have a surplice *(kesa),* begging bowl, or the other equipment normally required for life in the meditation hall. The young man had not even obtained the requisite permission of his Zen master to travel to Kamakura —apparently the adept had committed an offense so grave that his teacher categorically refused to meet with him.[7] Imakita provided the renegade with the necessities and allowed him to join the retreat, but concealed the young priest's checkered history from the other residents of the monastery. The abbot explained in a letter to a colleague that "if I now let this able-bodied monk out of my sight, he will surely fall into low society in Tokyo and return to lay life. When I observe the customs of the degenerate age that we live in today, [I see that] many are stumbling [and falling back] into the lay life.... In today's world, surely it is my job to take in hand even a single one of the Buddha's offspring and prevent him from falling away."[8]

Imakita attributed the weakness of young priests to poor training, financial difficulties, and, implicitly, to government policies that permitted immorality. He continued to worry about his monks' ability to withstand these challenges in the ensuing years. In 1882, he openly lamented the practice of clerical marriage and meat eating among the Rinzai clergy.[9] More than a decade after the marriage decree was issued, the breaking of celibacy remained a central issue in the Gozan community as a whole. A notice circulated by sect leaders in the Engakuji and Kenchōji communities in mid-1884 states that the lodging of women, including temporary visitors, within temple precincts must "absolutely be stopped."[10] The notice was accompanied by a set of rules drawn up earlier that year by the abbots of the seven Gozan lines and approved by the Home Ministry (Naimushō).[11] A commentary prefacing the rules warns that

> recently the ways of monks have been disorderly and a considerable number have broken the precepts and behaved wrongfully. Scandalous reports that should never have been heard are proliferating in newspapers and speeches.... At present the outer teachings are growing rampant by the day and are almost about to crush the territory of our Dharma underfoot. How, then, can we carelessly overlook [these matters]?[12] The key to preserving this [Dharma] lies in strictly maintaining the precepts and in cultivating the celibate life.[13]

The accompanying rules state in no uncertain terms that "even one's own mother may not lodge [in the temple precincts] unless one has received permission," and specifies terms of punishment for violators.[14]

The delineation of the male monastic domain remained a prominent topic in Rinzai discourse throughout the 1880s.[15] The government had implicitly reaffirmed the authority of the monastic precepts in 1878, when it announced that "edict number 133, which states that the clergy are free to eat meat and marry, only serves to abolish the state law that had prohibited such activities. In no way does the law have anything to do with sectarian regulations."[16] Yet Imakita and other Rinzai leaders remained fervently committed to the complete repeal of the infamous decree. In 1886, the Engakuji abbot declared in a memorial to prime minister Itō Hirobumi that the marriage edict had ushered in the degenerate age of the last Dharma. He argued that the new policy had gravely impaired the credibility of Buddhist priests as moral examplars for the Japanese people, and that the state should once again enforce strict celibacy throughout the monastic community.[17]

The Ministry of Doctrine's centralization and ideologization of religion through its Great Teaching Campaign is depicted in Rinzai discourse of the time as an equally critical challenge to the identity of monastic Buddhism, especially Zen Buddhism. Rinzai administrators disapproved of the government's efforts to reconceptualize their educational mission along "Shinto" lines, although many quietly acquiesced.[18] Imakita initially seems to have viewed the campaign as an intrusion on what he regarded as his real task, teaching Buddhism (although Satomichi Tokuo exaggerates when he asserts that the abbot preached Buddhism "in opposition to" the doctrinal instruction program's aims).[19] The Zen master's adaptation to his new role as a government preacher is probably representative of the many religious actors of the time who negotiated a compromise between their own credal agenda and the Three Standards ideology.[20] By his own account Imakita simply read off the Three Standards at the beginning and end of his talks, devoting most of his energy to the Buddhist message "in the middle," with occasional references to the official platform.[21] Shingaku preachers, as noted earlier, performed a similar ritual to meet the state's requirements.

Several Rinzai leaders nonetheless expressed anxiety about the impact of the preaching campaign on their sect's purported image as authentic Buddhist practice. Encouraged perhaps by the True Pure Land priest Shimaji Mokurai's public agitations against the government's religion policies in 1873, Rinzai spokespersons began to argue that further compromise of their sect's teachings would result in the demise of the Zen Buddhist discipline itself. In March 1874, the representatives of the seven Gozan lines signed a manifesto that contained the following statement.

> Since the spring of Meiji 5 [1872], when the Ministry of Doctrine was instituted, our followers have been appointed doctrinal instructors and have

devoted themselves to mastering completely the Three Standards of Instruction. They have been spreading our religious creed and instructing the
people far and wide.... However, from time to time, there have been those
who have misunderstood and put their own religious creed aside; they
have cooked up [the teachings of] the *kami* or [of] the Confucians, blurted
out whatever came to their minds, and muddled the Way. How can [this]
mixed-up teaching possibly consolidate people's hearts and prevent the incursion of the outer teachings? Especially in the case of our sect, it goes
without saying that one cannot afford to neglect practicing the way of Zen
(sanzen bendō) for even one day.[22]

Rather than criticize the government campaign openly, the Rinzai
leaders blamed careless members of the sect for replacing true Zen practice with a jumble of Shinto and Confucian ideas (a fair characterization
of the Three Standards ideology). They concluded that Zen would "be
swept clean off the earth" within a decade unless steps were taken to reform "this evil." In other words, the Rinzai rank-and-file were forgetting
their own religion because the government expected them constantly to
hold forth on non-Buddhist teachings. Zen priests who were allegedly
caught up in their new elocutionary role stood in danger of losing their
grounding in the special practices of the meditation hall *(zendō)*. The
writers of this manifesto subtly allude to the distinctive character of Zen
Buddhism vis-à-vis other Japanese Buddhist sects, which they implicitly
identify with secondary religious activities.

For much of its history in Japan, Rinzai had remained a system of
knowledge and practice tailored to the tastes of the privileged classes.
The oral presentation of Zen teachings by Rinzai priests to large, popular audiences was virtually unknown until the early modern period.
With the advent in the Tokugawa of vigorous preachers such as Bankei
Yōtaku (1622–1693) and the popularization of Hakuin-type Zen by
Shingaku preachers, Meiji Rinzai proselytizers could at least lay claim
to some precedents.[23] Even so, judging from the above manifesto, the
facility with which a few priests apparently took up their government-
anointed mission as sermonizers in the early 1870s did not sit well with
some sect leaders. Priests of the True Pure Land sect, which had emphasized active lay outreach from its origins, were equipped to handle the
new demand for homiletic performance; but members of the smaller
monastic sects like Rinzai that had downplayed popular preaching during the Tokugawa now confronted an unfamiliar challenge. The involvement of monks in public speaking seemed to some Meiji Rinzai leaders
inimical to the very identity of their sect.

Such apprehensions were common among various religious
teachers of the time. However, each group's spokespersons expressed

their preoccupations about the new policies in distinctive lexicons and selectively elaborated themes that they perceived as fundamental to their peculiar social identity. Rinzai abbots accordingly argued that Zen's special character derived primarily from an austere monastic lifestyle that allowed contact with the general public only within a prescribed ritual framework. The new proselytizing mission was inimical to this purist conception. One sectarian writer acknowledged the concern among the sect leadership that the new concentration on preaching (doctrinal instruction) might ultimately render the Rinzai teaching completely ineffective. Nevertheless, he cautioned, the sect would have to face the reality imposed on it: "[the government] has instructed us that each temple, down to the smallest branch [temple], is to be a preaching hall and that all temple abbots are to be considered preachers...."[24] Rinzai, even if reluctantly, was to be a preaching community.

The difficulty was not simply the undesirability of preaching non-Buddhist ideas on behalf of the government, but of preaching at all. Ōkubo Dōshū observes that "Buddhism until [the Meiji era] had not been sustained through proselytization; its power had been upheld by its various ties with the state. Consequently, it did not possess any standards for outward-directed proselytization. Among all the sects, Zen was the most deficient in this regard."[25] Even after the doctrinal instruction campaign ended and the issue of the ideological content of sermons became moot, Rinzai leaders as a whole did not invest much energy in devising new, popular presentations of their teachings. Indeed, in comparison with the leaders of other Buddhist groups, particularly the True Pure Land, but also the Sōtō, Shingon, Nichiren, and Pure Land sects, Rinzai administrators adopted a rather subdued approach to the dilemmas and debates of the time. Satomichi concludes that during the Meiji era most of the Zen leaders who had undergone the anti-Buddhism of the Restoration years simply "devoted their energies to preserving their interests *[kabu]* and producing one or two Zen followers."[26]

The Meditation-Hall Ideal

A number of Rinzai Zen leaders did participate to varying degrees in cooperative Buddhist efforts to mitigate the effects of undesirable government measures and to fend off the perceived threat of Christianity and secular Western ideologies. Yet Rinzai documents of the period also reveal a struggle for distinction that coexisted in tension with this pan-sectarian trend. The author cited above who expresses concern over the impact on the sect of proselytization says nothing, for example, about how the survival of the Rinzai monastic community was threatened by its diminished economic resources; the focus of distress in this discourse is rather the loss of a purportedly distinctive lifestyle in the face of secu-larizing pressures allegedly instigated by the state. The path of the Zen monk who bravely confronts the challenges of itinerant mendicancy and strict celibacy was thus held up in Rinzai writings of the time as repre-senting the authentic Buddhist way that must be preserved.

Other Buddhists, too, harked back to an imaginary ideal, located sometime before the Restoration, when "pure" monastics had been con-sistently celibate and vegetarian.[27] But Zen leaders staked a special claim on the image of the adept struggling in the meditation hall who, more than any other type of Buddhist, embodied the enlightened lifestyle of Śākyamuni Buddha. The same Rinzai commentator points out that "monasteries" *(sōrin)* or "monastic halls and meditation halls" *(sōdō zendō)* are unique to the Zen tradition.

> The work [that takes place in] these [halls] requires, not composing writ-ings and discourses, but simply understanding completely the true source of the Great Way and making clear the essence of the gods and the Bud-dha. Daily life involves eating and sleeping in the elements,[28] possessing one garment and one bowl, yearning for the simplicity of the old ways and not coveting alms under any circumstances, walking [in the streets] begging and barely maintaining one's life, and painfully exerting oneself with con-stant diligence day and night....[29]

The recollection of a golden age of Zen practice centered on the arduous life of the meditation hall was to some extent a remaking of reality, partly inspired by the need to rally demoralized monks of the time. The magnification of this way of life was by no means novel in Zen or Chan discourse, but in the early Meiji it seems to have intensified and become prominent in Rinzai debates over sectarian identity.

The meditation hall or *zendō* was a key symbol in these discus-sions. By the end of the Tokugawa, the Rinzai *zendō* was taken to rep-resent in reduced form the full-fledged monastic quarters of earlier times. The communal-style monastic hall *(sōdō),* modeled after the Song Chi-nese structures in which Chan monks had meditated, slept, and eaten their meals, had been the heart of the medieval Japanese Zen monas-tery.[30] After about the fifteenth century, however, these monastic halls gradually disappeared in Japan, partly because of the decentralizing ef-fect of the growing number of subtemples *(tatchū)* that were installed in monastery precincts. Especially in the Rinzai sect, which tended to em-phasize koan practice, master–disciple interchanges became the focal point of monastery life and the main site of training shifted from the highly regulated monastic hall to the master's quarters *(hōjō).*[31]

In the Edo period, the fortunes of temples fluctuated in response to their patrons' financial circumstances and fiscal policies. During the reforms of the Kyōhō era (1716–1735), shogunal edicts urged Tokugawa subjects to practice frugality and diligence; Zen monastics were exhorted to apply themselves assiduously to their practice. Members of some Gozan communities began to call for the revival of the monastic hall and the way of life associated with it, including regular seasonal retreats. However, the movement for the restoration of the *sōdō* was not fulfilled in the long term, partly because of economic difficulties.[32] The monastic halls that were eventually "restored" in the seventeenth and eighteenth centuries were mostly small meditation halls inspired by the Ōbaku structures of Ming China, rather than full-fledged communal *sōdō* used for eating and sleeping as well as meditating. Especially in the Rinzai sect, the communal-style halls completely disappeared, and even the smaller meditation halls did not appear until the second half of the Tokugawa period.[33]

After Imakita moved to Kamakura in 1877 to take up his duties as abbot of Engakuji on a full-time basis, he reopened the meditation hall for a seasonal retreat. This event is sometimes credited with ushering in several other *zendō* "revivals" in the early Meiji: that is, the reopening of these halls is interpreted not simply as the return of one or another temple facility to operational status, but as evidence of the renewal of Zen in response to the anti-Buddhist campaign of the first Meiji years.[34] However, as I have noted, a drive to restore monastic halls to their old function as central sites of practice in Zen monasteries was already under way in the Tokugawa period. Moreover, the Engakuji meditation hall had been active throughout the Bakumatsu period, and the 1877 reopening after a hiatus of only a few years was not necessarily remarkable. The trauma of the Restoration event and the new religion policies of the first Meiji years seem to have provoked a surge in discourse *about* the meditation hall, rather than a concerted movement to restore such halls.

The *zendō* had long been idealized. Along with its associated structures it was physically set apart and viewed by monastics and lay visitors alike as ritually different from the other parts of the temple complex. As Griffith Foulk remarks in regard to the Song Chan monastic hall, "[i]t is clear that the sangha hall [J. *sōdō*] was not only a vital center of monastic life and training, but that it also had a certain symbolic value, representing the monastery proper, that is, the home base of all the ordained monks who were full members of the community."[35] He emphasizes that although such structures for communal practice were not unique to Chan monasteries, the "quasi-historical" discourse produced by Song Chan representatives, which harked back to a golden age of Chan, convinced later interpreters that the monastic hall epitomized pristine Chan and Zen practice.[36] This interpretive phenomenon is replicated in the nineteenth-century Rinzai passage cited above, in which the meditation hall functions as a symbol of the praxical core of Buddhism that Zen adepts often claimed as their special domain vis-à-vis other Buddhist groups. Because of the symbolic quality of the meditation hall, Imakita's opening of the Engakuji hall, Shōbōgendō, has also lent itself to interpretation as a veritable Meiji restoration of the original spirit of Zen.

During the 1870s, when Rinzai priests were still adjusting to the enforced proselytization of non-Buddhist ideas and the decriminalization of clerical marriage, the meditation hall provided a powerful image of the special Zen "Way." Sectarian writers marshaled this image, both to exhort wayward monastics to persevere in their life of self-denial, and to reassert Zen Buddhism's claim to uniqueness in the religious and intellectual marketplace of the early Meiji. The aforementioned Rinzai author accordingly goes on to argue that Japanese Zen had a critical role to play in maintaining the authentic Dharma, which had already fallen by the wayside in its countries of origin. "I have heard that [by] now in India and China as well, those who have penetrated these depths are rare. The fact that this Way is transmitted solely in our Imperial Nation ... is due to the merit of the arduous exertions [that take place] in the meditation hall." The survival of Buddhism as a whole thus depended on the resuscitation of the meditation-hall way of life in Japan: if Rinzai monastics "abandoned this Dharma," the writer warned, it would probably become "extinct."[37] Here are glimmerings of that patriotic sense of mission which would later become conspicuous in certain sectors of the modern Zen Buddhist community.[38]

The rhetoric about the survival of Zen Buddhism that emerged in the 1870s and 1880s regenerated themes common in Zen theory from its origins in China. However, the old paradigms and polarities were now reproduced in response to specific Meiji conditions and used as a code that mediated the developing relationship between Rinzai practitioners and those conditions. Imakita Kōsen's writings exemplify this phenomenon. Soon after he began living in the Tokyo area, the abbot drafted a proposal paper in which he urged his peers in the Rinzai leadership to curb what he perceived as a growing tendency for monastics to engage in superficial intellectual studies.[39] In the paper he prepares the rhetorical ground for his recommendation by reflecting on "the way things were" when he was in his prime. Before the Restoration, he claims, the Rinzai sect had been a thriving religious community infused with the spirit of authentic Zen Buddhism; great masters and capable students had flocked to Zen monasteries, which flourished in every part of the country. Imakita pointedly notes that most Zen adepts of the time had revered the life of the meditation hall and had held in low regard the dwindling "textual" or "literary" schools *(moji no gakurin)*; they despised the members of these schools, calling them *shuryō bōzu* or "study-hall monks." Because this healthy attitude prevailed, the abbot implies, the "meditation-hall schools" *(zendōka)* had steadily flourished in the Tokugawa era.[40]

Early in the history of Japanese Zen, Dōgen had designated the *shuryō* as the building in which monks were to read the Mahayana sūtras and the words of the Zen patriarchs in order to "illuminate the mind through ancient teachings" *(kokyō shōshin)*. In his writings he explicitly contrasts the study hall with the monastic hall, in which students should directly "plumb the truth and practice the Way" *(kyūri bendō)*.[41] Dōgen evidently conceived of the study hall as a facility that complemented the monastic hall; one could refine the understanding attained while meditating in the latter by reading Buddhist scriptures in the former.[42] Over time, the Japanese *shuryō* turned into a common room that was used for a number of other purposes, including listening to talks by the master, drinking tea, consuming evening meals, and sleeping.[43] Yet it continued to be identified in Zen discourse as the site in the monastery that was intended for studying texts. This view informs Imakita's critical remark about the study-hall monks who belonged to the "literary" Zen schools in the Tokugawa. *Shuryō bōzu* in this context is synonymous with *gakurin bōzu* or *gakkō bōzu* (school monk)—all are derogatory terms for a monk who neglects Zen practice in favor of textual or doctrinal studies.[44]

Imakita's usage reveals his view of recent sectarian history, as well as a common polarity in Zen Buddhist thought. The study-hall monks of the late Tokugawa to whom he refers probably included, among others, the latter-day disciples of Zen master Kogetsu Zenzai (1667–1751).[45] Kogetsu followers had been active in Gozan temples during the eighteenth century, but their influence seems to have faded thereafter; the disciples of Hakuin Ekaku (1686–1769) are usually assumed to have dominated Rinzai institutions completely by the time of the Restoration.[46] However, some Kogetsu-line Zen masters were still training disciples in the 1860s and 1870s at Rinzai temples in the Kantō area— notably Engakuji, Kenchōji, and the latter's branch temple Chōtokuji.[47] Contemporary Hakuin followers apparently viewed Kogetsu followers as rivals and tended to derogate their style of practice; some charged that the Kamakura abbots were promoting "literary Zen."[48] Kogetsu monks were in fact known for their advocacy of a "combination of practice and study" *(dōgaku kenbi)*.[49] Imakita's reference to Tokugawa-era study-hall monks may thus have been an allusion to the persistent strand of textually oriented Kogetsu followers who inhabited the Engakuji community in the years just before his arrival in Kamakura.[50] However, when the abbot revived the study–meditation contrast in his proposals for internal Rinzai reform in the 1870s, his target was not simply a former school of Zen, or even a perceived drift toward Buddhist textual studies. He and other Rinzai reformers now aimed their rhetoric at an entirely new generation of study-hall monks—young men who were distracted by the new brands of knowledge proliferating in Meiji society.

Zen Buddhist Education

Rinzai leaders' concern about the changing identity of their sect found a substantial outlet in debates over monastic schooling. These discussions were not unrelated to the negotiations over learning and education that took place in other quarters of Japanese society during the 1870s and 1880s. In early 1869, members of the Shoshū Dōtoku Kaimei ([Buddhist] Ethical Alliance), a pan-sectarian coalition of leaders that had begun to meet in Kyoto the previous year, took up the issue of establishing new Buddhist schools; several sects had already opened their own schools right after the Restoration.[51] The association ultimately resolved that each sect should indeed create its own schools, but that supradenominational educational activities should also be organized.[52] Soon afterward, a pan-sectarian "general school" *(shoshū sōkō)* was established in Tokyo; another was set up in Fukui.[53]

Rinzai priests professed a keen interest in educational reform during this period. In 1869 the Kyoto Gozan temples organized the Hōkokushagaku ([sic]—Study Program of the Society for Repaying Obligations to the Nation), a rather grand scheme for cooperative study, internal reform, and defense against pernicious "outer" influences. The society mobilized a sizable staff of abbots who were to expound on the numerous Buddhist, Confucian, and historical texts specified in the program's curriculum.[54] In the meantime, various head temples set up their own study facilities; the Myōshinji line stands out for its early efforts in this regard.[55] After the Great Teaching Academy was abolished in May 1875 and religious groups were instructed to manage their own educational activities, sectarian schools of all stripes multiplied further.[56] The Rinzai lines (which at the time included Ōbaku) set up a facility called Tōkyō Jūzan Sōkō (Tokyo General School of the Ten Temples) in the precincts of Konji-in in Shiba.[57] At the recommendation of Ogino Dokuon, who was general abbot of the Rinzai sect at the time, Imakita Kōsen was appointed head of the new institution and, soon afterward, installed as abbot of Engakuji.[58] A train was now running between the capital and nearby Yokohama, enabling Imakita to commute between his two posts, though he apparently resided mostly in Tokyo during his tenure as school head.

The joint Rinzai institution did not last long. After the Ministry of Doctrine was dissolved in early 1877, the Rinzai lines separated and the General School was closed. Imakita professed relief at his emancipation from his academic responsibilities—he had apparently sought to resign even before the ministry closed.[59] When he opened the Engakuji meditation hall for a retreat a few months later, the Zen master reflected in verse that "formerly, I opened a variety store and traded in the dust of the capital; today the great criminal of the true Rinzai sect [a committed Zen practitioner] has returned to sit on the old mat [in the monastery]."[60] The reference to a "variety store" *(zatsuho)* in Tokyo was not simply poetic license. Imakita had not approved of the General School's aims, over which he apparently had little control. His implication that the Tokyo school was a shop that dealt in miscellaneous goods ("dust") is an oblique reference to its curriculum, which apparently catered to the demands of the Meiji marketplace.[61] The school's offerings during its short-lived existence are not known with any precision, but the corresponding Rinzai general school in Kyoto provided instruction in international law, theories of human rights, basic physics, and biblical studies —it is likely that the Tokyo school was characterized by the same breadth.[62] In any case, Imakita's tenure at the school turned the abbot against what he perceived as a Western-influenced, technological trend in Meiji higher education, which in his view had infected the Rinzai community with a fondness for intellectualistic activities and a neglect of practice.

Soon after the Rinzai general schools were founded, each prefecture reportedly followed up with "middle" and "elementary" academies *(chūkyōin, shōkyōin)*. We can gain some idea of the direction in which sectarian education was moving from the offerings of these regional schools. The elementary schools concentrated on teaching students how to write and how to "read off" both Buddhist and non-Buddhist texts, while the middle schools required pupils to study not only Buddhist and Confucian writings, but also works of history, geography, and astronomy.[63] Required readings in the middle-school courses included well-known contemporary works about Western culture and geography, notably Fukuzawa Yukichi's *Bunmeiron gairyaku* (Outline of a Theory of Civilization), Uchida Masao's popular *Yochi shiryaku* (World Compendium), and Nakamura Masanao's rendition of Smiles' *Self-Help (Saigoku risshi hen)*.[64]

From the outset Buddhist educators assimilated into their educational programs a good portion of the Western-influenced curricular content that was adopted by the new public schools in the first Meiji years.[65] After the Ministry of Doctrine was eliminated in 1877, however, a diversity of perspectives on educational issues rose to the fore within the Rinzai community, paralleling in some ways the contention over moral instruction in public schools that intensified in the late 1870s and 1880s. Imakita took the position that the Zen lines had gone wrong in their collaborative educational endeavors. In a draft of an address to his fellow Rinzai leaders he complained that "since that dubious General School was established in Tokyo, the sentiment of the whole sect has changed; [members] mistakenly believe that the Zen sect will not survive without relying on doctrinal studies."[66] After the school was founded, it seemed to the abbot, Zen monastics had lost their integrity and "thoughtlessly turned to temporary, transient human feelings."[67]

These remarks were directed at Kyoto Rinzai leaders who were arguing for a sectarian facility of higher education comparable to the Tokyo General School.[68] The sentiments in favor of another joint institution apparently were stronger in Kyoto than in the Kantō area, perhaps partly because of the history of cooperation among the Gozan temples in the western part of the country. Judging from the abbot's remarks to his peers, in any case, the proposed general school in Kyoto was quite different from the type of Zen school that he envisioned. Imakita argued that fascination with textual studies and "outer" learning (especially Western forms of knowledge) had contributed to the current decline in Rinzai monasteries, a situation that was aggravated by the recent decease of the older Zen masters who had been active in the late Tokugawa. Rinzai monastic membership was at an all-time low, Imakita believed, and the fate of the community was hanging by a thread. How could the sect members allow themselves to be "vainly pulled along by current trends and sentiments, remaining silent with their arms folded?"[69] If the sect did not start producing genuine masters, he warned, it would soon run out of successors to the Dharma: Zen Buddhism would simply collapse.[70]

Imakita utilized well-worn arguments to make his case against "generalists" in the sect who opposed his narrow focus on Zen practice. As we have seen, he drew a contrast between practice- and study-oriented approaches to Zen in his depiction of Tokugawa Rinzai schools. The abbot was well aware that the practice–doctrine opposition had fueled Zen debates throughout its history. In his proposal paper he cites the remarks of the great Zen master Daitō (Shūhō Myōchō, 1282–1338) to the effect that teaching students the path of "seeing one's nature" (*kenshō*)—as opposed to the path of gradual cultivation through doctrinal studies—was critical to the survival of Zen (and of Buddhism as a whole). Imakita claimed that Chan and Zen succeeded historically in China and Japan precisely because its practitioners understood the value of the "special transmission outside the teachings" and "seeing one's nature," and thus could offer people a form of learning that was *distinct* from that of other Buddhist sects (which the abbot identifies with gradualistic, discursive studies).[71] Imakita's vehement reaction to the idea of another Rinzai general school drew on the same rhetorical stock:

> I heard that already in October of last year, at the conclusion of the great assembly of the western [Zen monasteries] that was held in your region, it was resolved to build a cooperative school *(kyōritsu gakkō)* and to train new novices. I thought to myself: this evil of schools that [teach] gradual cultivation is really tremendous. We must do something to guard against it.[72]

The Engakuji abbot raised the concern that the planned system would encourage Zen students to become caught up in the "tangled learning [of words]" *(kattōgaku)* and that they would thus never be able to reach true liberation.[73] Once they had become imbued with preconceptions through inappropriate schooling, even committed monks who aspired to enlightenment and practiced in a meditation hall would always carry with them their "unfinished dreams" of engaging in theoretical studies. As a result, they would end up producing elaborate commentaries or theoretical analyses of Buddhist doctrines and would lose the ability to focus on their own religious transformation. Imakita ostensibly was worried, in other words, that early exposure to a broad-based curriculum would delay students' *kenshō*. Rather than immersing themselves at the outset in the lifelong task of studying the Buddhist scriptures and other writings, he argued, Zen students should devote themselves to contemplative practice centered on the koan that they received from their teachers, and thus liberate themselves from the constant cycle of birth and death.[74] From the abbot's perspective, the need for this kind of Zen practice had not been taken seriously in the overly general "academic schools" *(kyōkō)* that Rinzai leaders had established in the early Meiji years.

Reclaiming a term frequently used by Confucian scholars to critique textualist inclinations within their own circles, Imakita went on to fault the Zen adepts of his day for disliking the "practical learning" *(jitsugaku)* of seeing into one's nature. Instead of the "distinguished sword" of learning that had been bequeathed to them by the Zen patriarchs, contemporary students seemed more interested in "the dull swords of other schools."[75] Evidently speaking from his own experience at the Tokyo General School, Imakita asserted to his colleagues that students at the academic schools were satisfied with simply "pursuing the examination course and investigating the meaning of phrases." They tended to memorize a wide range of abstruse details in the hope of impressing others with the breadth of their erudition, he alleged, but in the end they would be unable to master Zen, in practice *or* in theory. Producing monastics of this kind, Imakita warned his peers, would not only deplete the sect's finances but fail to stem the decrease in numbers of students who were genuinely qualified to practice Buddhism. He therefore urged the sect leaders to revise their plans for a general school in Kyoto and to develop a creditable policy that would reverse the Rinzai sect's decline.[76]

In 1876, Rinzai leaders nonetheless installed a "university" or "advanced school" *(daikyōkō)* at Enpukuji, an important Myōshinji-line temple near Kyoto.[77] Soon afterward, Imakita inserted some notes into the margins of his proposal paper that indicate the details of the alternative instititution he envisioned.[78] He proposed a complete overhaul of the existing schools' aims and curricular structures, and the establishment of uniform standards in Rinzai schooling in general. Picking up on current public discourse about specialized schooling, the Engakuji abbot suggested that Zen institutions of higher learning should not be called "general schools" at all, but "specialized Zen schools" or "Zen seminaries" *(senmon Zen gakkō)*. His solution to the problem of an unfocused, theoretically oriented course of study was framed in terms similar to those used by Meiji officials who were unhappy with private academies' overly diffuse humanities curricula, even though the meanings of the two lexicons were radically different. Imakita used words like "practical" and "specialized" to denote educational goals that were religious, not utilitarian.

Imakita's advice to sectarian educators was specific. He recommended that novices and monks-in-training be clearly distinguished, with separate curricular categories and periods of study for each group. Novices would ideally enroll at the age of eighteen in the study hall *(shuryō)*, where they would spend three calendar years receiving instruction in "specialized Zen practice and theory" *(senmon gongaku)*. They would be examined on their studies every month, until their teachers approved their graduation; if they had not completed the required course after two summers, they would be asked to withdraw from the study hall.[79] The novitiate would be followed by a five-year course of study in the senior division of the seminary. In fact, those who wished had the option of transferring directly from the study hall to another Zen monastery to complete their training; Imakita apparently envisioned the upper division of the seminary as the equivalent of a bona fide meditation hall.

The Engakuji abbot accordingly drew a marked contrast between the study-hall novices and the advanced monastic students, whom he associated with the meditation hall. The study hall was to be located at a distance from the upper seminary, and its residents were to be called "novices" regardless of their age. Members of the upper division, on the other hand, were to be called "elders" or "seniors" (*jōza*, a traditional Buddhist title) and given seating precedence during group ceremonies and lectures. Imakita apparently intended that the seniors be committed monks who had been tonsured for several years and were familiar with the life of the meditation hall; their behavior was to exemplify the "original rules of the monastic sangha" *(sōrin no hon kiku)*. At the discretion of their teachers, senior monks who had "seen their natures" would be permitted to study and explicate Zen texts—but such permission was not to be easily granted. Even the most advanced monks would be encouraged to practice as much as possible rather than pursue textual studies. For novices, texts not included in the fixed reading list were out of the question.[80] In these ways the beginner, who read off texts and engaged in some practice, would be sharply distinguished from the committed Zen monk, who modeled the life of enlightenment. Although both seniors and novices would be required to attend nightly meditation during retreats, in Imakita's view the students who lived in the study hall clearly represented an earlier stage of religious understanding.

The distinction between the meditation hall and the study hall was thus not simply a rhetorical device used in Zen discourse to mark off the relative value of particular styles of religious activity. Nor were Imakita's proposed guidelines for the division of the Rinzai seminary merely an articulation of his concern for sequence, ritual order, and merit, important though these themes were in his vision of modern Zen training.[81] Participation in the life of the meditation hall is correlated in his discourse with enlightenment itself, and thus bears significant symbolic weight, as it does in the other Rinzai statements of the period that I have highlighted. We shall see in the next chapter that the image of the meditation hall also played an important role in the debate over lay practice that took place in the Engakuji community during Imakita's tenure.

The abbot's proposed school was a world away from the Tokyo and Kyoto general schools, whose curricula drew inspiration from secular courses of instruction and, if we are to credit Imakita's account, emphasized theoretical studies over practice. Apparently he disagreed strongly with his contemporaries in the Rinzai community in the late 1870s who advocated exposing students to Western studies for apologetical purposes.[82] Imakita fully affirmed these defensive aims: he became personally involved in anti-Christian and anti-Western ideological activities shortly afterward, as we shall see. Nevertheless, the Zen master insisted that Rinzai students place priority on meditation-hall practice over theoretical and cultural studies of any kind. His own recommendation of an intensive eight-year regimen of Zen practice may well have been modeled after the religious training he had undergone in the late Tokugawa. The implications of this regimen for prospective students were considerable; an adept who could not graduate from the meditation hall would never qualify as an authentic Zen teacher.[83] To some younger priests of the time, this seemingly narrow, long-term commitment to Zen "practical learning" no doubt seemed quite *impractical* and out of touch with the reality of contemporary Japanese society.

Ironically, nearly twenty years earlier, when Imakita was abbot of Yōkōji in Iwakuni, he had criticized Zen adepts for making light of book learning, and avowedly wrote his apologetical masterpiece, *Zenkai ichiran,* with the aim of encouraging students to ground their practice more thoroughly in discursive studies. He complained at the time that "students of the Zen school generally misunderstand the saying 'specially transmitted outside the teachings, without setting up words.' They do not enquire into the meaning of Buddhism or Confucianism: they swallow ideas whole, without chewing them fully ... [and] increasingly provoke the charge of 'silent Zen.'"[84] Yet by the late 1870s, the central problem in Zen education that Imakita depicted in his seminary proposal seemed quite the opposite.

The Rinzai leader's criticism of the general schools and his insistence on practice to the detriment of a broad-based curriculum for young priests was not an attack on either book learning or the study of foreign culture, however. Imakita was a trained Confucian scholar and retained an unceasing appreciation for the subtleties of written Chinese. He also read widely and attained familiarity with the new currents of thought that were circulating in the early Meiji era. In addition to perusing texts on Greek philosophy and European history, the abbot reportedly drew on Darwin and took copious notes on the works of such Western studies scholars as Nakae Chōmin (1847–1901). Suzuki says that some of Imakita's manuscripts contain marginal notes that translate the German and English terms for such ideas as spirit, body, and civilization.[85] The abbot was apparently a veritable bookworm, who continued reading even while interviewing his disciples in *sanzen.*[86] Indeed, evidence suggests that some Rinzai leaders came to regard the Engakuji style of practice in a critical light because it reportedly encouraged intellectual and cultural sophistication at the expense of Zen practice.[87] In any event, the Zen master did not argue against theoretical studies, or even Western studies per se. His objections to the general school curricula were aimed specifically at the institutionalization of "outer" forms of learning, whether Sino-Japanese or European, in advanced Zen training. He fought to preserve an inviolable domain for religious practice, but, as we shall see, he allocated alternative types of learning to other contexts or phases in the life of the student.

Imakita's preoccupation with practice over theory, or with "specialized" over "general" Zen schooling, could be interpreted as a Buddhist variation on the broader mid-Meiji backlash against utilitarian learning. In a discourse addressed to religious leaders in the 1880s, Imakita again articulated the moralist lament of the time that the rapid spread of modern technology in Meiji society (steamships, electric lines, postal services, printing, and so forth) had been accompanied by a decline in Japanese values and customs.[88] Depicting the Western societies of his day as troubling precedents to this type of moral degeneration,[89] the Zen master voiced sentiments in the religious domain that closely paralleled the dissatisfaction of Nishimura Shigeki and Motoda Eifu with the perceived amoral drift of Meiji education. Like these Confucian-inspired public educators, the abbot insisted that the implementation of technology be founded on personal cultivation. However, unlike them, he did not correlate this project with a transreligious "teaching of this world" or "creed of loyalty and morality." Instead, the master held up Zen practice as the most effective path to "internal enlightenment" *(naibu no kaika),* superior to the religionless cultivation theorized by his secular counterparts.

Restless Monks

Ultimately, it was members of the abbot's own religious community, not representatives of the secular sphere, who challenged his views on education most directly. Inoue Zenjō is no doubt justified in saying that from 1877, when Imakita began to reside permanently at Engakuji, the Kamakura temple became the leading Zen training center of the Kantō area.[90] The former Confucian scholar had ambitions for the Engakuji program; he hoped it would be a centerpiece in an internal campaign to reverse the rising tide of poor discipline that he perceived in the Buddhist sangha. Yet Imakita's efforts to revive monastic standards were not always adequate to the circumstances he faced; in his personal writings he admits that he was disappointed by some of his monks (though several eventually became important sectarian leaders).[91]

Imakita's favorite was unquestionably the young Shaku Sōen (1860–1919), a preference that inevitably led to tensions among Shaku's immediate peers. The young monk received Imakita's seal of approval unusually early (in spring 1883) and several months later was appointed head priest of Butsunichi-an. The latter was an important Engakuji subtemple closely associated with the monastic hall; by installing Shaku there, Imakita signaled that his protégé would succeed him as abbot of the head temple.[92] Miyaji Sōkai (Kan'ō; 1856–1923), who had begun practicing under Imakita in early 1880, was three and a half years older than Shaku. Yet by the spring of 1884, Miyaji was still a *tenzo* (cook), while Shaku had already assumed the status of *rōshi* (senior Zen master). During the next three seasonal retreats, Miyaji did not advance significantly.[93] One of Miyaji's later disciples recounted that

> Master [Miyaji] Sōkai practiced under Master [Imakita] Kōsen for many years, and as he was trying to complete the Great Matter, something happened in the monastic hall. He transcribed the verse "In the spring breeze, one tree has two kinds of branches; the southern branches face the warmth, the northern branches are cold," pasted it on the door of the cook's quarters, and abruptly departed.[94] It is said that the head of the cook's quarters [at that time] was [Shaku] Sōen. [Master Sōkai] fled to Master [Ogino] Dokuon of Kyoto and acquired his Dharma.[95]

As Inoue points out, by 1886—the year that Miyaji left Engakuji—Shaku was already studying in Tokyo and therefore could not have been head of the cook's quarters at the time.[96] However, the above account is probably correct in implying that Miyaji's restlessness was related to Shaku's rapid rise in status in the Engakuji community.

Miyaji's flight from his chilly "northern" treatment at the hands of Imakita, as the above remarks imply, was prompted by an incident that occurred in the monastery during the spring of 1886. The report that "something happened in the monastic hall" is confirmed by other documents of the time; news of the disturbance apparently spread quickly in Rinzai circles. Writing to Ogino Dokuon and the lay practitioner Yamaoka Tesshū (Tetsutarō; 1836–1888) on consecutive days in April 1886, Imakita tried to allay their apprehensions about rumors they had heard. (Yamaoka had apparently written to Imakita earlier, expressing concern over reports of trouble at Engakuji.) An extant draft of the abbot's response to Yamaoka relates that during the preceding (winter) retreat, two monks had initiated a movement to break up the Engakuji monastic community. The rebels, according to Imakita, were Miyaji Sōkai and his brother, Sōshuku; both had been practicing at Engakuji for some years.[97] Imakita speaks harshly of the pair, implying that they tended to waver in their religious commitment, possessed little capacity to follow the monastic path, and were full of arrogance and envy. He alleges that they had instigated serious discord in the Engakuji sangha: "I have heard that the incessant disputes among the monks have in each case been related to [the doings] of these rats." The Zen master had tried to straighten them out, he explains to Yamaoka, ever since he perceived that they were beginning to weaken in their commitment. From some months earlier he had begun to treat them more strictly, "raising the 'murderous sword'" when they came to his room for guidance and

FIGURE 8. A portrait of Imakita Kōsen, based on a photograph taken in his late years. Courtesy of Engakuji.

conveying to them "the compassionate thought that they should correct their self-centered minds" (figure 8).

Imakita's compassionate thoughts were apparently of no avail, for the two brothers secretly aroused "an evil aspiration" together. "From the middle of the last retreat they seduced and incited the lazy and immature among their companions and awaited the close of the retreat to break up the sangha. The two ... reached the point of falsely accusing even [Shaku Sō]en and myself...."[98] Imakita claimed that the pair had been preparing their companions to join them in a "strike" (in Inoue Zenjō's words), even while they curried favor with the abbot by presenting him with rice cakes (Imakita apparently had a sweet tooth).[99]

After the retreat ended, Imakita discovered the scheme and confronted the conspirators, but they merely adopted a stance of "outward submission and internal disobedience." In the end, the Zen master ordered all the monks who were directly involved in the disturbance to leave the monastery. Some simply moved across the street to the Engakuji-line temple, Jōchiji; they were allowed to return to Engakuji after they confessed and repented their errors. As indicated above, Miyaji initially went to practice under Ogino Dokuon in Kyoto, evidently with Imakita's consent.[100]

What prompted the monastic mutiny? Several younger monks who practiced under Imakita in the 1880s were not happy with the type of training they were receiving. In his letter drafts, the abbot says that the young men felt they were not being educated in a way that would enable them to cope with the changing times. It is not without significance that the 1886 disturbance took place soon after Shaku Sōen had begun studying at Fukuzawa Yukichi's school in Tokyo; Shaku's fellow monks probably felt the limitations of their own access to a "modern" education all the more keenly at this juncture. Imakita reports that Miyaji Sōkai and his companion had stirred up the other monks by making inflammatory statements about the monastic program, such as the following:

> In the present day and age, for young people to be in a monastery is to be in a fool's paradise. If one graduates quickly, one may indeed get something out of it. But to occupy oneself with this kind of ridiculous learning and be deprived of the best school years of one's life is not what a spirited Zen monk should do. To submit to the master's teaching, consume precious time, and not realize the foolishness of it, is truly [the behavior of] a dead beat *(shikan)*.[101]

The abbot, who goes on to excoriate the rebels further, no doubt exaggerates their sentiments in his rather apologetic remarks to his Rinzai peers. But his comments nevertheless pinpoint a key issue for young Buddhist monks of the time. By the mid-1880s, many had grown restless with the kind of educational regimen for which Imakita had lobbied so eloquently in his seminary proposal of the late 1870s. The abbot's chosen successor, Shaku Sōen, harbored similar sentiments. In 1885 Shaku had turned to Imakita's prominent lay follower, Torio Tokuan (Koyata; 1847–1905), for advice about enrolling in a Western studies school. Torio encouraged Shaku to proceed, but Imakita at first opposed the project—the abbot did not approve of his disciple's interest in Western culture.[102] As we have seen, Imakita was against including Western studies (Yōgaku) in the education of Zen monks. He predicted that if

FIGURE 9. Shaku Sōen during
a visit to America in 1905.
Reproduced from *Engakujishi,*
by Tamamura Takeji and
Inoue Zenjō. Courtesy of
Engakuji.

Shaku "would only open his heaven-endowed eyes wide, not stand in the
Western-smelling after-dust, reform his will, and exclusively master Chinese studies or [Buddhist] doctrinal studies, then in the future his brilliant reputation as a teacher of our sect without paragon in our country
will extend throughout the world."[103] But Shaku was a member of the
new generation, and Tokugawa-style Chinese learning and Buddhist
studies were not enough to satisfy his intellectual curiosity. He persisted
in his plans and soon enrolled in Fukuzawa's Keiōgijuku (figure 9).

It is notable that Imakita softened his opposition to his disciple's
pursuit of a broader education only after Torio Tokuan interceded for
the young monk and offered to help with the latter's expenses.[104] Imakita's lay associates often mediated alternative perspectives on certain
issues to the abbot. In fact, the master seems to have modified his opposition to a broad-based education for Zen monks as a whole in response
to Torio's encouragement—and perhaps also to Shaku Sōen's lobbying.
In the late 1880s, Imakita lent his efforts to the organization of an "educational society" *(kyōikugikai),* based at Engakuji, that would develop
a scholarship fund for members of the monastic community who wished
to study. Shaku's enrollment in Keiōgijuku probably inspired this proj-

ect. According to Kimura Junseki (Shaku's fellow priest at the time), after Shaku entered the academy he barely managed to pay the tuition and scrape by on ten yen a month. His patron Torio organized the Engakuji educational association, and Imakita was invited to head the group.[105] In that capacity the Zen master wrote a preface for the organization's bylaws in which he describes how a group of volunteers associated with the temple established the foundation on behalf of the Engakuji line. They raised funds, selected "a monk of exceptional talent" (presumably Shaku), and sent him off to "schools of discursive studies." The plan, Imakita indicates, was to have the future graduate return to establish a Zen school at Engakuji. The school would aim to educate not only members of the sect; it would be an institution of higher learning *(daikyōkō)* open to both monastics and laypeople—in short, a Zen Buddhist university.[106]

Although the establishment of private colleges or universities was still relatively unregulated during the early Meiji, because of the significant financial and human resources required, it was difficult to maintain an institution of this kind. Beginning in the 1880s, advanced private institutions *(senmongakkō)* were subjected to discriminatory policies by the government (such as denial of draft deferments to students); they began to suffer economically, and lost prestige in comparison with the emerging public system.[107] Because of their limited financial and human resources, these so-called specialized schools came to occupy the lowest rung in Meiji higher education (with a few prominent exceptions, such as Keiogijuku, Tōkyō Senmon Gakkō, and Dōshisha).[108] Denominational schools, especially Buddhist seminaries, which were backed by sectarian organizations that could provide continuing financial support, were in a more favorable position than the secular academies, which lacked built-in constituencies.[109] In addition, Buddhist schools of higher learning could presume on the unpaid services of the sect's clergy.[110] However, to Meiji citizens who believed that a modern, utilitarian education would lead to success in the world, sectarian schooling probably appealed far less than that offered by reputable secular institutions.

In any case, the planned Engakuji college was strikingly different from the traditional model the abbot had promoted a decade earlier. Imakita announced in his preface to the rules of the new academy that it would encompass both "Zen" and "discursive" or "verbal" studies. The latter type of learning was critical to a proper Buddhist education:

> Zen studies are the martial arts of Buddhist learning. The various types of learning that are founded on words *(ritsugen no shogaku)* are the cultural arts of Buddhist learning. We forge and temper students in these cultural and martial fires. They are the ultimate learning transmitted by the Buddha

and patriarchs of our school.... The phrase "not setting up words" has
circulated in our country since medieval times, and has been taken to mean
that Zen studies have nothing at all to do with words. This is greatly
mistaken.[111]

Imakita had come full circle. When the abbot was in Iwakuni in the
1860s he had complained that Zen monastics ignored the value of intellectual study.[112] In the years following the Meiji Restoration, Imakita
had anathematized the doctrinal and cultural emphasis of the Rinzai
general schools, implicitly comparing them to past "literary Zen" monasteries that had produced "study-hall monks." But by the late 1880s, he
was again pointing out the benefits of discursive activities for the Zen
Buddhist trainee. Moreover, although the extent to which the proposed
Engakuji college would have encompassed Western forms of learning is
not documented, given the interests of its proposed leader, Shaku Sōen,
we can safely assume that Imakita's approval of the plan indicated the
master's tacit acceptance of some such curricular content. In his last
years Imakita apparently began to conceive of advanced Zen education,
not only as a program of intensive religious practice centered on the
meditation hall, but also as a foundation for adult life in the secular
world—a seminary education, but one that would encompass doctrinal
or "verbal" studies as well as, possibly, a broad range of "outer" forms
of learning.

The contrasting positions that Imakita took over the years in regard to the correct balance between praxis and theoretical learning evidently had more to do with the immediate demands of each historical
(and rhetorical) moment than with a systematic Zen educational policy.
Each new context required a re-presentation of the balance between
practice and ideas. Rinzai leaders of the 1870s had focused their growing
apprehensions on the possible loss, in the face of multiplying outer influences, not simply of Buddhism as a whole, but of the distinctive Zen
path, symbolized by the meditation hall, that they identified as its essence. Imakita took that perspective further than some of his peers in his
emphasis on Zen practical learning as the primary strategy of sectarian
renewal. If considered in isolation, the abbot's 1870s insistence on intensive Zen practice might be interpreted as one last, desperate attempt
to preserve the ritual and moral distinction of the monk within the larger
sangha and society as a whole. However, in the face of alternative trends
in the younger monastic community the master apparently came to accept a larger view of Zen higher education. He continued to promote a
practice-centered program, but tacitly acknowledged that the fate of the
Buddhist monastery depended on its capacity to accommodate the new
brand of useful learning that held sway in the secular domain. By the

1880s Imakita was also more aware that potential donors to the temple fund (well-endowed laypeople) were more likely to support a broad-based type of sectarian education than the intensive focus on practice that the master had earlier advocated.

In the early chapters of this book I suggested that the members of several distinct groups in the late Tokugawa shared a preoccupation with establishing practicable systems of personal cultivation. In the social and political context of the time, the teachings generated by these groups offered interpretive sanctuaries in which members could project a modicum of control over their particular circumstances and, at least in theory, over the broader social environment. In the years after the Restoration, however, the preoccupation with the details of self-improvement was overshadowed in religious discourse by a drive to address issues of social and national improvement. The dominant concern in the 1870s seems to have been less about specific practices of bettering one's mind and body than about the meaning of practicality. Regardless of their affiliation, individuals or groups frequently used terms such as *"jitsugaku"* to identify certain spheres of knowledge and activity as more valuable than others. Sectarian leaders agreed with government officials and public intellectuals that "real learning" was indeed the key to success in life— even though each of these groups defined the content of that learning differently. The language of practicality became a hallmark of correctness, especially among the educated elites who shaped public opinion, although, as we shall see in a later chapter, representatives of less-enfranchised groups exploited this vocabulary for their own purposes.

CHAPTER 6
Koji Zen

THE CHANGES IN political life that took place in early Meiji society extended beyond the secular arena; new social structures emerged within and among individual religious organizations. Buddhist clergy struggled during this time to formulate new modes of political consciousness pertinent to their social circumstances just as did Meiji citizens generally. In August 1884 the government discontinued the doctrinal instruction campaign and gave sectarian directors *(kanchō)* the power to appoint or dismiss their own abbots. At the same time, it ordered each sect to submit its rules of internal organization to the government for approval. In the case of the Engakuji denomination, an especially important change in its internal rules was the introduction of more equitable relations between the head and branch temples with regard to the selection of leaders and the allocation of funds. A "national assembly" of delegates from each temple district was empowered to determine these and other denominational affairs.[1]

The *kanchō* system, in which one priest was vested with authority over almost all aspects of community life, nonetheless provided a check on egalitarian movements within the sangha. Official decentralization at the larger sectarian level did not necessarily defuse tensions within individual temple communities. The hierarchical patterns of action that Imakita maintained in his own monastic community during the early Meiji in fact fueled dissatisfaction among his monks. Some of the internal disputes that took place at Engakuji in the 1880s centered on the demands of ambitious young monks, as we saw in chapter 5. However, elite lay practitioners played an even more powerful role in temple affairs during this period. Scholars have argued that the dramatic anti-Buddhist drive of the first Restoration years prompted Buddhist leaders to try to reshape the identity of their religion so that it would no longer be susceptible to the old criticisms of corruption, economic dependency, anti-family ethics, social irrelevance, and foreignness.[2] In this vein it is sometimes implied that sect leaders enhanced the scale and quality of their outreach to laypeople as part of a deliberate strategy to render their teachings more relevant to the new age.[3] I prefer to interpret the expansion of lay Buddhism in the Meiji, not primarily as a reformist response by clerical leaders to the early attack on Buddhism (although in many cases it was undoubtedly this, too), but rather as part of a general trend among lay practitioners to exert more control over systems of religious knowledge and practice.

This and the next chapter shift the focus of our discussion from discourses about practical learning to a specific model of personal cultivation that appealed to educated Tokyo residents during the first half of the Meiji—the model of the lay Zen practitioner, as illustrated by individuals associated with the temple Engakuji. I begin with a brief summary of the notion of *koji Zen* and its distinction from general conceptions of lay Buddhism, with particular reference to Imakita Kōsen's stated views. I then discuss the economic and social factors that encouraged the growth of lay Zen at Engakuji during the 1870s and 1880s. The rest of the chapter is a history of the Kamakura lay practice from its origins in the Bakumatsu period through the first two Meiji decades. Chapter 7 continues the discussion of the lay program, focusing on specific practitioners and on lay–clerical relations within the Engakuji sangha.

The ideal relationship between the monastic and lay sectors of the Buddhist community in traditional Asia is often depicted as one of reciprocal support or exchange. Monks and nuns were presumably not engaged in raising families and maintaining households, and could therefore dedicate their time and energy to helping others along the path. By explicating the Buddhist teachings, performing specialized rituals, and living a lifestyle in accordance with the precepts, monastics ostensibly provided inspiration to the laity and gained merit on their behalf; in return, laypeople donated food to the monastic sangha (eventually land, buildings, and money as well). Of course, the actual boundaries between the lay and monastic sectors of early Buddhist societies were not nearly so clear-cut as this idealization implies.[4] Scholars have challenged the so-called two-tiered model of Indian Buddhism, according to which early practitioners belonged to either the monastic sangha or a large, undifferentiated class of laity. Schopen, for example, has marshaled significant evidence that monks and nuns were heavily involved in donating materials in connection with either *stūpa* or image worship from about the middle of the second century B.C.E. The popularization of later pre scriptive texts nonetheless led to the view that giving alms to monks was one of the most important ways in which laypeople in particular could accumulate merit and raise their spiritual status. The ritual of alms rounds thus came to be represented as a kind of transaction—an exchange of symbolic and economic capital between two presumably distinct socioreligious groups.

Modern scholars of East Asian Buddhism have been less concerted in their efforts to revise the conventional monastic–lay typology and to suggest a more nuanced understanding of nonmonastic roles.[5] There is little doubt, however, that lay practitioners carved out diverse roles for themselves in both the Chinese and Japanese sanghas; one of the best known is that of the *jushi* or *koji*. In China *jushi* originally meant a learned or virtuous man—not necessarily a Buddhist—who lived at home without serving in the government. A *jushi* might thus be a "retired" Confucian gentleman, a scholar-official who for political or ethical reasons chose not to serve the current administration. After Buddhism became prevalent in medieval China, the term *"jushi"* was also used to render the Sanskrit term *"gṛhapati"* (literally, the male head of a household, or property owner), and was understood to mean a committed Buddhist layman.[6] Moreover, a number of translated Mahayana texts, notably the *Vimalakīrti-nirdeśa Sūtra,* seemed to many Chinese to advocate the ideal of an enlightened layman—a person who managed to fulfill the bodhisattva ideal without ever relinquishing life in the "marketplace." Song and Ming Buddhist writers, taking inspiration from these accumulated associations of the term, explicitly characterized the *jushi* as a man who pursued the Buddhist path to enlightenment, did not seek office, behaved morally, and was endowed with material wealth.[7] Chan practitioners in particular were held up as models of enlightened lay behavior. Many were said to be well-versed not only in Buddhism, but also in Confucian and Daoist thought—along the lines of Han Yu (768–824) and Li Ao (772–841).[8]

In early Japan the term *"koji"* was used as an appellation for male lay practitioners (S. *upāsaka;* J. *ubasoku*), many of whom carried out austerities in the mountains.[9] In medieval times, committed practitioners continued to be distinguished by this title from the majority of laypeople, most of whom sought the ritual services of Buddhist priests but did not themselves carry out intensive religious disciplines.[10] As in China, Zen lay practitioners tended to be members of the privileged social sectors who were well-endowed or politically influential; Hōjō Tokiyori (1227–1263) is a prototype of this phenomenon.[11] The same tendency seems to have persisted in the Tokugawa period, when many Zen temples depended on the economic and political patronage of highly ranked samurai and daimyo (as well as on revenue from household parishioners or *danka*).

The clients of Rinzai temples were not highly organized in comparison with Buddhist groups such as the Pure Land and Nichiren sects, which generated active lay societies during the Edo period, although financial pressures prompted the creation of a few temple-based Rinzai groups later in the period. Zen-inspired ideas were widely popularized in the seventeenth and eighteenth centuries through vernacular literature and other media; the sermons, popular writings, and letters of such well-known Rinzai masters as Takuan Sōhō (1573–1646), Shidō Munan (1603–1676), Bankei, and Hakuin demonstrate a particular sensitivity to lay needs. Many lesser-known Rinzai teachers also encouraged serious lay practice.[12] Yet the main thrust of the Rinzai lay outreach, like that of other Buddhist denominations, remained the accommodation of local parishioners' routine ritual needs; systematic training in disciplines closely associated with Zen Buddhism (koan practice and meditation) was pursued by relatively small numbers of nonmonastic practitioners.

Imakita Kōsen had already attracted a coterie of dedicated lay followers during the Bakumatsu years, when he was in Iwakuni; his Confucian-Buddhist treatise, *Zenkai ichiran,* was addressed in large part to these trainees. He differentiated sharply between such committed practitioners and the laity as a whole. The abbot's view of the role of the lay "masses" was for the most part based on the aforementioned transactional model, according to which the exchange of alms for Dharma was integral to the life of the sangha. In a sermon directed to a large audience in the early Meiji, the abbot identifies stinginess as a form of greed that leads to evil and misfortune among laypeople. When Buddhist monastics practice the discipline of begging, he avers, they take responsibility for the "poison" of greed upon themselves and in return give donors an antidote—the Buddhist teachings.[13] When laypeople donate the rice or money they have saved up, the monks transfer back to them the truth that leads to liberation *(gedatsu)*—a truth that the monks have attained by performing ascetic disciplines.[14] Furthermore, when monks beg for alms they earn spiritual merit by destroying their own selfish inclinations and counteracting the greed and delusion of all sentient beings, and this merit in turn is transferred to the almsgivers. The Buddha, the Zen patriarchs, and worthy monastics throughout history, the abbot declares in his sermon, practiced the *upāya* (expedient means) of begging precisely in order to save laypeople.[15] Consequently, by giving alms, even people who do not perform any other religious devotions can advance toward Buddhahood.[16]

The lay donors, in this last sense, exert their own kind of power through the alms transaction. We recall Mauss' suggestion that the giving of gifts engenders the "obligation to reciprocate."[17] While the laity may appear to be passive recipients of the Dharma, in fact they procure access to religious capital, as it were, through seasonal exchanges. The repetition of this transaction, premised as it was on the continuing ritual distinction between the lay and monastic realms, effectively sustained the role division in the Buddhist sangha in a range of Asian historical contexts. Imakita never explicitly questioned this structure of relations, even in his later years. According to Suzuki, the Engakuji abbot maintained that regular Zen practice was suited only to a committed minority of believers—it was "something to be studied by specialists." Throughout his career Imakita refrained from propounding Zen teachings to the general public and concentrated instead on recounting miracle stories *(innen banashi)*, narratives that purport to illustrate the laws of karmic causality.[18] This approach to large-scale Buddhist education was routine in Japan as elsewhere in traditional Asia; preachers tailored their remarks to the perceived level of religious understanding of their audiences. Imakita no doubt felt that he could more effectively motivate his lay audiences to support the sangha *and* make progress in their religious lives by recounting intriguing "karma tales" than by expounding on a Rinzai classic such as the *Blue Cliff Record (Biyanlu)*.

The *koji,* however, were another matter. In his attempt to persuade Iwakuni officials and scholars to take up Zen practice in the 1860s, Imakita drew copiously on stories of Chinese Confucian paragons who allegedly came to realize the superiority of Buddhism or used it to gain a more authentic understanding of Confucian teachings. The examples he cites in *Zenkai ichiran* range from scholars who were versed in Buddhist as well as Confucian and Daoist traditions to reformist Neo-Confucian thinkers whose (supposed) innermost Buddhist faith had been glossed over by subsequent Neo-Confucian commentators. The Song scholar-official Zhang Shangying (Tianjue, 1043–1122), author of the *Hufalun* (In Defense of the Dharma), is representative of the former type.[19] In *Zenkai ichiran,* Imakita quotes Zhang's remarks to the effect that Buddhism is ultimately superior to Confucianism, along with various anecdotes that illustrate the high quality of Zhang's Buddhist practice. At the same time, he praises Zhang for having passed his civil service examination with the highest marks and having mastered the path of the government minister.[20] For Imakita, Zhang embodied several defining qualities of the *jushi* or *koji*: wide learning, skill in government service, dedication to Buddhist ideals. He was, in short, a working bodhisattva— one who pursued the path to enlightenment while remaining in the marketplace in order to help others. It is no surprise to learn from Imakita that Zhang first understood the "wondrous mysteries" of the Buddhist path when the Song scholar read the *Vimalakīrti Sūtra.*[21]

The abbot lists numerous other Chinese exemplars who decided to practice Chan despite (and, paradoxically, because of) their mastery of Confucian learning.[22] Several of these figures probably would not have acknowledged their alleged Buddhist inspiration. For Imakita's readers, however, the historical accuracy of his list of Confucian-Chan practitioners was less important than its cumulative hortatory weight: the sheer numbers of lay adepts who attained eminence throughout Chinese history demonstrated the universal validity of the *koji* paradigm.[23] In *Zenkai ichiran,* Imakita effectively cut an elite lay "tradition" out of Confucian cloth; in the Meiji era, he actively encouraged this model of personal cultivation among his followers.

Rinzai Temple Economy

The leading members of the lay program that Imakita oversaw in the Kantō area in the 1870s and 1880s indeed resembled the paradigm of the Zen Buddhist scholar-official that the abbot had enunciated during the Bakumatsu period. However, I am not suggesting a simple continuity between the two phenomena, whether intellectual or social. The blossoming of *koji Zen* in the Tokyo area in the early Meiji was a distinctive phenomenon that is best understood by considering not only cultural precedents but also the economic circumstances and political interests of the Engakuji community during the second half of the nineteenth century.

During the Edo period, lay financial support of the sangha was ensured by shogunal and domainal authorization of parish fees and temple-based commerce. However, by the early nineteenth century many Rinzai temples were undergoing significant pecuniary stress. The economies of the well-known Gozan temples of Kyoto and Kamakura were closely tied to the financial fortunes of their samurai and shogunal patrons, which deteriorated throughout the late Edo era. Some full-scale temple complexes attempted to supplement their income by soliciting additional funds from their parishioners through organized activities, but these provisional strategies did not in themselves restore financial stability. The fluctuation of domestic prices after foreign trade began in the last decades of the Tokugawa only exacerbated the precariousness of the large temple economies; by 1856, for example, Tōfukuji's reserves were depleted and it was forced to turn to other Gozan temples for assistance.[24] The Rinzai complexes that derived most of their income from temple fiefs were particularly hard hit during the Bakumatsu years. An 1865 Nanzenji document records that an unprecedented rise in prices forced its staff to reduce their clothing budget: members were thenceforth to use only surplices and *tabi* (socks) made from inexpensive cotton and hemp.[25]

These strains were nothing, however, compared to the economic reverberations of the Meiji transition. Immediately after the Restoration, Buddhist temples were ordered to make sizable contributions to the new government. Nanzenji and its Kyoto branch temples paid a total of 270 *ryō;* the government levied a heavy tax on Nanzenji's rice revenues as well.[26] But the complete loss of traditional sources of regular revenue was the most damaging in the long term. Tithes from parish families *(danka),* which had been collected under the auspices of the temple registration system, were now rendered voluntary. In the case of smaller ancestral temples *(bodaiji),* grants from hereditary samurai patrons who lost their feudal stipends after the Restoration simply disappeared; large institutions lost income from the temple-sponsored lotteries and other moneymaking activities that had sustained them during the Tokugawa.[27] Regular income from loan interest, for example, suddenly vanished after the Restoration. Previously, temples and shrines had generated revenue by arranging "nominal loan funds" *(meimoku-kin);* in effect, these institutions had functioned as banks, complete with official guarantors.[28] In early 1868 the new government completely proscribed nominal loans and forgave all related debts. An edict issued in the ninth month forbade the Kamakura Zen temples in particular from collecting on loans that their administrators had previously made in the name of the court or nobility to the residents of nearby Izu and Sagami.[29] Lender temples were not compensated for their sudden losses; Engakuji therefore lost its outstanding investment capital as well as the projected interest income.

The critical step in the economic redefinition of large religious institutions followed in early 1871. The state took possession of the so-called red-seal lands *(shuinchi)* that had been enfeoffed to temples and shrines by the Tokugawa shogunate, as well as all remaining "black-seal lands" *(kokuinchi)* granted to temples by domain lords that had not already been confiscated in 1869 (when domain lands were "returned" to the emperor).[30] The land possession had a severe impact on large Buddhist complexes, which had tended to control a great deal of property and thus to provide the upkeep of numerous substructures and personnel.[31] As a relatively well-endowed Rinzai head temple, Engakuji took heavy losses; all its land holdings were sequestered except the territory within its own immediate precincts.[32] The temples' forfeiture of these lands was temporarily mitigated by the distribution of the value of a portion of the yearly harvest from the confiscated properties to the associated institutions: in 1874 the government allocated ten-year stipends that were scheduled to diminish gradually until their termination in 1883.[33] But this provision merely softened the blow.

After Buddhist temples' loss of the red-seal lands, loan interest, and other traditional sources of revenue, the Meiji state's prohibition of mendicant rounds *(takuhatsu)* in the eleventh month of 1872 merely added insult to injury.[34] The measure probably had stronger repercussions in the Zen communities, which tended to place more emphasis on begging as a monastic discipline than most other Japanese Buddhist sects. The exact extent to which monastics actually carried out *takuhatsu* in the late Tokugawa cannot be stated with any precision without further local historical research, but the practice is believed to have been a regular feature of Zen monastic training programs.[35] Here I will simply cite the testimony of the Rinzai priest, Sakagami Shinjō, about his own experience of begging in the Bakumatsu years; his comments are impressionistic, but they do convey some sense of the social and economic characteristics of Zen mendicancy just prior to the Restoration.

Sakagami reports that monks of Sōgenji, an important Rinzai monastery in Bizen (today's southeastern Okayama prefecture), conducted officially approved alms rounds every autumn. Once Sōgenji received permission to make the rounds from the Office of Temples and Shrines, the domain's district supervisor would notify village headmen that two monks from the temple would carry out a mendicant tour for a period of one week in each area, and that villagers should arrange for the expedition to proceed smoothly.[36] Sakagami describes a begging tour he carried out in the late 1850s in preparation for a Sōgenji retreat as follows:

> We first reached the headman's precincts, and in accordance with the communication sent in advance from Maruyama Temple [Sōgenji] to the district superintendent, we announced that we were conducting a mendicant tour and that we would like to arrange [to do] this in the streets of the village. Depending on the number of households in the village, the headman would wrap up 10 or 15 *monme* [of cash], place it on a tray and offer it to us.... In places where there were many households and many [of them] were members of the Shingon sect, [the headman] would summon a guide, who would stand in front of us and announce that [this] was the cash [fund] for Maruyama Temple, whereupon [the donors] would offer us rice and cotton, or else 6 *bu* or 1 *monme* of the domain currency in a tray. The guide would take this, and after we toured the entire village we would have the guide sell the rice, cotton, and such, and render these into the domain currency [as well], whereupon we would then receive this [combined amount]. Our noon meals and lodging were provided by the headman. If the house in which we were to be lodged was unclean, he would change it for another. From what I heard, [the lodging fee] was 5 *gō* of unmilled rice for each [monk]. According to the monastery bookkeeper's accounts of the alms [received] at about that time, [the total amount] apparently came to more than 8 or 9 *ryō* of gold. However, the reality was that, even with an intake of 14 or 15 *ryō*, [the headman] would ordinarily give [only] half to the intinerant mendicants and would pocket the other half himself.[37]

The system of religious mendicancy that had grown up in the Tokugawa period was evidently a complex social arrangement rife with systematic abuse. Zen trainees were well aware that their income depended on cooperation, if not collusion, with the local authorities. Nevertheless, if we are to judge from this account, seasonal alms rounds were a genuine source of income for monastic adepts. The decree that eliminated mendicant rounds in 1872 thus surely aggravated the economic instability of the large monasteries that held seasonal retreats (which were generally funded at least in part by alms tours). Katō reports that when the new prefectural government in Gifu issued a ban on Buddhist mendicancy, it "deprived the training monasteries of their means of livelihood and caused terrible difficulties for those monasteries which had to support large numbers of monks."[38] The elimination of alms as a supplementary source of income was probably felt most immediately by the monastic adepts themselves; participation in some Zen retreats is said to have decreased in the immediate aftermath of the decree.[39]

The loss of income from mendicant rounds was nevertheless negligible compared to the forfeited revenues from the other traditional sources mentioned earlier. The significance of the ban on begging was probably more symbolic than economic. As we have seen, Rinzai leaders worried that Meiji religious policies would infringe on their sect's fundamental identity. Their response to the *takuhatsu* prohibition is a case in point. Imakita sent a petition to the Ministry of Doctrine through the offices of his "older brother in the Dharma," Ogino Dokuon (who headed the Great Teaching Academy at the time), in which he requested that the government rescind the ban.[40] The text seems to be no longer extant, but Imakita's arguments against the prohibition no doubt agreed with the sentiments expressed by his Rinzai peers. One sectarian spokesperson feared that monks who were "traveling the country" would simply quit, excusing themselves by saying that their monastic lifestyle, including alms begging, did not conform with "the law of civilization and enlightenment" promulgated by the government.[41] Like the doctrinal instruction campaign and the clerical marriage decree, Rinzai representatives interpreted the prohibition of begging as a threat to the integrity of the Zen lifestyle, rather than primarily as an economic setback or an intrusion into the sect's outreach activities.

Although the prohibition of alms rounds was rescinded nine years later, it was a significant step in the early Meiji rearrangement of lay–clerical relations. The ban meant that Buddhist clergy could no longer look to the outer world for social and economic authentication of their presumed long hours of meditation, ritual exactitude, and personal self-denial: they could no longer assume a relationship of reciprocal obligation with the local population.[42] Following upon the decrees that required clergy to register under the law as ordinary citizens with secular surnames, that removed long-established social privileges such as exemption from the draft, and that decriminalized clerical marriage and meat eating, the *takuhatsu* ban signaled to parishioners that temple personnel were little different from themselves.[43]

The state's diminution of the social and economic status of Buddhist institutions and personnel brought the importance of lay voluntarism into relief. Although the temple registration system had been eliminated, for most Meiji citizens their local temple, regardless of sect, remained the guardian of their ancestral heritage. Many parish families continued to guarantee the security of that heritage, which was visibly marked by memorial tablets or graves located within temple precincts, by making voluntary offerings. In the case of large temples or training centers, however, economic survival during the last third of the late nineteenth century depended not only on the contributions of hereditary parishioners but also on the generous support of well-endowed laypeople. These patrons were not limited to local residents; they often represented a broader geographical constituency. Especially in Buddhist communities like Rinzai, which had little history of systematic lay outreach, it was a minority of powerful sponsors who contributed most to the growth of lay activism during the 1870s and 1880s, rather than grass-roots organizations of local parishioners. Ikeda has been able to document only a negligible number of teaching assemblies *(kyōkai)* and lay societies *(kessha)* affiliated with the Rinzai sect during the years 1875–1889—three in all (in contrast to 128 in the Sōtō sect).[44]

Lay "activism" or "voluntarism" in the context of this discussion therefore does not mean massive attendance at sermons or seasonal rituals, but rather the cultivation by committed individuals of specific Zen Buddhist disciplines, often combined with significant donations of resources. I accordingly distinguish in this book between "lay practitioners," on the one hand, and "laypeople" or "laity," on the other. Whereas the laity in general attended regular ceremonies at their local temples, donated funds or goods, and in return expected the ritual services of their neighborhood priests, they did not ordinarily engage in koan practice or meditation under the guidance of a *rōshi* (Zen master). In contrast, *koji* (male lay practitioners) and *zenshi* (female lay practitioners) not only participated in seasonal rituals but also focused intensively on regular Zen practice with the ostensible aim of "seeing their natures" *(kenshō)*.[45] *Koji* and *zenshi* in this sense claimed special access to religious knowledge vis-à-vis the majority of parishioners. They constituted, in effect, a third section of the Zen sangha, located in religious status somewhere between priests and nuns, on the one hand, and the majority of laypeople, on the other. In the Engakuji community, the distinction between these practitioners and ordinary parishioners was explicitly reiterated through ritual events, beginning with the formal conferral of the title *"koji"* or *"zenshi"* along with new Dharma names *(hōmyō)* to those deemed to have made significant progress along the path. The designation often took place soon after the master had acknowledged the validity of the adept's initial insight into her or his nature.

The figure of the committed lay practitioner had long-established precedents in Buddhist and Chan history, but it was during the Meiji period that the terms *"koji Bukkyō"* and *"koji Zen"* came to connote an identifiable trend rather than simply the lifestyle of a few exceptional adepts.[46] The elimination of income from land holdings, revenues, loan interest, and other Edo-era temple enterprises forced institutions of the stature of Engakuji to reconceive their economic bases by the early eighties. At the same time, as we saw earlier, younger members of the Rinzai community argued for accommodation in sectarian education of the new "practical learning" that held sway in the secular sphere. The pressing need to develop new economic foundations and the growing demand for a practical model of personal cultivation both contributed to the emergence of the *koji* phenomenon in the mid-Meiji.

Lay Zen in the 1860s and 1870s

I have concentrated on economic factors in the rise of the new lay activism, but its social and political aspects were equally if not more important in the long term. In the early chapters of this book I pointed out that the cultivation theories promoted in the 1820s–1840s by Mizuno Nanboku, Yokoyama Marumitsu, Inoue Masakane, and their associates in the Kantō area had appealed to people from a range of low-to-middle social sectors, and that the most active and enduring members of their communities, like those of Shingaku, possessed at least modest social status or financial resources. The changing attitudes and needs of these groups factored into the religious rearrangements of the second half of the nineteenth century. In the Rinzai Buddhist context, some practitioners who originated in these sectors became leading members of Tokyo society; they began to assert greater control over temple affairs and to play a more active role in propagating Buddhist teachings than had been possible for laypeople during the Edo period. The rise in lay voluntarism in Rinzai as a whole cannot be quantified without further research; but there is little question that the Kamakura monasteries enjoyed a boom after the transfer of the capital to the east. It will become clear in the following pages that the growth of the Engakuji practice, in particular, was related to the development of a bureaucratic elite associated with the new government in Tokyo.

The Zen adepts who became influential in the Tokyo-Kamakura

sangha during the mid-Meiji era had constituted a network since the Bakumatsu period. Lay registers, biographies, letters, temple ledgers, and other miscellaneous records document that Zen practitioners organized religious activities among themselves in Edo and Kamakura at least from the early 1860s. I should add that although Imakita Kōsen stands out among Zen masters in this regard, he was not the only teacher of his time to encourage lay Zen, whether in Kamakura or elsewhere. The *koji* and *zenshi* who congregated in Kamakura in the late 1870s had been practicing together for some time even before the abbot arrived in Tokyo. Much of their religious activity had taken place not under temple auspices but in association with the Shingaku community. From the early decades of the nineteenth century, the Shingaku headquarters in Edo, Sanzensha, had provided a supportive environment to laypeople who wished to practice Zen.[47] Interested individuals could frequent the meetinghouse on their own terms, without sacrificing their work schedules or family responsibilities to a lengthy process of initiation and study, not to mention tonsure.

During the 1860s, a circle of educated individuals met regularly at Sanzensha. According to a Shingaku source:

> Tsumaki Seiheki, Yamaoka Tesshū, and others all practiced under Zen master Gan'ō. Because of this, sometimes they met at [Takahashi Kōsetsu's] house in Hongō [in Edo], and practiced the discipline of *zazen* together. In support of these [activities], Master [Kōsetsu] would lecture on the Buddhist sūtras or the records of [Zen] sayings, and foster the [practitioners'] commitment to the Way.[48]

Takahashi, it will be recalled, was the Shingaku master and practitioner of Tokyūjutsu (and probably of Tohokami) who "saw his nature" under Zen master Gan'ō Genshi in 1867, and who refused to compromise the Shingaku name when pressured by the Ministry of Doctine in the early 1870s.[49] Centering on Takahashi, the practitioners mentioned in the cited passage created an early node of the lay network that blossomed at Engakuji after the Restoration. Rinzai biographical sources confirm the central involvement of Yamaoka Tesshū in Gan'ō's following, which may have included as many as fifty lay practitioners, both men and women.[50]

The activities that Takahashi and his associates organized among themselves under Shingaku auspices in the last Tokugawa years constituted the beginnings of modern lay Zen in the Kantō area. It was not an uneventful transition. Lay Rinzai before and after the Restoration was characterized by an important difference—the Tokugawa socioreligious order precluded lay Zen teaching initiatives. The Rinzai establishment's disapproval of lay teaching was made quite clear to *koji* who aspired to greater authority within the sect. Even after Gan'ō certified the authenticity of his enlightenment, Takahashi found that he would not be permitted to teach Zen:

> On one occasion, in response to some friends' request, Takahashi lectured on the *Blue Cliff Record*. At the time, some common monks who resided in that district heard about this and, envious of Takahashi's high moral repute, sent a malicious report to the administrator of [their] head temple, Myōshinji.[51] Because of this, Myōshinji censured Zen master Gan'ō: "We have been informed that your disciple Takahashi has lectured on the *Blue Cliff Record*. You are surely aware that even monastics, unless they have reached the rank of a Zen teacher *[shike]*, are forbidden to lecture on the two works the *Record of Linji [Linjilu]* and the *Blue Cliff Record*. But if a layman privately expounds [on these works] he will have a bad name in our sect. You should prohibit this at once."

Gan'ō did not bother to argue with the Myōshinji bureaucracy. He sent a messenger to warn Takahashi that he was "extremely angry" and that the Shingaku teacher must repair at once to Chōtokuji (Gan'ō's residence at the time). When Takahashi arrived at the temple in trepidation, "his teacher sternly conveyed to him the import of the head temple's notice and confiscated his disciple's lecture notes."[52] However, the summons and the reprimand were staged for the benefit of the sect authorities, if we are to credit Takahashi's biography. Gan'ō had probably known all along that his disciple was expounding Zen texts at the Shingaku headquarters; it was Gan'ō, we recall, who had urged Takahashi to return to his duties at Sanzensha after the latter attained *kenshō*. The Zen master evidently felt that Shingaku was an effective gateway, or perhaps complement, to Buddhist practice. The day after Gan'ō scolded Takahashi, we are told, he called his follower back and quietly returned the notes to him, avowing that, in his opinion, Takahashi was sufficiently enlightened to transmit the Zen teaching. The master explained that he felt it would be a mistake to become involved in an intrasectarian dispute—as he put it, Buddhism meant "not fighting." He asked Takahashi simply to tolerate the Myōshinji restrictions on his teaching activities.[53] The Shingaku leader and his successors apparently continued (perhaps with a bit more circumspection) to give sermons on Rinzai canonical texts and to supervise meditation and koan practice at Sanzensha.

Under the auspices of an ostensibly Neo-Confucian system of personal cultivation, but with the active encouragement of nearby Zen masters, leading members of the Edo Shingaku community thus laid the groundwork for a Zen Buddhist program tailored to the needs of lay practitioners.[54] Following in Takahashi's footsteps, the Edo tradesman Kawajiri Hōkin (who, as mentioned earlier, was also active for several years in both the Tohokami and Shingaku communities) took up Zen practice under Gan'ō in 1867.[55] Three years later, after Kawajiri had become a Shingaku *tokō* (director), he commenced monthly sessions under Takahashi's supervision in which he engaged in the "contemplative discipline of quiet sitting" *(seiza kufū)* from dawn until ten o'clock at night every day for seven days at a time—in short, he regularly participated in *sesshin* or intensive Zen retreats.[56] Kawajiri reportedly maintained this monthly routine through October 1875, when he began practicing under Imakita Kōsen.[57] Kawajiri's fellow Tohokami and Shingaku practitioner, Mitani Ken'ō, also aspired to practice Zen; in 1871, three months after enrolling in Sanzensha, Mitani made his way to Gan'ō's training center.[58]

After Gan'ō died, these Shingaku-Tohokami-Tōkyū practitioners, along with the other Zen regulars in this network (such as the above-cited Yamaoka and Tsumaki), continued to practice together in Tokyo, apparently without clerical supervision. Once Imakita Kōsen arrived in Tokyo in 1875 to preside over the Rinzai General School, the people who had practiced under Gan'ō in Kamakura for several years and on their own at the Shingaku meetinghouse placed themselves under the new master's guidance.[59] Several of these individuals came to play pivotal roles in the modern Engakuji community. They and their associates were educated and, in some cases, socially prominent; all were endowed with financial resources, even if modest. Regular Zen practice required at least a modicum of time and money. Takahashi Kōsetsu, for example, was able to concentrate intensively on his quest for enlightenment during the 1860s in part because his wife, Ishiwata Takiko, supported him by running a tobacco shop in Edo.[60] Kawajiri Hōkin's dealership in tortoiseshell artifacts must have been well established: beginning in the 1860s, both he and his wife managed to attended seven-day Zen retreats every month, as well as to participate in various other Buddhist, Shingaku, and Misogi (Tohokami) activitites.

The first formal manifestation of this lay Zen activity in the Tokyo area after the Restoration was an association called Ryōmō Zensha (Ryōmō Zen Association) or Ryōmō Kyōkai (Ryōmō Society), founded in 1875 by the aforementioned Tosa Confucian scholar Okunomiya Zōsai. This eclectic figure played a pivotal role in the development of *koji Zen* in the first Meiji years.[61] As a young man, he had studied with Satō Issai and become a committed follower of Wang Yangming; the academy he supervised in Tosa attracted numerous young men who would later play important roles in Meiji society—notably the emerging liberal thinker, Nakae Chōmin (1847–1901). After the Restoration, Okunomiya worked in Tokyo for the Department of Shinto and subsequently for the Ministry of Doctrine.[62]

According to Okunomiya Zōsai's own account, as a young man he had dabbled in Zen Buddhism, visiting local temples and discussing the meaning of Buddhist texts with the priests.[63] Later, while working for the new government in Tokyo, the Tosa scholar revived his interest in contemplative practice, which by now he identified with both Neo-Confucian quiet sitting and Zen meditation. During this period Okunomiya apparently instructed his own students in contemplative practice; in a piece called "An Explanation of Quiet Sitting" *(Seiza setsu)* he sets out guidelines for his "companions"—probably mature students and colleagues who were interested in methods of personal cultivation.

> In general, the way to do quiet sitting is, in the first place, to enter a room, light a stick of incense, sit cross-legged, and arouse this mind [to a state of] exceptional, constant clarity, without directing your will toward anything. Once your will is not directed toward anything, your spirit will naturally return to a settled state, without depending on you to put it in order.... If you practice quiet sitting for three days, you will definitely reach a marvelous realm; but after four or five days, you had better use the disciplinary stick *(keisaku)*. Do not permit yourself to become languorous and distracted. After eating, be sure to walk for one hundred paces. You must not create dark turbidity [in your spirit] by ingesting a great quantity of sake or meat. When you lie down, you must not loosen your clothing. If you feel like sleeping, then [you should] immediately rouse yourself and get up. When you reach the seventh day, your spirit will overflow and your various afflictions will no longer be active....[64]

Okunomiya's ideas about "quiet sitting" clearly venture beyond those advocated by his erstwhile teacher, Satō Issai, who in more orthodox Neo-Confucian style had understood reading and reflection as integrated phases of a continuum of personal cultivation:

> When you read the classics, you should simply sit calmly, open the volume and cast your eyes over it; if you seek without fail in your mind [to understand] each item and each principle, you will comprehend them internally, and before you know it, you will grasp them for yourself *(jitoku)*.... You do not necessarily need to practice the discipline of a half-day [of quiet sitting and a half-day of reading].[65]

In contrast to Issai, Okunomiya prescribes a concentrated meditative session, complete with instructions for eating and walking, and injunctions to stay awake even when reclining. He is proposing, in short, a *sesshin* or Zen retreat, in which participants meditate almost continuously for seven days and nights. The cross-legged posture, the use of the Zen disciplinary stick, and the avoidance of alcohol and meat all confirm the nature of the Tosa scholar's "quiet sitting"—only the Zen master and the koan escape mention.

The addition of even these elements was soon facilitated, however. During his time at the Ministry of Doctrine, Okunomiya began to practice Zen on a regular basis under Imakita Kōsen.[66] The two men had met as early as 1873, when Imakita was still in Yamaguchi; at the time, the master invited Okunomiya to read his Confucian-Buddhist treatise, *Zenkai ichiran*. (The Tosa scholar subsequently helped to arrange permission for the book's publication with the Ministry of Doctrine.)[67] Once Imakita arrived in Tokyo to take over the Rinzai General School, Okunomiya and another prominent lay practitioner, Date Chihiro (Jitoku, 1803–1877), organized the Ryōmō Society and asked the Zen master to be its director.[68] The group's first meeting included a sermon by Imakita on the *Blue Cliff Record* and a statement of membership regulations.

The Ryōmō Society's rules, which Okunomiya Zōsai drew up, stipulated that: (1) members were free to discuss whatever they liked during meetings, with the exception of worldly affairs and matters related to government service; (2) meals would be limited to one bowl of rice, one small bottle of sake, and three vegetable side dishes per person (all of which would be funded by members' contributions); (3) participants would personify honesty and simplicity, and follow the proper rules of etiquette when entertaining guests and carrying out other protocols; and (4) new participants would be introduced by current members and would commit themselves to the aims of the group in the presence of the director at a specified time each month.[69]

Imakita has been repeatedly credited with the founding of this group,[70] but he was more of a mentor and guest lecturer than the driving force behind the Ryōmō Society. To be sure, in traditional East Asian style, leaders are not necessarily expected to involve themselves in the concrete, day-to-day details of the groups they head. Imakita's official biography (which is moderately hagiographical) depicts virtually all of his actions as seemly responses to requests from others rather than as projects or decisions that he personally initiated. Even so, the Ryōmō Society is not even mentioned in his self-approved biography. Other sources confirm that Okunomiya and Date were fully responsible for the creation and maintenance of this early *koji* group.[71]

Okunomiya and his companions were "men of culture" *(bunkajin)*—the breadth of their interests is confirmed by the society's activities. In the preamble to his rules, the Tosa scholar suggests that Ryōmō members practice Zen together and "illuminate each other" by sharing any insights they might attain; but the purpose of the group was not religious practice narrowly conceived. The members are advised, for example, to "express their commitment" through poetry and literary composition, and to "add interest" to their activities by enjoying koto music, calligraphy, painting, or the game of go. They might also compare ancient and recent Japanese poems, classifying the talents of various poets.[72] The Ryōmō Society, in other words, was a cultural association, a club for educated men who were interested in literary and aesthetic refinement as well as in Zen practice.[73]

The Ryōmō Society's honorary leader, Imakita, who was busily administering the Rinzai General School in Tokyo at this time, came into contact with numerous Meiji officials of middle to high rank during the period in which the group took shape. Not coincidentally, the Rinzai temple in Yushima where the society held its meetings was also the site of the General School. Furthermore, although injunctions against discussing political matters were not uncommon in religious and cultural groups both before and after the Restoration, the Ryōmō Society's explicit rule on this point suggests that political gossip was a genuine temptation for its members, no doubt because many of them were civil officials or other men of weight. Indeed, considering its membership, it is safe to assume that the Ryōmō Society functioned as a bonding group for Tokyo statesmen and intellectuals during their leisure time. Even if members conscientiously refrained from discussing government matters during the society meetings, they undoubtedly became better acquainted with each other by meditating together and sharing cultural hobbies on a regular basis. Tsunemitsu Kōnen avers that the group's "cultured lay practitioners" *(bunkajin koji)* included: (1) Yamaoka Tesshū (imperial palace minister, famed calligrapher and swordsman); (2) Torio Tokuan (highly ranked military leader, member of the Council of Elder Statesmen [Genrō-in], and future conservative activist); (3) Takahashi Deishū (1835–1903; former shogunal retainer and lance expert who helped Yamaoka and Katsu Kaishū [1823–1899] facilitate the shogun's bloodless exit from power);[74] (4) Nakae Chōmin (eminent liberal thinker and scholar of Western thought); (5) Kawajiri Hōkin (Shingaku leader, Misogikyō elder, Kabuki playwright, and successful businessman); and (6) Nakajima Nobuyuki (Chōjō, 1846–1899; former Kanagawa governor, member of the Council of Elder Statesmen, and future liberal party leader).[75]

Separate sources confirm that most if not all of these men indeed practiced Zen under Imakita in the 1870s, though given the central role played by Okunomiya and Date in the founding of the Ryōmō Society,

Tsunemitsu errs when he credits the above-listed figures with its initiation. The continuing involvement of Yamaoka, Torio, Kawajiri, and Nakajima in the Engakuji circle into the 1880s is well documented, and considering Nakae Chōmin's and Takahashi Deishū's personal connections with this core group, it is likely that they were Ryōmō practitioners for a time as well. Takahashi was Yamaoka's brother-in-law and close associate during the Restoration crisis; his writings include several poetry exchanges with both Imakita and Okunomiya Zōsai.[76] Nakae Chōmin, as mentioned earlier, had studied under Okunomiya in Tosa as a young man; he is believed to have become seriously interested in Zen while living in Tokyo during the mid-1870s (after his return from France)—the same years in which his teacher was running Ryōmō Kyōkai in the capital. Nakae's student, the socialist Kōtoku Shūsui (1871–1911), later testified that Nakae was interested in Zen Buddhism all his life.[77]

Lay Initiatives at Engakuji in the 1880s

The original Ryōmō association apparently served as a forum for social and religious interaction among a select group of officials, thinkers, and educators during a period when the Meiji government was still in a relatively open, formative phase. Several decades later, Imakita's successor, Shaku Sōen, asked his disciple, Shaku Sōkatsu (Tettō, 1870–1954), to organize a lay group under the same name.[78] The revived society was incorporated in 1925 and set up a training headquarters in Chiba prefecture in 1936; branch centers were founded in other parts of Japan, as well as in the West. By the time Sōkatsu died, the Ryōmō Society allegedly boasted several thousand members.[79] Considering this later expansion, Robert Sharf may be right when he says that Ryōmō Kyōkai "became the model for the urban lay meditation centers that were so influential in the propagation of Zen practice in the West." The twentieth-century incarnation, however, was far removed from the original group—a loosely conceived association of Confucian-educated officials and intellectuals more interested in the pleasures of occasional contemplation, poetry, and calligraphy than in systematic Zen proselytization. The Ryōmō Society of the 1870s functioned more importantly as a gathering place outside the public domain for politically connected individuals.[80]

After Okunomiya and Date died in 1877, the Ryōmō Society continued to thrive for a time, though it was eventually replaced by other arrangements initiated by the same core group of practitioners.[81] I noted earlier that after Imakita was relieved of his school responsibilities in Tokyo in 1877 he reopened the Engakuji meditation hall, Shōbōgendō, and held a winter retreat there.[82] According to accounts that have been

passed down orally in the Engakuji community, beginning with this retreat the new abbot allowed *koji* and *zenshi* to use the meditation hall
along with the monks.[83] The Zen master evidently permitted this inno-
vative practice on an unofficial basis: ordinarily, lay practitioners were
not allowed entry into Zen monastic quarters, especially the meditation
hall. Not unexpectedly, Imakita's biography is silent about the lay use of
the *zendō;* his chronologers merely state that in 1877 the master's lay
followers began to occupy a building in the temple precincts called Shōden'an.[84] The latter was simply a subtemple in the Engakuji grounds; it
was not located within the monastic quarters at all.[85] Male lay practitioners slept and ate in Shōden'an, and apparently also meditated there
along with the female practitioners when the meditation hall was closed.
Suzuki later recalled seeing Shingaku leader Kawajiri Hōkin practicing
for hours in Shōden'an when the younger man visited Engakuji in the
1890s.[86] By that time, the building had become the principal site for lay
meditation—a kind of lay *zendō*.

The approximate extent of Imakita's lay following during the early
As temple abbot, Imakita approved and encouraged the lay use of
the subtemple Shōden'an, but he did not initiate this special arrangement. According to his official biography, the "Tokyo *koji* borrowed
Shōden'an, named it Takuboku-en, and applied themselves to Zen practice."[87] The text's wording leaves no doubt that the lay practitioners
took the initiative in this project; with Imakita's blessing, they claimed
one of the temple buildings and publicly marked it as their domain by
renaming it.[88] The part Imakita played in both the founding of the
Ryōmō Society and the initial opening of Engakuji buildings to lay
practice thus appears to have been rather subdued, if not passive. There
is no evidence that he expended much energy in planning and supervising these events—in comparison, for example, with his involvement in
the rebuilding of the monks' meditation hall. The latter project is described in detail in his biography and formally recorded in his Chinese
works as well.[89] The abbot regarded the rebuilding of the meditation
hall as a far more important achievement than his unofficial concessions
to the *koji* and *zenshi*. The testimony of other sources reinforces this
picture. At least at Engakuji, the Rinzai lay outreach was more of an
"inreach" into the monastery by the *koji* and *zenshi* themselves.

The approximate extent of Imakita's lay following during the early
1880s is documented in a register that purports to record the names of
practitioners who attended an assembly at Engakuji in February 1881.[90]
The names of several lay patrons of the time who did not attend this
particular assembly are omitted from the register, but most of the leading
Engakuji *koji* of the 1870s and early 1880s are included: Kawajiri Hōkin, Yamaoka Tesshū, Nakajima Nobuyuki, Kitashiro Masaomi (Eishū),
Taguchi Tōkan, and Tsumaki Seiheki.[91] Engakuji historian Inoue Zenjō

reports that twenty-nine *koji* and nineteen *zenshi* are listed in this register.[92] Many of these people were instrumental in the rebuilding of the Engakuji meditation hall. Torio, Yamaoka, and Nakajima helped Imakita plan the reconstruction in early 1881, and along with other *koji* and priests put up funds for the project in the following amounts (in yen):[93]

Engakuji administrators *(jōjū)*	450
Imakita Kōsen	200
Yamaoka Tesshū	100
Nakajima Nobuyuki	100
Kawajiri Hōkin	100
Torio Tokuan	50
Kitashiro Masaomi	50

The *koji*'s contribution to the construction costs was almost 40 percent of the total compared with clerical contributions, although the above evidently represents only starting funds. In addition, Imakita prepared an essay for the donation register for the project (in which he again laments the "recent decline" of Zen and its lack of teachers) and personally traveled to Kyoto to solicit support from potential sponsors.[94] Fund-raising efforts of this nature continued until the hall was completed in July 1883. Imakita's biographers were careful to record the abbot's memories of the exertions associated with this project:

> Master [Imakita Kōsen] had aroused his resolve to accomplish this project in the middle of the fourth month of Meiji 14 [April 1881]. His hard work and concern were such that at times he made the rounds of the homes of the Tokyo *koji* and at times of the wealthy farmers of the villages in the vicinity; the pains he took went beyond the ordinary. The monks, too, divided into parties and during the intervals between retreats solicited donations from most of the temples and committed households.[95] During the retreats, every day they carried out the construction work or else transported loads, unmindful of the long, steep roads. There is no way to describe the hardships [they endured].[96]

Raising money to maintain a large temple complex like Engakuji was a pressing matter in the early Meiji and no doubt occupied a significant portion of time for both monastic and lay leaders. By the 1880s the Kamakura temple had nearly depleted its "diminishing stipend," and its staff were often expected to raise funds on behalf of Zen temples throughout the country as well as for their own. Imakita's well-positioned, educated lay followers were invaluable resources, particularly in the organization and financing of large projects such as the above restoration. The *koji* and *zenshi* regularly carried out fund-raising campaigns, whether to restore temple structures or to pay the recurring costs of running Engakuji and its associated activities; they also donated money to cover onetime costs, such as publications. A group of lay practitioners sponsored the printing of Imakita's *Muji no uta* (Songs about "Mu") in 1877; Tsumaki had the master's poetry collection, *Ondaigo*, published in 1878; and several lay disciples collaborated in funding reduced-size printings of the Buddhist canon on behalf of Engakuji in 1880 and 1885.[97] These followers not only helped cover the printing costs of Imakita's publications; they also dealt on his behalf with printers and book dealers, wrote prefaces for his writings, and (as we saw in the case of Okunomiya Zōsai) helped to acquire publication permits from the government.

All of these voluntary activities may be classified as merit-gaining efforts of the kind traditionally encouraged by Buddhist temples. However, the nature of the alms–merit transaction changed dramatically in the aftermath of the Restoration. After Engakuji's abrupt loss of regular income in the 1870s, lay voluntarism became indispensable to the temple's survival as a Zen educational center. Like other Buddhist institutions, Engakuji continued to meet some of its costs by appealing to local parishioners. In 1885, after a large, expensive commemoration ceremony was held at the temple in honor of its founder, Engakuji established a lay society with the stated goal of enrolling a hundred thousand members and raising 15,000 yen within fifteen years. Fund-raisers were to be selected from the priests and laypeople associated with Engakuji-line temples and sent out to canvass the surrounding areas. The collected amounts would be invested in real estate, bonds, and loans, and the resulting interest would be used to support temple restoration, education, emergency relief efforts, and the cost of ordinary ritual and lay activities.[98] However, donations from local parishioners probably supplied only a portion of these operating costs. The job of keeping the head temple solvent remained a challenge. Account records for 1892, the year Imakita died, show a deficit of over 183 yen.[99]

The role of wealthy lay patrons was therefore critical during this period—as indeed it had been in Japanese Buddhist communities of the past. The relationship between the Kamakura temple and its lay supporters during the nineteenth century is reminiscent in this regard of the close association between Zen institutions and their ruling-class sponsors during the Kamakura and Ashikaga periods. (The Kitsuregawa family, which maintained Engakuji during the Tokugawa era, was in fact lineally descended from the Ashikaga shoguns.)[100] In the Meiji, however, the economic support provided by Tokyo elites had a more spontaneous quality than those earlier hereditary arrangements; it was one element in a more complex relationship that included serious individual practice of Zen disciplines as well as participation in affiliated lay groups. In the case of Engakuji, practitioners not only made donations to temple funds but enrolled in its training program in greater numbers than ever before. As we shall see in subsequent chapters, they also joined associated political groups and took on leadership roles in Zen Buddhist educational programs. The next chapter will describe specific examples of *koji* leadership during this period and discuss the impact of the growing lay presence on the Engakuji community.

CHAPTER 7

Shifting Boundaries in the Sangha

THE INCREASED LAY activism of the Meiji period is sometimes called a "movement" *(undō),* but it was by no means a mass phenomenon. It was spearheaded in the Rinzai case by a select number of men who possessed significant status in the secular sphere. In the following pages I single out two individuals, Yamaoka Tesshū and Kawajiri Hōkin, who played a leading role in the formation of *koji Zen* in the Kantō area during the late nineteenth century. Shaku Sōen, their younger contemporary and fellow practitioner at Engakuji, later credited these two with laying the foundations for the success of Zen Buddhism in the twentieth century.[1] This chapter gives particular attention to Kawajiri's role in the expansion of lay Zen Buddhism through its assimilation of Shingaku; it then moves on to consider the impact of the growing lay practice on lay–clerical relations within the Engakuji community. In conclusion, I summarize patterns of gender and social identity in the temple program during the late 1880s and early 1890s. Enrollment records indicate that Imakita Kōsen's brand of Zen Buddhism appealed especially to promising young intellectuals who commuted to Kamakura from Tokyo.

Yamaoka is probably the best-known lay Zen practitioner of the early Meiji; he was prominent in artistic and political circles as well as in the religious world.[2] By birth the son of a shogunal retainer, he succeeded to the house of Yamaoka, a family that specialized in the art of the lance *(yari).* He trained in the shogunal school of military arts (Kōbusho) and by the early 1860s was supervising military recruits. During the Restoration, Yamaoka served as head of an auxiliary unit and as senior inspector *(ōmetsuke),* but he is best known for helping to negotiate the surrender of the Edo castle to Restoration forces. He also distinguished himself during this period by arranging the dissolution of the Shōgitai, a group of rebellious shogunal retainers who were unhappy with the Tokugawa regime's unconditional surrender. After the transition, Yamaoka served in a series of regional administrative posts and eventually joined the emperor's entourage. He advanced quickly in subsequent years, becoming palace minister of the first rank in 1881.[3]

Yamaoka was intensely involved in sword arts from his childhood; he eventually created his own "No-Sword Style" *(Mutōryū)* and opened a school called Shunpūkan. He was also one of the leading calligraphers of his day. Both calligraphy and sword practices have long been associated with Zen Buddhism in Japan, and the anecdotes that have grown up around Yamaoka not surprisingly depict his legendary accomplishments in these arts as evidence of his commitment to Zen practice.[4] The swordmaster was indeed well acquainted with the leading Rinzai masters of the day; in addition to Gan'ō, he practiced under Seijō Genshi (1816–1881), Yuri Tekisui (from whom he received the Zen seal of approval), and Ogino Dokuon; he maintained especially close relations with Imakita Kōsen.[5] Yamaoka's mastery of Zen Buddhism was accordingly unquestioned, and he taught numerous disciples of his own under the auspices of his sword school. He seems to have employed his calligraphic talents almost constantly in writing prefaces and other short pieces in order to raise funds on behalf of various Zen associates and their temple projects; he also sponsored two Zen temples of his own (Tesshūji in Shizuoka prefecture and Zenshōan in Tokyo). Modern sectarian historians depict Yamaoka as a highly qualified Zen master in his own right, not simply as an "outside protector" *(gegosha)* of the Dharma (a common rubric for powerful lay practitioners).[6]

Imakita was convinced of Yamaoka's special qualities; from the abbot's perspective, the swordmaster was virtually the paradigm of the enlightened Buddhist practitioner. Imakita seems to have regarded Yamaoka as a model for both monks and laity, if we are to judge from the master's reaction to the idea of his associate taking the tonsure. After Yamaoka reached the highest echelons of the imperial ministry in the early 1880s, he informed his lineal Zen master, Yuri Tekisui, that he wished to resign his government post and take orders together with his wife. By this time Yamaoka had already attained an advanced level of Zen practice, having passed through the requisite series of difficult koans. Yuri gave his approval to the plan and asked Imakita to do the same.

The Engakuji abbot refused. His written response to Yamaoka's request for tonsure conveys in no uncertain terms that the abbot was dismayed by the idea.[7] Imakita argues that everything one does, not just the monastic life, should be understood as the operation of the Buddha nature; he takes both Yamaoka and Yuri to task for not having a broader vision of the Buddhist path. The abbot warns Yamaoka not to become obsessed with the external manifestations of Buddhism, such as reading the scriptures, worshiping Buddha images, carrying out rituals, or collecting alms, thereby failing to grasp its deeper meaning. Imakita backed up his admonitions with examples of famous Chinese Buddhists who successfully practiced Chan without giving up their government positions. The vein of Imakita's writing recalls his apologetical arguments in *Zenkai ichiran,* which he had written twenty years earlier in order to persuade Bakumatsu scholar-officials that they should take up Zen Buddhist practice. The discourse of the enlightened gentleman-official served both to encourage Zen practice and to prevent it from being taken too far (into the monastery).

In his youth, Imakita had insisted on leaving his young wife, abandoning his career, and defying his family's wishes in order to take the tonsure. To be sure, in the Tokugawa period a scholar who seriously wished to master the Zen Buddhist path had no real choice other than life in the monastery. However, as Imakita grew older and witnessed the changes that took place after the Restoration, his views on the relative value of monastic and lay practice shifted. In his response to Yamaoka the abbot speaks of himself (with considerable poetic license) as a monk "hiding out in a country temple" who is "useless to the world."[8] Suzuki suggests that after years of Zen practice, by the 1880s the master had simply realized the inadequacies of a purely monastic education.[9] However, Imakita's proposals to Rinzai leaders regarding the institution of a Zen seminary (discussed in the preceding chapter) leave little doubt that in the late 1870s he still placed priority on traditional monastic training for young monks, to the exclusion of other kinds of education. Perhaps Suzuki, who never took the tonsure himself, read some of his own ideals into Imakita's position. It is more plausible to conclude that by the 1880s Imakita, still conservative in matters of monastic education, nevertheless could see the writing on the wall for the Rinzai sangha as a whole: the public activism of prominent lay practitioners like Yamaoka was essential to Buddhist prosperity.

Koji and *zenshi,* alongside the monastics and regular laity, were an indispensable third pillar of the Zen community in the new world of Meiji Japan. Lay practitioners provided economic sustenance, political connections, social prestige, and a broad, "enlightened" perspective on developments outside the temple gates. Even though Imakita believed that the religious training of young novices was critical to the survival of Zen Buddhism, he also came to recognize that talented, dedicated men like Yamaoka could probably do more good for the Dharma as *koji* than as monks—not least because the latter had no direct voice in political matters at this time (a point to which we shall return). Meiji Buddhist leaders like Imakita seem to have valued their lay disciples not only for their exemplary religious conduct, their economic resources, and their general savoir faire, but also—especially in the Tokyo area—for their

FIGURE 10. Kawajiri Hōkin. Reproduced from the frontispiece of *Kawajiri Hōkin sensei jiseki,* by Hayano Gankō (1911). Courtesy of Sanzensha, Tokyo.

public service. The old paradigm of the bodhisattva in the marketplace who exemplifies Confucian as well as Buddhist sensibilities seems to have taken on new meaning in the Meiji era.

Among the lay practitioners who frequented Engakuji, Imakita was personally closest to the businessman, playwright, and religious leader Kawajiri Hōkin (figure 10).[10] We saw earlier that the tortoiseshell crafts dealer was initiated into both the Tohokami teachings of Inoue Masa-kane and the Edo branch of Sekimon Shingaku in 1861, and in the following year began practicing Zen, first under Gan'ō and subsequently under Imakita. In the space of two or three years in his early twenties,

Kawajiri thus committed himself to three distinct systems of personal cultivation (and he maintained ties with all three groups throughout his life). Yet in the final analysis, Kawajiri seems to have been most zealous in his Zen practice. He and his wife, Esō (Kashima Sadako), were enthusiastic Zen practitioners; they each achieved *kenshō* while practicing under Imakita in 1876.[11] The couple's commitment to Zen was shared by their family; Kawajiri's mother, five sisters, and at least one adoptive brother, as well as Esō's younger sister, also practiced under Imakita.[12] After the abbot moved permanently to Kamakura in mid-1877, Kawajiri, Esō, and their relatives routinely attended the scheduled Zen retreats and practiced at Engakuji during the interludes between retreats as well.[13]

According to his Shingaku biographer, Kawajiri successfully navigated the most advanced phases of Zen training and had several enlightenment episodes after his first insight. In the mid-1880s, Imakita effusively praised Kawajiri for his mastery of Zen Buddhism: the abbot claimed that he had never heard of a layman who had "gone beyond" *(kōjō)* in his practice, as had Kawajiri.[14] The abbot was so pleased by Kawajiri's progress that he conferred upon him the original manuscript of his cherished masterpiece, *Zenkai ichiran;*[15] he also gave Kawajiri his seal of approval and designated the *koji* a successor to his Dharma—an unusual honor for a lay practitioner at the time. Far less information about Esō's religious progress is recorded; we are told simply that she mastered the "profound depths" of the Way at about the same time as her husband.[16]

Imakita's relationship with Kawajiri Hōkin was not narrowly focused on matters of religious practice—the two men were close friends.[17] The Kawajiri residence was a second home for Imakita whenever he visited the capital. In fact, the Zen master's visits to Tokyo were invariably related to his encounters with the *koji* and *zenshi*. His biography offers a sample list of these excursions: Imakita stayed at the Kawajiri residence in 1877, gave a two-week lecture series there on the *Record of Linji* in May 1880, spoke again on the *Record of Linji* at Kawajiri's Shingaku meetinghouse (Sanzensha) in October of that year, lectured for two weeks on the same text at Kawajiri's home in April 1881, and returned there for a similar engagement in the winter of 1882. The abbot stayed at the home of another faithful *koji*, Tsumaki Seiheki, while he expounded on Hakuin's *Dokugō shingyō* (Poison Words for the Heart) in the spring of 1884.[18] In the meantime, with Imakita's blessing, Kawajiri continued to hold the "quiet sitting" meetings at Sanzensha that his predecessor Takahashi Kōsetsu had initiated. Kawajiri also invited his friends and students to Zen retreats at his house in Ikenohashi, where (as at Sanzensha) he guided followers in *sanzen*.[19] On these occasions the Shingaku master expounded on a wide range of Zen classics, from the *Platform Sūtra of the Sixth Patriarch (Liuzu tanjing)* to Hakuin's writings.[20] By the end of the nineteenth century, he was a well-known Zen teacher who lectured frequently in various venues around the country as well as at several Tokyo locations.[21]

The most distinctive aspect of the *koji* phenomenon in the Meiji period is that unordained practitioners began to teach Buddhism, openly identified as such, at independent (nonclerical) facilities. In the 1870s and 1880s it was still rare for a layman to conduct *sanzen,* run his own retreats, and publicly interpret the Zen records; yet during these years Yamaoka Tesshū and Kawajiri Hōkin routinely engaged in these activities. They were de facto Rinzai masters of some repute. In his popular discourses, as we have seen, Imakita avowed that laypeople could best support the Dharma by offering alms to the monastic sangha. In practice, however, he distinguished between ordinary parishioners who attended seasonal temple functions and the adepts who regularly practiced Zen under his guidance. He seems to have believed that his male lay disciples could promote Zen teachings in the world as well as his monks, if not better. (I have seen no evidence that the Engakuji *zenshi* were involved in publicly transmitting Zen during this period.) Many of the Tokyo *koji* were indeed better educated (and probably better speakers) than the monastic personnel under Imakita's supervision.[22]

The first large-scale lay outreach in the Engakuji line is usually associated with Imakita's younger followers, especially Shaku Sōen and his protégés, Shaku Sōkatsu and D. T. Suzuki. Yet Kawajiri Hōkin, Imakita's friend and confidante, had routinized group lay Zen as many as twenty years earlier.[23] In doing so, he was following in the footsteps of his teacher, Takahashi Kōsetsu, who with Gan'ō's blessings had grafted Shingaku into Kamakura Rinzai Zen during the Bakumatsu era. However, Kawajiri went much further than his predecessors in bringing Shingaku and Rinzai interests together.

Shingaku's Zen Turn

Despite important pockets of support and even enthusiasm for the Shingaku program among certain Tokyo elites, Ishida Baigan's teachings, deprived of their raison d'être as an accessible form of Confucian-type learning, steadily lost appeal after the Restoration. In the 1880s the number of listeners who attended Shingaku talks decreased precipitously.[24] To make matters worse, in 1886 Sanzensha was forced to abandon its meetinghouse in Kanda in order to make way for a new train route through Tokyo. At the time, only two head lecturers were still active, and the few remaining Shingaku members lacked the resources to rebuild elsewhere. They decided to disband the group and give the building to their Shinto-sect affiliate, Taiseikyō, which was about to set up a new teaching center.[25] By the following year, only one Shingaku lecturer remained active in the Tokyo area. Four surviving elders of the group met at Kawajiri's house in Asakusa and reluctantly decided to discontinue regular Shingaku activities for the indefinite future.[26]

According to Kawajiri Hōkin's retrospective acccount, he and his companions felt that the main reason for Shingaku's decline after the Restoration was that it "failed to gain people" *(hito o ezaru)*. This problem in turn, they reasoned, derived from the fact that the customary Shingaku training system, *mikiki tebiki* (literally, "guidance in seeing and hearing"), no longer suited people's circumstances in the new age. The leaders concluded that Shingaku teaching methods should be modified to meet the new generation's needs and varying levels of commitment. In his narrative Kawajiri carefully marks his and his colleagues' respect for the training methods that Teshima Toan had systemized in Kyoto in the eighteenth century and that had been used in meetinghouses across Japan ever since. The near demise of Shingaku in the Tokyo area in their time, however, mandated that the venerable system be revised. The elders also agreed to correct the alleged misinterpretations of Ishida Baigan's ideas that had crept into Shingaku texts over the years.

The net result of the 1887 council was the decision to infuse Shingaku with Hakuin Zen. In December of that year the group opened a new meetinghouse in Kanda, and Kawajiri began to hold regular meditation sessions *(seizakai)*, lectures on Zen records, and *sanzen* consultations, in addition to traditional Shingaku talks *(dōwa)*. He also resuscitated Shingaku "support meetings" *(kaiho)* in an effort to stem the decline of the core membership (mostly lecturers and "elder companions," *rōyū*).[27] Kawajiri, the central figure in this shift, also believed that the group's *sakumon* or "problems" (functionally equivalent in Shingaku to Zen koans) had been corrupted through the gradual insertion of rationalizing, discriminative comments in the written record. He accordingly edited the *sakumon* in consultation with Imakita Kōsen; he similarly revised the central Shingaku training manual with an eye to Hakuin-style Zen praxis.[28] These "reforms" institutionalized the displacement of the pre-Meiji Shingaku educational program by the Hakuin Zen system of training (figure 11).

Once these measures were in place, Sanzensha began to hold one-week retreats centered on the "contemplative practice of quiet sitting" *(seiza kufū)*, in which students reviewed Ishida Baigan's "old cases" *(korei)*.[29] It comes as no surprise to learn from Kawajiri's retrospective account that audiences at Shingaku talks increased steadily after the revised program was instituted.[30] His disciple, Hayano Gankō, relates

FIGURE 11. A view of the *zazendō* (meditation room) used by Shingaku practitioners today. The characters on the calligraphy scroll read: "filial piety, deference, loyalty, and trust." Courtesy of Sanzensha, Tokyo.

along the same lines that several tens of people attended Sanzensha activities in the late 1880s, and that the number of people who "saw their natures" grew daily.[31] The one-hundred-and-fiftieth commemoration of Ishida Baigan's death, which took place in the early 1890s, allegedly attracted four hundred people.[32] It was also during this period that the wording used in the signs at the entrances to Sanzensha and the other Tokyo Shingaku centers was changed from *sekkyō* (doctrinal instruction) back to *dōwa* (talks on the Way).[33] The revival of Sanzensha was evidently an opportunity both to reinforce the close relations between Shingaku and Rinzai Zen and to throw off the lingering government-concocted rubrics that had been used to circumscribe Shingaku during the first two Meiji decades.

In addition to the Zen-informed redaction of Shingaku teaching texts and the introduction of Hakuin-style training methods at Sanzensha, Kawajiri undertook Zen-oriented rewritings of Shingaku narratives. He authored the biographies of all the major Edo/Tokyo Shingaku leaders of the mid-nineteenth century and compiled the important

Shingaku chronicle *Sanzensha nenpu* (A Chronological History of Sanzensha). We recall, for example, that according to Kawajiri's account, his
predecessor Takahashi had studied both Tōkyūjutsu-type divination and
a popular form of "Shinto," probably Tohokami, prior to his encounter
with Shingaku, and that he had reportedly discovered the "living mind"
of Confucian and Shingaku texts only after attaining *kenshō* under Zen
master Gan'ō. This narrative is probably based on information that
Takahashi had passed on to his Shingaku colleagues. However, Kawajiri
redacted the biography in 1895, long after he had become a prominent
Rinzai educator in his own right, and he not unexpectedly highlights the
salvific role of Zen Buddhism in the story line. Kawajiri relates, for example, that after Takahashi attained enlightenment under master Gan'ō,
his Shingaku mentor, Kumatani Tōshū, beseeched him to return to Sanzensha and resuscitate its program. Outsiders warned Takahashi that
Ishida Baigan's followers were now corrupt and hypocritical, and that he
should avoid "falling into the Shingaku hell."[34] When confronted with
these allegations, Kumatani confirmed that Shingaku was indeed in a sad
state—hence the need for a (Zen-inspired) leader like Takahashi. Moreover, it was not until Zen master Gan'ō approved of the project that
Takahashi moved back to Sanzensha.[35]

Kawajiri's rendition of the life of Shingaku teacher Mitani Ken'ō is
structured along the same lines. Mitani also practiced Zen in Kamakura
on a regular basis, and as his practice developed he, too, came to realize
that the Shingaku religious discipline was "truly not easy" and that
its mastery required a more profound level of understanding than most
people supposed.[36] Kawajiri reminds us through both these narratives
that serious engagement with the special Zen "transmission outside the
teachings" is a prerequisite for authentic understanding of the Shingaku
(and Confucian) path. The Shingaku master's own religious journey from
Tohokami to Shingaku to Zen was similarly depicted by his disciple
Hayano as an evolutionary process.

By emphasizing common structures in Meiji Shingaku biographies I
do not mean to imply that the stories of these men's lives of faith had no
basis in reality. Takahashi, Mitani, Kawajiri, and other nameless associates were inspired by a common stock of religious ideas and practices.
They organized elements from the same universe of possibilities into a
system of moral and religious cultivation that seemed appropriate to
their needs and to those of their listeners at the time. In the process of
moving from one religious formation to another, they apparently came
to the conclusion that Zen Buddhism offered the best framework for
successful personal and social development. At the same time, the stories
of Takahashi's, Mitani's, and Kawajiri's religious travels are clearly Zen-
inspired reconstructions of the events. All three figures are depicted as

attaining fulfillment at Engakuji only after having moved from prognos-ticatory systems to Tohokami to Shingaku. Their biographers tacitly claim that a full understanding of the Confucian-based Shingaku system is predicated on practice under the guidance of an ordained Zen master. This perspective is by now familiar. In Iwakuni during the 1860s, Im-akita Kōsen described how he had once been moved by his own post-Zen realization that Confucian learning was, after all, "not easy," and that it indeed encompassed the highest Zen insight. His Meiji disciples resounded this theme: only through Zen practice could Confucian learn-ing survive in the world as an authentic form of personal improvement.

With the demise of the Tokugawa order and the implementation of new religious control mechanisms by the early Meiji state, the clergy of the monastic Buddhist sects lost their monopoly of the transmission of sectarian doctrines and practices. However, in the Rinzai community the certification of lay practitioners' enlightenment, the granting of *koji* or *zenshi* status, and admission to a particular Dharma lineage remained clerical prerogatives. The peculiar relationship between the Kamakura Gozan abbots and the Shingaku community in Tokyo is illuminating in this regard. Kumatani relied on Zen master Gan'ō both to certify Taka-hashi's enlightenment and to authorize Takahashi to revive Shingaku. Similarly, Shingaku records explicitly justify Kawajiri's later revision of the Sanzensha training program by stating that Imakita authorized him to use "Hakuin's method" to instruct his members in Zen practice. Moreover, although several people reportedly attained *kenshō* under Kawajiri Hōkin's guidance in the early Meiji, many of them simulta-neously practiced in Kamakura and ultimately received their Dharma names from the Engakuji abbot. Indeed, all the Shingaku-Zen practi-tioners discussed here are portrayed in their biographies as lacking the capacity to sanction the transmission of the "living mind" on their own. Despite the fact that the Shingaku masters ran their own lay retreats and master–disciple consultations throughout the Bakumatsu and Meiji peri-ods, ultimately the authenticity of their transmission of Zen depended on the imprimatur of an ordained master—first Gan'ō, and later, Imakita. The legitimacy of the lay Zen enterprise thus remained contingent on priestly intervention. The tension between this reality and the new promi-nence of several activist *koji* contributed to the shifting and sometimes conflicted nature of lay–clerical relations in the Rinzai sangha.

Koji Zen in Territorial Perspective

The pattern of interaction that developed between the Tokyo lay practi-tioners and the Engakuji abbot concretely affected the latter's lifestyle and schedule, and therefore his relations with his monastic companions in Kamakura. By the early 1880s, Imakita had established a routine of staying in Tokyo for a week or two every spring and autumn in order to train groups of *koji* and *zenshi*. The monks back at Engakuji were not entirely happy with this arrangement. In the early months of 1884, Imakita wrote in some detail to Kawajiri Hōkin and Tsumaki Seiheki about tensions within the temple community. Apparently a *koji* named Kaneko Kō-ō, on behalf of all the Tokyo practitioners, had invited Imakita to visit the capital that spring and expound on Hakuin's *Kaian kokugo*. Imakita replied that he would have to forgo the trip this time. By way of explanation, he confided in Tsumaki that a disturbing incident had recently taken place at Engakuji:

> I have now discovered for the first time that the monks felt displeased from the beginning that I was going to the capital for a week each spring and autumn. Their feeling was that in administering my guidance I was sidelining the monks and giving priority to the *koji* and *zenshi*. This view is a complete misunderstanding—I love the monks. One or two of them, who had evil hearts, took a strong stand [against me], saying that I treated them in an unequal way that is unworthy of a Zen master....[37]

In a letter to Kawajiri written immediately afterward, Imakita expresses his feelings about the affair even more vividly.

> Allow me to inform you of this, confidentially. This is a secret. You are forbidden to speak about it—I have also asked Kōgaku [Shaku Sōen] to keep this a secret.... [T]here were one or two jealous monks who felt that in my heart I deeply loved the laymen and laywomen, and was neglecting the monks, and who misunderstood my way of treating them when they came to my chambers to receive guidance and with regard to various other things. They talked about these matters and stirred up the [other] monks— they were planning to break up the monastic community. At that point, thanks to the gods who protect the Dharma, the situation came to light and these monks were brought to shame. They are indeed wicked men who destroyed the harmony [of the sangha], so I ordered them to leave the monastery.[38]

The abbot adds that a number of other monks who had been involved in the incident also left Engakuji (about ten "obedient" ones remained).

Imakita was reluctant to have less experienced Zen practitioners hear of this disturbance—much less the public in general. Admitting that the affair had exposed his own failings as well as the weakness of his training program, he repeatedly urged Kawajiri to keep the matter in the strictest confidence:

> [P]lease keep this a secret. Since you, a venerable layman, are a Dharma-protecting god *(gohōjin)* who has practiced Zen for a long time, I am telling you [everything] without reserve. I am also revealing this secret to you with the thought that it may serve as an insight in the future. Absolutely do not speak of this to other people.[39]

Kawajiri was by now in a position of responsibility over the other Tokyo *koji* and *zenshi*—the people who maintained the Engakuji coffers as well as the temple's reputation in the capital. Imakita could ill afford to have these followers' commitment to Engakuji shaken by the realization that the resident priests were jealous of them and hostile to their needs.

If we are to credit Imakita's remarks in his letter to Tsumaki, such mutinies were not uncommon in Zen monasteries of the time; the abbot notes that similar rebellions had occurred that spring in three other monastic programs.[40] In any case, the monks' complaint about their "unequal" treatment vis-à-vis the lay disciples rings true. Traditional Zen training takes place within a hierarchical social framework, at least initially requiring what may seem to the novice to be utter submission to the master—a mental posture that is constantly reinforced by ritual prostrations, ordered seating arrangements, and regulated access to the master. Needless to say, Chan and Zen texts hold out the possibility of a complete reversal of this power relationship as the disciple achieves a higher degree of understanding. One has only to skim the pages of the *Record of Linji,* among other Chan classics, to encounter various bodily and verbal demonstrations of the meaninglessness of dualistic mental structures. Master and disciple are depicted as fair game for each other, presumably equal at the ultimate level of reality. Yet the everyday life of most Chan and Zen trainees was ordered by strict hierarchical convention; revolts in the monastery were surely nothing new in the Meiji period.

Each historical moment nonetheless provides fodder for a new formulation of the issues. We saw earlier that Rinzai leaders were anxious about the effect on the viability of their program of the government's new policies on clerical marriage, doctrinal instruction, and mendicant rounds. The leaders of the monastic sects as a whole opposed clerical marriage in particular with a tenacity that lasted into the twentieth century. However, as Jaffe points out, the lower ranks of the Buddhist clergy tended to harbor a different perspective.[41] Imakita's and other Rinzai leaders' repeated exclamations of dismay over the diminishing number and quality of monastic recruits in the early Meiji constituted a concerted rhetoric, as I have suggested, but this discourse was probably inspired in the first instance by reports of priests who had forsaken their vows of celibacy. Differences in status and power among members of the same

religious community affected the range of responses to other issues as
well. The incongruities and inconsistencies of Japanese monastery life
were felt most acutely by younger priests during the 1870s and early
1880s, when new theories of autonomy and equal rights were being
hotly debated in the public domain. Observing the lay practitioners' increasing freedom to enjoy the Engakuji master's company both inside and
outside the monastery in ways that were often denied to themselves, the
few monks who remained committed to life in the meditation hall despite
the inducements of Meiji society may well have concluded that the time
had come for equal rights in the religious community as in the secular.

Imakita himself recognized the resonance between the recent muti-
nous trend in Zen monasteries, the popular rights debates, and the current spate of rural insurrections that were putatively inspired by notions
of equality and freedom. He wondered whether his rebellious monks had
been influenced by the new egalitarian ethos. In his letter to Tsumaki, the
abbot remarks jocularly that "these [monastic disturbances] vaguely appear to be taking their cue from the rise of popular rights in the world—
ha ha!" Yet Imakita does not summarily dismiss the validity of such
sentiments among his monks; in fact, he duly acknowledges the need for
a new mode of relationship between Zen masters and their disciples:
"I, too, have come to a realization and have repented; from now on, I
am going to reform my way of treating the monks.... I definitely think
that in each matter concerning my disciples I must maintain strict equality...."[42] Neither Imakita nor his monks were oblivious to the implications of the early Meiji debate over popular rights. The age-old problem
of jealousy in the monastery was thus articulated in a language that
played on the contemporary relevance of these issues in society at large.

The lay practitioners, participants in the same socioreligious figuration, did not easily relinquish their own demands for religious "rights."
By the 1880s the mature *koji* and *zenshi* had come to expect, not only
seasonal Zen training sessions in Tokyo, but regular access to monastic
facilities in Kamakura. Questions of time and space accordingly became
flashpoints in the rising tension between the two segments of the Engakuji sangha during these years. For the monks, not only their abbot's
time (his sojourns in Tokyo), but also their own hallowed space (the
meditation hall) were at issue. Imakita had allowed his *koji* and *zenshi*
to practice in the meditation hall from the beginning of his residence at
Engakuji, but when the Tokyo practitioners, led by Kawajiri, asked to
practice in the hall in the spring of 1884, the abbot replied that he would
be unable to accommodate them. Some of the monks were upset about
his alleged neglect of them, Imakita explained, and he had been forced
to consult with the senior priests before making a decision on lay use of
the meditation hall that spring. Until this time the master had evidently

allowed lay practice in the meditation hall by fiat. Once "consulted," however, the monks refused on the grounds that the hall would be in use at the proposed time; they did not wish the *koji* and *zenshi* to practice at Engakuji at all that spring.[43]

In his letter to Kawajiri, Imakita offers a number of reasons for the priests' refusal to grant the Tokyo practitioners' request, including the intense manual labor *(samu)* that was planned for the spring; the monks would be particularly busy preparing for an upcoming exhibition of rare Buddhist treasures in Kamakura, to which Engakuji was scheduled to contribute. The assumption was that the *koji* and *zenshi* required special care during retreats; their inclusion in monastic activities that spring would be an added burden on the temple personnel. Imakita also reports in his letter the monks' concern that permitting lay practitioners to use the *zendō* might violate Buddhist monastic regulations. Allowing the *koji* and *zenshi* to practice alongside the monks would allegedly conflict with the "Buddhist prohibition of going out during a [monastic] retreat."[44] Kawajiri was commissioned to convey the news of the priests' refusal to the rest of the Tokyo *koji* and *zenshi*. By way of compensation, Imakita promised that he would persuade the senior monks to send him to Tokyo that fall to hold a special retreat for the lay practitioners.[45] In the meantime, he encouraged Kawajiri and his companions to visit the temple for short periods of practice on their own (probably in the aforementioned lay quarters, Takuboku-en).

The underlying premise of the various justifications that Imakita cites for the monks' decision was that their commitment to intensive Zen practice during retreats did not cohere with the presence of laypeople; since the *koji* and *zenshi* were held to lesser standards of religious discipline, their presence in the monastic quarters would distract the monks or somehow dilute the power of their Zen practice. The Engakuji priests had apparently concluded that they should reclaim their "traditional" domain, the meditation hall. Ever since Imakita had given the lay adepts access to the *zendō* in 1877, the boundaries between the monastic and lay domains at the temple had become ambiguous. Sack reminds us that "human spatial relations are the results of influence and power."[46] The intrusion of the *koji* and *zenshi* into the heart of the monastic domain appeared to augment lay control of Engakuji and its religious resources. At issue for the monastics was not only physical dominion over the *zendō* structure and its schedule of use but the integrity and prestige of the austere religious lifestyle that it symbolized. They accordingly objected to *any* lay retreat that spring—not only to Imakita's usual spring program in Tokyo, but to any practice session within the Engakuji precincts—much less in the meditation hall, which represented the monks' last enclave of ascetic power.

Aware of the precarious nature of his authority in the Engakuji sangha after the recent unrest, Imakita chose on this occasion to acquiesce. His expulsion of a few rebellious individuals from the Kamakura monastery had not entirely dispelled his monastic followers' dissatisfaction with his administrative style; even the "obedient" individuals who remained at the temple evidently harbored apprehensions about the lay demands. The Engakuji priests accordingly exerted their "popular rights," in Imakita's parlance. By denying lay access to the meditation hall, the monks implemented, in effect, a territorial strategy that strengthened their internal political standing. By drawing a line around the meditation hall, even temporarily, the priests implicitly deprived the *koji* and *zenshi* of a specific form of experiential knowledge, and thus power (or, in Bourdieu's parlance, symbolic capital). The request to use the meditation hall was not merely a demand for the greater convenience or aesthetic satisfaction of practicing in a sacred area; in early-Meiji Rinzai discourse, as we have seen, life in the hall symbolized the essence of Zen training. Sack tells us that human territoriality is a geographical expression of social power that invariably involves a process of classification by area. "When using territoriality, the parent [does] not have to tell the children what they should not touch. They [are] simply not allowed in the room."[47] By banning lay practitioners from the meditation hall in 1884, the Engakuji monks not only reasserted their authority, but managed to avoid (for a time) confronting the detailed reality of their changing relations with the *koji* and *zenshi*.

The abbot's routinization of seasonal lay retreats in the capital, paralleling the monks' winter and summer retreats, and the lay practitioners' regular access to the *zendō* were two important moves in the negotiation of time and space that took place in the Engakuji sangha in the 1880s. To be sure, Zen masters in Japan had long held practice sessions that were open to committed lay practitioners, both at their own and other temples, but the majority of participants in such assemblies during the Tokugawa had been monks and nuns. The Shingaku Zen gatherings and Okunomiya's Ryōmō Society meetings in Tokyo in the 1860s and 1870s had ushered in a new, less temple-centered type of practice in the Kantō area. Imakita's institution of seasonal training sessions designed specifically for the Tokyo *koji* and *zenshi* regularized this urban Zen phenomenon. However, the abbot's periodic dislocation, together with his disregard for traditional boundaries within the temple grounds, raised questions about the true locus of authority in Engakuji and, by implication, in the sangha as a whole. These tensions persisted for some years. We saw in the previous chapter that in 1886, about two years after the meditation-hall dispute, younger Engakuji monks came into conflict with the abbot over the quality of their education. These two episodes were part of a series of disagreements between Imakita and his monks that apparently did not dissipate until at least 1887.

New Boundaries

The debates over lay and monastic prerogatives that took place in the 1880s in Kamakura were part of a general rearrangement of social relations that occurred in Buddhist communities in the early Meiji era. Buddhist historians have long credited the lay activism of the time with the veritable survival of the religion after the Restoration: for example, the Buddhist educator Katō Totsudō remarked in 1933 that "for the most part Meiji Buddhism was sustained by laypeople."[48] Even in their own time, the *koji* (one hears nothing of the *zenshi*) were held up by some observers as exemplars of enlightened practice; they were emblematic of a larger shift from what was depicted in public discourse as the parasitic, corrupt Buddhism of the Edo period to a modern, practical Buddhism that transcended outdated divisions between lay and clerical. In the early 1890s the Sōtō Zen writer Takada Dōken (1858–1923) seemed to argue along these lines when he advocated the idea that the *koji* was a "lay bodhisattva" who "in appearance has not yet attained the realm of liberation, but who in his mind is already seeking this great Way." Ikeda detects in this apparent exaltation of the *koji* an implicit criticism of organized clerical Buddhism.[49] Ketelaar similarly highlights Takada's theory of a "common" or "united" Buddhism *(tsū Bukkyō)* that "would not rely on any single sect for its form or meaning but rather would draw directly from the 'essence of Buddhism itself.'" The new common Buddhism would purportedly transcend not only sectarian divisions but the division between clerical and lay members. In Ketelaar's rendition, Takada believed that "[t]here is ... no 'occupational' distinction between priests and lay persons. Leaving the world *(shukke)* or dwelling within the world *(zaike)* is not merely a matter of corporeal displays but is contingent upon the unity of the body/mind *(shinjin)* and its relation to the teachings themselves." Takada thus "lionized" the model of the lay Buddhist, represented by such paragons as Vimalakīrti and Prince Shōtoku, as "the practical ideal of a modern Buddhism."[50]

The *koji* were indeed depicted in Meiji discourse as peculiarly qualified to bring about a true revival of Buddhism in the modern, secular world because, like Vimalakīrti, they had mastered the art of acting freely in that world while remaining in constant service to the Dharma. There was another side, however, to this public glorification of the lay practitioner. Ikeda and Ketelaar notwithstanding, Takada's tribute to legendary lay bodhisattvas was accompanied by sharp criticism of the contemporary *koji* phenomenon in Japan. He denounced the casual way in which unqualified people were appropriating the appellation *"koji"*:

> Especially in recent times it seems to have become the fashion of the mo-
> ment to use a *koji* name. It has reached the point where everyone imagin-
> able uses a *koji* name on some pretext or other, whether [the person]
> merely gives speeches on Buddhism as a hobby—in a dilettantish way—
> holds a lecture, writes a book about Buddhism, researches a Buddhist text,
> carries out some enterprise for the Buddhist community, uses his influence
> [on its behalf], or firmly places his faith in Buddhism. . . .[51]

Takada goes on to complain that the *koji* rubric was being utilized not
only by uncommitted Buddhists, but even by Christians and atheists who
had no understanding of what it really meant.[52] As far as the Sōtō writer
was concerned, the high estimation of *koji* Buddhism during his time was
largely due to the efforts of "one or two powerful gentlemen *[jinshi]*,"
who in the wake of the anti-Buddhist campaign of the first Meiji years
had spontaneously designated themselves *koji* and invested themselves
in the public promotion of Buddhism. This popularization of the title
had come at a price, however. According to Takada, it was now impossible to distinguish which of the multiplying *koji* were authentic Buddhist
practitioners.[53]

    Takada notes that the title *"koji"* was part of continental Asian
usage even before the spread of Buddhism, and that for the most part it
had simply designated gentlemen of moral character who pursued some
form of the Way. However, he argued, since *"koji"* later evolved into a
term that possessed specific Buddhist connotations, it should not now be
bandied about without regard for its meaning.[54] Drawing on the same
apologetical stock that had served Imakita, Takada holds up Su Shi,
Huang Tingjian, and Zhang Shangying as paradigmatic Chinese lay
Buddhists.[55] The title *"koji,"* in the author's view, was meant to indicate
respect for devout Buddhist laymen like these—hence the Zen custom
of granting the title to practitioners by way of certifying their religious
commitment. From Takada's perspective, the number of genuine *koji*
in Meiji society, contrary to appearances, was thus rather small. Even
though numerous authentic *koji* had indeed mastered the "profound
principles" of Buddhism in the past and during his own time, he warns,
"we should remember that [their numbers] do not match those of the
assured gentlemen who have left home *(shukke daijōbu no shi)*." The
Buddhist priest, or "assured gentleman" had attained a level of awakening or liberation from "the cycle of life and death," and was free of "the
dust of the secular world," but the *koji* was still immersed in the world
of delusion.[56]

    Support for the new *koji* phenomenon was evidently qualified even among priests who vigorously advocated a modernized, "common" Buddhism. In the final analysis, even the most committed lay practitioners were not considered to be on a par with ordained clergy. Takada, for one, was far from doing away with the distinction between lay practitioners and clergy. If anything, his interpretation of the popularization of the term *"koji"* in Meiji society suggests that at least some priests perceived the Buddhist establishment to be losing control of the processes of religious authentication; the perception was probably exacerbated by the appropriation of Buddhist language by Christians and others for their own purposes. The priestly institution, in Takada's view, needed to re-assert its authority over the conferral of the title *"koji"* and, by implication, over the lay members of the Buddhist sangha.

The concern about the long-term significance of the *koji* phenomenon was one vector in the larger debate over clerical status and identity that took place in Meiji Japan. The very meaning of the terminology used to designate the social position of the Buddhist clergy was transformed during this period, as Jaffe points out. "The changes in clerical status [in the early 1870s] made it increasingly difficult for the clergy to argue that ordination meant 'leaving home.'"[57] What with the normalization of the clergy's social status and the vitiation of monastic identity by the clerical marriage decrees, the growing prominence of lay leaders in the sangha no doubt added to some priests' sense that their customary life-world was vanishing. I should add that it was not only in the monastic sects that conflicts arose between the two divisions of the sangha. Ikeda tells us that tensions between lay and clerical members of the Honganji True Pure Land sect rose appreciably in the late 1880s; during this period the sect's revisions of its regulations for teaching assemblies and lay societies show that "the former spirit of 'oneness between clergy and laity' *(sōzoku ittai)* had fundamentally collapsed."[58] Disputes between members of the clergy and laity during this period were not peculiar to Engakuji.

The intramural tensions in the Kamakura monastery did not have a revolutionary impact in the long term. The 1884 conflict over the meditation hall cleared the ground for a slightly reformed style of relations between the two sectors of the Engakuji community, but it did not lead to a lessening of clerical control of religious authentication. The debate that took place at Engakuji over the use of the meditation hall seems to have resulted primarily in attempts to formalize and modulate lay conduct in the monastery. The need for regulation of the lay practitioners' behavior no doubt appeared more pressing to the Engakuji priests as the lay adepts' numbers expanded during the last years of Imakita's life. The abbot's second lay register, which covers the period from August 1885 through July 1891, contains 367 names in all; an additional number of lay followers who did not sign the register practiced at Engakuji during these years as well.[59]

The regularization of the lay program is documented in the 1885 preface to the register, which contains a set of rules for the *koji* dormitory (Takuboku-en) issued by the monastery administration. The content of the rules confirms that the lay practice of the mid-1880s had grown away from the more informal groupings of Imakita's first years in the Kantō area. The text opens with a call for religious commitment: "We all wish to spur ourselves on, arouse a strong faith, practice intensively under the guidance of the master, and completely invest ourselves in seated meditation. It is essential that we not regard these [aims] at all lightly."[60] A subsequent article affirms that mature members who have been practicing for a long time are responsible for enforcing the group's regulations and that their instructions are authorized by the abbot. The number of *koji* and *zenshi* who were practicing at the temple was now large enough to allow some sort of differentiation or channeling of authority among them, based on seniority.

Most of the rules, however, deal with external details. Those who used the lay quarters were expected to pay their keep by supplying rice and firewood to the temple treasurer once a week; they were also required to follow the customary rules of the "school" *(gakurin)* for disposition of bedding and for eating, and to clean the floors inside and outside Takuboku-en. The practitioners were further warned not to read books in bed or leave them scattered around the dormitory. Moreover, insofar as Takuboku-en was "a pure building of the head temple" *(honzan seijō garan),* its inhabitants were expected to refrain from eating or drinking anything "unclean," that is, anything that would contravene monastic strictures, particularly meat and alcohol.[61] Residents of Takuboku-en were also warned not to visit local shops or buy food and beverages when they were walking outside the temple gates, not to be "hurried and disorderly" when entering and leaving the boardinghouse, and not to waste time chatting with each other.[62] Such activities would normally have been forbidden to the monastic residents of Engakuji, and perhaps the lay practitioners' indulgence in these vices during past monastery sojourns had been irksome to the monks.[63] However, the rules' position on the central issue, the use of the meditation hall, seems to represent a concession by the monastic community. It is reiterated in no uncertain terms that "during retreats one is absolutely required to present oneself in the meditation hall for meditation." Apparently the monks' opposition to lay use of the *zendō* had subsided in the year and some months since the Tokyo *koji* were refused access in 1884.

The guidelines for Okunomiya Zōsai's earlier lay society, Ryōmō Kyōkai, provide an instructive contrast to the 1885 rules. Unlike the latter, the Ryōmō precepts refer to playing go, reading poetry, and practicing calligraphy during group meetings; they also allow modest consumption of alcohol and meat. The different tone of the two sets of rules is of course related to the fact that Rinshōin, the site of the Ryōmō meetings, was not a full-fledged Rinzai monastery, nor did the society members lodge there overnight. But the emergence in the 1885 code of a narrower focus on group discipline and an implicit preoccupation with not violating monastic sensibilities was also a response to the growing prominence of the lay program and the recent internal troubles at Engakuji. Significantly, it was not until after the 1884 monastic "strike" that any rules at all were established for the lay residence at Engakuji, even though the Tokyo practitioners had begun to use Takuboku-en as many as eight years earlier. The incident seems to have alerted both the lay and monastic sectors of the community to the need for clearer boundaries. The resultant codification marked a compromise between the monks' presumption of authority, expressed in territorial terms, and the lay practitioners' demand for access to that authority. In the final analysis, the *koji* and *zenshi* retained their prerogative to use the meditation hall, but they were required to follow a more rigorous standard of behavior while in residence.

Gender and Social Identity in the Engakuji Lay Program

The rules for the lay quarters are notably silent about issues pertinent to the *zenshi*. The code refers generically to the comportment of the *koji*, even though some of the rules presumably were applicable to both groups, since men and women practiced together in Takuboku-en and in the meditation hall. Women were a relatively strong presence in the Engakuji program during the Meiji. Forty-two of the practitioners listed in Imakita's 1885 lay register are women, and at least thirty-one of these recorded their *dōgō* or religious names: in other words, about two-thirds of the women listed in the register were mature practitioners who had already attained *zenshi* status. In contrast, only about one-third of the 103 men listed in the register had attained the status of *koji*. Contrary to Fields' supposition, women apparently did not have to wait until Shaku Sōkatsu revived the Ryōmō Society in the twentieth century to practice Zen in any numbers.[64] In fact, the Engakuji *zenshi*'s religious commitment appears to have been proportionally stronger than that of their male companions.

Many of these women were the mothers, wives, and sisters of the *koji* who frequented Engakuji. Zen Buddhist practice is often depicted as an individual pursuit, but in this particular context it was clearly a family affair, much like other forms of religious activity in Japan. However (and not unexpectedly, given the prevalent tendency among Japanese men of the time to be reticent about their female associates and relatives), neither Imakita nor his leading *koji* refer extensively in their writings to the *zenshi*. The abbot mentions a few female followers in his correspondence: Tsumaki Ayako (Seiheki's wife), her daughter, Suda Eyū; Izawa Ochiyo; and Kawajiri Esō.[65] All of these women were married to men who practiced under Imakita. In his letters the abbot expresses high regard especially for Esō's religious practice and commitment, including her study of the *Diamond Sūtra* and her daily devotions to the bodhisattvic deity Kannon. Elsewhere he testifies that Esō unfailingly accompanied Kawajiri every time he came to Engakuji to practice (spanning a period of more than ten years, at the time of Imakita's writing).[66] In other correspondence the Zen master urges Tsumaki Ayako to practice *zazen,* and vigorously encourages several of the *zenshi* to come to Kamakura; he carefully reassures them that "arrangements for lodging and board will be quite easily settled ahead of time."[67] Imakita thus genuinely welcomed the participation of women in the Engakuji program.

Given that traditional Buddhist regulations prohibited women from entering monastic precincts, it is surprising to find that female lay practitioners were routinely allowed to practice in the Engakuji meditation hall along with monks during the early Meiji. As we saw earlier, strictures against female visitors to the monastery had been repeatedly iterated by Engakuji-line administrators in the aftermath of the clerical marriage decree (although these injunctions presumably targeted women associated with individual priests, not the *zenshi*). Yet the available evidence about the lay program of this time indicates that although the *zenshi* and *koji* slept in different buildings, the women practitioners indeed practiced along with the *koji* as a group, and thus shared the meditation hall with the monks during retreats. Perhaps the presence of female practitioners in the monastic quarters was one of the reasons Imakita's monks lost patience with lay demands in 1884; the *zendō* was, after all, a long-established male domain in the Gozan Zen community. Imakita's (and his successors') liberalization of the *vinaya* in this regard appears to be distinctive. According to Inoue Zenjō, unlike the Kyoto Gozan institutions, Engakuji has permitted female practitioners to use its *zendō* ever since Imakita's time (except for the aforementioned hiatus in the mid-1880s, when the monks refused access to all lay practitioners). Inoue reports that even in 1937, when he was practicing at Tenryūji in Kyoto, women were strictly prohibited from entering its *zendō*.[68]

Faure has commented that "[d]espite—or because of—the theoretical equality it posits between the sexes, Chan [Zen] was an essentially masculine discourse, defined by its patriarchal tradition: for all the talk about robes, there are no women, no matriarchs there."[69] Attitudes at

Engakuji during the Meiji epitomize this tension between theoretical and practical equality among men and women in the Zen sangha. In the text of a portrait inscription that Imakita wrote for Kawajiri Hōkin and Esō, he quotes at length from the well-known passage in the *Vimalakīrti Sūtra* in which the arhat Śāriputra, personifying Hinayana ignorance, confronts an enlightened goddess. The deity demonstrates to him that, at the ultimate level of truth, the distinction between male or female does not exist: gender is simply a provisional attribute.[70] Taking this passage as his cue, Imakita wrote: "In body and mind, the Kawajiris, husband and wife, are neither the same nor different."[71] He identifies Esō and her husband with an ultimate, transsexual reality, and thus depicts them as equal and complimentary in value. In actuality, however, judging from temple records, none of the *zenshi* occupied leadership roles of any kind in the Engakuji circle, although they were probably active volunteers, especially in fund-raising efforts.

There is no question that after the Restoration the Kamakura monastery began to welcome more women into the higher tiers of its religious program; indeed, many of Imakita's longtime female followers may have invited their sons, husbands, or brothers to practice Zen with them in Kamakura. The modest rise in female participation, especially during the 1880s (and 1890s, judging from Shaku Sōen's lay register), perhaps indicates a loosening of traditional prejudices about women's religious capacities—in Japanese society at large as well as within the Rinzai monastery.[72] It must be said, however, that the diligence of the *zenshi* did not alter the public status quo; even the most accomplished among them, Esō, is for the most part a silent presence in the history of this community. Perhaps in some historical settings "the impulse for an egalitarian Chan seems to have come largely from lay circles," but in this particular context, similar attitudes toward women seem to have characterized both the lay and the monastic sectors.[73] The Tokyo *zenshi* were more avid practitioners of Zen than their grandmothers had been, but their growing presence at Engakuji was not accompanied by any deterioration of the Zen Buddhist "masculine discourse." Several of the men who practiced alongside their mothers and wives at Engakuji were involved, as we shall see, in promoting social agendas that, on the contrary, had distinctly conservative implications for the position of women in Meiji society.

Many of the Zen practitioners included in Imakita's 1885 register belonged to a younger set who had no firsthand knowledge of the Tokugawa world. Both the older and younger adepts, however, tended to have similar social origins and occupations. Like Imakita's mature followers, the young people who began practicing at Engakuji in the late 1880s interacted with each other in other social contexts; some were related to the older generation of practitioners through family ties. One of the most active and influential *koji* of this period was Hayakawa Senkichirō (Setsudō; 1863–1922), the son of a samurai from Kanazawa (in Ishikawa prefecture), who had traveled to England during the early Meiji years. His mother, Katsumi, began practicing at Engakuji in 1883; she received her *zenshi* name (Eshō) from Imakita during a retreat several years later.[74] In the early 1890s, Hayakawa was a secretary in the Ministry of the Treasury, but he began working for the Mitsui company in 1900 and eventually became executive director of the Mitsui network of enterprises. Hayakawa was also the head of Kuchōkan, a Tokyo boardinghouse for samurai-descent students from Ishikawa, which he cofounded along with Hōjō Tokiyuki (Chikuu; 1858–1929).

Hōjō was another Engakuji regular, and his mother, Toshi, was a longtime disciple of Imakita. In the mid-1880s the young Hōjō was teaching math in Kanazawa at a highly ranked secondary institution; he went on to become an eminent educator, serving in such capacities as president of Tōhoku University and head of Gakushūin. Two years after Imakita died, Hōjō edited and published the abbot's offical biography *(Sōryōkutsu nenpu)* in consultation with Shaku Sōen. Like many of Imakita's younger followers, Hōjō retained his ties to the Engakuji practice into the twentieth century. D. T. Suzuki (Suzuki Daisetsu Teitarō, 1870–1966) was Hōjō's student in Ishikawa, and later attributed his initial interest in Zen to his schoolteacher[75] Hayakawa, however, first invited the young man to practice at Engakuji; Suzuki formally joined Imakita's lay practice in 1891 and, as is well known, went on to become the preeminent popularizer of Zen Buddhism in the West.

Suzuki is only one of the more famous members of an elite group of young people, closely associated with Hōjō and Hayakawa, who began to practice Zen at Engakuji during Imakita's late years.[76] In the late 1880s and early 1890s, young men flocked to Tokyo from all over the country in quest of higher schooling, whether at Tokyo Imperial University or at one of the reputable private schools in the capital. The Imperial University students in particular, who were cultivated for positions in the central government, tended to remain in the capital after graduation.[77] A number of these students and graduates seem to have found a home away from home in Kamakura. In addition to the Ishikawa students already mentioned, this young Zen circle included Suzuki Masaya (Shinjō; 1861–1922), who later became the director of Sumitomo; his brother Akizuki Satsuo (Kidō), later the Japanese ambassador to Belgium; and Toki Hiroshi (Zōge), who worked for Tokyo First National Bank. Another member of this group, Hiranuma Kiichirō (Kige; 1867–1952), had a long and peculiarly illustrious career. After distinguishing himself in the judiciary, Hiranuma headed the Privy Council, served as prime minister (briefly, in 1939), and even lived to be imprisoned as a "class A" war criminal after the Pacific War. Hirayama Sentarō, Kawamura Yoshimasa, and Suga Torao (Mui) were also part of this network of promising Zen *koji*.[78]

In diary entries dating to the late 1880s, Hōjō mentions Hayakawa, Suzuki Masaya, and Toki almost daily; he also refers frequently to Hiranuma, Hirayama, Kawamura, and Suga. This group of friends apparently continued to thrive in the 1890s and beyond. Suga, for example, invited the great writer Natsume Sōseki (1867–1916) to Engakuji to practice Zen under Shaku Sōen in 1894.[79] Natsume's close friend, Yoneyama Hosaburō (Tennen), also began to practice at Engakuji during Imakita's last years. This circle reportedly also included such future luminaries as Ichiki Kitokurō (1867–1944), who became a Tokyo University professor and served prominently in several government ministries; Hayashi Gonsuke (1860–1939), later a leading Foreign Ministry official; and Uchida Kōsai (1865–1936), who served as foreign minister under several administrations in the twentieth century.[80]

The members of this group were not just former schoolmates, but intimates. Several of them organized educational activities together; they also took walks together, visited each other's homes in Tokyo, attended the same funerals and weddings, and engaged in long discussions about the importance of educating young people for the future of Japan.[81] One of the most regular ways in which these emerging leaders nurtured their commitment to a shared vision of the future was by practicing Zen together. Hōjō records at least four occasions during 1889 in which he attended Zen sessions under Imakita with various members of this group.[82] Other participants in the Engakuji lay practice (not necessarily connected with the Hōjō group) were similarly involved in educational or intellectual activities. Many were enrolled in secondary or specialized schools *(senmongakkō),* and some had studied abroad; a good number were already employed as schoolteachers and newspaper reporters. A significant contingent was composed of military-academy students and other individuals connected to the navy or army.

I have been able to confirm the identity of only a minority of persons who, because of the importance of their positions or connections, are mentioned in a source other than Imakita's register. Consequently, this social profile of the Engakuji lay circle in the late 1880s and early 1890s may be skewed in favor of its prominent members. It is safe to conclude, however, that the Kamakura program attracted a good number of educated people who commuted from their workplaces, schools, or homes in Tokyo. (A majority of the lay registrants listed Tokyo as their current address, although many also came from other areas near Kamakura, such as the Izu peninsula and Yokohama.)

The growth of the Engakuji lay practice during the late nineteenth century may be attributed to a number of factors, mundane and other. First, the centralization of national affairs in Tokyo led to greater interest in nearby resorts where urbanites could spend a few scenic days away from the busy capital. Practitioners no doubt enjoyed the authenticity of Kamakura, a traditional pilgrimage center full of Buddhist temples, not to mention the famous Hachiman Shrine. As we have seen, a good number of these adepts were enterprising young men destined to occupy leading positions in Japanese society; they may have found the Kamakura excursions an opportunity to step outside their daily routine and bond with others of like interests. In addition, the opening in 1889 of a Kamakura station on the new Yokozuka railway line greatly facilitated transportation for these Tokyo visitors;[83] previously, the trip reportedly required two hours by boat from Tokyo (Shinbashi) to Kamakura.[84]

Although Imakita did not necessarily initiate or organize this migration of practitioners in the late 1880s, his friendly treatment of the Tokyo *koji* and *zenshi,* later enhanced by Shaku Sōen's own charisma, undoubtedly also contributed to the popularity of the Engakuji program. The abbot's relatively late tonsure after a career as a Confucian scholar perhaps lent him what Katsu Kaishū disdainfully called "a rather secular air"[85]—yet this very openness to the nonreligious life may well have attracted the abbot's urban following. Indeed, a key factor in Imakita's personal appeal, both to the older *koji* who had been educated in the Tokugawa and to the younger men who pursued successful careers in the early twentieth century, was the abbot's reputation for Confucian learning. It is telling in this regard that Imakita's younger contemporary, Rinzai master Nantenbō (Tōshū Zenchū; 1839–1925), considered Engakuji-line teachers suspect because of their association with the urban intelligentsia.[86] Ironically, one of Nantenbō's own lay disciples, the aforementioned Hiranuma Kiichirō, claimed that he left his master's Tokyo program to practice in Kamakura precisely because of Imakita's alleged intellectual abilities. Hiranuma later commented, "I did not take to [Nantenbō] because he had no learning *[gakumon].*" The one-time prime minister firmly believed that Imakita was the most learned Zen master of the late nineteenth century because, after all, "he was originally a Confucian scholar and engaged in Chinese learning."[87]

Imakita's personal reputation for learning was only one factor in the success of the Kamakura program, however. After his death in 1892, the well-traveled Shaku Sōen, who was trained in both Chinese and Western forms of learning, proved even more effective than his teacher in attracting urban intellectuals to the Kamakura resort.[88] The quest for learning, however defined, was a common theme among up-and-coming young people during this period. Many, like Hiranuma, continued to echo the old conceit that learning was, by definition, Confucian studies. Perhaps the type of Confucian-flavored Zen taught at Engakuji in the late nineteenth century drew men like Hiranuma, Hōjō, and even the young D. T. Suzuki because it appeared to offer them a time-honored form of personal improvement during a period in which such "traditions" were newly attractive—the same period in which Motoda, Nishimura, and other public educators successfully lobbied for the return of Confucian education under other names. Katō once remarked that in the immediate aftermath of the anti-Buddhist campaign of the first Meiji years, even people who had formerly been well-disposed toward Buddhism were "ashamed to enter the temple gates," but that by the mid-Meiji, members of the younger generation (who had been educated in the new school system) began to evince a new interest in Buddhist "learning."[89] The style of Zen practice that Imakita advocated may have attracted educational elites partly because of its perceived affinity with older systems of moral improvement.

In the final analysis, however, the Engakuji program was successful in the Meiji period because it was open-ended enough to encompass, not only traditional conceptions of personal cultivation, but also the more utilitarian interpretations that were in vogue at this time. The figures who were most active in the Engakuji community during the first two Meiji decades, such as Yamaoka, Kawajiri, and Torio Tokuan, recall the age-old ideal of the well-endowed lay bodhisattva, active in the marketplace. This ideal was not inconsistent with the new practical learning that was promoted in Meiji public discourse as the key to success. Imakita's Tokyo *koji*, many of whom were involved in government or education, seem to have exemplified the model of the "man of culture" that was taking shape at this time in the Japanese public imagination: an educated, even cosmopolitan individual who combined rigorous personal discipline with social and political involvement. The younger generation of lay disciples, such as Hōjō, Hiranuma, and D. T. Suzuki, integrated the professional and moral dimensions of *gakumon* even more successfully than their predecessors. During the late Meiji, a growing number of these gentlemen-bodhisattvas put their cultural and political capital to work in service of both the Dharma and the nation.

CHAPTER 8

The Great Synthesis

DURING THE SAME years in which lay practitioners were making their presence felt in long-standing Buddhist institutions like Engakuji, the members of less-established communities were reconceiving their socio-religious identities through a state-sponsored process of centralization, leading in several cases to their official designation as "Shinto sects." These Meiji groupings were highly diverse. Some originated in the activities of charismatic leaders whose ideas and practices had developed into identifiable religious systems before the end of the Tokugawa period. These popular, often syncretic movements, which have come to be called "Shinto-derived new religions" *(Shintōkei shinshūkyō)*, found the quest for recognition in the Meiji era an uphill battle. Even if they had managed, whether by subterfuge or circumstance, to retain some sort of chimeric self-identity during their underground years in the preceding regime, they now succeeded in surviving as religious bodies only at a cost to that identity, by affiliating with more powerful, government-approved religious bodies.[1]

A number of smaller Tokugawa groups placed themselves under the jurisdiction of the "umbrella" sects associated with "sect Shinto" *(kyōha Shintō)*.[2] These sects were not inspired by the revelations of charismatic founders but were deliberately created by nativist enthusiasts in the aftermath of the Great Teaching Campaign. Their organizers were mostly former shogunal officials or state-appointed "shrine administrators" (in Hardacre's parlance) who took upon themselves the task of constructing one or another version of the true Japanese faith. The government encouraged the formation of these associations in the interests of raising money and human resources for its ideological campaign in the 1870s. In contrast to the new religions, which were founded with the aim of resolving the pressing spiritual and physical needs of their constituents, the umbrella Shinto sects were designed in the first place to promote a national creed.[3] Their teachings were generally framed by the ideology of the Three Standards of Instruction and often referred to shrine rituals and ancient Japanese narratives. However, they also comprehended pre-Meiji strains of thought and practice that had far less claim to the appellation "Shinto"—whether Confucian teachings, yin-yang philosophy, prognostication, meditation, or mountain devotionalism.

Murakami Shigeyoshi expresses the consensus of many twentieth-century scholars in his remark that "the lumping together of these religions of diverse origins under the rubric of sect Shinto was an artificial, policy-type measure taken by the government in order to establish state Shinto *[kokka Shintō]*."[4] At the same time, however, numerous religious associations *(kō* or *kōsha)* that had been outlawed in the Tokugawa period welcomed the opportunity to legitimize their activities by reconfiguring themselves under the auspices of the Great Teaching Campaign and, ultimately, sect Shinto.[5] A good deal of voluntarism and self-interest on the part of these preexisting groups therefore figured in the "lumping together." Although sect Shinto clearly served the state's centralizing needs and the ideological ambitions of nativist leaders, it was also shaped by the interests of the various groups that made up the particular sects. This chapter describes the formation of a classic administrative sect of this kind, Shintō Taiseikyō, and summarizes its founder's general aims and understanding of personal cultivation. The story of the origins of Taiseikyō demonstrates the role of pre-Meiji social and religious formations in the creation of the Shinto sects: the groups highlighted earlier in this book were instrumental in the emergence of this particular sect.

Our knowledge of the formation of Taiseikyō is in fact based largely on information associated with the groups that initially composed it, as well as on biographical materials related to its founder. Tohokami is especially important in this regard; the story of Inoue Masakane's followers in the first Meiji years may even be considered a prehistory of Taiseikyō. After the Meiji state lifted the shogunal ban against Inoue's teachings in 1869, his followers began to lobby for official recognition of the group as a religious body. Tōgū Chiwaki (1833–1897), a Hachiman shrine priest of Shimotsuke who had become a disciple of Murakoshi Morikazu in 1856, opened a temporary training center in Tokyo and initiated procedures to obtain authorization of the movement from the Department of Shinto (Jingikan).[6] Tōgū was a trained nativist: he had studied in Hirata Kanetane's school in late 1868 and under another Hirata disciple, Inō Hidenori (1805–1877), in 1869.[7] Records indicate that, like other post-Tokugawa religious leaders of the time, he sought to render his group's teachings more compatible with the early Meiji government's nativist stance. In a Tohokami manual that he wrote in 1870, for example, Tōgū requires members to possess certain works of Hirata

Atsutane.[8] During this period he also enlisted the help of Onari (Masakane's widow), Murakoshi Morikazu, and another Tohokami elder, Nozawa Kanenori, in "documenting" the transmission of the Tohokami teachings from the great nativist scholar Kamo Mabuchi to Inoue Masakane (via the latter's father).[9]

Just after the Ministry of Doctrine was established, Tōgū and other Tohokami members submitted a petition formally requesting public recognition of the group; they claimed a membership of over three thousand in the Tokyo area. Three months later the ministry duly recognized Inoue's followers under the name "Tohokami-kō";[10] Nozawa, Tōgū, and another colleague were appointed doctrinal instructors and given charge of the group. It is worth noting that Tōgū reportedly recommended Nozawa for the highest rank because of the latter's longtime connections with Honjō Munehide, who was now a prominent ministry official.[11] Honjō indeed helped facilitate the ministry's approval of Tohokami, just as he did in the case of Shingaku. Soon after the Tohokami petition was granted, the former daimyo summoned Inoue's followers to his residence to celebrate the good news with them.[12]

Tohokami members benefited in other ways from Honjō Munehide's connections. He is believed to have introduced Inoue's teachings to the future founder of Taiseikyō, Hirayama Seisai (1815–1890).[13] Hirayama, the second son of a *kendō* master of Mutsu domain, had studied Chinese learning under the Confucian scholar Asaka Gonsai (1791–1860) and nativism under Maeda Natsukage (1793–1864).[14] In his mid-thirties the young samurai succeeded to the position of his father-in-law, a shogunal retainer in charge of minor construction projects, and thereafter advanced through a series of posts in the Bakufu. In 1852 he was assigned to help the shogunate in foreign relations, and by 1866 had become a superintendent in the Office of Foreign Affairs (*gaikoku bugyō*). He remained loyal to the shogunal side during the events leading up to the Restoration and consequently was sentenced to house arrest by the new Meiji state. Hirayama accordingly moved to Shizuoka (following the Tokugawa family) and opened a Chinese studies school there, but he was soon pardoned and given complete freedom to travel. After the Ministry of Doctrine opened in Tokyo, Hirayama was appointed a doctrinal instructor; in 1873 he became head priest of the Hikawa Shrine (in Saitama prefecture) and in 1875 (concurrently) priest of the important Hie Shrine.[15]

Honjō Munehide and Hirayama Seisai may have been on friendly terms from before the Restoration, as both men dealt with foreign affairs on behalf of the shogunate during its last years. Alternatively, Honjō may have came into contact with Hirayama and imparted the Tohokami teachings to him immediately after the Restoration (in Shizuoka or Tokyo).[16] The two probably cemented their relations during the early 1870s, when both worked at the Ministry of Doctrine and served as major shrine priests. In any event, Hirayama clearly favored the Tohokami/Misogikyō community throughout his career as a priest and sect leader. Tokoyo Nagatane (1832–1886), another Shinto figure of the time, confirms in his writings that the Tohokami group played a central role in Hirayama's Taisei organization.[17] Furthermore, perhaps through his connections with the Honjō household, during the early 1870s Hirayama had become closely acquainted with the Tohokami teacher Tōgū Chiwaki, who like himself served as both doctrinal instructor and shrine priest during this period. Tōgū became acting priest *(gon-negi)* of the Hikawa Shrine late in 1873, the same year that Hirayama was appointed head priest of the institution; other Tohokami members also served in the shrine's administration.[18] Apparently with Hirayama's cooperation, Tōgū set up a religious program at the Hikawa Shrine that was based on Inoue's Masakane's teachings.

During this period Tohokami-kō was a transitory alliance rather than a unified religious community. Inoue's followers had pursued their mission in separate locations under the shadow of the shogunal prohibition for nearly three decades, and by the early 1870s they had split into a number of groups, each led by an independent-minded leader. In the Kantō area many believers were part of the Honjō-Tōgū network, but others followed the lead of Masakane's senior disciple, Sakata Kaneyasu. After the Restoration, Sakata had pursued his own quest for a modern, legal version of Masakane's teachings. The former village headman successfully lobbied to have the group's name changed from Tohokami to Misogi, and by the end of 1876, according to one source, the Bureau of Shinto Affairs (Shintō Jimukyoku) appointed him leader of "Misogi Kōsha."[19] During the same year, perhaps in order to safeguard his own lineage further, Sakata also gained permission from the bureau to lead a group of Misogi followers under the auspices of a government-approved association called Ishin Kyōkai. However, in 1877 the bureau appointed Hirayama Seisai to supervise the entire Misogi movement; with Hirayama's encouragement the various faction leaders decided to appoint Tōgū as the community's director *(honshachō)*. Sakata Kaneyasu and several other teachers were relegated to the status of group leaders *(shachō)*.[20]

Needless to say, Sakata was unhappy with this arrangement and the factionalization of the Misogi community intensified. Tensions peaked when the various groups of Inoue's followers failed to agree on the procedures for reburying the founder's remains in 1878 and for building a shrine dedicated to him in the following years.[21] The ultimate effect of these conflicts was the alienation of Sakata's group (which later came to be called "Misogikyō") from Tōgū's followers, who continued to work closely with Hirayama and the Honjō household. The latter was now headed by Honjō's oldest son, Munetake (Jōan; 1846–1893), the head priest of Kono Shrine in Miyazu and an erstwhile doctrinal instructor in his own right. In an apparent attempt to preserve the movement's integrity, in early 1879 Munetake established a clearinghouse for all the Misogi groups, called the Bureau of Misogikyō Affairs (Misogikyō Jimukyoku). However, Sakata formally withdrew from the association later that year and concentrated on building up his following in Ishin Kyōkai.[22]

Hirayama now took the opportunity to initiate his own organization, initially called Taisei Kyōkai (Teaching Association of the Great Synthesis). The remaining members of the Misogikyō Bureau placed themselves under Hirayama's jurisdiction; they reported to him regarding administrative and educational matters, rather than directly to the Bureau of Shinto Affairs, as they had done previously.[23] This arrangement was politically convenient for Hirayama's close associate, Honjō Munetake. Both Hirayama and Honjō were now well-known figures in the Shinto world. Hirayama had participated actively in efforts to resolve the disagreements among shrine administrators in the 1870s that culminated in the so-called pantheon dispute *(saijin ronsō)* between the Ise and Izumo shrine factions.[24] Honjō had taken the Izumo side, thereby placing himself in opposition to the Bureau of Shinto Affairs, which was dominated by the Ise faction.[25] Honjō Munetake's allocation of his and Tōgū's Misogi followers to Hirayama's new Taisei group may have been a strategy to bypass the local office of the bureau, which would otherwise have directly controlled the administration of his members' activities.

In the pantheon debate Hirayama publicly adopted a neutral stance.[26] In a memorial to the government he argued that the choice of deities to be worshiped in each shrine or teaching association should depend on the preferences of its parishioners.[27] To be sure, the Shinto leader's conciliatory attitude during this controversy may not have been completely disinterested; his accommodating attitude toward Honjō's pro-Izumo activism facilitated a large influx of Inoue Masakane's followers into his budding organization, thereby providing it with a necessary economic foundation. Later, as we shall see, Hirayama and his successors overlooked debatable aspects of other Taisei enrollees, probably also for economic reasons.

Yet whether Hirayama was a genuine universalist at heart or simply prevaricated for his own reasons during the pantheon dispute, his advocacy of a Shinto informed by individual religious preferences, rather than by a set orthopraxy, was eminently consistent with the premises of

Taisei Kyōkai.[28] In early 1882, when the Home Ministry prohibited imperial and national shrine priests from serving as doctrinal instructors, Hirayama joined several other shrine administrators of the time in resigning his priestly status in order to devote himself fully to his group's proselytizing activities. Later that year the Taisei association was officially designated a Shinto sect (initially called Shintō Taiseiha; later, Taiseikyō).[29]

The Purpose of Taiseikyō

The ideas propagated by Taiseikyō and the other umbrella Shinto sects were largely determined in their formative stages by the defensive ideological aims of the Great Teaching Campaign of the 1870s, in which their leaders generally played a prominent role. In an 1885 manifesto of the aims of Taiseikyō, Hirayama argued that Shinto was clearly the supreme way of humankind, but that its tenets were not yet firmly established in Japan, even though the Meiji government had encouraged its development. This state of affairs, Hirayama warned, did not augur well for protecting the populace from erroneous foreign ideas.[30] Like many other social educators of the time, the Taiseikyō leader affirmed the potential benefits of Western systems of knowledge. As far as he was concerned, it was the will of the gods that the Japanese people utilize Western legal, military, and scientific methods. He insisted, for example, that the native deities Ōkuni-nushi and Sukuna-hikona had first established the laws of medicine and incantation, as recorded in the ancient chronicles, but allowed that other viable medical knowledge had later been introduced into Japan from China and the Western countries.[31] In other words, although all things originally derived from the Japanese gods, with the passing of time and the changing of historical conditions, different forms of knowledge had been and could be successfully assimilated into the pristine heritage, including Western practical knowledge. In a similar vein, Hirayama allowed that sages had appeared in every country, indeed that all cultures offered workable religious alternatives —but in the final analysis, the Shinto and Confucian teachings were supreme.[32]

The stated aim of Taiseikyō was thus to combine Confucian teachings, the scientific insights of the West, and Japanese forms of learning— in other words, to illuminate the people of Japan by means of their own traditions combined with the best of foreign civilization.[33] Needless to say, this synthesis did not include Christian teachings. Hirayama characterized Christianity as a harmful body of ideas and practices that posed the ultimate threat to Japanese moral integrity and national security. The main purpose of popular education, from the Shinto leader's perspective, was in fact to oppose the presumed influence of Christian ideas. Like the voluntary Buddhist associations of the time (discussed in the next chapter), Hirayama's "Great Synthesis" was less concerned with the enactment of a body of teachings than with their propagation. An article in the *Tōkyō Yokohama Mainichi* newspaper, published just before the Taisei association was officially designated a Shinto sect, reported that Hirayama's stated objective in forming the group was to refute Christianity. As the sect's members grew in number, according to the writer, Hirayama planned to expand his anti-Christian campaign to Kyushu and Shikoku, and eventually as far as Korea and China.[34]

The Taisei leader's strategic plan is a classic example of the defensive stance toward foreign ideologies that characterized mid-Meiji religious discourse as a whole. From this perspective, Taiseikyō appears to have been simply an expedient grouping of plausible Japanese religious traditions in the battle for the public mind. The eclectic presentation of the group stands out in retrospect as its most distinctive feature. Hirayama Seisai's adopted son, Hirayama Seishin, 1854–1929 (a prominent Meiji and Taishō government official in his own right), later commented that "the reason why [the group] was named Taiseikyō is that it means gathering together and bringing to completion. According to my late father's way of thinking, the aim was to draw in various kinds of phenomena, no matter what, gather them together, and gradually refine them."[35] The "gathering together" was not directed by Hirayama's perception of affinities among preexisting religious strands or even by his own religious predilections. Although his earlier connections with the Tohokami community facilitated the initial formation of Taiseikyō as an organization, from the outset the umbrella sect did not possess a clear religious identity. After the founder's death a multiplicity of additional units were funneled into the sect that in turn had little or no relation to the early coalition of the 1870s and early 1880s. The forces driving this agglomeration were partly economic: a greater number of affiliates would generate more revenue for the sect through membership fees. By the late Meiji, numerous little-known associations operated under the sect's umbrella, some of which had minimal if any religious purpose (such as poetry societies). According to one account, over one hundred groups were affiliated with Taiseikyō by the beginning of the Taishō period (1912); the organization devolved into a mere administrative structure with little identity of its own, comparable in this regard to the amorphous cooperative, Shintō Honkyōku.[36]

Given its eclectic character, the Taiseikyō enterprise, as Inoue Nobutaka demonstrates, provides a useful lens on the groping for the meaning of "Shinto" that took place in the early Meiji.[37] "Shinto" in Hirayama's definition apparently encompassed any Japanese cultural system

that was not otherwise identified with an established sect. However, because Taiseikyō was organized in this "smorgasbord fashion," it was
constantly dogged by the problem of which groups it should allow under
its umbrella.[38]

> The organizing method that [Hirayama] Seisai adopted was an extraordi-
> narily liberal one in which religious groups that based their existence on
> various popular beliefs were ultimately included in the Shinto sect. It can-
> not be denied that because he had an overly inclusive attitude, encompass-
> ing groups like Tōkyūjutsu and sundry others that one would generally
> hesitate to include in the category of "Shinto," Taiseikyō turned out to be
> an incoherent religious body. However, the question of what sort of reli-
> gious group or sodality should be included in the category of Shinto was
> quite difficult to answer....[39]

Hirayama's lenient construal of "Shinto" in the 1880s certainly
laid the foundation for his sect's irretrievable loss of identity by the early
twentieth century (although other factors also contributed to the degeneration).[40] However, in the early stages of its development Taiseikyō was
not devoid of a certain coherence, quite apart from the ideological parameters that it had inherited from the doctrinal instruction campaign.
The association was spearheaded in the late 1870s and early 1880s by a
few primary partners that shared both social and religious interests. It is
not by accident that following the remarks cited above, Hirayama's
son Seishin adds that his father had enlisted all sorts of groups in the
formation of Taiseikyō, "whether Misogi or Tōkyū or Shingaku."[41] The
Meiji alliance among these three units, as I have indicated in earlier
chapters, was prefigured in a series of exchanges and overlapping affiliations among their Edo-area members that dated from at least the Tenpō
era. Under the circumstances, I differ with Inoue Nobutaka in his implication that Hirayama's early inclusion in Taiseikyō of such groups as
Tōkyūjutsu contributed to the sect's lack of coherence.

A closer look at the ideologies and social groups that dominated
the initial Taisei coalition reveals that it was driven, not only by the cultural nationalism that infused numerous religious organizations of the
day or by the centralizing policies of the Meiji state, but also by the
interests of a specific sector of mid-Meiji society. In the first place, its
leading members shared a common way of thinking about personal improvement. Inoue Nobutaka correctly emphasizes that one unmistakable
pillar of the Taisei structure of thought was Confucian moral cultivation.
In this respect it was similar, of course, to other Meiji Shinto organizations, such as the Shūseiha sect founded by Nitta Kuniteru (1829–1902).
The leaders of the umbrella sects in general (who were mostly of samurai

background) routinely used Confucian language to articulate their ethical ideas.[42]

However, the role of Confucian modes of thought in these administrative organizations went beyond supplying ethical injunctions. Hirayama's teachings are a case in point. In his "True Meaning of the Fundamental Teachings" *(Honkyō shinketsu)*, the Shinto leader indicates how one should go about cultivating oneself *(mi o osamuru)*:

> The essence of cultivating one's person lies in "being careful when one is alone" *[hitori o tsutsushimi]* and "practicing sincerity to the utmost" *[sei o itasu]*. The essence of "being careful when one is alone" and "practicing sincerity to the utmost," in turn, is that one must always examine one's self, reflect quietly, ponder thoughtfully, and put things into action in each situation—whether one is in a dark room by oneself, in the government offices or imperial court, in the midst of a thousand troops or ten thousand cavalry, ill to the point of death, or [simply] during the ordinary affairs of daily life.[43]

This is a vintage Neo-Confucian program of personal improvement: conscientious examination of one's own actions and thoughts, whether in private or public.[44] The passages Hirayama glosses are set phrases from the *Great Learning* and the *Doctrine of the Mean*. They were no doubt comfortingly familiar to educated men of his generation, but probably seemed rather abstract to the average follower of Tōkyūjutsu, Misogikyō, or even the Confucian-flavored Shingaku. The Taisei leader's description of the methods people should use to cultivate themselves is somewhat more concrete. However, we have no evidence that Taiseikyō members indeed carried out these practices; the methods Hirayama describes probably reflect his own idealized views more than the actual religious life of Taiseikyō members.[45]

> One should settle one's body in a relaxed way on a soft seat, placing one's hips on the seat and keeping one's knees more than one *shaku* apart; one should direct one's spirit into the area just below the navel *[tanden kikai]* and join one's hands below the abdomen, with the right hand above and the left hand below. One's eyes should turn downward, half-open, gazing at the tip of one's nose, or else one may face the sword, imperial seal, or mirror that is in front of the [sanctuary of the] god. One should then exhale all the sins and defilements [accumulated] since one fell into this world, the deluded ideas, distracting thoughts, and old nitrogenous ethers *[chisso no koki]* that destroy the body; and subsequently inhale the fundamental, authentic essence of the divine, pure spirit and the new oxygenous ethers *[sanso no shinki]* that nourish human beings and all things. One

stores this [spirit] in the area below the navel, in the hips and legs, and in the arch of the foot. One should dissolve one's ties to all things and abandon one's self, entrusting it to the gods of heaven and earth. Counting one exhalation and one inhalation as a breath, one should complete fifty breaths each time. (The nose is the gate of heaven, it governs inhalation; the mouth is the door of earth, it governs exhalation.) However, after one has matured [in this practice] one can complete one hundred, two hundred, or three hundred breaths [at a time]. Value is placed on a greater number of breaths.[46]

Much of the above is a description of the Nagayo method of breathing advocated by the Tohokami founder Inoue Masakane and his teacher, the physiognomist Mizuno Nanboku. Hirayama also alludes to the physically based cultivation of vital humors *(ki)* that informed Tokugawa systems of personal well-being. In other writings, like his Tōkyū associates, Hirayama draws on Song Neo-Confucian ideas about the difference between material dispositions *(kishitsu)* and original nature in order to account for differences in people's characters and to justify the idea that it is possible to improve one's personality.[47] Parts of Hirayama's guidelines on posture also resonate strongly with Zen-type meditative techniques that were practiced in the Tokugawa era by lay adepts—whether Shingaku followers or individual scholars such as Okunomiya Zōsai.[48]

The Tokugawa practitioners of Tohokami, Tōkyūjutsu, and Shingaku had created and enacted holistic programs of personal improvement that involved varying degrees of attention to meditation, breathing, and physical/ritual purification. These discourses are brought together in Hirayama's "Shinto" cultivation praxis. It is worth noting that the enactment of the above regimen in front of the three imperial regalia—one of the few recognizably Shinto elements in his proposal—is presented merely as one option among others. From this perspective, the teachings of the "Great Synthesis" appear to be simply a Meiji variation on the theme of attaining well-being through the practice of personal disciplines—one more contribution to a medley that was played in Japan throughout the nineteenth century.

It is rather on the level of social organization that this and other sect-Shinto groupings of the time gain significance. Taiseikyō was the formalization of a network of preexisting groups in the name of Shinto—a vaguely religious coalition ultimately held together by political and economic need. It is true that we have little firm documentation of the early Meiji history of the Taisei member groups and the concatenation of events that led to their alliance under the umbrella of Hirayama's organization. Yet it is clear that the Honjō-Tōgū branch of Inoue Masakane's

followers constituted the dominant stratum of the early Taisei membership, and that Tōkyūjutsu and Shingaku were also key partners in the
original alliance.

The Dynamics of Affiliation

Denominational accounts offer a modicum of information about the enrollment of the last two groups in Taiseikyō. In February 1873 the Meiji
government (presumably the Ministry of Doctrine) informed the contemporary head of Tōkyūjutsu, Sano Kazumaru, that it would conduct
an investigation of the group—most likely in response to the association's
request for official recognition. Sano was required to submit detailed
documentation of the Tōkyū founder's social status and teachings to
the authorities. He accordingly presented the government with a statement of the "Twelve Personalities" theory, the founder's principal written
work *(Aki no arashi)* and other writings, and Sano's own account of the
group's teachings on character development. The leader included the
following remarks in his written report:

> Our founder [Yokoyama] Marumitsu attained the profound, secret trans-
> mission of the Twelve Personalities of Tengen[jutsu], after which he thor-
> oughly mastered the principles of the Twelve Personalities. Later, as many
> people know, after many years of effort he brought to light the principles
> for transforming the human body and the dispositions; these [principles]
> are the doctrines of a distinct school that does not derive from [any of] the
> three teachings (Shinto, Confucian, Buddhist).
>
> After your investigation is complete, I hope that you will by all
> means sanction Tōkyūjutsu, in accordance with the request that I hereby
> submit. I will answer any questions that may arise.[49]

According to modern Tōkyū chronologers, extant records indicate that
the response to Sano's request was very positive: the government official
in charge (unidentified) concluded that the group's teachings deserved to
be widely circulated.[50] Tōkyūjutsu was thus permitted to pursue its activities, though always within the parameters of the government's ideological campaign; in May 1873 Sano Kazumaru proceeded to the Great
Teaching Academy in Shiba and was appointed a doctrinal instructor.
Niinomi Harumitsu and other Tōkyū teachers were similarly licensed.[51]

The various Tōkyū cells, each of which was led by one of Yokoyama Marumitsu's direct disciples, apparently subsisted for the next
several years by affiliating in turn with one or another group that was
already authorized by the government. In early 1878, Tōkyū leaders
requested permission from both the Tokyo district authorities and the

Home Ministry to form a separate society for the propagation of Maru-mitsu's teachings; approval was granted in July of the same year, re-portedly with the backing of a local official who was versed in Tōkyū-jutsu.[52] In 1879 "Tōkyū Kōsha" was officially recognized and placed under the direction of Sano Kazumaru (other Tōkyū communities soon followed suit; each attained recognition as a separate *kōsha*).[53] Niinomi Harumitsu's group alone, which (like the Sakata branch of Misogikyō) had affiliated with Ishin Kyōkai, now boasted a membership of two thousand.

The Tōkyū network, or parts of it, continued to thrive. By 1881 Niinomi's group had reached a membership of 3,750. Sano began to hold two-day Tōkyū training sessions three times a month, in response to demand. Seating space reportedly became cramped as the divination group drew ever larger audiences in the 1880s.[54] Modern Tōkyū histor-ians assert that, because of its growing membership, the government de-cided to appoint a general supervisor for the group. The man chosen for the task was Suwa Chūsei, an officer in the Home Ministry and a prom-inent Shinto leader. Evidently the Tōkyū elders had a say in this ap-pointment, for Suwa also happened to be a zealous Tōkyū practitioner and a close associate of the senior Tōkyū teacher, Yoshikawa Ichigen (1826–1909).[55] Suwa was also acquainted with the Taisei-Misogi leader, Honjō Munetake, with whom he had sided in the earlier pantheon controversy.[56]

Tōkyū sources indicate that many members of Hirayama's newly formed Taisei society spontaneously enrolled in Tōkyūjutsu during this period; the mutual imbrication of Tohokami and Tōkyūjutsu practi-tioners that had occurred in Edo during the late Tokugawa years seems to have persisted in the Meiji era. However, in spite of its prominent connections and the popularity of its teachings, Tōkyūjutsu was unable to attain the status of an autonomous sect. Given the increasing overlap between Tōkyūjutsu and Taiseikyō members, the Tōkyū leaders eventu-ally concluded that they had no choice but to affiliate with Hirayama's organization in order to ensure their group's prosperity and status. With the approval of Sano and the other Tōkyū elders, Yoshikawa Ichigen formally placed Yokoyama Marumitsu's followers under the authority of Taiseikyō in May 1883.[57] Modern Tōkyu historians explain this de-cision on the grounds that the community simply did not have enough power to become an independent legal entity at the time.[58] The subtext seems to be that Tōkyūjutsu was far more popular than the umbrella sect Taiseikyō, but Yoshikawa and his associates lacked the political cachet of powerful shrine administrators like Hirayama Seisai. That Tōkyū had no choice but to join the Taisei organization even when the latter was losing members to it may seem odd, but given the logistics of the Shinto world at the time, in which nonmainstream religious and cultural groups survived mostly through a strategy of selective affiliation with authorized bodies, it is not implausible. The umbrella Shinto sects legitimized less powerful groups like Tōkyūjutsu in return for the latter's membership numbers and fees.

Tōkyū chronologers for their part are adamant that the group's affiliation with Taiseikyō was purely for legitimizing purposes, and that Tōkyū teachers "never said a word" to their members about "the Taisei doctrines": they concentrated solely on teaching Tōkyūjutsu and "completely ignored" the so-called Shinto tenets of their parent group.[59]

> Because a policy that emphasized state Shinto was being implemented in Japan, even though Tōkyū was not a religion, given the condition that it could not really conduct its activities publicly unless it contrived to proselytize in affiliation with a Shinto-designated religious body, it reluctantly placed itself under the umbrella of that religious body [Taiseikyō]. Until August 1945, when the war ended, for the most part it was forced to adopt this type of arrangement.[60]

Judging from such statements in the group's chief publication, *Tōkyū,* today's practitioners are keen to disassociate their movement from its Shinto history. The authors repeatedly point out that despite Yoshikawa Ichigen's official rise through the ranks of the doctrinal instructor system, he occupied himself only with Tōkyū education, not with the Taiseikyō ("Shinto") platform. Moreover, like their Shingaku colleagues, to this day the Tōkyū spokespersons prefer to identify their teachings as a secular form of personal cultivation rather than as "religion." In the twentieth century both groups registered with the government as "corporate juridical persons" *(shadan hōjin),* rather than as "religious juridical persons" *(shūkyō hōjin).*

It may well be that Tōkyū teachers in the 1880s were able to propagate their message without regard to the ideological and ritual framework of their sponsoring organization. The Taisei association appears to have been quite loosely administered from its origins. However, Tōkyūjutsu's relative autonomy was also premised on the fundamental compatibility of its ideas and practices with Hirayama's program of personal cultivation. Modern Tōkyū chroniclers seem oblivious to the fact that from at least the Bakumatsu era some of Yokoyama Marumitsu's followers doubled as leading members of other groups that later played an important part in the Taisei association—namely, Tohokami and Shingaku. Hirayama himself, like the Bakumatsu Shingaku teachers, may very well have dabbled in Tōkyū practices in his youth; Nishikawa Kōjiro, a Taishō-period writer, avers that Hirayama studied under Sano

Kazumaru, though the allegation remains unverified.[61] In any event, it seems likely that the teachings of Tōkyūjutsu and Taiseikyō were not as mutually exclusive as the spokespersons of the divination system imply. For Tōkyū members of the Meiji period, the most alien aspect of the Taisei program was probably its ad hoc pantheon of Shinto gods and related rituals.

Whether because of or despite its Taisei affiliation, the Tōkyū movement maintained a modest but healthy constituency during the Meiji period, operating as a federation of separate groups (known as the Sano Kōsha, Yoshikawa Kōsha, and so forth, after the names of each unit's leader), some of which in turn formed their own regional branches *(bunkai).*[62] The movement's popularity seems to have peaked in the late Meiji and Taishō periods; Yoshikawa, who traveled throughout Japan for teaching purposes, reportedly had 13,500 followers at the time of his death in 1909.[63] Extant Tōkyū-related publications, which languish on the shelves of used bookstores in Tokyo today, date overwhelmingly from this period.

The standard account of Shingaku's affiliation with Taiseikyō is similiar to that of Tōkyūjutsu: Ishida Baigan's followers affiliated with Hirayama's organizaton purely from necessity. It is generally assumed that, for Shingaku as for other nonestablished groups, its Shinto metamorphosis was a transient identity required by the sociopolitical pressures of the time. This view is not incorrect, but, as I have suggested, voluntary ties between members of Shingaku and other interpretive groups long predated the sect-Shinto phenomenon and were directly related to the Shingaku leaders' ultimate choice of an umbrella group in the Meiji.

The successful negotiations between Shingaku and the government regarding its name and other issues of identity in the early 1870s (reviewed in chapter 4) were in themselves not sufficient to ensure the group's autonomy during this period, given its reduced size. Shingaku cooperation with Hirayama's group began in 1878 when Kaiseisha (a Shingaku meetinghouse in Tokyo) affiliated itself with "Taiseikyō."[64] The Tokyo headquarters, Sanzensha, followed suit in early 1880; when Hirayama inaugurated Taisei instruction in February of that year, the program included Shingaku talks.[65] Before long, Shingaku centers in Gifu, Shizuoka, Gunma, and the Osaka area also affiliated with Taiseikyō.[66] Hirayama continued to sponsor and participate personally in Shingaku instructional programs through the 1880s. Inoue Nobutaka points out that although the Taisei leader was constantly involved in teaching in one form or another throughout his life, his public lectures probably did not attract large audiences.[67] He reportedly tended to depict moral values as abstract ideals in the rather dry style of Tokugawa

Confucian scholars instead of seeking to relate these ideals to the concrete concerns of ordinary people. The Taiseikyō proselytizing program was probably invigorated by the inclusion of Shingaku sermons, which listeners generally found engrossing.

An important feature of Taiseikyō in the early Meiji was the close relationship between the Misogi and Shingaku member groups, personified by Kawajiri Hōkin. Kawajiri was not only an energetic religious educator, comfortable in multiple denominational contexts; he was also an amateur playwright. The Kawajiri family had generously patronized the Ichikawa Danjūrō line of Kabuki performers since the mid-seventeenth century, and Kawajiri proudly continued this tradition. The Shingaku leader was excessively fond of the theater—he allegedly attended three performances of each play and was on friendly terms with several actors.[68] He was also involved in the Society for Theater Reform (Engeki Kairyō Kai), which was founded in 1886 by several political, business, and cultural luminaries under the direction of the well-known Meiji official Suematsu Kenchō (1855–1920).[69]

It was partly through his scriptwriting that the Shingaku leader helped shape the Taisei-Misogi system. Kawajiri began to publish play scripts in 1883 (initially under an alias) and wrote more than twenty during his lifetime.[70] His plays are said to have been infused with such traditional values as loyalty, filial piety, and humaneness. The Shingaku leader apparently had a special flair for evoking the sentiments of "moral duty and human emotion" *(giri ninjō)*, a classic Japanese contrast that had inspired much Edo-period drama.[71] Kawajiri's use of dramatic narrative to convey moral values in an engaging fashion (a typical Shingaku skill) is well in evidence in the aforementioned play based on Inoue Masakane's life ("The Eternally Fragrant Shrine of Umeda").

"Umeda" reads unusually well as a narrative. It presents a dramatic, moving account of the early Tohokami community—one with which the Taisei-Misogi practitioners of the time generally concurred.[72] The characterization of Uneme/Chizen is significant in this regard. She is endowed in the play with the status of a martyr who suffered for the teaching alongside the founder. At the same time, perhaps picking up on earlier representations of Chizen as an opponent of superstition and spiritualistic practices, Kawajiri enhances her function as a voice of reason and political caution within the religious community (figure 12). In his script, when several Tohokami followers urge an aggressive approach to spreading Inoue Masakane's teachings—ringing bells, beating drums, and loudly chanting the purification formula—Chizen discourages them, saying she fears further government persecution should the members attract public attention.[73] When prospective recruits query her about the details of her teaching, she advises them simply to chant *To ho kami emi*

FIGURE 12. Chizen (Miura Uneme), a leader of the Tohokami community during the 1840s and 1850s. Woodblock print contained in *Inoue Masakane shindenki*, ed. Inoue Sukekane (1877).

tame. They persist, demanding to know whether the Tohokami system also encompasses a mystical transmission *(shinpi no tsutae)*—whereupon she acknowledges only that "ritual techniques" *(shikihō)* are taught. Finally, when one of the novices says he has heard that the Tohokami group possesses some sort of "auspicious water" *(arigatai omizu)* that is reputed to cure the blind and the lame, and adds that he would like to drink it in order to cure his lumbago, Chizen flatly denies that the community distributes any such thing. In Kawajiri's rendition she has difficulty in convincing her listeners that she is not secretly harboring any miraculous healing water: they insist that she must be hiding something from them. In a Kabuki-style dramatic reversal, the recruits are then revealed to be local patrolmen who had infiltrated the group in order to trick Chizen into disclosing her supposed illicit practices.[74]

It becomes clear in the play that during the Bakumatsu era Tohokami members were afraid to speak to nonmembers about the teaching because of the possibility of this kind of surveillance.[75] Rumors of "auspicious water" were indeed a red flag to the authorities in both the late Tokugawa and the Meiji periods. Water had long been revered in Japan for its life-supporting and cleansing qualities, and thus easily lent itself to religious elaborations. The term "divine water" *(jinsui)* indicated water offered to a deity at an altar or shrine, or simply a stream, pond, or other body of water that was located in a sacred site. Insofar as deities were believed to use this water or even dwell in it, in traditional Japan it was often considered to have miraculous qualities—especially curative powers.[76]

During the nineteenth century, the followers of devotional movements regarded the possession or production of such healing waters as a mark of their leaders' religious authenticity, while the authorities interpreted it a sign of their heterodoxy. Tokugawa officials in charge of monitoring religious groups may well have used undercover agents in the way depicted in Kawajiri's play to confirm the practice of healing in nonestablished congregations. During the Edo period the issues at stake were probably more economic than ideological, given the implicit sanction of healing practices within the more established sects, on the one hand, and the opposition of professional physicians and other therapists to the upstart healing systems of the time, on the other.[77] In the Meiji, however, a new layer of discourse was utilized to elaborate the opprobrium against these practices. The use of healing water was no longer simply a violation of the state's social controls or an infringement on the prerogatives of professional healers; it was evidence of a perverse stagnation in the unenlightened ways of the past.

Healing as practiced by charismatic religious leaders did not cohere with the visions of a newly civilized Japan that educated elites projected during the early Meiji. In his play, Kawajiri accordingly persuades us that Inoue Masakane's teachings, properly understood, did not contain illegal or improper *(fusei)* elements. We are told that during the founder's lifetime "peasants who had no understanding caused a commotion with their bells and drums" (while chanting the Tohokami formula); they ignored the remonstrations of the group's leaders and refused to grasp the danger in which they were thereby placing both the founder and themselves. In the aftermath of Masakane's first arrest, according to the play, these "peasants" were a major source of anxiety for the senior Tohokami members. In one scene, Murakoshi Masahisa and Chizen worry openly that these followers' shallow comprehension will precipitate the failure of the founder's mission.[78]

Inoue Masakane did not employ "auspicious water" or any other such material aids in his healing practice on a routine basis, as far as extant documents reveal, nor did he advocate such methods to followers in his letters. Sanctified water was apparently stored at Tohokami meeting sites, but it was used primarily in initiatory rituals rather than as a healing potion.[79] The principal focus of Masakane's health-care system was breath regulation, as we saw in chapter 3. Nevertheless, the use of water in healing was not uncommon in religious groups at the time;[80] some Tohokami members may have engaged in the practice, especially after the founder's death, when the movement became highly decentralized. The Office of Temples and Shrines apparently suspected as much in the 1850s, if we are to credit Kawajiri's play script. In any case, it is clear from the Shingaku master's rendition that by the mid-1880s he and his Taisei-Misogi audience had excluded the use of healing water from the early Tohokami story. By means of this and other interpretive modulations, in both "Umeda" and other writings the Zen *koji* persuasively depicts the Misogi community (and, by implication, Taiseikyō) as having been from its origins a civilized form of moral and religious cultivation that was eminently suited to the new age.[81] Any unconventional or rowdy elements in the early movement are simply attributed to lower-class members.

A similar interpretive approach informed Kawajiri Hōkin's treatment of other "folk" religious practices in the history of the early Tohokami community. As we saw in chapter 3, in Inoue Masakane's own quite detailed description of his rainmaking on Miyakejima, he does not depict it either as a capitulation to popular pressures or as a premeditated, *upāya*-like recruitment strategy. In Kawajiri's Kabuki play, however, Masakane agrees to bring rain to Miyakejima only after the islanders repeatedly and strenuously supplicate him, and with significant reluctance at that. The founder's decision is justified in the script by the arguments that rainmaking had a respectable history in both China and Japan, that other religious leaders had engaged in the practice, and most important, that if Masakane refused, the island people would resent him and his teaching would decline.[82] Kawajiri thus characterizes both the use of healing water and rainmaking as forms of *upāya* that Inoue used to recruit members only when absolutely necessary. In other words, the founder's reliance on magical practices was portrayed in the 1880s as exceptional and not at all representative of the regular Misogi program of cultivation.

During the Tokugawa as well as the early Meiji, for most people access to spiritual therapies represented their last hope of recovery from debilitating disease and death. To the more educated, however, practices of this kind epitomized the ignorance and credulity of the masses, which could best be countered by directing people toward a more reasonable and seemly form of personal betterment. In the end, as we shall see in chapter 10, it was not the Misogi branch of Taiseikyō (which came to be viewed as a fairly respectable system of religious cultivation), but a younger member of Hirayama's Shinto federation that contributed most dramatically to the growing public debate in Meiji Japan over the acceptability of religious healing. The three member groups of the Taisei organization treated in this chapter—Misogikyō, Tōkyūjutsu, and Shingaku—not only shared the assumption that health and prosperity are closely related to the cultivation of personal well-being through discreet meditative and purification practices, but also participated in a common social network that predated their Meiji partnership. These commonalities lend some weight to the view that even the most amorphous-seeming Shinto sects were not simply expedient, random, or forced unions, but further elaborations of voluntarist Tokugawa networks.

CHAPTER 9

Enlightened Conservatives

PUBLIC DISCOURSE ABOUT the future of Japan took on a singular urgency in Meiji society during the 1880s. Many of those who had lived through the Restoration of 1868 became increasingly concerned in the ensuing years about the rapid changes taking place in the country and their implications for the national cultural identity. Now they also faced the prospect of constitutional government and a national assembly. In Carol Gluck's words, "for those who lived through it, the decade of the eighties had a headlong forward thrust. For every backward glance toward the changes that had transpired in the recent past, there were scores of eyes fixed upon the future, in particular on the year 1890, when the first elected national assembly would inaugurate a new political system."[1]

Religious practitioners were especially fixated on the future; sectarian representatives participated vigorously in debates about Japan's emerging cultural identity, particularly when they believed the prospects of their respective organizations were at stake. The history in the 1880s of the interpretive groups we have surveyed in the preceding pages, whether these were inspired in the Tokugawa by Shinto-type purification practices, divination systems, or popular forms of Zen or Confucian learning, must be understood in terms of this political thrust. These and other religious groups had now been exposed for years, along with the rest of Japan, to the dizzying series of social and cultural innovations that the Meiji state had promoted in the name of "civilization and enlightenment." In the 1880s representatives of many such communities, like the Confucian-minded public educators mentioned earlier, called for a return to values and practices they depicted as time-honored Japanese traditions. The mentality of these sectarian leaders is invariably characterized by modern scholars as conservative (as well as nationalistic and anti-Christian). However, a close look at specific groupings reveals a spectrum of positions among their members, ranging from simple traditionalism to conscious political ideology, both conservative and liberal.

Karl Mannheim once pointed out that conservatism is a conscious, reflective response to particular changes—a deliberate counterproposal to progressive movements. Conservatives retain elements of the older way of thinking but reformulate them, consciously placing them in a new intellectual framework. In other words, conservatism is a creative synthesis that is necessarily influenced by the ideas of the opposing ("progressive") movement.[2] It can therefore be distinguished from traditionalism, which Mannheim says is simply an unconscious, psychological predisposition—an "instinctive" fear of innovation based on attachment to old ways. Whereas the traditionalist is unreflectively attached to older patterns of life and thought, the conservative proposes, in effect, a new system. Recent histories of conservatism in the European historical context similarly reiterate that "conservatism arose not *against* the Enlightenment but *within* it."[3]

The notion of conservatism as a novel configuration of old and new ideas is useful for understanding the political and ideological patterns that characterized socioreligious figurations during the early Meiji. Many "conservative" spokespersons of groups that originated before the Meiji were in fact eager to prove that they were not fusty throwbacks to an earlier time, but inspired creators of a new ideology that would guide the Japanese people into the modern age. In this chapter I discuss the political attitudes of several members of the Engakuji circle, liberals as well as conservatives, but with special attention to the emergence of a conservative consensus in the late 1880s. The later part of the chapter demonstrates that these Zen practitioners were core members of a multireligious coalition that promoted social conservatism and nationalism in the late nineteenth century.

Suzuki comments in his monograph, *Imakita Kōsen*, that his erstwhile teacher was less concerned with the political developments of his time than with the improvement of monastic training and the spread of the Zen teaching.[4] Imakita certainly did not become involved, for example, in public debates about state policy toward Buddhism, as did his younger Buddhist contemporaries, Shimaji Mokurai and Ōuchi Seiran (1845–1918). Nor do we hear of Imakita sparring with government officials during the first Meiji years, as did his Rinzai colleague, Ogino Dokuon.[5] Moreover, Imakita rarely mentions political events in his writings except in the context of remarks about religious or educational issues. Nevertheless, the abbot developed a distinct, if understated, political persona during his Meiji years.

There are few surprises here. Like many Buddhist priests who were born and educated during the Tokugawa period, Imakita affirmed common Confucian and Shinto-type values throughout his life. He maintained the importance of loyalty and filial piety as standards of social conduct and routinely expressed reverence for the Japanese gods and their imperial "descendants."[6] In practice, Imakita adopted an attitude of modest deference to the authorities, whether the pre-Restoration government of Iwakuni domain or the Meiji state.[7] After he took up his posts in the capital as head of the Rinzai General School and in nearby Kamakura as abbot of Engakuji, his contacts with government personnel greatly increased—we have already noted his friendly relations with early Meiji officials and his continuing popularity among career-minded youth who resided in Tokyo in the 1880s and early 1890s.[8] As a prominent abbot and de facto representative of the early Meiji government,[9] Imakita not unexpectedly demonstrated respect for the imperial institution; indeed, his personal reverence for the emperor appears to have been quite heartfelt. His follower Hiranuma Kiichirō later recalled that "[w]hen ... the imperial train passed in front of the Engakuji gate, [Imakita] Kōsen would dress up and [as a sign of respect] kneel on the ground in front of the gate without wearing anything on his feet. Once when it was raining he [even] went without *tabi* [socks]...."[10]

The Zen master was not unaware of the diverse political currents swirling around Kamakura in the late 1870s and the 1880s; during this time the campaign for popular rights burgeoned into a "movement for freedom and people's rights" *(jiyū minken undō)* that included numerous local groups in Kanagawa prefecture.[11] The early leaders of this movement were mostly ex-samurai who had been excluded from power, but in the late 1870s, many village headmen, landlords, and small-scale entrepreneurs joined the campaign.[12] During the same period, peasant dissatisfaction with the effects of the land tax reform of 1873 exploded in a series of village protests.

One such disturbance, allegedly "the best-known, and certainly the bloodiest, dispute over proprietary rights" of the time,[13] is believed to have fueled the organizational development of opposition movements in the Kamakura area.[14] In 1878, in a nearby town called Shindo, a man named Matsuki Chōemon took possession of pawned land after deceptively appropriating the rightful owner's seal. The peasant who owned the land failed to gain redress through the courts and was ordered to pay an exorbitant amount in legal costs and arrears. In desperation, a group of his supporters decided to take matters into their own hands. Twenty-five peasants, led by a man named Kanmuri Yaemon, reportedly set fire to and broke into the Matsuki home in Shindo, assaulting its residents. By the time the blaze was put out, Matsuki and seven household members were dead. Kanmuri and his companions were arrested, charged, and found guilty—but they were regarded as heroes by their fellow villagers. Before long, farming people in the surrounding districts organized a movement in support of the accused and petitioned the prefectural

FIGURE 13. Imakita Kōsen presents a petition for clemency to the authorities in Kanagawa on behalf of Kanmuri Yaemon and his fellow prisoners. A wood-block print in a popular account of the Shindo uprising written by Itō Ichitarō in 1880. Reproduced in *Ishin nōmin hōkitan,* ed. Ono Takeo.

governor, Nomura Yasushi (1842–1909), to commute the prisoners' sentences.[15]

Several religious leaders in the Kanagawa area, including Imakita Kōsen, joined the Shindo campaign and formally asked the governor to spare the lives of Kanmuri and his companions. Imakita's biography records that the abbot "had an audience with the governor and earnestly made the appeal" (figure 13).[16] The Engakuji abbot was sufficiently in tune with community sentiments to be willing to assist in this kind of crisis. He was not unsympathetic to the injustices and hardships that less-privileged people suffered during the early Meiji period. However, Imakita became involved in the Shindo movement simply as one among many community leaders; for the most part, like other Meiji Buddhist leaders he kept aloof from popular opposition groups.[17] His primary local acquaintances seem to have been privileged members of the rural population, whom he sometimes canvassed for funds to support the monastery.[18] The Zen master's writings and biography do not indicate that he was involved in social welfare, or indeed in much interaction with poor people at all, except in preaching to them occasionally. In 1885, when many Kanagawa peasants were desperately poor as a result of poor harvests, deflationary monetary policies, land taxes, and usurious moneylending practices, the Zen master insisted to a general lay audience at Engakuji that the famine of the previous season was due to their "lack of faith in the True Dharma," which was manifest in their failure to give donations to the monastic sangha (meaning, in this context, Engakuji). He did allow that, if some people were too poor to give alms, they could express their commitment to the Dharma by encouraging others to donate.[19]

Even though Imakita maintained an attitude of detachment from the popular-rights movement itself, like other Meiji citizens, he was affected by the public debate over representative government and did not fail to make his own contribution to it. The abbot worried especially about the implications of current political developments for the Buddhist sangha. Soon after the government's announcement in 1881 that a national diet would be established, he argued in an address to the Rinzai clerical community that the assembly would be a turning point for Japan —especially, he hoped, for Buddhist Japan.[20] We saw earlier that in Imakita's view the monastic community had declined since the Restoration, both in numbers and in the quality of its members; in his address he duly expresses dismay over the prevalence of meat eating and marrying by Rinzai priests. He ostensibly holds the clergy responsible for this behavior, but obliquely implicates the government for its interference in Buddhist affairs. To his mind, the government need not have issued the 1872 clerical marriage decree: after all, the sangha had its own regulations.[21] As Imakita points out, the government had certainly not decriminalized clerical marriage and meat eating because of concern for the well-being of the monks.

Without directly criticizing the Meiji administration, the Engakuji abbot thus manages to depict it as a kind of seductive "big brother" who was tempting weak monks with its libertarian policies. He uses the prospect of a national assembly as an opportunity to caution the clergy to improve their behavior: should they fail, the assembly might take legislative action against the sangha on the grounds of its corruption.[22] On the other hand, if the monks succeeded in reforming themselves, the future diet might even make Buddhism the state religion. Like others caught up in the national identity debates of the time, Imakita assumed that his own religious system was surely the best candidate for an ideology that could, as he puts it, protect Japan from "evil teachings" (such as Christianity). But in order to meet the challenge of the heterodox teachings that were "trampling on our Dharma-territory and plundering the followers of our sect," Zen Buddhists would have to follow the precepts —and, in other words, ignore the infamous clerical marriage decree.[23]

Along with the many Japanese who openly participated in the popular-rights movements, by the early 1880s the abbot was apparently convinced of the value of some form of representative government. He welcomed the coming assembly despite the possible risks to Buddhism; once the diet was in place, he imagined, intelligent people would think more seriously about the significance of religion and evaluate the behavior of its representatives in an informed manner.[24] He optimistically depicted the future assembly as a forum for free debate, where important issues would be openly discussed. The Rinzai abbot had often hesitated in the face of innovation, whether it was anti-Bakufu activism in the last Tokugawa years, opposition to Meiji government policies, or his own disciples' yearning for a modern education. But in the 1880s he responded in a more explicit and deliberate manner to the sociopolitical challenges of his time. He continued to articulate traditional ideas, but within the context of a new appreciation of the proposed political structures. To use Mannheim's language, Imakita had evolved into a "primitive" conservative.[25] He had begun to participate, quietly but actively, in the construction of conservative ideologies. The Engakuji abbot's deliberate role in this process is confirmed by his involvement in his followers' activities.

Before turning to these later developments, I should emphasize that during the 1870s the Engakuji *koji* were still rather fluid in their political associations and represented a range of views. Two regular practitioners of the time, Okunomiya Zōsai and Nakajima Nobuyuki, are well known for their liberal political activism. Okunomiya, the cofounder of the Ryōmō Society, had formed his political persona in the same Bakumatsu Tosa milieu that produced several liberal party leaders, notably Itagaki Taisuke (1837–1919).[26] When Itagaki became governor of Kōchi some months after the Restoration, Okunomiya returned home from Tokyo to help with educational reforms and to implement the Department of Shinto's proselytization campaign.[27] It is worth nothing that Okunomiya was also assigned to "edify" members of the still-outlawed Kirishitan community, who were being held in Kōchi in the aftermath of the 1867 Urakami suppression.[28] In the process of preparing for these indoctrination activities, the Confucian scholar became versed in translated Christian texts and related Western writings.[29] Although he was a proselytizer of the Restoration government's ideology, Okunomiya was not necessarily an anti-Christian zealot; he maintained an intellectual curiosity about Christianity in the years leading up to the formation of the Ryōmo Society.

Okunomiya became involved in the emerging movement for freedom and popular rights during the same period. After the 1873 split in the Meiji governing circle over the Korea controversy, Itagaki and his circle formed a political group called Aikoku Kōtō (Patriotic Party). Okunomiya attended the group's early planning meetings and joined Itagaki, Gōtō Shōjirō (1838–1897), Etō Shinpei (1834–1874), and several others in signing the party's inaugural pledge in January 1874. It was Okunomiya who edited the draft of the group's famous memorial to the government that called for the establishment of a popularly elected assembly.[30] Moreover, the Tosa scholar seems to have maintained his connection with this circle until his death three years later. We noted earlier the report that Nakae Chōmin, the popular-rights theorist and founding member of the Liberal Party, had studied with Okunomiya in Tosa and later became involved in his teacher's Zen society in Tokyo. Okunomiya's son, Okunomiya Kenshi (1856–1911), also joined the popular-rights movement during this period.[31]

The prominent liberal leader Nakajima Nobuyuki was another Ryōmō Society practitioner. Like Okunomiya, Nakajima was a Tosa samurai who had opposed the pro-Tokugawa faction that had dominated domain politics in the mid-1860s.[32] After the Meiji transition, he occupied a series of posts in the new government (most notably the governorship of Kanagawa in 1872), but soon became absorbed in the emerging popular-rights movement. In 1881, Nakajima became vice president of Itagaki's Liberal Party (Jiyūtō); the following year he organized another liberal group, the so-called Constitutional Party (Rikkenseitō).[33] One of the first events sponsored by Nakajima's party was a speech in Osaka called "The Path for Women" *(Fujo no michi),* delivered by the aforementioned feminist pioneer, Kishida Toshiko.[34] Kishida and Nakajima apparently developed a close relationship while on a boat trip with Nakajima's friend Mutsu Munemitsu in late 1883; they spent more time together the following year and decided to marry shortly thereafter.[35] In the meantime, Nakajima's Constitutional Party dissolved, but he and Kishida continued their efforts on behalf of liberal causes.

I have not seen any evidence of Nakajima's active involvement in Engakuji affairs after the spring of 1881. He probably did not stop practicing under Imakita or supporting temple fund-raising projects all at once; his immersion in political activism may have prevented him from visiting the temple as frequently as he had in the late 1870s, when he worked in the capital. However, Nakajima's diminishing presence in the Engakuji community may also reflect his evolving political sensibilities. By the mid-1880s he differed sharply with his fellow *koji* on key political issues. Paralleling the divisiveness that characterized political discourse in the public domain at this time, the ideologies promoted by Nakajima and Kishida, on the one hand, and by Imakita's other prominent lay followers, on the other, stood in stark opposition to each other. In the mid-1880s Kawajiri Hōkin, Yamaoka Tesshū, Torio Tokuan (discussed below), and, less visibly, the Engakuji abbot himself, were actively involved in promoting conservative social agenda and polemicizing against Christianity; Nakajima and Kishida, in contrast, were baptized into the Congregational church during these years.[36] Furthermore, although we have no way of verifying whether Nakajima fully shared his wife's ideas, given the couple's common political sympathies and their reportedly harmonious marriage, it is likely that he supported her affirmation of equal rights for women. Kishida's discourse on the position of women was radically different, however, from the one that Nakajima's Dharma companions propagated in the 1880s.

Kawajiri Hōkin's Discourse on Equal Rights and His Alliance with Tani Kanjō

The issue of equal rights provides a useful template for gauging the social philosophy of members of the Engakuji community during this time. In 1884 Kawajiri Hōkin published an extended disquisition, called "On Internal Civilization" *(Naibu bunmeiron),* in which he argues that Japanese citizens should pay more attention to the personal, moral dimension of "civilization," as opposed to what he perceived as the current infatuation with Western-type technology. A section of the treatise, titled "The Equal Rights of Men and Women" *(Danjo dōken),* provides an illuminating contrast to Kishida Toshiko's speeches and writings.[37] Both thinkers were thoroughly familiar with the arguments that had been raised in the early Meiji debate over equal rights.[38] In a series called "To My Compatriot Sisters" *(Dōhō shimai ni tsugu)* published in the same year as Kawajiri's treatise, Kishida refutes several of the propositions that typify conservative discourse of this time on the position of women, and that inform Kawajiri's stance in particular.[39]

Kawajiri argues that the putative Japanese tradition of "honoring men and despising women" (which Kishida excoriated) represents a timeless truth that recent critics had overlooked.[40] He avers that in the remote past the Japanese people had indeed followed "the true principle of equal rights for men and women," but that they had now become oblivious to their native heritage and were mistakenly derogating the alleged inequality of the past.[41] The Shingaku leader further implies that the West is the source of this deplorable trend (in general his treatise is interspersed with arguments for the liberality of Japanese customs as opposed to such Western practices as slavery). Kawajiri's central message, however, is that equal rights are not established by human law, but are naturally endowed in human beings. Following a strained but familiar line of reasoning, he argues that, like heaven and earth (or one's head and one's feet), the relationship between the two sexes is one of relative position, not of fundamental value. He cites the *Book of Changes* by way of explanation:

> "The Way of heaven was established and was called 'yin' and 'yang.' The Way of earth was established and was called 'weak' and 'strong.'" Yang and strong are the virtues of heaven, while weak and yin are the virtues of earth.... Moreover, if one categorizes these in [terms of] rank, heaven comes first and earth after. Heaven does not intend to be master, [but] spontaneously takes the position of master. Earth does not intend to follow, but is endowed with the principle of following. This is simply the reality of nature....[42]

Kawajiri goes on to extend the yin-yang paradigm to water and fire. Just as fire can boil water, so water can extinguish fire; these are simply unconscious, spontaneous processes that derive from the inherent nature of the two substances. Neither fire nor water, then, is prior in value.

Perhaps we can take Kawajiri to mean that neither sex has more intrinsic value than the other; extrapolating from the water-fire analogy, perhaps he would allow that in the human realm as well, sometimes one pole predominates and sometimes the other. But this is never made explicit.[43] Instead, the *koji* simply reiterates that insofar as men are yang, they are *naturally* respected, and insofar as women are yin, they are *naturally* depreciated. Female–male relations, in short, must be modeled on nature—the yin-yang pattern in its conventional interpretation is thus the correct standard of "equal rights" for both parties. What Kawajiri meant by "nature" was in fact the social status quo of the time.

The Shingaku master does not dwell much on the idea that biological differences are the basis for male superiority. He acknowledges that men possess greater physical strength than women, but insists that weakness and strength are both part of the cosmic structure of the universe, and thus equal in value. Following this reasoning, Kawajiri again concludes that the sexes are already equal by nature.[44] Kishida, in contrast, unambiguously dismisses physical strength as a criterion of value; she points out that if physical force is a priority, then (in Siever's rendition) "sumo wrestlers should become councillors of state."[45] The two thinkers' responses to the presumed cultural superiority of men follow the same pattern. Kawajiri hedges. He does not absolutely deny the potential of women to match men intellectually, but lamely observes that "a woman who excels men is one in a hundred or a thousand" and insists that this imbalance has nothing to do with the problem of equal rights. "Intelligence and stupidity are intelligence and stupidity; in terms of rights, there is no inequality at all."[46] Kishida, for her part, introduces the culture argument to show that the two issues are indeed closely related. Any apparent differences in "mental power" *(seishinryoku)* between the sexes is not inborn, she points out, but the gradual effect of the disparity in their schooling and social training.[47]

Like other moralists of his time (and ours), as a way of refuting the validity of equal rights legislation Kawajiri raises the specter of marriage relationships gone hopelessly awry. "Equal rights between men and women will become a fence that will cut off harmony and love between husbands and wives." He fulminates against the "superficial" attitude of equal rights supporters who are fixated on mere semantics without comprehending social realities and who insist on an "uncontrollable independence" for women that will have dire consequences for Japanese society.[48] Needless to say, the impact on the family of the proposed legislation was a constant point of reference in the Meiji debate over women's rights.[49] Kishida was well-acquainted with these alarmist predictions of family disruption; in her writings she responds that, on the contrary, once rights were equalized, husbands and wives would love each other all the more deeply.[50] Instead of issuing commands to their wives, husbands would consult with them in a spirit of cooperation, and as a result couples "would invariably take delight in each other and would attain the highest joy of humankind."[51]

The Zen *koji* takes a moderate tone in his essay in regard to allegations that women had an insatiable desire for power and that if given equal rights they would become difficult to control. He observes that supporters of this view justified it by referring to Confucius' remark that "[w]omen and people of low birth are very hard to deal with. If you are friendly with them, they get out of hand, and if you keep your distance, they resent it" *(Analects* 17:25).[52] But he goes on to interpret the line simply as an admonition to gentlemen to behave properly, not as a statement of women's inferiority.[53] Kawajiri further argues that when a woman dominates a man, it is because the man lusts after "temporary" pleasures. In doing so, the man cedes his "rights" or power *(ken)* to the woman and voluntarily becomes her puppet. The implication, however, is that women are by nature incapable of dominating men in any event (without the latter's cooperation).

In sum, regardless of the particular issue, the Shingaku-Zen leader consistently returns in his essay to the premise that women and men are naturally equal and consequently there is no need for legislation to correct the purported imbalance. "The equal rights of men and women are not something established by human beings," Kawajiri concludes, "they are the fixed principles of nature."[54] This appeal to "fixed" natural laws characterizes conservative thought across cultural contexts; speaking of

Euro-American precedents, Muller observes that "a recurrent temptation of conservative theorists is to conflate culture with nature, to treat
'second nature' as 'nature' in order to make the contingent appear inevitable."[55] Kawajiri's employment of naturalistic metaphors to make the
existing mores of his time seem inevitable indeed seem to epitomize
the conservative mentality according to which, in Mannheim's words,
"[m]eaning and reality, norm and existence, are not separate."[56] In contrast to Kishida, who calls for the concerted establishment of equal rights
in Japan, and thus points up the gap between norm and existence in
Mannheim's sense, for Kawajiri the norm *is* the existent reality—one
merely has to acknowledge its presence in nature and model one's behavior after it.[57]

The Shingaku master's argument for the preservation of patriarchal
customs was not mere nostalgia or traditionalism; it was a directed response to specific proposals for change that liberals like Kishida and
Nakajima were promoting in the public domain. By publicizing the idea
(among other propositions in his treatise) that gender roles were "sure
and fixed, outside human construction, part of the natural or divine
order," Kawajiri joined his more prominent companions in transforming
the Engakuji circle from a group of urbane, eclectic Buddhist gentlemen
in the 1870s into a conservative ideological force in the 1880s.[58]

The Engakuji *koji* propagated their philosophy not only through
occasional writings but also through organized activities. In Kawajiri's
case, the Shingaku organization supplied a ready-made structure for the
public dissemination of social morality. Although the Tokyo Shingaku
group became greatly attenuated after the Restoration, its remaining
members made a modest contribution to moral education in the capital
during the 1880s. Kawajiri and his Shingaku-Zen colleagues were assisted in this regard by a key political figure of the time: Tani Kanjō (or
Tani Tateki; 1837–1911). Tani's connection to Shingaku activism is best
understood in the context of the broader political developments of the
1880s.

Like Torio Tokuan, Tani was one of the "Four Discontented Generals" who resigned from active service at the end of the 1870s in protest
against the reorganization of the army by Yamagata Aritomo (1838–
1922) and Katsura Tarō (1847–1913).[59] The four generals would later
become leading figures in the "Movement for the Preservation of the
National Essence" *(kokusui hozonshugi),* a conservative movement that
opposed the Westernization policy of the Meiji government and its
approach to revising the unequal treaties.[60] In the early 1880s the generals and their supporters in fact shared common ground with the Liberal Party in their calls for internal government reform, but they differed
with Itagaki and his supporters on the pace and methods of the proposed

reforms. Tani, in particular, argued for organizational changes rather than a complete replacement of the central government, and proposed the eventual rather than immediate institution of a national diet.[61] In September 1881 he and his associates founded an avowedly centrist group called the "Impartial Party" (Chūseitō) to promote their ideas.[62] The generals also formed a group called Getsuyōkai, which publicly opposed the policies of Itō Hirobumi and Yamagata Aritomo; its members sent a memorial to the emperor that vigorously argued against the concentration of all power (legislative, judicial, and executive) in the cabinet.[63] They recommended that the Council of Elder Statesmen be given the power to pass laws independently of the cabinet, and that it be made more representative by adding delegates to it from local assemblies.[64]

Tani, Torio, and their associates are usually called "conservative" because they opposed the emerging liberal parties of the time, and I follow the same convention here. However, the thrust of their 1881 memorial was progressive insofar as it called for a more broad-based national political structure than that envisioned by the oligarchy. The Getsuyōkai position was duly inspired by such Japanese "traditions" as the notion of a direct relationship between the emperor and the people, but this emphasis was now part of a new synthesis that included the idea of popular representation. The resultant conservatism was thus not an attempt either to preserve the status quo or to reinstate a past model of government. The generals and their sympathizers opposed the party activities associated with the people's rights movement, but they shared with its members the vision of a more representative political order.

The founders of Tani's Impartial Party overlapped with the members of a more informal group that the Tosa general also sponsored during this time, known simply as the "Tani League" (Kokuren). The League reportedly consisted of ten people, including the well-known political figure Sasaki Takayuki (1830–1910), a close associate of Tani who also originated in Tosa.[65] It was through this elite group, which was more concerned with public edification than with direct political activity, that Tani cooperated with the Shingaku community in Tokyo. The general and his associates recruited Kawajiri, Mitani Ken'ō, and Kumatani Tōshū to carry out a campaign of moral education in the Tokyo area. According to Shingaku sources, Tani personally sponsored regular Shingaku lectures from 1882 to 1886 and invited the principal Shingaku teachers to give "talks on the Way" at his residence in Tokyo. In addition, the members of the Tani League each donated ten yen every month to help Shingaku fund the propagation of its teachings.[66] On occasion, Tani also invited the Shingaku-Zen teachers to hold educational sessions designed especially for high-ranking individuals (these events were not open to the general public).[67]

Tani Kanjō was well connected at court. In 1884 he was appointed president of Gakushūin, the aforementioned Confucian-oriented school for nobility that had now come under the control of the Ministry of the Imperial Household (Kunaishō). The general was also a leading administrator of Shibun Gakkai, allegedly "the most important Confucian organization in Japan in the years from 1880 to 1918."[68] Smith notes that the success of this society's activities in the 1880s (lectures, publications, and a short-lived school) owed much to its close connections with the imperial family; the emperor's advisor Motoda Eifu was an active supporter.[69] It is not surprising to learn that members of the imperial family also attended the special Shingaku lectures that Tani sponsored. Shingaku chronologers are probably not exaggerating when they state that on one occasion these luminaries were so moved by the Shingaku talks that they treated the speakers magnificently afterward, donating generously to the Shingaku fund. Tani also sponsored large Shingaku meetings open to the general public in various locations throughout the capital during the early 1880s. Following Shingaku custom, the talks were held once a month in a continuous series that lasted three days; Tani himself usually gave a speech on the first day of each series. The Taiseikyō director, Hirayama Seisai, also joined the Shingaku teachers in giving lectures on these occasions. All the sessions reportedly attracted capacity audiences.[70]

Illuminating the Way

Unlike Tani, Torio did not simply sponsor the ideological activities carried out by members of the Engakuji circle but was a committed Buddhist leader of those activities. I have related elsewhere that Torio was a thorn in the side of the Meiji oligarchs; he opposed them on a range of issues, especially their refusal to broaden the powers of the proposed national diet (figure 14).[71] At the same time, the former general was a central figure in the Zen community: he gave generously to temple fundraising projects, mentored young monks like Shaku Sōen, recruited Zen practitioners, ran educational programs, wrote disquisitions on Buddhism, and held Zen practice meetings in his home. Torio was especially effective, however, in creating broad-based ideological organizations.

At a September 1883 meeting of the Shibun Gakkai, Torio announced his intention to form a Buddhist society dedicated to "protecting the nation" *(gokoku).*[72] He and Yamaoka Tesshū formally initiated the new group, called Myōdō Kyōkai (Society for Illuminating the Way), early the following year. Imakita Kōsen agreed to speak once a month to the members, beginning with an inaugural sermon on the *Blue Cliff Record*.[73] Numerous other prominent Buddhist leaders also held forth at

FIGURE 14. General Torio Koyata (Tokuan). Reproduced from the frontispiece of *Tokuan zensho*, ed. Tokuan-kai (1911).

the group's meetings, which took place twice a month in the Rinzai temple, Rinshōin; Ogino Dokuon, Sakagami Shinjō, Seki Mugaku, Shaku Unshō, Hara Tanzan (1819–1892), and Shaku Sōen gave lectures on Zen texts in particular.[74]

Myōdō Kyōkai aimed to promote Japanese religious and moral culture under the rubric of a nonsectarian Buddhism. In this regard, it was part of a general Meiji trend—Ikeda Eishun has identified over 220 pan-Buddhist groups that were founded from 1882 to 1887. The Myōdō Society alone instituted thirty-three centers and branches (located in eleven prefectures) during its founding year.[75] Like several other Buddhist societies of this time, the group supported Fukuda Gyōkai's monastic reforms and emphasized lay ethical discipline, as articulated in such formulae as the Four Obligations and the Ten Precepts.[76] Torio's principal aim in founding the group, however, was to "defend" Japan from pernicious, foreign-influenced currents of thought that he believed denied the fundamental truths of Buddhism.[77]

As the Myōdō Society's name implies, Torio, Yamaoka, and their colleagues planned to concentrate on "illuminating" the correct way of life for Meiji citizens rather than on facilitating religious praxis. The chief task of Myōdō Society members was therefore didactic in nature. According to Torio, preserving Japan's cultural and religious identity meant actively fighting against those who held "wrong views" as well as edifying persons who were ignorant of the "right views" (Buddhist teachings).[78] Publicly upholding Buddhism was, in his view, critical to the national well-being: failure to do so would have far-reaching effects at every level of society. By "wrong views," Torio meant not only the (presumably Christian) idea of a "creator god" and the idea of "self-love" (a reference to the utilitarian philosophies of Hobbes and Spinoza),[79] but also trademark Neo-Confucian ideas such as "the principle of Heaven" and "human nature and principles" (with which Torio generally disagreed). The Myōdō Society's educational campaign was thus directed not only against newfangled Western trends, but also against "false" ideas that had long been familiar to Japanese educational elites. When people believed in these theories, Torio complained, they were dreaming.[80]

Given the aim of the society, its members were expected to be committed Buddhist practitioners, if not experienced teachers (both lay and monastic). In this regard, too, the Myōdō Society was similar to the pan-Buddhist "teaching assemblies" or societies *(kyōkai)* that had begun to appear in the mid-1870s.[81] Yet by the mid-1880s these groups seem to have viewed their didactic mission with a greater sense of urgency. During the early Meiji, as Kenneth Pyle remarks, "the belief that the course of Western civilization represented the universal path of man's progress was so pervasive that the term *bunmei* (civilization) was often used as a synonym for *seiyō bunmei* (Western civilization)...." At the same time, many individuals and groups sought to redefine these key terms—to change people's very understanding of what it meant to be "civilized."[82] Torio indeed laments in his writings that the phrase "civilization and enlightenment" was being bandied about too much, and that society members should strive to remove this confusion by clarifying the meaning of "civilization."[83] The general's remarks leave no doubt that society members were to consider this civilizing project their patriotic duty: the phrase "protecting the nation" is implicitly identified in Torio's discourse with "enlightening the nation" and "illuminating the Way." In fact, the group's founding principles were originally titled "Rules of the Society for Protecting the Nation" *(Gokoku kyōkai kiyaku).* Apparently the phrase "protecting the nation" provoked negative reactions in some quarters; citing the need for "good *upāya*," the organizers accordingly changed it to "illuminating the Way."[84]

In spite of the name change, the society's nationalistic tone did not escape the central government. In March 1884, representatives of the seven Gozan denominations were summoned to the Home Ministry for a consultation over the clerical rules that each sect had recently submitted to the government for approval. The remarks that Vice-Minister Hijikata Hisamoto (1833–1918) made to the assembled Zen priests epitomize the "civilization and enlightenment" mentality against which Torio and his confreres had been planning their assault. Hijikata emphasized the importance of modeling Japanese institutions and culture after "European civilization" in order to foster a political climate conducive to revising the so-called unequal treaties. He reminded the Buddhist leaders that, since European laws and educational methods were for the most part "based on Christianity," Japan's emulation of European culture would inevitably involve some acceptance of Christian values. He also pointed out that the Europeans who currently served as advisors in the Japanese cabinet and in the Ministries of Education and Justice were Christians, and that the European states would not accept any treaty revisions that did not "safeguard their security and happiness." The central government did not seek to disestablish Japan's Shinto, Confucian, or Buddhist teachings, but if representatives of any of these teachings were to oppose the national aim of "reform," Hijikata warned, the government would take steps to deprive them of any role in the legal and educational domains. The vice-minister did not mince words on this point:

> If we wish publicly to permit Christianity, to turn to Western customs, and to confirm the view of the people of the Western countries that our Japan is the "Europe of Asia," then it is essential that as much as possible we not allow the followers of Shinto, Confucianism, and Buddhism to generate sentiments of aversion for Christianity....
>
> Therefore, such [associations] as the alarmist group, the Society for Illuminating the Way (Myōdō Shōkai *[sic]*), are in fact at cross-purposes with these government aims and are bringing great harm to the nation. Under the circumstances, when [even] those in high government offices repeatedly stir up the sentiments of people who belong to these groups, [their conduct] must by all rights be regarded as an obstruction to the state.[85]

Hijikata's warning to the sectarian leaders pinpoints the disjunction between the perspectives of the ruling oligarchy and of the emerging conservative opposition, whose members were growing increasingly restless with the government's treaty revision strategy. As we have seen, the leaders of several conservative subgroups possessed close ties to particular religious communities; as Hijikata indicates, some also held "high government" positions. Given the timing of his remarks (about a month after the Myōdō Society was founded), he may have been referring specifically to the group's well-known founders, Torio and Yamaoka, as well as to other Meiji officials who were involved in its activities. The comments were undoubtedly also a tacit rebuke of Imakita and the other Gozan leaders associated with the society. The government was quite aware of the political function of these ostensibly nonpolitical organizations.

In spite of Hijikata's warning, the association between members of the Engakuji circle and conservative critics of the government grew stronger during the ensuing years. In 1887 the government's efforts (led by Inoue Kaoru, 1836–1915) to revise the unequal treaties between Japan and the Western powers engendered a new wave of protests from a range of political groups; demands for freedom of speech and the reduction of the land tax became strident. The controversy over the government's treaty-revision strategy, in Pyle's words, "galvanized conservative opposition to *bunmei kaika* views" and led to greater preoccupation with the cultural autonomy of Japan.[86]

Torio and his former military colleague Tani Kanjō, both of whom had returned from tours of Europe earlier that year, reacted strongly. Tani, who had served as minister of trade and agriculture since 1885, submitted his resignation in June and attacked the government's treaty-revision plan in a memorial the following month. He regarded the proposed revisions as a humiliating submission to foreign demands and an affront to Japan's national integrity.[87] He also criticized the secretive way in which Inoue Kaoru had been conducting the treaty negotiations, and emphasized the importance of allowing public opinion to play a role in resolving the matter.[88] Torio for his part circulated a secret memorandum in which he again argued for radical expansion of the powers of the Council of Elder Statesmen.[89] He also proposed that "all of the people should be free to express their opinions publicly on political matters," and that "[t]he newspaper regulations should be revised, and the gates of public discussion opened...."[90] Even after the government responded to the protests against the treaty-revision plan and the calls for free speech by issuing the Peace Preservation Law (which further restricted public assembly and banned protest leaders from Tokyo), Torio continued to fight in the Council of Elder Statesmen—and later, in the Privy Council—for the right of representation and other civil liberties (though with little success).[91]

In these repeated calls for freedom of speech and a more representative governmental process, neither Tani nor Torio fits the stereotype of the rigid conservative who passionately seeks to maintain existing institutions.[92] Teters warns that Torio, in particular, confounds our tendency to label the individuals who opposed Westernizing trends in early Meiji Japan as conservative without considering the complexities of their thought.[93] More recently, Swale has suggested that we refer to this variety of mid-Meiji conservatism (or *kokusuishugi*) as "progressive conservatism," because even though its advocates insisted on the maintenance of social order and particular traditions, they "countenanced a variety of modifications to the institutions and customs of the polity."[94] Pyle for his part describes the emergence in the late 1880s of a "moderate" conservatism, especially among younger intellectuals and writers who were opposed to a revival of tradition for its own sake but argued coherently for the need to acknowledge cultural differences among nations and to preserve the unique spirit of Japanese civilization (the "national essence," *kokusui*).[95] Pyle distinguishes this moderate conservatism from the formulations espoused in the early 1880s by older civic ideologues (Nishimura Shigeki and Motoda Eifu come to mind). On this point he quotes the Meiji critic Yamaji Aizan (1864–1917), who purportedly speaks for the "new generation" of conservatives:

> Whereas the conservatism that appeared in 1881 and 1882 was nothing more than a rebirth of Chinese learning, the conservatism of the late 1880s represented the development of national consciousness. Of course, in the latter case, many backwoods priests and Confucianists were delighted to plunge into the movement, but ... the leaders of the group had an understanding of Western culture.[96]

Torio, Tani, Kawajiri, Imakita, and a number of other conservative figures in the Engakuji network of the late 1880s were not members of the new generation of public intellectuals highlighted by Pyle (and Yamaji), most of whom were born in the 1860s or later. On the other hand, they were not simply "backwoods priests and Confucianists" either.[97] Like the younger conservatives, they combined an "enlightened" openness to selected Westernizing reforms with a strong insistence on the need to protect the integrity of Japanese culture. The Meiji conservatives as a whole were a highly variegated group whose differences cannot be fully explained in terms of either age or religious ideology. Furthermore, some of the older conservatives changed their views over time. A "rebirth of Chinese learning" may well have compelled these figures in the early 1880s, but their trajectory gradually became far more complex and ambitious. In the mid-1880s Torio, Kawajiri, and the other members of this older group began publicizing time-honored moral and religious values, not out of nostalgia, but in order to counter what they saw as the unchecked spread of socially liberal ideas. In anticipation of constitutional government, they also began to campaign for a distinctive Japanese polity inspired by the "national essence" ideal of a direct relationship between the emperor and the Japanese people (which would not be subject to interference by the cabinet). This vision encompassed the institution of political mechanisms, such as representative government and free speech, that are ordinarily considered progressive.[98]

By the late 1880s these members of the Engakuji circle and their supporters thus became, in Mannheim's sense, mature political conservatives who synthesized elements of tradition and innovation. At the same time, the practitioners who had been associated with the popular-rights movement or liberal party activities (such as Nakajima) were no longer a visible presence in the Engakuji program. The political character of the temple-based community had shifted (along with the rest of Japan) from a fluid mixture of diverse ideas in the 1870s to a spectrum of conservatisms, ranging from Kawajiri's social morality to Torio's more nuanced conservative discourse. It is important to note, however, that all of the men discussed above, regardless of their particular positions in the ideological game field of the time, practiced Zen *and* esteemed political activism. Okunomiya and Nakajima, on the one hand, and Kawajiri, Yamaoka, and Torio, on the other, pursued a type of personal development that they believed would give them insight into the enlightened Buddha-nature. Yet they also assumed that this personal cultivation cohered with, even enhanced, their activities in the public domain. None of the Tokyo *koji* promoted Confucian doctrines per se; Torio, for one, explicitly criticized Neo-Confucian ideas. However, he and the other Tokyo *koji* of his generation had been educated as samurai, in the Confucian texts. They assumed, as had Fukuzawa Yukichi, that cultivating oneself in order to "govern the nation and bring peace to the world" was a sine qua non for the successful man in modern Japan.

The enterprise of learning in the sense of moral or religious self-improvement was for the most part no longer articulated in terms of these classical paradigms or, for that matter, grounded in social structures that identified themselves with a Confucian body of knowledge. The rubric "Confucianism" and its associated language was consciously excluded from the public discourse of even its most ardent advocates. The activism of the Tokyo *koji* and their associates was instead framed in terms of the new practical learning—a form of personal improvement that comprehended moral discipline, mastery of useful forms of knowledge, and engagement in the public sphere. It was an open-ended model of human action that proved attractive not only to Zen Buddhists, of course, but to a broad range of other religious practitioners during the late nineteenth century.

The Three Teachings in Parallel

Several of the figures discussed above formed political alliances with members of other religious groups who possessed a similar vision of human fulfillment. The Tokyo *koji* of the 1880s shared ideological and/or religious interests with the leaders of Shingaku, the Taisei branch of Misogikyō, and Tōkyūjutsu. The core members of these groups knew each other well and in some cases were the same individuals. They constituted an evolving yet remarkably stable socioreligious network, elements of which originated before the Restoration. All agreed on the fundamental aims (if not the details) of "learning" or personal cultivation, and in the 1880s they began working together to spread these ideas through systematic activism.

The representatives of these groups documented their shared commitment through collaborative publishing efforts. The most telling example is a set of prefaces and postfaces written from 1882 to 1884 in support of "On Internal Civilization," the disquisition in which Kawajiri Hōkin propounds his views on equal rights legislation and other social issues of the day. Appended to the treatise are introductory or concluding laudations of the Shingaku master's discourse by (among others): the Engakuji abbots (Imakita and Shaku Sōen); the Tenryūji abbot, Yuri Tekisui; the leading Tokyo *koji* (Tsumaki, Yamaoka, Torio, and Takahashi Deishū); the Tokyo Shingaku teachers (Kumatani and Mitani); and the Taisei-Misogi administrator, Murakoshi Kaneyoshi.[99] The most prominent person to recommend Kawajiri's treatise to readers was the conservative political figure and avid Shingaku sponsor Tani Kanjō.

The convergence of interests of the Shingaku, Rinzai, and Shinto communities that these people represented and the concerted nature of their efforts to influence public opinion in Japan are confirmed by an association they created in the immediate aftermath of the political crisis that was provoked in late 1887 by the government's treaty-revision policy. The new group was ambitiously named Dai Nihon Kokkyō Daidōsha—literally, "Society of the Great Way of the Great Japanese National Teaching." Yamaoka and the Misogi leader, Honjō Munetake, formally sponsored the creation of Daidōsha and invited Torio to direct it. By this time Honjō Munetake was both the general director of the Taisei branch of Misogikyō and the vice-director of Taiseikyō (he worked closely with Hirayama until the latter's death in 1890). He had been promoting Shinto causes in the public sphere for several years, but apparently also cultivated an interest in Buddhism (his Engakuji associates called him "Jōan koji").

The Myōdō Society was still active at this time, but Torio and his associates apparently felt the need for a more broad-based movement. In fact, the entire Myōdō membership was automatically enrolled in Daidōsha when the latter was officially inaugurated in January 1888;[100] the society's leaders simply transferred their administrative responsibilities to the new group. The de facto head of Daidōsha was Torio's student, the former Shinto priest Kawai Kiyomaru (1848–1917).[101] Kawai had practiced Zen for a number of years under Torio's supervision; he also served as a Myōdō Society administrator and as the editor of the Buddhist group's magazine, *Myōdō kyōkai zasshi*.[102] He now took his place in Daidōsha as executive secretary and editor-in-chief of its journal, *Daidō sōshi;* when the new magazine commenced publication in July 1888, Kawai simply merged it with the Myōdō publication.[103]

Several members of the Engakuji circle joined Yamaoka and Torio in Daidōsha activities. Kawajiri Hōkin frequently lectured at the group's meetings and regularly published transcripts of his Shingaku talks as well as commentaries on Daoist ideas in the Daidōsha journal.[104] Imakita Kōsen wrote an essay in celebration of Daidōsha's progress in which he praised Kawai's literary skills and affirmed the editor's critical view of Christianity. A series of other pieces by the abbot and his successor, Shaku Sōen, appear in the pages of *Daidō sōshi*.[105] Zen master Ogino Dokuon, close to seventy years old at the time, enthusiastically supported the new movement. He promised Kawai that when he attended Buddhist leadership meetings each month he would persuade the abbots of the various denominations to join the new society.[106] But the Daidōsha network ranged far beyond the Rinzai Zen community; it was backed by a wide variety of religious leaders and scholars from all over Japan. Numerous well-known Buddhist figures and top Shinto leaders enrolled in Daidōsha and/or wrote for its magazine.[107] A number of scholars who identified themselves primarily with Confucian studies also vigorously supported the Society of the Great Japanese Way.[108]

In short, Daidōsha was significantly more universalistic in its aspirations than the Buddhist Myōdō Society had been. It was also more overtly nationalistic and anti-Christian. The members of the society sought to advance the idea that the true creed of the Japanese people was a balanced configuration of Shinto, Confucian, and Buddhist traditions. In a kind of politicized version of the Tokugawa discourse that had been popularized by Shingaku preachers, the Daidōsha founders proclaimed that the three teachings were all the "Great Japanese Way" and differed only in name. Suzuki later took a dim view of the group; it appeared to him to advocate an indistinctive "syncretism" much like "the beliefs of the Japanese people before the Restoration."[109] The society's platform indeed had the semblance of an intellectual bricolage, insofar as it seemed to marshal together whatever Japanese religious systems were at hand to create a "national teaching." However, the mixture was not genuinely indiscriminate; as we shall see in the next chapter, it excluded an entire swath of Japanese religious culture.

Kawai Kiyomaru was anxious to clarify that Daidōsha's message was *not*, in fact, a regenerated version of the pre-Meiji "three teachings combined in one" *(sankyō itchi)*. To his mind, the ideal Japanese creed was based on a compartmental model, called *sankyō heikō* or "three teachings in parallel," in which each major tradition represented a specific domain of expertise—a kind of religious division of labor. Kawai believed that Shinto provided inspiration for the maintenance of the Japanese polity *(kokutai)*, the Confucian teachings supplied guidance in administrative and ethical matters, and Buddhism was a resource for personal emancipation.[110]

Pace both Kawai and his biographer, this compartmental vision coheres nicely with Shingaku and other three-teachings discourses of the Tokugawa. In general, these discourses had *not* been based on a combinatory paradigm in which all the religious traditions supposedly blended together into a unified whole. Kawai's insistence on the novelty of Daidōsha's three-teachings model vis-à-vis pre-Meiji precedents was part of the general tendency of the time to characterize preexisting cultural formations as new or reformed, and therefore uniquely appropriate to the demands of a modernizing Japan. The leaders of Daidōsha implicitly claimed distinction for their doctrine by stressing (not unlike Meiji Shingaku teachers) that the Restoration government's policies had destroyed Japan's age-old religious "harmony" by causing the various communities to turn against each other.[111] The systematic exaltation of Shinto by nativist-inspired officials in the first Meiji years, the associated downgrading of Buddhist status and infrastructure, and the public criticism and educational displacement of Confucian learning had, in fact, transformed the structure of Japanese religious culture. However, Kawai and his Daidōsha colleagues emphasized the agonistic quality of the recent relations between the respective communities, not simply out of yearning for an imagined past, but as justification for their further claim that the early Meiji religious friction had damaged Japan's cultural integrity and therefore its ability to defend itself against the incursion of European ideologies. The argument for a fresh configuration of "traditional" Japanese religious harmony was thus one more plank in the group's nationalistic platform.

Daidōsha was a movement of its time. In its early phase the society claimed a membership of over thirty thousand throughout the country (though it later declined greatly).[112] A flurry of similar organizations appeared in the years just prior to the promulgation of the constitution and the inauguration of the national diet. In 1889 Ōuchi Seiran founded a Buddhist ideological coalition called Sonnō Hōbutsu Daidōdan (Great Association for Revering the Emperor and Venerating the Buddha).[113] Nishimura Shigeki's Nihon Kōdōkai (Society of the Vast Japanese Way) had originated in the 1870s, but began propagating its program of traditional morality much more actively during the late 1880s.[114] Seikyō-sha, the chief organ of the conservative National Essence Movement *(kokusuishugi)*, appeared in 1887 (the writers of its well-known journal, *Nihonjin*, expressed support for the formation of Daidōsha).[115] *Nihon*, the conservative journal favored by Tani Kanjō, also began publication during this period.[116]

The Daidōsha leaders, for their part, were full of enthusiasm for their mission. Honjō Munetake gave a talk to the society's Osaka members in early 1889 that vividly expresses the tone of the group. In the transcript of his speech (published in *Daidō sōshi*) the Taisei-Misogi leader laments the spiritual vacuum that he believed had emerged in Japan in the wake of its recent overemphasis on technological progress. He expresses delight, however, that the treaty-revision problem had recently stirred up the country's "nationalistic forces" *(kokkashugi no seiryoku)*, and explicitly affirms the value of the National Essence Movement in this regard. Declaring that Daidōsha's vision of the three teachings could indeed save the Japanese people from their fatal attraction to evil religions, he concludes by warning his audience that Japan was at a turning point, and that their active efforts were needed. "Exert yourselves, my friends!" he urged his listeners, "the time has come!"[117] The tone of urgency, the marked reference to "nationalistic forces" as a resource for cultural renewal, and the explicit affirmation of the aims of the National Essence Movement are all indicative of the political currents that had been set in motion in 1887 by Tani, Torio, and the many other "enlightened" conservatives of the time.

I have concentrated here on the role of the Engakuji–Taisei circuit in the ideological surge of the mid-Meiji. The links between the groups and individuals in this network could certainly be construed as religious or philosophical—we have noted the resonance between Taisei–Misogi ideas of self-purification and the Neo Confucian–Shingaku–Zen concern with inner discipline. However, the religious nature of these linkages was little in evidence as debates began in the national assembly in the 1890s. The Daidōsha alliance was conspicuous, rather, for its political flavor. Kawai, who handled public relations for the group, was at pains more than once to deny allegations about Daidōsha's political aims.[118] The Society of the Great Japanese Way was rumored to be in cahoots with the Impartial Conservative Party (Hoshu Chūseitō), which the Daidosha director, Torio Tokuan, had just founded; journalists insinuated that *Daidō sōshi* was simply a mouthpiece for Torio's party.[119] In response Kawai insisted on the distinction between Daidōsha, a "purely doctrinal" or "religious" society *(junsui no kyōhōsha)*, and the Impartial Party, a "purely political society" *(junsui no seijisha)*. The two groups were different in purpose because political groups were created to oppose other political parties, whereas "our Society of the Great Way," the former Shinto priest declared, "arose to oppose foreign doctrines." Daidōsha members thus did not engage in "political" activities such as lobbying national assembly members.[120] Kawai, who was also a member of Torio's Impartial Party, understandably did not address the possibility that participants in the Daidōsha movement wielded significant political power simply by virtue of their duplicate membership in the corollary party—much as today's Sōka Gakkai adherents allegedly determine the Kōmeitō platform on certain issues.

Daidōsha's stated abstention from direct political action was not necessarily voluntary. As Kawai reminded his critics, because Daidōsha was a religious-educational movement, its leading members were mostly clergy and schoolteachers; as such, they were ineligible for election and therefore could not possibly influence the outcome of policy debates in the diet.[121] The former Shinto priest's exchanges with commentators on this point were part of an ongoing public debate over the separation of religion and state that intensified in the late 1880s after a number of politically charged religious organizations like Daidōsha became active. The Meiji government had earlier forbidden teachers, students, military personnel, and several other groups from participating in political discussions. The passage in 1889 of a law that deprived members of religious orders from standing for election to the lower house further polarized the debate.[122]

The ultimate effect of these and similar strictures, as Gluck points out, was not to dampen political activity, but to give it another name.[123] Groups like Daidōsha and Ōuchi's Daidōdan were now the chief public organs through which Shinto and Buddhist priests could voice their interests in a collective fashion. Under the circumstances, the members of these organizations presented their views as religious and educational propositions rather than as straight political platforms, but they were inspired by the same assumptions that informed conservative political alliances of the time—namely, that Japanese moral and religious traditions should be publicly promoted, and that the spread of Western ideologies, especially Christianity, should be actively resisted.

Scholars have called our attention to the function in contemporary East Asia of "informal politics"—interpersonal activities, prompted by shared, often unarticulated political dispositions, that occur outside the framework of formal institutions and rules. This kind of activism may take place in any number of unofficial venues and social groups, such as "labor unions, churches and sects, professional societies, business and trade associations, fraternal organizations, recreational clubs, civic service associations,... social welfare councils, communes and other 'collectivist' organizations."[124] Especially in the case of religious groups, participation in common beliefs and rituals often encourages shared attitudes toward events in the secular sphere; religious societies have served as arenas for the formation of political bonds outside the domain of the state in any number of cultures. The Meiji government's prohibition of direct political action by clergy and teachers only served to enhance the political importance of informal groupings in this regard. Because "religious" groups like Myōdō Kyōkai and Daidōsha were relatively well organized and imbued with a common sense of mission, they probably played a disproportionately large role in the informal political activities that surged in Japan during the late 1880s.

CHAPTER 10

The Enemy Within

FOR THE LEADERS of the Society of the Great Japanese Way, who campaigned to convince the public that a broad configuration of Shinto, Confucian, and Buddhist teachings was Japan's true civic creed, the question of religious acceptability was presumably not a matter of particular doctrines and practices. The collaborative, pan-sectarian impulses of the time indeed allowed much leeway in the construction of models of social and religious behavior. However, the driving force behind the formation of Daidōsha and other such coalitions of the time was fundamentally political and ideological in nature rather than religious ecumenism for its own sake. Such campaigns accordingly demanded the public identification and thus exclusion of specific cultural practices as undesirable forms of religion.

This chapter concerns the rise and fall of the new religion, Renmonkyō. The story of this short-lived group shows how public moralists of the late nineteenth century used the new religious movements of the time to demarcate their vision of a Japanese religious orthodoxy. Earlier, I emphasized the voluntaristic nature of the formation of Taiseikyō by its early members, Misogikyō, Shingaku, and Tōkyūjutsu. However, other associations came under the jurisdiction of the umbrella sect in a far more constrained and fortuitous manner. Renmonkyō was one of these "extraneous" Taiseikyō affiliates.

The representatives of Daidōsha and like-minded ideologues used the new religions as whipping boys in their discursive circumscription of the modern Japanese ideal. Kawai Kiyomaru's "Discourse on Tenrikyō" *(Tenrikyōron)*, published in the Daidōsha journal in late 1893, is an eloquent example of this type of exercise.[1] Although the discourse focuses on Tenrikyō, it serves as an excellent introduction to attitudes toward the new religions in general that prevailed in certain quarters of Japanese society during the early 1890s, and thus to the debate that arose over Renmonkyō, in particular. The piece purports to describe a dialogue between Kawai and a Tenrikyō elder, who is identified as a direct disciple of Nakayama Miki. The Tenri teacher is allowed considerable opportunity to explain the group's teachings about, for example, the deities its members revere, before Kawai steps in to refute the belief system from his "Shinto" perspective. The discussion also takes up the notion that Japan is the center of the world (with which Kawai generally agrees)—an idea that for Tenri members is premised on the holiness of the site where Miki received her original revelation (a belief that Kawai dismisses).[2]

It is not until after the Tenri elder lauds the healing powers of his group's teachings that Kawai moves in for the kill. The Daidōsha leader characterizes Tenrikyō as an implausible, superstitious group of practices and ridicules its leaders' hopes of converting all the people of Japan, to say nothing of the world.[3] Kawai then states his definitive argument:

> Are you aware of the national condition? Let us consider, for example, the debate between those who advocate mixed residence in the country's interior and those who oppose it.[4] This national crisis is gradually closing in on us. What if one day we open up the interior and permit foreigners to dwell mixed in [with Japanese]? Among the various kinds of national troubles that this will cause, the most fearful will be the struggle between religions. Consider the proud and scornful sentiments of the foreign residents. Imagine the sight of foreign religious teachers blathering on here in our country! Imagine the actuality of Japanese believers in foreign religions selling out our country and enticing in the enemy![5]

The Daidōsha leader paints an alarming picture of the churches that the "foreign religious teachers" (Christian ministers) would build all over Japan and the innumerable converts they would make by "stealing the faith of our people." In the end, the Shinto shrines, the Buddhist temples, the very spirit of Japan would die: the country would be left defenseless against the "Western army of the crucifix." The Daidōsha leader depicts the envisioned religious onslaught in strikingly military terms.

Kawai's message to the Tenrikyō teacher turns out to be the same as the guiding purpose of the Society of the Great Japanese Way. The only way to prevent the coming crisis, Kawai argues, is to make sure that the Japanese people understand the true principles of their own national creed and are willing to give their lives for their nation.[6] Tenrikyō is working at cross-purposes with these aims, according to Kawai, because it promotes its own inferior deity, Tenri-ō *(sic)*, and presumptiously plans to defraud the great majority of the Japanese people. "What you teach is different [from Christianity]," Kawai concedes, "but insofar as you confuse people's minds, you are committing exactly the same crime as those foreign religious teachers who incite a small number of believers and conspire [with them] to rob the faith of an enormous number of our people."[7]

In the Daidōsha leader's discourse Nakayama Miki's followers emerge as de facto accomplices of the enemy. The Tenrikyō elder did not simply lack a proper public spirit: to Kawai's mind, he was a veritable traitor to his country: "One who ... forgets public matters to follow his own private concerns is a wicked depredator who imparts poison universally to all the people, without caring whom, and brings disaster to our Emperor."[8] Given their deviation from the religious preferences of the majority, the leaders of Tenrikyō and other heterodox groups were evidently as guilty of lèse-majesté as Uchimura Kanzō (1861–1930), the Christian activist who had famously refused to bow before the Imperial Rescript on Education two years earlier.

In 1893 the acceptability of any religious system was increasingly depicted as a matter of patriotic spirit. Kawai appeals overtly to the idea that foreign/Christian ideas were the ultimate threat to Japan's well-being. However, his argument contains a tacit assumption to the effect that certain *native* beliefs and practices detracted from Japan's claim to be a civilized (and therefore powerful) country in which magic and superstition no longer held sway. In contrast to the Meiroku Society debaters of the 1870s, Kawai makes no allusion to European theories of religious evolution according to which popular devotional practices and mythologies would gradually give way, as education advanced, to more abstract, rational-seeming forms of personal development. Yet similar premises are at work in his discourse. The spread in the 1880s of groups like Tenrikyō, Maruyamakyō, and Renmonkyō, all of which promoted healing practices during a time when disease was rampant in Japan, had rendered palpable the customary division in the religious world between the preferences of educated sectarian leaders, government officials, and public intellectuals (now including journalists), on the one hand, and ordinary working folk, on the other. The heightening of nationalistic sentiment elicited by the treaty-revision debates of the late 1880s and the growing consciousness of Japan as a military power on the Asian continent in the 1890s brought this socioreligious division into focus.

Sarah Thal has identified a similar dynamic in relation to the Kotohira (Konpira) religious movement of the time. She traces a growing disjunction in the Meiji between the priests of the main Kotohira shrine in Shikoku and the large numbers of ordinary people who genuinely looked to the shrine's deity for assistance with their problems. On the eve of the Sino-Japanese War, Thal remarks, "[t]he religious landscape of Meiji Japan was ... framed as a contrast between two ideals: the decorous, Shinto enactment of a proto-middle-class social morality, and the individual pursuit of miraculous aspirations. Only with the impetus of the war would the two extremes be reconciled in a new configuration."[9] She concludes that the two components of the Meiji religious picture indeed "publicly merged" during Japan's wars with China and Russia at the end of the nineteenth century.[10]

Large mergers often involve layoffs, however. For the nonestablished religious groups of the time, which (unlike the Konpira association) lacked firm sociopolitical and territorial foundations, the pressure to conform to the new definitions of "Shinto," "religion," and "learning" that had been pushed by the state and publicized by civic ideologues proved in some cases overwhelming. As we have seen, nonmainstream religious associations gained a degree of legitimacy in the 1880s by affiliating with various Shinto sects; some of these groups gradually attained social acceptance, though at a cost to the integrity of their teachings. Others, however, deteriorated and eventually ceased to exist.[11]

Renmonkyō is a case in point. The group originated in Kyushu in the activities of a peasant woman called Shimamura Mitsu (1831–1904) (figure 15).[12] As a young woman Mitsu lived for a time in a small Nichiren-sect temple in the town of Ogura, where she reportedly learned divination, exorcism, and shamanic practices from a neighborhood woman and quickly gained a reputation for her accurate prediction of the rice exchange rates. In 1847 Mitsu married a local tofu dealer called Shimamura Otokichi, but continued to pursue her religious interests. Soon she began studying the teachings of the *Lotus Sūtra* under a man named Yanagida Ichibei (Sonyū; 1794–1877), a local samurai who devoted much of his time to religious and educational activities.[13]

Yanagida is reverently called *senshi,* "former teacher," in later Renmon accounts; Mitsu is said to have considered him the "second Nichiren" (and herself the third). Yanagida's main message was the "Wondrous Dharma of Things" *(Ji no myōhō),* an idea that was presumably inspired by Nichiren's interpretation of the Tendai doctrine of "three thousand realms in one thought-moment" *(ichinen sanzen).*[14] Nichiren had posited that while it may have been appropriate during the time of earlier Tendai masters to use the method of "principle" *(ri)* in contemplating the truth of the "three thousand realms in one thought-moment," in his own age of the final Dharma *(mappō),* people needed to use the method of "actuality" (in Stone's rendition) or actual phenomena *(ji).*[15] In effect, Nichiren's "actuality" meant the concrete forms of practice that he advocated, most notably reverence to the *Lotus Sūtra* as articulated in the saying, *Namu myōhō renge kyō* (I name the Sūtra of the Lotus Blossom of the Wondrous Dharma).[16]

We do not know the precise reasoning or experiences that led Yanagida and his follower Mitsu to advocate reverence for the "Wondrous Dharma of Things." They may well have understood the idea to imply

FIGURE 15. Shimamura Mitsu, the founder of Renmonkyō.
Undated photograph contained in *Renmonkyō suibōshi,* by Oku
Takenori.

the immediate presence of Buddhahood or enlightenment within the
world of relative phenomena. On the other hand, according to an inscription on the back of a stone monument in Ogura that Mitsu constructed in 1889 in commemoration of her teacher, Yanagida had taught
her that "my Wondrous Dharma is not the Wondrous Dharma of the
Buddha, but the Way of the natural, true law that completely envelopes
and penetrates the entire universe."[17] Of course, even the contents of this
rare primary source cannot be taken at face value; by the late eighties
Mitsu and her associates were keenly aware of the need to downplay the
Buddhist dimensions of their teachings. The closing verse at the end of

this inscription accordingly announces in no uncertain terms that "the Wondrous Dharma is not the Buddhist teachings" and praises the "great jewel-torch of Shinto."[18] In any event, judging from the inscription as well as other fragmentary and secondhand descriptions of the Renmon teaching that are extant today, Renmon members of the time seem to have understood the "Wondrous Dharma of Things" less as a formulation of Nichiren's specific teachings than as the generalized proposition that truth and goodness inhere in all phenomena—including human beings, who under the correct conditions can return to their pure, original state. This emphasis on innate goodness or Buddha-nature may have been accompanied by a corollary discourse on moral and physical cultivation.

Yanagida may in fact have offered some type of moral instruction to the local people of Ogura. An account of the Renmon group later submitted to the Meiji government cites a report to the effect that Yanagida "had studied some sort of learning of the mind [shingaku] and had assembled numerous people and provided guidance to them."[19] More than one source states that he claimed to transmit a version of "practical learning" (jitsugaku). Yanagida's interpretation of the meaning of this phrase is unclear, but given his samurai education it probably encompassed the thrust of the pre-Meiji Neo-Confucian idea that learning is a matter of moral or spiritual discipline, not simply intellectual study. Renmonkyō members apparently interpreted Yanagida's jitsugaku along these lines in 1892:

> Our former teacher, Old Man Yanagida, pondered deeply and disciplined himself silently for ten years; he thoroughly investigated and mastered the most profound truth of all things. Transcending words and language, he discovered a practical learning based on the original source of the divine principle [shinri]. This is the "Wondrous Dharma of Things" that we teach in our religion today.[20]

Mitsu and her followers went on to define jitsugaku more specifically:

> The essentials of what we call "practical learning" are to purify and refine people's spirits, to preserve the original nature endowed by the gods of heaven, to save people who because of disease or disaster die young or suffer long-term illnesses and thus cannot fulfill the needs of our nation, and to have [people] completely fulfill their obligations [to their ancestors].[21]

This is one of the more tangible descriptions of practical learning that we have encountered in the Meiji context; it includes not only the conventional Neo-Confucian sense of cultivating one's inner states for the sake of the whole, but also the specific activity of succoring the ill. Mitsu's understanding of practical learning in the 1890s is reminiscent, in fact, of Inoue Masakane's insistence in the 1840s on healing, feeding, and edifying others while at the same time purifying oneself by chanting *To ho kami emi tame*. Yet such therapeutically oriented interpretations of "learning" did not appeal to the emerging middle classes of the Meiji any more than they had to the shogunal authorities. Recent interpreters of practical learning had identified it with the pursuit of professional, scientific forms of knowledge rather than with personal cultivation—not to mention relief of the ill and the indigent. The implicit distinction between *gaku* and *kyō*, we saw earlier, was used in Meiji discourse to differentiate systems of personal improvement or education. In the 1890s Yanagida's and Mitsu's use of the word "learning" to refer to their activities struck "enlightened" observers as ludicrous. "Learning" *(gaku)*, one critic of Renmonkyō remarked in disdain, is based on knowledge, whereas "religion" *(kyō)* is based on faith.[22]

Like other founders of new religions (and indeed shamanic figures in Northeast Asia in general), it was not until Mitsu miraculously recovered from a serious illness after following Yanagida's instructions that she fully committed herself to her calling. She began to spread the word that if one had faith in the Wondrous Dharma of Things and drank "divine water" *(jinsui)*, one would need neither doctors nor medicine to cure one's illnesses, and would enjoy other benefits as well. In time, Mitsu began distributing to her followers not only quantities of water that she had sanctified but also pieces of paper inscribed in her own hand with the words *"Ji no myōhō"* (Wondrous Dharma of Things). The members reportedly treated these slips as divine dwelling objects *(shintai)* or wore them on their persons as protective talismans. They evidently regarded Ji no myōhō as both a deity and a mantric articulation of truth. According to one account, the main ritual of the group during the mid-Meiji consisted of reciting five times in succession *Ji no myōhō, namu myōhō renge kyō* (Wondrous Dharma of Things, I pay homage to the Sūtra of the Lotus of the Wondrous Dharma), clapping one's hands, and paying obeisance to Ji no myōhō.[23] Mitsu's followers reportedly performed these rituals and recited passages from the *Lotus Sūtra* in front of an altar overhung by a scroll that displayed the words *"Ji no myōhō."* They also are said to have practiced forms of ritual cleansing and expurgation *(misogi harae)* inspired by the Nakatomi purification rites,[24] although the group may have inserted these rituals into its praxis in order to authenticate its Shinto identity.

We have little further information about the teachings that Yanagida transmitted to Mitsu or that she later developed on her own. After

Yanagida passed away in the 1870s, Mitsu and his other disciples opened a religious center in Ogura, where she offered healing and other ritual services to her growing following. The founder allegedly encouraged members to engage in some sort of ritual confinement *(okomori)*, a practice that may have led to rumors of men and women spending the night in the same quarters. Needless to say, these early activities in Ogura were not authorized by the government, and before long Mitsu was arrested and her followers dispersed. In 1878 she set up another teaching site under the rubric of a center for the study of political ideals *(seigaku kōdansho)*, where she continued to preach about the Wondrous Dharma and to distribute miraculous healing water to the ill. When one of her patients (the young son of a wealthy Ogura merchant) suddenly died, Mitsu was again detained by the police, this time for several months. Upon her release she nevertheless took up her religious and healing activities once again.

Syncretic Buddhist-Shinto rituals and healing-exorcistic activities, both of which Mitsu appears to have practiced, had been explicitly banned during the first Meiji years, and even after the collapse of the Great Teaching Campaign, the creed of the Three Standards of Instruction and the central state's policy of civilization and enlightenment continued to define the parameters of acceptable religious activities. Moreover, unlike Shingaku, Tōkyūjutsu, and Tohokami, the Renmon group had not been included in the doctrinal instruction campaign and therefore still lacked a connection to an authorized religious organization in the late 1870s. While some associations were welcomed or even actively recruited by nativist-inspired shrine administrators who sought to build up their own sects in the early Meiji, newer or less conventional groups like Renmonkyō had to fight for legitimation in the newly partitioned "Shinto" and "Buddhist" world.

The founder began actively to pursue legalization for her organization in 1882, when she traveled to Tokyo and made overtures to possible Shinto-sect affiliates. In the meantime she opened a Tokyo worship site (initially in Kanda, then in Shitaya) and began to give out healing water— a practice that attracted droves of followers that summer, when cholera was raging in the capital.[25] Soon Mitsu and the group's manager, Honda Hachirō, were summoned to the police station; they were prohibited from distributing the sanctified water, fined, and imprisoned. After their release they redoubled their efforts to legitimize the group's activities. An attempt to affiliate with Shinshūkyō fell through, but Taiseikyō (which had just attained the status of an independent Shinto sect) accepted the Kyushu-based movement into its fold. Mitsu was ranked a doctrinal instructor candidate and appointed the head of her group, which was officially titled "Taiseikyō Renmon Kōsha."

These credentials greatly facilitated the spread of Renmonkyō. The movement expanded rapidly throughout Japan, especially in Tokyo, the Chūgoku region, and the northern part of Kyushu.[26] During the mid-1880s the movement is believed to have been comparable in scale to Tenrikyō, Konkōkyō, and Maruyamakyō; it peaked toward the end of the decade, when the membership reportedly reached about nine hundred thousand, with ninety-two teaching sites in operation throughout the country. These numbers may be somewhat inflated, but there is little doubt that the Renmon movement gained hundreds of thousands of followers during these years.[27] Moreover, although Mitsu's followers were mostly of commoner ancestry, aristocrats and former samurai were also well represented. A written statement of faith in Renmonkyō, dated August 11, 1886, was signed by eight former samurai, eight members of the nobility, and one commoner.[28] A Renmonkyō register of 1888–1889 allegedly contained the names of thirty-six members of the nobility (*kazoku*), some of whom enjoyed national repute (such as the aforementioned Tōkyū supervisor, Suwa Chūsei, and the wife of the prominent official, Hijikata Hisamoto).[29] It is worth noting that the donors who funded the aforementioned stone monument in Ogura in 1889 each gave at least 100 yen; they included such figures as the noted navy general Kawamura Sumiyoshi (1836–1904).[30]

One of the most important factors in the explosive growth of Mitsu's movement, as indicated above, was the spread of cholera in the larger Tokyo area. The cholera epidemic of 1858 had left two hundred thousand dead in Edo, and in 1879 there had been a serious resurgence of the disease. When another outbreak occurred in 1882 (the year Mitsu arrived from Kyushu), the fear of cholera in the capital is said to have been intense.[31] Oku Takenori warns that we cannot necessarily assume a specific, chronological correspondence between the spread of cholera and (for example) the number of Renmon sites that were established in a particular area, as Takeda Dōshō argues, but there is no question that the movement's boom in the mid-1880s (like that of other healing religions) was related to the spread of the illness.[32]

People in nineteenth-century Japan adopted various methods in order to cope with the personal devastation caused by epidemics, including soliciting the services of exorcists and carrying out communal rituals designed to ward off the the disease (so-called cholera festivals, *korera matsuri*).[33] Soon after the Restoration the government initiated a public-health policy that was informed by Western medicinal principles, but it was not successfully implemented on a large scale during the early Meiji. Most people could not afford effective medical treatment, even if they happened to have access to it; as Takeda points out, Renmonkyō's healing water was far less expensive at two *sen* per month.[34] Yet the conflict between official policy and people's approach to health care involved more than economics. As Susan Burns puts it, "the establishment of the new public health system required the reordering of the socio-cultural understanding of sickness and health, of the body and the practices to which it was subject."[35] Many people in the early Meiji period, as in the Tokugawa, assumed an integral connection between physical health and spiritual well-being, and resisted the government's attempts to control health care by excluding it from the domain of religion and ritual. Insofar as Mitsu and her associates encouraged followers to imbibe the sacred water distributed by the group rather than rely on doctors and medicines, they presented a challenge to the state's civilization policies.[36] It was probably in response to the growing popularity of these and other unofficial strategies for dealing with epidemics that in 1882 the central state reiterated its earlier warning that religious teachers were permitted to carry out incantations and exorcistic rituals for sick people who requested them only if the latter were already under the care of a physician.[37]

After the Renmon movement grew popular in the 1880s it therefore suffered more and more government harassment on the grounds of its alleged healing practices. However, the state was only one contributor to the increasing pressure on the movement, and not always an effective one at that. The years in which Renmonkyō reached its greatest numbers were the same in which social conservatives moved into high gear in their battle for the Japanese public mind. The group's heterodox presentation indeed seems to have caught the attention of writers and publicists just as the political climate in Japan was shifting from the conservatism of the late 1880s to the new nationalism of the 1890s. In 1891 the popular writer Ozaki Kōyō (1867–1903) fanned the flames of the incipient controversy surrounding the movement when he published a novella in installments in the *Yomiuri shinbun* called "Red and White Poison Dumplings" *(Kōhaku dokumanjū)*. The series is a tale of nefarious doings, supposedly inspired by the inside story of Renmonkyō.[38] (The title alludes to the way in which the innate evil of the group was disguised by an attractive outer image—like the red bean paste buried in the middle of white rice-flour dumplings.) During the ensuing years, Renmonkyō became the target of a widespread public-relations assault: members of the press, intellectuals, and leaders of established religious communities universally denounced it as a "perverted, evil teaching" *(inshi jakyō)*.

The Campaign against Renmonkyō

The hardening of public opinion about devotional movements like Renmonkyō was inextricably related to the political climate of the 1890s.

The outbreak of the Sino-Japanese War in 1894 brought nationalistic sentiments to their peak; the cultural openness and liberal attitudes of the first Meiji years were seemingly displaced.[39] The intensification of national consciousness is well documented in the press, which by 1890 had become quite sophisticated, independent, and not least, profit-oriented. *Yorozu chōhō,* which catered to the working classes, stands out among the many newspapers that contributed to the ideological process of the time. This so-called paper of the Tokyoites *(Edokko shinbun)* was cheaper, shorter, and more readable than the more established papers; it reached a circulation of over nine million by 1893 (although not without indulging in sensationalism and inaccurate reporting).[40]

Yorozu chōhō was not a "political" newspaper; it reported on political affairs, but it did not consistently promote a particular platform of causes, as did some of the larger Meiji papers.[41] It participated energetically, however, in the production of discourses of social morality and nationalism during the 1890s. One of *Yorozu*'s most distinctive contributions to this process was its concentrated use of religion as a gauge of Japanese civic propriety. During the months just before and during Japan's war with China, the newspaper conducted a prolonged and concerted campaign against Renmonkyō. Day after day, for a period of about nine months, the paper featured critical articles about Mitsu and her following, usually on the front page and often accompanied in the same issue by supplementary pieces on a related topic. The main series about the movement, "The Perverted Religion, Renmon Kyōkai" *(Inshi Renmon Kyōkai),* published in ninety-four installments, purported to describe the origins and general history of the movement and its founder. Other running features included, for example, an ostensible exposé of the corrupt relationship between Renmonkyō and *Kaishin shinbun* (a prominent newspaper aligned with Ōkuma Shigenobu's Progressive Party), a disquisition on the threat to Shinto posed by new groups like Renmonkyō, and an extended editorial on why the movement should simply be abolished. Countless requests for retraction from the Renmon organization, on the one hand, and numerous letters of appreciation (ostensibly from readers) for *Yorozu*'s illumination of the "truth" about the group, on the other, also appeared in the paper with regularity. Separate reports on the group's practices, its relationship with Taiseikyō, the legal wrangling between Renmonkyō and *Yorozu chōhō,* and reprints of other newspapers' critical coverage of the movement were added as the campaign heated up in the late spring of 1894.

It is difficult to account for the spectacular length and singular focus of *Yorozu*'s attack on Shimamura Mitsu and her followers until one casts an eye on the rest of the paper. The campaign against Renmonkyō was not simply an expression of the moral indignation of the paper's opinionated editor, Kuroiwa Ruikō (Shūroku, 1862–1920).[42] Side by side with the Renmonkyō articles, other running stories and intriguing tales appear in installments in each issue, often accompanied by engaging illustrations of the particular "episode" of the day.[43] The serial publication of dramatic novelettes and titillating narratives was one of the chief devices that *Yorozu chōhō* and other emerging newspapers of the time used to attract and hold their readers' interest. "The Perverted Religion, Renmon Kyōkai," which appeared nearly every day from April to June 1994, exemplifies an early Japanese journalistic genre that aimed to satisfy the public demand for a suspense-ridden, long-lasting, and (best of all) "true" story.

The charges brought against Mitsu and her followers in *Yorozu chōhō* fall into roughly four categories: personal immorality, fraudulent and corrupt money practices, illicit healing, and religious heterodoxy and heteropraxy. The founder is depicted from the beginning of her career, indeed even as a young girl before she turned to religion, as incorrigibly promiscuous; her shamed, despairing parents are said to have finally disowned her. According to the *Yorozu* account, the young Mitsu managed to seduce virtually every man with whom she became acquainted, from the local youths to her own teacher, Yanagida. All of this sexual activity naturally led to unwanted pregnancies, at least one of which allegedly produced an illegitimate child.[44] Later, the story went, Mitsu used the same powers of persuasion to make her way in Tokyo. *Yorozu* writers asserted, for example, that in order to acquire legal status for her group Mitsu became intimate with a certain Hara Kurasuke, a subordinate of Hirayama Seisai; by promising Hara various bonuses (including a young wife from Kyushu), Mitsu convinced him to intercede for her with the Taisei leader.[45] The *Yorozu* writers also repeatedly accused the Renmon leader and her followers of moneymaking scams and bribery. The most common charge in this category was that the group sold fake healing water and talismans to people who were seeking a cure for their illnesses. The bribery accusations were somewhat more elaborate. For example, *Kaishin shinbun* was said to have taken payoffs from Renmonkyō, apparently because it failed to attack the group as fiercely as other papers of the time.[46]

The alleged Renmon practice of having people drink "divine water" in lieu of undergoing medical treatment was a major focus of the press campaign. The publicized complaints about the group's healing practices apparently prompted the Tokyo police to carry out an analysis of the water that was being distributed at local Renmon worship centers. When the results showed that the substance was not poisonous (as some had suspected), *Yorozu chōhō* insisted that the investigation had, contrary to its ostensible purpose, served only to legitimate the group.

Regardless of whether Renmonkyō sold pure or impure water to its followers, the press writers argued, it was clearly an evil religion that
should never have been legalized in the first place. The investigation did
reveal traces of ammonia in the water, presumably added for disinfective
purposes; the authorites announced that it was not potable and prohibited Renmon practitioners from distributing it.[47] In the ensuing days,
Yorozu writers nevertheless continued to protest the government's strategy; they asserted that Renmonkyō was now storing and selling the outlawed water clandestinely, and called on the authorities to enforce the
prohibition more vigorously.[48]

The paper's critical attitude toward the government's handling of
the Renmonkyō affair, on this occasion and others, illustrates a trend in
which members of emerging professional groups in Tokyo claimed moral
superiority vis-à-vis the state bureaucracy and appointed themselves the
true educators of the less-privileged classes.[49] *Yorozu chōhō* was especially aggressive in exposing the misdoings of high-ranking elites and officials during the 1890s. The paper's editor, Kuroiwa, utilized an emerging brand of "investigative reporting" to contrast the allegedly corrupt
habits of government representatives with the purportedly reasonable,
"practical" concerns of his hard-working constituents. *Yorozu* readers,
according to Kuroiwa, were "people who are busy, people who work in
the daytime and pay their oil bills in the evening, people who need reading that is easy."[50] The reading was "easy" not merely in terms of its
textual presentation but because it played on the disposition of the
working classes to challenge the prerogatives of official and hereditary
elites. *Yorozu* and other newspapers of this kind became popular in the
late nineteenth century in part because of this polemical social stance.
From this perspective, the attack on Renmonkyō was not simply a narrow assault on certain unconventional practices: religious propriety was
one of the key issues that educated urbanites used to distinguish themselves as the moral arbiters of the day.[51]

The doctrinal presentation of Renmonkyō was another press target. A quarter of a century after the nativist-inspired campaign to "separate gods and Buddhas," contributors to the debate over Renmonkyō
depicted the division between Shinto and Buddhism as an incontrovert-
ible reality. Even though Renmonkyō had been duly affiliated with
Shinto Taiseikyō since 1882, its Shinto credentials were now angrily
called into question. Self-appointed defenders of the native faith complained that the group's Buddhist coloration should have disqualified it
at the outset for inclusion in Taiseikyō. Whether Shinto be defined as
nonreligious reverence of the imperial ancestors or as sectarian worship
of *kami*, the commentators declared, Mitsu and her teachings clearly did
not measure up.[52] The chief premise in either case, as in Kawai's dis-

course on Tenrikyō, was that the superstitious beliefs and occult rituals of the group conflicted with contemporary rationality. "Today's religion," *Yorozu* writers declared, must conform with "the common knowledge of our age."

> What Renmonkyō teaches is not adequate to satisfy the knowledge of people who have received the common education of our time.... [W]hat [the Renmon teachers] say is nothing more than that one must firmly believe in the "Wondrous Dharma of Things." If one believes in it, then physically one will have good fortune, one's whole family will prosper, and one will enjoy the protection and miraculous benefits of the God of the Wondrous Dharma (Myōhōjin).[53]

The grounding of one's fortune and prosperity on faith in this unfamiliar god was evidently not enough to qualify the Renmon system as either "Shinto" or "religion"—much less "learning," as we saw earlier. All of these categories were now used in public discourse to exclude heterodox groups from the domain of reasonable and respectable forms of personal cultivation.

The Shinto sects of the day lost little time in joining the assault on Mitsu's group, despite its official ties with their presumed peer, Taiseikyō. Representatives of Jingūkyō and Shinshūkyō called for urgent action to be taken against the Renmon movement. The director of Shinshūkyō, Yoshimura Masamochi (who was also involved in Daidōsha), had rejected Mitsu's application for affiliation with his sect years earlier; now he raised the alarm about the impact of Renmonkyō on Shinto as a whole. He depicted the new group as a fearful threat to the very integrity of Japan:

> Just at this time, foreign enemies like Christianity are invading the customs and teachings of our country. How can the people of our nation neglect to defend themselves against this [enemy] for [even] one day?... Right now we who are responsible for the customs and teachings of our own country must unite in heart, create a single, powerful regiment, and counter the foreign enemy. However, even within the ranks of our own people, there are already ugly, unclean things like Renmonkyō.

Yoshimura's language eerily previews twentieth-century discourses (both Asian and European) that predicated successful nationhood on religious sanitation. Before vanquishing the external enemy, the Shinto leader concluded, it was imperative first to "destroy these hideous, filthy traitors."[54] Yoshimura, like his Daidōsha colleague Kawai and other

Japanese patriots of the time, in effect argued that domestic religious cleansing was the prerequisite for any successful defense against the foreign threat. In the above passage, the enemy is identified as Christianity, but in the early 1890s this kind of rhetoric also fueled the public imagination of the foreign *military* challenges Japan was facing.

Buddhist leaders were just as distressed as their Shinto colleagues over the spread of the new religions, not least because of the potential loss of their own parishioners to these groups. The well-read Buddhist paper *Meikyō shinshi* urged the Home Ministry to dissolve Renmonkyō and groups like it as soon as possible, lest they irreparably damage the customs and mentality of the Japanese people.[55] Nichiren-sect leaders sharply denounced Mitsu's use of the vocabulary of Lotus Buddhism and reiterated that her group had absolutely no connection with the great Nichiren or his teachings. The Pure Land Buddhist newspaper *Jōdo kyōhō* ran a month-long series of articles called "Yōkyō Taiji" (Stamp Out Strange Religions) that took special aim at Renmonkyō.[56] The Gakushikai (Scholars Society), a Buddhist studies group founded by such luminaries of the late Meiji Buddhist world as Nanjō Bun'yū (1849–1927), Murakami Senshō (1851–1929), and Kiyozawa Manshi (1863–1903), took up the critique in a more sophisticated style.[57] Its members devoted a significant portion of their inaugural meeting to the topic "Policies toward Tenrikyō and Renmonkyō."[58]

In addition to elucidating one of the processes through which publicists, intellectuals, and established sectarian leaders delineated the parameters of acceptable religion in Meiji Japan, the campaign against Renmonkyō sheds invaluable light on the internal dynamics of the umbrella Shinto sects. The relationship between Renmonkyō and Taiseikyō became a matter of public debate in 1894. The defenders of Shinto openly chastized the Taisei organization for its apparent indifference to the corruption and heterodoxy of one of its members. How could this Shinto sect, commentators demanded, maintain in its very midst a group that showed little evidence of worshiping authentic Japanese deities or of using ancient Japanese language in its ceremonies—not to mention that it contravened legal injunctions against the use of incantations and rituals for healing and rejected modern medical treatment? In response, rather than defending Mitsu and her group, other Taisei affiliates became just as preoccupied with Renmonkyō's alleged evils as the rest of the religious establishment, if not more. After two weeks of the *Yorozu* series, members of the "Great Misogikyō Youth Association of Japan" (Dai Nippon Misogikyō Seinenkai) demanded that the headquarters of Taiseikyō take decisive action against Renmonkyō and announced its own lecture meeting on the campaign to abolish the group.[59] The fact that the Misogi community, a founding member of the Taisei coalition, publicly called for action against its own affiliate is one more testimony to the Shinto sect's highly decentralized nature.

Information contained in the *Yorozu chōhō* must be used with caution, but the few feature articles in the paper that discuss Taiseikyō in detail are at least not obviously fictionalized in the style of the main Renmon narrative. Reporters attest in these articles that, when queried about the origins of the relationship between Taiseikyō and the Renmon group, the Taisei general manager, Katō Naokane, informed them that twelve years earlier the Shinto sect had accepted the Kyushu group into its jurisdiction on the basis of Mitsu's avowal that her followers worshiped the Taisei Shinto pantheon.[60] However, Katō allegedly added that, unlike the other Taisei member groups, Renmonkyō had never requested the attendance of the Taisei director on occasions of religious worship, and since the latter rarely visited the group, he had not really known what was going on.[61] This rather limp defense of Hirayama, if taken at face value, suggests that the relationship between Taiseikyō and Renmonkyō was nominal from the outset, consisting only of economic and administrative cooperation. Another negative article insinuates that the Taiseikyō leader (again, presumably Hirayama) had originally accepted the Renmon group despite his misgivings about its Buddhist-Shinto character because of the movement's potential as a source of revenue.[62]

The Taisei administration was clearly disturbed by the public allegations about its own integrity. Katō told reporters that the director, Isobe Saishin (Hirayama's successor), planned to look into the charges thoroughly and to consult with his organization's "highly ranked patrons" *(sanjo no kazokura)* about the matter. According to the *Yorozu* account, the Taisei leaders conceded that for a Shinto sect to include a group whose members recited the formula "Wondrous Dharma of Things" was awkward, and they "had no words to excuse it."[63] The net effect of this kind of reportage, needless to say, was to depict the Taiseikyō adminstrators as inept if not unprincipled. Misogikyō was inevitably tarred with the same brush. Katō was the son-in-law of the revered Misogi founder and the heir of the Misogi elder, Katō Kanehide; at the time of the controversy he was head of the Taisei branch of Misogikyō (having suceeded Honjō Munetake).

According to *Yorozu chōhō* writers, the Department of Shrines and Temples of the Home Ministry was alarmed by the paper's "investigative" reports and summoned the Taisei leader for questioning.[64] However, in the end it was not the authorities, but Kuroiwa and his cohort who exerted the most pressure on the umbrella sect to account for its wayward affiliate. Allegations that the Taisei leaders' reluctance to take decisive action against Renmonkyō stemmed from their fear of losing its membership fees were repeated in numerous *Yorozu* articles during this period. In some versions the person who comes in most directly for this charge is Hirayama's successor, Isobe, while in others, it is Katō, the Misogi head. In either case the relationship between the Taisei leadership and Renmonkyō is characterized as thoroughly corrupt. One writer indignantly concluded that

> Taiseikyō is truly being driven to its own death. It is not just Renmonkyō that is a non-creed *(mukyōshi)* which mixes up Shinto and Buddhism; Taiseikyō is also a non-creed that mixes up Shinto and Buddhism. Taisei-kyō cannot rank itself alongside the other Shinto sects as a form of Shinto: it is not qualified to call itself "Shinto"![65]

The public pressure had its effect. On April 30, a few days after these accusations were printed, Isobe rescinded Shimamura Mitsu's status as a Major Doctrinal Instructor *(Daikyosei)*. But the *Yorozu chōhō* writers did not let up. They accused Taiseikyō of simply devolving Mitsu's teaching credentials to her heir, Shimamura Shinshū, instead of dissolving the group entirely, because the sect wished to preserve one of its main sources of revenue.[66] The charges of corruption against both Renmonkyō and Taiseikyō thus continued to multiply. *Yorozu* alleged, for example, that Renmonkyō had once attempted to attain the status of an independent Shinto sect (and thereby leave Taiseikyō), but that the Taisei leaders had insisted on a huge "severance" payment of 4,000 yen (1,000 according to some accounts). When Renmon's application for sect status to the Home Ministry failed, the Taisei leaders reportedly refused to return the money.[67] *Yorozu* writers also claimed that Mitsu had bribed the Taisei administrators to take the lesser action of removing her rank rather than acquiesce to the calls for her group's dissolution; according to this account, Isobe and Katō split the payoff of 500 yen between them.[68]

It is impossible to disprove or prove any of these insinuations. There is surely some truth, however, in the inference that Taiseikyō was reluctant to expel Renmonkyō because of the anticipated loss of membership, and thus income. We have already noted that the relationship between the umbrella Shinto sects and their secondary member groups was often more economic and administrative than religious in nature. Contemporary enrollments in the primary Taisei groups—Shingaku, Misogikyō, and Tōkyujutsu—were relatively insignificant in comparison with Mitsu's following of several hundreds of thousands.[69] The prospect of losing these members may well have deterred the Taisei administrators from cutting their ties with Renmonkyō. In any event, the *Yorozu* allegations that Isobe and Katō had accepted a bribe from Mitsu prompted an indignant demand by Isobe for a retraction. The next issue of the paper included a statement by Isobe (in tiny print) denying that he had received the said monies from Renmonkyō, or indeed that he or Katō exerted any undue influence on the Taisei policy toward the Renmon group.[70] A few days later, Isobe instituted a set of reforms for Renmonkyō. The rules were duly printed in *Yorozu chōhō*, but not on the front page, and with little fanfare.

The new guidelines were not particularly radical or controversial. Members were advised, for example, not to place the jar labeled "divine water" in front of the altar, to continue to perform the "great purification" *(ōharae)* rituals, to chant Shinto prayers, and to place a Shinto purification wand *(gohei)* near the altar. These measures were designed to downplay—though not quite forbid—the group's healing practices and to refurbish Renmonkyō's (and by extension, Taiseikyō's) Shinto qualifications. In addition, Isobe strictly prohibited evening meetings, no doubt in order to parry reports of the group's nighttime sexual misdoings. Renmon teachers were further cautioned to give central place to the Three Standards of Instruction and to moral values in their sermons. However, the rules omit any mention of the practice of reciting the "Wondrous Dharma of Things" or of the distribution of healing water —the two components of the group's praxis that the press and established religious leaders had most harshly criticized.[71] Under the circumstances, the response of the Taisei organization to the accusations against its member group was quite modest—perhaps an indication that the retention of the Renmon followers within the Taisei fold was indeed economically crucial.

Although the outbreak of the Sino-Japanese War in the summer of 1894 shifted public attention away from Renmonkyō, demands on the Taisei leader to dissolve the group continued. Later that year, when Isobe quietly reinstated Mitsu's Taiseikyō teaching credentials, he was vituperated by the press and again accused of taking bribes. Increasingly vulnerable after months of controversy, Isobe was now under pressure from the government as well; in November the Home Ministry not only rejected his request for authorization of Mitsu's reinstatement but summarily relieved him of his duties as director of Taiseikyō.[72] In the following month the ministry assigned Misogi leaders Tōgū Chiwaki and Murakoshi Kaneyoshi responsibility for administering the umbrella sect.[73]

Yorozu chōhō led the charge, but it did not have a monopoly on the campaign against Shimamura Mitsu and her associates. Negative reports about Renmonkyō, many derived from the same source or simply borrowed directly from the pages of *Yorozu*, abounded in newspapers across the spectrum during the early 1890s. The *Jiyū shinbun, Mainichi shinbun, Yomiuri shinbun, Chūō shinbun, Kokumin shinbun, Niroku shinpō,* and *Miyako shinbun,* to name only a few national-level papers, universally printed derogatory reports and editorials about the group. It is important to note that these papers were not aligned with one party or government faction, but represented the entire range of political views.[74] The anti-Renmon frenzy was not a liberal or a conservative campaign, but simply one episode in a wide-ranging ideological process that propelled itself to a consensus, seemingly of its own accord, once *Yorozu* pulled the trigger. I should add that although the newspapers took the lead in this campaign, the public attacks on Mitsu's group were oral as well as written. Lecture meetings on the evils of Renmonkyō and strategies to abolish it were held frequently in Tokyo in the mid-1890s (and duly announced in advance in the press). The fate of the group was apparently even debated in the national assembly; a Liberal Party representative made a motion to the effect that the Home Ministry should disband the group. His arguments drew on the same litany of complaints that *Yorozu* had publicized: Renmonkyō did not qualify as a genuine religion; it illegally distributed healing water, heartlessly defrauding followers and preventing them from receiving proper medical care; its leaders were immoral; and finally, it was not "Shinto" because its praxis centered on the *Lotus Sūtra.*[75]

Mitsu's movement declined drastically in the late 1890s, and in the twentieth century it disappeared altogether. It is unlikely that Renmonkyō would have imploded so quickly if it had not been subjected to the public-relations assault described above, but significant internal problems also contributed to the fragmentation of the movement. Takeda stresses that Mitsu lacked a personal experience of revelation or divine possession comparable to those enjoyed by the founders of contemporary new religions such as Tenrikyō, Konkōkyō, and Ōmotokyō; she did not project the charisma of a "living god" *(ikigami)* and therefore was unable to maintain the cohesion of her community in the long term. In this view, Mitsu had simply inherited Yanagida's "philosophy"; her teachings were accordingly rather shallow and idealistic in nature, without a significant focus on the problem of personal salvation.[76] The group's weak organizational structure may have been more instrumental in its decline, however. Mitsu and her associates were unable to establish a firm administrative foundation before the group mushroomed in the 1880s. People turned to the group in despair over their illnesses, hoping to be cured by its holy water, but most of these individuals did not maintain their commitment to the Renmon teachings in the aftermath of their "treatment" (in contrast with analogous recruits to the Tenri and Konkō groups, as Takeda points out). The fickleness of these Renmon followers is probably related to the dearth of skilled leaders in the group at the time. Many influential members apparently dropped out of the movement quite abruptly when it was attacked in the press in the 1890s. In the ensuing years Mitsu's hereditary successors also died prematurely; the resultant vacuum led to disputes over administration and property—and, eventually, to a permanent split between the Shimamura family and Taiseikyō.[77]

The Modulation of Orthodoxy

The primary members of the Taiseikyō organization—Misogikyō, Shingaku, and Tōkyūjutsu—shared fundamental assumptions about the nature of personal cultivation, despite their distinctive practices. Renmonkyō and other ad hoc members of the federation were not necessarily participants in that consensus. Even among the primary members, disparity in doctrines and rituals invited a kind of leveling in which some coalition partners reinterpreted their affiliates' histories or practices in the direction of their own interests. Kawajiri Hōkin, who "updated" Shingaku training manuals and biographies from a Hakuin Zen perspective, made an analogous contribution to the history of Tohokami by emphasizing elements in his Misogi writings that would appeal to an educated, "modern" audience. These individual adaptations were not a response to demands made by Hirayama or other sectarian administrators. As Taiseikyō's 1890s critics correctly pointed out, the sect did not enforce strict conformity with a set of ritual and ideological standards. Even after Hirayama had died and the political climate in Japan evolved from cultural conservatism to outright nationalism, Taiseikyō did not become a tightly knit group commanded by a strong leader who persuaded his constituent units to advance some sort of uniform ideology. Indeed, by the outbreak of the war with China, Hirayama's "Great Synthesis" had degenerated into a fragmented assocation of unrelated groups, each intent on pursuing its own agenda and bound together only by political and economic necessity. Shingaku and Misogi leaders Kawajiri Hōkin and Honjō Munctake were probably able to contribute to the shaping of religious orthodoxy in Japan more effectively through Daidōsha, a voluntary ideological association that originated outside the state, than through the rather emasculated, semiofficial Shinto sect to which they both necessarily belonged.

I have focused in this chapter on the story of Renmonkyō because of its relationship to the history of the Taisei–Engakuji network that has occupied us, in one aspect or another, throughout this book. However, the attack on Mitsu and her followers is more broadly significant for its illustration of the Meiji debate over the new religious movements as a whole—a debate that became conspicuous in public discourse during the months leading up to Japan's first modern war. Other healing religions that spread widely during the disease-ridden early Meiji were subjected to the same opprobrium. The Tenri, Konkō, and Maruyama movements had each been authorized to teach in affiliation with an official Shinto sect, but as in the case of Renmonkyō this nominal legalization did not mitigate their suppression. Local and state authorities repeatedly arrested and otherwise harassed the leaders of all these movements throughout the early Meiji years. In contrast with the umbrella Shinto sects, by the end of the 1880s none of these popular movements had attained the status of an autonomous religious body.[78]

Once the press took up the cause of orthodoxy in earnest in the 1890s, the new religions were lumped together in public discourse as repugnant, unwholesome phenomena that threatened the moral fiber of the Japanese nation. The *Jiyū shinbun* called for the immediate abolition of "these four perverted religions—Konkō, Renmon, Tenri, and Tenrin."[79] *Yorozu chōhō* printed a chart titled "Investigation into the Social Status of the Founders of Strange Religions" *(Yōkyō kaikisha no mibun shirabe)* that highlighted (among various unidentified groups) Renmon, Tenri, Maruyama, and Konkō.[80] In much the same vein, *Kokumin shinbun* demanded to know why, if Renmon, Tenri, and the various other depraved associations that were spreading evil in the world were indeed "part of Shinto," their respective Shinto-sect directors did not fulfill their civic responsibility to control and reform them?[81]

During the early Meiji, the practitioners of the new devotional movements were accused mainly of illicit healing, immorality, and other "uncivilized" practices. In the early 1890s, critics launched the same charges, but used the language of nationalism to edge public opinion further in the direction of preferred standards of cultural practice. The Daidōsha leader, Kawai, the Shinshūkyō director, Yoshimura, and the other public moralists quoted earlier energetically upheld the ideal of an unalloyed national creed as war approached on the continent; their comments are simply a few examples of the rhetorical identification of internal dissent with an external enemy that became a common discourse during this time. By identifying an "other" within their own midst— Japanese citizens who could serve, in Gluck's apt phrase, as "metaphorical foreigners"[82]—these and other ideologues could more effectively modulate the moral and civic sensibilities of the urban workers who avidly bought up copies of tabloids like *Yorozu chōhō* during the formative years of Japanese imperialism.

In the first few chapters of this book I emphasized that, although the creators of Nanboku physiognomy, Tōkyūjutsu, and Tohokami all paid lip service to conventional Neo-Confucian paradigms of social and individual development, they each redefined "learning" in the direction of tangible, often physiologically oriented practices. In the figuration of that particular time, they played the part of creative reformers of the available discourses of personal cultivation. The physical dimension of self-improvement was not necessarily missing from more elite formulations. Kaibara Ekiken's explicit concern with diet and health, mentioned in chapter 2, is only one of the more prominent examples of this way of thinking among Tokugawa Confucian scholars, many of whom doubled as physicians. Nevertheless, taken as a whole, in contrast to more educated discourses of personal well-being, the systems we examined tended to place more stress on the bodily aspects of "cultivating one's person" than on the ordering of inner states.

It is important to note that this disaffection with the abstractness of the scholarly paradigm of self-improvement and the concomitant interest in such processes as eating and breathing did not necessarily translate into devotional movements centered on powerful or unfamiliar gods. None of the cultivation groups in our Tokugawa survey were inspired by a charismatic leader who derived authority from experiences of divine possession, or who advocated practices designed to foster miraculous benefits such as healing. It is true that Inoue Masakane was a man of demonstrated religious commitment who ostensibly placed his greatest emphasis on the importance of faith in the divine, but the program of practice that he actually promoted (and that his later followers enhanced in this regard) rested in the final analysis on the initiative of the individual. Inoue's followers were not passionate devotees of unorthodox gods —unlike the worshipers of Tenrin-ō, Ji no myōhō, Konkō, and Moto no chichihaha (the Maruyama deity), Tohokami practitioners paid obeisance to Amaterasu and other textually authorized Shinto deities. The latter usually functioned as relatively impersonal objects of ritual attendance, not as possessing agents or as all-powerful healing forces.

Religious groups led by distinctive leaders who claimed special access to divine authority and miraculous curative powers played a negative defining role in the emergence of a public consensus about religion in modern Japan.[83] "Orthodoxy is best defined by what it chooses to exclude," as Sheldon Garon puts it.[84] The issue that comes sharply to the fore in the late Meiji, and that differentiates the eventual middle-class orthodoxy from formulations more attractive to less-privileged sectors of Japanese society, is not necessarily an interest in the physical dimension of personal well-being per se, but rather the acceptability of devotion to a single charismatic leader and/or deity.

Even though Mitsu did not claim to have been possessed by her god, she purported to be infused with a unique divine power that commanded a submission of faith from her followers. This stance of devotional surrender differs from (though it is not necessarily incompatible with) notions of religious transformation that emphasize the role of the subject. The latter seem to have become more widespread in the middle strata of Japanese society in the late nineteenth century, partly through the proliferation of the print media. Unlike Yokoyama Marumitsu, Mizuno Nanboku, Inoue Masakane, Imakita Kōsen, and their Meiji followers, Shimamura Mitsu steadfastly emphasized simple faith in her deity; as far as one can determine from the few sources available, the Renmon understanding of "practical learning" did not encompass a regimen of psychological or physical disciplines that encouraged individuals to control their own (and thus, society's) well-being.

It was the perceived surrender (not only credal, but also economic and sexual) to devotionalist leaders like Mitsu that most disturbed the Meiji "men of maturity" who envisioned systems of personal development more conducive to national unity. During the late nineteenth century, social educators and sectarian leaders eagerly engaged in defining what they understood to be reasonably intelligent and practical forms of personal improvement that would contribute to Japan's (and their own) success in the world. Associations that continued to derive their primary inspiration from the revelatory experiences of charismatic founders— especially, but not exclusively, female founders—were held up as counterexamples to this vision of genuine learning and social order.

The relationship between personal cultivation and devotion in the religious life of any individual or group is never absolute or static, but rather a constantly shifting dialectic. Ideological currents in late-nineteenth-century Japan nonetheless seem to have fueled the public imagination of a binary opposition between these two modes, and in the ensuing decades the state took steps to enliven the contrast for its own purposes.[85]

AFTERWORD

In the Tokugawa milieu treated early in this book, Confucian scholars, Buddhist priests, morality preachers, fortune-tellers, and new-religion founders promoted their teachings by referring to paradigms of personal cultivation that all took for granted. They shared a certain perception of the world in which they lived, a perception that was at the same time modulated in accordance with each one's social environment and interests.[1] For these individuals and their followers, the quest was not to modify the existing order directly, but to show how the pursuit of each one's particular proposal would lead to the fulfillment of the common vision of personal and social perfection.

It is problematic to use the term "conservatism" with reference to this type of situation, in which, as Huntington says, "[e]ach group attempts to show that its policies are more in accord with the common ideals than those of the other group."[2] A broad-based, fundamental challenge to the established institutions of the time that could provoke the rise of a conservative ideology in the social strata from which these groups emerged was absent in early-nineteenth-century Japan. It must be said, however, that these Tokugawa interpretive systems were premised on ideas that are associated with conservatism in its classic Burkean definition: the notion that evil derives from the inner condition or behavior of individuals rather than from established social institutions, and the idea that the community is more important than the individual.[3] These two assumptions seem to inform much of the historical conversation investigated in this book. In the Tokugawa context, many persons elaborated upon these ideas by referring to well-known Confucian passages; some defined them in reaction to Chinese textual traditions, which they depicted as irrelevant to the practical concerns of daily life.

The striving for practical forms of cultivation was eminently compatible with this protoconservative mentality. Disciplines of self-improvement did not require the adoption of new ideational elements or the acceptance of new institutions; many Tokugawa educators understood practical learning simply as a more experiential and, in some versions, workable approach to personal reform. This moral or religious understanding of practical learning persisted in the discourse of various Meiji teachers, whether the educated abbot Imakita Kōsen, or the new-religion founder, Shimamura Mitsu. Even when Meiji intellectuals and government leaders called for a new, technologically oriented practical learning, the emphasis was not on a type of knowledge that sought to shape or challenge the existing social order, but on a more efficient system of bettering the individual as a component in the national collective. Ultimately, the model of the successful man that inspired urban elites in the late nineteenth century drew on both meanings of practical learning: personal reform or discipline, on the one hand, and professional education in the service of the whole, on the other.

The emerging middle classes of this period had absorbed the ethos of individual career success that was popularized in the early Meiji; at the same time, as David Ambaras notes, they had "inherited traditions that stressed the importance of intellectual and moral cultivation geared to public service and the improvement of people's lives."[4] With the elimination of the Confucian academy, a modernized ideal of the gentleman who personifies both moral and practical excellence found a foothold in certain quarters of the established Buddhist community. Despite the loss of income, personnel, and social status of large temples in the immediate aftermath of the Restoration, they were still an imposing presence in Meiji society. These institutions were able to provide, as in the past, not only sites for shared religious activities, but, more important, foundations of social stability that encouraged the development of human networks beyond the religious domain. Communities like Engakuji played a role in the emergence of political movements in Meiji Japan in part because they offered venues for the formation of social bonds.

As a temple of historical significance located in a resort town within commuting distance of the seat of the nation's political power, Engakuji was particularly well-positioned in this regard. To be sure, the demands of its lay constituency had to be balanced against the needs of its priests through social and territorial negotiation. Ultimately, however, the temple community served the aims of its Tokyo constituents well. Engakuji Zen was an attractive form of personal refinement in the Meiji period. It provided both a nostalgic continuity with the Neo-Confucian and Buddhist enterprises of the past and a flexible religious lifestyle that seemed compatible with the new practicalism of the day—including the affirmation (muted though it was) of female religious practice. Especially for the younger practitioners who were educated in the second half of the nineteenth century, Zen Buddhism may have seemed an acceptable phase in the transformation of religion into moral philosophy that the enlightenment thinkers had envisioned for Japan. It is not without significance that increasing numbers of educated urbanites were drawn to Zen practice in the mid-1890s, just as public disapprobation of the "irrational" new religions became conspicuous in the nationalistic climate leading up to Japan's first modern war.[5] It is worth noting in this regard that many members of the same stratum of urban society were attracted to Protestant Christian ideals during these years,[6] and that missionaries living in Tokyo in the late Meiji supported these middle-class moralists in the campaign against the new religions.[7]

At the same time, the traditional relationship between priests and laypeople was not fundamentally transformed in the early to mid-Meiji years. Rinzai Zen in particular never became a mass movement; in the Kantō area, it continued to attract mostly educated urban dwellers.[8] Yet the number of such practitioners is probably less significant than their eventual social influence. These Buddhist adepts shared a common religious and moral foundation as they made their way into the upper and middle levels of twentieth-century Japanese society: they became government officials, bankers, company managers, teachers, military officers, thinkers, politicians, and writers. Several, notably D. T. Suzuki, profoundly influenced modern Japanese and Western interpretations of the Zen Buddhist teachings.

As I have implied throughout this book, we cannot successfully characterize any community in terms of a single religious system. The members of the network we have examined sought fulfillment in Shinto-type purification rituals, divination practices, and Confucian or Shingaku cultivation, as well as in Zen Buddhism.[9] Ultimately, the representatives of these religious systems created a web of interlocking figurations that extended quite beyond any particular "tradition." By the turn of the nineteenth century, they not only shared a common vision of personal and social well-being, but also cooperated in promoting it as a Japanese orthodoxy.

NOTES

A list of the abbreviations used in the notes precedes the bibliography.

Introduction

1. Roger Chartier, "Intellectual History or Sociocultural History?" 45.

2. Most of these studies concentrate on the later phase of the nineteenth-century transition; several focus on a single issue. Recent English-language studies that purport to depict an aspect of Meiji Buddhism or Shinto as a whole are: James E. Ketelaar, *Of Heretics and Martyrs;* Notto Thelle, *Buddhism and Christianity;* Richard Jaffe, *Neither Monk nor Layman;* and Helen Hardacre, *Shintō and the State*—though the coverage of the last two works extends beyond the Meiji period. Sarah E. Thal's "Rearranging the Landscape of the Gods," is an in-depth study of the "Shinto" phase of the history of Konpira/Kotohira devotionalism during the Meiji. For a recent local history of Japanese religious life that discusses both late-Edo and early-Meiji developments, see Hardacre's *Religion and Society in Nineteenth-Century Japan.*

3. The disjunction characterizes both Western and Japanese historical scholarship; for a discussion of contributing factors in the case of European and American studies of early modern Japanese religion, see my "Tokugawa Religious History," 39–41, 63.

4. Norbert Elias, *What Is Sociology?* 130–131.

5. Winston Davis, *Japanese Religion and Society,* 33.

6. "Dispositions" here is loosely inspired by the idea of "mental habits" or "social habitus," terms used by Erwin Panofsky in *Gothic Architecture and Scholasticism,* e.g., 20–21, and by Elias in *The Society of Individuals.* Pierre Bourdieu takes up the notion of habitus more intensively; for a definition see, e.g., his *The Logic of Practice,* 53.

7. Lucien Goldmann borrows the term "world vision" from Gyorgy Lukács to mean "the whole complex of ideas, aspirations and feelings which links together the members of a social group ... and which opposes them to members of other social groups" (Goldmann, *The Hidden God,* 17). My own use of the term "world vision" is not meant to imply that the mentalities highlighted in this book *necessarily* opposed their representatives to members of other social groups.

8. See Carlo Ginzburg, *The Cheese and the Worms.*

9. Soon after the Restoration, the Meiji government issued decrees (in 1872 and 1873) that permitted Buddhist monks and nuns to eat meat, grow their hair out, and lead married lives. Many Buddhist clerics, especially Shinto-shrine Buddhist priests *(shasō)*, were forcibly laicized in early Meiji, and many low-ranking temple priests voluntarily broke their commitment to a celibate life. In this context, the criteria for the application to Buddhists of the terms "lay" *(zaike)* and "monastic" *(shukke)* demand clarification. To refer to individuals who retain formal ecclesiastic duties but no longer follow the precept of celibacy as "monastics," "monks," or "nuns" is incoherent or at least ambiguous. However, in this book I treat primarily the first two decades of the Meiji era, when clerical marriage was not yet widespread or accepted (particularly not in the Rinzai sect, with which I am mostly concerned). I therefore refer to Buddhist priests and nuns as "monastics" insofar as they still avowedly followed the celibate lifestyle. When referring to later historical contexts, in which greater numbers of ordained Buddhist practitioners took up the married lifestyle, I use the term "clerics" or "clergy," following Jaffe *(Neither Monk nor Layman)*. I use the word "lay" to refer to Buddhists who were *not* ordained priests, monks, or nuns—whether married or unmarried.

10. Yasumaru Yoshio argues that the leaders of popular religious and moral movements of the eighteenth and nineteenth centuries consistently stressed the power of individual moral cultivation in the construction of a better world; see especially his *Nihon no kindaika to minshū shisō.* Hardacre in turn suggests that Neo-Confucian themes of self-cultivation may have influenced the worldview of the new lay-oriented movements that originated in this period; see her *Kurozumikyo,* 10–14, and chapter 1, passim. Harootunian argues that a "restorationist" drive toward self-sufficiency characterized a broad spectrum of interpretive groups—nativism, Mito studies, and Western learning, as well as the new religions *(Things Seen and Unseen,* 329). As it pertains to groups other than nativism, this thesis is worked out in more detail in Harootunian's essay, "Late Tokugawa Culture and Thought."

11. By "school Shinto" I mean especially the schools that dominated shrine administration during the Edo period, viz. the Yoshida and Shirakawa houses, as well as the Suika and Watarai schools.

12. See, e.g., Suzanne Desan, *Reclaiming the Sacred,* 76–121, for a discussion of anticlerical motifs in revolutionary France.

Chapter 1: The Fertility of Dead Words

1. The classic example of this interpretation in English is Robert Bellah's *Tokugawa Religion.* Harootunian also emphasizes the nativist valuation of work in his *Things Seen and Unseen.* See also Eiji Takemura, *The Perception of Work in Tokugawa Japan.* The idea of a common ethical stock or "core values" *(tsūzoku dōtoku)* was elaborated by Yasumaru Yoshio in his *Nihon no kindaika to minshū shukyō.* For an interpretation in English of a Japanese popular movement of the nineteenth century that draws on Yasumaru's notion, see Emily Ooms, *Women and Millenarian Protest in Meiji Japan,* esp. 33–44; and for a

summary of critiques of the meaningfulness of "core values" in the study of this field, see Helen Hardacre, *Kurozumikyō*, 42–43, esp. n. 20.

2. Harootunian, *Things Seen*, 70.

3. See ibid., 85, and for Harootunian's mention of Norinaga's phrases, 60. For the Japanese original of the latter, see *Motoori Norinaga zenshū*, ed. Ono Susumu, 5:388.

4. Harootunian, *Things Seen*, 188. Hirata Atsutane's attitude toward language and textual studies must also be understood in the context of his disagreements with rival nativists who emphasized philological methods. See Mark McNally, "The *Sandaikō* Debate," *Japanese Journal of Religious Studies* 29.3–4 (2002): 359–378.

5. See, e.g., the comments of Motoori Uchitō (1792–1855) on "Kogakuyō," by Motoori Ōhira (1756–1833), in *Motoori Norinaga zenshū*, ed. Motoori Toyokai, *kan* 6 *(furoku)*: 535.

6. *Things Seen*, 178. In general, Harootunian is referring here to the views of both Motoori Norinaga and Hirata Atsutane. It is unclear to me whether the further clause, that ordinary people "had remained outside the Neo-Confucian field of knowledge," is intended to represent the nativist view or Harootunian's own perspective.

7. Ibid., 179. Harootunian is drawing on Claude Lévi-Strauss here; he cites *Structural Anthropology* (New York: Basic Books, 1963), 216.

8. See Nakamura Yukihiko's essay "Kinsei kōki jugakkai no dōkō," in NST, 47:479–498, for a typology of late-Tokugawa Confucian studies, which includes the trend toward textual studies, among others. "Neo-Confucianism" in Harootunian's usage presumably indicates the scholarship inspired primarily by Zhu Xi (1130–1200) and Wang Yangming (1472–1529), the preeminent Neo-Confucian scholars of the Song (960–1279) and Ming (1368–1644) periods of China, respectively.

9. Jinsai's approach was known as Kogigaku (study of ancient meanings) and Sorai's, Kobunjigaku (study of ancient texts). Yamaga Sōkō (1622–1685) is usually depicted as the founding figure of Kogaku.

10. Kanaya Osamu, "Nihon kōshōgaku no seiritsu," 77. Kochūgaku refers in the strict sense to the work of scholars who analyzed and elaborated on pre-Song Confucian commentaries, while Kōshōgaku was a broader movement of critical textual studies whose proponents took inspiration from late Ming and early Qing scholarship.

11. See Nakamura, "Kinsei kōki," 483, 484–485.

12. Ibid., 487.

13. He began to characterize the Kōshōgaku scholars as wont to read the *Analects* or the *Mencius* without enacting the ideas therein—unlike physicians, who in his view put into practice the ideas they found in texts (Kanaya, "Kōshōgaku," 72–73). Kanaya documents the close relations between evidential studies scholars and physicians; many Kōshōgaku figures were themselves doctors. See ibid., e.g., 56.

14. Kinjō explains his change of mind in his *Gosō manpitsu (kan* 1), in *Nihon zuihitsu zenshū* 17:95–96; for his explicit criticism of Itō Jinsai and Ogyū Sorai, see, e.g., ibid., 99–100. See also Kanaya, "Kōshōgaku," 74.

15. Cited in Kanaya, "Kōshōgaku," 74, from Ōta Kinjō, *Kyūkeidan,* vol. 1.

16. Kinugasa Yasuki, *Kinsei Nihon no Jukyō to bunka,* 198.

17. *Igai Keishō sensei shokan shū, kan* 1, p. 9.; cited in Kanaya, "Kōshō-gaku," 74. Igai Keisho is ordinarily classified as a proponent of Kochūgaku, but like other eclectics he drew on diverse Confucian commentarial traditions.

18. Ishikawa Ken, *Sekimon Shingaku shi no kenkyū,* 1359; see also Ōta Kinjō, *Gosō manpitsu kōhen,* in *Nihon zuihitsu zenshū* 17:164. Izu corresponds to eastern Shizuoka prefecture.

19. Kinugasa, *Kinsei Nihon,* 200.

20. Toan was the successor to Ishida Baigan (1685–1744), the founder of the Shingaku movement. For details about him and his teachings, see Sawada, *Confucian Values,* esp. chaps. 2 and 3.

21. *Igai shokan, kan* 2, pp. 57–58.

22. Nakamura, "Kinsei kōki," 486.

23. Michael Kinski, "Moral Disposition and Personal Autonomy," 54–55. For a full-length study of Kenzan and his ideas, see Kinski's *Knochen des Weges.* The evidentialists and eclectics are conventionally classified as distinct schools (see, e.g., *Kinsei Kangakusha denki chosaku jiten* ed. Seki Giichirō and Seki Yoshinao), but in reality the two movements overlapped. Kanaya offers a rationale for the distinction between the eclectics and evidentialists in his "Kō-shōgaku," 78–79. See also Nakamura, "Kinsei Kōki," 484–485.

24. This characteristic of the Setchūgaku scholars is discussed by Sagara Tōru in his *Kinsei Nihon Jukyō undō no keifu;* see especially 180–183.

25. A majority of students at Kangien were non-samurai, mostly Buddhist priests and wealthy commoners; see Richard Rubinger, *Private Academies of Tokugawa Japan,* 93–95. For a supplementary study of Tansō and his school, see Marleen Kassel's *Tokugawa Confucian Education.*

26. The comment is contained in Tansō's *Jurinhyō,* 1.

27. See Takehiko Okada, "Neo-Confucianism in Nineteenth-Century Japan," 215–250, regarding this interchange.

28. Okada, "Neo-Confucianism," 218.

29. Several later Tokugawa scholars identified with specific Chinese thinkers; Okada, "Neo-Confucianism," 226–227. On the learning of the mind, see de Bary, *Neo-Confucian Orthodoxy,* and idem, *The Message of the Mind.*

30. The revival of interest in the workings of the mind has also been interpreted as an escapist response to the sociopolitical disorder of the period; cf. Nakamura, "Kinsei kōki," 493.

31. Pace Okada, "Neo-Confucianism," 230, discourse about personal cultivation in late-Tokugawa Confucian circles owed much to Issai's writings and teachings. He was a central figure at the Shōheikō throughout the first half of the nineteenth century, exposing many budding scholars and administrators to his views. His writings circulated extensively, even after his death in 1859—notably his magnum opus, *Genshi shiroku.*

32. Cited from Satō Issai, "Saigyo jō," in *Shūo gappen (furoku), Kusumoto Tanzan, Sekisui zenshū* (Fukuoka-shi: Ashi Shobō, 1975; 1981 repr.), and trans. Okada, "Neo-Confucianism," 230.

33. Cited in Nakamura, "Kinsei kōki," 492, apparently from Shūyō's *Dokuga shorō ikō.*

34. See, e.g., *Genshi banroku,* no. 75; NST, 46:258b (Japanese text on 121); and *Genshiroku,* no. 24, NST, 46:220a (12).

35. See *Genshi banroku,* no. 23; NST, 46:255a (111).

36. Sagara, *"Genshi shiroku,"* 710; see Sato Issai, *Genshi tetsuroku,* nos. 17 and 19, in NST, 46:275a (171). "Man" here renders Issai's term *shi,* which variously denotes a samurai, male leader, or scholar.

37. Sagara, *"Genshi shiroku,"* 710; see also *Genshi banroku,* no. 4; NST, 46:254a (109).

38. *Genshiroku,* no. 120; NST, 47:227a (30). Issai stresses the corollary relation between mental/emotional and physical health in, e.g., no. 20, NST, 46:220a (12); no. 112; NST, 46:225b (27); and *Genshi kōroku,* no. 21; NST, 46:238b (62). On this point, see also Sagara, *"Genshi shiroku,"* 716.

39. In addition to Fujizawa, Imakita studied with the Zhu Xi scholar and literary writer Shinozaki Shōchiku (1781–1851), a student of Koga Seiri (1750–1817), and with the poet Hirose Kyokusō (1807–1863), Tansō's brother.

40. *Zenkai ichiran,* ed. Morinaga Sōkō, 137. SKN, the primary source for Imakita's life, contains a detailed account of his religious practice after he took the tonsure. He did not adopt the name Kōsen until he became a monk.

41. Imakita practiced primarily under Rinzai masters Daisetsu Jōen (1797–1855) and Gisan Zenrai (1802–1878); he received the seal of approval from Gisan and became the latter's Dharma-successor *(hassu).*

42. For a modern reproduction of the Chinese text, as well as modern and classical Japanese renditions with annotations, see *Zenkai ichiran,* ed. Morinaga Sōkō. (Citations below refer to the Chinese text in this edition.) *Zenkai ichiran* was completed in 1862 but first published in a block-print edition in 1874.

43. Imakita, *Zenkai ichiran,* 151.

44. Ibid., 240.

45. Ibid., 170. Imakita reserves his most vehement criticism for the representatives of the Sorai school. See ibid., 203; 204.

46. Trans. D. C. Lau, 111, with orthographic modifications.

47. Imakita, *Zenkai ichiran,* 239–240.

48. Ibid., 202.

49. Ibid., 202. See *Analects* 15:2, trans. Lau, 13, for the "single thread" passage.

50. Though creative, Imakita's arguments in *Zenkai ichiran* are not necessarily original; he draws on his extensive knowledge of Chinese Buddhist apologetical writings.

51. Trans. Lau, 146, with orthographic modifications.

52. Imakita, *Zenkai ichiran,* 271.

53. Imakita criticized not only Sorai followers but the other Tokugawa Confucian schools. He sympathized most with the views of Wang Yangming; see, e.g., *Zenkai ichiran,* 244–245.

54. Ibid., 175.

55. Confucius, *Confucian Analects, the Great Learning, and the Doctrine of the Mean,* trans. James Legge, 388.

56. Imakita, *Zenkai ichiran,* 257.

57. Another testimony in this vein about the value of Confucius' teachings appears in ibid., 173.

58. See Antonio Gramsci, *Gli intellettuali e l'organizzazione della cultura,* 9; and John Fulton, "Religion and Politics in Gramsci," 204–205.

59. Imakita, *Zenkai ichiran,* 173–174.

60. Harootunian, *Things Seen,* 179.

61. Ibid., 187.

62. See ibid., 17, re the nativist "reworking" of earlier culture.

63. For Harootunian's expressions, see *Things Seen,* 336.

64. Pierre Bourdieu, *Language and Symbolic Power,* 39.

65. The notion that language is embedded in a particular community goes back at least to Ferdinand de Saussure, who emphasized that "language is not complete in any speaker, but exists fully only in a collectivity" (cited in Fred Dallmayr, *Language and Politics,* 58). The thrust of "linguistic community" is close to that of "speech community" (It. *la comunità linguistica*) as the latter term is used in the field of sociolinguistics, but has the advantage of allowing for both the written and oral dimensions of communication. For a definition of "speech community," see J. Gumperz, "The Speech Community," 219. Here I do not use the term "linguistic community" in the conventional sense to mean a specific national or ethnic community that shares a common language (e.g., standard Japanese vs. dialects), but in a broader, almost metaphorical sense to mean a class of individuals and groups that are competent in the lexicons and linguistic patterns through which a particular cultural system is regularly articulated.

66. Religious language "manages to speak to all groups and all groups speak it...." Bourdieu, *Language and Symbolic Power,* 40.

67. Gumperz, "Speech Community," 222.

68. Regarding the late-eighteenth-century formalization of a set curriculum for Shingaku educational activities, see Sawada, *Confucian Values,* 151–155.

69. See, e.g., Ishikawa Ken, *Sekimon Shingaku,* 1062–1063. Administrative conflicts also grew in number during this period.

70. Information about Takahashi Kōsetsu is based on "Takahashi Kōsetsu sensei jiseki ryaku," contained in the 1895 block-print edition of SSJR. A copy of the latter was kindly provided to me by the current director of Sanzensha in Tokyo, Koyama Shikei.

71. SSJR, 1a–2a.

72. SSJR, 2b.

73. SSJR, 3a. Kumatani Tōshū's allusion (*Analects* 6:25 or 12:15) elides Confucius' implication that one should integrate one's cultural learning by means of the rites. Lau renders the entire passage as follows: "'The gentleman widely versed in culture but brought back to essentials by the rites can, I suppose, be relied upon not to turn against what he stood for.'" *Analects,* 115. For Waley's version, see his *The Analects of Confucius,* 121.

74. "Replies" here refers to the "solutions" or answers to Shingaku study

questions or "problems" *(sakumon)* that Baigan (and later Shingaku masters) offered to their students. See Sawada, *Confucian Values,* 94–98.

75. *Kakku* is a Zen term for words that function in such a way as to lead one to a level of consciousness that is beyond dualistic discrimination and which in that sense faithfully express the operation of the realm of enlightenment. The contrast between "living words" (Ch. *huoju*) and "dead words" (Ch. *siju*) in Chan is discussed in the context of koan practice in Robert E. Buswell, "The 'Short-Cut' Approach of *K'an-hua* Meditation," esp. 348–349.

76. *Analects* 2:7–8.

77. SSJR, 3a–b.

78. The construction of early-Meiji Shingaku biographies is discussed in chapter 7.

79. For a succinct essay on Sorai's thought, see Samuel Yamashita, "Nature and Artifice in the Writings of Ogyū Sorai (1666–1728)"; and idem, *Master Sorai's Responsals,* 16–25. For Sorai's exclusion of a "metaphysical" dimension of the Way (whether in terms of "nature," "heaven," or "principle"), see Olivier Ansart, *L'Empire du rite,* 72–74.

80. SSJR, 3b–4a.

81. Ibid., 4a; 4b lists three other Buddhist teachers under whom Takahashi practiced.

82. The master duly confirmed that Takahashi had "seen his nature" *(kenshō);* the latter underwent a symbolic tonsure ritual at this point, but retained his lay status (SSJR, 5a).

83. "Rays of wisdom" is an interpretive rendition of *kōmyō,* literally "shining light," which in a Buddhist context means the rays of wisdom and compassion that radiate from a Buddha or bodhisattva's body.

84. SSJR, 9b. The resemblance between the two experiences is perhaps not entirely coincidental; Takahashi's Meiji biographer, as we shall see in later chapters, was Imakita's chief lay disciple.

85. Cf. Ephesians 2:1; Romans 11:11.

86. SSJR, 10a. Even at this juncture, however, Takahashi reportedly felt that he had not yet attained a sufficient degree of enlightenment; it was only after further intensive practice in 1869 under Zen master Zenmyō Hōshū (1802–1872) of Tōzenji (in today's Gifu prefecture) that he attained confidence in his level of understanding. See SSJR, 8b–9a.

Chapter 2: Divination as Cultivation

1. For contemporary practices, see Suzuki Kentarō, "Divination in Contemporary Japan," esp. 253n. Contemporary diviners may also emphasize the agency of the client (ibid., 252n.).

2. Ian Reader and George J. Tanabe, Jr., *Practically Religious,* 110. Material in brackets added.

3. The founder did not begin using the name Marumitsu until 1843; his common name was Sannosuke.

4. For these traditions, see the current Tōkyūjutsu organization's comprehensive publication, Nihon Tōdōkai, ed., *Tōkyū,* 11.

5. "Tengen Tōkyūjutsu no taika—ko Yoshikawa Intetsu-ō," *Hōchi shinbun*, Oct. 2, 1909. The subject of the article (an obituary) is Yoshikawa Ichigen (1826–1909).

6. Biographical information is relatively more available. I have relied on the few secondary accounts that I have found, some of which contain reproductions of early Tōkyū texts. Late-Meiji and early-twentieth-century Tōkyū writings represent a wide variety of interpretations, analysis of which must await a future study. I have limited my comments here to sources associated only with the founder and his immediate disciples.

7. Strictly speaking, the compound "kaiun" does not only denote the transitive action of a subject on a direct object—" 'to open up luck' in the sense of bringing or making good luck," as the authors state in the passage cited earlier (Reader and Tanabe, *Practically Religious*, 110). "Opening" *(kai)* may also describe the unfolding action of the destiny itself. The improvement may indeed take place in relation to the individual's efforts (or the latter's karma), but the possibility of simple chance playing a part is not excluded.

8. Here I follow the unsigned 1900 newspaper article "Tōkyūjutsu," *Hōchi shinbun*, 1900, reproduced in Nihon Tōdōkai, *Tōkyū*, 207.

9. Cited in Nihon Tōdōkai, *Tōkyū*, 118.

10. Ibid., 119.

11. See Sawada, *Confucian Values*, 31, 50, for the Shingaku version of this strategy.

12. According to Nihon Tōdōkai, *Tōkyū*, 14, Marumitsu attracted more than a thousand disciples; Marumitsu himself claimed more than double this number.

13. For the shogunal role in the so-called Tenpō reforms, see Harold Bolitho, "The Tempō Era," esp. 139–155. Buddhist and Shinto institutions had long been under shogunal control; for a general survey of the mechanisms and laws that the early Tokugawa government used in this regard, see Tamamuro Fumio, *Edo bakufu no shūkyō tōsei*. Sakamoto Masahisa situates the increasing regulation of so-called popular religious groups in the Edo area during this period within the shogunate's broader urban initiatives; see his "Kinsei kōki no Edo ni okeru shūkyōsha tosei to toshi mondai." I am indebted to Hayashi Makoto for bringing my attention to this useful essay.

14. Access to such archives seems to be restricted to long-time members of the Tōkyū group. The following summary of Marumitsu's interview with the shogunal authorities is based on an abridged reproduction of a document titled "Tōkyūjutsu benmei," in Yokoyama Masamitsu, "Tōso no ushiro-sugata o otte," cited in Nihon Tōdōkai, *Tōkyū*, 122–127.

15. Cited in Nihon Tōdōkai, *Tōkyū*, 124.

16. Marumitsu reported that fees for the three levels of inititation were respectively 200 *hiki*, 300 *hiki*, and 1,000 *hiki* of *zeni* (cash), but added that people occasionally joined for only 100 *hiki*, and that some paid in goods rather than cash ("Tōkyūjutsu benmeisho," cited in Nihon Tōdōkai, *Tōkyū*, 124–125). Rates fluctuated, and it is difficult to estimate the purchasing power of these monetary amounts with any accuracy. However, according to the stated prices for rice, in Edo in 1848 for 200 *hiki* one could buy 1.1 *koku* of rice; for 300 *hiki*,

1.6 *koku*; and for the highest initiation fee of 1,000 *hiki*, about 5.5 *koku* of rice. (I am counting 25 *mon* for 1 *hiki*, .015 silver *monme* for 1 *mon*, and using the Kaei 1 exchange price of 1 *koku* per 1.076 *ryō*, at 63.76 *monme* per gold *ryō*. One *koku* is about 180 liters or 5 bushels. See *Iwanami Nihonshi jiten*, 1616–1617.) Seasonal fees were much less, but could be high: domain lords and bannermen were allowed to pay whatever they felt was appropriate.

17. The Twelve Personalities are discussed below. The Twelve Branches and Ten Stems *(jikkan jūnishi)* constitute the Chinese counting system that was used for calculating dates and times in traditional East Asia.

18. Nihon Tōdōkai, *Tōkyū*, 125. I do not have access to independent sources that could confirm this.

19. Ibid.

20. Yokoyama Masamitsu, cited in Nihon Tōdōkai, *Tōkyū*, 125.

21. Ibid., 127.

22. Nihon Tōdōkai, *Tōkyū*, 108.

23. For biographical details about the six successors, see ibid., 142–176. According to Nishikawa Kōjirō, *Reigen kizui Shintō kyōsō den* (Tokyo: Eirakudō Shoten, 1914), 121–125 (cited in Inoue Nobutaka, "Bakushin," 275n48), the so-called Four Teachers of Tōkyūjutsu (Marumitsu' successors) were Sano Kazumaru, Aoki Sogan, Iida Katsumi, and Niinomi Harumitsu.

24. "Tōkyūjutsu benmei," cited in Nihon Tōdōkai, *Tōkyū*, 124.

25. One modern observer of Tōkyūjutsu suggests that this social insularity is one of the reasons why the group never became well known; see Nihon Tōdōkai, *Tōkyū*, 214.

26. Studies of samurai income during the late Tokugawa indicate that their increasing poverty was the result of the growing financial demands on them combined with a stationary income. See, e.g., Kōzō Yamamura's study of bannermen income in his *A Study of Samurai Income*, 41–48. On samurai poverty during the 1830s and early 1840s, the period when Tōkyūjutsu began to take hold, see also Bolitho, "The Tenpō Era," esp. 127.

27. Nihon Tōdōkai, *Tōkyū*, 164–165.

28. The *fudasashi* was an officer commissioned by shogunal retainers to supervise rice storage and trade in Edo.

29. Sensōji was a center of entertainment and commerce as well as religious activity during the late Tokugawa. For a full-length study, see Nam-lin Hur, *Prayer and Play in Late Tokugawa Japan*.

30. For this very sparse information about Aibara Teisan, see Nihon Tōdōkai, *Tōkyū*, 157–159.

31. Nihon Tōdōkai, *Tōkyū*, 13, 99–100.

32. Scholars have given little concerted attention to the wide range of prognostication practices that were used in early modern Japan. For a brief review of Edo divination systems, see Kidō Gennosuke, "Edo jidai no uranai yogensha," 105–115. I am grateful to Hayashi Makoto for providing me with this article.

33. The term *"honshin"* is attributed to Marumitsu in the entry "Tōkyūjutsu," in *Kōjien*.

34. For a discussion of Zhu Xi's understanding of hexagram divination and its relation to self-cultivation, see Joseph Adler, "Chu Hsi and Divination."

35. Translation adapted from Chan, *Sourcebook in Chinese Philosophy,* 624–625. I have changed "man" and "men" to "person" and "people," respectively.

36. Both *Tōeishū* and *Aki no arashi* are distributed as pamphlets, usually to members only. The latter text is reproduced in Nihon Tōdōkai, *Tōkyū,* 706–710.

37. See *Aki no arashi,* in Nihon Tōdōkai, *Tōkyū,* 707.

38. Ibid., 708.

39. Ibid., 709.

40. Ibid., 709–710.

41. Nihon Tōdōkai, *Tōkyū,* 101. This line is another loose allusion to the idea of "clarifying the bright virtue" contained in the opening chapter of the *Great Learning.* Marumitsu assumed the validity of the larger social implications of Confucian cultivation paradigms as well. See, e.g., his praise of the domain lord Kurushima Maruichi for reforming himself and thereby exerting a beneficial influence on the people in his domain (ibid., 151). Neo-Confucian ideas similarly informed the teachings of the founder's immediate disciples. E.g., paraphrases of the views of Aoki Sogan, in ibid., 155, touch on such themes as the self-centered mind and the unity of oneself with all things of creation.

42. Nanboku's dates of birth and death are disputed. I follow modern biographers Makino Masayasu and Tanaka Ichirō, who conclude that the traditional dating of 1757–1843 is erroneous; see Makino and Tanaka, *Mizuno Nanboku to sono shisō,* 22, 124, 128. Kidō for his part suggests 1757–1834; "Edo jidai no uranai yogensha," 113. Nanboku's original family name was Ono; for a list of other personal names he allegedly used at various times during his life, see Kidō, "Edo jidai." The physiognomist's life is also the subject of a historical novel, *Damatte suwareba—kansōshi Mizuno Nanboku ichidai,* by Kōsaka Jirō. I am indebted to Yokoyama Toshio for bringing this book to my attention.

43. Some of this information is contained in a brief entry on Mizuno Nanboku, in the anecdotal biographical compilation by Masada Yoshihiko, *Naniwa jinketsu dan,* cited in Makino and Tanaka, *Mizuno,* 20. See also Sugata Masaaki, *Fukugan no Shintōkatachi,* 82–83.

44. See Makino and Tanaka, *Mizuno,* 23–25; 29; Sugata, *Fukugan,* 84.

45. For Mizuno Nanboku's comments on his Daoist-type cultivation, see his *Shūshinroku,* 226–227. See also Sugata, *Fukugan,* 85.

46. The compilation was imported to Japan in 1651. Livia Kohn gives a detailed introduction to the Chinese textual tradition in "A Textbook of Physiognomy."

47. Makino and Tanaka, *Mizuno,* 25; 26; in the authors' judgment, Shingon, Tendai, and Zen clergy tended to be especially well versed in physiognomic lore.

48. See Makino and Tanaka, *Mizuno,* 40–45, for a 1788 list of Nanboku's disciples; and the authors' comments, 45.

49. Makino and Tanaka, *Mizuno,* 28–29. The adoption of Buddhist monastic dress was not uncommon among itinerant raconteurs and other traveling speakers in the Tokugawa period.

50. Makino and Tanaka quote Nanboku's own comment as the primary

source for the *koji* appellation event but do not specify to which of his writings they are referring; *Mizuno,* 47–48. Nanboku presumably practiced under Jiun while the latter was residing in Kōkiji, a Shingon temple at the foot of Mount Katsuragi in Ōsaka-fu, from 1776 until his death in 1804. See the timeline in Kinami Takuchi, *Jiun Sonja,* 232.

51. Cited in Makino and Tanaka, *Mizuno,* 27f.

52. See Makino and Tanaka, *Mizuno,* 36–37, for examples of detailed interpretations of physical features contained in the *Nanboku sōhō zenpen;* and Sugata, *Fukugan,* 88.

53. Mizuno Nanboku, preface to *Shūshinroku,* a selection of commentaries that represent Nanboku's mature thought (completed in 1812); reproduced in Makino and Tanaka, *Mizuno,* 175.

54. Mizuno Nanboku, *Nanboku sōhō kōhen, kan* 2, "Kesshoku no bu benron," cited in Makino and Tanaka, *Mizuno,* 33. For the classic Neo-Confucian articulation of the idea of being one body with the universe, see Zhang Zai's "Western Inscription" *(Ximing)* in de Bary and Bloom, eds., *Sources of Chinese Tradition* 1:683.

55. Makino and Tanaka, *Mizuno,* 50. The date of Nanboku's visit to Ise is unknown; Sugata judges it to be sometime between 1808 and 1810. The latter's account differs from Makino and Tanaka's in regard to the number of days that Nanboku fasted; see *Fukugan,* 91–92. For Edo-period interpretations of the identity of Toyouke (or Toyuke), see Mark Teeuwen, *Watarai Shintō,* 319–322.

56. Mizuno, *Shūshinroku,* preface, cited in Makino and Tanaka, 52.

57. Mizuno, *Shūshinroku,* 179.

58. Ibid., 182–183.

59. Kaibara Ekiken, *Yōjōkun, Wazoku dōjikun,* 64.

60. Ibid., 66, 88, 93.

61. Mizuno, *Shūshinroku,* 215.

62. A locus classicus for the idea that hidden virtue leads to "manifest reward" (J. *yōhō*) is the *Huainanzi, juan* 18, renjian xun. See D. C. Lau, ed., *A Concordance to the Huainanzi,* 189, line 12.

63. *Practically Religious,* 181–182.

64. Mizuno, *Shūshinroku,* 204–205.

65. Mizuno Nanboku believed that meat eating led to undesirable interchange with the vital energies of the animal consumed, although he allowed that moderate intake was not problematic for certain people. See *Shūshinroku,* 193–194; see also Sugata, *Fukugan,* 94. For Ekiken's advice on meat consumption, see, e.g., *Yōjōkun,* 70.

66. Mizuno, *Shūshinroku,* 215.

67. Ibid., 195, 196. Similar statements regarding the conservation of resources appear in ibid., 184, 197, 198.

68. See Nanboku's positive appraisal of a dissipate man who nevertheless valued natural resources in *Shūshinroku,* 195. He discourses in a similar vein in response to a questioner in ibid., 211. Nanboku's counsel on how to use money is contained in ibid., 187–188.

69. Ibid., 184–185. Rice harvests determined the value of currency during the Tokugawa, which accordingly tended to fluctuate greatly.

70. For references to the "Rice Bodhisattva" in the writings of the leader of the mountain devotional sect Fujidō, see, e.g., Sangyō Rokuō, *Sangyō Rokuō-ku otsutae,* cited in Miyazaki Fumiko, "'Furikawari' to 'Miroku no miyo,'" 328–329.

71. Mizuno, *Shūshinroku,* 189.

72. Re Atsutane's view of work, worship, and consumption, see Harootunian, *Things Seen,* 212–214.

73. Mizuno, *Shūshinroku,* 216.

74. Ibid., 189.

75. Pierre Bourdieu discusses symbolic capital and its relationship to material or economic capital in, e.g., his *The Logic of Practice,* 112–121; see also Bourdieu's *The Field of Cultural Production,* 75.

76. Mizuno, *Shūshinroku,* 187.

77. Ibid., 189.

78. Ibid., 179, 180. Nanboku considered wives who ate sparingly and still managed to dominate their husbands to be an incorrigibly evil species.

79. Claude Lévi-Strauss, *The Savage Mind,* 17.

80. *Meitoku* (Ch. *mingde*) is a key word in the opening section of the *Great Learning. Konton* refers to the inchoate state of the world before it divided into heaven and earth, a theme that is prominent in the *Shintō gobusho* (Five Books of Shinto). See Mark Teeuwen, *Watarai Shinto,* 255–262, for a discussion of the role of the Five Books in mid-Tokugawa Shinto thought. (Edo-period interpretations of the idea of *konton* or "primeval chaos" are mentioned in numerous places in Teeuwen's book, beginning with that of Hayashi Razan, 1583–1657, on p. 210).

81. Mizuno, *Shūshinroku, kan* 4, cited in Makino and Tanaka, 93.

82. See Lévi-Strauss, *Savage Mind,* 19. Lévi-Strauss uses the idea of an intellectual bricolage to elucidate what he calls "mythical thought." By borrowing his terminology here I do not mean to imply that Nanboku's thought was necessarily "mythical," or that it involved a building up of "structures."

83. A figurative expression that means merely imitating knowledge that is bequeathed by predecessors without making any creative contribution to it.

84. That is, clarifying the bright virtue, renewing (or loving) the people, and abiding in the highest good.

85. Mizuno, *Shūshinroku,* 203.

86. Ibid., 244.

87. Ibid., 249.

88. Ibid., 218–219.

89. Makino and Tanaka, *Mizuno,* 101; the source, *Chirizuka-dan,* part 2, is cited on p. 165 without further publication information or dating.

90. Makino and Tanaka, *Mizuno,* 163–164.

91. Konjin was the traditional deity of directions in Onmyōdō; violation of taboos associated with Konjin were popularly believed to result in family deaths and other disasters. *Nisshu seiten* may refer to the art of determining the correct day or period for carrying out certain actions: *nisshū* seems to mean "choosing an [auspicious] day," while *seiten* indicates the "revolution of the stars" or constellations. The above passage is cited in Makino and Tanaka, *Mi-*

zuno, 165, from Hakuga's *Yami no akebono;* Hakuga goes on to cite the early Confucian philosopher Xunzi's critique of divination. See also ibid., 102–103.

92. For Sadanobu's comments, see his *Kagetsu sōshi,* 415, 426, 430, 430–431. According to Makino and Tanaka, *Mizuno,* 165–166, Yamagata Bantō's critique is in his *Yume no shiro* (1820), but no page is given. (*Yume no shiro* contains Bantō's rationalist-type discourse on Copernican theory, Buddhism, native Japanese beliefs, and other issues of the day.) I have not found the alleged reference to *kansō* in the edition of that work contained in NST, 43:141–616.

93. Mizuno, preface to *Shūshinroku,* in Makino and Tanaka, *Mizuno,* 176.

94. Mizuno, *Shūshinroku,* 250.

95. *Kinsei kijin den,* 137–138. Kōkei seems to be referring to a contemporary, i.e., a late-eighteenth-century figure.

96. Mizuno, *Shūshinroku,* 188–189. *Kanki* refers to the vital energies associated with the liver.

97. Mizuno, *Shūshinroku,* 252.

98. Makino and Tanaka, *Mizuno,* 93.

99. Nanboku discusses how to dissolve a poor karmic legacy by performing the "hidden virtue" of reducing one's food intake, in *Shūshinroku,* 194–195.

100. Cited and translated into modern Japanese from Nanboku's *Nanboku sōhō zenpen (kan 5),* in Makino and Tanaka, *Mizuno,* 57. The idea that one's physical appearance derived from the state of one's mind had precedents in several Chinese discourses. See Makino and Tanaka, *Mizuno,* 78, for examples from Buddhist and Confucian texts. The authors give a more detailed history of Chinese physiognomy in their appendix, 136–146.

101. Another reference to the text of the *Great Learning.* Cited in Makino and Tanaka, *Mizuno,* 170, from *Shūshinroku, kan* 2.

Chapter 3: Breathing as Purification

1. From 1872 to 1876, the movement as a whole was designated "Tohokami-kō"; one branch adopted the modern name "Misogikyō" after 1876. Although I use "Tohokami" to refer to Masakane's teaching and organizaton prior to 1876, it should be noted that the founder and early members of the movement did not use this rubric. Masakane tended to call his teaching "Shintō," or, sometimes, "Yuiitsu Shintō."

2. In addition to the sources cited below, I am indebted for chronological details about Inoue Masakane's life to the charts, time lines, and biographical name lists in Ogihara Minori, *Inoue Masakane monchū shi benran.*

3. Tetsuyo belonged to the Dharma lineage of Mokuan Shōtō (Ch. Muan Xingtong, 1611–1648). The style of Chinese medicine that Masakane learned from Isono Kōdō was based on the teachings of Nagata Tokuhon (1513–1630). Mitsubashi Ken, "Inoue Jinja no seiritsu," 6, dates Masakane's study under Kōdō from 1809.

4. Masakane mentions both Isono Kōdō and Nanboku in *Ikunshū,* 108.

5. Inoue Masakane, *Shintō yuuitsu mondō sho* [hereafter *Mondō*], 6–7; see also Ogihara, "Misogikyō no gyōhō" (no pagination).

6. Ch. *Zhouyi,* an alternative title of the *Book of Changes.*

7. See Sakata Yasuyoshi, "Kaidai," 9–11. For Masakane's own account see his *Mondō, 6–7.*

8. Inoue Masakane, *Ikunshū, 52.*

9. Ibid., *Ikunshū, 78.*

10. Sakata, "Kaidai," 19. Masakane may have been exposed to Hirata's ideas via the Shirakawa school of Shinto, mentioned below.

11. Masakane's follower Murakoshi Morikazu (1813–1880) asserts this transmission in his hagiography of the Tohokami leader, "Jingidō chūkō Masakane reijinki," 26.

12. Inoue Masakane, *Ikunshū, 53.*

13. Ibid., 53. See also Murakoshi Morikazu, "Jingidō," 26, 29, re Masakane's alleged Zen practice.

14. Inoue Masakane, *Mondō, 39.*

15. For the account of the dream, see Inoue Masakane, *Ikunshū, 53.*

16. The term *"tokudō"* may also refer specifically to enlightenment in the Buddhist sense. Shūzan was a physician and retainer of the house of Nijō.

17. The source for this last tradition is Okifuji Tarō et al., eds., *Kyōso Inoue Masakane daijin jitsudenki, kan* 1, 40a. According to an earlier account, in 1824 Masakane received a "Shinto" transmission from Iyo, the daughter of Imai Buntoku, a Takamatsu domain retainer. Inoue Sukekane, *Inoue Masakane shindenki, kan* 1, 2a. The *Jitsudenki* authors, however, explicitly deny that Iyo was the central figure in Masakane's initiation, and suggest that she and Buntoku's wife were simply Teishō's "Dharma disciples." Okifuji, ibid., *kan* 1, 41a.

18. See, e.g., *Tabako no uraba,* 315, 317–318. Other sources state that in the same year he formally studied under Sochō, the abbot of Manioji, a Buddhist temple in Echigo (southern Niigata prefecture). Ogihara, "Misogi kyōso Inoue Masakane no tsuma—Anzai Onari," 9.

19. The source is Okifuji, *Jitsudenki,* 41a. The text suggests that Teishō may have received her transmission from the Takada branch of this group, which was active in Shimōsa at the time. Ogihara Minori believes that the *otoriage* ritual practiced in the Okura movement resembled the purification ritual that Masakane eventually advocated. On Masakane's debt to Pure Land Buddhism, see Ogihara, "Gyōhō," and Sakata, "Kaidai," 22.

20. For Masakane's usage, see his *Mondō, 39.*

21. Inoue Masakane, *Mondō, 38–39.*

22. The Shirakawa house was a hereditary Shinto family associated with the court in Kyoto. For a brief account, see "Hakke Shintō," Kokugakuin daigaku, ed., *Shintō jiten,* 441–442. The details of the Shirakawa teachings during the late Tokugawa are not well known. The school is believed to have been primarily concerned with ritual practices; its theoretical discourses were probably borrowed from the Yoshida and Suika schools of Shinto.

23. *Misogi* and *harae* were originally two distinct phases or events in the native Japanese ritual system, but they came to be paired together, especially in usage that refers to the Great Purification *(ōharae)* ritual.

24. See, e.g., Sakata, "Kaidai," 20.

25. "Shirakawa ke," 48–49. Nakayama Shūji (1821–1881), the oldest son of the Tenrikyō founder, Nakayama Miki (1798–1887), obtained a license from

the Yoshida house in 1867; Oguri Junko, *Nihon no kindai shakai to Tenrikyō*, 286. The founder of Konkōkyō, Kawate Bunjirō (Konkō Daijin, 1814–1883), acquired permission from the Shirakawa school to carry out shrine rituals in 1864 and became a Shirakawa priest in 1867. Murakami Shigeyoshi, *Nihon shūkyō jiten*, 314b.

26. Musashi corresponds to today's Tokyo, Saitama, and part of Kanagawa prefectures. The Shinmei Shrine is located today in Umeda, a neighborhood in the Tokyo ward of Adachi.

27. Hardacre, *Kurozumikyō*, 68.

28. Murakoshi, "Jingidō," 30.

29. Ogihara, "Shirakawa ke," 51–53.

30. Minamiōji's appeal is reproduced in Ogihara, "Shirakawa ke," 54. It is dated the twenty-sixth day of the twelfth month of Tenpō 12.

31. Sakata, "Kaidai," 22.

32. The arrest took place on the twelfth day of the eleventh month of Tenpō 13. A few weeks later, Masakane's early disciple Honjō Munehide formally registered his name in the Shirakawa lineage and transferred a considerable amount of money to the institution. Munehide's younger brother Shirō, his relative Okitsu Tadasuke (Sakyō), and the latter's retainer Katō Kanehide (Yahachi) also affiliated with the Hakke school at this time and made appropriate "donations." Sugiyama Shūzan had already enrolled in the Shirakawa house in 1836; another important follower, Itō Kaname (1806–1877), registered in late 1842. Masakane's disciples Nozawa Kanenori (1814–1875) and Ōkino Kazue affiliated in 1841. Documentation of the Shirakawa enrollments of several of these practitioners is contained in Kondō Yoshihiro, comp., *Shirakawa ke monjin chō*, 372. See also Ogihara, *Benran*, 6, 9.

33. Katō Kanehide apparently had a good rapport with the Shirakawa Edo representative, Minamiōji. For details, including a reproduction of Kanehide's appeal to the Shirakawa in the name of all four Honjō associates, and the total amount of the Tohokami contributions to the Shinto school, see Ogihara, "Shirakawa ke," 57–59.

34. The Shirakawa document, dated the fourteenth day of the twelfth month of Tenpō 13, is reproduced in ibid., 60–61.

35. The excerpt from the announcement of Masakane's sentence translated here is contained in Asō Masaichi, *Zōho Inoue Masakane-ō zaitōki*, 94–95.

36. Sakata, "Kaidai," 20.

37. Endō Jun, "Bakumatsu shakai to shūkyōteki fukkō undō," 151–152, 153–154. (My thanks to Ogihara Minori for bringing this useful article to my attention.) See also Takano Toshihiko, "Idō suru mibun," for a discussion of the acquisition of shrine priestly status by Fuji pilgrimage guides.

38. The drive apparently gained momentum from Hirata Atsutane's activism. The Shirakawa school affirmed the validity of Tohokami activities during the same years in which Minamiōji Sahyōe and other followers of Atsutane were gathering strength in the Edo office. See Endō, "Bakumatsu shakai," 138–143, 145–151, 155–164, 170, n. 30; and re Minamiōji Sahyōe, Ogihara, "Shirakawa ke," 55. The Tohokami leader and Shirakawa priest Katō Kanehide was also a nativist; see Kondō, *Shirakawa chō*, 377a; Ogihara, *Benran*, 12, 13.

39. According to some accounts, breathing exercises may also have been transmitted in the Shirakawa school; e.g., Sugata, *Fukugan,* 86 and 88. Both Nanboku and Masakane may have learned some form of breath modulation in the context of their Buddhist practices as well.

40. Zen master Hakuin Ekaku's *Yasen kanna* is the classic Tokugawa-era expression of this way of thinking. For an annotated modern edition, see Izuyama Kakudō, ed., *Yasen Kanna.* It is translated into English in R. D. M. Shaw and William Schiffer, "Chat on a Boat in the Evening." See Norman Waddell, *Wild Ivy,* 87–112, for a recent translation of a later version of this work.

41. *Fukurokuju,* which I have translated here as "fortune, wealth, and long life," is the name of one of the traditional gods of luck. For this comment and the preceding account of Nanboku's thought, see his *Shūshinroku,* 247–248.

42. See, e.g., Kawajiri Hōkin, "Yorozuyo ni kaoru Umeda no kamigaki," *Michizuke* 24, 6.1 (1992): 11. I draw loosely here and below on Kawajiri's Kabuki play script, which dramatizes the early history of Misogikyō. The work was first published in the second month of 1887, but was probably written several years earlier. The first performance was warmly welcomed by Misogi members; the newspaper *Tōkyō nichinichi shinbun* reported that followers queued up for seats at the play's premiere in Tokyo in early 1888. Several of these members were personally acquainted with the people upon whom the play's characters were modeled; some "characters" were still alive. Although fictionalized in some details and hagiographical in tone, the script is probably faithful to the main events of Inoue Masakane's life as recollected by the first generation of his followers.

43. See, e.g., Inoue Masakane, *Ikunshū,* 64, 98.

44. The nativist Ōkuni Takamasa (1792–1871) identified this formula with *Amatsu norito no futonorito,* a prayer recorded in volume 8 of the *Engishiki;* NST 50:549b. For brief details on the origins and uses of this formula, see *Shintō jiten,* 354, 392; *Shintō daijiten* 3:235, 2:127b; and NST, 50:410n.

45. According to one interpretation, *to ho* is an alternative version of *tohoko* (halberd, or sword); *kami,* of *kagami* (mirror); and *tame,* of *tama* (jewel).

46. Inoue Masakane, *Mondō,* 45; Ogihara, "Gyōhō."

47. Even the well-known Kamo Shrine priest and Shinto popularizer Umetsuji Norikiyo (Kamo no Norikiyo, 1798–1861), who met with Masakane on Miyakejima in 1847 while on his way to his own place of exile (Hachijōjima), does not escape this judgment. Masakane calls him a "savant" who does not possess the authentic transmission of faith; *Ikunshū,* 76, 77, 91. On Norikiyo, see Ogihara Minori, "Kamo no Norikiyo," in *Shintō jiten,* 505; and Sugata, *Fukugan,* 19–39.

48. One version of the formula's meaning is "God grants us blessings, expels [evil from us], and purifies us." See, however, Harootunian, *Things Seen,* 337–340, for reflections on Ōkuni Takamasa's distinctive interpretation of the first five words of the formula.

49. Inoue Masakane, *Mondō,* 3. In modern Misogikyō groups, when new members reach this point in the ritual, they are told that they have completed their initial purification and are admitted to a private meeting with the group leader, during which they formally receive the transmission of faith, an event

marked by a secret ritual and the distribution of sacred water. In addition to Masakane's writings, for details on Tohokami and Misogikyō practices, I have consulted Matsuno Junkō's *Shinshūkyō jiten*, 409–410; and Ogihara, "Gyōhō."

50. *Shinjin* is preceded by two preliminary phases of religious experience, *kishin* (joyful mind) and *goshin* (awakened mind). Inoue Masakane, *Ikunshū*, 104. See below, n. 52.

51. Masakane avers that the formula was originally pronounced by the Japanese emperors in daily rituals in order to induce Amaterasu to manifest her power. Inoue Masakane, *Ikunshū*, 76–77.

52. Masakane's leading followers were expected to become versed in the protocols for creating sacred water *(jinsui no koto)*, for certifying members' completion of the first stages of the purification discipline *(kigoshin no koto)*, and for carrying out the transmission-of-faith ceremony *(norito no den)*. See Inoue Masakane, *Ikunshū*, 104; Ogihara, "Gyōhō."

53. *Monoimi* denotes restriction of food intake and abstention from conduct considered taboo or impure for a specified period of time. The secondary report, contained in *Miyakejima nendai kenbunki*, a local history, is cited by Ikeda Shindō in his *Miyakejima no rekishi to minzoku*, 243. (My thanks to Ogihara Minori for this reference.) Inoue Masakane's own account of the incident is contained in his *Ikunshū*, 88–89.

54. Ogihara, *Benran*, 10, dates the beginning of Masakane's prayers at the Kisaki Shrine the nineteenth day of the seventh month of 1845; on the twenty-sixth day of the same month Masakane began his confinement on Mount Senzu (Senzu-san).

55. For a full-length treatment of the *genze riyaku* theme in the contemporary Japanese context, see Ian Reader and George Tanabe, *Practically Religious*.

56. See, e.g., Inoue Masakane, *Ikunshū*, 64.

57. E.g., ibid., 67.

58. Ibid., 87, 90.

59. Ibid., 100, 105.

60. Ibid., 98.

61. Ibid., 108.

62. Ibid., 108.

63. Inoue Masakane, *Mondō*, 3.

64. Sukuna-hikona no mikoto is said to have granted humankind preventive incantations *(kinju)*, and Ōnamuchi no mikoto, methods for curing illnesses; *Ikunshū*, 107–108. For the locus classicus, see Iida Takesato, ed., *Nihon shoki tsūshaku* 1:608; W. G. Aston, trans., *Nihongi*, 59–60.

65. The founder was apparently using this technique by at least 1826; see Inoue Masakane, *Tabako no uraba*, 318, 319, 320.

66. Regarding healing practices in Misogikyo, see Ogihara, "Gyōhō." Ogihara has iterated to me (personal letter, July 30, 1997) that *kantsū* was used only to supplement the main purification discipline, and in this sense was not a major focus of the Misogi program. It is likely, however, that at least the *promise* of healing played a significant part in attracting first-time followers to the Umeda Shrine. For a contemporary example of healing in a new religion by "blowing

breath" on patients, see Watanabe Masako and Igeta Midori, "Healing in the New Religions," 176–177.

67. Inoue Masakane, *Ikunshū*, 108.

68. For comments on healing in other new religions of this period, see Hardacre, *Kurozumikyō*, 55ff.; cf. Hardacre, "The Transformation of Healing." Oguri discusses various aspects of Nakayama Miki's healing activities in *Nihon no kindaika*, 41, 193–195. See also Satō Hiroshi, "Tenrikyō," 359b.

69. I have seen no evidence that Masakane's and his followers' healing practices in the Edo area incurred the enmity of established professional healers, as did the practices of Kurozumi Munetada in Okayama. Cf. Hardacre, *Kurozumikyō*, 55–56.

70. Inoue Masakane, *Ikunshū*, 108.

71. Winston Davis, *Dojo*, 214.

72. The Tohokami leader's disciples are believed to have transported his mail secretly to and from the island and the mainland. Ogihara, personal communication, November 29, 1998.

73. See, e.g., Inoue Masakane, *Ikunshū*, 77, 82, 286; idem, *Mondō*, 5, 14, 33, 41.

74. Inoue Masakane, *Mondō*, 5.

75. Ibid., 24.

76. Inoue Masakane, *Ikunshū*, 50.

77. Ibid., 102. See also idem, *Mondō*, 5.

78. Ibid., 103. See also 68, in which Masakane cites the *Doctrine of the Mean* (Ch. *Zhongyong*) to justify this equation of the purification ritual with the cultivation ideal, and idem, *Mondō*, 3, 20.

79. Inoue Masakane, *Ikunshū*, 82.

80. Ibid., 69.

81. *Onore ni kaeru* is an allusion to *Analects* 12.1.

82. Inoue Masakane, *Mondō*, 24.

83. Inoue Masakane, *Ikunshū*, 180.

84. Ibid., 180.

85. Inoue Masakane, *Mondō*, 8.

86. Ibid., 9.

87. See also Inoue Masakane, *Ikunshū*, 194.

88. Masakane implies that this single-minded approach is the main reason why he calls his system *yuiitsu*, the "single" or "one and only" teaching; Inoue Masakane, *Ikunshū*, 85. I must correct my earlier implication that Masakane's use of the term "Yuiitsu Shinto" is an oblique claim to the tradition formulated by Yoshida Kanetomo (1435–1515). Having consulted with Ogihara Minori and read more of Masakane's writings, it seems unlikely to me now that the founder was consciously alluding to the Yoshida school. Cf. Sawada, "Mind and Morality," 111–112.

89. Inoue Masakane, *Ikunshū*, 98.

90. Ibid., 66.

91. Inoue Masakane, *Mondō*, 27.

92. Ibid., 31.

93. Bankei's sermons were an important source of inspiration for Toan. See Sawada, *Confucian Values,* 59–61.

94. Kobayashi Junji, "Kinsei ni okeru 'kokoro no gensetsu,'" esp. 166f. and 173.

95. Chizen probably took the tonsure in order to facilitate her proselytization of Tohokami after Masakane's exile; nuns faced fewer travel restrictions than other women in Tokugawa society. For an informative account of Chizen's life, see Ogihara Minori, "Miura Chizen." Chizen's close disciple, Murakoshi Morikazu (1813–1880), provides some firsthand details about the nun in his "Jingidō."

96. Ogihara, "Miura Chizen," 15, 19n. For more on Chizen's Kōzuke period, see Murakoshi, "Jingidō," 31.

97. Murakoshi, "Jingidō," 33.

98. Ibid., 32–33. Ogihara notes that Chizen reportedly adopted the same "rational" *(gōritekina)* approach to other members' problems as well; "Miura Chizen," 17.

99. Hardacre has identified this so-called mind-as-mirror attitude as a characteristic pattern of action in modern Japanese new religions; *Kurozumikyō,* 22–23.

100. Hardacre, *Kurozumikyō,* 17–18.

101. For the above paraphrase and quotation, see Nozawa Kanenori, "Nakatomi no harai ryakuge," 1, 2, respectively.

102. Gumperz, "Speech Community," 227.

103. Harootunian, "Late Tokugawa Culture and Thought," 253.

104. Bourdieu, *Language and Symbolic Power,* 55.

105. Gumperz, "The Speech Community," 226.

106. The repeated suppression of the movement probably stifled this incipient social welfare in Tohokami before the Restoration. Some followers apparently carried out relief work in the Meiji, however; see, e.g., Tōgu Kanemaro, comp., *Tōgū Chiwaki daijin nenpu,* 28, 32.

107. Sakata, "Kaidai," 21; see also Sawada, "Mind and Morality," 115.

108. Kawajiri, "Yorozuyo," *Michizuke* 36, 6.1 (1993): 18–19, 20–21.

109. Ogihara, "Miura Chizen," 8–9.

110. The latter had been adopted into another headman family, the Sakata of Hokima (a prosperous farming village, located at what is now the center of Adachi ward in Tokyo).

111. See Ogihara, "Meiji zenki," 57; Kondō, *Shirakawa chō,* 382b and 387a. Katō Kanehide and Shōji Naotane (1779–1857, the Akimoto house swordsmith) had received Shirakawa credentials in 1847; Ogihara, *Benran,* 11, 13.

112. Ogihara, "Meiji zenki," 57

113. Ibid.

114. Ogihara suggests that the group's continuing interactions with the Shirakawa institution during this period helped it survive until the Meiji government finally recognized it in 1872; "Shirakawa ke," 47–48, 65–66.

115. Tōgū, comp., *Tōgū Chiwaki daijin nenpu,* 5. He also built sleeping quarters for members in his residence.

116. Honjō Munehide is officially recorded among Masakane's followers in 1840, when the Tohokami leader was priest of the Umeda Shinmei Shrine. See, e.g, Inoue Nobutaka, "Bakushin," 260. Here I follow Ogihara, *Benran,* 32.

117. Kawajiri, "Yorozuyo," *Michizuke* 24, 10.1 (1991): 11–12.

118. Kawajiri, "Yorozuyo," *Michizuke* 31, 10.1 (1992): 14.

119. During the second expedition, Munehide inititated early negotiations with Chōshū for a truce without first obtaining authorization from his commander. As a result, the daimyo lost his position as senior councilor and was placed under house arrest until after the Restoration. *Konsaisu jinmei jiten: Nihon hen,* 1018.

120. The source is *Heikaku no kyōka katsudō nenpu;* see Ishikawa Ken, *Sekimon Shingaku shi no kenkyū,* 1047, 1103.

121. Ishikawa, *Sekimon Shingaku,* 1220.

122. Ishikawa cites three separate sources for this point: *Shibata Yūō katsudō nenpu; Miyazu kigyō;* and *Tango kigyō. Sekimon Shingaku,* 1220.

123. The source is *Shingaku shonyū zendō tebiki jinmei;* see Ishikawa, *Sekimon Shingaku,* 1058.

124. Ishikawa, *Sekimon Shingaku,* 1060.

125. Ibid., 1068. The source of the latter report is the writings of the aforementioned Shingaku teacher, Nakamura Tokusui.

126. The *sansha inkan,* literally "Seal of the Three Meetinghouses," was a required credential for Shingaku teachers in the late Tokugawa.

127. Ogihara Minori and I realized Tarasawa Okaemon's "double identity" during a conversation in June 1999. Okaemon is included among the Tohokami members who were appointed leaders in Inoue Masakane's 1845 letter from Miyakejima; Inoue Masakane, *Ikunshū,* 104–105.

128. SSJR, 15a.

129. Ibid., 2b.

130. Ibid., 15a.

131. Hayano Gankō, ed., *Kawajiri Hōkin sensei jiseki,* 3.

132. SSJR, 20b–21b. For Mitani's Tōkyū studies, see ibid., 24a.

133. Kanetomo evidently inherited the family name of his mother, Fukuda Saku (mentioned earlier in this chapter). I am indebted to Ogihara Minori for identifying Fukuda Kanetomo's place in the Tohokami community for me.

134. These areas correspond to today's Fukushima, Miyashiro, Iwate, Aomori, and part of Akita prefectures.

135. Mitani Ken'ō eventually resigned his Tohokami/Misogikyō teaching responsibilities (no date or reasons are given). SSJR, 21b–22a.

Chapter 4: The Parameters of Learning

1. Apter and Saich, *Revolutionary Discourse in Mao's Republic,* xi, speak in this vein of the ways in which people create languages to interpret and also transcend their circumstances.

2. Ketelaar gives sustained attention to the shifting meanings of words in the early Meiji debates about religion and government in his book *Of Heretics;* see his comments about *kyō* on 125. Hardacre, *Shinto and the State,* esp. 63–65, provides a succinct account of the evolution of the notion of religion with par-

ticular reference to Shinto. Rubinger discusses "the development of a new vocabulary of educational organization" with special reference to the term *"gakkō"* (school) in his "Education," 210–211.

3. See Stephen Vlastos, ed., *The Invention of Modern Japan,* and especially Vlastos' introduction to the same volume, "Tradition: Past/Present Culture and Modern Japanese History," 1–16, for a useful discussion of some of the issues involved in the application of the notion of "invention of tradition" in the Japanese context.

4. For information in the above paragraph, I have relied especially on Motoyama Yukihiko, "The Political Background of Early Meiji Educational Policy," in Motoyama, *Proliferating Talent,* esp. 84–90. Here and below I have also consulted the original Japanese version of this essay, in Motoyama, *Kindai Nihon no seiji to kyōiku,* 1–70. The nativist officials that Iwakura appointed were Yano Harumichi (1823–1887), Tamamatsu Misao (1810–1872), and Hirata Kanetane (1799–1880).

5. Inoue Hisao, *Gakusei ronkō,* 5.

6. The original Daigakuryō was a court school that provided instruction in the Confucian classics to officials from about the eighth century to the eleventh century.

7. For an additional perspective on the educational vision of Yano and his colleagues during the first Meiji years, see Harootunian, *Things Seen,* 396–398. See Motoyama, *Proliferating Talent,* 92, and Ōkubo Toshiaki, *Nihon no daigaku,* 178–180, for details regarding the *Gakushasei.*

8. Motoyama, *Proliferating Talent,* 92–93.

9. For more on Iwakura's evolving positions, see Inoue Hisao, *Gakusei ronkō,* 72–76.

10. See Motoyama, *Proliferating Talent,* 99–101. For developments in the struggle during the ensuing months of 1868, see Ōkubo Toshiaki, *Nihon no daigaku,* 181.

11. Motoyama, *Proliferating Talent,* 128–129. For more details regarding the Daigakkō's founding and internal organization, see Ōkubo Toshiaki, *Nihon no daigaku,* esp. 184–192.

12. The curricular changes were set out in the "University Regulations" *(Daigakkō kisoku),* issued in the seventh month of 1869. Kōdōgaku was promoted by Hasegawa Akimichi (1815–1897), a Mito scholar. As Inoue Hisao points out, its central place in the new regulations indicates that the nativist faction was already in retreat at this point; *Gakusei ronkō,* 13–14. On Hasegawa's ideas, see also Motoyama, *Proliferating Talent,* 103.

13. Motoyama, *Proliferating Talent,* 131–132. There were precedents for the reverence of native gods as patrons of learning, but it was not a systematic practice in Japanese schools until the early Meiji; Ōkubo Toshiaki, *Nihon no daigaku,* 179–180. In the Edo period, Confucian rites had been regularly performed in the Hall of Sages (Seidō), a temple attached to the Shōheikō, but these had ceased in 1868. *Nihon jugaku nenpyō,* 431; cited in Warren Smith, *Confucianism in Modern Japan,* 42.

14. Ōkubo Toshiaki, *Nihon no daigaku,* 193–195. Motoyama, *Proliferating Talent,* 132.

15. The Daigakkō was renamed Daigaku at this time.

16. These 1870 rules were called "University Regulations and Middle and Elementary School Regulations" *(Daigaku kisoku oyobi chūshōgaku kisoku).* Shinto-type studies, ethics (under the rubric *shūshin*), and Chinese studies, as well as historical and literary studies, were retained at the Main College. See Ōkubo Toshiaki, *Nihon no daigaku,* 196–198, for more details.

17. See Motoyama, *Proliferating Talent,* 135–139, and Ōkubo Toshiaki, *Nihon no daigaku,* 198–199, for the final phase of the struggle for control of the university; and Rubinger, "Education," 202–204, for a succinct account of the early attempts to systemize public higher education.

18. Motoyama takes this position in "The Political Background of Early Meiji Educational Policy," in his *Proliferating Talent,* 83–147. Ōkubo Toshiaki, one of Motoyama's sources in the same essay, similarly avers that conflicts over such external details as the Chinese classical curriculum and seasonal Confucian rituals masked larger factional conflicts that arose in the aftermath of the recent political changes; *Nihon no daigaku,* 195.

19. Motoyama, *Proliferating Talent,* 140.

20. Strictly speaking, the Monbushō did not become a "ministry" until the cabinet system was established in 1885.

21. Motoyama, *Proliferating Talent,* 146. This directive was addressed to the South College (Daigaku Nankō), the successor to the Western studies institute.

22. For a perspective on the history of the modern Japanese academy that emphasizes continuities between critical Sinology and Tokugawa-era evidential learning, see De-min Tao, "Shigeno Yasutsugu," in Hardacre and Kern, eds., *New Directions in the Study of Meiji Japan,* 373–382.

23. Rubinger, "Education," 208. The general aims of the new system are set out in the preamble to the code, translated in Herbert Passin, *Society and Education in Japan,* 209–211.

24. Cited in Araki Ryūtarō, "Nihon ni okeru Yōmeigaku no keifu (2)," 412.

25. *Book of Changes,* Qian hexagram, Wenyan commentary. Wilhelm trans., *The I Ching,* 380.

26. *Zhongyong,* chap. 20, sec. 18. Shimada Kenji, ed. *Daigaku Chūyō* 2:145. Translation adapted from Chan, ed., *A Sourcebook in Chinese Philosophy,* 107. In the original text the maxims refer to the study of how to be sincere.

27. The sources for these sayings are *Mencius* 4B:14 and *Analects* 14:24, respectively. For a fuller discussion of these themes, see especially de Bary, *Learning for Oneself,* and idem, *The Liberal Tradition in China.*

28. *Doctrine of the Mean,* chap. 1, sec. 1.

29. A locus classicus for the compound *kyōiku* is contained in *Mencius* 7A:20.

30. "Wakayama-ken Jinjō Shihangakkō," dated Nov. 15, 1887, in *Mori Arinori zenshū* 1:580; translation in Ivan Hall, *Mori Arinori,* 411. Hall notes that in this context Mori's *gakumon* may also be rendered "higher learning," in contrast to *kyōiku,* "common learning." It is worth noting that educator Takada

Sanae (1860–1938) later blamed Mori for having introduced into public discourse the notion of a national, as distinct from an individual, education; "Kokkateki kyōiku," 259.

31. Cf. the early Fukuzawa Yukichi (1834–1901), who affirms the value of doubt in the intellectual process in his *Gakumon no susume*, but ties it to European rather than Confucian culture. Dilworth and Hirano, trans., *An Encouragement of Learning*, 93; see also Motoyama, *Proliferating Talent*, 256.

32. Harootunian, *Things Seen*.

33. See Shively, "Motoda Eifu," in *Confucianism in Action*, 302.

34. Kiyohara Sadao, *Kaishū Nihon dōtoku shi*, 619.

35. Section One, *An Encouragement of Learning*; trans. Dilworth and Hirano, 1–2. According to his postface, 7, Fukuzawa wrote this section in 1871.

36. For a survey of earlier Tokugawa interpretations of *jitsugaku*, see Minamoto Ryōen's classic study, *Kinsei shoki jitsugaku shisō no kenkyū*, and in English, his "*Jitsugaku* and Empirical Rationalism."

37. See, e.g., Matsumoto Sannosuke, "Atarashii gakumon," 426–428; and Harootunian, *Things Seen*, 403.

38. The custom of using the term "real" or "practical" to exalt one's own system of thought at the expense of "empty" types of knowledge dates at least to the Song period. See Minamoto Ryōen, "'Jitsugaku,'" 379. De Bary discusses Fukuzawa's and Tsuda Mamichi's uses of the term "*jitsugaku*" in the passages cited here in his "Introduction," 1–2.

39. Trans. Braisted, *Meiroku zasshi*, 38, with modifications; viz., *gogyō seiri* probably refers to two systems of thought (as above), not, as Braisted has it, to the "theory of the five elements [Sung Confucianism]." I have also substituted "learning" for "studies" (both render the term *gaku*) throughout for the sake of coherence in the present discussion. Braisted correctly identifies "intuitive knowledge" with the Wang Yangming school. Tsuda's remarks appear in an undated issue of the Meiroku journal from the early 1870s. See Ōkubo Toshiaki, ed., *Meiroku zasshi* 1.3:7a. Motoyama points out that Fukuzawa and Tsuda had different views of *jitsugaku*; *Proliferating Talent*, 267.

40. Tōkyō Teitoku Daigaku, ed., *Tōkyō Teikoku Daigaku gojūnen shi*, 1:188. Translation in Motoyama, *Proliferating Talent*, 146; material in brackets is added.

41. For a discussion of the "general vs. vocational" dichotomy in post-Tokugawa education discourse, see Passin, *Society and Education*, 92.

42. Ōkubo Toshiaki, *Nihon no daigaku*, 217.

43. Cited in ibid., 216.

44. The guidelines are cited in ibid., 216. See also Kyōikushi Hensankai, ed., *Meiji ikō kyōiku* 1:560–561.

45. For the early deemphasis on humanistic fields in Tokyo University (which was eventually redressed), see Ōkubo Toshiaki, *Nihon no daigaku*, 225, 233–234.

46. See Rubinger, "Education," 218–223, re private schools founded in the 1870s. The sectarian schools (which Rubinger does not mention) were "private" in the sense that they were self-funded. See Kyōikushi, *Meiji ikō kyōiku*

1:712–713, for brief information on Buddhist and Christian *senmongakkō* established in this period. For the history of Japanese "specialized schools," see Amano Ikuo, *Kyūsei senmongakkō*.

47. Cited in Ōkubo Toshiaki, *Nihon no daigaku*, 213, and translated in Passin, *Society and Education*, 210–211. See also Earl Kinmonth, *The Self-Made Man in Meiji Japanese Thought*, 55.

48. See Kinmonth, *The Self-Made Man*, 50–51, esp. 56–57, for comments on the samurai view of self-advancement; and Ronald Dore, *Education in Tokugawa Japan*, 312. The value of learning was a common theme in popular didactic texts of the Tokugawa era, such as the *Jitsugokyō*; Sawada, *Confucian Values*, 119.

49. Motoyama, *Proliferating Talent*, 245.

50. See Kinmonth, *Self-Made Man*, esp. 32–35, 37, 46–48.

51. Itō Hirobumi, "Kyōiku-gi," September 1879; cited and translated in Passin, *Society and Education*, 233, from Kokumin Seishin Bunka Kenkyūjo, ed., *Kyōiku chokugo kanpatsu kankei shiryō-shū* (Tokyo, 1940), 1:5–9. For the original text I have consulted Shunpōkō Tsuishōkai, ed., *Itō Hirobumi den* 2:153.

52. Motoda's statement is titled "Kyōgaku taishi." The translation appears in Passin, *Society and Education*, 226–228; the source cited is Mombushō, ed., *Gakusei 80-Nen-shi* (Tokyo, 1955), 715–716. I have used the reproduction in Kaigo Tokiomi, *Motoda Eifu*, 51–53.

53. Many of the private academies that emerged in the mid-1870s were connected with the movement for freedom and popular rights (*jiyu minken undō*), including the aforementioned Risshisha in Tosa. The political atmosphere in these schools, which offered instruction in European law, politics, and economics, troubled government leaders such as Motoda, who referred to them as "political discussion gangs." Rubinger, "Education," 221.

54. *Genshi tetsuroku*, no. 19; NST 46:171.

55. Kishida's date of birth is given in standard biographies as Bunkyū 3, which would correspond to 1863 or early 1864; other sources, however, suggest that she was born in Ban'en 1 (1860 or early 1861). The former date seems somewhat less likely, though not impossible; it would mean that Kishida was appointed to her court position at the age of fifteen or sixteen. See Nishikawa Yuko, *Hana no imoto—Kishida Toshiko-den* (Tokyo: Shinchōsha, 1986), cited by Mioko Fujieda, "Japan's First Phase of Feminism," 338n3.

56. Sōma Kokkō, *Meiji shoki no sanjosei*, 40; Itoya Toshio, *Josei kaihō no senkushatachi*, 20. Kishida's later lectures on the *Mencius* at the Ferris Japanese-English Girls School in Yokohama were also very popular with the students; ibid., 76.

57. Rendered into English by Sharon L. Sievers, *Flowers in Salt*, 34. A more literal translation is: "Not one matter of business [takes place] at court, laughter and chatter multiplies all day long. Brocade garments satisfy the palace women, their graceful beauty dazzles more than does the spring. The court is like a paradise of immortals—in a daze, remote from the dust of the world." The verses are contained in Sōma Kokkō, *Meiji shoki*, 40–41. See also Itoya, *Josei kaihō*, 21.

58. Han Tuizhi is Han Yu (768–824), one of the so-called eight great poets of the Tang and Song periods.

59. "Hakoiri musume," *Jiyū shinbun* 411 (Nov. 20, 1883): 3b; a modernized Japanese rendition appears in Itoya, *Josei kaihō,* 40–41.

60. I have based my English translation of this passage on the earliest printed version, contained in *Jiyū shinbun* 411 (Nov. 20, 1883): 3a. Itoya's Japanese rendition of these lines in his *Josei kaihō,* 39, is overly interpretive.

61. "Hakoiri musume," *Jiyū shinbun* 412 (Nov. 21, 1883): 2c; Itoya, *Josei kaihō,* 42.

62. "Hakoiri musume," *Jiyū shinbun* 412 (Nov. 21, 1883): 2d; Itoya, *Josei kaihō,* 43. *Tentei* (Ch. *tiandi*) ordinarily means a creator god, such as the ancient Chinese Shangdi. Here Kishida presumably uses the term synonymously with *ten* (heaven), i.e., the natural or cosmic order; but she may also be alluding to the Christian concept of deity.

63. "Hakoiri musume," *Jiyū shinbun* 412 (Nov. 21, 1883): 2d; Itoya, *Josei kaihō,* 45.

64. See, e.g., *Mencius* 7B:14.

65. According to Itoya, the police charged Kishida because some hecklers in the audience (3,400 people) interpreted her remarks about girls being confined to boxes as an allusion to civil liberties restrictions; Itoya, *Josei kaihō,* 45. Sievers, however, emphasizes that Kishida's speeches about women during the early 1880s were not simply metaphorical discussions of general popular-rights issues, as some historians have assumed; *Flowers in Salt,* 45, 205n43.

66. On the debate over the meaning of practical education, see Passin, *Society and Education,* 92–93; and ibid., 226–228, for Motoda's views on the proper balance between moral and technical training, as expressed in his 1879 "Kyōgaku taishi." Nishimura Shigeki in turn suggested that society needed teachers and scholars who were broadly trained in Western as well as Sino-Japanese subjects, not just "traditional pedantic Confucianists"; but like Motoda he viewed the ideal educator in a Neo-Confucian light as one who had "undertaken the study of cultivating peace of mind." Nishimura's remarks are contained in his 1889 memorial to the Minister of Education; *Hakuō Sōsho* 1:422–433; trans. Donald Shively, "Nishimura Shigeki," 238–239.

67. Martin Collcutt, "The Legacy of Confucianism in Japan," 147–148. See also Passin, *Society and Education,* 81–86. Established educators who had been critical of late Tokugawa textualist trends and emphasized the value of personal, experiential learning reacted even more negatively to the utilitarian interpretation of *gakumon* that informed the early Meiji "civilization and enlightenment" campaign. See, e.g., Araki, "Nihon ni okeru Yōmeigaku no keifu" (2), 415.

68. Nishimura began his lobbying efforts in 1875 and continued to campaign along these lines into the 1880s along with Motoda and others; Hall, *Mori Arinori,* 351. Shively's "Nishimura Shigeki" is a nuanced account of the evolution of Nishimura's ideas and activism.

69. Fukuzawa also persisted in his polemics against Confucian thought into the 1880s. See his "Butsurigaku no yōyō," *Jiji shinpō* editorial, dated March 22, 1882, reproduced in *Fukuzawa Yukichi zenshū,* 8:50–51. As minister of

education in the 1880s, Mori Arinori argued against having *any* system of beliefs dominate the nation's school curriculum; Hall, *Mori Arinori*, 438.

70. An "official translation" of the rescript appears in The Centre for East Asian Cultural Studies, ed., *Meiji Japan through Contemporary Sources*, 3:128.

71. As Gluck has shown, the rescript laid the foundation for decades of creative ideological interpretation; see her *Japan's Modern Myths*, especially 102–156.

72. See Yamashita, "Confucianism and the Japanese State, 1904–1945," 141, 143.

73. Hikaku Shisōshi Kenkyūkai, ed., *Meiji shisōka no shūkyō kan*, 16–17. Regarding the Buddhist origins of the term *"shūkyō,"* see Ketelaar's note, *Of Heretics*, 240n120; he cites Aihara Ichirōsuke, "Yakugo 'Shūkyō' no seiritsu," *Shūkyōgaku kiyō* 5 (1938): 1–15.

74. The use of *"shūkyō"* to translate "religion" dates at least from the translation of American foreign relations documents regarding the Urakami Kirishitan problem, viz., from 1867–1868. Haga Shōji, *Meiji ishin to shūkyō*, 381. See Ketelaar's detailed note on this issue, *Of Heretics*, 240n121, in which he cites Suzuki Norihisa, *Meiji shūkyō shichō no kenkyū*, 16.

75. See Mori, "Shūkyō," in *Meiroku zasshi*, 220–229 (no. 6, pt. 4; April 28, 1874); Fukuzawa often uses the term in such works as *Gakumon no susume no hyō* and *Bunmeiron no gairyaku*. See Hikaku, ed., *Meiji shisōka*, 4–28, for details on the various early renditions and eventual dominance of *"shūkyō."*

76. Haga, *Meiji ishin*, 379.

77. Ketelaar, *Of Heretics*, 41.

78. Fukuchi, *Shūkyōron*, published April 25, 1883; cited and paraphrased in Haga, *Meiji ishin*, 382.

79. Ōkubo Toshiaki, ed., *Meiroku zasshi*, 1:417 (issue no. 13, pt. 2; pub. June 1874). Trans. Braisted, *Meiroku zasshi*, 167.

80. Fukuzawa adopted this stance in such early works as *Gakumon no susume;* however, by the 1880s he came to see Buddhism as a viable defense against the spread of Christianity in Japan, and in his later years was drawn to True Pure Land and Zen Buddhism. Hikaku, ed., *Meiji shisōka*, 69.

81. Fukuzawa Yukichi, "Dokkyō no setsu," *Fukuzawa Yukichi zenshū*, 9:283.

82. Tsuda Sōkichi, "Preface," xii, xvi.

83. In English, see, e.g., Tsuda, "Preface," xii; or Watanabe Hiroshi, "They Are Almost the Same as the Ancient Three Dynasties," 130–131.

84. Fukuzawa, "Jukyōshugi," *Fukuzawa Yukichi zenshū*, 9:274. Trans. Eiichi Kiyooka, *Fukuzawa Yukichi on Education*, 196; material in brackets added.

85. Haga, *Meiji ishin*, 389. For Nishimura's views on religion, Haga cites "Nihon shūkyōron," in *Hakuō sōsho*, pt. 2, 102–103. Cf. Kozaki Hiromichi, who drew on Herbert Spencer to interpret Confucianism as a "preparation" for Christianity in Japan; Helen Ballhatchet, "Confucianism and Christianity in Meiji Japan," esp. 354; 358–362.

86. Hikaku, ed., *Meiji shisōka*, 104–105, 107. See also Kiyohara Sadao,

Kaishū Nihon dōtoku shi, 628–632. Nishi Amane similarly theorized that religious traditions would lose influence as the Japanese people became more educated; Ōkubo Toshiaki, ed., *Meiroku zasshi,* 1:210–211 (no. 6, pt. 2; n.d.).

87. Braisted trans., *Meiroku zasshi* (issues 22 and 25), 279 and 312, respectively. As Braisted implies, Sakatani distinguished *seikyō* from *shūkyō* or *hōkyō* (to which he also allowed a role in moral education); ibid. 286n.

88. See Matsumura, "Yōmeigakusha Okunomiya Zōsai," 166. Okunomiya was inspired by the historicist approach of the Shinto scholar Yoshimi Yukikazu (Kyōken; 1673–1761). For information on Yukikazu and his ideas, see Yasaki Hiroshi, "Yoshimi Yoshikazu," in *Shintō jiten,* 540d; and Teeuwen, *Watarai Shintō,* 313–340.

89. Cited in Kataoka Yakichi, "Nakano Kenmei," 173–174.

90. For nativist/Shinto leaders' disavowals of the religious quality of Shinto, see Hardacre, *Shintō and the State,* 66.

91. Karakasa Shinzō, "Haishinron," 254.

92. The Kaishintō or "Progressive Party" was founded in 1882 by Ōkuma Shigenobu (1838–1922).

93. Asano Ken, "Shūkyōron," 255–258.

94. Asano Ken, "Jigoku gokuraku ron," 260–261.

95. Trans. Ketelaar, *Of Heretics,* 100; cited from *Meiji ishin shinbutsu bunri shiryō,* 6 vols. (Tokyo: Iwanami Shoten, 1926), 3:102. In his rebuttal to this manifesto, the True Pure Land priest Shimaji Mokurai (1838–1911), who had originally lobbied for the establishment of the Ministry of Doctrine, assumes that the Kyoto protest was the work of a "worthless Confucian." Trans. Ketelaar, *Of Heretics,* 102; cited from *Kyōtō-fu no kenpakusho o yomu,* in Futaba Kenko and Mineshima Hideo, eds., *Shimaji Mokurai zenshū,* 5 vols. (Kyoto: Honganji Shuppan, 1973), 1:205–218. Ketelaar says the letter was probably written by the anti-Buddhist Kyoto official Uemura Masanao; *Of Heretics,* 254n32.

96. *Of Heretics,* 41.

97. Bourdieu, *The Logic of Practice,* 53.

98. For a discussion of one Confucian scholar's interpretation of spiritual beings, see John A. Tucker's "Ghosts and Spirits in Tokugawa Japan."

99. Gluck, *Japan's Modern Myths,* 123.

100. Ibid., 123. Her sources for Inoue Kowashi's comments are "Ōshū mohō o hi to suru setsu" (1874 or 1875); and "Jukyō o zonzu" (1881–1882), in *Inoue Kowashi den,* 1:47–54, 3:497–500, respectively.

101. Trans. Shively, "Motoda Eifu," 327. The Japanese text is Motoda Eifu, "Kyōiku-gi fugi," in Kaigo Tokiomi, *Motoda Eifu,* 143.

102. Motoda Eifu, "Mori bunsō ni taisuru kyōiku ikensho," contained in Kaigo, *Motoda Eifu,* 207–209. In this personalized response to Mori's education policy, Motoda writes, "although I believe in Confucius, this is not comparable to Buddhists paying obeisance to Shakya [Buddha] or Christians placing their faith in Jesus."

103. Motoda, "Mori ikensho," 209.

104. Imakita Kōsen, cited in Suzuki, *Imakita Kōsen,* 97, 98.

105. "Shūkyō," in Suzuki, *Imakita Kōsen,* 184–185.

106. The Shingaku leader Kawajiri Hōkin expresses similar views in his *Naibu bunmeiron, kan* 3, 85–86.

107. These remarks are excerpted from a memorial to the Minister of Education; trans. Shively, "Nishimura Shigeki," 238, from *Hakuō sōsho* 1:422–423.

108. Gluck, *Japan's Modern Myths*, 125–126; material in brackets added. Gluck's sources for Tokutomi's reaction to the rescript are "Shigeno Yasutsugu-shi ayamareri," *Kokumin no tomo*, no. 100 (Nov. 13, 1890): 42–43, and for his earlier criticism of Confucianism, *Shin Nihon no seinen* (1885), in *Meiji bungaku zenshū* 34:125–137. For the journalist's comments, Gluck cites *Tōkyō nichinichi shinbun*, Nov. 13, 1890; and for Inoue Kowashi's views on the issue, his "Rinri to seirigaku to no kankei," *Nihon*, Nov. 7, 1890.

109. Shimaji Mokurai exemplifies this line of argument in the early 1870s; see Ketelaar, *Of Heretics*, 127.

110. Ketelaar (*Of Heretics*, 87–135) discusses the Ministry of Doctrine's instructional campaign in detail. On p. 106 he renders the Three Standards of Instruction as follows: "1. Comply with the commands to revere the kami and love the nation. 2. Illuminate the principle of heaven and the way of man. 3. Serve the Emperor and faithfully maintain the will of the court."

111. *Mencius* 6A:11, trans. Lau, 167. On this theme in Shingaku, see Sawada, *Confucian Values*, e.g., 51–52.

112. Sawada, *Confucian Values*, esp. 145–150.

113. The five moral relations are those between ruler and minister, parent and child, husband and wife, older and younger brothers, and among friends.

114. SN, 8b. *Kōsatsu* continued to be posted by the Meiji government (under the auspices of the Dajōkan) until February 1873. Harafuji, "Kōsatsu," *Kokushi daijiten*, 5:353.

115. SN, 8b.

116. See, e.g., Ōshima Urin, "Shingaku wagōka," 63.

117. See, for example, Allan Grapard's *Protocol of the Gods*, 237–258, for a discussion of the effects of Restoration religion policies on an important Buddhist-Shinto ritual complex.

118. SN, 17b.

119. An important factor in this policy was concern about the influence of Christian schooling. See Takeda Michio, "Meiji zenki no Bukkyō kyōiku," 86–87.

120. I have not yet identified Oharai-kō or Kaseki-kō; the former was evidently a Shinto-type purification group. Ontake and Yudono are famous sacred mountains, which, like Fuji, were central sites for worship associations *(kō)*. Seigaku, if understood as the "learning of human nature," may have been a Neo-Confucian–inspired society.

121. Yokushō Sannin [pen name], "Shintō shokō—ryūkō—," *Shinbun shūsei Meiji hennenshi*, 1:515.

122. SSJR, 10b.

123. By *"kokuten"* Takahashi probably meant such "Shinto" texts as the ancient chronicles *(Kojiki, Nihon shoki)* or the *Shintō gobusho*.

124. SSJR, 10b–11a.

125. See Sawada, *Confucian Values,* 50.

126. Takahashi's response to the Ministry of Doctrine detailed here and below is recorded by his disciple and successor, Kawajiri Hōkin, in the chronological biography, "Takahashi jiseki ryaku," contained in SSJR, 1a–16b. The account must be interpreted with care, not only because it is semihagiographical, but also because it is based on Kawajiri's and other Meiji followers' recollections of what Takahashi told them rather than on the original written text (which may have been lost in a fire in the early Meiji). All in all, however, the account offers valuable insight into one of the numerous smaller struggles that took place when religious groups were drafted into the Great Teaching Campaign in the early 1870s; at the very least, the narrative shows how Meiji Shingaku members construed this pivotal moment in their movement's history.

127. SSJR, 11b–12a.

128. SSJR, 12a. I have been unable to locate the memorial among Shingaku or government records.

129. Honjō is identified in Shingaku records as a Major Doctrinal Instructor. According to Inoue Nobutaka, however, who follows *Shaji torishirabe ruisan,* in the second half of 1873 Honjō was still a Middle Doctrinal Instructor; *Kyōha Shintō,* 348.

130. Yokushō Sannin, "Shintō shokō."

131. For this information about Honjō's speaking tours, see Inoue Nobutaka, *Kyōha Shintō,* 348, and his chart on 349, where he summarizes records of Jingū Kyōkai proselytization contained in the *Shaji torishirabe ruisan.*

132. SN, 17b. See also SSJR, 12a. These comments are very likely an interpolated summary of the ministry's position, not a verbatim report of Honjō's remarks on the occasion. It is worth noting, incidentally, that although the Meiji government decriminalized eating meat and marrying by Buddhist priests in 1872, presumably before this meeting took place, the Shingaku narrative nevertheless uses these practices to distinguish Buddhist laity from monastics.

133. SN, 17b.

134. SSJR, 12a.

135. See SN, 43a, 45a.

136. SN, 45b.

Chapter 5: Practical Learning in the Meditation Hall

1. These events are covered in English in several works; see especially Ketelaar, *Of Heretics,* 43–86; and, for a succinct account, Collcutt, "Buddhism," 150–163.

2. This decree (n. 133) is commonly referred to as the *nikujiki saitai* (literally, "eating meat and having wives") decree.

3. See Richard Jaffe's *Neither Monk nor Layman* for an excellent, full-scale analysis of the conditions that led to the decree, its impact, and the debates that raged in its aftermath in the Meiji and Taishō periods.

4. Cited in Sakurai, *Nanzenjishi,* 689. No source or date is given. The Gozan temples of Kyoto included Tenryūji, Shōkokuji, Nanzenji, Tōfukuji, and Kenninji.

5. E, 626.

6. Inoue Zenjō, who amply treats many other aspects of life at Engakuji in the period, says little about the actual impact of clerical marriage in the temple community or in Rinzai as a whole. In private conversations with me, he has dated the acceptance of married abbots at Engakuji to the early twentieth century—though even at that time it carried a stigma. Inoue, the former abbot of Tōkeiji (an Engakuji branch temple), has been exceptionally forthright about this and other controversial points in Engakuji history, both in his writings and in personal communications with me.

7. The monk's master was a former abbot of Mannenji, a temple in Yamaguchi.

8. Imakita Kōsen, draft letter to Gyoku-ō (unidentified); the manuscript probably dates to the early or mid-1880s.

9. "Sōryo kokkai junbiron," 168, 170.

10. KSKS, 1:197.

11. The seven lines were identified with the Gozan head temples in Kyoto and those of Kamakura (Engakuji and Kenchōji). From September 1877 until August 1884, these seven lines maintained a joint business office and elected a rotating "representative abbot" *(kanchō sōdai)* each year (E, 630). Myōshinji, Daitokuji, and the Ōbaku sect became separate institutions in 1877 when the Ministry of Doctrine was abolished.

12. "Outer teachings" refers to non-Buddhist systems, whether Confucian, Shinto, Daoist, or other, whereas "inner teachings" denotes Buddhist doctrines. In this context, "outer teachings" probably means Christianity, in particular.

13. The rules and the attached caution are dated May 1884; the regulations had been drawn up in February and were approved by the government in March of that year (KSKS, 1:197–198).

14. KSKS, 1:199.

15. The concomitant degeneration of the female monastic domain in Rinzai (such as it was) was marked more in practice than in discourse during the nineteenth century. Tōkeiji, formerly an independent temple, officially affiliated with Engakuji in 1872; its identity as a convent deteriorated quickly thereafter—the last Tōkeiji abbess died in 1902; E, 637–638. See also Inoue Zenjō, *Kakekomidera: Matsugaoka Tōkeiji no jishi to jihō*, 77–79.

16. I owe this information, as well as the translation of the addendum to the *nikujiki saitai* edict, to Richard Jaffe, *Neither Monk nor Layman*, 158.

17. I refer here to a copy of an untitled and unpaginated manuscript draft of the memorial, dated August 1886, which was kindly provided to me by Inoue Zenjō. For a brief summary of the contents of this memorial, see E, 736. I have not located the final version of the memorial in such collections as Irokawa and Gabe, eds. *Meiji kenpakusho shūsei*, and cannot confirm that Imakita in fact submitted it to the government.

18. Ogino Dokuon, along with the Sōjiji abbot, Morotake Ekidō (1805–1879), is said to have lodged a formal protest against the Ministry of Doctrine's restriction of Buddhist content in campaign sermons; Kawakami, *Myōshinjishi*, 775. Ogino's forceful efforts to persuade the ministry and the Kyoto government to lift the ban on Buddhist content is recounted in KZSD, 3:151–152.

19. Satomichi Tokuo, "Meiji ishin ni okeru Bukkyō," 71–72. My thanks to Silvio Vita for bringing this essay to my attention.

20. In response to reports that some priests were rather loose in their interpretation of the Three Standards, official warnings were issued in late 1872 and 1873. (For the Japanese text of these cautions, see Sakurai, *Nanzenjishi,* 691–692 and 692–693, respectively.) Ketelaar, *Of Heretics,* 123–124, offers a detailed discussion of Buddhist interpretations of the Three Standards and their derivative themes.

21. See Satomichi, "Meiji ishin," 70–71.

22. Cited in E, 43, from "Kōshi shokiroku," presumably an internal Engakuji document.

23. Re the popularization of Zen in early Tokugawa, see Sawada, *Confucian Values,* 23ff.; and for Shingaku teachers' Hakuin-type formulations, see ibid., e.g., 93–98.

24. Anonymous, "Zen Rinzaishū fukyō no gi ni tsuki ryakui," in E, 642; quoted from "Ruki," no. 4, apparently an internal Engakuji document. The author is unknown; Inoue suggests that it may be Ogino Dokuon or a Rinzai administrator who was influenced by him. The statement evidently originated during the period that the Rinzai lines were treated as a unitary sect, i.e., 1873–1877.

25. Ōkubo Dōshū, "Meiji Bukkyō no saiken," 235.

26. In Satomichi's view, "Zen" (he seems to mean especially Rinzai) leaders probably reacted as other Buddhists did to the upheaval of the Restoration, but were unable to express those reactions effectively, perhaps because of their purported emphasis on a "self-powered, personal enactment" of Buddhism. Satomichi, "Meiji ishin," 63–64.

27. Bernard Faure suggests that the Buddhist insistence on monastic celibacy, articulated through criticisms of lax monks, was part of a rhetoric that exalted an imaginary tradition in several historical contexts. See his *The Red Thread,* e.g., 153–157.

28. Literally, "eating the wind and sleeping in the dew."

29. Anonymous, "Zen Rinzaishū," cited in E, 642.

30. For an edifying discussion of Song Chan monastic structures and their functions, see Foulk, "Myth, Ritual, and Monastic Practice," 147–208. The monastic or sangha hall is described on pages 183–186.

31. Other factors in the shift may have been the involuntary destruction of early temple structures, intramural friction over the selection of abbots, and the general decline in the quality of Zen practice that accompanied the rise of "cultural Zen" after the period of the Southern and Northern dynasties. See Yokoyama, *Zen no kenchiku,* 177; and Tamamura Takeji, "Kenchōji no rekishi," 789 (3067).

32. Sakurai, *Nanzenjishi,* 630–635, 637. The Kyoto Gozan finally resolved to hold summer retreats on a rotating basis, thereby relieving each temple from a portion of the yearly financial burden. This system lasted from 1734 to 1867.

33. Yokoyama, *Zen no kenchiku,* 178–179, 187–189; Collcutt, *Five*

Mountains, 215. Sōtō reformers of the seventeenth and eighteenth centuries were somewhat more successful in reviving the full-scale monastic hall. Re the timing of the establishment of the Engakuji and Kenchōji *zendō* in the Tokugawa period, see Tamamura, "Kenchōji no rekishi," 796, 798 (3076), and for the Kyoto meditation halls, Ogisu Jundō, "Meiji igo no Myōshinji," 779.

34. E.g., Satomichi, "Meiji ishin," 66–67. Cf. Ogisu, "Myōshinji," 779.

35. Foulk, "Myth, Ritual," 184.

36. Ibid., 147–149, 185, and passim.

37. Anonymous, "Zen Rinzaishū," cited in E, 642–643.

38. For discussion of nationalistic overtones in prewar Japanese Zen communities, see, e.g., Heisig and Maraldo, eds., *Rude Awakenings,* and Sharf, "Zen Nationalism." Cf. also Mohr, "Japanese Zen Schools," 197–199, who argues for a nuanced understanding of the nationalist sentiments of late-Meiji Zen leaders.

39. The essay is reproduced under the title "Kengi" in Suzuki, *Imakita Kōsen,* 174–181. Excerpts also appear in E, 651, and Satomichi, "Meiji ishin," 73–75. Satomichi suggests that the main essay was completed while Imakita was still head of the Rinzai General School in Tokyo (Tōkyō Jūzan Sōkō), viz. 1875–1877, an inference with which I am inclined to agree. Suzuki notes that the proposed regulations, which follow the main text in his modern edition, are written into the margins of the original document in cursive style; they may not have been included in the final version or even made public. Suzuki, ibid., 179, 181.

40. Imakita, "Kengi," 175. Suzuki glosses *shuryō* in this context as *gakurin,* schoolrooms or study halls. See also Collcutt, *Five Mountains,* 215–218, re "reading rooms." *Zendōka* may also be rendered as "meditation-hall masters."

41. For these statements by Dōgen, see especially the *Jūundō shiki* section of the *Shōbōgenzō,* in *Sōtōshū zensho* 1 (Shūgen 1): 54; and *Kichijōzan Eiheiji shuryō shingi,* in ibid., 1:611.

42. See Foulk, "Myth, Ritual," 186–187, for a description of the common quarters (study hall) in Song Chan monasteries.

43. Yokoyama, *Zen no kenchiku,* 196.

44. Similarly, *sōrin bōzu* or *sōdō bōzu* (monastery monk) denotes an adept who is entirely taken up with the monastic life, out of touch with contemporary society, ignorant of socially oriented Buddhist practices, and/or unversed in doctrinal learning. See *Shinpan Zengaku daijiten,* 163d, "Gakkō bōzu."

45. Imakita identifies the "literary" schools of Zen with masters who taught in Kyushu and Shikoku, areas associated with the Kogetsu school; "Kengi," 174–175. For brief details on Kogetsu Zen, see Takenuki Genshō, *Nihon Zenshūshi,* 265–267; Michel Mohr, *Traité de l'inépuisable lampe,* 1:26–28; Furuta Shōkin, *Kinsei no Zensha,* 148–155; and Akiyama Kanji, *Shamon Hakuin,* 146–151.

46. See, e.g., Dumoulin, *Zen Buddhism,* 393.

47. See Tamamura Takeji, "Kenchōji to Engakuji no idō," 393–394 (2671–2672). Seisetsu Shūcho (1745–1820), a lineal heir of Kogetsu Zenzai, revitalized Zen practice at Engakuji in the early nineteenth century. On Seisetsu,

see KSZD, 1:121–124; Furuta Shōkin, *Kinsei no Zensha,* 56–166; E, esp. 425–455; and Takenuki, *Nihon Zenshūshi,* 266–267.

48. Ogino Dokuon criticized in this vein Kaigan Dōkaku (1798–1872), the teacher of the Kogetsu-line abbot Suzumura Keisō (1818–1873), who taught at Engakuji from the late 1860s until 1873. See KZSD, 1:235; and E, 619. Sakagami Shinjō (Sōsen; 1842–1914) also exemplifies Hakuin monks' critical stance toward the Kogetsu-line "Kamakura Zen" of the Bakumatsu period; Sakagami, *Keikyokuroku,* 108. Sakagami practiced in the early 1860s at Engakuji under Seisetsu's Dharma-heir Tōkai Shōshun; on Tōkai, see KZSD, 1:189–190.

49. Kawakami, *Myōshinjishi,* 646; Furuta, *Kinsei no Zensha,* 148–150; see also Tamamura, "Kenchōji no rekishi," 796.

50. After Tōkai died in 1865, Chikuin Shōin (1796–1867), also of the Kogetsu line, began to give sermons at Engakuji; E, 617. He was followed by Kansō Bonjin (1812–1880), Yūhō Zetan, and Suzumura Keisō.

51. For details especially on the True Pure Land and Pure Land schools that appeared in the late 1860s and early 1870s, see Takeda Michio, "Meiji zenki," 85–86.

52. The decision was taken in the tenth month of 1869. Yamamoto Tetsuo, "Meiji shoki ni okeru sōryo," 146. See also Takeda, "Meiji zenki," 82–84, regarding the Shoshū Dōtoku Kaimei, which remained active until 1873.

53. The Tokyo school was founded in the third month of 1870; Yamamoto, "Meiji shoki," 148. See also Tsuji Zennosuke, *Nihon Bukkyōshi no mondai,* 99–102, and Takeda, "Meiji zenki," 84, re Buddhist "general schools" in the early Meiji.

54. Sakurai, *Nanzenjishi,* 704–705, treats the details of the program.

55. The head temple founded a small school called Hannyarin within its precincts in 1872, purportedly to provide students with an "ordinary" course of study in preparation for full-scale Zen training; Ogisu, "Myōshinji," 789. Hanazono University today includes a Zen preparatory residence called Hannyarin, inhabited by college students who are planning to undergo full-scale monastic training after their graduation. (My thanks to Victor S. Hori for this information.)

56. In 1875 the Sōtō sect established the Sōtōshū Senmon Gakkō in Tokyo, which ultimately developed into Komazawa University in 1925; see Takenuki, *Nihon Zenshūshi,* 285–286. Takeda, "Meiji zenki," 87, briefly lists other Buddhist schools that appeared in the late 1870s.

57. E, 643. The school was moved to the site of Rinshōin in Yushima a month after it opened.

58. Imakita moved to Tokyo from Iwakuni in April 1875 and opened the school in June. SKN, 12a. Re Ogino's recommendation of Imakita for the Engakuji post, see the remarks of Kimura Junseki, in Nagao Sōshiki, ed., *Sōen zenji to sono shūi,* 279–280.

59. SKN, 15a.

60. Cited in E, 651.

61. "Dust" is often used in Buddhist texts to indicate the "defiled," worldly realm of existence.

62. See Sakurai, *Nanzenjishi,* 708; and E, 651.

63. For more details on the Rinzai schools, see Takenuki, *Nihon no Zenshūshi,* 285. This system lasted until 1881, when the cooperative Rinzai Sect Office was eliminated and the various lines set up their own separate schooling systems.

64. Reading *Yochi shiryaku* for *Yochi shiyō,* and *Saigoku risshi hen* for *Saigoku risshi den.* See Sakurai, *Nanzenjishi,* 706–708, for a detailed presentation of the Rinzai elementary and middle-school curricula.

65. This trend continued; see Yamamoto, "Meiji shoki," 149.

66. Imakita, "Kengi," 175.

67. Ibid., 177.

68. Imakita may have been responding to the Kyoto abbots' plan for the Daikyōkō that was founded in 1876.

69. "With their arms folded" is an interpretive translation of *te o futokoro ni shite.*

70. Imakita, "Kengi," 175.

71. Imakita places particular emphasis on the Song Chan context in this regard; "Kengi," 176, 177. The debate between the relative value of practice and doctrinal studies has a long history in East Asian Buddhism. For some well-known Buddhist masters' attempts to reconcile the two dimensions of the Buddhist path, see Peter Gregory, "Sudden Enlightenment Followed by Gradual Cultivation," and Robert Buswell, *Tracing Back the Radiance,* esp. 57–62.

72. Imakita, "Kengi," in Suzuki, *Imakita Kōsen,* 177. If these remarks refer to the proposed general school that was ultimately established in Kyoto in 1876, when Imakita was still head of the Tokyo general school, the assembly he mentions would have taken place in October 1875.

73. Imakita, "Kengi," 177–178.

74. Ibid., 178.

75. Ibid., 177.

76. Ibid., 178, 179.

77. This facility seems to have been negatively affected by the closure of the Tokyo general school in 1877, but Rinzai leaders apparently revived it in 1879. Myōshinji abandoned the cooperative Kyoto arrangement that year and instituted its own study facility (which after many transitions, divisions, and name modifications, evolved into today's Hanazono University). On the Myōshinji school system, see Ogisu, "Myōshinji," 789; Takenuki, *Nihon no Zenshūshi,* 286; Sakurai, *Nanzenjishi,* 705, 708.

78. The notes are undated, but Imakita states at the outset that "recently in the eastern and western capitals [Tokyo and Kyoto] schools have been established and new novices of the whole sect are trained and educated," so he probably added these remarks sometime in 1876/1877—i.e., soon after the Kyoto general school opened. Imakita, "Guan setsumoku hidari no gotoshi," 179.

79. Imakita does not specify the contents of the novices' curriculum itself, but he does mention that the students were to be instructed primarily in "reading off" the required texts. "Guan setsumoku," 180–181.

80. For the above details, see ibid., 180, 181.

81. In addition to the formalities that marked off junior and senior monks,

Imakita suggested that outstanding students receive awards, a device that enhanced merit differentiation within the community.

82. Re Hōkokushagaku, see, e.g., Sakurai, *Nanzenjishi*, 703–705, and 708 re the Kyoto Daikyōkō curriculum.

83. Upon completion of the seminary course, students would receive written certificates *(jireisho)*, after which they would be free to practice elsewhere. Without these documents, Imakita suggested, monks should not be permitted to assume responsibilities at any Rinzai institution. Imakita, "Kengi," 179–180.

84. Imakita, *Zenkai ichiran, kan* 1, "Reigen," 2a; Morinaga, ed., *Zenkai ichiran*, 126–127. See Sawada, "Religious Conflict," 214.

85. Suzuki, *Imakita Kōsen*, 91, 92; and see Imakita, "Bunmei to shūkyō," 182.

86. Izuyama Kakudō, "Kaisetsu," 312.

87. See Mohr, "Japanese Zen Schools," 188, 192; we shall return to this point in chapter 7.

88. The discourse is reproduced in Suzuki, *Imakita Kōsen*, 181–185.

89. "Bunmei," 182. He justifies his view by citing the writings of Xenophon (d. 355? B.C.E.) and the German historian Barthold G. Niebuhr (1776–1831); see Suzuki, *Imakita Kōsen*, 187nn40, 41.

90. *Engakujishi*, 651.

91. Daikyū Sōetsu (Mineo; 1860–1954) became abbot of Heirinji and Myōshinji; Hirota Tenshin (Jikyō; 1856–1924) became a later abbot of Engakuji, then Tōfukuji; and Sugawara Jiho (Jusen) became the abbot of Kenchōji. E, 659.

92. SKN, 20b.

93. He served as *shōji* (monastic hall attendant), *tenzo*, and then *shōji* again. E, 660.

94. According to Inoue Zenjō (E, 660), the verse is by Su Shi (Dongpo; 1036–1101) and is contained in *Zenrin kushū*. Iriya Yoshitaka, however, says these lines (in reverse order) are from a verse in the "early plum blossom" poem of the wife of Liu Yuanzai; he cites *Shiren yuxie*, 20. *Zengo jiten*, 357a.

95. Following "Shōbō rekidai no denki," evidently an internal temple document, cited by E, 659; the comments were written by Miyaji's disciple, Nishida Daikyō (Sōgen).

96. E, 659.

97. Both had studied under a Confucian scholar in Nagoya called Satō Bokusan (1801–1891) and had come to Engakuji from Higashi Kannonji in Mikawa (eastern Aichi prefecture). Miyaji's life is briefly summarized in KZSD, 3:480–482.

98. Imakita, draft letter to Yamaoka, written April 25, 1886.

99. Inoue Zenjō, "Kōsen rōshi no shokan no shitagaki," 2. For anecdotes about Imakita's love of sweets and other "worldly" defects, see Izuyama, "Kaisetsu," 318.

100. Draft letter to Yamaoka; for the version of this incident contained in a draft of a similar letter to Ogino Dokuon, see E, 660–661. Miyaji Sōkai was eventually rehabilitated and later succeeded Shaku Sōen as abbot of Engakuji.

The feminist activist and writer Hiratsuka Raichō (1886–1971), who practiced in Kamakura during the early twentieth century, apparently also had a dim view of Miyaji. See Michel Mohr, "Japanese Zen Schools," 190.

101. Draft letter to Yamaoka.

102. See his letters to Shaku in Nagao, ed., *Sōen Zenji to sono shūi,* 16–21; and Suzuki, *Imakita Kōsen,* 76.

103. Undated letter to Shaku Sōen, in Nagao, ed., *Sōen Zenji to sono shūi,* 21.

104. For Torio's response to Shaku Sōen's request for help, dated May 17, 1887, see Nagao, comp., *Sōen Zenji to sono shūi,* 49–50 (the year of the letter appears to be misdated by two years). See also Nagao, ed., *Sōen Zenji shokan shū,* 17, for Shaku's own testimony about Torio's support for his decision to attend Keiōgijuku, in his March 20, 1895, letter to the Engakuji priest, Ogawa Dōkai (Zokutōan).

105. Kimura, in Nagao, ed. *Sōen Zenji to sono shūi,* 281.

106. "Kyōikugikō shingi jo"; SK 3:29b. Based on Shaku's placing of the text in SK, the preface was probably written in 1887, perhaps a few months before Shaku finished his course of studies at Keiōgijuku.

107. They also came under increasing government supervision. Amano, *Senmongakkō,* 41. The ultimate effect of these policies was a "two-layer structure" in Japanese higher education; Rubinger, "Education," 227. For details, see Amano, *Senmongakkō,* 31–37; 75–107.

108. Amano, *Senmongakkō,* 77.

109. Ibid., 78–79. Most of these nondenominational schools ended up relying on tuition fees for their upkeep.

110. Ibid., 95.

111. SK, 3:29a. *"Ritsugen"* usually means the expression of one's ideas or opinions—especially ideas that one expresses well for the sake of posterity. Given Imakita's subsequent remarks, however, by *"ritsugen no shogaku"* he simply means forms of learning that are articulated in words, as opposed to practices or gestures.

112. Sawada, "Religious Conflict," 214.

Chapter 6: Koji Zen

1. The Engakuji denomination's code was finalized in 1885; E, 674–676. During the Edo period, the abbots of head temples had the largest say in intra-sectarian decisions, including the appointment of branch-temple staff. For a useful recent description of the head-branch temple system during the early Tokugawa period, see Williams, "Representations of Zen," 41–49.

2. For a detailed study of this phenomenon and the ensuing Buddhist reconstruction strategies, I refer the reader once again to Ketelaar's *Of Heretics and Martyrs.*

3. See Notto Thelle, *Buddhism and Christianity,* 110; Martin Collcutt, "Buddhism: The Threat of Eradication," 165. Ketelaar does not focus on the development of lay Buddhist movements, though he cites the late Meiji writer Takada Dōken's apparent idealization of the lay Buddhist, *Of Heretics and Martyrs,* 185 (discussed below).

4. Gregory Schopen, "Two Problems in the History of Indian Buddhism," 23–26. This essay appears in edited form in Schopen's *Bones, Stones, and Buddhist Monks*, 23–55; see 30–34 in the later version. Reginald Ray has suggested that a group of "forest renunciants" coexisted and interacted with both the lay and the settled monastic communities during the formative phases of Mahayana Buddhism. See Ray, *Buddhist Saints in India*, and the related review article by Charles Prebish, "Ideal Types in Indian Buddhism."

5. Timothy Brook devotes sustained attention to the ways in which lay patrons defined their relationship to the monastic sangha in the Ming period, in his *Praying for Power*. Keyworth also highlights the importance of elite lay practitioners as an identifiable group in his "Transmitting the Lamp of Learning in Classical Chan Buddhism," 111–141.

6. The term also came to be used as an honorific suffix to male literary names, a custom followed by not a few writers in Japan. For a systematic discussion of these and other nuances of the term in Sanskrit, Chinese, and Japanese, see *Bukkyōgo daijiten*, 346c–d. For information on the history of *jushi Chan* and *koji Zen*, see also *Zengaku daijiten*, 342a–b. Keyworth offers documentation of appearances of the term *"jushi"* in various early and later Buddhist Chinese sources; "Transmitting the Lamp," 112–116.

7. ZZ, 64:356a (no. 1261) from *Xuedou zuying ji* [J. *Setchō soei shū*] (1032 preface), *juan* 1, contained in *Zuting shiyuan* [J. *Sotei jien*] (pub. 1154), *juan* 3.

8. Needless to say, the "Chan" qualifications of these figures is highly debatable; on Li Ao's alleged Chan inclinations, e.g., see Timothy Barrett, *Li Ao*, 33–57. Other famous laymen associated with Chan were, e.g., Wang Wei (ca. 701–761), Bo Juyi (772–846), and Su Shi (1036–1101). See below for further examples of well-known *jushi* cited by Imakita Kōsen. Numerous hagiographies of Chinese Buddhist laypeople are contained in the Ming compilation, *Jushi fendeng lu* (2 *juan*, comp. Zhu Shien, published in 1610); contained in ZZ, 86:573–613 (no. 1607); and in the Qing collection, *Jushi zhuan* (56 *juan*, comp. Peng Jiqing, published in 1775); contained in ZZ, 88:180–291 (no. 1646). Keyworth provides a convenient table that enumerates details about the *jushi* treated in the *Jushi fendeng lu* in his "Transmitting the Lamp," 116–130.

9. The term *"koji"* also came to be affixed to the name of deceased Buddhists. *"Daishi,"* the formal term for an *upāsikā* (J. *ubai*) or a female lay practitioner, was an honorific suffix to a deceased laywoman's name. By the early modern period, the conferral of posthumous rank suffixes *(igō)* and precept names *(kaimyō)* came to depend largely on the social status and, especially, the degree of economic support the deceased had given to his or her temple. See Williams, "Representations of Zen," 231–245.

10. E.g., in the late fifteenth century, Sōtō laypeople from a wide range of social backgrounds received personal precept-lineage charts *(kechimyaku)* when they participated in "mass ordination ceremonies" *(jukaie)*, but they did not necessarily practice Zen extensively. See William Bodiford, *Sōtō Zen in Medieval Japan*, 172, 180–181, 184.

11. See Collcutt, *Five Mountains*, 57–58.

12. KZSD recounts the biographical details of twenty-two notable lay

practitioners who practiced under Rinzai masters during the Edo and early Meiji periods.

13. Imakita, "Takuhatsu kuyō no kudoku," 234–235. Greed, in the Buddhist view, is the first of the Three Poisons (followed by anger and ignorance) and one of the causes of falling into the Three Evil Realms (the lowest realms of karmic existence).

14. Imakita, "Takuhatsu," 236.

15. Ibid., 237.

16. Ibid., 236–237. For a classical articulation of this axiom, see, e.g. *The Scripture of the Lotus Blossom of the Fine Dharma,* trans. Leon Hurvitz, 38–39.

17. Marcel Mauss, *The Gift,* 18.

18. Suzuki, *Imakita,* 53, says that many handwritten records of Imakita's "karmic relations" talks are extant; see also Izuyama, "Kaisetsu," 317. Suzuki, *Imakita,* 242–249, reproduces the text of one of Imakita's popular sermons, "Kanzeon Bosatsu reigen no setsu," given in 1876 at Konji-in in Tokyo.

19. Zhang practiced Chan under the poet Su Shi's friend, Donglin Changzong (1025–1091) and inherited the Dharma of Doushuai Congyue (1044–1091). For a discussion of Zhang, see Robert M. Gimello, "Chang Shang-ying," esp. 91–97.

20. Imakita, *Zenkai ichiran,* 146, 147 (sec. 21); see also 227, 228 (sec. 65), and 251, 252 (sec. 75), for other references to Zhang.

21. *Zenkai ichiran,* 146, 147 (sec. 21).

22. He cites as examples such scholars, poets, thinkers, and officials as Wang Zong (584–618); Pei Xiu (797–820); Liu Zongyuan (773–819); Zhou Dunyi (1017–1073); Yang Yi (974–1020); Huang Tingjian (1045–1105); Zhao Mengfu (1254–1322); Wang Yangming; and Wen Zhengming (1470–1559). See Morinaga, ed., *Zenkai ichiran,* 147–148 (n. 21); 161–162 (n. 28); 166–167 (n. 31); 227 (n. 65); and 244–248 (nos. 73–74), for these and similar references. Regarding Imakita's apologetic strategy in this work, see Sawada, "Religious Conflict," 212–216.

23. For discussion of a contemporaneous critique of Imakita's Buddhist interpretation of Neo-Confucian thinkers, see Sawada, "Religious Conflict," esp. 217–223.

24. Sakurai, *Nanzenjishi,* 663, 664.

25. Ibid., 684.

26. Ibid., 681–682. The general levy on Buddhist temples was issued in the fourth month of 1868. With rice at a nominal price of 586 silver *monme* per *koku* in Edo, in 1868, 270 *ryō* would have purchased only 28 *koku* (ca. 138.5 bushels).

27. See NBKH, 406–438, re temple lotteries and moneylending systems in the Tokugawa; cf. also Sakurai, *Nanzenjishi,* 681. The loss of the "black-seal lands" that had traditionally provided revenue to ancestral temples in most cases was not compensated by any interim measures such as temporary stipends. This was also true of temples that had close relations with the Tokugawa family; see NBKK, 307.

28. The seed money for the loan funds originated in resources granted by

the shogunate or other official patrons under the rubric of temple restoration. Because of their official sanction, interest payment on these loans was virtually guaranteed, which made them an attractive option for "investors" who wished to put their money to work (Takekoshi Yosaburō, *Nihon keizaishi,* 9:325; NBKH, 419). In the late eighteenth century the shogunate began to crack down on the practice, but with little effect. Takekoshi, *Nihon Keizaishi,* 9:332; NBKH, 426–429.

29. NBKH, 437.

30. For more details, see NBKK, 306. In 1875, additional land that had been considered to be within temple/shrine precincts in 1871 was newly designated as being outside the precincts and confiscated. Ibid., 307–308.

31. See NBKK, 308. The Tendai, Shingon, Rinzai, Ji, and Pure Land sects suffered proportionally greater losses than the Nichiren, Sōtō, and True Pure Land sects, which had generally relied less on shogunal and domainal fiefs for their upkeep. Tamamuro Taijō argues that the True Pure Land sect was able to play a leading role in early Meiji Buddhism because it suffered least from these temple eliminations and land confiscations. NBKK, 309.

32. Regarding Engakuji, see E, 610–611. Again, larger institutions took greater losses. Inoue Zenjō says that Engakuji lost an income of 144 *kanmon* when its land was confiscated, but the much wealthier Hachiman shrine of Kamakura lost 840 *kanmon.* By the same token, Engakuji's smaller branch temples suffered fewer losses during the anti-Buddhist years than did the head temple. E, 622–623.

33. The diminishing stipends were calculated based on a sum corresponding to one-fourth of the actual income from the 1874 harvest; one-half of this amount was given to the temples in the first year, and a sum reduced by one-tenth of the base fund per year was granted for each of the remaining nine years (NBKK, 307). See Sakurai, *Nanzenjishi,* 685–686, for details on the impact of this system on Nanzenji in Kyoto.

34. For a reproduction of the text of the decree (no. 25), see Date Mitsuyoshi, ed., *Nihon shūkyō seido shiryō ruijukō,* 632; it was rescinded by decree no. 8, issued by the Home Ministry in 1881.

35. Regarding *takuhatsu,* especially its Buddhist textual sources, see "Bunne," in Lévi and Takakusu, eds., *Hōbōgirin,* Premier Fascicule, 158–169. My thanks to Victor Hori for this reference.

36. Sakagami, *Keikyokuroku,* 100.

37. Ibid., 101–102. It is difficult to estimate the exact purchasing power of the sums that Sakagami specifies. Each domain's economy and monetary system possessed its own characteristics, and prices varied greatly during the Bakumatsu period. However, for comparative purposes, we may consider that, based on Edo rice prices and money rates for 1858 (Ansei 5), a donation of 10 to 15 *monme* of copper *zeni* would have been worth only about one-third to one-half a British cup of rice; 1 *monme* of silver at Edo rates would have bought about 255 cc. of rice (1.42 *gō*). An intake of 8 to 9 gold *ryō* for the entire tour would have purchased about one and one-half bushels of rice; 14 to 15 *ryō,* about two and one-half bushels. The monks would have had to visit many households in order to cover their retreat expenses after they paid their lodging fees of 5 *gō* of rice

(ca. 902 cc.) each and the headman took his cut. For the rates used, see *Iwanami Nihonshi jiten*, 1616–1617.

38. Katō Shōshun, "'A Lineage of Dullards,'" 157.

39. The drop in numbers of monks at Kaiundō, Imakita's Zen training center in Yamaguchi in the early 1870s, may have been related to the initial impact of this prohibition on the monks' resources (Inoue, *Engakujishi*, 646; see SKN, 11b). The Engakuji monastic program registered a similar drop in late 1872 and early 1873.

40. Imakita's petition was reportedly submitted in the winter of 1872; SKN, 11b. It is not contained in Irokawa and Gabe, eds., *Meiji kenpakusho shūsei*, vol. 2, which covers memorials submitted to the government during 1872–1873.

41. Anonymous, "Zen Rinzaishū," cited in E, 642.

42. Even after the interdiction was lifted nine years later in 1881, Buddhist mendicancy was never again practiced in Japan on its former scale. Today, alms rounds are still a required feature of Rinzai monastic training, but they are much reduced in scale and highly ritualized.

43. See Jaffe, *Neither Monk nor Layman*, 58–94, for an analysis of the implications of the new household registration system for the Buddhist clergy.

44. Ikeda Eishun, "Teaching Assemblies and Lay Societies," 35.

45. The female counterpart of *koji* is, strictly speaking, *nyokoji* or *daishi*, but in contrast to *zenshi*, these terms are rarely used in the Rinzai texts that I cite. In this study I therefore use *zenshi*, a title that may be peculiar to the Engakuji denomination.

46. Japanese scholars have depicted the broader contours of the Meiji *koji* phenomenon as a whole, which was led by a number of prominent figures, such as Ōuchi Seiran (1845–1918) and Inoue Enryō (1858–1919). Ōkubo Dōshū lists a number of well-known *koji*, including Torio Tokuan and Yamaoka Tesshū, discussed below; "Meiji Bukkyō," 235. Ikeda discusses lay Buddhist groups in several works, especially *Meiji Bukkyō kyōkai kessha shi no kenkyū* and, in translation, "Teaching Assemblies and Lay Societies." Kashiwahara Yūsen deals with the growth of the lay practice in broad terms in his *Nihon Bukkyōshi: Kindai*, 95–112. Although dated, another essay worth consulting is Katō Totsudō, "Meiji jidai no zaike Bukkyō."

47. See Sawada, *Confucian Values*, 39–41, re the Zen Buddhist predilections of the Sanzensha founder, Nakazawa Dōni. "Sanzen" in the name Sanzensha is both a classical Confucian allusion and a play on the phrase "practicing Zen."

48. SSJR, 5a. Although no dates are given, the placement of this account in Takahashi's biography suggests that it refers to events in early 1867 or thereabouts, before Gan'ō moved to Nanzenji, and Takahashi, for his part, to Sanzensha. Tsumaki also used the names Shōji and Yorinori.

49. Gan'ō had practiced at Kenchōji under the Kogetsu-line master Shinjō Genmyō (1772–1841) and inherited the Dharma of Shinjō's successor, Setsudō Genkatsu (d. 1853). Gan'ō resided at the temple Chōtokuji in Shibamura (in today's Saitama prefecture) and was also abbot of Kenchōji from about 1860 to

1868, after which he was appointed to Nanzenji in Kyoto. See ZD, 283b; KZSD, 1:165–166.

50. According to Kenchōji registers, in 1868 and still in 1872 Gan'ō had charge of ten *koji.* KSKS, 423. KZSD, 1:166, however, states that Gan'ō had about fifty lay disciples his late years.

51. It is not clear to me why Myōshinji became involved; perhaps it held jurisdiction over the site in which Takahashi lectured. Gan'ō himself was associated with the Gozan temple Kenchōji (and later, Nanzenji), not Myōshinji— although he was a lineal descendant of Kogetsu Zenzai, who had originally been affiliated with Myōshinji.

52. For this and the above passage, see SSJR, 5b–6a.

53. SSJR, 6a.

54. For fuller discussion of the role of Zen ideas and practices in Shingaku during the Tokugawa period, see Sawada, *Confucian Values,* chaps. 3, 4, and 5.

55. Hayano Gankō, *Kawajiri Hōkin sensei jiseki,* 3b. Kawajiri's first koan was Zhaozhou's Wu (J. *Mu*); he received the name Hōgin from Gan'ō at about this time (Imakita later had him change the pronunciation to Hōkin; Izuyama, "Kaisetsu," 313).

56. Rinzai *sesshin* is a period of intensive training that usually involves extended meditation. It sometimes includes a number of private interviews between master and student, and may involve working on a koan.

57. Hayano, *Kawajiri jiseki,* 3b–4a.

58. Mitani allegedly met Gan'ō in the eighth month of 1871; SSJR, 22b–23a. Mitani was also certified as a Shingaku teacher; in late 1872 he was designated a doctrinal instructor. SSJR, 25a.

59. Imakita acknowledged Mitani Ken'ō's understanding of Zen by giving him the name Sōyaku in June 1878. Mitani also practiced under Yuri Tekisui of Tenryūji and Ekkei Shuken (1810–1884) of Myōshinji. SSJR, 23b.

60. SSJR, 4a.

61. For more details about Okunomiya and his ideas, see Matsumura Iwao, "Yōmeigakusha Okunomiya Zōsai"; Inoue Tetsujirō, *Nihon Yōmeigakusha,* 357–359; KZBD, 1:316–317; Takase, *Satō Issai,* 743–750; *Meiji ishin jinmei jiten,* 238; Kataoka Yakichi, "Nakano Kenmei"; and Itoya, *Okunomiya Kenshi,* 13–15.

62. Okunomiya's tenure at the Ministry of Doctrine dates from the sixth month of Meiji 5 (1872). Matsumura says he resigned in early 1877 and spent his remaining days teaching in the capital; "Yōmeigakusha," 159. Cf. Nihon Shiseki Kyōkai, ed., *Hyakukan rireki,* which dates his tenure only to January of Meiji 9 (1876).

63. "Tsuisōki," cited in Matsumura, "Yōmeigakusha," 165. Okunomiya later practiced under a master called Daikyū of the Sōtō temple, Shinnyoji, in Tosa (Kōchi), and under Kyōdō Etan (1809–1895) of the Rinzai temple Shōfukuji in Hyōgo. KZSD, 1:317.

64. Okunomiya Zōsai's writings remain unpublished. The above excerpt is translated from the text of "Seizasetsu" reproduced in Matsumura, "Yōmeigakusha," 165.

65. *Genshi banroku,* no. 74; NST, 46:258 (121). The last line is an allusion to Zhu Xi's instructions to one of his students about quiet sitting in *Zhuzi yulei, juan* 116, sec. 55. For the primary text, I have consulted SGT, 6:302–303.

66. Okunomiya eventually attained *kenshō* after working through the koans known as "Doushuai's Three Barriers" (Ch. *Doushuai sanguan*); Suzuki, *Imakita,* 64, 73n19.

67. *Zenkai ichiran* was published with official approval in May 1876; it had been issued in a block-print edition in 1874 in Yamaguchi, but the Ministry of Doctrine apparently required republication permission; SKN, 14a. The Meiji government's regulation of publications commenced in early 1868; in 1872, the Ministry of Doctrine was given jurisdiction over books considered to be in its domain (religion and ethics). For details, see Richard H. Mitchell, *Censorship in Imperial Japan,* esp. 19, 21, 32, 50–52, 80.

68. Date, once a highly ranked official of Wakayama domain, had studied under Motoori Norinaga's son, Motoori Ōhira (1756–1833), and distinguished himself as a poet and historian. He practiced Zen under Rinzai master Ekkei Shuken; for details, see KZSD, 1:314–315. Date's son was the well-known Meiji official Mutsu Munemitsu (1844–1897). On the latter, see Marius Jansen, "Mutsu Munemitsu"; see also Mutsu's well-known work, *Kenkenroku,* translated by Gordon Berger.

69. The last article adds, rather cryptically, that steps should be taken to prevent vulgar guests *(zokkaku)* from infringing upon the refined interests *(gakyō)* of the group. "Ryōmō shakai yaku," dated November 21, 1875; cited in Matsumura, "Yōmeigakusha," 174, and paraphrased in E, 662.

70. Sharf, "The Zen of Japanese Nationalism," 148n14. Sharf cites Fields, *How the Swans Came to the Lake,* 177 (the correct page number is 175); Fields and/or Sharf may also be following Miura and Sasaki, *Zen Dust,* 225.

71. See Okunomiya's biographical materials, listed above, as well as Imakita's eulogy of Okunomiya, SK, 2:37a, in which the abbot says that the Ryōmō Society greatly assisted him in fulfilling his educational aims.

72. Cited in Matsumura, "Yōmeigakusha," 174.

73. I have encountered no mention of women in association with this group in the 1870s, though Kawajiri Esō (mentioned below) regularly practiced at Engakuji from the mid-1870s.

74. After the shogunate fell, Takahashi withdrew from public life; little is known about his activities during the Meiji period. See, e.g., the popular treatment by Matsumoto Ken'ichi, *Bakumatsu no sanshū,* 156–160.

75. Tsunemitsu also lists Taguchi Tōkan, possibly the same Tōkan *koji* who is identified as Tanouchi Itsuo in Imakita's 1885 lay register (discussed below). *Meiji no Bukkyōsha,* 2:110.

76. The Confucian scholar and translator Nakamura Masanao (Keiu) also participated in these literary conversations. See, e.g., Takahashi Deishū, *Deishū ikō,* 9.

77. Kōtoku Shūsui, *Chōmin sensei, Chōmin sensei gyōjōki,* 30. For interpretations of Nakae's alleged Zen inspiration, see, e.g., Ueyama Shunpei, "Chōmin no tetsugaku shisō," 39; and Funayama Shin'ichi, *Meiji tetsugaku shi kenkyū,* 174.

78. Judging from Sasaki's account, Shaku Sōen approached Sōkatsu about the group when the latter was about twenty-nine years old, i.e., in about 1898. For comments on this event and on the later development of the Ryōmō association, see Sasaki, *Cat's Yawn*, 23. I am grateful to Michel Mohr for this reference.

79. E, 758n.

80. Moreover, the Shingaku center, Sanzensha, though not formally identified with the Rinzai establishment, long predated the Ryōmō Society in teaching Zen to laypeople in an organized fashion. Sharf's further suggestion that Ryōmō Kyōkai was "the first Zen center in modern Japan explicitly dedicated to teaching meditation to laypersons" must be qualified accordingly. (His statement may be inspired in turn by Fields' declaration that "[n]othing like [Ryōmō Kyōkai] had ever existed in Japan"; Fields, *How the Swans*, 177.) For Sharf's remarks, see his "Japanese Nationalism," 148n14.

81. E, 662.

82. E, 650.

83. Engakuji historian Inoue Zenjō has reiterated this point to me both in person and in a letter dated May 26, 1995.

84. SKN, 15a. Sharf says that Imakita opened "the newly constructed Zen hall at Engakuji to lay students wishing to practice Zen meditation"; "Zen Nationalism," 112. (I assume that "Zen hall" is a translation of *zendō*.) However, the meditation hall, Shōbōgendō, was not rebuilt until 1883; SKN, 19a. Soon afterward (probably during the spring of 1884), this building actually became *less* accessible to lay practitioners for a time, a development discussed below. The assumption that the meditation hall was rebuilt in the 1870s may derive from confusion between Shōbōgendō and Shōden'an, the lay quarters.

85. A precedent in the Song Chinese context for a lay quarters of this kind may be a structure in one monastery of the time called the "eastern bank" (Ch. *dongpo*), apparently named after the lay practitioner and poet Su Dongpo; see Foulk, "Myth, Ritual," 187.

86. Suzuki reportedly said that the pillar in Shōden'an against which Kawajiri leaned while meditating bore a stain made by his hair oil over the years. See Izuyama Kakudō, "'Zazen no michi,'" 4. In 1923 Shōden'an was destroyed by the great Kantō earthquake, but was later restored. From about 1912 to 1945, Suzuki himself resided in Shōden'an. In 1946 he moved to the building that now houses the Matsugaoka Archives (Matsugaoka Bunko) on the slope overlooking Tōkeiji. Shōden'an was renovated and has since served as the Engakuji abbot's quarters. This update on the erstwhile lay quarters was provided to me by Inoue Zenjō in a letter dated May 26, 1995.

87. SKN, 15a.

88. The original calligraphy for the Takuboku-en entrance plaque is still displayed today in the Engakuji building Ichigeki-tei, where Imakita spent his last years.

89. Neither Ryōmō Kyōkai nor Takuboku-en are formally acknowledged in SK, to my knowledge, though Imakita expresses gratitude to Okunomiya Zōsai for founding the Ryōmō Society in the aforementioned eulogy, SK, 2:37a. Takuboku-en is mentioned only in the brief SKN reference quoted above and in later accounts that draw on it.

90. *Bōroshū e kōshū meiseki.* This register is now lost or misplaced (Inoue Zenjō, personal communication, 1994). Imakita held the assembly in early 1881 to commemorate the seventeenth anniversary of the death of the aforementioned Engakuji abbot, Tōkai Shōshun. Tōkai, a disciple of Seisetsu Shūcho, was the compiler of *Bōroshū,* a collection of Seisetsu's poems. In addition to the lay practitioners, the 1881 assembly drew over a hundred monastics. SKN, 17a.

91. Kitashiro was a judge of the third rank who had been associated with Okunomiya Zōsai's school in Tosa in the 1860s; see SKN, 17b, and Takase, *Satō Issai,* 746. Tsumaki was an official in the Ministry of Education who (as noted earlier) had practiced with this Zen group from before the Restoration.

92. E, 662.

93. SKN, 18a, 19b; E, 654.

94. SKN, 18a. For the text of Imakita's preface to the donation register, dated April 1881, see Imakita, "Engakuji zendō saiken hokki kanjinjō," 8a; partially cited in E, 654.

95. Presumably these solicitation rounds took place privately or only after the prohibition of public mendicancy was lifted in 1881.

96. SKN, 19b.

97. SKN, 14a–b, 16a, 16b, 22a. *Ondaigo* might be rendered "A Drink of the Purest Nectar."

98. The lay society was called Butsuge Shari Jūmannin-kō (The Buddha's Tooth-Relic Associaton of One Hundred Thousand Members). See "Meiji jūhachi nen: Engakuji jūmannin-kō," document no. 10 in KSKS, 210–213. The document is held in the Engakuji collection, according to the editors.

99. "Meiji nijūgo nen: Engakuji kaikei," document no. 11 in KSKS, 215.

100. The Kitsuregawa were a Kantō branch of the Ashikaga clan. Tamamura Takeji, "Kenchōji to Engakuji no idō," 391 (2669).

Chapter 7: Shifting Boundaries in the Sangha

1. Shaku Sōen, "Furoku," 1b–2a; see also 2b–3a.

2. For information on Yamaoka, I have consulted KZSD, 1:318–326; Tsunemitsu, *Meiji no Bukkyōsha,* 2:150–159; Zen Bunka Kenkyūsho, ed., *Meiji no Zenshō,* 155–172; Matsumoto Ken'ichi, *Bakumatsu no sanshū;* and *Meiji ishin jinmei jiten,* 1028–1029.

3. Yamaoka's rapid move into the service of the Meiji emperor was criticized by fellow Tokugawa retainers; Matsumoto, *Bakumatsu no sanshū,* 118–119.

4. See, e.g., John Stevens' *The Sword of No-Sword* and Ōmori Sōgen's *Yamaoka Tesshū* for summaries of popular stories about Yamaoka along these lines. For the following information, see E, 662.

5. Yamaoka's name appears frequently in Imakita's writings and personal letters, as well as in documents related to other Engakuji *koji.* He wrote a preface for the abbot's *Shōju rōnin sugyō roku,* published in 1877; a preface for a reprint of Hakuin's *Kaian kokugo* in 1885; an advance solicitation essay for Imakita's chronological biography, *Sōryōkutsu nenpu;* and a preface for a donation register to fund the publication of Imakita's complete Chinese works, *Sōryō kōroku* (both in 1886).

6. See, e.g., Zen Bunka Kenkyūsho, ed., *Meiji no Zenshō,* 155–172, and Tsunemitsu, *Meiji no Bukkyōsha,* 2:150–159. The coverage of Yamaoka in KZSD, 1:318–326 is unusually detailed compared to the treatment of other *koji.*

7. See "Yamaoka Tesshū koji kōin ni wa shite, iken o teisuru jo," SK, 3:11b–12a; and Suzuki, *Imakita,* 15–17, for a Japanese translation.

8. SK, 3:12a; see also Suzuki, *Imakita,* 17.

9. Suzuki, *Imakita,* 13.

10. The most detailed biographical source for Kawajiri Hōkin and his wife, Esō, is Hayano, *Kawajiri Hōkin sensei jiseki,* of which a block-print edition is held in the Sanzensha collection. See also KZSD, 3:511–515; Izuyama Kakudō, "'Zen no hayamichi,'" and E, 662–663.

11. Imakita gave Kawajiri the lineal Dharma name Sōsei, and his wife the name Esō, in acknowledgment of their 1876 attainments. See *Kawajiri jiseki,* 4b; E, 663.

12. Several of these family members are enrolled in the Engakuji 1885 lay register, "Sōryōkutsu ejō koji zenshi meishi." The original register is held in the Engakuji collection at Tōkeiji in Kamakura; it has been reproduced in modern print in KSKS, 390–401. See also KZSD, 3:512 and E, 663–664.

13. Hayano, *Kawajiri jiseki,* 5a. See also Shaku Sōen, "Furoku," 2b–3a.

14. Cited in E, 663. Michel Mohr translates *kōjō* in Rinzai texts of the late Tokugawa as *le dépassement;* the term is also used in a more specific sense to mean a highly advanced stage of koan practice. For a fuller discussion, see Mohr, *Traité de l'inépuisable lampe,* 2:513–515n851. Kawajiri is also said to have studied under Ekkei Shuken and Yuri Tekisui. For details about Kawajiri's Zen practice, see Hayano, *Kawajiri jiseki,* 5a–5b.

15. The draft of Imakita's letter to Kawajiri on this occasion, dated October 9, probably 1886, is held in the Engakuji collection; see E, 663.

16. Imakita marked the couple's achievements by giving Kawajiri the literary name Bōroan, and altering the second character of Esō's name. The abbot also wrote an inscription for a painting of the couple to commemorate the occasion; see *Kawajiri jiseki,* 5b–6b.

17. Draft letter to Kawajiri, no. 2, written November 24, perhaps 1884.

18. SKN, 15a, 16b, 17a, 17b, 19a, 21a.

19. For mention of the *sesshin* retreats, see Hayano, *Kawajiri jiseki,* 5a.

20. See Hayano, *Kawajiri jiseki,* 10a, for an extensive list of the Zen Buddhist works that Kawajiri regularly explicated.

21. On these occasions, Kawajiri invariably received practitioners in *sanzen* and gave Shingaku *dōwa;* his audiences at these talks are said to have reached the several hundreds. He also offered his services to non-Buddhist groups, including Hōtoku and Misogikyō-related organizations. Hayano, *Kawajiri jiseki,* 10b–11b.

22. Katō Totsudō suggests that monks' teaching skills in general compared poorly with those of lay activists during the early Meiji; "Meiji jidai," 137.

23. Inoue Zenjō and Izuyama Kakudō have duly noted the contribution to Rinzai history of the Shingaku/Misogikyō leader. E, 663; Izuyama, "'Zazen no hayamichi.'" However, whether because Kawajiri lacked a high profile or social rank (in comparison with Yamaoka or Torio), or because he was closely

identified with Shingaku and Misogikyō, for the most part the role he played in the Meiji popularization of Zen has been overlooked.

24. SN, 19a.

25. The structure apparently was disassembled and reassembled elsewhere. In return, Taiseikyō provided Shingaku with a promissory note to the effect that it would contribute 200 yen toward the cost of rebuilding Sanzensha in the future. SN, 24b; the note appears on 25a.

26. SN, 26b. The four included Kawajiri, Kumatani, and Mitani.

27. *Kawajiri jiseki,* 7a. The Sanzensha *kōsha* was moved to Shitaya (in Tokyo's Taito-ku) in 1891.

28. *Kawajiri jiseki,* 7a; Izuyama, "Kaisetsu," 314. The manual is *Kenmon shijū hassoku,* attributed to Teshima Toan. For a fuller description of Shingaku *sakumon,* see Sawada, *Confucian Values,* 93–98.

29. *Seiza kufū* is a characteristic Shingaku expression. It should be emphasized that *seiza* was not consistently identified in Shingaku with *zazen* (or Shingaku *sakumon* with Zen *koan*) until the mid-nineteenth century, although the overlap in meaning of the terms originated in the discourse of eighteenth-century Shingaku leaders. See Sawada, *Confucian Values,* 99–109, for a discussion of Shingaku contemplative praxis.

30. SN, 27a–b.

31. Hayano, *Kawajiri jiseki,* 6b–7a.

32. SN, 40a.

33. SN, 18a, 27b.

34. SSJR, 6b.

35. SSJR, 7a–b.

36. SSJR, 23b.

37. Draft letter to Tsumaki, most likely written during the early part of March 1884. Imakita also cites the "great change" of the central government as a reason for postponing the Zen lectures; he makes a similar remark in a letter to Tsumaki's wife, Ayako, and connects it with her husband's possible dismissal (from the Ministry of Education); draft letter to Tsumaki Ayako, probably written in spring 1884. It is unclear to me what Imakita means by the "great change" in the government; it is possible that the letter is misdated by a year and that he is referring to the institution of the cabinet system, which took place in 1885.

38. Draft letter to Kawajiri, no. 1, probably written in early March 1884.

39. Ibid.

40. Imakita identifies the monasteries as Tokugenji in Nagoya, Enpukuji in today's southern Kyoto prefecture, and Tenryūji in Kyoto.

41. Jaffe, *Neither Monk nor Layman,* 164.

42. Draft letter to Tsumaki.

43. Draft letter to Kawajiri, no. 1. Based on his research into this and other correspondence of the time, Inoue has concluded that Imakita allowed the lay practitioners to use the meditation hall continuously from 1877 until 1884, when the monks pressured him to stop the practice. Inoue Zenjō, letter to the author, May 26, 1995.

44. Presumably the lay practitioners' freedom to leave the monastery would infringe on the rule of seclusion for retreat participants.

45. Draft letter to Kawajiri, no. 1.

46. Robert Sack, *Human Territoriality*, 26.

47. Sack, *Human Territoriality*, 21.

48. Katō, "Meiji jidai," 136.

49. Ikeda Eishun, "Kindai shakai ni okeru Bukkyō no jittai," 251. Ikeda cites "Koji shinron," *Meikyō shinshi*, n. 2860, but the passage he quotes actually appears in issue no. 2865.

50. Ketelaar, *Of Heretics*, 185. Ketelaar draws here on Takada's *Tsū Bukkyō anshin* (Tokyo: Bukkyōkan, 1904), 7, 23–24, 29.

51. Takada, "Koji shinron," pt. 1, *Meikyō shinshi*, no. 2859 (March 12, 1891): 3.

52. Ibid., pt. 2, *Meikyō shinshi*, no. 2860 (March 14, 1891): 5. For Takada's related criticism of the use of *"sōryo"* to mean Christian teachers, see ibid., pt. 4, *Meikyō shinshi*, no. 2863 (March 20, 1891): 6.

53. Ibid., pt. 2, *Meikyō shinshi*, no. 2860 (March 14, 1891): 4.

54. Ibid., *Meikyō shinshi*, no. 2862 (March 18, 1891): 6.

55. Ibid., *Meikyō shinshi*, no. 2865 (March 24, 1891): 6, 7.

56. It is in the context of these considerations that Takada goes on to make the remark cited above, that "although in appearance the true *koji* has not yet attained the realm of liberation, in his mind he is already seeking this great Way...." Ibid., 7.

57. Jaffe, *Neither Monk nor Layman*, 93.

58. Ikeda, "Teaching Assemblies," 34.

59. Engakuji, "Sōryōkutsu ejō koji zenshi meishi." Inoue Zenjō counts 348 practitioners in all, perhaps because he omits names that are crossed out; *Engakujishi*, 664. See also his comment in Inoue Zenjō, *Suzuki shokan*, 116n4.

60. Engakuji, "Kojiryō seiki" (unpaginated).

61. Regulations pertaining to the monks' study hall ordinarily prohibited the introduction of these and other substances. See, e.g., Dōgen's stipulations in his "Kichijōsan Eiheiji shuryō shingi," in *Dōgen Zenji zenshū*, 6:82; trans. Leighton and Okumura, *Dōgen's Pure Standards*, 114.

62. Engakuji, "Kojiryō seiki."

63. Again, Zen monks had been forbidden by Dōgen to "have discussion with tradesmen," "conversations about worldly affairs," or to violate "dignified decorum" in or near the study hall. *Dōgen Zenji zenshū*, 6:76, 78; trans. Leighton and Okumura, *Dōgen's Pure Standards*, 110, 111, 112, respectively.

64. Rick Fields, *How the Swans*, 175.

65. Draft letter to Tsumaki.

66. "Kawajiri nikoji zōsan," SK, 3:28a; or *Kawajiri jiseki*, 5b.

67. Draft letter to Tsumaki. During the late 1870s and 1880s, when the male lay practitioners lodged in Takuboku-en while practicing at Engakuji, the *zenshi* apparently boarded at Tōkeiji (across the street from Engakuji), which was nominally still a convent at the time. This custom continued after Shaku Sōen took charge of Engakuji in the 1890s (E, 756). For discussion of Tōkeiji

in its capacity as "divorce temple" during the Edo period, see Inoue Zenjō's writings, such as *Kakekomi-dera;* Sachiko Kaneko and Robert E. Morrell, "Sanctuary: Kamakura's Tōkeiji Convent"; and Diana E. Wright, "The Power of Religion/The Religion of Power."

68. Inoue Zenjō, letter to the author, April 28, 1997. Today, longtime lay practitioners, both men and women, routinely practice in the Engakuji *zendō* during retreats. Regular summer and winter retreats, as well as Saturday and Sunday sessions, have been held for lay practitioners since 1964; E, 757.

69. Faure, *Rhetoric of Immediacy,* 242.

70. For an English translation, see Robert Thurman, *The Holy Teaching of Vimalakīrti,* 62.

71. SK, 3:28b; *Kawajiri jiseki,* 6b.

72. For Shaku's lay register, which includes the names of lay practitioners who enrolled in his program from 1892 to 1899, see Engakuji, "Ryōgakutsu ejō koji zenshi meibo."

73. Faure, *Rhetoric of Immediacy,* 244. Faure's view of the differentiation between lay and monastic positions on social issues resonates with that of Winston Davis, who traces liberalizing influences in the Meiji sangha to lay movements. Cf. also Sharf, who argues that the understanding of Zen Buddhism disseminated by D. T. Suzuki and later lay Zen intellectuals differed significantly from the "traditional Buddhist" concerns of monastic practitioners; see, respectively, Davis, *Japanese Religion and Society,* 166–167; and Sharf, "Whose Zen?" 43. See Sawada, "Political Waves in the Zen Sea," 142, for more detailed remarks on this issue.

74. See Hayakawa Senkichiro's reminiscences about his mother and Shaku Sōen in Nagao, ed., *Sōen Zenji to sono shūi,* 38–39.

75. D. T. Suzuki, "An Autobiographical Account," 16–17.

76. E.g., Okamoto Keijirō (Hakuun), who lists the Kuchōkan as his Tokyo address. For Suzuki's and Okamoto's names, see entry nos. 340 and 211, respectively, in "Sōryōkutsu meishi" (my numeration). Suzuki is listed as "Suzuki Teitarō."

77. Amano, *Senmongakkō,* 121–122.

78. See Hōjō Tokiyuki, *Kakudō hen'ei,* 346b. (I am much indebted to Michiko Yusa for sharing the latter source and her knowledge about Hōjō Tokiyuki with me.) Kawamura became a justice on the Supreme Court; Suzuki, *Imakita Kōsen,* 18.

79. Natsume Sōseki is listed in Shaku Sōen's lay register, "Ryōgakutsu meibo"; KSKS, 1:407b.

80. Komiya Toyotaka, *Natsume Sōseki,* 1:245–246; Yoneyama may have encouraged Sōseki to read Imakita's *Zenkai ichiran.* Ichiki and Yoneyama are also listed in Engakuji, "Sōryōkutsu meishi," entry nos. 172 and 183, respectively (my numeration).

81. For an example of the last activity, see Hōjō, *Kakudō hen'ei,* 343b–344a, 348a.

82. Hōjō, *Kakudō hen'ei,* 346b–347b, 348a, 349a–350a, 358a–358b.

83. See Suzuki, "An Autobiographical Account," 19. Inoue Zenjō dates the opening of the station to June 16, 1889; E, 736. Suzuki nevertheless walked

all night (for lack of funds?) from Tokyo to Kamakura when he first went to Engakuji to practice Zen in 1891. Inoue, ed., *Suzuki shokan*, 112.

84. Hōjō, *Kakudō hen'ei*, 346b.

85. Katsu Kaishū, *Hikawa Seiwa*, 106. My thanks to Michiko Yusa for bringing this passage to my attention.

86. Mohr, "Japanese Zen Schools," 192.

87. Hiranuma Kiichirō, *Hiranuma Kiichirō kaikoroku*, 65, based on oral remarks made on May 5, 1942. Yamaoka Tesshū, who also practiced under Nantenbō, apparently introduced Hiranuma to him. Hiranuma calls Nantenbō's temple in Ichigaya "Kōrinji," presumably a mistaken rendition of Dōrinji. Cf. Mohr, "Japanese Zen Schools," 185.

88. Within three years, 330 people had signed Shaku's lay register. See E, 755–756. In the early twentieth century, students from universities in the Tokyo area (such as Waseda and Keiō) continued to form Zen societies that met for practice in Tokyo and Kamakura.

89. Katō, "Meiji jidai," 136, 137.

Chapter 8: The Great Synthesis

1. A number of syncretic Tokugawa groups never became Shinto sects. Some reconfigured themselves as nonreligious entities rather than give up their original character; an example is Fujidō Kōshinkō. See Okada Hiroshi, "Jikkō-kyō to Fujidō Kōshinkō," 306–311. (See also below, p. 323, n. 11.) Others were subsumed by Buddhist organizations; the syncretic group Nyoraikyō, which affiliated with the Sōtō sect, never fully recovered its original identity.

2. Inoue Nobutaka, a leading scholar in the field of Shinto-derived religions and sects, discusses the coverage of the conventional categories *Shintōkei shinshūkyō* and *kyōha Shintō* in his *Kyōha Shintō no keisei*, 114–115.

3. Inoue Nobutaka, *Kyōha Shintō*, 118. Typical examples of these administrative sects are Shinshūkyō, Shintō Taiseikyō, Shintō Shūseiha, and Shintō Honkyoku.

4. Murakami, "Bakumatsu ishinki no minshū shūkyō," in 567.

5. The "General Guidelines for Teaching Associations" *(Kyōkai tai-i)*, issued in 1873, set out rules for the formation of these groups; they are reproduced in Miyachi, "Shūkyō kankei," 456. On the nature and function of *kō* in the Tokugawa period, see Sakurai Tokutarō, *Nihon minkan shinkōron*, 159–202; and for brief consideration of the *kō*-type structure in early Meiji groups, see Kozawa Hiroshi, " 'Kō' to 'kyōdan.' "

6. See Tōgū, comp., *Tōgū nenpu*, 5.

7. Ibid., 7, 8.

8. Ogihara, "Meiji zenki," 58–59. The works were Hirata's *Dōmō nyūgakumon* and *Miyabi kami ondenki*.

9. Tōgū, *Tōgū nenpu*, 11–12.

10. The request was granted on the twenty-second day of the eighth month of 1872. Ogihara, "Meiji zenki," 59.

11. Tōgū, *Tōgū nenpu*, 11–12. At the time, Honjō had the rank of *chū-kyōsei* (intermediate doctrinal instructor).

12. Documentation of the meeting is reproduced in Ogihara, "Meiji zenki," 76.

13. For details about Hirayama I have consulted Tanaka Yoshitō, "Shintō Taiseikyō no kenkyū," originally published as a separate volume in 1936 and reprinted in his collection, *Shintō jūsanpa no kenkyū;* Inoue Nobutaka, "Hirayama Seisai"; idem, "Bakushin kara ishinki Shintōka e," as well as the slightly revised and expanded version of the latter essay in Inoue's *Kyōha Shintō,* 305–339. A recent work that draws on the above scholarship as well as on primary sources is Kamata Tōji, *Hirayama Seisai to Meiji no Shintō.*

14. Hirayama also studied under the Neo-Confucian scholar Kuwabara Bokurin; Inoue Nobutaka, *Kyōha Shintō,* 308. Bokurin's dates (1750–1804) in *Kinsei kangakusha denki chosaku daijiten,* ed. Seki and Seki, are apparently erroneous.

15. The Hikawa shrine, as Hardacre notes, was "important as the site of the imperial proclamation of the Charter Oath and intended to serve as the tutelary shrine of all Tokyo"; *Shintō and the State,* 68. Both the Hikawa and the Hie shrines received imperial shrine *(kanpei taisha)* status. For basic information on these shrines, see *Shintō jiten,* 669. For unknown reasons, Hirayama resigned his post at the Hikawa Shrine a year after his appointment, but he was reinstated in 1876 and continued as priest of both the Hikawa and Hie shrines. Hardacre's statement, *Shintō and the State,* that Hirayama was "appointed" to the Hikawa Shrine in 1876 must be qualified accordingly.

16. Inoue Nobutaka, "Bakushin," 260–261.

17. Tokoyo, *Shinkyō soshiki monogatari,* 408b–409a.

18. Tōgū, *Tōgū nenpu,* 17. According to Ogihara, the Tohokami follower Murakoshi Kaneyoshi (younger brother of Inoue's direct disciple, Murakoshi Masahisa, and future Taiseikyō general affairs manager) also served as a Hikawa Shrine priest during these years. Ogihara Minori, electronic mail to the author, January 9, 2002.

19. Tōgū, *Tōgū nenpu,* 18.

20. Ogihara, "Meiji zenki," 60–61. The name "Misogi Kōsha" was changed to "Misogi Kyōsha" at this time, according to Tōgū, *Tōgū nenpu,* 18; cf. Inoue, "Bakushin," 267–268.

21. Sakata Kaneyasu ultimately withdrew his support for the reburial plan; the specific reasons are not clear. See Ogihara, "Meiji zenki," 61.

22. Tōgū, *Togu nenpu,* 20–21; Inoue Nobutaka, "Bakushin," 271.

23. Tōgū, *Tōgū nenpu,* 22. The bureau became the administrative center for Shinto activities after the Daikyōin was dismantled in 1875.

24. The Ise group promoted the exclusive worship of the three creation deities (Ame-no-minaka-nushi, Takami-musubi, and Kami-musubi) and Amaterasu, whereas the leader of the Izumo faction insisted on the inclusion of Ōkuninushi in the pantheon. See Hardacre, *Shintō and the State,* 48–51, for a succinct summary of this controversy. For examples of Hirayama's efforts to occupy the middle ground in this dispute, see, e.g., Fujii Sadafumi, *Meiji Kokugaku hasseishi no kenkyū,* 56, 62. Fujii provides an exhaustive analysis of the affair as well as reproductions of several pertinent primary texts.

25. See Irokawa and Gabe, *Meiji kenpakusho shūsei,* 6:243–246, for

Honjō Munetake's 1880 memorial on the status of the Bureau of Shinto Affairs; his numerous memorials and petitions, critical of Tanaka Yoritsune (1836–1897), the Ise faction's leader, are reproduced in Fujii, *Meiji Kokugaku,* 53, 296–297, 364–369, 406–409, and 394–396.

26. See Fujii, *Meiji Kokugaku,* 489. If this view is correct, Hardacre's statement that "Hirayama opposed the Izumo side" should be qualified. (Incidentally, he devoted himself thereafter to Taiseikyō—"Taishakyō" is a misprint.) Hardacre, *Shintō and the State,* 69.

27. The memorial (undated) is reproduced in Fujii, *Meiji Kokugaku,* 490–492.

28. Fujii makes this point in *Meiji Kokugaku,* 489.

29. Hirayama had previously doubled as the administrator of Ontakekyō, a mountain devotional group; it affiliated with Taisei Kyōkai from 1880 until late 1882. In a separate development, the Sakata faction of Inoue's followers attained recognition during this period under the name "Shintō Misogiha" as an affiliate of the Taishakyō sect and, from 1884, of the Bureau of Shintō Affairs. In 1894, when Sakata's son Yasuji became director, this branch of Inoue's followers attained the status of an independent sect called Misogikyō. For the vicissitudes of the Misogi factions in the early Meiji I have drawn (here and below) on a transcription of Ogihara's oral presentation, "Misogikyō kaiso Sakata Kaneyasu," n.p., and on his published article, "Meiji zenki," especially 60–63. Details concerning internal changes in the Tōgū branch of Misogi from the late 1880s until Tōgū's death in 1897 are recorded in Tōgū, *Tōgū nenpu.*

30. Inoue Nobutaka, *Kyōha Shintō,* 326.

31. See Inoue Nobutaka's paraphrase of Hirayama's writings in "Bakushin," 282, or idem, *Kyōha Shintō,* 328. A modern Japanese translation of the Chinese text of Hirayama's *Honkyō shinketsu* appears in Kamata, *Hirayama Seisai,* 189–200.

32. See Hirayama's remarks, cited in Tanaka Yoshito, "Taiseikyō," 5.

33. Inoue Nobutaka, "Bakushin," 278–279; or idem, *Kyōha Shintō,* 326–327. Similar sentiments are expressed in Hirayama's *Taiseikyō kyōki,* cited at length in Tanaka, "Taiseikyō," 15.

34. Cited in Inoue Nobutaka, "Bakushin," 273; idem, *Kyōha Shintō,* 321.

35. Hirayama Seishin, "Hirayama Seisai jiseki no gaiyō," cited in Inoue Nobutaka, "Bakushin," 271.

36. Inoue Nobutaka, "Bakushin," 275; idem, *Kyōha Shintō,* 324. Inoue cites Nishikawa Kōjirō, *Reigen kizui Shintō kyōsō den,* 106, re the late Meiji influx.

37. Inoue Nobutaka, "Bakushin," 290.

38. Ibid., 291. "Smorgasbord" is a loose rendition of Inoue's *takatsuki,* which literally means a one-legged table or pedestal upon which food is displayed and offered. The category is part of his typology of the organizing principles of nineteenth-century Japanese sects; see his *Kyōha Shintō,* 124–127.

39. Inoue Nobutaka, *Kyōha Shintō,* 334.

40. Hirayama's failure to generate a hereditary leadership for Taiseikyō may be related to this problem; Inoue Nobutaka, "Bakushin," 294.

41. "Hirayama Seisai jiseki no gaiyō," cited in Inoue, "Bakushin," 271.

42. Inoue, "Bakushin," 294–295. See also idem, *Kyōha Shintō*, 117. On Shinto priests' employment of conventional moral notions (often identified with Confucian ideas) in their sermons during this period, see also Hardacre, *Shintō and the State*, 72–73.

43. *Honkyō shinketsu*, Gaihen, chap. 5; cited in Tanaka, "Taiseikyō," 34. The locus classicus of "being careful when one is alone" is the *Doctrine of the Mean*, chap. 1, or the *Great Learning*, commentary, chap. 6. The passage about practicing sincerity could be interpreted as an allusion to the *Doctrine of the Mean*, esp. chaps. 22, 23, 24, 26, and 32.

44. By "vintage Neo-Confucian" I mean especially the interpretations of the so-called Cheng-Zhu school of the Song period that dominated Tokugawa Confucian academies.

45. Inoue Nobutaka, *Kyōha Shintō*, 329–331.

46. Hirayama Seisai, *Shūdō shinpō*, cited in Tanaka, "Taiseikyō," 39. This text was not published until 1912; a Japanese translation is contained in Kamata, *Hirayama Seisai*, 201–225.

47. Tanaka, "Taiseikyō," 48; see also 49–50.

48. Like today's Shingaku practitioners, Hirayama does not insist on the lotus position, which was usually associated with Zen meditation in the monastic context. For Shingaku contemplative practices, see Sawada, *Confucian Values*, 99–109.

49. Cited in Nihon Tōdōkai, ed., *Tōkyū*, 17, in modern Japanese translation. I have had no access to the original text.

50. Ibid., 17.

51. See, e.g., ibid., 170.

52. The official, Nakamura Mitsuyoshi, was a Tokyo prefecture clerk; Nihon Tōdōkai, *Tōkyū*, 172–173.

53. Ibid., 18, 169–170.

54. Ibid., 19, 148.

55. Yoshikawa had practiced under the founder from 1845 to 1854, and thereafter under Sano Kazumaru. He was the son of a shogunal retainer, but had been adopted by a wealthy master of Nō and tea ceremony in the service of shogun Tokugawa Ieyoshi (r. 1837–1853).

56. See Fujii, *Meiji kokugaku*, 283, 376–377, 489.

57. Nihon Tōdōkai, *Tōkyū*, 173–174.

58. Ibid., 173.

59. Ibid., 22–23.

60. Ibid., 24.

61. Cited in Inoue Nobutaka, "Bakushin," 275. I have not had access to Nishikawa's work.

62. Nihon Tōdōkai, *Tōkyū*, 24. E.g., in 1889, Yoshikawa Ichigen received permission to set up his own group, called "Taiseikyō Tōkyū Yoshikawa Kō-sha." Ibid., 175.

63. Ibid., 23–24.

64. SN, 16b. Unless there is a slight error in the dating, we may take "Taiseikyō" here to mean the branch of the Misogi community that Hirayama

had taken under his wing in 1877; it was not designated "Taisei Kyōkai" until October 1879.

65. SN, 17b–18.

66. The historically important Kyoto headquarters, Meirinsha, did not affiliate. A list of the meetinghouses that joined Taiseikyō is provided in SN, 24a. It is not clear when Shingaku officially disassociated from Taiseikyō; it is not named in lists of Taisei member groups of the Taishō and early Shōwa periods. The current director of Sanzensha, Koyama Shikei, believes that Shingaku became a corporate juridical person before the Pacific War.

67. Inoue Nobutaka, "Bakushin," 276–277, 294–295.

68. Kawajiri Seitan, "Bōfu Kawajiri Hōkin no kotodomo," 46; 41. On one occasion Kawajiri reportedly insisted on seeing a performance of *Chūshingura* even though his house had burned down earlier that day.

69. Suematsu was the son-in-law of Itō Hirobumi, in whose cabinet he later served; he and Kawajiri allegedly coauthored the play *Shōnankō*; Kawajiri Seitan, "Bōfu," 48, 50. The Society for Theater Reform sought to implement changes to Japanese theater inspired by Western practices, ranging from the improvement of staging facilities to the removal of the ban against women on stage. Kawajiri's vigorous opposition to equal rights legislation evidently did not prevent him from supporting greater freedom for women in the public sphere.

70. Kawajiri Seitan, "Bōfu," 42. A list of Kawajiri Hōkin's plays appears in ibid., 49–50.

71. Ibid., 48.

72. Inoue Masakane's Meiji followers, as noted earlier, received the play warmly. In the last act, set in the early 1880s, the leaders of the Honjō-Tōgū faction (Murakoshi Kaneyoshi, Honjō Munetake, Tōgū Chiwaki, and Fukuda Kanetomo, among others) are depicted in attendance at the new Umeda Shrine in Tokyo. Kawajiri, "Yorozuyo," *Michizuke* 42, 4.1 (1994): 18–21.

73. Kawajiri, "Yorozuyo," *Michizuke* 23, 8.1 (1991): 12.

74. Ibid., 13.

75. E.g., Kawajiri, "Yorozuyo," *Michizuke* 28, 6.1 (1992): 14.

76. Igeta Midori, "Shinsui, Jinsui," 294.

77. Medical therapies were practiced professionally (for a fee) by doctors of Chinese medicine, Buddhist priests, and *yamabushi* (Shūgendō practitioners). On the conflict between these established professionals and the new healing religions, see Helen Hardacre, "Conflict between Shugendō and the New Religions of Bakumatsu Japan"; and her *Kurozumikyō*, 55–56. See Williams, "Representations of Zen," 119–161, for a detailed discussion of the role of medicine and healing in the growth of the Sōtō Zen sect in Tokugawa Japan.

78. Kawajiri, "Yorozuyo," *Michizuke* 24, 10.1 (1991): 10.

79. See Inoue Masakane, *Ikunshū*, 104; and Ogihara, "Misogikyō no gyōhō."

80. Healing water was used, for example, by Kurozumi Munetada and his followers; see Hardacre, *Kurozumikyō*, 55n; cf. 85. Tenrikyō was also accused of distributing sanctified water for healing purposes.

81. In his Misogi writings Kawajiri also dwells on aspects of Masakane's

thought that he perceived as compatible with or similar to Zen Buddhist cultivation. See, e.g., "Yorozuyo," *Michizuke*, 24, 6.1 (1992): 11; and his lecture on a text attributed to Inoue Masakane, presented on June 8, 1907, at "Misogi Kyō-kai" in Tokyo and transcribed under the title *Nashinoko no ofumi.*

82. Kawajiri, "Yorozuyo," *Michizuke* 39, 12.1 (1993): 22–24.

Chapter 9: Enlightened Conservatives

1. Gluck, *Japan's Modern Myths,* 21.

2. Mannheim, "Conservative Thought," 145–147, 153, 157. Mannheim's reflections on the nature of conservatism referred to an entirely different historical context than that of Meiji Japan, and his approach to the study of knowledge is based on philosophical premises that I do not necessarily share. But I believe some of his categories and distinctions are useful for analyzing early Meiji thought. Attempts to apply Mannheim's notion of political conservatism to early Meiji date at least to Matsumoto Sannosuke's 1958 essay, "Meiji zenki hoshu-shugi shisō."

3. Jerry Z. Muller, ed., *Conservatism,* 24.

4. Suzuki, *Imakita Kōsen,* 47–48. The following sketch of Imakita's political identity is a reduced version of the material in Sawada, "Political Waves," 119–129.

5. See KZSD, 3:151–152, re Ogino's altercations with the Ministry of Doctrine and the Kyoto government during the doctrinal instruction campaign; see also Ogisu Jundō, "Ogino Dokuon," 112.

6. For Imakita's acceptance of elements of the Meiji "Shinto" ideology, see Suzuki, *Imakita Kōsen,* 110–111.

7. For more details on Imakita's early political attitudes, see Sawada, "Religious Conflict," esp. 226–228.

8. The contacts with government leaders began soon after Imakita's arrival in Tokyo. See, e.g., SKN, 14a, and SKN, 15b.

9. Imakita's appointments at the Rinzai General School and Engakuji were sanctioned by the Ministry of Doctrine; he attained the rank of Provisional Major Instructor *(Gon-daikyōsei)* in 1880. SKN, 17a.

10. Hiranuma, *Hiranuma kaikōroku,* 69.

11. Irokawa Daikichi has written about some of these Kanagawa groups, most notably in his *Meiji no bunka,* available in translation as *The Culture of the Meiji Period.*

12. Vlastos, "Opposition Movements in Early Meiji, 1868–1885," 406.

13. Ibid., 379–380.

14. Nakamaru, *Kanagawa-ken no rekishi,* 237.

15. For this summary of the Shindo uprising, I have consulted a number of sources; for an accessible account, see Nakamaru, *Kanagawa-ken no rekishi,* 236–237. Nakamaru erroneously dates the incident October 26, Meiji 10 [1877]. The disturbance in fact took place on October 26, 1878; the petition was first presented to Nomura on November 11 of that year. For the petition, see "Tangansho," in KKS, 17b.

16. SKN, 16b. Imakita's petition, dated consistently with the SKN account, is reproduced in Hiratsuka-shi, ed., *Hiratsuka-shi shi 5: Kindai,* 1:442–

443. The brief petition that Imakita and two other prominent Kanagawa abbots presented in May 1879 is distinct from the aforementioned original petition of 1878 (the version reproduced in KKS, 16–22), which was signed by numerous local Buddhist and Shinto priests.

17. Buddhist leaders of the time generally kept their distance from the popular-rights movement itself. See Yoshida Kyūichi, *Nihon kindai Bukkyō shakaishi kenkyū*, 1:94–95.

18. See, e.g., SKN, 19b, for Imakita's solicitation of wealthy farmers in the Kamakura area during the early 1880s.

19. SKN, 23b.

20. Imakita, "Sōryo kokkai junbiron"; Suzuki, *Imakita Kōsen*, 167–174, supplies the Japanese text. Imakita was sectarian abbot at the time he wrote this essay (1882).

21. He does not allude to the aforementioned 1878 addendum to the marriage decree; no doubt for rhetorical reasons, the abbot simply refers back to the notorious 1872 decree in an effort to persuade his monks that the state was *still* testing their moral caliber.

22. Imakita, "Sōryo kokka," 169.

23. Ibid., 173, 174.

24. Ibid., 172.

25. Mannheim uses the term "primitive" to refer to a traditionalist who has just begun to develop a conscious political conservatism. "Conservative Thought," 173–174.

26. For comments on Okunomiya's plural sources of inspiration, see Matsumura, "Yōmeigakusha," 175; Takase, *Satō Issai*, 748. He had been a fervent supporter of the movement for imperial restoration, and attracted a significant following of young anti-shogunal zealots while teaching at the domain school in the 1860s. (Takase lists their names in *Satō Issai*, 746.) For an outline of the political factions in Tosa at this time, see Motoyama, *Proliferating Talent*, 154. The pro-shogunal faction in the Tosa government had Okunomiya dismissed from his teaching post in 1865, but he was reemployed in 1869. For the above details, see esp. Takase, *Satō Issai*, 745–746.

27. This information is based on Okunomiya's own account; cited in Matsumura, "Yōmeigakusha," 159. See also Takase, *Satō Issai*, 747.

28. He served in this capacity during the second half of 1871 (Kataoka, "Nakano Kenmei," 163). For a reproduction of one of Okunomiya's discourses to the Kirishitan, see ibid., 176–182.

29. See Kataoka, "Nakano Kenmei," 169–170, for a partial list of works on which Okunomiya drew in his discourses on Christianity.

30. See Itagaki Taisuke, comp., *Jiyūtōshi*, 1:87–88, 356–358. The memorial, *Minsen giin setsuritsu kenpakusho*, was submitted to the Sain that year; its first draft was prepared by Furusawa Shigeru (1847–1911). Regarding Okunomiya's role in these early popular rights activities, see Takase, *Satō Issai*, 47; *Meiji ishin jinmei jiten*, 238; *Nihon rekishi jiten*, 2:361; *Dai jinmei jiten*, 5:463; and Itoya Toshio, *Okunomiya Kenshi*, 12.

31. Kenshi later became a well-known socialist who was executed along with Nakae's student Kōtoku Shūsui (1871–1911) in the aftermath of the High

Treason Incident *(Taigyaku jiken)* of 1910. *Konsaisu jinmei jiten,* 253; Itoya, *Okunomiya Kenshi,* 6–7.

32. Nakajima left Tosa in 1864 to confer with other anti-shogunal activists in Suō (eastern Yamaguchi). Like Okunomiya, he may have met Imakita Kōsen (who resided in Suō at the time) before the latter became abbot of Engakuji.

33. For the above biographical details, I have relied on Itoya, *Jōsei kaihō,* 62. Nakajima's activities are also recorded in Itagaki, *Jiyūtōshi;* for the Rikkenseitō founding, see 2:87.

34. A few details about this event are described in Itoya, *Jōsei kaihō,* 28–29. The talk was given on April 1, 1882.

35. Nakajima had earlier been married to Mutsu's younger sister and Date Jitoku's daughter, Date Hatsuho, but she had died, leaving him three sons. Sōma Kokkō has suggested that the marriage between Kishida and Nakajima remained platonic, possibly because Nakajima developed some sort of physical problem; *Meiji shoki,* 58–59. Most accounts agree, in any case, that Kishida and Nakajima enjoyed a marriage of mutual respect and friendship.

36. Itoya, *Nihon kaihō,* 70. Suzuki Yūko, ed., *Kishida Toshiko kenkyū,* 148, dates the baptism to July 18, 1886.

37. For Kawajiri's essay, see his *Naibu bunmeiron,* 2:16–55. For a useful analysis of Kishida's activities and ideas in the context of the emerging feminist movement of the time, see Sievers, *Flowers in Salt,* especially 33–48.

38. See Sievers, *Flowers in Salt,* 10–25, for a succinct discussion of the debate as it developed in the 1870s, especially as recorded in the writings of Fukuzawa Yukichi, Mori Arinori, Nakamura Masanao, and other members of the Meiroku Society.

39. The series was originally published in ten installments, dating from May 18 to June 22, 1884, in the Liberal Party's mouthpiece, *Jiyū no tomoshibi;* it is contained in *Nihon fujin mondai shiryō shūsei* 8 (Shichō 1): 103–113. Excerpts appear in Itoya, *Nihon no kaihō,* 65–69.

40. For Kishida's remarks on the saying, see her "Dōhō shimai ni tsugu," 103.

41. Kawajiri, *Naibu bunmeiron,* 2:50.

42. Ibid., 2:18. The opening quotation is from the *Yijing* (chap. 2, "Remarks on Trigrams").

43. Kawajiri, *Naibu bunmeiron,* 2:18–19.

44. Ibid., 2:35.

45. Kishida, "Dōhō shimai," 103; trans. Sievers, *Flowers in Salt,* 39.

46. Kawajiri, *Naibu bunmeiron,* 2:36.

47. Kishida, "Dōhō shimai," 105.

48. Kawajiri, *Naibu bunmeiron,* 2:50.

49. Kawajiri, for example, argued that the practice of concubinage was justified, when necessary, by the imperative of family reproductive integrity— another unchangeable natural law; *Naibu bunmeiron,* 2:26–27; 29. Re the debate over this issue in the late 1870s and 1880s, see Kiyohara, *Kaishū Nihon,* 623f., and Sievers, *Flowers in Salt,* 18–22.

50. Kishida, "Dōhō shimai," 110.

51. Ibid., 112.

52. Confucius, *Analects,* trans. Waley, 216–217; cf. Lau's translation, 148.

53. Kawajiri adds that "there is already an explanation for this in the commentaries of Zhu Xi"; *Naibu bunmeiron,* 36–37. Presumably he means Zhu's commentary on the line in *Sishu jiju;* see SGT, 7:437a, 317.

54. Kawajiri, *Naibu bunmeiron,* 2:38. Kawajiri also comes out in favor of the traditional division of labor (whereby wives are confined to domestic duties) and against the idea that equal rights require a division of family property between spouses, or equitable divorce rights. Confucian ideologues had argued along similar lines in earlier ages and in other East Asian contexts, in the face of popular customs that allowed women more leeway. See, e.g., Martina Deuchler, *The Confucian Transformation of Korea,* 231–281.

55. Muller, "Introduction," 20. "Second nature" is a phrase used in Western conservative discourse to mean cultural habits or customs that are internalized to the point where they are no longer consciously deliberated upon.

56. Mannheim, *Ideology and Utopia,* 232.

57. Cf. Mannheim, *Ideology and Utopia,* 234–235.

58. The quoted words are borrowed from Joan W. Scott, "Gender," 1073.

59. The other two generals were Miura Gorō (1846–1926) and Soga Sukenori (1843–1935). See Barbara Teters, "The Genrō In," 367; and Sawada, "Political Waves," 133. On some of the changes that were implemented in the military, see Roger F. Hackett, *Yamagata Aritomo,* 63, 82–83.

60. Teters, "Genrō In," 367. The movement is often referred to by the abbreviated term "Kokusuishugi."

61. Hirao Michio, *Shishaku Tani kanjō den,* 505. For a detailed discussion of the development of Tani's brand of conservatism, see Motoyama, *Proliferating Talent,* 195–237.

62. For the founding platform of the party, see Hirao, *Shishaku Tani,* 506.

63. The text of the 1881 memorial is contained in ibid., 502–503.

64. Teters, "Genrō In," 368–369. See also Motoyama, *Proliferating Talent,* 207.

65. Sasaki's diary, *Hogohiroi Sasaki Takayuki nikki,* contains numerous references to and correspondence with Tani, as well as with Motoda Eifu, who was agitating in support of Confucian-based values in primary education during these years. The league also included individuals called "Kita," "Nakamura," "Sano," and "Kawamura" (full names are not given in the text). SN, 18b.

66. Hayano, *Kawajiri jiseki,* 10b. SN, 18a–18b, dates the start of these talks from 1883 rather than 1882.

67. One such series of talks took place in the precincts of the important Hie Shrine, with which the Taiseikyō leader, Hirayama Seisai, was associated. I have not verified the Tani sponsorship of Shingaku in sources other than the Shingaku records themselves.

68. Smith, *Confucianism,* 57.

69. Ibid., 58–63. After Motoda passed away in 1891, the group apparently received much less support from the imperial circle.

70. For the information in the above paragraph, see SN, 18b. The princes

who attended included Kitashirakawa-no-miya Yoshihisa Shinnō (1847–1895), an army lieutenant colonel at the time, and Fushimi-no-miya Sadanaru (1858–1925), a military man who became closely connected to the Meiji and Taishō emperors.

71. Sawada, "Political Waves," 131–144.

72. The announcement was noted in the *Tōkyō nichinichi shinbun;* Kotani Yoshizō, *Kawai Kiyomaru den,* 118. The society reportedly evolved from a lay practice group that had met at Torio's house since 1876.

73. SKN, 21a.

74. According to KZSD, 3:155–156, Ogino gave a lecture for the group at Rinshōin in March 1882, but the year must be erroneous, since the Myōdō Society was not founded until 1884. Sakagami reports preaching to the group at Konji-in in Shiba; *Keikyokuroku,* 165. Titles of lectures by other abbots are listed in Kotani, *Kawai Kiyomaru den,* 148f. Seki Mugaku was the abbot of Myōshinji at the time.

75. See Ikeda, *Meiji Bukkyō,* 95, and 113–115, where he lists the various Myōdō Kyōkai centers that were announced in the journal *Meikyō shinshi.* The local branches of Myōdō Kyōkai kept in close touch with their headquarters and propagated the same or similar ideas. Another example of this type of group is Wakeikai, associated with Ōuchi Seiran; ibid., 122–123.

76. Ikeda, *Meiji Bukkyō,* 60. For Fukuda's reform movement, see Jaffe, *Neither Monk nor Layman,* 117–118. The Four Obligations, *shion,* are owed to one's parents, the ruler of one's country, all sentient beings, and the Three Treasures (Buddha, Dharma, Sangha). The Ten Precepts are prohibitions against killing, stealing, adultery, lying, frivolous language, slander, equivocation, greed, anger, and wrong views (as translated by Paul Watt, "Jiun Sonja"). This formula, popularized in the Tokugawa period by the Shingon-Ritsu monk Jiun Onkō (1718–1804), was a common refrain in early Meiji Buddhist circles; Jiun's *Jūzen hōgo* (Dharma Talks on the Ten Precepts) was widely used as a teaching text at this time (Ikeda, *Meiji Bukkyō,* 126). The founding principles of the Myōdō Society are contained in Torio's *Myōdō kyōkai yōryō kaisetsu* (published April 5, 1884).

77. Torio, *Myōdō kaisetsu,* 295b.

78. Ibid., 297a–b.

79. See ibid., 305a.

80. Ibid., 299a.

81. In the first Meiji years the term *"kyōkai"* was used in government edicts to indicate religious groups that propagated ideas within the framework of its Shinto-type doctrinal instruction system, but Buddhist teachers soon began to use the term to indicate (literally) "teaching assemblies" formed under sectarian auspices. Ikeda, "Teaching Assemblies," 12.

82. Pyle, *The New Generation in Meiji Japan,* 148 (with orthographic modifications).

83. Torio, *Myōdō kaisetsu,* 296b.

84. Ibid., 295b.

85. KSKS, 1:200–201. The preface to the written record of Hijikata's oral address indicates that the meeting with him took place on March 25, 1884. (The

address was apparently circulated to the seven Rinzai lines along with the newly approved sect regulations.) Despite the appearance in the text of "Myōdō Shō-kai" instead of "Myōdō Kyōkai," the content, context, and timing of his remarks indicate that Hijikata is indeed referring to Torio's group; the Chinese character *shō* was probably mistakenly substituted for *kyō* in the transcription or later reproductions of the text. Moreover, the substitution of *shō*, which means to illuminate, does not significantly change the meaning of the group's name.

86. Kenneth Pyle, "Conservatism," 690.

87. An English translation of Tani's memorial against the treaty revision plan, dated July 3, 1887, appears in The Centre for East Asian Cultural Studies, comp., *Meiji Japan through Contemporary Sources*, 3:162–172. See also Motoyama, *Proliferating Talent*, 226–229, for Tani's denunciation of government policies in a separate statement of this time; and Pyle, *New Generation*, 102–105.

88. Trans. in Centre for East Asian Cultural Studies, *Meiji Japan*, 3:171.

89. See Teters, "Genrō In," 373–374.

90. Trans. Teters, ibid., 374.

91. In the Privy Council he eventually won the future diet the power to initiate legislation. Ibid., 367.

92. See Huntington, "Conservatism," 455, for a characterization of this view of conservatism.

93. Teters, "Genrō In," 378. See also Tamamuro Taijō's similar qualification of Torio's conservatism; NBKK, 341.

94. Alistair Swale, *The Political Thought of Mori Arinori*, 7.

95. Pyle, "Conservatism," 690–692.

96. Trans. Pyle, *The New Generation*, 108. Yamaji was an associate of Tokutomi Sohō, one of the key players in Pyle's "new generation."

97. These phrases are more precisely rendered by W. J. Boot as "abbots of mountain temples, old Shinto priests, and Confucian scholars nostalgic for the study of the classics"; see his rendition of the entire Yamaji passage in Motoyama, *Proliferating Talent*, 234.

98. Torio himself was at pains to point out that his conservatism was not a stifling traditionalism; see his "Hoshu to wa nanzo ya," *Tokuan zenshū*, 3.

99. Murakoshi Kaneyoshi was the son and cousin of Inoue Masakane's followers Murakoshi Masahisa and Sakata Kaneyasu, respectively. He was named the head of the Murakoshi branch of Taiseikyō Misogikyō (Taiseikyō Misogikyō Hon'in Bunkyōkai) in 1889.

100. Hashimoto Itsuo, "Butsudō soku gedatsu mon jōkan kaisetsu," 8.

101. Kotani, *Kawai Kiyomaru*, 175.

102. *Shintō jiten*, 506a.

103. According to one account, Kawai served in the Myōdō Society from its origins; others say he joined in 1886; Hashimoto, "Butsudō," 8. Kotani Yoshizō argues that Kawai joined Myōdō a month after it was founded; Kotani, *Kawai Kiyomaru*, 119.

104. Hayano, *Kawajiri jiseki*, 10a. Kawajiri was also the appointed lecturer on Zhuangzi at the school later founded by Daidōsha. See Hashimoto, "Shisō oyobi shutō hen kaisetsu," 7; and KKZ, 10:282.

105. For Imakita's praise of Kawai, see SK, 3:30a–31a. A piece by Shaku Sōen appears, e.g., in *Daidō sōshi* 3.21 (March 25, 1890). Re the latter's participation in Daidōsha, see also Kotani, *Kawai Kiyomaru,* 168.

106. Kotani gives a modern Japanese translation of these remarks but cites no source; Kotani, *Kawai Kiyomaru,* 159.

107. Buddhist leaders who contributed to Daidōsha or to its journal included Hara Tanzan (1819–1892), Shimaji Mokurai, Shaku Unshō, Yuri Tekisui, Fukuda Gyōkai, and the Sōtō priest Nishiari Bokusan (1811–1910). Shinto leaders involved in Daidōsha included Yoshimura Masamochi (1839–1915), Inaba Masakuni, Tanaka Yoritsune, Ōtori Sessō, and Senge Takatomi, among others. See Kotani, *Kawai Kiyomaru,* 162–163, 205. For sample essays by Fukuda Gyōkai and Inaba Masakuni, see *Daidō sōshi* 1.2 (August 25, 1988); and 1.9 (March 25, 1889), respectively.

108. Kotani, *Kawai Kiyomaru,* 169. Examples of Confucian scholars involved in the group are Fujizawa Nangaku (1842–1920) and Higashi Takusha (1832–1891). Fujizawa was the oldest son of Imakita's erstwhile teacher, Fujizawa Tōgai. Higashi was a Wang Yangming scholar who once criticized Imakita for his Buddhistic rendition of Neo-Confucian traditions; see Sawada, "Religious Conflict."

109. *Imakita Kōsen,* 64; see also Izuyama Kakudō's comments on Suzuki's remarks in his "Kaisetsu," 314–315. Re Daidōsha, see also Gluck, *Modern Myths,* 22.

110. See Kotani, *Kawai Kiyomaru,* 176.

111. Kawai's mentor Torio articulated views along these lines in the mid-1880s when both men were involved in the Myōdō Society. Kotani, *Kawai Kiyomaru,* 153.

112. Smith, *Confucianism,* 67.

113. Daidōdan was originally sponsored by Shimaji Mokurai and Inoue Enryō; Kashiwahara Yūsen, *Nihon Bukkyōshi: Kindai,* 62. See Notto Thelle's *Buddhism and Christianity in Japan,* esp. 101–109, for a review of several of these nationalistic Buddhist groups. Winston Davis offers a typology of Meiji Buddhist movements in his *Japanese Religion and Society,* 161–170.

114. For a description, see Smith, *Confucianism,* 64–65; and Kiyohara, *Kaishū Nihon,* 626, 639.

115. *Nihonjin* 32; cited in Kotani, *Kawai Kiyomaru,* 169. Pyle's *New Generation* includes detailed discussions of the ideas of the leading Seikyōsha members.

116. Pyle, *New Generation,* 93. For a succinct summary of the "nativist" movements of this period in their political context, see Donald Shively, "The Japanization of Middle Meiji."

117. *Daidō sōshi* 2.18 (Feb. 25, 1889): 5–13 (the quoted lines appear on the last page).

118. See Kawai's "Daidōsha to seitō no kankei" and his "Seitō kankei ni tsuite."

119. Torio established the Impartial Conservative Party in 1888, but his student Kawai avers that the party was not formed until a year after Daidōsha was initiated. Kawai also states that Torio did not become a leader of Daidōsha

until August 1888, after Yamaoka Tesshū passed away. However, Torio's name appears alongside those of Yamaoka and Honjō on Daidōsha's founding statement, dated January 1888. Both of Kawai's claims may be part of the Shinto leader's argument that Daidōsha was unrelated to Torio's Hoshu Chūseitō. See KKZ, 1:172 and 1:6, respectively.

120. KKZ, 1:165, 168. The group's founding rules duly declare that its fundamental aim is to encourage Japanese citizens to "return" to their national creed. See KKZ, 1:4.

121. KKZ, 1:167.

122. Haga, *Meiji ishin to shūkyō,* 222–223. The law in question was *Shūgiin giin senkyo hō.* Gluck comments on government efforts to keep schoolteachers out of politics in her *Modern Myths,* 52.

123. Gluck, *Modern Myths,* 51.

124. For reflections on the notion of informal politics, see Haruhiro Fukui, "Introduction." The above list of unofficial groups (cited by Fukui on p. 2) is drawn from David Knoke, "The Political Economies of Associations," 212.

Chapter 10: The Enemy Within

1. "Tenrikyōron," *Daidō sōshi* 66 (December 1893); the dialogue is reproduced in KKZ, 9:234–249.

2. The site was the location of Miki's house and of the sacred pillar (*kanrodai,* literally "sweet-dew platform"). The stone structure is believed to mark the site of the world's creation and of a future eschatological outpouring of divine blessings or "nectar."

3. KKZ, 9:241–242.

4. The proposition of *naichi zakkyoron,* or "mixed residence in the interior," was that foreigners should be allowed to live alongside the Japanese in any part of the country rather than being confined to restricted areas, as they had been theretofore. The provision for opening up residence rights to foreigners, included in the treaty-revision proposals of 1889 and in Mutsu Munemitsu's 1893 proposals, provoked strong political opposition.

5. KKZ, 9:243.

6. Ibid., 244.

7. Ibid., 246.

8. Ibid., 248–249.

9. Thal, "Rearranging the Landscape of the Gods," 271.

10. Ibid., 327.

11. Hardacre offers an excellent analysis of the transformation of the older new religions, especially Kurozumikyō and Konkōkyō, through their participation in the Shinto-based ideological processes of the early Meiji; see her *Shinto and the State,* 51–59. For insights into the cost to Fujidō (a branch of which became the Shinto sect Jikkōkyō), see the works of Miyazaki Fumiko, especially "Bakumatsu ishinki ni okeru minshū shūkyō no hen'yō"; "The Formation of Emperor Worship in the New Religions"; and "Taikyō senpu no jidai no shin shūkyō"; as well as Okada, "Jikkōkyō to Fujidō Kōshinkō."

12. Mitsu's birth, marriage, and death dates have been verified by Hiruma Tane; see Oku Takenori, *Renmonkyō suibōshi,* 28. The death year 1914, which

appears in Murakami's *Nihon shūkyō jiten,* 376, is erroneous. The reliability of information about this group, especially its founder, is problematic because of the extreme dearth of extant primary sources. The few secondary accounts available are all based on more or less cautious interpretation of the chief source, a sensationalistic newspaper series called "Inshi Renmon Kyōkai," published in *Yorozu Chōhō.* I have drawn directly on the *Yorozu* articles only for ostensible points of fact that seem plausible despite the paper's overtly negative bias. My rendition of the group's history also benefits from several modern Japanese scholars' analyses of this source and investigations of other fragmentary documents. See Murakami, *Nihon shūkyō jiten,* 375–378; Takeda Dōshō [Michio], "Renmonkyō no hōkai katei no kenkyū" (published in English under the title "The Fall of Renmonkyō, and Its Place in the History of Meiji-Period Religions," in Inoue Nobutaka, ed., *New Religions,* 25–57); Takeda's "Nihon kindai ni okeru shinshūkyō kyōdan no tenkai katei," 123–134; and Oku, *Renmonkyō suibōshi.* See also Takeda's "Nihon kindai no shinshūkyō tenkai katei" and his "*Yorozu chōhō* ni yoru Renmonkyō kōgeki kyanpein." Murakami's treatment, in the work cited above and in the "Renmonkyō" section of his "Kindai shakai seiritsuki no shinshūkyō" (coauthored with Oguchi Takeichi), is not as accurate as that of Takeda or Oku. For turn-of-the-century accounts of Renmonkyō in English, see A. Lloyd, "The Remmon Kyō," and D. C. Greene, "Remmon Kyō Kwai." Both of these authors draw on the group's official publications of the time and first-person accounts as well as the *Yorozu Chōhō* series, but their treatment of Renmonkyō is fraught with Christian missiological concerns and other biases.

    13. "Renmon inshi no beppō," *Yorozu Chōhō,* May 1, 1894. Murakami's use of *sui* for the second character of Yanagida's literary name is an error; he also mistakenly renders Mitsu's husband's name as Kōkichi instead of Otokichi. The name of Mitsu's eventual movement, *renmon,* allegedly derives from a passage in the *Lotus Sūtra* in which laypeople who accept the sūtra are called *renmon kyōshu* (leaders of the Lotus School); see Murakami, "Renmonkyō," 376, 377.

    14. Murakami, "Renmonkyō," 376, 377. According to one (unverified) account, Yanagida was clandestinely involved in the Fuju-fuse line of Nichiren Buddhism, which had been outlawed by domain authorities. "Yanagida Ichibei no ryakureki," *Yorozu Chōhō,* May 1, 1894.

    15. As Jacqueline Stone explains, Nichiren's teaching of "the three thousand realms in a single thought-moment in actuality" *(ji no ichinen sanzen)* "represents a shift in perspective, in which enlightenment is understood, not as the fruit of a process of cultivation having beginning, middle, and end, but as inherent from the outset." See her *Original Enlightenment,* 266. I am indebted to Jackie Stone for her assistance in confirming this specific connection between Nichiren's ideas and the Renmonkyō message.

    16. Stone, *Original Enlightenment,* 267.

    17. The inscription is reproduced in full in Yonetsu Saburō, "Renmonkyō ni tsuite," 310.

    18. Ibid.

    19. Cited in Oku, *Renmonkyō,* 52.

20. Quoted in "Inshi o kaisan sezunba Shintō o ikansen," *Yorozu Chōhō*, April 25, 1894, apparently from "Renmonkyō taiyō," a statement issued by Renmonkyō in its publication, *Fushō* 3 (May 1892). The latter is also cited by Takeda, "Nihon kindai," 6, and Oku, *Renmonkyō*, 57, 58.

21. *Fushō* 3 (May 1892), cited by Takeda, "Nihon kindai," 6, and Oku, *Renmonkyō*, 58.

22. "Inshi o kaisan sezunba," *Yorozu Chōhō*, April 25, 1894. Ultimately, the writer of this article does not allow that Renmonkyō is a bona fide "religion" either.

23. The second clause of the chant is the *daimoku* (sacred title); its recitation is a central feature of the religious practice of Nichiren Buddhists.

24. Murakami, *Nihon shūkyō*, 377.

25. Ibid., 376.

26. In 1885 Mitsu moved her headquarters to Shiba in Tokyo, though she later transferred it back to Ogura; she also set up teaching academies in Nagasaki and Okayama. Oku, *Renmonkyō*, provides a chart showing the location and founding dates of Renmon regional centers from 1885 to 1896, based on a Taiseikyō document.

27. Oku, *Renmonkyō*, 107, bases this judgment on a judicious analysis of the various available reports and studies, especially the works of Takeda.

28. Ibid., 115.

29. Half of the names in the register belonged to women. This information is not necessarily reliable, given its source. As part of his argument against Renmonkyō, the journalist who reported the discovery of this register emphasizes that virtually all of the people on the list (which was reprinted in the paper) had left the group long ago. "Fuki," *Yorozu Chōhō*, May 8, 1894.

30. The highly ranked Kawamura became an advisor in the imperial entourage in 1885 and a member of the Privy Council in 1888.

31. Oku, *Renmonkyō*, 72, apparently following Tatsukawa Shōji, *Kinsei byōsōshi*. Cf. Susan Burns, "Constructing the National Body," 20, who cites an earlier work by the same author to the effect that only around a hundred thousand died in Edo during the 1858 epidemic.

32. Oku, *Renmonkyō*, 76; Takeda posits a correlation between the progress of the illness and the movement's success in his "Renmonkyō no hōkai katei."

33. Hartmut Rotermund gives a rich account of the religious practices associated with smallpox epidemics in the late Tokugawa and the contemporary critiques of those practices, in *Hōsōgami ou la petite vérole aisément*. See Oku, *Renmonkyō*, 70–71, regarding the 1858 cholera festivals; in some cases, forced quarantines and other health control measures provoked social disturbances or "cholera riots"; ibid., 82–83.

34. Takeda, "Renmonkyō hōkai," 31.

35. Burns, "Constructing the National Body," 27.

36. Renmon documents indicate that the group may indeed have taken this approach; Oku, *Renmonkyō*, 82.

37. The Meiji laws against healing practices are edict number 33, issued by the Ministry of Doctrine on June 7, 1874, and edict number 3, issued by the

Home Ministry on July 10, 1882. The texts are reproduced in Miyachi, "Shūkyō kankei hōrei ichiran," 461 and 481, respectively.

38. The series was published in two parts: from October 1 to November 20, and December 6 to 8, respectively; Fukuda Kiyohito, ed., *Ozaki Kōyō shū*, 418. According to Ozaki's student Izumi Kyōka, when the story began appearing in the paper it was advertised on illustrated billboards in the street; "Kōyō sensei," an interview with Izumi Kyōka and Oguri Fūchō, contained in ibid., 363.

39. Pyle, "Conservatism," 695.

40. See Huffman, *Creating a Public*, 197, 193–194, and 456n206, for this information.

41. Ibid., 187.

42. On Kuroiwa and his predilections, see ibid., 191–195.

43. *Yorozu*'s almost obsessive series on the Sōma affair in 1893 is perhaps the classic example of installment reportage of this kind. Huffman, *Creating a Public*, 194, contains a concise summary of the affair; see also Burns, "Constructing the National Body," 42–44.

44. "Inshi Renmon Kyōkai," no. 2, *Yorozu chōhō*, March 29, 1984.

45. Ibid., no. 8, *Yorozu chōhō*, April 5, 1894. The promised wife was reportedly the younger sister of Honda Hachirō, Mitsu's second-in-command.

46. See "*Kaishin shinbun* to Renmonkyō," *Yorozu chōhō*, April 20, 1894; and "*Kaishin shinbun* no shūwai," *Yorozu chōhō*, April 24, 1894.

47. "Renmon no mizu" and "Renmonkyō ni kansuru Tōkyō fucho no ikō," *Yorozu chōhō*, May 5, 1894.

48. "Renmonkyō nao mizu o uru," *Yorozu chōhō*, May 11, 1894.

49. This dynamic is persuasively described by David Ambaras in "Social Knowledge, Cultural Capital, and the New Middle Class in Japan, 1895–1912."

50. Cited and translated in Huffman, *Creating a Public*, 173.

51. Sexuality was another of these differentiating issues; Ambaras, "Social Knowledge," 27.

52. Both of these definitions are used as criteria to exclude Renmonkyō from Shinto in the three-part series, "Inshi o kaisan sezunba," which appears in three consecutive issues of *Yorozu chōhō*, April 24–26, 1894.

53. "Inshi o kaisan sezunba," *Yorozu chōhō*, April 25, 1894.

54. Yoshimura's remarks, cited from *Nihon shintsūsha (sic)*, are contained in "Shintō imada otoroezu," *Yorozu chōhō*, April 29, 1894.

55. Reported in "Renmon Kyōkai to kaku shinbun," *Yorozu chōhō*, April 20, 1894.

56. The series ran from April 15 to May 15, 1894 (issues 177–180); Takeda, "Renmonkyō hōkai," 35.

57. All three of these scholars were True Pure Land Buddhists; Nanjō and Kiyozawa were priests.

58. Sakurai Masashi, *Meiji shūkyōshi kenkyū*, 397–398, lists the topics of the meeting cited in *Zenshū* 21 (November 1896). The part of the meeting devoted to discussion of Renmonkyō was titled "The Doctrines of Renmonkyō and the Circumstances of its Diffusion."

59. "Misogikyō Seinenkai," *Yorozu chōhō*, April 15, 1894.

60. According to some reports, the deity Ji no myōhō came to be equated in Renmonkyō with the three Shinto creation deities—perhaps in response to charges that the group was not genuinely "Shinto."

61. "Taiseikyō kanchō no kushin," *Yorozu chōhō*, April 12, 1894.

62. "Inshi o kaisan sezunba," *Yorozu chōhō*, April 26, 1894. One of the few neutral sources extant today shows only that Hirayama actively supported the group in its early years as an affiliate. See Oku, *Renmonkyō*, 97.

63. "Taiseikyō kanchō no kushin," *Yorozu chōhō*, April 12, 1894.

64. "Taisekyō kanchō no shōkan," *Yorozu chōhō*, April 12, 1894.

65. "Taiseikyō wa kaiwan no yū naki ka," *Yorozu chōhō*, April 27, 1894.

66. "Honshoku chidatsu no kontan," *Yorozu chōhō*, May 3, 1894.

67. "Renmon to Taiseikyō," *Yorozu chōhō*, May 4, 1894; the report is cited from *Dokuritsu tsūshinsha.*

68. "Renmonkyō ni taisuru Taiseikyō no naibu," *Yorozu chōhō*, May 6, 1894.

69. The Taisei–Misogi organization seems to have been the largest of the three primary member groups; according to a chart inserted in the back of Asō, *Zōho Inoue Masakane-ō zaitōki*, it claimed 1,139 teaching staff in 1890 (membership numbers are not recorded). In the late nineteenth century Tōkyūjutsu may have attracted several thousand members in all (see chapter 8). In 1893 Sanzensha, the Shingaku headquarters in Tokyo, reported 120 "students" and twenty-two staff members; SN, 41a–b.

70. "Torikeshi seikyū," *Yorozu chōhō*, May 8, 1894.

71. "Renmonkyō no daikaikaku," *Yorozu chōhō*, May 10, 1894.

72. Oku, *Renmonkyō*, 156–157.

73. Tōgū, *Tōgū nenpu*, 30. Tōgū and Murakoshi held joint leadership over Taiseikyō for about one year. Kamata, *Hirayama Seisai*, 235.

74. *Jiyū* was associated with the Liberal Party, *Mainichi* and *Yomiuri* with the Progressive Party, and *Chūō* with the Satsuma faction in the government; Huffman categorizes the *Kokumin, Niroku, Kokkai*, and apparently *Miyako* (for which Kuroiwa had worked in the early 1890s), as "neutral." *Creating a Press*, 186, 187.

75. "Renmon jiken Teikoku gikai ni agaran," *Yorozu chōhō*, May 6, 1894.

76. Takeda, "Nihon kindai," 131.

77. Ibid., 129, 130. According to the twentieth-century account of Shimamura Fujisuke (a member of Mitsu's husband's family who became vice-director of the group after the founder died), when Mitsu passed away in 1904, Shimamura Senshū—the son of Shimamura Shinshū (who died young) and thus Mitsu's hereditary successor—was only eleven years old. A faction of Renmon followers allied with the Taiseikyō leadership took the opportunity to install a Renmon leader of its own choice. Because of the elimination of the group's hereditary leadership, after a period of court litigation between the Taisei and Shimamura factions, the latter lost control of the main Renmon worship site and other properties, including Mitsu's family holdings. When Renmonkyō formally requested independence from Taiseikyō in the early twentieth century, because of these losses it was unable to come up with the requisite "donation" for the

change in status (Yonetsu Saburō, "Renmonkyō ni tsuite," 306–307). With the premature death of Senshū in 1931 (and of Fujisuke himself in 1961), the Shimamura branch of Renmonkyō ceased to exist; the remaining Renmon followers were effectively absorbed by Taiseikyō. For more details, see Takeda, "Renmonkyō hokai," 26–27.

78. See Oku, *Renmonkyō,* 66. Like Renmonkyō, in addition to being pressured by the authorities, during the late nineteenth century Tenrikyō was hounded by press writers and religious leaders. The charges were nearly identical to those brought against Renmonkyō: irrational and fraudulent healing practices (including allegations that its sacred water was poisonous), sexual immorality, misuse of money, and (as we saw in Kawai's discourse), lack of patriotism. Re the healing water issue, see, e.g., Oguri, *Nihon no kindai,* 211, 219–220. Polemicists also declared that Tenrikyō was "just like Renmonkyō" because its deity was neither Buddhist nor Shinto. Cited in ibid., 220–221.

79. Reprinted in "Renmon Kyōkai ni tsuki kakushinbun no hitchū," *Yorozu chōhō,* April 10, 1894. Both "Tenri" and "Tenrin" indicate the movement associated with Nakayama Miki. In 1880 the group had affiliated with a Shingon Buddhist temple, under the name Tenrin-ō Kōsha; in 1885, Miki's followers affiliated with Shintō Honkyoku under the name Tenri Kyōkai.

80. *Yorozu chōhō,* May 4, 1894.

81. "Renmon Kyōkai to kakushinbun," *Yorozu chōhō,* April 13, 1894.

82. Gluck uses the term "metaphorical foreigners" to describe the analogous function of Japanese Christians in Meiji ideologies; *Japan's Modern Myths,* 135.

83. Christianity served this function in the self-definition processes of both sect-Shinto and Buddhist communities in the early to mid-Meiji. See Inoue Nobutaka, *Kyōha Shintō,* 336–337; and Notto Thelle, *Buddhism and Christianity,* 95–111.

84. Sheldon Garon, "State and Religion, 1912–1945," 285; or idem, *Molding Japanese Minds,* 70.

85. See Garon, *Molding Japanese Minds,* 60–87, for a lucid analysis of twentieth-century persecutions of the new religions, especially Ōmotokyō. The prime minister and Engakuji *koji,* Hiranuma Kiichirō, concisely expressed the state's position in 1939 when he warned a diet committee that "all religions must be one with the ideal of our national polity; they cannot be at odds with the spirit of our Imperial Way." Cited and translated in ibid., 85.

Afterword

1. For the notion of a shared yet socially differentiated awareness of the world, see Antonio Gramsci's remarks on *il senso comune;* in, e.g., *The Gramsci Reader,* 343–344.

2. Huntington, "Conservatism," 458. Swale nevertheless argues for the application of the term to such "prototypes" as Sakuma Shōzan and Yokoi Shōnan; *Political Thought,* 8–11.

3. These and other elements of Edmund Burke's definition of conservatism are paraphrased by Huntington, "Conservatism," 456. Burke attributed evil more precisely to human nature.

4. Ambaras, "Social Knowledge," 8.

5. In comparison with the early Meiji period, more people began to practice at Zen temples, to read Zen Buddhist publications, and to join societies aimed at the practice or spread of Zen Buddhism. For examples in the Engakuji context, see Sakurai, *Meiji shūkyōshi,* 398–399, and E, 757.

6. Ambaras, "Social Knowledge," 11.

7. The Reverend D. C. Greene reports that he was friendly with "Tokusaburo Hachihama," the author of "the well-known book whose English title is 'Superstitious Japan'" and of a similarly enlightened piece on Renmonkyō. Greene, "Remmon Kyō Kwai," 19, 20.

8. Yoshida Kyūichi summarizes the factors that prevented Buddhism in general from taking hold among the middle classes during the mid-Meiji; *Nihon kindai shakai to Bukkyō,* esp. 125–128.

9. The network continued to evolve in the twentieth century. The continuing affinity between lay Rinzai practice and Misogikyō, for example, is illustrated by the activities of Ogura Tetsuju (1865–1944), a senior disciple of Yamaoka Tesshū who inspired the founding of Jūkyūkai—a Misogi splinter group that survives today. For details, see Ogura Tetsuju-shi Kenshōkai, ed., *Ogura Tetsuju sensei,* esp. 443–449.

GLOSSARY

This list includes most personal names and terms used in the text and notes, as well as selected place-names and titles. Prewar forms of Chinese characters are used for Japanese terms and names that originated before 1946.

Aibara Teisan　相原貞三
Aikoku Kōtō　愛國公黨
Aki no arashi　阿氣の顕支（秋の嵐）
Akimoto　秋元
Akizuki Satsuo (Kidō)　秋月左都夫
　　（毅堂）
akushō shishin　悪性私心
Amaterasu　天照
Amatsu norito no futonorito　天津
　　祝詞太諄辭
Ame-no-minaka-nushi　天之御中主
Andō Magane　安藤眞鐵
anjin ryūmei　安心立命
Anzai Masahisa　安西正久
Aoki Sogan　青木十丸
Arai Hakuga　新井白蛾
Arai Hakuseki　新井白石
Arakawa Sayū　荒川佐右
arigatai omizu　有難いお水
Asai Sen'an　淺井仙庵
Asaka Gonsai　安積艮斎
Asano Ken　淺野乾
Bakufu　幕府
Ban Kōkei　伴蒿蹊
Bankei Yōtaku　盤珪永琢
benxin (J. *honshin*)　本心
Biyanlu　碧巖録
bodaiji　菩提寺
bonbu　凡夫

bonnō mayoi　煩惱迷い
Bōroshū e kōshū meiseki　忘路集會
　　闔集名籍
bu　分
bunkai　分會
bunkajin　文化人
bunkajin koji　文化人居士
bunmei　文明
bunmei kaika　文明開化
Bunmeiron gairyaku　文明論概略
Butsuge Shari Jūmannin-kō　佛牙
　　舍利十萬人講
Butsunichi-an　佛日庵
buzoku　部属
Chan jushi　禪居士
Cheng　程
chi　智
chinkon　鎭魂
chishiki　知識
chisso no koki　窒素の故氣
Chizen　知善
chō　町
chōnin　町人
Chōtokuji　長徳寺
Chōya shinbun　朝野新聞
chū o toru　中を取[る]
chūgishū　忠義宗
chūkyōin　中教院
Chūō shinbun　中央新聞

330

chūsei no shinto　忠誠の信徒

chūseishugi　中正主義

Chūseitō　中正黨

Dai Nihon Kokkyō Daidōsha
　　大日本國教大道社

Dai Nippon Misogikyō Seinenkai
　　大日本禊教青年會

Daidō sōshi　大道叢誌

Daidōsha　大道社

Daigakkō　大學校

Daigakkō kisoku　大學校規則

Daigaku　大學

Daigaku Honkō　大學本校

Daigaku kisoku oyobi chūshōgaku
　　kisoku　大學規則及び中小學
　　規則

Daigaku Nankō　大學南校

Daigakuryō　大學療

Daigakuryō-dai　大學寮代

Daikyōin　大教院

daikyōkō　大教校

Daikyōsei　大教正

Daikyū　大休

Daikyū Sōetsu (Mineo)　大休宗悦
　　（峯尾）

daimoku　題目

dairin　大輪

Daisetsu Jōen　大拙承演

daishi　大姉

Daitō (Shūhō Myōchō)　大燈
　　（宗峰妙超）

Dajōkan　太政官

Danjo dōken　男女同権

danka　檀家

Date Chihiro (Jitoku)　伊達千廣
　　（自得）

Date Hatsuho　伊達初穂

Daxue (J. *Daigaku*)　大學

Dazai Shundai　太宰春臺

dōgaku kenbi　道學兼備

Dōgen　道元

dōgō　道号

Dokugo shingyō　毒語心經

Dōmō nyūgakumon　童蒙入學門

Donglin Changzong　東林常總

Dongshan Liangjie　洞山良价

dongpo　東坡

Dōrinji　道林寺

dōshin　道心

dōtoku　道徳

Doushuai Congyue　兜率從悦

Doushuai sanguan　兜率三関

dōwa　道話

Echigo　越後

Echizen　越前

Edokko shinbun　江戸っ子新聞

Ekkei Shuken　越溪守謙

Engakuji　圓覺寺

Engeki Kairyō Kai　演劇改良會

Engishiki　延喜式

Enpukuji　圓福寺

Etō Shinpei　江藤新平

fu (fun)　奮

fudasashi　札差

Fujidō Kōshinkō　不二道孝心講

Fujikō　富士講

Fujizawa Nangaku　藤澤南嶽

Fujizawa Tōgai　藤澤東咳

Fujiwara Seika　藤原惺窩

Fujo no michi　婦女の道

Fuju-fuse　不受不施

fuki dokuritsu　不羈獨立

fukoku kyōhei　富國強兵

Fukuchi Gen'ichirō　福地源一郎

Fukuda Gyōkai　福田行誠

Fukuda Kanetomo　福田鐵知

Fukuda Saku　福田さく

fukurokuju　福禄寿

Fukushima Taneomi　副島種臣

Fukuzawa Yukichi　福澤諭吉

Furukawa Mitsura　古川躬行

fusei　不正

Fushimi-no-miya Sadanaru
　　伏見宮貞愛

futsūgaku　普通學

gaikoku bugyō　外國奉行

gakkō bōzu　學校房主

gaku　學

gaku　樂

gakubu　學部

gakumon　學問

Gakumon no susume　学問のすすめ

gakurin 學林

gakurin bōzu 學林房主

Gakusei 學制

gakusha 學者

Gakushasei 學舎制

Gakushikai 學師會

Gakushūin 學習院

gakyō 雅興

Gan'ō Genshi 願翁元志

gedatsu 解脱

gegosha 外護者

Genrō-in 元老院

genze riyaku 現世利益

Getsuyōkai 月曜會

giri ninjō 義理人情

Gisan Zenrai 儀山善来

gō 合

gogyō seiri 五行性理

gohei 御幣

gohō 御法

gohōjin 護法神

gojō 五常

gōketsu 豪傑

gokoku 護國

gokoku 五穀

Gokoku kyōkai kiyaku 護國協會
規約

Gon-daikyōsei 權大教正

gon-negi 權禰宜

gorin 五輪

gōritekina 合理的な

goshin 悟心

Gōtō Shōjirō 後藤象二郎

gotsuza 兀座

Gozan 五山

Hachijōjima 八丈島

Hachiman 八幡

Hagi 萩

haikai 俳諧

hakarai 計らい

Hakke 伯家

Hakke Shintō 伯家神道

Hakuin Ekaku 白隱慧鶴

Han Yu 韓愈

Hara Kurasuke 原倉助

Hara Tanzan 原担山

harae 祓え

harae shugyō 祓修行

Hasegawa Akimichi 長谷川昭道

hassu 法嗣

hatake 畑

hatamoto 旗本

hatsu musubi 初産靈

hatsumei 發明

Hayakawa Katsumi (Eshō) 早川勝見
(惠勝)

Hayakawa Senkichirō (Setsudō)
早川千吉郎 (雪堂)

Hayashi Gonsuke 林權助

Hie 日枝

Higashi Takusha 東澤瀉

Hijikata Hisamoto 土方久元

Hikawa 氷川

hiki 匹

Hiranuma Kiichirō (Kige) 平沼騏
一郎 (機外)

Hirata Atsutane 平田篤胤

Hirata Kanetane 平田銕胤

Hiratsuka Raicho 平塚らいてう

Hirayama Seisai 平山省齋

Hirayama Seishin 平山成信

Hirayama Sentarō 平山詮太郎

Hirose Kyokusō 廣瀬旭荘

Hirose Tansō 廣瀬淡窓

Hirota Tenshin (Jikyō) 廣田天眞
(慈教)

Hiruma Tane 昼間種

hito o ezaru 人ヲ得ザル

hitori o tsutushimi 獨を愼み

Hitotsugi 一つ木

ho (hō) 豐

hō no ko 法の子

Hōchi shinbun 報知新聞

hodokoshi 施し

hōiki 法域

hōjō 方丈

Hōjō Tokimune 北條時宗

Hōjō Tokiyori 北條時頼

Hōjō Tokiyuki (Chikuu) 北條時敬
(竹塢)

Hōjō Toshi 北條トシ

Hōki 伯耆

Hokima　保木間

hokku　發句

Hōkokushagaku　報國社學

hōkyō　法教

hōmyō　法名

Honda Hachirō　本田八郎

Hōnen　法然

Honjō Munehide (Matsudaira
　Hidejirō)　本荘宗秀
　(松平秀次郎)

Honjō Munetake (Jōan)　本荘宗武
　(成庵)

honkyōgaku　本教學

Honkyō shinketsu　本教眞訣

honshachō　本社長

honshin　本心

honshin o shiru　本心を知る

honzan seijō no garan　本山清淨伽藍

Hoshigaoka　星ケ岡

hoshu　保守

Hoshu Chūseitō　保守中正黨

Hōtoku　報徳

Hufa lun　護法論

Hyōbushō　兵部省

Ichigeki-tei　一撃亭

Ichikawa Danjūrō　市川團十郎

Ichiki Kitokurō　一木喜徳郎

ichinen sanzen　一念三千

Igai Keisho　猪飼敬所

igō　位号

Iida Katsumi　飯田勝美

ikigami　生き神

ikita kotoba　生言

iku　育

Imai Buntoku　今井文徳

Imai Iyo　今井伊豫

Imakita Kōsen (Sōon; Sōryōkutsu;
　Kyoshū)　今北洪川 (宗温;
　蒼龍窟; 虚舟)

imina　諱

Inaba Masakuni　稲葉正邦

innen banashi　因縁話

innen kahō　因縁果報

Inō Hidenori　伊能頴則

Inoue Enryō　井上圓了

Inoue Hatsu　井上初

Inoue Kaoru　井上馨

Inoue Kinga　井上金峨

Inoue Kowashi　井上毅

Inoue Masakane (Shūeki; Shikibu)
　井上正鐵 (周易; 式部)

inshi jakyō　淫祠邪教

Inshi Renmon Kyōkai　淫祠蓮門教會

intoku　陰徳

Ippen　一遍

Ishida Baigan　石田梅巖

Ishin Kyōkai　惟神教會

Ishiwata Takiko　石綿瀧子

Isobe Saishin　磯部最信

Isono Kōdō　磯野弘道

Itagaki Taisuke　板垣退助

Itō Hirobumi　伊藤博文

Itō Ichitarō　伊東市太郎

Itō Jinsai　伊藤仁齋

Itō Kaname (Sukekata)　伊藤要人
　(祐像)

Itō Rokurōbei　伊藤六郎兵衛

Itō Tōgai　伊藤東涯

Itoko　糸子

Iwakura Tomomi　巖倉具視

Iwase Shunga　岩瀬春雅

Izawa Ochiyo　伊澤おちよ

Izumi Kyōka　泉鏡花

Izumo　出雲

jashūmon　邪宗門

ji　事

Ji　時

ji no ichinen sanzen　事の一念三千

Ji no myōhō　事の妙法

*Ji no myōhō, namu myōhō renge
　kyō*　事の妙法南無妙法蓮華經

jikkan jūnishi　十干十二支

Jikkokyō　實行教

Jingū Kyōkai　神宮教會

Jingukyō　神宮教

jinriki　神力

jinshi　人士

Jinsilu　近思録

jinsui [shinsui; jinzui]　神水

jinsui no koto　神水の事

jireisho　辭令書

jisha bugyō　寺社奉行

jitoku; Ch. *zide* 自得

jitsu 實

jitsugaku 實學

Jiun Onkō 慈雲飲光

jiyū minken undō 自由民權運動

Jiyū shinbun 自由新聞

Jiyūtō 自由黨

Jōchiji 淨智寺

Jōdo Kyōhō 淨土教報

jōe 淨衣

Jōfukuji 乘福寺

jōjū 常住

Jōkōji 淨光寺

jōza 上座

Judō 儒道

jukaie 授戒會

Jukyō 儒教

Jūkyūkai 十九会

jūnikyū 十二宮

junsui no kyōhōsha 純粹の教法社

junsui no seijisha 純粹の政治社

jusha 儒者

jushi 居士

Jushi fendeng lu 居士分燈録

Jushi zhuan 居士傳

kabu 株

kagami 鏡

Kagiya Kumata 鍵屋熊太

kagura 神樂

kai 開

Kaian kokugo 槐安國語

Kaibara Ekiken 貝原益軒

Kaigan Dōkaku 晦巖道廓

kaiho 會輔

Kaijō 海常

kaimyō 戒名

Kaiseisha 開成舎

Kaishin shinbun 改進新聞

Kaishintō 改進黨

kaiun 開運

Kaiun Tōkyūjutsu 開運淘宮術

kakku; Ch. *huoju* 活句

kakure nenbutsu 隠れ念佛

kami 神

Kami no yo 神の代

Kami-musubi 神皇産靈

Kamo 賀茂

Kamo Mabuchi 鴨眞淵

kanchō 管長

kanchō sōdai 管長總代

kandai na 寛大な

Kaneko Kōō 金子洪翁

kangaku 漢學

kanki 肝氣

kanmon 貫文

Kanmuri Yaemon 冠彌右衛門

kanpei taisha 官幣大社

kanrodai 甘露臺

kansō 觀相

Kansō Bonjin 貫宗梵心

kansōhō 觀相法

kantsū 感通

Kaseki-kō 嘉石講

Katayama Kenzan 片山兼山

Katō Hiroyuki 加藤弘之

Katō Kanehide (Yahachi) 加藤鐵秀
   (彌八)

Katō Naokane 加藤直鐵

Katō Yūji 加藤勇二

Katsu Kaishū 勝海舟

Katsura Tarō 桂太郎

kattōgaku 葛藤學

Kawai Kiyomaru 河會清丸

Kawajiri Esō (Kashima Sadako)
   川尻惠聰 (鹿島貞子)

Kawajiri Hōkin (Yoshisuke; Sōsei;
   Bōrōan) 川尻 (寶岑義祐;
   宗静; 忘路庵)

Kawamura Sumiyoshi 川村純義

Kawamura Yoshimasa 河村善益

Kawase Kan'emon 川瀬勘右衛門

Kawate Bunjirō (Konkō Daijin)
   川手文治郎 (金光大神)

kazoku 華族

kechimyaku 血脈

kegare fujō 穢れ不淨

Keigi setchū 經義折衷

Keiōgijuku 慶應義塾

keisaku 警策

keizaigaku to shūshingaku 經濟學
   と修身學

kekki 血気

ken 權

Kenchōji 建長寺

kendō 劍道

Kenmon shijū hassoku 見聞四十八則

kenshō 見性

kesa 袈裟

kessha 結社

Kesshoku no bu benron 血色之部辯論

kigoshin no koto 喜悟心の事

Kikuchi Tōsai 菊池冬齋

Kimura Junseki 木村潤石

kinju 禁呪

Kinkazan 金華山

Kisaki Daimyōjin 后大明神

Kishida Toshiko 岸田俊子

kishin 喜心

kishitsu 氣質

kishitsu henka no shugyō 氣質變化の修行

Kita Tadasu 城多董

Kitashirakawa-no-miya Yoshihisa Shinnō 北白川宮能久親王

Kitashiro Masaomi (Eishū) 北代正臣 (瀛洲)

kitoku 奇得

Kitsuregawa 喜連川

Kiyozawa Manshi 清澤満之

kō 講

Kobuku 巨福

Kobunjigaku 古文辭學

Kochūgaku 古注學

Kōdō 皇道

Kōdōgaku 皇道學

Kōfu 甲府

Koga Seiri 古賀精里

Kogaku 古學

Kogetsu Zenzai 古月禪材

Kogigaku 古義學

Kōhaku dokumanjū 紅白毒饅頭

koji 居士

kōji no gaku 口耳の學

koji Zen 居士禪

Kojiki 古事記

Kōjimachi 麴町

kōjō 向上

Kōkiji 高貴寺

Kokin waka shū 古今和歌集

kokka Shintō 國家神道

kokkashugi no seiryoku 國家主義の勢力

kokkyō 國教

kokoro no gensetsu 心の言説

kokoro no manabi 心の學び

koku 石

Kokubō Kaigi 國防會議

Kokugaku 國學

Kokugaku shugyō 國學修行

kokuinchi 黒印地

Kokumin Shinbun 國民新聞

kokurei 穀靈

Kokuren 谷連

kokusui 國粹

kokusui hozonshugi 國粹保存主義

kokusuishugi 國粹主義

kokutai 國體

kokuten 國典

kokyō shōshin 古教照心

kokyū no hō 呼吸の法

Komatsu-no-miya 小松宮

kōmyō 光明

Kondō Heikaku 近藤平格

Konjin 金神

Konkō 金光

Konkōkyō 金光教

Konpira 金毘羅

konton 混沌

korei 古例

korera ikki コレラ一揆

korera matsuri コレラ祭

Kōrinji 光林寺

kōsatsu 高札

kōsha 講舎

Kōshōgaku 考證學

kotodama 言霊

Kotohira 金刀比羅; 琴平

kōun 幸運

Koyama Shikei 小山止敬

Kōzuke 上野

Kuchōkan 久徴館

kufū 工夫

Kumatani Tōshū 熊谷東洲

kumigashira　組頭

Kunaishō　宮内省

Kuroiwa Ruikō (Shūroku)
　　黒巖涙香 (周六)

kūron　空論

Kurozumi　黒住

Kurozumi Munetada　黒住宗忠

Kurozumikyō　黒住教

Kurushima Maruichi　久留島丸一

kuse　癖

Kuwabara Bokurin　桑原北林

kyō; oshie (Ch. *jiao*)　教

Kyōbu daikōgi　教部大講義

Kyōbu taifu　教部大輔

Kyōbushō　教部省

Kyōdō Etan　匡道慧潭

kyōdō jimu tōdori　教導事務頭取

kyōdōshoku　教導職

kyogaku　虛學

kyōge betsuden furyū monji
　　教外別傳不立文字

kyōha Shintō　教派神道

kyōhō　教法

kyōhō no bubun　教法の部分

kyōhōkoku　教法國

kyōiku　教育

Kyōiku chokugo　教育勅語

kyōikugikai　教育義會

Kyōikurei　教育令

kyōkai　教會

Kyōkai tai-i　教會大意

kyōmon　教門

kyōritsu gakkō　共立學校

kyōto shinto　教徒信徒

Kyōto shoshidai　京都所司代

kyū; miya　宮

kyūri bendō　究理辨道

Li Ao　李翱

Linjilu　臨濟錄

Liuzu tanjing　六祖壇經

Lunyu　論語

Maeda Natsukage　前田夏蔭

Mainichi shinbun　每日新聞

magokoro　眞心

makoto; sei　誠

makoto no kokoro　眞心

Maniōji　摩尼王寺

Mannenji　萬年寺

mappō　末法

Maruyama　丸山

Maruyamakyō　丸山教

Matsu　まつ

Matsudaira Muneakira　松平宗發

Matsudaira Sadanobu　松平定信

Matsuki Chōemon　松木長右衞門

matsuri　祭り; 政り [*sic*]

Meikyō shinshi　明教新誌

meimoku-kin　名目金

Meirinsha　明倫舍

meitoku　明德

meitoku o akiraka ni suru　明德
　　を明らかにする

mi o mamori　身を守り

mi o osameru　身を修める

mi o osamuru　身を修むる

mikiki tebiki　見聞手引

Minagawa Kien　皆川淇園

Minamiōji Sahyōe　南大路左兵衞

Mino　美濃

Minsen giin setsuritsu kenpakusho
　　民選議院設立建白書

misogi　禊

misogi harae　身滌祓除

misogi harai　禊祓い

Misogi Kōsha　禊講舍

Misogi Kyōkai　禊教會

Misogi Kyōsha　禊教社

Misogikyō　禊教

Misogikyō Jimukyoku　禊教事務局

Mitani Ken'ō (Sōyaku)　三谷謙翁
　　(宗益)

Miura Gorō　三浦梧樓

Miura Hayato　三浦隼人

Miura Uneme (Chizen)　三浦采女
　　(知善)

Miyabi kami ondenki　宮比神御傳記

Miyaji Sōkai (Kan'ō)　宮路宗海
　　(函應)

Miyakejima　三宅島

Miyakejima nendai kenbunki　三宅
　　島年代見聞記

Miyako shinbun　都新聞

Mizuno Nanboku (Kumata) 水野南北 (熊太)

moji 文字

moji no gakurin 文字の學林

Mokuan Shōtō (Ch. Muan Xingtong) 木庵性瑫

mokujiki 木食

mon (Ch. *wen*) 問

mon 文

Monbushō 文部省

monjin 門人

monme 匁; 文目

monoimi 物忌

monoshiri 物知り

Mori Arinori 森有禮

Morotake Ekidō (Sengai) 諸嶽奕堂 (栴崖)

Moto no chichihaha 元の父母

Motoda Eifu [Motoda Nagazane] 元田永孚

Motoori Norinaga 本居宣長

Motoori Ōhira 本居大平

Motoori Toyokai 本居豊頴

Motoori Uchitō 本居内遠

muga 無我

Mugaku Sogen (Ch. Wuxue Zuyuan) 無學祖元

Muji no uta 無字の歌

mukyōshi 無教旨

Munetada Shintō 宗忠神道

Murakami Senshō 村上専精

Murakoshi Kaneyoshi 村越鐵喜

Murakoshi Masahisa 村越正久

Murakoshi Morikazu 村越守一

Musashi 武蔵

musō 無相

musubi 産靈

Mutōryū 無刀流

Mutsu 陸奥

Mutsu Munemitsu 陸奥宗光

Myōdō Kyōkai 明道教會

Myōdō kyōkai zasshi 明道教會雑誌

Myōdō Shōkai 明道照會

Myōhōjin 妙法神

Naganuma Sawaemon 長沼澤右衛門

Nagata Tokuhon 永田徳本

Nagayo no den 永世の傳

naibu no kaika 内部の開花

naichi zakkyoron 内地雑居論

Naimushō 内務省

Nakae Chōmin 中江兆民

Nakae Tōju 中江藤樹

Nakajima Nobuyuki (Chōjō) 中島信行 (長城)

Nakamura Masanao (Keiu) 中村正直 (敬宇)

Nakamura Mitsuyoshi 中村光賢

Nakamura Ryōtai 中村龍袋

Nakamura Tokusui 中村徳水

Nakatomi no harae 中臣祓

Nakatomi sanshu no harae 中臣三種の祓え

Nakayama Miki 中山みき

Nakayama Shūji 中山秀司

Nakazawa Dōni 中澤道二

Namu Amida Butsu 南無阿彌陀佛

Nanboku sōhō kōhen 南北相法後編

Nanboku sōhō zenpen 南北相法前編

Nanjō Bun'yū 南条文雄

Nantenbō (Tōshū Zenchū) 南天棒 (鄧州全忠)

nanushi 名主

Natsume Sōseki 夏目漱石

nenbutsu 念佛

Nichiren 日蓮

Nihon Kōdōkai 日本弘道會

Nihon shoki 日本書紀

Nihongi 日本紀

Niinomi Harumitsu 新家春三

Nikkō 日光

nikujiki saitai 肉食妻帶

Ninigi 瓊瓊杵

ninsoku yoseba 人足寄場

Niroku shinpō 二六新報

Nishi Amane 西周

Nishiari Bokusan (Kinei) 西有穆山 (瑾英)

Nishida Daikyō (Sōgen) 西田大狂 (宗玄)

Nishikawa Kōjirō　西川光次郎
Nishimura Shigeki　西村茂木
nisshu seiten　日取星転
Nitta Kuniteru　新田邦光
Noriko　法子
norito　祝詞
norito no den　法止の傳
Nozawa Kanenori　野澤鐵教
nyokoji　女居士
Nyoraikyō　如来教
Ōbaku　黄檗
Ogawa Dōkai (Zokutōan)
　　小川棠谿 (續燈庵)
Ogino Dokuon　荻野獨園
Ogyū Sorai　荻生徂徠
ōharae　大祓え
Oharai-kō　御祓講
Ōkino Kazue　大木野主計
Okitsu Tadasuke (Sakyō)　興津忠祐
　　(左京)
okomori　御籠り
okotae　御答
Ōkuma Shigenobu　大隈重信
Ōkuni Takamasa　大國隆正
Ōkuni-nushi　大國主
Okuno Nanboku (Marumichi;
　　Genkisai)　奥野南卜 (丸道;
　　源龜斎)
Okunomiya Kenshi　奥宮健之
Okunomiya Zōsai (Masayoshi)
　　奥宮慥斎 (正由)
Okura　御蔵
ōmetsuke　大目付
Ōmotokyō　大本教
Ōnamuchi no mikoto　大己貴尊
Onari　男也
Ondaigo　飲醍醐
Onmyōdō　陰陽道
Onna daigaku　女大學
Onna shōgaku　女小學
Ono　小埜
onore ni kaeru　己に復る
Ontake-kō　御嶽講
Ontakekyō　御嶽教
osa　オサ
Ōsaka jōdai　大坂城代

oshi　御師
Ōshima Urin　大島有隣
Ōta Kinjō　大田錦城
Ōtori Sessō　鴻雪爪
otoriage　おとりあげ
Ōtsu　大津
Ōuchi Seiran　大内青巒
Ozaki Kōyō　尾崎紅葉
Peng Jiqing　彭際清
qi (J. *ki*)　氣
re (ren)　煉
rei　禮
renmon　蓮門
renmon kyōshu　蓮門教主
Renmonkyō　蓮門教
ri　理
ri　里
rigaku　理學
Rikkenseitō　立憲政黨
Rinshōin　麟祥院
Rinzai　臨濟
risshin shusse　立身出世
Risshisha　立志社
ritsugen no shogaku　立言之諸學
rōjū　老中
roku　禄
roku kaiden　六皆傳
rokudō　六道
rōshi　老師
rōyū　老友
ryō　兩
Ryōmō Kyōkai　兩忘協會
Ryōmō Zensha　兩忘禪社
saido no michi　濟度の道
Saigō Takamori　西郷隆盛
Saigoku risshi hen　西國立志編
saijin ronsō　祭神論爭
Sain　佐院
sairei　祭礼
saisei itchi　祭政一致
Sakagami Shinjō (Sōsen)　坂上眞淨
　　(宗詮)
Sakamoto Ryōma　坂本龍馬
Sakata Kaneyasu　坂田鐵安
Sakata Masayasu　坂田正安
Sakata Yasuji　坂田安治

Sakata Yasuyoshi　坂田安儀
Sakatani Shiroshi　阪谷素
sakumon　策問
samu　作務
sangai　三界
Sanjo no kazokura　賛助の華族等
sanjō no kyōsoku　三条の教則
sankyō heikō　三教並行
sankyō itchi　三教一致
Sannō　三王
Sano Kazumaru　佐野量丸
sanrin　三輪
sansha inkan　三舎印鑑
sanshu no harae　三種祓
sanshu no kandakara　三種の神寶
sanso no shinki　酸素の新氣
sanzen　參禪
sanzen bendō　參禪辨道
Sanzensha　參前舍
Sasaki Takayuki　佐々木高行
Satō Bokusan　佐藤牧山
Satō Issai　佐藤一齋
segaikyō　世外教
sei o itasu　誠を致す
Seidō　聖堂
Seigaku　性學
seigaku kōdansho　政學講談所
Seijō Genshi　星定元志
seikyō　政教
seikyō　世教
seikyō itchi　政教一致
Seikyōsha　政教社
Seisetsu Shūcho　誠拙周樗
seishin　精神
seishinryoku　精神力
seito　生徒
seiyō bunmei　西洋文明
seiza　靜坐
seizu kufū　靜坐工夫
Seiza setsu　靜坐説
seizakai　靜坐會
Seki Mugaku　関無學
Sekimon no shinpō　石門の心法
sekiten　釋奠
sekkyō　説教
sen　錢

Senge Takatomi　千家尊福
senkyōshi　宣教師
senmon　專門
senmon gongaku　專門勤學
senmon no gakkō　專門ノ學校
senmon Zen gakkō　專門禪學校
senmongakkō　專門學校
senmongaku　專門學
sensei　先生
senshi　先師
Sensōji　淺草寺
Senzu　泉津
sesshin　攝心
setchū　折衷; 折中
Setchūgaku　折衷學
Setsudō Genkatsu　拙堂元劼
shachō　社長
shadan hōjin　社団法人
Shaji torishirabe ruisan　社寺取調
　　　類纂
shaku　尺
Shaku Sōen (Kōgaku)　釋宗演
　　　(洪嶽)
Shaku Sōkatsu (Tettō)　釋宗活
　　　(輟翁)
Shaku Unshō　釋雲照
shashu　舍主
shasō　社僧
shayaku　社約
Shenxiang quanpian　神相全編
shi　士
shiatsu ryōhō　指圧療法
Shibata Yūō　柴田遊翁
Shibun Gakkai　斯文學會
Shidō Munan　至道無難
shihan gakkō　師範學校
shijin　士人
shikan　死漢
shike　師家
shiki　式
shikihō　式法
Shimaji Mokurai　島地黙雷
Shimamura Fujisuke　島村藤助
Shimamura Mitsu　島村みつ
Shimamura Otokichi　島村音吉
Shimamura Senshū　島村仙修

Shimamura Shinshū　島村信修
Shimo-kinegawa　下木下川
Shimōsa　下總
Shimotsuke　下野
shin　神
shin　心
shinbutsu bunri　神佛分離
Shinbutsu hanzen rei　神佛判然令
shinda kotoba　死言
shinden　神傳
shingaku (Ch. *xinxue*)　心學
shingaku　神學
Shingaku shugyō　心學修行
shingi iryū　新義異流
Shingon　眞言
shinjin　信心
shinjin　身心
shinjin ekō　信心廻向
shinjin gōitsu　神人合一
shinjin tokudō　信心得道
Shinjō Genmyō　眞淨元苗
shinjutsu　心術
shinjutsu no gaku　心術の學
shinka　心火
shinki　心氣
shinkyō　神教
shinkyō shūshin　神教修身
Shinmei　神明
Shinozaki Shōchiku　篠崎小竹
shinpi no koto　深秘ノ事
shinpi no tsutae　神秘の傳え
shinpō　心法
shinri　神理
shinshūkyō　新宗教
Shinshūkyō　神習教
shintai　神體
Shintō　神道
Shintō gobusho　神道五部書
Shintō Honkyoku　神道本局
Shintō Misogiha　神道禊派
Shintō Shūseiha　神道修成派
Shintō Taiseiha　神道大成派
Shintō Taiseikyō　神道大成教
Shintōkei shinshūkyō　神道系新宗教
shinzen　神前
shion　四恩

Shirakawa　白川
Shirō　四郎
shisei　至誠
Shōbōgendō　正法眼堂
Shōden'an　正傳庵
Shōhei Gakkō　昌平學校
Shōheikō　昌平黌
shōji　聖侍
Shōji Naotane　荘司直胤
shōjin　小人
Shōju rōnin sugyō roku
　　　　正受老人崇行錄
shoku　食
Shoku Bosatsu　食菩薩
shōkyōin　小教院
Shōnankō　小楠公
shoshi no gaku　書肆の學
Shoshū Dōtoku Kaimei
　　　　諸宗道徳會盟
shoshū sōkō　諸宗總黌
Shōzokuin　正續院
Shūdō shinpō　修道眞法
Shūgiin giin senkyohō
　　　　衆議院議員選挙法
shūha Shintō　宗派神道
shuinchi　朱印地
shukke　出家
shukke daijōbu no shi
　　　　出家大丈夫の士
shūkyō　宗教
shūkyō hōjin　宗教法人
shūmon　宗門
Shunpūkan　春風館
shuryō　衆寮
shuryō bōzu　衆寮坊主
Shūseiha　修成派
shūshi　宗旨
shūshin　修身
Shūyōdan　修養團
siju　死句
Sochō　祖超
sōdō　僧堂
sōdō bōzu　僧堂房主
sōdō zendō　僧堂禪堂
Soga Sukenori　曽我祐準
Sōgenji　曹源寺

sōhō 相法

Sonnō Hōbutsu Daidōdan
尊皇奉佛大同團

sōrin 叢林

sōrin bōzu 叢林房主

sōrin no hon kiku 叢林の本規矩

sōryo 僧侶

Sōshuku 宗叔

sōzoku ittai 僧俗一體

Su Shi (Dongpo) 蘇軾 (東坡)

Suda Eyū 須田惠優

Suematsu Kenchō 末松謙澄

Suga Torao (Mui) 菅虎雄 (無為)

Sugawara Jiho (Jusen) 菅原時保
(壽仙)

Sugiyama Shūzan 杉山秀三

Suika 垂加

Sukuna-hikona no mikoto 少彦名尊

Suō 周防

Suwa Chūsei 諏訪忠誠

Suzuki Daisetsu (Teitarō) 鈴木大拙
(貞太郎)

Suzuki Masaya (Shinjō) 鈴木馬左也
(真清)

Suzumura Keisō 鈴村荊叢

tabi 足袋

Taguchi Tōkan 田口透關

Taigyaku jiken 大逆事件

Taikyō senpu undō 大教宣布運動

Taisei Kyōkai 大成教會

Taiseikyō 大成教

Taiseikyō kyōki 大成教教規

Taiseikyō Misogikyō Hon'in
Bunkyōkai 大成教禊教本院
分教會

Taiseikyō Renmon Kōsha
大成教蓮門講舎

Taiseikyō Renmonkyō 大成教蓮門教

Taiseikyō Tokyu Yoshikawa Kosha
大成教淘宮吉川講舎

Taishakyō 大社教

Takahashi Deishū 高橋泥舟

Takahashi Kōsetsu (Tokusaburō)
高橋好雲 (徳三郎)

Takami musubi 高御産靈

Takashima Kaemon 高島嘉右衛門

takatsuki 高坏

Takuan Sōhō 澤庵宗彭

Takuboku-en 澤木園

takuhatsu 托鉢

takuhatsu junkai 托鉢巡回

tama 玉

Tamamatsu Misao 玉松操

tamashibi 魂火

Tanaka Yoritsune 田中頼庸

tanden 丹田

tanden kikai 丹田氣海

Tani Kanjō [Tani Tateki] 谷干城

Taniguchi Masaharu 谷口雅春

Tarasawa Okaemon 樗澤岡右衛門

tariki 他力

tatchū 塔頭

Tatebayashi 館林

te o futokoro ni shite 手を懐にして

Teishō ていせう

tenchi no ri 天地の理

tenchi no shinri 天地の眞理

tendō 天道

Tengen Tōkyūjutsu 天源淘宮術

Tengengaku 天源學

Tengenjutsu 天源術

Tenkai 天海

Tenri 天理

Tenri Kyōkai 天理教會

Tenri-ō 天理王

Tenrikyō 天理教

Tenrin 天輪

Tenrin-ō Kōsha 轉輪王講社

tenroku 天録

Tenryūji 天龍寺

tentei (Ch. *tiandi*) 天帝

tenzo 典座

terakoya 寺子屋

terauke 寺請

Teshima Toan 手島堵庵

Tetsuyo Zenni 鉄輿禪尼

tō 淘

To ho kami emi tame 吐菩加美
依身多女

*To ho kami emi tame, harai tamai
kiyome tamau* 吐菩加美依身
多女，祓賜比清女給布

Tōdōkai　淘道会
Tōeishū　淘詠集
Tōgū Chiwaki　東宮千別
Tohokami　吐菩加美
Tohokami-kō　吐菩加美講
tohoko　とほこ
Tōkai Shōshun　東海昌暾
Tōkeiji　東慶寺
Toki Hiroshi (Zōge)　土岐横 (象外)
tokō　都講
Tokoyo Nagatane　常世長胤
tokudō　得道
Tokugawa Ieyasu　徳川家康
Tokugawa Ieyoshi　徳川家慶
Tokugenji　徳源寺
Tokutomi Sohō　徳富蘇峰
Tōkyō Jūzan Sōkō　東京十山總黌
Tōkyō nichinichi shinbun　東京
　　日日新聞
Tōkyō Yokohama mainichi shinbun
　　東京横濱毎日新聞
Tōkyū Kōsha　淘宮講社
Tōkyūjutsu　淘宮術
Tōkyūjutsu benmei　淘宮術辯明
Torio Tokuan (Koyata)　鳥尾徳庵
　　(小彌太)
Tōso no ushiro-sugata o otte　陶祖
　　の後姿を追って
Tōtaku (Shōjōkōji)　藤澤 (清浄光寺)
Toyouke; Toyuke　豊受
tsū Bukkyō　通佛教
Tsuda Mamichi　津田眞道
Tsukada Taihō　塚田大峯
tsukimono　附物
Tsumaki Ayako　妻木綾子
Tsumaki Seiheki (Shōji; Yorinori)
　　妻木棲碧 (笑而; 頼矩)
tsūzoku dōtoku　通俗道徳
tsuzumi　鼓
ubai　優婆夷
ubasoku　優婆塞
uchibito　内人
Uchida Kōsai　内田康哉
Uchimura Kanzō　内村鑑三
ui-musubi　初産靈

Umeda　梅田
Umeda Shinmei　梅田神明
Umetsuji Norikiyo (Kamo no
　　Norikiyo)　梅辻規清
　　(鴨の規清)
undō　運動
Uneme　采女
unsei (*sic*)　運性 (*sic*)
waga mi　我身
waga omoi　我おもい
waka　和歌
Wang Yangming (Shouren)
　　王陽明 (守仁)
Warongo　和論語
Watarai　度会
wei ji zhi xue　為己之學
wuxing　五行
Xiaoxue　小學
Ximing　西銘
xing (J. *sei*)　性
xue　學
xuewen　學問
yamabushi　山伏
Yamagata Aritomo　山縣有朋
Yamagata Bantō　山方蟠桃
Yamaji Aizan　山路愛山
Yamaoka Tesshū (Tetsutarō)
　　山岡鐵舟 (鐵太郎)
Yami no akebono　闇の曙
Yanagida Ichibei (Sonyū)
　　柳田市兵衛 (素入)
Yano Harumichi [Yano Gendō]
　　矢野玄道
yari　槍
yasuku oki sōrō koto　安く置候事
Yochi shiryaku　輿地誌略
Yōgaku　洋學
yōhō　陽報
yōjō　養生
yōka　陽火
Yōkōji　永興寺
Yokoyama Marumitsu (Shunkisai;
　　Sannosuke)　横山丸三 (春龜斎;
　　三之助)
Yokoyama Masamitsu　横山正三

Yokushō Sannin　沃燋山人
Yōkyō kaikisha no mibun shirabe
　　妖教開基者の身分調
Yōkyō Taiji　妖教退治
Yomiuri shinbun　讀賣新聞
yonageru　淘げる
Yoneyama Hosaburō (Tennen)
　　米山保三郎 (天然)
Yorozu chōhō　萬朝報
Yoshida　吉田
Yoshida Kanetomo　吉田兼倶
Yoshikawa Ichigen　吉川一元
Yoshimi Yukikazu　吉見幸和
Yoshimura Masamochi　芳村正秉
Yoshimura Shūyō　吉村秋陽
Yudonosan-kō　湯殿山講
Yūhō Zetan　融峰是坦
yuiitsu　唯一
yuiitsu Shintō　唯一神道
Yuri Tekisui (Giboku)　由利滴水
　　(宜牧)
Yushima　湯島

zaihon　財本
zaike　在家
zange　懺悔
zatsuho　雑舗
zazen　坐禪
zendō　禪堂
zendōka [*zendōke*]　禪堂家
zeni　錢
Zenmyō Hōshū　禪苗蓬洲
zenshi　禪子
Zenshōan　全生庵
Zhang Shangying (Tianjue; Wujin)
　　張商英 (天覺; 無盡)
Zhang Zai　張載
Zhongyong　中庸
Zhouyi　周易
Zhu Shien　朱時恩
Zhu Xi　朱熹
zide　自得
zokkaku　俗客
Zuiōji　瑞応寺

BIBLIOGRAPHY

Works in Japanese and Chinese

Unless otherwise noted, the city of publication is Tokyo.

WORKS CITED BY ABBREVIATIONS

E　　Tamamura Takeji 玉村竹二 and Inoue Zenjō 井上禪定. *Engakujishi* 圓覚寺史. Shunjūsha, 1964.

KKS　Kanagawa-ken shi, Shiryō hen 神奈川県史資料編 13, *Kindai, gendai* 近代現代 3: *Shakai* 社会. Ed. Kanagawa-ken Shi Henshūshitsu 神奈川県史編集室. Yokohama: Kanagawa-ken, 1977.

KKZ　Kawai Kiyomaru 川合清丸. *Kawai Kiyomaru zenshū* 川合清丸全集. Ed. Hashimoto Itsuo 橋本五雄. 1931. Reprint. Kawai Kiyomaru Zenshū Kankōkai, 1933.

KSKS　Kamakura-shi shi, Kindai shiryō hen 鎌倉市史近代資料編 1. Ed. Kamakura-shi Shi Hensan Iinkai 鎌倉市史編纂委員会. Kamakura: Yoshikawa Kōbunkan, 1988.

KZSD　Kinsei Zenrin sōbō den 近世禪林僧寶傳. Comp. Ogino Dokuon 荻野独園 and Obatake Buntei 小畠文鼎. 3 vols. Vol. 1 originally published in 1890, vols. 2–3 in 1938. Reprint. Kyoto: Shibunkaku, 1973.

NBKH　Tsuji Zennosuke 辻善之助. *Nihon Bukkyōshi* 日本仏教史. Vol. 10: *Kinsei hen* 近世編 4. 1955. Iwanami Shoten, 1960.

NBKK　Tamamuro Taijō 玉室諦成. *Nihon Bukkyōshi* 日本仏教史 III: *Kinsei kindai hen* 近世近代編. Hōzōkan, 1967.

NKST　Nihon kindai shisō taikei 日本近代思想体系. Ed. Katō Shūichi 加藤周一 et al. 24 vols. Iwanami Shoten, 1988–1992.
　　　　Vol. 5: *Shūkyō to kokka* 宗教と国家. Ed. Yasumaru Yoshio 安丸良夫 and Miyachi Masato 宮地正人. 1988. Reprint. 1996.
　　　　Vol. 10: *Gakumon to chishikijin* 学問と知識人. Ed. Matsumoto Sannosuke 松本三之介 and Yamamuro Shin'ichi 山室信一. 1988.

NST　　Nihon shisō taikei 日本思想体系. Ed. Ienaga Saburō 家永三郎 et al. 67 vols. Iwanami Shoten, 1970–1982.
　　　　Vol. 43: *Tominaga Nakamoto, Yamagata Bantō* 富永仲基・山片蟠桃. Ed. Mizuta Norihisa 水田紀久 and Arisaka Takamichi 有坂隆道. 1973.

Vol. 46: *Satō Issai, Ōshio Chūsai* 佐藤一斎・大塩中斎. Ed. Sagara Tōru 相良亨, Mizoguchi Yūzō 溝口雄三, and Fukunaga Mitsuji 福永光司. 1980.

Vol. 47: *Kinsei kōki juka shū* 近世後期儒家集. Ed. Nakamura Yukihiko 中村幸彦 and Okada Takehiko 岡田武彦. 1972.

Vol. 50: *Hirata Atsutane, Ban Nobutomo, Ōkuni Takamasa* 平田篤胤・伴信友・大国隆正. Ed. Tahara Tsuguo 田原嗣郎, Seki Akira 関晃, and Haga Noboru 芳賀登. 1973.

Vol. 67: *Minshū shūkyō no shisō* 民衆宗教の思想. Ed. Murakami Shigeyoshi 村上重良 and Yasumaru Yoshio 安丸良夫. 1971. Reprint. 1973.

SGT   *Shushigaku taikei* 朱子学体系. 15 vols. Meitoku Shuppansha, 1974– .

Vol. 6: Zhu Xi 朱熹. *Shushi gorui [Ch. Zhuzi yulei]* 朱子語類. Ed. Okada Takehiko 岡田武彦 et al. 1981.

Vols. 7–8: Zhu Xi 朱熹. *Shisho shūchū [Ch. Sishu jiju]* 四書集註. Ed. Suzuki Yoshijirō 鈴木由次郎. 1974.

SK   Imakita Kōsen 今北洪川. *Sōryō kōroku* 蒼龍広録. Ed. Shaku Sōen 釈宗演. *5 kan.* 1892. Block print.

SKN   Hōjō Tokiyuki 北條時敬 and Shaku Sōen 釋宗演. *Sōryōkutsu nenpu* 蒼龍窟年譜. 1894. Block print.

SN   "Sanzensha nenpu" 三前舎年譜. Comp. Kawajiri Hōkin 川尻寶岑. Sanzensha, 1896. Manuscript.

SSJR Kawajiri Hōkin 川尻寶岑. *Sekimon sanshi jiseki ryaku* 石門三師事蹟略. Sanzensha, 1895. Block print.

T   *Taishō shinshū daizōkyō* 大正新修大藏經. Ed. Takakusu Junjirō 高楠順次郎. 85 vols. Taishō Issaikyō Kankōkai, 1924–1934.

ZZ   *Shinsan dai Nihon zoku zōkyō* 新算大日本續藏經. Ed. Kawamura Kōshō 河村孝照. 90 vols. Kokusho Kankōkai, 1975–1989.

UNPUBLISHED MANUSCRIPTS AND BLOCK-PRINT EDITIONS

Engakuji 圓覺寺. "Kojiryō seiki" 居士寮制規. 1885. Manuscript. Engakuji collection, Tōkeiji.

———. "Sōryōkutsu ejō koji zenshi meishi" 蒼龍窟會上居士禪子名刺. 1885–1891. Manuscript. Engakuji collection, Tōkeiji.

Hayano Gankō [Hakuin] 早野元光[柏蔭]. *Kawajiri Hōkin sensei jiseki* 川尻寶岑先生事蹟. Sanzensha, 1911. Block print.

Imakita Kōsen 今北洪川. (The originals of the following drafts are held in the Engakuji collection in Tōkeiji 東慶寺, Kamakura, and have been dated by Inoue Zenjō.)

Draft letter to Gyoku-ō 玉應. Early or mid-1880s. Manuscript.

Draft letter to Kawajiri 川尻, no. 1. March 1884. Manuscript.

Draft letter to Kawajiri, no. 2. November 24, 1884. Manuscript.

Draft letter to Tsumaki 妻木. Early March, 1884. Manuscript.

Draft letter to Tsumaki Ayako 妻木綾子. Spring 1884. Manuscript.

Draft letter to Yamaoka 山岡. Late April 1886. Manuscript.

———. "Engakuji zendō saiken hokki kanjinjō" 圓覺寺禪堂再建發起勸進帖. SK, 3:8a–b.

———. "Kawajiri nikoji zōsan" 川尻二居士像賛. SK, 3:28a; and Hayano, *Kawajiri Hōkin sensei jiseki*, 5b.

———. "Kyōikugikō shingi jo" 教育義礑精規序. SK, 3:29a–b.

———. "Naikaku sōri daijin hakushaku Itō Hirobumi dono" 内閣總理大臣伯爵伊藤博文殿. 1886. Manuscript. Engakuji collection, Tōkeiji.

———. "Seishū tōheisai o harau saibun" 祓西洲鬪兵災祭文. SK, 3:37b.

———. *Zenkai ichiran* 禪海一瀾. Yamaguchi, 1874. Block print.

———. "Yamaoka Tesshū koji kōin ni wa shite, iken o teisuru jo" 和山岡鐵舟居士高韻呈意見序. SK, 3:11b–12a.

Inoue Sukekane 井上祐鐵, ed. *Inoue Masakane shindenki* 井上正鐵眞傳記. 3 *kan*. 1877. Block print.

Kawajiri Hōkin [Yoshisuke] 川尻寶岑[義祐]. *Naibu bunmeiron* 内部文明論. 3 *kan*. Kakumeidō, 1884. Block print.

Ogino Dokuon 荻野独園. "Kōsen hōhin nenpu jo" 洪川法兄年譜序. 1893. In SKN, 1a–2b. Block print.

Okifuji Tarō 小木藤太郎 et al., eds. *Kyōso Inoue Masakane daijin jitsudenki* 教祖井上正鐵大人實傳記. 2 vols. Misogi Dairoku Kyōin, 1895. Block print.

Shaku Sōen [Kōgaku] 釋宗演[洪嶽]. "Furoku" 付録. In Hayano, *Kawajiri Hōkin sensei jiseki*. Transcript of an oral address given November 20, 1910.

PRIMARY SOURCES

Asano Ken 淺野乾. "Jigoku gokuraku ron" 地獄極樂論. *Chōya shinbun* 朝野新聞, Oct. 11, 1877. Reproduced in NKST, 5:260–261.

———. "Shūkyōron" 宗教論. *Chōya shinbun* 朝野新聞, Sept. 10, 1876. Reproduced in NKST, 5:255–258.

Asō Masaichi 麻生正一, ed. *Zōho Inoue Masakane-ō zaitōki* 増補井上正鐵翁在島記. 1890. Reprint. Wadō Shuppan, 1989.

Ban Kōkei 伴蒿蹊. *Kanden bunshō* 閑田文章. Kenkyūsha gakusei bunko 310. Ed. Tachibana Munetoshi 橘宗利. Kenkyūsha, 1940.

———. *Kinsei kijin den, zoku kinsei kijin den* 近世畸人傳・續近世畸人傳. Ed. Munemasa Isō 宗政五十緒. Heibonsha, 1972.

Date Mitsuyoshi 伊達光美, ed. *Nihon shūkyō seido shiryō ruijukō* 日本宗教制度史料類聚考. Ganshōdō, 1930.

Dōgen 道元. *Kichijōsan Eiheiji shuryō shingi* 吉祥山永平寺衆寮箴規. *Dōgen Zenji zenshū* 道元禪師全集, ed. Kagamishima Genryū 鏡島元隆. 7 vols. Shunjūsha, 1988–1993. 6:82. Also contained in *Sōtōshū zensho* 曹洞宗全書, ed. Sōtōshū Zensho Kankōkai 曹洞宗全書刊行会. 18 vols. 1929–1938. Reprint. Sōtōshū Zensho Kankōkai, 1970–1973. 1 (Shūgen 宗源 1): 611–614.

———. *Shōbōgenzō Jūundō shiki* 正法眼藏重雲堂式. *Sōtōshu zenshō* 曹洞宗全書. Ed. Sōtōshū Zensho Kankōkai 曹洞宗全書刊行会. 18 vols. 1929–1938. Reprint. Sōtōshū Zensho Kankōkai, 1970–1973. 1 (Shūgen 宗源 1): 53–56.

Engakuji 圓覺寺. "Meiji jūhachi nen: Engakuji jūmannin-kō" 明治十八年〜圓覺寺十萬人講. KSKS, 210–213.

———. "Meiji nijūgo nen: Engakuji kaikei" 明治二十五年〜圓覺寺會計. KSKS, 213–215.

———. "Ryōgakutsu ejō koji zenshi meibo" 楞伽窟會上居士禪子名簿. KSKS, 401–423.

————. "Sōryōkutsu ejō koji zenshi meishi" 蒼龍窟會上居士禪子名刺. KSKS, 390–401.

Fukuzawa Yukichi 福澤諭吉. *Fukuzawa Yukichi zenshū* 福澤諭吉全集. Ed. Keiōgi-juku 慶応義塾. 22 vols. 1958–1971. Reprint. Iwanami Shoten, 1969–1971.

Hakuin Ekaku 白隱慧鶴. *Yasen Kanna* 夜船閑話. Ed. Izuyama Kakudō 伊豆山格堂. 1983. Reprint. Shunjūsha, 1994.

Hijikata Hisamoto 土方久本. "Naimu taifu Hijikata Hisamoto dono kōensho 内務大輔土方久本殿口演書. KSKS, 200–201.

Hiranuma Kiichirō 平沼騏一郎. *Hiranuma Kiichirō kaikoroku* 平沼騏一郎回顧録. Hiranuma Kiichirō Kaikoroku Hensan Iinkai, 1955.

Hirose Tansō 廣瀬淡窓. *Jurinhyō* 儒林評. *Nihon Jurin sōsho* 日本儒林叢書, ed. Seki Giichirō 関儀一郎. 14 vols. 1927–1938. Reprint. Ōtori Shuppan, 1971. Vol. 3 (Shiden shokan bu 史傳書簡部). No continuous pagination.

Hōjō Tokiyuki 北條時敬. *Kakudō hen'ei* 廓堂片影. Ed. Nishida Kitarō 西田幾多郎. Kyōiku Kenkyūkai, 1931.

———— and Shaku Sōen 釋宗演. *Sōryōkutsu nenpu (wayaku)* 蒼龍窟年譜 (和訳). Translated into Japanese by Hokohonara Myōrei 鉾之原美鈴. Kyoto: Daishuin Chokushinkai, 1982.

Igai Keisho 猪飼敬所. *Igai Keisho sensei shokan shū* 猪飼敬所先生書翰集. In *Nihon Jurin sōsho* 儒林叢書, ed. Seki Giichirō 関儀一郎. 14 vols. 1927–1938. Reprint. Ōtori Shuppan, 1971. Vol. 3 (Shiden shokan bu 史傳書簡部). No continuous pagination.

Iida Takesato 飯田武郷, ed. *Nihon shoki tsūshaku* 日本書紀通釋. 5 vols. and index. 1940. Reprint.

Imakita Kōsen. "Bunmei to shūkyō" 文明と宗教. In Suzuki Daisetsu, [Teitarō] *(Gekidōki Meiji no Kōso) Imakita Kōsen,* 181–185. 1944. Reprint. Shunjūsha, 1992.

————. "Guan setsumoku hidari no gotoshi" 愚案節目如左. In Suzuki Daisetsu, *Imakita Kōsen,* 179–181.

————. "Kanzeon Bosatsu reigen no setsu" 觀世音菩薩霊驗の説. In Suzuki Daisetsu, *Imakita Kōsen,* 242–249.

————. "Kengi" 建議 (Proposal). In Suzuki Daisetsu, *Imakita Kōsen,* 174–181.

————. "Sōryo kokkai junbiron" 僧侶國會準備論. In Suzuki Daisetsu, *Imakita Kosen,* 167–174.

————. "Takuhatsu kuyō no kudoku" 托鉢供養の功徳. In Suzuki Daisetsu, *Imakita Kōsen,* 234–242.

————. *Zenkai ichiran* 禪海一瀾. Ed. Morinaga Sōkō 盛永宗興. Hakujusha, 1987.

Inoue Masakane 井上正鐵. *Ikunshū* 遺訓集. In Kurozumi Tadaaki and Sakata Yasuyoshi, eds., *Shoka Shintō,* 2:48–312. Shinto Taikei Hensankai, 1982–1988.

————. *Shintō yuiitsu mondō sho* 神道唯一問答書. In Kurozumi and Sakata, eds., *Shoka Shintō,* 2:2–45.

————. *Tabako no uraba* 煙草の裏葉. In Kurozumi and Sakata, eds., *Shoka Shintō,* 2:314–330.

Irokawa Daikichi 色川大吉 and Gabe Masao 我部正男, eds. *Meiji kenpakusho shūsei* 明治建白書集成. 9 vols. Chikuma Shobō, 1986–2000.

Itagaki Taisuke 板垣退助, comp. *Jiyūtōshi* 自由党史. 3 vols. Ed. Tōyama Shigeki 遠山茂樹 and Satō Shigerō 佐藤誠朗. 1958. Reprint. Iwanami Shoten, 1967.

Itō Hirobumi 伊藤博文. "Kyōiku-gi" 教育儀. In *Itō Hirobumi den* 伊藤博文傳, ed. Shunpō-kō Tsuishōkai 春畝公追頌會, 2:149–157. 3 vols. 1940. Reprint. Tōseisha, 1944.

Izumi Kyōka 泉鏡花. "Kōyō sensei" 紅葉先生. In *Ozaki Kōyō shū* 尾崎紅葉集, ed. Fukuda Kiyohito 福田清人, 361–375. Meiji bungaku zenshū 18. Chikuma Shobō, 1965.

Kaibara Ekiken 貝原益軒. *Yōjōkun, Wazoku dōjikun* 養生訓和俗童子訓. Ed. Ishikawa Ken 石川謙. 1961. Reprint. Iwanami Shoten, 1998.

Karakasa Shinzō 唐笠眞藏. "Haishinron" 排神論. *Chōya shinbun* 朝野新聞, Jan. 29, 1876. Reproduced in NKST, 5:254–255.

Katsu Kaishū 勝海舟. *Hikawa Seiwa* 氷川清話. Ed. Etō Jun 江藤淳 et al. Kōdansha, 1974.

Kawai Kiyomaru 川合清丸. "Daidōsha to seitō no kankei" 大道社と政黨の關係. KKZ, 1:165–171.

———. "Kawajiri Hōkin rōkoji o itamu" 悼川尻寶岑老居士. KKZ, 10:281–284.

———. "Nihon Kokkyō Daidōsha setsuritsu taii" 日本國教大道社設立大意. KKZ, 1:1–6.

———. "Seitō kankei ni tsuite" 政黨關係に就いて. KKZ, 8:63–69.

———. "Seitō kankei ni tsuki shakoku" 政黨關係に付社告. KKZ, 1:172.

———. "Tenrikyōron" 天理教論. KKZ, 9:234–249.

Kawajiri Hōkin [Yoshisuke] 川尻寶岑[義祐]. *Nashinoko no ofumi* 梨子の御文. Misogi Kyōkai, 1908.

———. *Yorozuyo ni kaoru Umeda no kamigaki* 萬代に薫る梅田の神垣. Kakumeidō, 1908.

———. "Yorozuyo ni kaoru Umeda no kamigaki" 萬代に薫る梅田の神垣. *Michizuke* みちづけ 23–42 (Aug. 1, 1991–March 1, 1994), in 15 installments published approximately bimonthly.

Kishida Toshiko 岸田俊子. "Dōhō shimai ni tsugu" 同胞姉妹に告ぐ. In *Nihon fujin mondai shiryō shūsei* 日本婦人問題資料集成, ed. Maruoka Hideko 丸岡秀子. 1976. Reprint. Domesu Shuppan, 1978. 8 (Shichō 思潮 1): 103–113.

———. "Hakoiri musume" 箱入娘. *Jiyū shinbun* 自由新聞 411 (Nov. 20, 1883). A modern Japanese rendition appears in Itoya Toshio, *Josei kaihō no senkushatachi—Nakajima Toshiko to Fukuda Hideko*. Shimizu Shoin, 1975.

Kondō Yoshihiro 近藤善博, comp. *Shirakawa ke monjin chō* 白川家門人帳. Osaka: Seibundō, 1972.

Kurozumi Tadaaki 黒住忠明 and Sakata Yasuyoshi 坂田安儀, eds. *Shoka Shintō* 諸家神道. 2 vols. *Shinto Taikei, ronsetsu hen* 神道体系論説編 27–28. Shinto Taikei Hensankai, 1982–1988. No continuous pagination.

Kyōikushi Hensankai 教育史編纂會, ed. *Meiji ikō kyōiku seido hattatsushi* 明治以降教育制度發達史. 12 vols. Ryūginsha, 1938–1939.

Matsudaira Sadanobu 松平定信. *Kagetsu sōshi* 花月双紙. In *Nihon zuihitsu taisei* 日本随筆大成, *dai san ki* 第三期, ed. Nihon Zuihitsu Taisei Henshūbu. 24 volumes. 1929. Reprint. Yoshikawa Kōbunkan, 1976. 1:387–468.

Mizuno Nanboku 水野南北. "Nanboku sōhō gokui bassui jijo" 南北相法極意抜粋自序. In Makino Masayasu and Tanaka Ichirō, *Naniwa no sō hijiri—Mizuno Nanboku to sono shisō,* 175–176. Osaka: Ōsaka Shunjūsha, 1988.

———. *Shūshinroku* 修身録. In Makino and Tanaka, *Mizuno Nanboku to sono shisō,* 173–265.

Mori Arinori 森有礼. *Mori Arinori zenshū* 森有礼全集. Ed. Ōkubo Toshiaki 大久保利謙. 3 vols. Senbundō, 1972.

———. "Shūkyō" 宗教. *Meiroku zasshi* 明六雑誌 6, pt. 4 (April 28, 1874). In Yamamuro Shin'ichi and Nakanome Tōru, eds., *Meiroku zasshi,* 220–229. Iwanami Shoten, 1999.

Motoda Eifu [Nagazane] 元田永孚. "Kyōgaku taishi" 教學大旨. In Kaigo Tokiomi, *Motoda Eifu,* 51–53. Reprint. Bunkyō Shoin, 1943.

———. "Mori bunsō ni taisuru kyōiku ikenshō" 森文相に対する教育意見書. In Kaigo Tokiomi, *Motoda Eifu,* 207–209.

Motoori Norinaga 本居宣長. *Motoori Norinaga zenshū* 本居宣長全集. Ed. Motoori Toyokai 本居豊穎. 7 vols. Yoshikawa Hanshichi, 1901–1904.

———. *Motoori Norinaga zenshū* 本居宣長全集. Ed. Ono Susumu 小野晋. Chikuma Shobō, 1970.

Motoori Ōhira 本居大平. "Kogakuyō" 古學要. *Motoori Ōhira zenshū* 本居大平全集. Contained in Motoori, *Motoori Norinaga zenshū,* ed. Motoori Toyokai. 6 *(furoku)*: 531–545.

Murakoshi Morikazu 村越守一. "Jingidō chūkō Masakane reijinki" 神祇道中興正鐡霊神記. In *Inoue Masakane chokumon kabunshū* 井上正鐡直門歌文集, ed. Ogihara Minori 荻原稔, 23–35. Inoue Masakane Kenkyūkai, 1991.

Nagao Daigaku [Sōshiki] 長尾大學[宗軾], ed. *Sōen zenji shokan shū* 宗演禪師書翰集. Nimatsudō, 1931.

Nagao Sōshiki 長尾宗軾, ed. *Sōen zenji to sono shūi* 宗演禪師と其周圍. Kokushi Kōshūkai, 1923.

Nihon Shiseki Kyōkaisō 日本史籍協會叢, ed. *Hyakukan Rireki* 百官履歴. 1928. Reprint. Tōkyō Daigaku Shuppankai, 1973.

Nishimura Shigeki 西村茂樹. *Hakuō Sōsho* 泊翁叢書. 2 vols. 1909. Reprint. Nihon Kōdōkai Hakubunkan, 1912.

Nozawa Kanenori 野澤鐡教. *Nakatomi no harai ryakuge* 中臣祓略解. In *Inoue Masakane chokumon kabunshū* 井上正鐡直門歌文集, ed. Ogihara Minori 荻原稔, 1–19. Inoue Masakane Kenkyūkai, 1991.

Ōshima, Urin 大島有隣. *Shingaku wagōka* 心學和合歌. In *Shingaku—Ōshima Urin, Sekiguchi Hosen—(Dai isshū)* 心学〜大島有隣、関口保宣 (第一集), ed. Sugito-machi Bunkazai Senmon Iinkai 杉戸町文化財専門委員会, 63–67. Kyōdo shiryō 郷土史料 12. Sugito-machi, Saitama-ken: Sugito-machi Kyōiku Iinkai, 1984.

Ōta Kinjō 大田錦城. *Gosō manpitsu* 梧窗漫筆. 6 *kan*. In *Nihon zuihitsu zenshū* 日本随筆全集. 20 vols. Kokumin Tosho, 1927–1930. 17:1–320.

Sakagami Shinjō [Sōsen] 坂上眞淨[宗詮]. *Keikyokuroku* 荊棘録. Seikenji, 1915.

Sasaki Takayuki 佐々木高行. *Hogohiroi Sasaki Takayuki nikki* 保古飛呂比佐々木高行日記. 12 vols. Tōkyō Daigaku Shuppankai, 1979.

Satō Issai 佐藤一齋. *Genshi banroku* 言志晩録. NST, 46:107–165, 254–273.

———. *Genshi kōroku* 言志後録. NST, 46:57–106, 237–253.

———. *Genshi shiroku* 言志四録. NST, 46:7–356.

———. *Genshi tetsuroku* 言志耋録. NST, 46:167–218, 274–290.

———. *Genshiroku* 言志録. NST, 46:9–56, 219–236.

Suzuki Daisetsu [Teitarō] 鈴木大拙 [貞太郎]. *Suzuki Daisetsu mikōkai shokan* 鈴木大拙未公開書翰. Ed. Inoue Zenjō 井上禪定 and Zen Bunka Kenkyūsho 禅文化研究所. Kyoto: Zen Bunka Kenkyūsho, 1989.

Takada Dōken 高田道見. "Koji shinron" 居士新論. *Meikyō shinshi* 2859–2865 (March 12–24, 1891). A series in five parts.

Takada Sanae 高田早苗. "Kokkateki kyōiku to kojinteki kyōiku" 國家的教育と個人的教育. *Yomiuri shinbun* 讀賣新聞, May 28, 1890. Reproduced in NKST, 10:258–260.

Takahashi Deishū 高橋泥舟. *Deishū ikō* 泥舟遺稿. Ed. Abe Masato 阿部正人. Kokkōsha, 1903.

"Tangansho" 嘆願書. KKS, 17b.

Tōgū Kanemaro 東宮鐵真呂, comp. *Tōgū Chiwaki daijin nenpu* 東宮千別大人年譜. Tōgū Kanemaro, 1901.

Tokoyo Nagatane 常世永胤. *Shinkyō soshiki monogatari* 神教組織物語. Ed. Sakamoto Koremaru 阪本是丸. NKST, 5:361–422.

Torio Tokuan [Koyata] 鳥尾徳庵 [小弥太]. "Hoshu to wa nanzo ya" 保守とは何ぞや. In Torio, *Tokuan zenshū zokuhen narabi ni nenpu*, ed. Soda Fumiho. Tokuan-Kai, 1934.

———. *Myōdō kyōkai yōryō kaisetsu* 明道教會要領解説. In *Meiji bunka zenshū* 明治文化全集. 28 vols. Hyōronsha, 1928–1930. 11:295–306.

———. *Tokuan zensho* 徳庵全書. Ed. Tokuan-kai 徳庵會. Shūeisha Kōjō, 1911.

———. *Tokuan zenshū zokuhen narabini nenpu* 徳庵全集續編並年譜. Ed. Soda Fumiho 曽田文甫. Tokuan-kai, 1934. No continuous pagination.

Yamagata Bantō 山片蟠桃. *Yume no shiro* 夢の代. NST, 43:141–616.

Yamamuro Shin'ichi 山室信一 and Nakanome Tōru 中野目徹, eds. *Meiroku zasshi* 明六雑誌. Iwanami Shoten, 1999.

Yokushō Sannin 沃燋山人. "Shintō shokō—ryūkō—" 神道諸講一流行. *Nichiyō shinbun* 日曜新聞 51 (11.1872). Reproduced in *Shinbun shūsei Meiji hennenshi* 新聞集成明治編年史. 15 vols. Rinsensha, 1924. 1:515.

SECONDARY SOURCES

Akiyama Kanji 秋山寛治. *Shamon Hakuin* 沙門白隠. Shizuoka-shi: Akiyama Aiko, 1983.

Amano Ikuo 天野郁夫, *Kyūsei senmongakkō: Kindaika e no yakuwari o minaosu* 旧制専門学校～近代化への役割を見直す. Nihon Keizai Shinbunsha, 1978.

Araki Ryūtarō 荒木龍太郎. "Nihon ni okeru Yōmeigaku no keifu (2)—Bakumatsu Meiji zenki o chūshin ni—" 日本における陽明学の系譜（二）～幕末明治前期を中心に. In *Yōmeigaku no sekai* 陽明学の世界, ed. Okada Takehiko 岡田武彦, 406–422. Meitoku Shuppansha, 1986.

Endō Jun 遠藤潤. "Bakumatsu shakai to shūkyōteki fukko undō—Shirakawa ke to Hirata Kokugaku—Furukawa Mitsura o shūten to shite" 幕末社会と宗教的復古運動～白川家と平田国学―古川躬行を焦点として. *Kokugakuin daigaku Nihon bunka kenkyūsho kiyō* 国学院大学日本文花研究所紀要 83 (March 1999): 135–178.

Fujii Sadafumi 藤井貞文. *Meiji Kokugaku hasseishi no kenkyū* 明治国学発生史 の研究. Yoshikawa Kōbunkan, 1975.

Fukuda Kiyoto 福田清人, ed. *Ozaki Kōyō shū* 尾崎紅葉集. Meiji bungaku zenshū 18. Chikuma Shōbō, 1965.

Funayama Shin'ichi 船山信一. *Meiji tetsugaku shi kenkyū* 明治哲学史研究. Kyoto: Mineruva Shobō, 1959.

Furuta Shōkin 古田紹欽. *Kinsei no Zensha* 近世の禪者. Furuta Shōkin chosaku shū 5. Kodansha, 1981.

Haga Shōji 羽賀祥二. *Meiji ishin to shūkyō* 明治維新と宗教. Chikuma Shobō, 1994.

Harafuji Hiroshi 腹藤弘司. "Kōsatsu" 高札. In *Kokushi daijiten*, 5:351–353.

Hashimoto Itsuo 橋本五雄. "Butsudō soku gedatsu mon jōkan kaisetsu" 佛道即 解脱門上巻解説. KKZ, 5:1–10.

———. "Shisō oyobi shutō hen kaisetsu" 詞藻及手束篇解説. KKZ, 10:1–8.

Hikaku Shisōshi Kenkyūkai 比較思想史研究会, ed. *Meiji shisōka no shūkyō kan* 明治思想家の宗教観. Ōkura Shuppan, 1975.

Hirao Michio 平尾道雄. *Shishaku Tani kanjō den* 子爵谷干城傳. Zōsonsha, 1981.

Hiratsuka-shi 平塚市, ed. *Hiratsuka-shi shi* 平塚市史 5: *Shiryō hen: Kindai* 資料 編近代 1. Hiratsuka: Hiratsuka-shi, 1987.

Igeta Midori 井桁碧. "Shinsui, jinsui" 神水. In *Nihon minzoku shūkyō jiten* 日本 民俗宗教辞典, 293–294.

Ikeda Eishun 池田英俊. "Kindai shakai ni okeru Bukkyō no jittai" 近代社会にお ける仏教の実体. In *Ajia Bukkyōshi, Nihon hen* アジア仏教史日本編 8: *Kindai Bukkyō* 近代仏教 —*Seiji to shūkyō to minshū* 政治と宗教と民衆, ed. Nakamura Hajime 中村元, Kasahara Kazuo 笠原一男, Kaneoka Shūyū 金岡秀友 et al., 203–292. Kōsei Shuppansha, 1972.

———. *Meiji Bukkyō kyōkai kessha shi no kenkyū* 明治仏教教会結社史の研究. Tōsui Shobō, 1994.

———. *Meiji no shinbukkyō undō* 明治の新仏教運動. Yoshikawa Kōbunkan, 1976.

Ikeda Shindō 池田信道. *Miyakejima no rekishi to minzoku* 三宅島の歴史と民俗. Dentō to Gendaisha, 1983.

Inoue Hisao 井上久雄. *Gakusei ronkō* 学制論考. Kazama Shobō, 1963.

Inoue Nobutaka 井上順孝. "Bakushin kara ishinki Shintōka e—Hirayama Seisai no zahyō tenkan" 幕臣から維新期神道家へ～平山省斎の座標転換. In *Nihongata seikyō kankei no tanjō* 日本型政教関係の誕生, ed. Inoue Nobutaka and Sakamoto Koremaru 坂本是丸, 245–304. Daiichi Shobō, 1987. A revised version of this essay appears in Inoue Nobutaka, *Kyōha Shintō no keisei*, 305–339.

———. "Hirayama Seisai" 平山省斉. In *Shintō jiten*, ed. Kokugakuin Daigaku, 528.

———. *Kyōha Shintō no keisei* 教派神道の形成. Kōbundō, 1991.

———, ed. *Kindai Nihon no shūkyō to kyōiku—Nihon no shūkyō kyōiku no rekishi to genjō* 近代日本の宗教と教育～日本の宗教教育の歴史と現状. Kōbundō, 1997.

Inoue Tetsujirō 井上哲次郎. *Nihon Yōmeigakusha no tetsugaku* 日本陽明學者の哲學. Toyamabō, 1938.

Inoue Zenjō 井上禪定. *Kakekomi-dera* 駆込寺: *Matsugaoka Tōkeiji no jishi to jihō* 松ヶ岡東慶寺の寺史と寺法. Koyama Shoten, 1955.

———. "Kōsen rōshi no shokan no shitagaki" 洪川老師の書簡の下書き. Insert appended to the fourth printing of Suzuki Daisetsu, *Imakita Kōsen,* dated Sept. 30, 1963.

Ishikawa Ken 石川謙. *Sekimon Shingaku shi no kenkyū* 石門心学史の研究. Iwanami Shoten, 1966.

Itoya Toshio 絲屋寿雄. *Josei kaihō no senkushatachi—Nakajima Toshiko to Fukuda Hideko* 女性解放の先駆者たち～中島俊子と福田英子. Shimizu Shoin, 1975.

———. *Okunomiya Kenshi* 奥宮建之. Kinokuniya Shoten, 1972.

Izuyama Kakudō 伊豆山格堂 [Zentarō 善太郎]. "Kaisetsu" 解説. In Suzuki Daisetsu, *Imakita Kōsen,* 309–319.

———. "Kawajiri Hōkin 'Zazen no hayamichi' fukkan ni atarite" 川尻宝岑「座禅の捷径」復刊に当たりて. *Daijō Zen* 大乗禅 48.8 (1971): 3–7.

Kaigo Tokiomi 海後宗臣. *Motoda Eifu* 元田永孚. Nihon kyōiku sentetsu sōsho 19. 1942. Reprint. Bunkyō Shoin, 1943.

Kamakura-shi Shi Hensan Iinkai 鎌倉市史編纂委員会, ed. *Kamakura-shi shi: Kindai tsūshi hen* 鎌倉市史―近代通史編. Kamakura: Yoshikawa Kōbunkan, 1994.

Kamata Tōji 鎌田東二. *Hirayama Seisai to Meiji no Shintō* 平山省斎と明治の神道. Shunjūsha, 2002.

Kanaya Osamu 金谷治. "Nihon kōshōgaku no seiritsu—Ōta Kinjō o chūshin to shite" 日本考証学の成立～大田錦城を中心として. In *Edo kōki no hikaku bunka kenkyū* 江戸後期の比較文化研究, ed. Minamoto Ryōen 源了圓, 38–88. Perikansha, 1990.

Kashiwahara Yūsen 柏原祐泉. *Nihon Bukkyōshi: Kindai* 日本仏教史―近代. Yoshikawa Kōbunkan, 1990.

Kataoka Yakichi 片岡弥吉. "Nakano Kenmei no Kōchi junshi to Okunomiya Zōsai no Kirishitan kyōyū" 中野健明の高知巡視と奥宮慥斎のキリシタン教論. *Kirishitan kenkyū* キリシタン研究 5, ed. Kirishitan Bunka Kenkyūkai キリシタン文化研究会, 151–183. Yoshikawa Kōbunkan, 1959.

Katō Totsudō 加藤咄堂. "Meiji jidai no zaike Bukkyō" 明治時代の在家佛教. *Gendai Bukkyō* 現代佛教 (1933): 132–137.

Kawai Kiyomaru Zenshū Kankōkai 川合清丸全集刊行會. "Kaisetsu: Bukkyō enzetou" 解説: 佛教演説. KKZ, 5; prefatory pages 8–10.

Kawajiri Seitan 川尻清潭. "Bōfu Kawajiri Hōkin no kotodomo—Shiroto no kaita jōen kyakuhon" 亡父川尻寶岑の事ども～素人の書いた上演脚本. *Geijutsuden* 芸術殿 2.10 (1932): 40–50.

Kawakami Kosan 川上孤山. *Myōshinjishi* 妙心寺史. Kyoto: Shibunkaku, 1975.

Kidō Gennosuke 紀藤元之介. "Edo jidai no uranai yogensha" 江戸時代の占い予言者. *Nihon shisōshi gaku* 日本思想史学 30 (1998): 105–115.

Kinami Takuchi 木南卓一. *Jiun Sonja: Shōgai to sono kotoba* 慈雲尊者―生涯と その言葉. 1961. Reprint. Kyoto: Sanmitsudō, 1979.

Kinugasa, Yasuki 衣笠安喜. *Kinsei Nihon no Jukyō to bunka* 近世日本の儒教と 文化. Kyoto: Shibunkaku Shuppan, 1990.

Kiyohara Sadao 清原貞雄. *Kaishū Nihon dōtoku shi* 改修日本道徳史. Chūbunkan Shoten, 1937.

Kobayashi Junji 小林准士. "Kinsei ni okeru 'kokoro no gensetsu'" 近世における 「心の言説」. *Edo no Shisō* 6, ed. Koyasu Nobukuni 子安宣邦, 158–178. Perikansha, 1997.

Komiya Toyotaka 小宮豊隆. *Natsume Sōseki* 夏目漱石. 3 vols. 1953. Reprint. Iwanami Shoten, 1966.

Kōsaka Jirō 神坂次郎. *Damatte suwareba—kansōshi Mizuno Nanboku ichidai* だまってすわれば―観相師水野南北一代. Shinchōsha, 1988.

Kotani Yoshizō 小谷恵造. *Kawai Kiyomaru den* 川合清丸伝. Tottori: Fuji Shoten, 1998.

Kōtoku Shūsui 幸徳秋水. *Chōmin sensei: Chōmin sensei gyōjōki* 兆民先生～兆民 先生行状記. 1902. Iwanami Shoten, 1960.

Kozawa Hiroshi 小沢浩. "'Kō' to 'kyōdan'" 「講」と「教団」. *Furoku* 付録 (*Geppō* 月報 4), 4–6. Appended to NKST, 5.

Makino Masayasu 牧野正恭 and Tanaka Ichirō 田中一郎. *Naniwa no sō hijiri* 浪 速の相聖―*Mizuno Nanboku to sono shisō* 水野南北とその思想. Ōsaka shunjū sōsho 2. Osaka: Ōsaka Shunjūsha, 1988.

Matsumoto Ken'ichi 松本健一. *Bakumatsu no sanshū* 幕末の三舟: *Kaishū, Tesshū, Deishū no ikikata* 海舟・手舟・泥舟の生き方. Kodansha, 1996.

Matsumoto Sannosuke 松本三之介. "Atarashii gakumon no keisei to chishikijin: Sakatani Shiroshi, Nakamura Keiu, Fukuzawa Yukichi o chūshin ni—" 新しい学問の形成と知識人―阪谷素・中村敬宇・福沢諭吉を中心に―. NKST, 10:424–464.

———. "Meiji zenki hoshushugi shisō no ichi danmen: Seiji to dōtoku no mondai o chūshin ni" 明治前期保守主義思想の一断面～政治と道徳の問題を中心 に. In *Meiji zenhanki no nashonarizumu* 明治前半期のナショナリズム, ed. Sakata Yoshio 坂田吉雄, 129–164. Miraisha, 1958.

Matsumura Iwao 松村巌. "Yōmeigakusha Okunomiya Zōsai" 陽明學者奥宮慥 齋. *Tosa shidan* 土佐史談 40:158–179.

Minamoto Ryōen 源了円. *Kinsei shoki jitsugaku shisō no kenkyū* 近世初期實學 思想の研究. Sōbunsha, 1980.

Mitsubashi Ken 三橋健. "Inoue Jinja no seiritsu" 井上神社の成立. *Shintō Taikei Geppō* 神道体系月報, 21:5–9. Inserted in Kurozumi Tadaaki and Sakata Yasuyoshi, eds., *Shoka Shintō*.

Miyachi Masato 宮地正人. "Shūkyō kankei hōrei ichiran" 宗教関係法令一覧. NKST, 5:423–488.

Miyazaki Fumiko 宮崎ふみ子. "Bakumatsu ishinki ni okeru minshū shūkyō no hen'yō—Fujidō no baai" 幕末維新期に於ける民衆宗教の変容～不二道の 場合. In *Nihon kinseishi ronshū* 日本近世史論集, 2:371–403. Yoshikawa Kōbunkan, 1984.

———. "'Furikawari' to 'Miroku no miyo'—'Sangyō Rokuō-ku no otsutae' ni okeru yonaori—"「ふりかわり」と「みろくの御世」〜「参行六王価御伝」における世直り. In *Minkan shinkō to minshū shūkyō* 民間信仰と民衆宗教, ed. Miyata Noboru 宮田登 and Tsukamoto Manabu 塚本学. Yoshikawa Kōbunkan, 1994.

———. "Taikyō senpu no jidai no shinshūkyō—Jikkōsha no baai" 大教宣布の時代の新宗教〜実行社の場合. In *Meiji Nihon no seijika gunzō* 明治日本の政治家群像, ed. Fukuchi Atsushi 福地惇 and Sasaki Takashi 佐々木隆, 61–97. Yoshikawa Kōbunkan, 1993.

Motoyama Yukihiko 本山幸彦. *Kindai Nihon no seiji to kyōiku* 近代日本の政治と教育. Kyoto: Mineruva Shobō, 1972.

Murakami Shigeyoshi 村上重良. "Bakumatsu ishinki no minshū shūkyō ni tsuite" 幕末維新期の民衆宗教について. In NST, 67:563–570.

———. *Nihon shūkyō jiten* 日本宗教事典. 1988. Reprint. Kōdansha, 1993.

Murakami Shigeyoshi and Oguchi Takeichi 小口偉一. "Renmonkyō" 連門教. In "Kindai shakai seiritsuki no shinshūkyō" 近代社会成立期の新宗教, *Nihon shūkyōshi kōza* 日本宗教史講座 3: *Shūkyō to minshū seikatsu* 宗教と民衆生活, ed. Ienaga Saburō 家永三郎 et al., 227–230. 1959. Revised edition. San'ichi Shobō, 1963.

Nakamaru Kazunori 中丸和伯. *Kanagawa-ken no rekishi* 神奈川県の歴史. Yamagawa Shuppansha, 1974.

Nakamura Yukihiko 中村幸彦. "Kinsei kōki jugakkai no dōkō" 近世後期儒学会の動向. NST, 47:479–498.

Nihon Tōdōkai 日本陶道会, ed. *Tōkyū* 陶宮. Nihon Tōdōkai, 1994.

Ogihara Minori 荻原稔. *Inoue Masakane monchū shi benran* 井上正鐵門中史便覧. Umeda Shinmeigū, 1990. Pamphlet.

———. "Misogikyō kaiso Sakata Kaneyasu" 禊教開祖坂田鐵安. Unpublished paper.

———. "Misogikyō no gyōhō" 禊教の行法. Unpublished paper presented at the Nihon Shūkyō Gakkai, Kokugakuin Daigaku, Sept. 21, 1996.

———. "Shirakawa ke to Edo no monjin—Tenpō nenkan no Inoue Masakane entō o megutte." 白川家と江戸の門人〜天保年間の井上正鐵遠島をめぐって. *Shintō shūkyō* 神道宗教 143 (1991): 43–69.

———, ed. *Inoue Masakane chokumon kabunshū* 井上正鐵直門歌文集. Inoue Masakane Kenkyūkai, 1991.

Ogisu Jundō 荻須純道. "Meiji igo no Myōshinji" 明治以後の妙心寺. In Kawakami Kosan, *Myōshinjishi* 妙心寺史, 103–117.

———. "Ogino Dokuon: Haibutsu kishaku ni kōshita gohōsha Zen" 荻野独園: 排仏毀釈に抗した護法者禅. In *Meiji no Zenshō* 明治の禅匠, ed. Zen Bunka Kenkyūsho 禅文化研究所, 101–118.

Ogura Tetsuju-shi Kenshōkai 小倉鐵樹帥顕彰会, ed. *Ogura Tetsuju sensei* 小倉鐵樹先生. Ōmimachi, Nishi Kubiki, Niigata-ken: Ogura Tetsuju-shi Kenshōkai, 1989.

Oguri Junko 小栗純子. *Nihon no kindai shakai to Tenrikyō* 日本の近代社会と天理教. 1969. Reprint. Hyōronsha, 1986.

Okada Hiroshi 岡田博. "Jikkōkyō to Fujidō Kōshinkō" 実行教と不二道孝心講. In *Fuji Sengen shinkō* 富士浅間信仰, ed. Hirano Eiji 平野榮次, 283–312. Yuzankaku, 1987.

Oku Takenori 奥武則. *Renmonkyō suibōshi* 連門教衰亡史. Gendai Kikakushitsu, 1988.

Ōkubo Dōshū 大久保道舟. "Meiji Bukkyō no saiken to koji no katsuyaku—toku ni Ōuchi Seiran koji ni tsuite" 明治仏教の再建と居士の活躍～特に大内青巒居士について. *Kōza kindai Bukkyō* 講座近代仏教 2 (1961): 232–239.

Ōkubo Toshiaki 大久保利謙. *Nihon no daigaku* 日本の大学. Tamagawa Daigaku Shuppanbu, 1997.

Ōmori Sōgen 大森曽玄. *Yamaoka Tesshū* 山岡鐵舟. 1983. Reprint. Shunjūsha, 1993.

Ono Takeo 小野武夫, ed. *Ishin nōmin hōkitan* 維新農民蜂起譚. Tōkō Shoin, 1965.

Sagara Tōru 相良亨. *"Genshi shiroku to Senshindō sakki"* 「言志四録」と「洗心洞箚記. In NST, 46:709–738.

———. *Kinsei Nihon Jukyō undō no keifu* 近世日本儒教運動の系譜. Kōbundō, 1955.

Sakamoto Masahisa 坂本忠久. "Kinsei kōki no Edo ni okeru shūkyōsha tōsei to toshi mondai" 近世後期の江戸における宗教者統制と都市問題. *Hisutoria* ヒストリア 137 (1992): 52–70.

Sakata Yasuyoshi 坂田安儀. "Kaidai" 解題. In Kurozumi Tadaaki and Sakata Yasuyoshi, eds., *Shoka Shintō,* 2:9–29.

Sakurai Keiyū 桜井景雄. *Nanzenjishi* 南禅寺史. 2 vols. Kyoto: Hōzōkan, 1977.

Sakurai Masashi 櫻井匡. *Meiji shūkyōshi kenkyū* 明治宗教史研究. Shunjūsha, 1971.

Sakurai Tokutarō 桜井徳太郎. *Nihon minkan shinkōron* 日本民間信仰論. 1973. Revised edition. Kōbundō, 1982.

Satomichi Tokuo 里道徳雄. "Meiji ishin ni okeru Bukkyō—Unshō to Kōsen" 明治維新に於ける佛教～雲照と洪川. *Ōkurayama ronshū* 大倉山論集 28 (1990): 45–81.

Shimada Kenji 島田虔次, ed. *Daigaku Chūyō* 大学中庸. 2 vols. Asahi Shinbunsha, 1978.

Sōma Kokkō 相馬黒光. *Meiji shoki no sanjosei* 明治初期の三女性: *Nakajima Shōen, Wakamatsu Shizuko, Kiyomizu Shikin* 中島湘煙・若松賤子・清水紫琴. Kōseikaku, 1940.

Sugata Masaaki 菅田正昭. *Fukugan no Shintōkatachi* 複眼の神道家たち. Hachiman Shoten, 1987.

Suzuki Daisetsu [Teitarō] 鈴木大拙 [貞太郎]. *(Gekidōki Meiji no kōsō) Imakita Kōsen* (激動期明治の高僧)今北洪川. 1944. Reprint with additional material in a new edition. Shunjūsha, 1992.

Suzuki Norihisa 鈴木範久. *Meiji shūkyō shichō no kenkyū* 明治宗教思潮の研究. Tokyo Daigaku Shuppan, 1979.

Suzuki Yūko 鈴木裕子, ed. *Kishida Toshiko kenkyū bunken mokuroku* 岸田俊子研究文献目録. Fuji Shuppan, 1986.

Takano Toshihiko 高埜利彦. "Idō suru mibun—shinshoku to hyakushō no aida" 移動する身分―神職と百姓の間―. Nihon no kinsei 日本の近世 7. Chūō Kōronsha, 1992.

Takase Daijirō 高瀬大治郎. *Satō Issai to sono monjin* 佐藤一齊とその門人. Nan'yōdō Honten, 1922.

Takeda Dōshō [Michio] 武田道生. "Meiji zenki no Bukkyō kyōiku no mezashita mono—sōryo yōsei kyōiku to ippan joshi kyōiku" 明治前期の仏教教育の目指したもの〜僧侶養成教育と一般女子教育. In *Shūkyō to kyōiku* 宗教と教育, ed. Inoue Nobutaka 井上順孝, 81–103.

———. "Nihon kindai ni okeru shinshūkyō kyōdan no tenkai katei—Renmonkyō no hōkai yōin no bunseki o tōshite" 日本近代に於ける新宗教教団の展開過程〜蓮門教の崩壊要因の分析を通して. *Taishō daigaku daigakuin kenkyū ronshū* 大正大学大学院研究論集 8 (1984): 123–134.

———. "Nihon kindai no shinshūkyō tenkai katei" 日本近代の新宗教展開過程. *Bukkyō ronsō* 仏教論爭 27 (1983).

———. "Renmonkyō no hōkai katei no kenkyū—Meiji shūkyōshi ni okeru Renmonkyō no ichi" 蓮門教の崩壊過程の研究〜明治宗教史に於ける蓮門教の位置. *Nihon Bukkyō* 日本仏教 59 (1983): 23–41. Translated into English by Norman Havens under the title "The Fall of Renmonkyō, and Its Place in the History of Meiji-Period Religions," in *New Religions*, ed. Inoue Nobutaka, 25–57.

———. "*Yorozu chōhō* ni yoru Renmonkyō kōgeki kyanpein" 「万朝報」による蓮門教抗撃キャンペイン. *Kokugakuin daigaku Nihon bunka kenkyūjo kiyō* 国学院大学日本文化研究所紀要 63 (1989).

Takekoshi Yosaburō 竹越與三郎. *Nihon keizaishi* 日本經濟史. 10 vols. 1934–1935. Reprint. Heibonsha, 1946–1948.

Takenuki Genshō 竹貫玄勝. *Nihon Zenshūshi* 日本禅宗史. Daizō Shuppan, 1989.

Tamamura Takeji 玉村竹二. "Kenchōji no rekishi" 建長寺の歴史. In Tamamura Takeji, *Nihon Zenshūshi ronshū* 日本禅宗史論集, 2B:787–798. 2 vols. Kyoto: Shinbunkaku, 1981.

———. "Kenchōji to Engakuji no idō" 建長寺と圓覚寺の異同. In Tamamura Takeji, *Nihon Zenshūshi ronshū,* 2B:389–394. 2 vols. Kyoto: Shibunkaku, 1980.

Tamamuro Fumio 玉室文雄. *Edo bakufu no shūkyō tōsei* 江戸幕府の宗教統制. Nihonjin no kōdō to shisō 16. 1971. Reprint. Hyōronsha, 1986.

Tanaka Yoshitō 田中義能. "Shintō Taiseikyō no kenkyū" 神道大成教の研究. 1935. Reprinted in Tanaka Yoshitō, *Shintō jūsanpa no kenkyū* 神道十三派の研究. 2 vols. Daiichi Shobō, 1987. Vol. 1. No continuous pagination.

Tōkyō Teikoku Daigaku 東京帝國大學, ed. *Tōkyō Teikoku Daigaku gojūnen shi* 東京帝國大學五十年史. Teikoku Daigaku, 1932.

Tsuji Zennosuke 辻善之助. *Nihon Bukkyōshi no mondai* 日本仏教史の問題. Ritsubun Shoin, 1949.

Tsunemitsu Kōnen 常光浩然. *Meiji no Bukkyōsha* 明治の仏教者. 2 vols. Shunjūsha, 1968.

Ueyama Shunpei 上山春平. "Chōmin no tetsugaku shisō" 兆民の哲学思想. In Kuwabara Takeo 桑原武夫, *Nakae Chōmin no kenkyū* 仲江兆民の研究. Iwanami Shoten, 1966.

Yamamoto Tetsuo 山本哲生. "Meiji shoki ni okeru sōryo to kyōiku to o meguru shosō" 明治初期における僧侶と教育とを回る諸相. In *Ronshū Nihon Bukkyōshi* 論集日本仏教史 8: *Meiji jidai* 明治時代, ed. Ikeda Eishun 池田英俊, 139–161. Yuzankaku, 1987.

Yasumaru Yoshio 安丸良夫. *Nihon no kindaika to minshū shūkyō* 日本の近代化 と民衆宗教. Aoki Shoten, 1974.

Yokoyama Hideya 横山秀哉. *Zen no kenchiku* 禅の建築. Shōkokusha, 1967.

Yonetsu Saburō 米津三郎. "Renmonkyō ni tsuite" 蓮門教について. *Kiroku* 記録 20 (1980): 49 (299)–64 (314). Published by Ogura Kyōdoshikai.

Yoshida Kyūichi 吉田久一. *Nihon kindai Bukkyō shakaishi kenkyū* 日本近代仏 教社会史研究. 2 vols. Yoshida Kyūichi chosakushū 5–6. Kawashima Shoten, 1991.

———. *Nihon no kindai shakai to Bukkyō* 日本の近代社会と仏教. 1970. Reprint. Hyōronsha, 1990.

Yuri Jun'ichi 柚利淳一. *Maruyama kyōso otsutae* 丸山教祖御伝え. Maruyamakyō Honchō Shuppanbu, 1955.

Zen Bunka Kenkyūsho 禅文化研究所, ed. *Meiji no Zenshō* 明治の禅匠. Kyoto: Zen Bunka Kenkyūsho, 1981.

DICTIONARIES

Bukkyōgo daijiten 佛教語大辞典. Reduced-size ed. (*shukusatsuban* 縮刷版). Ed. Nakamura Hajime 中村元. 1981. Reprint. Tōkyō Shoseki, 1985.

Dai jinmei jiten 大人名事典. 10 vols. 1953–1955. Reprint. Heibonsha, 1962.

Iwanami Nihonshi jiten 岩波日本史辞典. Ed. Ishikami Eiichi 石上英一 et al. Iwanami Shoten, 1999.

Kinsei kangakusha denki chosaku daijiten fu keifu nenpyō 近世漢學者傳記著作 大辭典付系譜年表. Ed. Seki Giichirō 關儀一郎 and Seki Yoshinao 關義直. 1943. 3d ed. Inoue Shoten and Rinrōkaku Shoten, 1971.

Kōjien 広辞苑. Ed. Niimura Izuru 新村出. 5th ed. Electronic book version. Iwanami Shoten, 1999.

Kokushi daijiten 国史大辞典. 20 vols. Yoshikawa Kōbunkan, 1985.

Konsaisu jinmei jiten: Nihon hen コンサイス人名辞典―日本編. Ed. Ueda Masaaki 上田正昭 et al. 1976. Reprint. Sanseidō, 1983.

Meiji ishin jinmei jiten 明治維新人名辞典. Ed. Nihon Rekishi Gakkai 日本歴史学 会. Yoshikawa Kōbunkan, 1981.

Nihon minzoku shūkyō jiten 日本民俗宗教辞典. Ed. Sasaki Kōken 佐々木宏幹, Miyata Noboru 宮田登, and Yamaori Tetsuo 山折哲雄. Tōkyōdō Shuppan, 1998.

Nihon rekishi jiten 日本歴史事典. Ed. Wakamori Tarō 和歌森太郎. Jitsugyō no Nihonsha, 1958.

Nihonshi jiten 日本史辞典. Ed. Uno Shun'ichi 宇野俊一 et al. Kadokawa Shoten, 1997.

Shinpan Zengaku daijiten 新版禅学大辞典. Ed. Komazawa Daigaku Zengaku Daijiten Hensanjo 駒沢大学禅学大辞典編纂所. Daishūkan Shoten, 1985.

Shinshūkyō jiten 新宗教事典. Reduced-size ed. (*shukusatsuban* 縮刷版). Ed. Inoue Nobutaka 井上順孝 et al. Kōbundō, 1994.

Shinshūkyō jiten 新宗教辞典. By Matsuno Junkō 松野純孝. 1984. 3d ed. Tōkyōdō, 1987.

Shintō daijiten 神道大辞典. 3 vols. Kyoto: Rinsen Shōten, 1969.

Shintō jiten 神道事典. Ed. Kokugakuin Daigaku Nihon Bunka Kenkyūsho 国学院大学日本文化研究所. Kōbundō, 1994.

Zengo jiten 禅語辞典. Ed. Iriya Yoshitaka 入谷義高. Kyoto: Shibunkaku, 1991.

Works in European Languages

Adler, Joseph A. "Chu Hsi and Divination." In Kidder Smith, Jr., Peter K. Bol, Joseph A. Adler, and Don J. Wyatt, *Song Dynasty Uses of the I Ching,* 169–205. Princeton, NJ: Princeton University Press, 1990.

Ambaras, David R. "Social Knowledge, Cultural Capital, and the New Middle Class in Japan, 1895–1912." *Journal of Japanese Studies* 24.1 (1998): 1–33.

Ansart, Olivier. *L'Empire du rite: La pensée politique d'Ogyū Sorai, Japon 1666–1728.* Geneva and Paris: Droz, 1998.

Apter, David E., and Tony Saich. *Revolutionary Discourse in Mao's Republic.* Cambridge, MA: Harvard University Press, 1994.

Aston, W. G., trans. *Nihongi: Chronicles of Japan from the Earliest Times to* A.D. *697.* Two volumes in one. Rutland, VT, and Tokyo: Charles E. Tuttle Co., 1972.

Ballhatchet, Helen. "Confucianism and Christianity in Meiji Japan: The Case of Kozaki Hiromichi." *Journal of the Royal Asiatic Society of Great Britain and Ireland* 2 (1988): 349–369.

Baroni, Helen. *Ōbaku Zen: The Emergence of the Third Sect of Zen in Early Tokugawa Japan.* Honolulu: University of Hawai'i Press, 2000.

Barrett, Timothy H. *Li Ao: Buddhist, Taoist, or Neo-Confucian?* Oxford and New York: Oxford University Press, 1992.

Bellah, Robert N. *Tokugawa Religion: The Values of Pre-Industrial Japan.* 1957. Reprinted with a new introduction under the title *Tokugawa Religion: The Cultural Roots of Modern Japan.* New York: Free Press, 1985.

Berger, Gordon Mark, trans. *Kenkenroku: A Diplomatic Record of the Sino-Japanese War, 1894–95.* Princeton, NJ, and Tokyo: Princeton University Press and University of Tokyo Press, 1982.

Bodiford, William. *Sōtō Zen in Medieval Japan.* Honolulu: University of Hawai'i, 1993.

Bolitho, Harold. "The Tempō Era." In *The Cambridge History of Japan, Volume Five: The Nineteenth Century,* ed. Marius B. Jansen, 116–167. Cambridge: Cambridge University Press, 1989.

Bourdieu, Pierre. *The Field of Cultural Production.* New York: Columbia University Press, 1993.

———. *Language and Symbolic Power.* Trans. G. Raymond and M. Adamson. Oxford: Polity Press, 1991.

———. *The Logic of Practice.* Trans. Richard Nice. Stanford, CA: Stanford University Press, 1990.

Braisted, William Reynolds, trans. *Meiroku zasshi: Journal of the Japanese Enlightenment.* Cambridge, MA: Harvard University Press, 1976.

Breen, John. "Shintoists in Restoration Japan (1868–1872): Towards a Reassessment." *Modern Asian Studies* 24.3 (1990): 579–602.

Brook, Timothy. *Praying for Power: Buddhism and the Formation of Gentry Society in Late-Ming China*. Cambridge, MA, and London: Council on East Asian Studies, Harvard University, and the Harvard-Yenching Institute, 1993.

Burns, Susan L. "Constructing the National Body: Public Health and the Nation in Nineteenth–Century Japan." In *Nation Work: Asian Elites and National Identities,* ed. Timothy Brook and Andre Schmid, 17–50. Ann Arbor: University of Michigan Press, 2000.

Buswell, Robert E. "The 'Short-Cut' Approach of *K'an-hua* Meditation: The Evolution of Practical Subitism in Chinese Ch'an Buddhism." In *Sudden and Gradual: Approaches to Enlightenment in Chinese Thought,* ed. Peter N. Gregory, 321–377. Honolulu: University of Hawai'i Press, 1987.

———. *Tracing Back the Radiance: Chinul's Korean Way of Zen*. Honolulu: University of Hawai'i Press, 1991.

The Centre for East Asian Cultural Studies, comp. *Meiji Japan through Contemporary Sources*. 3 vols. Tokyo: The Centre for East Asian Cultural Studies, 1969–1972.

Chan, Wing-tsit. *Sourcebook in Chinese Philosophy*. Princeton, NJ: Princeton University Press, 1963.

Chartier, Roger. "Intellectual History or Sociocultural History? The French Trajectories." Trans. Jane Kaplan. In *Modern European Intellectual History: Reappraisals and New Perspectives,* ed. Dominick LaCapra and Steven L. Kaplan, 13–46. Ithaca, NY: Cornell University Press, 1982.

Collcutt, Martin. "Buddhism: The Threat of Eradication." In *Japan in Transition from Tokugawa to Meiji,* ed. Marius B. Jansen and Gilbert Rozman, 143–167. Princeton, NJ: Princeton University Press, 1986.

———. *Five Mountains: The Rinzai Zen Monastic Institution in Medieval Japan*. Cambridge, MA: Harvard University Press, 1981.

———. "The Legacy of Confucianism in Japan." In *The East Asian Region: Confucian Heritage and Its Modern Adaptation,* ed. Gilbert Rozman, 111–154. Princeton, NJ: Princeton University Press, 1991.

Confucius. *The Analects*. Trans. D. C. Lau. New York: Penguin Books, 1979.

———. *The Analects of Confucius*. Trans. Arthur Waley. New York: Random House, 1938.

———. *Confucian Analects, Great Learning and the Doctrine of the Mean*. Trans. James Legge. 1893. Reprint of 2d rev. ed. New York: Dover Publications, 1971.

Dallmayr, Fred. *Language and Politics*. Notre Dame, IN: University of Notre Dame Press, 1984.

Davis, Winston. *Dojo: Magic and Exorcism in Modern Japan*. Stanford, CA: Stanford University Press, 1980.

———. *Japanese Religion and Society: Paradigms of Structure and Change*. Albany: SUNY Press, 1992.

de Bary, W. Theodore. "Introduction." In *Principle and Practicality: Essays in Neo-Confucianism and Practical Learning,* ed. W. Theodore de Bary and Irene Bloom, 1–36. New York: Columbia University Press, 1979.

———. *Learning for Oneself: Essays on the Individual in Neo-Confucian Thought.* New York: Columbia University Press, 1991.

———. *The Liberal Tradition in China.* New York: Columbia University Press, 1983.

———. *The Message of the Mind in Neo-Confucianism.* New York: Columbia University Press, 1989.

———. *Neo-Confucian Orthodoxy and the Learning of the Mind-and-Heart.* New York: Columbia University Press, 1981.

de Bary, W. Theodore, and Irene Bloom, eds. *Principle and Practicality: Essays in Neo-Confucianism and Practical Learning.* New York: Columbia University Press, 1979.

———. *Sources of Chinese Tradition: From Earliest Times to 1600.* 2d ed. Volume 1. New York: Columbia University Press, 1999.

Desan, Suzanne. *Reclaiming the Sacred: Lay Religion and Popular Politics in Revolutionary France.* Ithaca, NY, and London: Cornell University Press, 1990.

Deuchler, Martina. *The Confucian Transformation of Korea: A Study of Society and Ideology.* Cambridge, MA, and London: Council on East Asian Studies, Harvard University, 1992.

Dore, Ronald. *Education in Tokugawa Japan.* 1965. Reprint. London: Athlone Press, 1984.

Dōgen. *Dōgen's Pure Standards for the Zen Community: A Translation of Eihei Shingi.* Ed. Taigen Daniel Leighton. Trans. T. D. Leighton and Shōhaku Okumura. Albany: State University of New York Press, 1996.

Dumoulin, Heinrich. *Zen Buddhism: A History—Volume 2, Japan.* Trans. James W. Heisig and Paul Knitter. New York and London: Macmillan Publishing Company and Collier Macmillan Publishers, 1990.

Elias, Norbert. *The Society of Individuals.* Ed. Michael Schröter. Trans. Edmund Jephcott. Cambridge, MA: Basil Blackwell, 1991.

———. *What Is Sociology?* Trans. S. Mennell and G. Morrissey. New York: Columbia University Press, 1978.

Faure, Bernard. *The Red Thread: Buddhist Approaches to Sexuality.* Princeton, NJ: Princeton University Press, 1998.

———. *The Rhetoric of Immediacy: A Cultural Critique of the Chan/Zen Tradition.* Princeton, NJ: Princeton University Press, 1991.

Fields, Rick. *How the Swans Came to the Lake: A Narrative History of Buddhism in America.* Boston: Shambhala, 1981.

Foulk, T. Griffith. "Myth, Ritual, and Monastic Practice in Sung Ch'an Buddhism." *Religion and Society in T'ang and Sung China,* ed. Patricia Buckley Ebrey and Peter N. Gregory, 147–208. Honolulu: University of Hawai'i Press, 1993.

Fujieda, Mioko. "Japan's First Phase of Feminism." In *Japanese Women: New Feminist Perspectives on the Past, Present, and Future,* ed. Kumiko Fujimura-Fanselow and Atsuko Kameda, 323–341. New York: The Feminist Press, 1995.

Fukui, Haruhiro. "Introduction: On the Significance of Informal Politics." In *Informal Politics in East Asia,* ed. Lowell Dittmer, Haruhiro Fukui, and Peter N. S. Lee, 1–19. Cambridge: Cambridge University Press, 2000.

Fukuzawa Yukichi. *An Encouragement of Learning*. Trans. David A. Dilworth and Hirano Umeyo. Tokyo: Sophia University Press, 1969.

———. *An Outline of a Theory of Civilization*. Trans. David A. Dilworth and G. Cameron Hurst. Tokyo: Sophia University Press, 1973.

Fulton, John. "Religion and Politics in Gramsci: An Introduction." *Sociological Analysis* 48.3 (1987): 197–216.

Garon, Sheldon. *Molding Japanese Minds: The State in Everyday Life*, 60–87. Princeton, NJ: Princeton University Press, 1997.

———. "State and Religion, 1912–1945." *Journal of Japanese Studies* 12.2 (Summer 1986): 273–302. A revised version of this essay appears in Sheldon Garon, *Molding Japanese Minds: The State in Everyday Life*, 60–87.

Gimello, Robert M. "Chang Shang-ying on Wu-t'ai shan." In *Pilgrims and Sacred Sites in China*, ed. Susan Naquin and Chün-fang Yü, 89–149. Berkeley, Los Angeles, Oxford: University of California Press, 1992.

Ginzburg, Carlo. *The Cheese and the Worms: The Cosmos of a Sixteenth-Century Miller*. Trans. John and Anne Tedeschi. New York: Penguin Books, 1982. Originally published as *Il formaggio e i vermi: Il cosmo di un mugnaio del '500*. N.p.: Giulio Einaudi Editore, 1976.

Gluck, Carol. *Japan's Modern Myths: Ideology in the Late Meiji Period*. Princeton, NJ: Princeton University Press, 1985.

Goldmann, Lucien. *The Hidden God: A Study of Tragic Vision in the* Pensées *of Pascal and the Tragedies of Racine*. New York: The Humanities Press, 1964.

Gramsci, Antonio. *Gli intellettuali e l'organizzazione della cultura*. N.p.: Giulio Einaudi Editore, 1949.

———. *The Gramsci Reader: Selected Writings 1916–1935*. Ed. David Forgacs. New York: New York University Press, 2000.

Greene, D. C. "Remmon Kyō Kwai." *Transactions of the Asiatic Society of Japan* 29 (1901): 17–33.

Gregory, Peter N. "Sudden Enlightenment Followed by Gradual Cultivation: Tsung-Mi's Analysis of Mind." In *Sudden and Gradual: Approaches to Enlightenment in Chinese Thought*, ed. Peter N. Gregory, 279–320. Honolulu: University of Hawai'i Press, 1987.

Gumperz, J. "The Speech Community." In *Language and Social Context: Selected Readings*, ed. Pier Paolo Giglioli, 219–231. Harmondsworth, Eng.: Penguin Books, 1972. Originally published in *International Encyclopedia of the Social Sciences*, 381–386. New York: MacMillan, 1968.

Hackett, Roger F. *Yamagata Aritomo in the Rise of Modern Japan, 1838–1922*. Cambridge, MA: Harvard University Press, 1971.

Hakuin Ekaku. "Chat on a Boat in the Evening." Trans. R. D. M. Shaw and William Schiffer. *Monumenta Nipponica* 13.1–2 (1956): 101–127.

———. *Wild Ivy: The Spiritual Autobiography of Zen Master Hakuin*. Trans. Norman Waddell. Boston: Shambhala Publications, 1999.

Hall, Ivan Parker. *Mori Arinori*. Cambridge, MA: Harvard University Press, 1973.

Hardacre, Helen. "Conflict between Shugendō and the New Religions of Bakumatsu Japan." *Japanese Journal of Religious Studies* 21.2–3 (1994): 137–166.

————. *Kurozumikyō and the New Religions of Japan.* Princeton, NJ: Princeton University Press, 1986.

————. *Religion and Society in Nineteenth-Century Japan: A Study of the Southern Kantō Region, Using Late Edo and Early Meiji Gazetteers.* Ann Arbor, MI: Center for Japanese Studies, University of Michigan, 2002.

————. *Shintō and the State, 1868–1988.* Princeton, NJ: Princeton University Press, 1989.

————. "The Transformation of Healing in the Japanese New Religions." *History of Religions* 20 (May 1982): 305–319.

Harootunian. "Late Tokugawa Culture and Thought." In *The Cambridge History of Japan, Volume Five: The Nineteenth Century,* ed. Marius B. Jansen, 168–258. Cambridge: Cambridge University Press, 1989.

————. *Things Seen and Unseen: Discourse and Ideology in Tokugawa Nativism.* Chicago: University of Chicago Press, 1988.

Heisig, James W., and John C. Maraldo, eds. *Rude Awakenings: Zen, the Kyoto School, and the Question of Nationalism.* Honolulu: University of Hawai'i Press, 1995.

Huffman, James L. *Creating a Public: People and Press in Meiji Japan.* Honolulu: University of Hawai'i Press, 1997.

Huntington, Samuel P. "Conservatism as an Ideology." *American Political Science Review* 51 (1957): 454–473.

Hur, Nam-lin. *Prayer and Play in Late Tokugawa Japan.* Cambridge, MA: Harvard University Press, 2000.

Hurvitz, Leon, trans. *The Scripture of the Lotus Blossom of the Fine Dharma.* New York: Columbia University Press, 1976.

Ikeda Eishun. "Teaching Assemblies and Lay Societies in the Formation of Modern Sectarian Buddhism." *Japanese Journal of Religious Studies* 25.1–2 (Spring 1998): 11–44.

Inoue Nobutaka, ed. *New Religions.* Trans. Norman Havens. Contemporary Papers in Japanese Religions 2. Tokyo: Institute for Japanese Culture and Classics, Kokugakuin University, 1991.

Irokawa Daikichi. *The Culture of the Meiji Period.* Ed. Marius Jansen. Princeton, NJ: Princeton University Press, 1985.

Jaffe, Richard. *Neither Monk nor Layman: Clerical Marriage in Japanese Buddhism.* Princeton, NJ: Princeton University Press, 2001.

Jansen, Marius B., ed. *The Cambridge History of Japan, Volume Five: The Nineteenth Century.* Cambridge: Cambridge University Press, 1989.

————. "Mutsu Munemitsu." In *Personality in Japanese History,* ed. Albert M. Craig and Donald H. Shively, 309–334. Berkeley, CA: University of California Press, 1970.

Kanagawa Prefectural Government, ed. *The History of Kanagawa.* Yokohama: Kanagawa Prefectural Government, 1985.

Kaneko, Sachiko, and Robert E. Morrell. "Sanctuary: Kamakura's Tōkeiji Convent." *Japanese Journal of Religious Studies* 10.2–3 (June–September 1983): 195–228.

Kassel, Marleen. *Tokugawa Confucian Education: The Kangien Academy of Hirose Tansō (1782–1856).* Albany: State University of New York Press, 1996.

Katō, Shōshun. "'A Lineage of Dullards': Zen Master Tōjū Reisō and His Associates." *Japanese Journal of Religious Studies* 25.1–2 (Spring 1998): 151–165.

Ketelaar, James E. *Of Heretics and Martyrs: Buddhism and Its Persecution.* Princeton, NJ: Princeton University Press, 1990.

Keyworth, George Albert, III. "Transmitting the Lamp of Learning in Classical Chan Buddhism: Juefan Huihong (1071–1128) and Literary Chan." Ph.D. diss. University of California, Los Angeles, 2001.

Kinmonth, Earl. *The Self-Made Man in Meiji Japanese Thought.* Berkeley, CA: University of California Press, 1981.

Kinski, Michael. *Knochen des Weges. Katayama Kenzan als Vertreter des eklektischen Konfuzianismus im Japan des 18. Jahrunderts.* Wiesbaden: Otto Harrassowitz, 1996.

———. "Moral Disposition and Personal Autonomy: Kayatama Kenzan as a Representative of Eighteenth-Century Eclectic Confucianism." *Japanese Religions* 22 (1997): 47–64.

Knoke, David. "The Political Economies of Associations." *Research in Political Sociology: A Research Annual,* ed. Richard G. Braungart and Margaret Braungart, 1:211–242. Greenwood, CN, and London: JAI Press, 1985.

Kohn, Livia. "A Textbook of Physiognomy: The Tradition of the *Shenxiang quanbian.*" *Asian Folklore Studies* 45 (1986): 227–258.

Lau, D. C., ed. *A Concordance to the Huainanzi.* Hong Kong: The Commercial Press Ltd., 1992.

Lévi, Sylvain, and Takakusu Junjirō, eds. *Hōbōgirin: Dictionnaire encycopédique du Bouddhisme d'après les sources Chinoises et Japonaises.* Premier fascicule: A—Bombai. Tokyo: Maison franco-japonaise, 1929–1930.

Lévi-Strauss, Claude. *The Savage Mind.* Chicago: University of Chicago Press, 1966.

Lloyd, A. "The Remmon Kyō." *Transactions of the Asiatic Society of Japan* 29 (1901): 1–16.

Mannheim, Karl. "Conservative Thought." In *From Karl Mannheim,* ed. Kurt H. Wolff, 132–222. New York: Oxford University Press, 1971.

———. *Ideology and Utopia.* 1936. Reprint. San Diego and New York: Harcourt, Brace, and Co., 1985.

Mauss, Marcel. *The Gift: The Form and Reason for Exchange in Archaic Societies.* Trans. W. D. Halls. New York and London: W. W. Norton, 1990.

McNally, Mark. "The *Sandaikō* Debate: The Issue of Orthodoxy in Late Tokugawa Nativism." *Japanese Journal of Religious Studies* 29.3–4 (2002): 359–378.

Mencius. *Mencius.* Trans. D. C. Lau. New York: Penguin Books, 1970.

Minamoto, Ryōen. "*Jitsugaku* and Empirical Rationalism in the First Half of the Tokugawa Period." In *Principle and Practicality: Essays in Neo-Confucianism and Practical Learning,* ed. W. Theodore de Bary and Irene Bloom, 375–469. New York: Columbia University Press, 1979.

Mitchell, Richard H. *Censorship in Imperial Japan.* Princeton, NJ: Princeton University Press, 1963.

Miura Isshū and Ruth Fuller Sasaki. *Zen Dust: The History of the Koan and*

Koan Study in Rinzai (Lin-chi) Zen. Kyoto: First Zen Institute of America in Japan, 1966.

Miyazaki Fumiko. "The Formation of Emperor Worship in the New Religions— The Case of Fujidō." *Japanese Journal of Religious Studies* 17.2–3 (1990): 281–314.

Mohr, Michel. "Japanese Zen Schools and the Transition to Meiji: A Plurality of Responses in the Nineteenth Century." *Japanese Journal of Religious Studies* 25.1–2 (Spring 1998): 167–213.

———. *Traité de l'inépuisable lampe: Tōrei et sa vision de l'éveil.* Mélanges chinois et bouddhiques 28. 2 vols. Brussels: Institute Belge des Hautes Études Chinoises, 1997.

Morris, Ivan, trans. *The Pillowbook of Sei Shōnagon.* New York: Penguin Books, 1967.

Motoyama, Yukihiko. *Proliferating Talent: Essays on Politics, Thought, and Education in the Meiji Era.* Ed. J. S. A. Elisonas and Richard Rubinger. Honolulu: University of Hawai'i Press, 1997.

Muller, Jerry Z., ed. *Conservatism: An Anthology of Political Thought from David Hume to the Present.* Princeton, NJ: Princeton University Press, 1997.

———. "Introduction: What Is Conservative Social and Political Thought?" In *Conservatism: An Anthology of Political Thought from David Hume to the Present,* ed. Jerry Z. Muller, 3–31. Princeton: Princeton University Press, 1997.

Nosco, Peter ed. *Confucianism and Tokugawa Culture.* Princeton, NJ: Princeton University Press, 1984.

Okada, Takehiko. "Neo-Confucianism in Nineteenth-Century Japan." In *Confucianism and Tokugawa Culture,* ed. Peter Nosco, 215–250. Princeton, NJ: Princeton University Press, 1984.

Ooms, Emily. *Women and Millenarian Protest in Meiji Japan: Deguchi Nao and Ōmotokyō.* Ithaca, NY: Cornell East Asia Program, 1993.

Panofsky, Erwin. *Gothic Architecture and Scholasticism.* 1951. Reprint. Cleveland and New York: The World Publishing Co., 1957.

Passin, Herbert. *Society and Education in Japan.* 1965. Reprint. Tokyo: Kodansha International, 1982.

Paul, Diana. *Women in Buddhism: Images of the Feminine in the Mahāyāna Tradition.* 1979. 2d ed. Berkeley: University of California Press, 1985.

Prebish, Charles. "Ideal Types in Indian Buddhism: A New Paradigm." *Journal of the American Oriental Society* 114.4 (1995): 651–666.

Pyle, Kenneth. "Meiji Conservatism." In *The Cambridge History of Japan, Volume Five: The Nineteenth Century,* ed. Marius B. Jansen, 674–720. Cambridge, MA: Cambridge University Press, 1989.

———. *The New Generation in Meiji Japan: Problems of Cultural Identity, 1885– 1895.* Stanford, CA: Stanford University Press, 1969.

Ray, Reginald A. *Buddhist Saints in India: A Study of Buddhist Values and Orientations.* New York: Oxford University Press, 1994.

Reader, Ian, and George J. Tanabe, Jr. *Practically Religious: Worldly Benefits and the Common Religion of Japan.* Honolulu: University of Hawai'i Press, 1998.

Rotermund, Hartmut. *Hōsōgami ou la petite vérole aisément: Matériaux pour l'étude des épidémies dans le Japon des XVIIIe, XIXe siècles.* Paris: Maisonneuve et Larose, 1991.

Rubinger, Richard. "Education: From One Room to One System." In *Japan in Transition from Tokugawa to Meiji,* ed. Marius B. Jansen and Gilbert Rozman, 195–230. Princeton, NJ: Princeton University Press, 1986.

———. *Private Academies of Tokugawa Japan.* Princeton, NJ: Princeton University Press, 1982.

Sack, Robert David. *Human Territoriality: Its Theory and History.* Cambridge: Cambridge University Press, 1986.

Sasaki, Shigetsu. *Cat's Yawn: A Zen Miscellany.* New York: First Zen Institute of America, 1947.

Sawada, Janine [Tasca] Anderson. *Confucian Values and Popular Zen: Sekimon Shingaku in Eighteenth-Century Japan.* Honolulu: University of Hawai'i Press, 1993.

———. "Mind and Morality in Nineteenth-Century Japanese Religions: Misogi-kyō and Maruyama-kyō." *Philosophy East and West* 48.1 (Spring 1998): 115–116.

———. "Religious Conflict in Bakumatsu Japan: Zen Master Imakita Kōsen and Confucian Scholar Higashi Takusha. *Japanese Journal of Religious Studies* 21 (June–September 1994): 211–230.

———. "Tokugawa Religious History: Studies in Western Languages." *Early Modern Japan: An Interdisciplinary Journal* 10.1 (Spring 2002): 39–64.

Schopen, Gregory. "Two Problems in the History of Indian Buddhism: The Layman/Monk Distinction and the Doctrines of the Transference of Merit." *Studien zur Indologie und Iranistik,* Heft 10 (1985): 9–47. Republished with stylistic changes in the author's *Bones, Stones, and Buddhist Monks: Collected Papers on the Archaeology, Epigraphy, and Texts of Monastic Buddhism in India,* 23–55. Honolulu: University of Hawai'i Press, 1997.

Scott, Joan W. "Gender: A Useful Category of Historical Analysis." *American Historical Review* 91.5 (1986): 1053–1075.

Sharf, Robert. "The Zen of Japanese Nationalism." In *The Curators of the Buddha: The Study of Buddhism under Colonialism,* ed. Donald S. Lopez, Jr., 107–160. Chicago: University of Chicago Press, 1995. An earlier version of this article appears in *History of Religions* 33.1 (1993): 1–43.

———. "Whose Zen? Zen Nationalism Revisited." In *Rude Awakenings: Zen, the Kyoto School, and the Question of Nationalism,* ed. James W. Heisig and John Maraldo, 40–51. Honolulu: University of Hawai'i Press, 1994.

Shively, Donald H. "The Japanization of Middle Meiji." In *Tradition and Modernization in Japanese Culture,* ed. Donald H. Shively, 77–119. Princeton, NJ: Princeton University Press, 1971.

———. "Motoda Eifu: Confucian Lecturer to the Meiji Emperor." In *Confucianism in Action,* ed. David S. Nivison and Arthur F. Weight, 302–373. Stanford, CA: Stanford University Press, 1959.

———. "Nishimura Shigeki: A Confucian View of Modernization." In *Changing*

Japanese Attitudes Toward Modernization, ed. Marius B. Jansen, 193–241. Princeton: Princeton University Press, 1965.

Sievers, Sharon L. *Flowers in Salt: The Beginnings of Feminist Consciousness in Modern Japan.* Stanford, CA: Stanford University Press, 1983.

Smith, Warren W., Jr. *Confucianism in Modern Japan: A Study of Conservatism in Japanese Intellectual History.* 2d ed. Tokyo: Hokuseido Press, 1973.

Stevens, John. *The Sword of No-Sword: Life of the Master Warrior Tesshu.* Boulder and London: Shambhala, 1984.

Stone, Jacqueline I. *Original Enlightenment and the Transformation of Medieval Japanese Buddhism.* Honolulu: University of Hawai'i Press, 1999.

Suzuki, D. T. [Daisetsu Teitarō]. "An Autobiographical Account." In *A Zen Life: D. T. Suzuki Remembered,* ed. Masao Abe, 13–26. Tokyo: Weatherhill, 1986.

Suzuki, Kentarō. "Divination in Contemporary Japan: A General Overview and an Analysis of Survey Results." *Japanese Journal of Religious Studies* 22.3–4 (1995): 249–266.

Swale, Alistair. *The Political Thought of Mori Arinori: A Study in Meiji Conservatism.* Richmond, Surrey: Japan Library, 2000.

Takemura, Eiji. *The Perception of Work in Tokugawa Japan: A Study of Ishida Baigan and Ninomiya Sontoku.* Lanham, MD, and Oxford: University Press of America, 1997.

Tao, De-min. "Shigeno Yasutsugu as an Advocate of 'Practical Sinology' in Meiji Japan." In *New Directions in the Study of Meiji Japan,* ed. Helen Hardacre and Adam L. Kern, 373–382. Leiden, New York, and Cologne: Brill, 1997.

Teeuwen, Mark. *Watarai Shintō: An Intellectual History of the Outer Shrine of Ise.* Leiden: Research School CNWS, 1996.

Teters, Barbara. "The Genrō In and the National Essence Movement." *Pacific Historical Review* 31 (1962): 359–378.

Thal, Sarah E. "Rearranging the Landscape of the Gods." Ph.D. diss., Columbia University, 1999.

Thelle, Notto. *Buddhism and Christianity in Japan: From Conflict to Dialogue, 1854–1899.* Honolulu: University of Hawai'i Press, 1987.

Thurman, Robert A. F. *The Holy Teaching of Vimalakīrti: A Mahāyāna Scripture.* University Park and London: The Pennsylvania State University Press, 1976.

Tsuda Sōkichi. "Preface." In Fukuzawa Yukichi, *An Outline of a Theory of Civilization,* ix–xxiii.

Tucker, John A. "Ghosts and Spirits in Tokugawa Japan: The Confucian Views of Itō Jinsai," *Japanese Religions* 21 (1996): 229–251.

Vlastos, Stephen. "Opposition Movements in Early Meiji, 1868–1885." In *The Cambridge History of Japan, Volume Five: The Nineteenth Century,* ed. Marius B. Jansen, 367–431. Cambridge: Cambridge University Press, 1989.

―――. "Tradition: Past/Present Culture and Modern Japanese History." In *The Invention of Modern Japan,* ed. Stephen Vlastos, 1–16. Berkeley, CA: University of California Press, 1999.

―――., ed. *The Invention of Modern Japan.* Berkeley, CA: University of California Press, 1999.

Watanabe, Hiroshi. "They Are Almost the Same as the Ancient Three Dynasties: The West as Seen through Confucian Eyes in Nineteenth-Century Japan." In *Confucian Traditions in East Asian Modernity: Moral Education and Economic Culture in Japan and the Four Mini-Dragons,* ed. Tu Wei-ming, 119–131. Cambridge, MA: Harvard University Press, 1996.

Watanabe Masako and Igeta Midori. "Healing in the New Religions: Charisma and 'Holy Water.'" In *New Religions,* ed. Inoue Nobutaka, 162–264. Tokyo: Institute for Japanese Culture and Classics, Kokugakuin University, 1991.

Watt, Paul B. "Jiun Sonja (1718–1804): A Response to Confucianism in the Context of Buddhist Reform." In *Confucianism and Tokugawa Culture,* ed. Peter Nosco, 188–214. Princeton, NJ: Princeton University Press, 1984.

Wilhelm, Richard, trans. *The I Ching or Book of Changes.* Rendered into English by Cary F. Baynes. 3d ed. Princeton, NJ: Princeton University Press, 1967.

Williams, Duncan R. "Representations of Zen: An Institutional and Social History of Sōtō Zen Buddhism in Edo Japan." Ph.D. diss., Harvard University, 2000.

Wright, Diana E. "The Power of Religion/The Religion of Power: Religious Activities as Upāya for Women of the Edo Period, the Case of Mantokuji." Ph.D. diss., University of Toronto, 1996.

Yamamura, Kōzō. *A Study of Samurai Income and Entrepreneurship: Quantitative Analyses of Economic and Social Aspects of the Samurai in Tokugawa and Meiji Japan.* Cambridge, MA: Harvard University Press, 1974.

Yamashita, Samuel Hideo. "Confucianism and the Japanese State, 1904–1945." In *Confucian Traditions in East Asian Modernity: Moral Education and Economic Culture in Japan and the Four Mini-Dragons,* ed. Tu Wei-ming, 132–154. Cambridge, MA: Harvard University Press, 1996.

———. *Master Sorai's Responsals: An Annotated Translation of* Sorai sensei tōmonsho. Honolulu: University of Hawai'i Press, 1994.

———. "Nature and Artifice in the Writings of Ogyū Sorai (1666–1728)." In *Confucianism and Tokugawa Culture,* ed. Peter Nosco, 138–165. Princeton, NJ: Princeton University Press, 1984.

Zhang Zai. "The 'Western Inscription' ('Ximing')." In *Sources of Chinese Tradition,* ed. W. Theodore de Bary and Irene Bloom, 1:683–684. New York: Columbia University Press, 1999.

INDEX

About the Author

Janine Tasca Sawada, who was born in New York and raised in Europe, received her doctorate in religion from Columbia University. Among her publications is *Confucian Values and Popular Zen: Sekimon Shingaku in Eighteen-Century Japan*. She currently teaches at the University of Iowa.